LAWSUIT

STUART M. SPEISER

Oct 8, 1982

To Jackie Wells —
 I thought that working
for Mike Flynn you might
not get to learn about
real litigation —
 Good Luck in law school
 Don Maddox

Horizon Press ‖ New York

Library of Congress Catalog Card Number: 80–82239
ISBN: 0–8180–2200–0 (cloth);
0–8180–2201–9 (paper)

Manufactured in the United States of America

Published by Horizon Press
156 Fifth Avenue
New York 10010

11   10   9   8   7   6   5   4   3   2   1

To AWG—
world's greatest lefthanded catcher

CONTENTS

Preface

Let us begin our survey of civil litigation with the popular image of lawyers and lawsuits. We could use Shakespeare, Dickens, Carl Sandburg, or Jimmy Carter; but my own favorite is Ambrose Bierce. Here are some pertinent definitions from his famous 1911 book, *The Devil's Dictionary:*

> LAWYER: One skilled in circumvention of the law.
> LITIGANT: A person about to give up his skin for the hope of retaining his bones.
> LITIGATION: A machine which you go into as a pig and come out as a sausage.
> IMPUNITY: Wealth.

In our quest for an understanding of litigation, we shall consider some specific lawsuits—the "case method" used by all American law schools. Keep Ambrose's definitions in mind, and at the end, try to judge how accurately they describe lawsuits of the 1980s.

All of the trial excerpts that follow have been taken from the official court reporters' minutes, but because lawyers do not always speak in sentences and court reporters occasionally miss a word, I have edited these excerpts without changing their substance.

Citations of major cases, books, and articles mentioned in the text (as well as others which may be of interest) will be found in the Notes, starting on age 599.

I have recounted the exploits of dozens of lawyers, and my only regret is that I did not have the space to mention all the lawyers who have contributed so much to the march of history described here. Only by merciless cutting of a manuscript which started at twice its present length, have I produced what I hope is a readable book. Therefore it should be understood that the cases and lawyers mentioned here were chosen as examples, and have many counterparts in other courtrooms throughout the nation.

New York, N.Y.   STUART M. SPEISER

April 2, 1980

Chapter 1

RALPH NADER v. GENERAL MOTORS CORP.

A Routine Investigation

Ralph Nader put the telephone to his ear. The man's voice on the other end sounded snide and threatening: *"Why don't you go back to Connecticut, buddy-boy!"* Then the phone clicked and the line went dead before Nader could say anything.

It was three thirty in the morning, but Nader had not been asleep. He had been working through the night preparing his testimony for Senator Abraham Ribicoff's subcommittee on auto safety. He was scheduled to be the first witness that morning, Thursday, February 10, 1966. The threatening call was at least the sixth of its kind that night.

Altogether there had been more than two dozen of these calls in the preceding two weeks, and they were building up in intensity. Some were merely designed to annoy him: "Mr. Nader, this is Pan American . . . (click)." "Mr. Nader, please pick up the parcel at Railway Express . . . (click)." "Is this Mr. Nader? Can you hear me? Can you hear me? I can't hear you, I can't hear you." "Cut it out. Cut it out. You're going to cut me off, you're going to cut me off (click)." Some of the voices were male and some female. All of the calls came at night, to Dorothy Remington's rooming house on 19th Street in northwest Washington, where Nader was living.

The calls became a nightly event during the early days of February 1966, after the Senate announced that Nader was going to testify in favor of automobile safety legislation and that he was going to expose automobile defects that threatened the safety of the American public. Some of the intimidating calls were more specific: "You're supposed to know all about cars. Well, why don't you come and help me? I can't get mine started." "You are fighting a losing battle, friend. You can't win. You can only lose." "Why don't you change your field of interest?"

The calls unsettled Nader enough to make him lose several pounds from his already thin frame. Other strange things had happened to confirm his suspicion that somebody was prying into his affairs in an effort to discourage him, or worse. In his dramatic testimony before a Senate hearing a few weeks after the "Buddy-Boy" call, he described his reactions to intimidation and prying by an unseen adversary:

> One never has a chance to confront the adversary, in a sense. It is faceless, it is insidious, and individuals, not only myself, individuals can be destroyed in this manner, quite apart from discomfort. And so I was quite fearful of what was going to be the end of this. How was this information going to be used, and whether there was going to be even more overt foul play, perhaps of a physical nature. . . . I don't intimidate easily, but I must confess that one begins to have second thoughts of the penalties and the pain which must be incurred in working in this area.

When he received these nocturnal phone calls in 1966, Ralph Nader was a 32-year-old lawyer living alone in a Washington rooming house, supporting himself by free-lance writing. He was born and raised in Winsted, Connecticut, where his Lebanese-American parents owned and operated a restaurant. He graduated *magna cum laude* from Princeton University in 1955 and went on to the Harvard Law School. There he found the curriculum slanted toward the needs of the large corporate law firms that recruited most of the law school graduates. Nader was more interested in using the law to improve society, and he did not take the trouble to distinguish himself academically. In his senior year, he devoted a lot of time to writing a term paper on auto safety for the law school seminar in medico-legal problems. His paper concentrated on automobile design defects, which Nader felt were causing thousands of deaths and millions of injuries annually. His thesis was that, because the four automobile-manufacturing giants were not accountable to the

American public, they should be required by federal legislation to manu-facture safer automobiles and to install safety devices which were al-ready within the technical capability of the industry.

After graduating from the Harvard Law School in 1958, Nader served a six-months tour of active duty in the Army Reserve at Fort Dix, N.J. Then he was in private law practice at Hartford, Connecticut, from 1960 to 1964. But the urge to start a crusade for auto safety was overwhelming, and in 1964 he left Hartford and moved to the rooming house in Washington. At first he did free-lance writing on auto safety for the *Christian Science Monitor*. Then he became a consultant and re-searcher for Daniel P. Moynihan, assistant secretary of labor in the Johnson administration, and later ambassador to the United Nations and senator from New York. Moynihan was himself one of the earliest ad-vocates of federal legislation that would force improvement in auto safety.

By 1964, Senator Abraham A. Ribicoff of Connecticut had be-come interested in auto-safety legislation. As governor of Connecticut from 1955 to 1961, Ribicoff had become known as "Mr. Auto Safety," largely because of his tough enforcement of speeding and reckless driv-ing laws. But even though suspension of Connecticut driver's licenses rose from less to 400 to more than 10,000 per year, there was no sig-nificant drop in the accident rate. This experience convinced Ribicoff that there was more to solving the problem of auto safety than the im-position of punishment for reckless driving. As chairman of the Senate Subcommittee on Executive Reorganization, he decided to hold hearings on auto-safety problems. By using these hearings to focus attention on the role of the automobile as well as the driver in road accidents, Ribicoff hoped to get Congress to support auto-design safety legisla-tion.

Late in 1964, Jerome Sonosky, chief counsel to the Ribicoff sub-committee, learned of Nader's promising work on auto safety and in-vited him in for a talk. As a result, Nader became a voluntary, unpaid adviser to the Ribicoff subcommittee staff. He worked with Sonosky and other staff members to prepare for public hearings which were held in March and July of 1965. During the July 1965 hearings, many em-barrassing questions were put to General Motors' chairman, Frederick G. Donner, and to its president, James M. Roche. Nader helped to pre-pare these questions, which directed congressional attention to the fact that the automobile industry was spending very little on safety research.

During 1964 and 1965, Nader worked on the manuscript of *Unsafe at Any Speed,* a book that presented his conclusions about auto design defects, concentrating on General Motors' Chevrolet Corvair as an ex-ample of irresponsible and dangerous auto design. He was determined to explode the myth that traffic deaths were inevitably caused by careless driving, by "the nut behind the wheel." He wrote that it was possible to design automobiles in which the occupants are less exposed to the impact of accidents, and that many accidents could be avoided completely by elementary considerations of safety design. He accused the automobile industry of concentrating on styling and deliberately neglecting available safety items, such as padded dashboards and energy-absorbing steering columns and bumpers. Nader blamed the manufacturers for many of the 50,000 deaths and 5 million injuries that occurred on the U.S. highways every year.

In his book, Nader claimed that the 1960–1963 Corvair (the sporty rear-engine compact that was one of General Motors' best sellers) was a menace to life and limb because GM had ignored one of its own leading engineers, Maurice Olley, whose written report had warned of the inherent hazards of this type of rear-engined auto. Nader revealed that 'he Corvair had a marked tendency to get out of control and to roll over, especially when cornering. He claimed that many Corvair accidents were caused by the tendency of the outside rear wheel to "tuck under" the chassis during turns. He charged that the management of General Motors concealed these defects from the public and did not correct them until the 1964 model year, even though they had been aware of the dangers and the corrective action required much earlier.

By the time his book was published in November 1965, the name of Ralph Nader was well known to high officials of General Motors. On January 6, 1966, Nader held a press conference at the Sheraton Cadillac Hotel in Detroit to discuss his book. He invited each of the big four automobile manufacturers to send representatives to join the discussion, but none accepted. In a press release declining the invitation, General Motors made it clear that they disagreed with the conclusions of Nader's book, but went on to invite Nader to discuss his ideas with GM's engineers at the GM Technical Center in Warren, Michigan. Nader accepted the invitation, and a date was set for him to meet GM officials at Warren on January 14, 1966.

In the interim, on January 7, Nader went to Des Moines, Iowa, to testify at hearings held by State Attorney General Lawrence Scalise, who had developed an interest in auto safety as part of his larger concern for consumer protection. Under an Iowa law that authorized the attorney general to hold hearings on defective merchandise sold in that state, Scalise scheduled hearings on auto safety and invited a number of authorities, including officials of each of the American auto manufacturers. The manufacturers declined to testify, but they sent a lot of observers, and they authorized Karl M. Richards of the Automobile Manufacturers Association to testify on behalf of the industry.

During the course of the hearings, Richards questioned Nader: "I am rather curious to know what your connection is here. You are not a citizen of Iowa. Who pays your expenses out here?" Nader replied that his out-of-pocket expenses were reimbursed by the state of Iowa, as was the case with all the other witnesses.

Nader stayed at the Kirkwood Hotel in Des Moines for a week, from January 7 to January 13. Several times during those days he noticed a man who seemed to be keeping an eye on him. Nader saw the man twice in the lobby and once near his room. Toward the end of the hearings, he became uneasy enough about the man's presence to inform Attorney General Scalise. The attorney general ordered an investigation, but the hearings ended before any evidence could be found, and Nader's suspicions about the man shadowing him were never confirmed.

With the Kirkwood Hotel surveillance still in his mind, Nader carried his lonely crusade to the General Motors Technical Center at Warren, Michigan, on Friday, January 14, 1966. He was ushered into the office of Edward N. Cole, then executive vice president of General Motors and later to serve as president from 1967 to 1974. Along with Cole, Nader met several other GM officials, including assistant general counsel Louis H. Bridenstine, who was holding a copy of *Unsafe at Any Speed*. It was bristling with paper clips that Bridenstine had used to mark important pages. All of the GM executives were cordial and insisted on putting everything on a first-name basis. They told Nader that they would move to a nearby conference room for a presentation on the design and handling characteristics of the Corvair. As a prelude to this presentation, Bridenstine asked Nader whether he represented any plaintiffs who were suing General Motors for injuries suffered in Corvair accidents. There were more than a hundred such "products liability" suits pending in various states. They claimed that GM had been negligent in the design of the Corvair, and that, under the emerging legal doctrine of strict product liability, GM was liable for injuries suffered by Corvair occupants due to design defects, whether or not the plaintiffs could prove that such defects were caused by negligence. Bridenstine told Nader that he didn't have any reason to believe that Nader was involved in the Corvair litigation as an attorney or as a consultant, but he wanted to hear this from Nader's own lips. Nader told Bridenstine that he was not involved in the Corvair litigation in any way. This cleared the way for the group to move along to the conference room for the presentation. There they showed Nader films of the Corvair in action and presented illustrated lectures by GM engineers, all designed to show that the Corvair was safe.

They also took Nader on a tour of the GM proving ground, where cars are wrung out to test them for defects and performance limitations. According to Nader, Edward Cole gestured toward the vast private roadways and research facilities and asked, "Why don't you come over and join us, and put your ideas to work here?" Nader says that Cole brought up this subject three times during the Warren visit, but that he simply ignored Cole's suggestions.

The Corvair presentation did not supply Nader with any new facts. He remained convinced that the 1960–1963 Corvair was a public menace, and he concluded that the purpose of the invitation to the Warren proving ground, apart from its value as a public relations ploy to indicate that GM took a benign attitude toward its critics, was to buy him off and silence his criticism by putting him on the GM payroll.

On the day that Nader visited the GM proving ground (January 14, 1966), Senator Ribicoff's staff notified the press that his subcommittee would resume its auto safety hearings early in February, and that Ralph Nader would be a principal witness. Although Nader had worked behind the scenes with the subcommittee staff to prepare for the previous hearings in March and July of 1965, this would be the first time that Nader would step into the public spotlight as a witness. Later in January 1966, Ribicoff announced that the hearings would resume on February 10th. It was about that time that Nader started receiving the anonymous late-night phone calls. By then, he was quite apprehensive about the innuendo of the calls. Billions of dollars were at stake in auto safety legislation. The forces that he had challenged were the strongest private adversaries in the world. One out of every five jobs in the United States depended on the production, sale, or maintenance of automobiles. In Nader's mind, only the automobile manufacturers would be interested in harassing him. He felt that they had tried to buy him off at Warren, Michigan. Now that he had refused to join them, how far would they go in the other direction? How could he stop them? How could he even identify them? These questions disturbed him as he was working through the night and early morning in preparation for the high point of his crusade, his Senate testimony on February 10.

After a sleepless night, Nader appeared as the first witness before Senator Ribicoff's subcommittee. Also present were Senators Robert Kennedy of New York, Carl Curtis of Nebraska, Jacob Javits of New York, and Millard Simpson of Wyoming. Promptly at 10 A.M., Senator Ribicoff opened the hearing and introduced the main witness:

> We have invited Ralph Nader to appear today because he is the author of a recently published book about traffic safety, called *Unsafe at Any Speed*.
> It is a provocative book. It is a book which has some very serious things to say about the design and manufacture of motor vehicles now operating on the nation's highways. It is a book which raises serious questions about current public policy in regard to traffic safety. We welcome Mr. Nader here today.

Nader took the witness chair and held it for the better part of three hours. His testimony and exhibits cover 137 printed pages of the hearing record. He expounded the theories that he had first presented in *Un-*

safe at Any Speed and responded to spirited questioning by the senators present.

February 11, 1966, the day after Nader's first appearance as a witness before the Ribicoff subcommittee, produced one of those comedies of error which seem to ensure that the United States will land on its feet, even when the clowns are running the show. It was an incident that contained striking parallels to the burglary of the Watergate headquarters of the Democratic National Committee six years later. On February 11, Nader went to the New Senate Office Building (later renamed the Dirksen Senate Office Building) to record a television interview. He arrived at about 1:30 P.M. and went into the television studio on the ground floor, where he remained for about half an hour. As he left the studio, he took the elevator, intending to go down to the basement to eat in the cafeteria. However, he pushed the wrong button and the elevator took him upstairs. Realizing his mistake, he quickly took the elevator down to the basement. Unknown to Nader and to the world in general, he was being followed at that time by two private detectives from New York. But his inadvertent upward trip in the elevator and his rapid reversal of direction had apparently shaked off those bloodhounds, although Nader could have had no intention of doing so.

Having lost their quarry, the private detectives went up to building guard Marshall Speake, described Nader and asked the guard if he knew where in the building Nader had gone. They also disclosed to the guard that they had been following Nader around the country. The guard became suspicious and called in a Capitol Police lieutenant, who promptly told the private eyes that they were not allowed to follow people in the Senate Office Building and that they had better leave immediately, which they did. A little while later, the building guard, Marshall Speake, saw Nader as he was leaving the building and told him about this incident. Thus, for the first time, Nader's long-held suspicions were confirmed: somebody was actually following him. But who was it? Who had hired these two men, and what were they up to? How could he expose them and stop them?

Nader did not go to the police or any other governmental authorities since he had no clue to the identity of the people following him. He decided that his best bet was the Washington press corps. He turned to Morton Mintz, an investigative reporter for the *Washington Post*. On Sunday, February 13, Mintz wrote the first press account of the surveillance of Ralph Nader, a small article with the headline, "Car Safety Critic Nader Reports Being Tailed."

In the week that followed the fiasco in the New Senate Office Building, Nader began to put more little pieces together. He learned that investigators had interviewed some of his past associates, under the pretext of checking his qualifications for an important job. Professor

Thomas F. Lambert, Jr., editor in chief of the *Journal of the Association of Trial Lawyers of America* in Cambridge, Massachusetts, wrote Nader a warm letter, describing such a pre-employment interview and wishing him success in his new job. Similar interviews were reported by Professor Harold Berman, with whom Nader had worked during his student days at the Harvard Law School; by George Athanson, a Hartford attorney for whom Nader had worked; by Peter N. Kinder, Nader's classmate at Princeton and Harvard Law School; and by Dr. Eugene Sweeney, a former faculty colleague of Nader at the University of Hartford. Dorothy Remington, the landlady of Nader's rooming house, was also visited, as were Charles Hale and Charles Fedora of Hirsch and Co. in Washington, where Nader had a small brokerage account. In his conversations with some of those interviewed, Nader learned that the inquiries delved deeply into his private life. Questions were asked about drinking, narcotics, sex, and anti-Semitism. Nader felt a web tightening around him, but he had no idea how to fight it. He kept talking to journalists, hoping that somehow they could force a disclosure of the investigators' identity.

On Sunday, February 20, the campaign touched Nader personally. That evening he walked from his rooming house to the Drug Fair drugstore a few blocks away and was standing at the magazine rack when he was approached by an attractive young brunette whom he had never seen before. She walked up to him and said, "Pardon me, I know this sounds a little forward—I hope you don't mind, but can I talk to you?" Before Nader could say anything, she told him that she and some friends often got together to discuss foreign affairs and that they wanted to get all kinds of viewpoints. She asked Nader if he would join them. He declined politely, but the woman persisted. She said that there was to be a meeting that very night, and repeated her invitation. Nader replied that he was simply not interested, and turned his back. The woman then left the drugstore without inviting any of its other patrons to discuss foreign affairs.

The next day, Monday, February 21, Nader flew from Washington to Philadelphia to appear on television in the Mike Douglas Show. He was booked on a 3:30 P.M. flight back to Washington, which he barely had time to make. As he hurried through the gate a minute or two before 3:30, he noticed that two men who were sitting on a bench near the gate got up and followed him aboard the plane, taking seats near him in the economy section. By this time, he was on his guard. After landing in Washington, Nader moved quickly down the ramp and took evasive action to shake off the two men who he felt were pursuing him.

Arriving back at his rooming house, Nader found a telegram waiting for him. It was from his Harvard Law School classmate Frederick Hughes Condon. Condon had been crippled for life in an automobile accident, and it was to him that Nader had dedicated *Unsafe at Any*

Speed. The telegram asked Nader to call Condon that night at his home in Concord, New Hampshire. Nader telephoned Condon at one o'clock in the morning and learned that Condon had been interviewed in his office in Concord on February 21 by one Vincent Gillen. Condon was alarmed by the nature of the questioning, even though Gillen had told Condon that Nader was being considered for an important job. Condon warned Nader that someone was hiring investigators to travel about and question people about Nader's personal life in such matters as sex, anti-Semitism, drinking, narcotics, finances, driving history, and his relationship with Senator Ribicoff. This news did not make Nader sleep any better, but at least he had a name. Again he turned to the press, giving journalists Gillen's name in the hope that they could find out for whom Gillen was working.

On Wednesday, February 23, the female arm of the campaign struck again. Nader had stopped in a Safeway store near his rooming house to buy a package of cookies. As he was making his selection of cookies, an attractive blond woman in her twenties who wore slacks came up to him and said, "Excuse me, but I need some help. I've got to move something heavy into my apartment. There's no one to help me. I wonder if I can get you to give me a hand. It won't take much time. Will you help?" Nader excused himself politely, saying that he was already late for a meeting. The woman tried again. "Please—it won't take long." Nader said that he was sorry but he was simply not in a position to help her. At this point the girl turned and walked out quickly, even though there were at least half a dozen other unaccompanied men in the store who appeared to be capable of moving something heavy into her apartment.

On Friday, March 4, Nader's counterattack through the press began to bear fruit. He had given the whole story to James Ridgeway, an investigative reporter for the *New Republic,* and now Ridgeway had written a three-page article on it under the title "The Dick." It reported the harassing telephone calls and the reasons Nader had for thinking he was being followed in the Kirkwood Hotel in Des Moines, Iowa, and during his return from the Mike Douglas Show in Philadelphia. It described the ouster of the private eyes from the New Senate Office Building, the two encounters with young women, and the prying interviews of Nader's friends, including Condon's questioning by Gillen. Ridgeway's associate, David Sanford, had interviewed detective Gillen on the telephone. Though Gillen told Sanford he had been hired by an unnamed client to investigate Nader because he was being considered for an important job, Gillen was evidently not too convincing. The *New Republic* article quoted several comments by Gillen which seemed to imply that the investigation was the consequence of statements Nader had made in his book, *Unsafe at Any Speed.*

The Ridgeway article in the *New Republic* for March 12, 1966, was on the newsstands by March 4. It stirred other journalists into action. On Sunday, March 6, the *New York Times* and the *New York Herald Tribune* ran stories about Nader's charges. They quoted Nader as believing that the automobile industry was attempting to harass and discredit him because of his book and his testimony before the Ribicoff subcommittee. The *Times* article said, "Spokesmen for the major manufacturers in Detroit dismissed Mr. Nader's charge as ridiculous. Several indicated they believed that the investigation wouldn't be worth the trouble."

Now Senator Ribicoff took a hand. On March 8, he announced on the floor of the Senate that the harassment of Nader, as alleged in the press, was "an extremely serious matter," and that he was asking the Department of Justice to investigate the possibility that there had been an attempt to intimidate or impede a witness before a Congressional committee, which would be a violation of the federal criminal law. Senator Gaylord Nelson of Wisconsin, although he was not a member of the Ribicoff subcommittee, joined Senator Ribicoff's request for a Justice Department investigation, calling the treatment of Nader "a filthy business."

Now the fat was in the fire, and the press would no longer be content with anonymous denials by "industry spokesmen." Reporters bombarded auto company officials with requests for more definitive answers to Nader's charges. The break came on March 9 when John S. Bugas, vice president of the Ford Motor Company, gave a statement to the press flatly denying that Ford had ever been involved in any investigation or harassment of Ralph Nader. This gave the reporters the opening wedge they needed. That same day, they pressed executives of the other three major auto manufacturers for similar statements. Chrysler and American Motors immediately released statements similar to Ford's. But throughout the day, General Motors refused to comment. Then, shortly after 11 P.M. Detroit time (when most of the nation's morning newspapers had published their first editions), General Motors issued the following press release:

> General Motors said today that following the publication of Mr. Ralph Nader's criticisms of the Corvair in writings and public appearances in support of his book "Unsafe at Any Speed," the office of its general counsel initiated a routine investigation through a reputable law firm to determine whether Ralph Nader was acting on behalf of litigants or their attorneys in Corvair design cases pending against General Motors. The investigation was prompted by Mr. Nader's extreme criticism of the Corvair in his writings, press conferences, TV and other public appearances. Mr. Nader's statements coincided with similar publicity by some attorneys handling such litigation.
>
> It is a well known and accepted practice in the legal pro-

fession to investigate claims and persons making claims in the product liability field, such as in the pending Corvair design cases.

The investigation was limited only to Mr. Nader's qualifications, background, expertise and association with such attorneys. It did not include any of the alleged harassment or intimidation recently reported in the press. If Mr. Nader has been subjected to any of the incidents and harassment mentioned by him in newspaper stories, such incidents were in no way associated with General Motors' legitimate investigation of his interest in pending litigation.

At General Motors' invitation, Mr. Nader spent a day at the GM Technical Center, Warren, Michigan, early in January visiting with General Motors executives and engineers. He was shown a number of engineering and research testing and development programs in the field of automotive safety. A number of the accusations in his book were discussed at length, and a presentation was made of the evidence used in the successful defense of the only two Corvair lawsuits tried.

Mr. Nader expressed appreciation for the courtesy in providing him with detailed information, but he nevertheless continued the same line of attack on the design of the Corvair in a number of subsequent press conferences, TV and other appearances. This behavior lends support to General Motors' belief that there is a connection between Mr. Nader and plaintiffs' counsel in pending Corvair design litigation.

Thus, General Motors was forced by the press to disclose that it had indeed initiated an investigation of Ralph Nader. The General Motors press release made the Nader investigation a front-page story throughout the country, and it was also covered by television network news. Nader denied publicly that he had represented any plaintiffs in the Corvair suits and said that he had suspended his law practice for the duration of his auto safety crusade.

On March 10, Senator Ribicoff announced on the floor of the Senate that he was requesting Nader, the president of General Motors, and the "detective agencies" to appear before his subcommittee on March 22. He said that he would expect a public explanation of the alleged harassment of a Senate committee witness. Senators Robert Kennedy and Gaylord Nelson joined in Senator Ribicoff's request. Senator Nelson said:

> This raises grave and serious questions of national significance. What are we coming to when a great and powerful corporation will engage in such unethical and scandalous activity in an effort to discredit a citizen who is a witness before a Congressional committee!
>
> If great corporations can engage in this kind of intimidation, it is an assault upon freedom in America. No average citi-

zen can face up to a corporation the size of General Motors
which sets out to destroy him.

But the Senate and the entire world were soon to learn that General
Motors had not selected an "average citizen" to intimidate.

Mr. Roche
Apologizes

The March 22 hearing was held in the Senate Caucus Room, scene of
many famous encounters, including Senator Sam Ervin's 1973 Watergate hearings. The room was packed to capacity and the television
cameras were grinding away as Senator Ribicoff called the hearing to
order at 10 A.M. The first witness was James M. Roche, president of
General Motors, a tall, pale, white-haired man who wore rimless glasses
and had the appearance and the demeanor of a kindly clergyman. On
his right sat his lawyer, Theodore C. Sorensen, former special adviser to
the late President John F. Kennedy, and now a partner in the New York
law firm of Paul, Weiss, Rifkind, Wharton and Garrison. Sorensen was
a good friend of Senator Ribicoff and of Senator Robert F. Kennedy,
who also sat on the subcommittee. In addition to Ribicoff and Kennedy,
the panel consisted of Senators Henry M. Jackson of Washington, Fred
R. Harris of Oklahoma, and Milward L. Simpson of Wyoming.

Pursuant to Senate custom, Roche was allowed to read a prepared
statement after he was sworn as a witness. His statement went right to
the heart of the matter:

> As president of General Motors, I hold myself fully respon-
> sible for any action authorized or initiated by any officer of the
> corporation which may have had any bearing on the incidents
> related to our investigation of Mr. Nader. I did not know of the
> investigation when it was initiated and I did not approve it.
> While there can be no disagreement over General Motors'
> legal right to ascertain necessary facts preparatory to litigation,
> as I shall discuss in a moment, I am not here to excuse, condone,
> or justify in any way our investigating Mr. Nader. To the extent
> that General Motors bears responsibility, I want to apologize
> here and now to the members of this subcommittee and Mr.
> Nader. I sincerely hope that these apologies will be accepted. Cer-
> tainly I bear Mr. Nader no ill will.
> To the best of my knowledge—and I have made every ef-
> fort to obtain all the facts since learning about this some 2 weeks

ago—the investigation initiated by General Motors, contrary to some speculation, did *not* employ detectives giving false names, did *not* employ Allied Investigations, Inc., did *not* use recording devices during interviews, did *not* follow Mr. Nader in Iowa and Pennsylvania, did *not* have him under surveillance during the day he testified before this subcommittee, did *not* follow him in any private place, and did *not* constantly ring his private telephone number late at night with false statements or anonymous warnings.

At the time the investigation was initiated last November, Mr. Nader's book had not yet been published, he had *not* appeared nor was he scheduled to appear as a witness before this subcommittee and he was *not* regarded to anyone's knowledge as a consultant to this subcommittee. In short, this investigation was wholly unrelated to the proceedings of this subcommittee and Mr. Nader's connections with them.

There has been no attempt by, and it has at no time been the intention of, General Motors Corp., or any of its officers or employees to annoy, harass, embarrass, threaten, injure or intimidate Mr. Nader, to invade his privacy, to defame his character, or to hinder, impugn, coerce, or prevent his testimony before this or any other legislative body. Nor was any attempt made along those lines with respect to any other critic of General Motors.

I personally have no interest whatsoever in knowing Mr. Nader's political beliefs, his religious beliefs and attitudes, his credit rating or his personal habits regarding sex, alcohol, or any other subject. Nor for the record was any derogatory information of any kind along any of these lines turned up in this investigation.

Roche went on to explain that GM's general counsel, Aloysius F. Power, was troubled by what he saw as a concerted effort by the plaintiffs' lawyers handling the Corvair claims to try their cases in the press, using sensational publicity that might influence juries against the Corvair. Since Nader had kicked up more adverse publicity against the Corvair than anyone else, GM decided (according to Roche) to investigate Nader to find out whether he was connected with the Corvair litigation as a plaintiff's attorney, a potential expert witness, or a consultant. They made a brief inquiry in his home town (Winsted, Connecticut) but were not able to get much information. Since they had a Washington address for him, the GM general counsel had requested a Washington attorney, one Richard Danner, "to secure an investigation of the facts needed." Roche went on:

Mr. Danner secured the services of Vincent Gillen Associates, an investigation agency in New York City, a decision which was not ratified by or made known to me. Nor was I informed of the pre-employment investigative methods which would be employed by Mr. Gillen and his associates. Most of the information gathered in this effort, which was terminated last month, was, not surprisingly, irrelevant for the very narrow purposes which our general counsel had originally intended.

When Roche had read his statement, Senator Ribicoff commended him for his forthrightness, as did Senator Kennedy. He was then questioned by Senators Ribicoff, Kennedy, Simpson, and Harris. The senators brought out the fact that the investigation had strayed far beyond any reasonable connection with the Corvair litigation. Each time this was brought up, Roche admitted the straying but said that it was done by the detective agency without his knowledge. He gave the impression that if he or any other officer of General Motors had known that the investigation was going so far afield, he would have stopped it immediately. Senator Harris pursued this line of questioning:

> Senator HARRIS: You are saying then that your own legal staff —no one in GM to your knowledge knew in advance that this investigation would go into facts that were not required to prepare the lawsuit; is that what you say?
> Mr. ROCHE: To my knowledge I don't think that was contemplated; no, sir.
> Senator HARRIS: And then who did make that decision? Who made the decision that extraneous matters would be investigated?
> Mr. ROCHE: I think that that decision was made by the people who were conducting the investigation.
> Senator HARRIS: They, just on their own, decided to do more than was required?
> Mr. ROCHE: I have been informed that the pre-employment pretext, as it has been referred to, was decided to be the basis for the investigation, and that decision, insofar as I know, was made by the investigating agency.
> Senator HARRIS: And no one else knew about that before they did it on their own?
> Mr. ROCHE: Not to my knowledge; no, sir.
> Senator HARRIS: Nobody within GM?
> Mr. ROCHE: Not to my knowledge.
> Senator HARRIS: Nobody within your general counsel's office?
> Mr. ROCHE: Not to my knowledge.

So GM's line of defense became clear. They were forced to own up to a thick stack of Gillen's investigation reports, including interviews with more than 60 people who had been asked the most searching personal questions about Nader. But GM portrayed itself as an innocent victim of an overzealous detective, who went far beyond the very limited investigation that was authorized and ran up a bill of $6,700. Despite Roche's allegations that he and other officers of General Motors had no idea that the investigation was going to become a smear job, he magnanimously apologized to the Senate and to Nader for any inconvenience involved. But it was a very carefully worded apology. Although it satisfied the senators to have the president of the world's most powerful corporation apologize to them and assure them that no offense was intended, Roche's testimony would be of limited use to Nader if he decided to sue General Motors. Roche had held himself responsible for "any action authorized or initiated by any officer" of General Motors, but he had said that the offensive Gillen tactics were *not* authorized or initiated by any officer. His apology was specifically limited "to the extent that General Motors bears responsibility," but he went on to claim that General Motors had no responsibility for the investigation because it was, in legal parlance, an "unauthorized frolic" by detective Gillen.

The hearing went on for more than six hours, but GM's line of defense never deviated from Roche's opening statement. On the whole, the senators seemed to be satisfied with the apology, and their questioning did not break down GM's defense.

Roche was followed in the witness chair by GM's general counsel, Aloysius F. Power. His testimony echoed Roche's version. He described the Corvair litigation in greater detail, putting into the record many newspaper articles which quoted press statements by plaintiff's lawyers that were similar to those in Nader's book, *Unsafe at Any Speed.* He was cross–examined by Senators Ribicoff and Kennedy, but he stuck to the position that he knew nothing about the direction that the investigation was taking and that, as far as he was concerned, it was a perfectly legitimate defense of GM's products to investigate an attorney who appeared to have some connection with the Corvair litigation. He, too, branded Gillen's investigation as an unauthorized frolic.

When Power took the stand, he was accompanied by Louis H. Bridenstine, assistant general counsel; Miss Eileen Murphy of the General Motors legal department; and attorney Richard G. Danner of Washington. All of them took the oath at the same time. Bridenstine was questioned briefly by Senators Kennedy and Harris, and he admitted that the investigation went beyond its original intention, but again he placed the blame for this squarely on the overzealous detective, Gillen.

After Bridenstine's testimony, the hearing adjourned at 1:05 P.M., to resume after lunch. At 2:00 P.M., Ralph Nader took the stand. He started with a prepared statement that was designed to inspire a much broader inquiry than the senators were prepared to undertake:

> I am responsible for my actions, but who is responsible for those of General Motors? An individual's capital is basically his integrity. He can lose only once. A corporation can lose many

times and not be affected. This unequal contest between the individual and any complex organization, whether it is a corporation, a union, government, or other group, is something which bears the closest scrutiny in order to try to protect the individual from such invasions.

The requirement of a just social order is that responsibility shall lie where the power of decision rests. But the law has never caught up with the development of the large corporate unit. Deliberate acts emanate from the sprawling and indeterminable shelter of the corporate organization. Too often the responsibility for an act is not imputable to those whose decisions enable it to be set in motion. The president of General Motors can say he did not know of the specific decision to launch such an investigation. But is he not responsible in some way for the general corporate policy which permits such investigations to be launched by lower–level management without proper guidelines? The office of the general counsel can put forth a document outlining the limits of a "routine" investigation merely to protect the interest of the company's shareholders. A second shield in front of the corporate shield comes in the form of a law firm commissioned in the nonlegal task of hiring a private detective agency. In this case, apparently, GM did not wish to hire agents directly. The enthusiasm of their detectives, the law firm would have us believe, were unauthorized frolics and detours. Besides, the law firm could assume responsibility in the last analysis, since there was little burden to such an assumption. Aside from the Federal statute under which this subcommittee is proceeding in this matter, there are few sanctions to protect the principle of privacy in American society against such new challenges largely unforeseen by the Founding Fathers.

Nader testified that he had been out of law practice for the past two years, had repeatedly turned down invitations to handle cases, and had absolutely no connection with the Corvair products liability litigation. He acknowledged that had been mentioned in a newsletter of the Association of Trial Lawyers of America (ATLA) as a lawyer who had information on the Corvair, but explained that ATLA had listed him because they knew he would furnish whatever information he had to anyone free of charge as a public service. He took the opportunity to insert into the Senate record several voluminous exhibits which were very damaging to the safety image of the Corvair, and they probably helped to bring about its later demise. Among these documents was a patent issued November 3, 1959, application for which had been filed May 19, 1956, by engineer Maurice Olley of General Motors. This patent proved that for at least three years before they put the Corvair on the market, GM had been aware of the dangers of its swing-axle suspension and of the changes necessary to make its design safe.

Senator Kennedy asked Nader a question that must have occurred to many of those watching the hearing:

> Senator KENNEDY: Now I would like to ask you perhaps just one final question. Why are you doing all of this, Mr. Nader? Mr. NADER: I think the initial difficulty in answering that question, Senator, can be put in this way. If I was engaged in activities for the prevention of cruelty to animals, nobody would ever ask me that question. Because I happen to have a scale of my priorities which lead me to engage in activities for the prevention of cruelty to humans, my motivations are constantly inquired into.
>
> Basically, the motivation is simply this: When I see, as I have seen, people decapitated, crushed, bloodied, and broken— and that is what we are really talking about in auto safety when we get down to it, it is the fatalities and the horrible carnage involved—when I see that on highways, as I have seen all over the country, going back many years, I ask myself, what can the genius of man do to avoid it? And, frankly, I think this country and the auto industry are abundantly endowed with the genius of man to provide an engineering environment of both highway and vehicle which will protect the occupants from the consequences of their errors, and which will avoid the very perpetuation of these errors in the first place by a humane automotive and highway design.

Following Nader's testimony, Washington attorney Richard G. Danner took the stand. He explained how he had been called by Eileen Murphy of the GM legal department to arrange for an investigation of Nader. He echoed the statements of Roche, Power, and Bridenstine, that the sole purpose of the investigation was to find out what connection Nader had with the Corvair litigation, and that the excursion beyond those guidelines was purely the work of detective Gillen. It had been arranged that Danner would engage Gillen as an investigator, that all GM instructions to Gillen would come through Danner, and all reports submitted by Gillen would be sent to Danner for transmittal to General Motors. He denied issuing any instructions to make any harassing phone calls to Nader or to use women to entice or trap him.

The final witness was the detective himself, Vincent Gillen. He read an expansive prepared statement in which he gave many details of his accomplishments, including his election as president of the parent-teachers association at his daughter's high school in Brooklyn. He denied that he had trailed Nader in Iowa, and said that he had not been brought into the case until January 13, 1966 (the day Nader left Iowa for Warren, Michigan). He also denied making harassing phone calls, using women as lures, and following Nader from Philadelphia to Washington after the Mike Douglas TV show. Gillen insisted that the surveillance of Nader and questioning of more than 60 of his associates were necessary parts of the "pre-employment pretext" which he had chosen as the best way of carrying out General Motors' instructions to determine Nader's connection with the Corvair litigation. He sensed that he was being made the fall guy, and he was not going to take it lying down. He almost torpedoed the General Motors defense by trying to justify his actions as being within his instructions. But by this time the entire subcommittee had typed him as the villain of the piece. Senators Ribicoff and Kennedy questioned him heatedly, and then allowed Roche to repeat his statement that the investigation was not within the intentions or instructions of General Motors.

When Gillen finished his prepared statement, Senator Ribicoff said:

> Mr. Gillen, this has been very revealing testimony. By the time you finished, I can imagine that Mr. Roche wondered why General Motors spent $6,700.

When Gillen complained that he was being smeared and that he had done a good job for his client, Senator Ribicoff said:

> Well, that is up to General Motors to indicate whether you did or not. I think, frankly, you have done General Motors a disservice, you have done Nader a disservice, and I think as I read this testimony and what you have sent down, I think a lot of people who hire detectives throw their money away, getting nothing for it.

After Gillen's testimony, Roche took the stand again and reiterated his opening statement. He assured the subcommittee that the mistakes of the Nader case would not be repeated—and it was clear that the mistake he referred to was the hiring of Gillen. Senators Ribicoff, Kennedy, and Harris again commended Roche for his candor and "sensitive appreciation" of the situation.

On that note, Senator Ribicoff closed the hearing at 5:15 P.M. Roche had put himself across as a corporate statesman whose company had been victimized by Gillen. The subcommittee accepted Roche's position that the target of the investigation had been Nader's connection with the Corvair litigation, and that the deviation from this legitimate concern was the idea and the fault of Gillen alone.

Although Eileen Murphy of the GM legal department had been sworn as a witness along with Power and Bridenstine, and it was clear that she was the one who gave GM's investigation instructions to Danner for delivery to Gillen, she was never asked what those instructions were. Neither was she or any other General Motors official asked to produce any documents showing the instructions that had been given by General Motors for the Nader investigation. She was not questioned, and she made no statement.

The subcommittee staff members were satisfied that they had put General Motors in its place. They also felt that the whole Nader incident had given a strong impetus to passage of federal auto safety legislation. Nader emerged from the hearings as a hero. Every witness confirmed the fact that the $6,700 spent by General Motors had turned up absolutely nothing the least bit questionable about Nader. Few people could survive such an inquisition without the slightest blemish. As Senator Ribicoff said during the hearings:

> And may I say to you, Mr. Nader, that I have read these reports very carefully, and you and your family can be proud, because they put you through the mill and they haven't found a damn thing out against you.

Ralph Nader emerged as a person whose only motive was the public good, as one who was devoting himself to a crusade that could not bring him any financial gain. All the GM witnesses admitted that no connection was discovered between Nader and the Corvair attorneys. That evening, all news programs on national television carried Nader's denunciation and Roche's apology. As Charles McCarry wrote in his 1972 book, *Citizen Nader:*

> The subcommittee did something for Nader that the Senate had never done for an individual in the history of the nation. It certified his virtue, gave birth to him as a public figure, and equipped him with an image that has remained a combination of the best qualities of Lincoln of Illinois and David of I Samuel 17.

The subcommittee hearing did all that for Nader, but as we were to discover, it did little to help any lawsuit that Nader might bring against GM.

The Dream Case

While Senator Ribicoff and his subcommittee staff were ecstatic over the outcome of the March 22 hearing, Ralph Nader was more reserved. He knew that big corporations could play the waiting game, and that General Motors would emerge unharmed after the memory of Roche's apology had faded.

Away from the glare of the television lights and the questions of angry senators, GM officials could treat the Nader affair less defensively. At their annual meeting in Detroit on May 20, 1966, GM Board Chairman Frederick G. Donner told the shareholders that the Nader investigation went beyond the intention of GM's general counsel and that it delved into Nader's personal life only because of "the ineptitude of an over-zealous gumshoe."

After the March 22 hearing, Nader immediately turned to the task of putting more teeth into the administration's proposed auto safety legislation, hoping his newly won prestige and GM's public embarrassment would help his lobbying efforts. GM was not off the hook entirely, since the Justice Department was looking into possible violations of federal statutes prohibiting interference with a Senate witness, as Senator Ribicoff had requested on March 8, 1966. But on June 1, Assistant Attorney General Fred M. Vinson, Jr., notified Senator Ribicoff that the Justice Department was not able to find evidence sufficient to support a criminal prosecution.

On June 1, Nader asked Jerome Sonosky, chief counsel of the Ribicoff subcommittee, for a copy of the Gillen investigation report that had been produced by GM for the March 22 hearing. Sonosky told Nader that the only copy produced for the subcommittee had been returned to GM's counsel, Theodore Sorensen. Nader was not satisfied with this reply, and he took his request to Senator Ribicoff. Finally Senator Ribicoff advised Nader that the subcommittee did have a copy of the Gillen report after all, but that they decided to retain it as confidential Senate property and to send it to the National Archives, where it would not be available to Nader or to the public. Nader was most unhappy that he was not allowed to see the reports of the detectives who had questioned more than 60 people about him. Apart from his personal curiosity about the content of these interviews, he wanted our firm to study them so that we could advise him of any legal remedies that he might have against GM and Gillen.

My first contact with Ralph Nader had been in 1957, when he was an editor of the *Harvard Law Record,* the weekly Harvard Law School newspaper (not to be confused with the more scholarly *Harvard Law Review*). Although he was still a law student then, he had come upon an injustice that many practicing lawyers were unaware of: the Warsaw Convention, an international treaty which limited damages for injury and death on international airline flights to a mere $8,300 per passenger. I was flattered to receive an invitation from Ralph to write an article on the Warsaw Convention for the *Harvard Law Record.* It was published in 1959, and I heard nothing further of Ralph Nader for the next six years.

Then, one day early in 1965 (several months before publication of his book and the ensuing GM investigation) he came to our office to have lunch with me and Paul Rheingold, a Harvard Law classmate of his who had recently joined our firm. Nader was about six foot four, slender, with intense dark eyes and a shy but friendly manner. Friendly, that is, until the conversation turned to auto safety. As we ate lunch at the cavernous old Oyster Bar in Grand Central Terminal, he told us that he was working on his own to promote federal auto safety legislation. He exclaimed that the nation's biggest industry, automobile manufacturing, was one of the least regulated, and that there were absolutely no federal auto safety standards to protect the public. As he warmed up to his subject, his tone became indignant, almost belligerent. With his fists waving and his dark eyes flashing, Ralph lectured to us. "Do you realize that there are close to 50,000 people killed in automobile accidents every year in this country, and only about 1,000 killed in airplanes, even including private planes? Yet anyone can build an automobile that's a death trap for its occupants, without any government standards or regulations. But if you try to build the smallest airplane, there are volumes of federal standards and safety regulations that every manufacturer has to comply with!"

I found this intense young man a little disturbing. He made me feel guilty because there were safety standards for aircraft and not for autos, even though I was not responsible for either condition. I felt an immediate urge to drop my fork, rise from my seat of comfort, and follow him into the streets to prevent the 50,000 auto deaths. To Ralph Nader in 1965, the lack of auto safety regulation was a shocking situation that cried out for immediate correction *by him* and other public-spirited lawyers, despite the combined opposition of General Motors, Ford, Chrysler, and American Motors. He said that the federal regulation of airplane manufacturing was a strong argument for auto legislation, and since I was an aviation law specialist and had written several books on the subject, he asked if I would help by providing him with historical background on aviation regulation. My offhand reaction was that he was out of his mind to think that any individual lawyer (or even an army of lawyers) could buck the auto manufacturers. But I was so impressed by his selfless attitude and by his genuine indignation that I got caught up in the spirit of his game. I agreed that we would try to help him to develop the analogy between federal aviation regulation that existed and the federal auto safety legislation that was needed.

We gave him some information on federal aviation regulation, and I instructed our Washington office to help him whenever he requested it, since our staff there included lawyers who had previously worked for federal aviation agencies. At Ralph's request, we supplied some information to senatorial staff researchers who were working on auto safety legislation. However, I doubt that this aviation material played any significant role in getting auto safety legislation enacted. For that, the nation can thank Senator Ribicoff, Ralph Nader, General Motors, and the detectives who lost Nader's trail in the New Senate Office Building.

Following our 1965 Oyster Bar luncheon, the next time I saw Ralph's face was on a television screen on March 22, 1966. That was the day James Roche delivered his carefully worded apology to Ralph and the Ribicoff subcommittee. As the worldwide television audience watched this happy ending of a modern David and Goliath encounter, I thought of it as only a beginning—as the beginning of a fascinating lawsuit. In view of our past relationship, I felt that when Ralph was ready to sue he would call us. It never occurred to me that he would have the slightest doubt about suing. But I knew very little about Ralph Nader then.

During the next few months, we had several discussions with Ralph. The first thing he wanted to know was how much time he had to make up his mind whether to sue. He was preoccupied with the auto safety bill which was then in the home stretch, and he had decided not to jeopardize its passage by filing a lawsuit. We advised him that under the laws of some of the states involved in the case, the statute of limitations expired one year from the time of the wrongful act. Since it appeared that GM had started investigating Ralph in November 1965, he would have to start suit in November 1966 to stay safely within the one-year statute of limitations.

By the summer of 1966, it was apparent from our discussions that the question of whether to sue was causing Ralph real agony. He was totally dedicated to the consumer safety crusade. He was influenced by investigative reporters, some of whom felt that Ralph's image would be tarnished by suing, and that his auto safety activities in the future would be interpreted as support tactics for his lawsuit. We spent many hours discussing these points. I tried to convince him that he could protect his image by announcing at the start of the lawsuit that the proceeds would be dedicated to supporting his public-interest work. I argued that the whole country was shocked at General Motors' attempt to silence him; that everyone was expecting him to sue; and that, rather than looking on the suit with disfavor, most people would admire his courage in taking on GM in the courts. Ralph came up with strong reasons of his own for suing: he wanted all the facts brought out, so that the whole world would be able to see the extent of GM's involvement; and he wanted to widen the law's protection against corporate harassment so that future consumer advocates would not have to rely upon acts of personal courage for survival.

On the minus side was the uncertainty of the proposed remedy. Our research indicated that Ralph's main claim against General Motors would come under the heading of "invasion of privacy." It appears in all the textbooks as a well established cause of action, but it had proven to be more of a plaything for law professors than a means of collecting damages. We researched the reported decisions of all state and federal courts and found only twelve cases in which damages had been awarded for invasion of privacy. The awards ranged from $250 to a high of only $12,500, and in some states, including New York, the protection of privacy was very narrow. Ralph himself pointed out that, while GM had the worst of motives, they had unwittingly increased the sales of his book (his major source of income at the time) and had helped him to become a national hero much in demand as a lecturer and television personality.

I told Ralph I was sure GM expected to be sued and that they were probably prepared to pay a large sum, much larger than any previous award, to bury their mistakes; and that I was reasonably certain this sum would be large enough to keep Ralph's crusades going for years. This prospect was attractive to him because he had no financial support at the time, and he feared that the auto giants would nullify any federal auto safety legislation enacted unless he could build an organization that would help to enforce it.

As we came closer to the one-year deadline, a large hurdle was cleared away. On September 9, 1966, Senator Ribicoff and Ralph Nader were honored guests at the White House, looking on as President Lyndon Johnson signed the National Traffic and Motor Vehicle Safety Act into law. At last Ralph could give his full attention to deciding whether to sue. Although he still had strong doubts, our arguments finally prevailed, and he authorized us to file suit. We agreed to take the case on a contingent fee basis. If we won or settled the case, we would receive as our fee one-third of the amount recovered up to $300,000 and 30 percent of any recovery above $300,000. We would advance all expenses, and would not get them back until the case was concluded. And in the event that GM filed any counterclaims against Ralph (such as claims that his book or other statements libeled or slandered GM's products), we would defend him without any further fees.

Having almost exhausted our powers of persuasion in the task of overcoming the client's doubts about suing, we turned quickly to fashioning the important first shot at the enemy: the *complaint* that would be filed in court to start the lawsuit. I had begun to draft that complaint in my mind on March 22, 1966, as I watched the television news showing Ralph at the Ribicoff subcommittee hearing. Ralph had not retained us, I had not read any of the Ribicoff subcommittee hearing transcript, I was—to say the least—rusty on the law of privacy and had never handled an invasion of privacy case; but none of these obstacles kept me from visualizing *Nader v. General Motors* as the perfect tort case.

Torts are wrongful acts that are not necessarily crimes; they involve money damages in compensation for a violation of some legal duty (other than breach of contract) owed by the defendant to the plaintiff. Most tort suits are based on negligence, such as auto accidents, where the defendant violates the legal duty to use reasonable care for the safety of others on the road. Other important torts are defamation (libel and slander), false imprisonment, assault and battery, malicious prosecution, invasion of privacy, and misrepresentation. Some torts, such as assault and battery, may also be criminal offenses, but the battered plaintiff still has the right to sue the attacker for damages in a civil tort action.

The tort lawyer's dream of the perfect case usually involves a completely pure plaintiff (such as a nun) who has been injured outrageously by a "target defendant": someone who makes a ready target for the jury's righteous indignation and can also pay a large judgment (such as a drunken millionaire playboy driving an expensive sports car at breakneck speed). But almost always, there is something to spoil the dream tort case.

As I watched James Roche apologize to Ralph Nader on nationwide television, I was convinced that we had the dream case at last. Whatever Ralph Nader had become to idol–hungry admirers—knight in shining armor, champion of the consumer, the last honest man, even a sex symbol—in my narrow sights he was one thing above all else: the perfect plaintiff. And General Motors was a perfect target defendant: hated by millions of disgruntled car owners and unlikely to get sympathy from a jury when it came to fixing damages. To be handed the representation of the perfect plaintiff against the ultimate target defendant in a classic David–Goliath confrontation that had climaxed in a nationally televised apology was the final realization of this dream.

My exuberance was dampened a bit when I read the full transcript of the Ribicoff subcommittee hearing. GM's lawyers had handled the situation cleverly in anticipation of a Nader lawsuit. Roche's apology was not what it had seemed to be in the brief television vignette; he had not admitted that GM had done anything to harm Nader, and he had succeeded in placing the blame on an unauthorized frolic by detective Gillen. Well, no case is perfect, I thought; we'll get around those problems somehow. But I really came back to earth with a thud when I sat down with Al Gans to discuss the fruits of his preliminary research. I had assumed that we would have no difficulty in getting to the point of presenting Ralph's case to a jury, but Al found so many potential legal obstacles that I was not so sure that we would ever reach that crucial milestone. Unless we could clear all the hurdles that Al had spotted, the case could be thrown out at the pleading stage (because of legal deficiencies in our complaint) before the facts were ever presented to a jury.

Our Secret Weapon

Since Alfred W. Gans is one of the main characters in this story, I must digress a moment to describe him. Al is easily the leading scholar and researcher in our firm, and when he speaks, the rest of us take notes. Indeed, we call him our secret weapon, although his scholarly accomplishments are hardly a secret.

He looks the part of a judge right out of Hollywood central casting—tall, white-haired, distinguished—and he actually played the judge in an educational film produced by the American Arbitration Association. For many years prior to joining our firm, he was managing editor of *American Law Reports,* the most exhaustively annotated set of legal reference books, known to lawyers as *ALR.* As a regular business exercise, he read every court decision published in England and the United States—state and federal courts at the trial and appellate levels—plus at least fifty law reviews and other publications. After speed-reading through these thousands of pages each week, he would assign various cases to his large staff of editors for write-up in *ALR* and other publications. He has a photographic memory which he can apply to a printed page after a glance. For years, the publishers of *ALR* used him as a sort of traveling circus act at Bar Association conventions. He would stand at a blackboard hour after hour during lectures by professors and practicing lawyers, and whenever they mentioned a specific point of law, he would chalk up citations of leading cases and authorities on the legal point involved, mostly from memory. I never heard of anyone finding a mistake on his blackboard. Al's ability to speed-read and absorb thousands of pages of text is not confined to law. He gobbles up novels, newspapers, magazines, at the same pace and is a fountain of knowledge in history, chemistry, philately, Russian literature, and baseball.

An incident in Al's career as an Air Force Captain in World War II will show the kind of stuff he is made of. Early in the war, he was assigned to the Judge Advocate (legal) department of the Air Transport Command in Alaska. At that time our forces in Alaska were commanded by General Simon Bolivar Buckner, a spit-and-polish type officer from a family with a long military tradition. When Buckner took over the Alaska command, it was not formally designated a combat zone, and service men were allowed to have their wives and other dependents living with them. But General Buckner did not relish the idea of running a potential combat command amid civilian trappings. In 1943, even though the Japanese were in the process of being ousted from Kiska and Attu and the prospects of combat in Alaska were becoming remote, General Buckner decided that he would send all wives and dependents of servicemen back to the continental United States. There were rumors that this move was inspired by high-ranking officers who had managed to create some Arctic warmth through liaisons with Eskimo girl-friends.

To complete the formal orders that would return the civilians to the continental United States, General Buckner had to obtain the endorsements of the judge advocates of the command, certifying that he had the legal power to give such an order. All of the other members of the Judge Advocate staff endorsed General Buckner's order automatically, but Captain Al Gans refused to do so. In fact, he wrote a short treatise on constitutional law, advising the general that he had no power to "deport" American citizens from Alaska because Alaska was not in a combat zone and its civilian government was functioning. This caused an immediate explosion at the highest level. The Staff Judge Advocate, a colonel who was the highest ranking military lawyer in Alaska confronted Captain Gans with: "Who the hell are you, a lousy captain, telling a general officer that he can't do what he wants to do? Don't you know you're in the Army? You'd better endorse General Buckner's order immediately!'

General Buckner and his staff were to find out what they were up against when they sent that same order to Captain Gans once again for endorsement. In return, they received an even more elaborate essay on constitutional law, which included this gem from the Civil War era Supreme Court decision in *Ex parte Milligan:*

> The Constitution of the United States is a law for rulers
> and people equally in war and in peace, and covers with the
> shield of its protection all classes of men, at all times, and under
> all circumstances.

Shortly thereafter General Buckner was completely stymied when a group of civilian dependents filed suit in the federal district court at Anchorage and obtained a ruling that denied the Army's power to deport them, and on exactly the grounds stated in Captain Gans's message to the general. Needless to say, Al Gans never advanced beyond the rank of captain (until his discharge as a major), and since he was already as close to Siberia as his superiors could station him, the Judge Advocate department was content to leave him there for the rest of the war.

When Al Gans had read the Ribicoff subcommittee's transcript of the Nader-GM testimony and the other notes in our files, he told me that our first problem would be to establish a legal cause of action against General Motors. One would think that the bizarre investigation and harassment of Nader would automatically have given Ralph the right to recover damages from GM and Gillen. Unfortunately, our legal system does not quite work that way.

The United States, Great Britain and the former and present members of the British Commonwealth are known as *common law* countries, but most countries have a legal system that evolved from the older Roman law. In this book, we will use the term *Roman law* for the legal systems of France, Germany, Mexico, Japan, and other countries that do not operate under the common law system. Roman law is also known as *civil law,* because the Romans used that term to distinguish their secular law from ecclesiastical law. But we will use the term *civil law* here as it is commonly used in America: to distinguish between criminal and non-criminal law.

Under the common law system, judges proclaim the law from case to case. Even when cases fall within statutes enacted by the legislature, common law judges have the power to interpret these statutes. A judge's decision then becomes the law by *stare decisis*—by setting a precedent that other judges are bound to follow. Roman law countries depend more upon written codes and much less upon judicial decisions to develop the law. The common law is supposed to be more flexible and adaptable to changing conditions than the Roman law system. In common law countries, the courts have the inherent power to break new ground when novel questions of law arise. However, this is not as easy as it sounds.

As a rule, this power to declare new principles of common law is exercised only by judges of the highest appellate courts. In the lower courts, where cases are actually tried, the judges feel bound by precedent, and it is very unusual for them to overrule a prior appellate decision or declare a new principle of law. So a lawyer who files a complaint based on a novel theory of law is likely to get from defendant's attorneys a stack of papers with the ominous title, DEFENDANT'S MOTION TO DISMISS COMPLAINT FOR FAILURE TO STATE A CAUSE OF ACTION. This motion, often called a demurrer, will be argued before a judge of the trial court; and if the plaintiff's lawyer cannot fit his claim into one of the established categories of existing law, the chances are overwhelming that the judge will dismiss the case—just like that, without a trial or any hearing on the facts. Then the plaintiff's lawyer must carry the case to an appellate court, or more likely to two successive levels of appellate courts, in an effort to pioneer a new cause of action. Only if the plaintiff wins these expensive appeals will the plaintiff be allowed to go back to the trial court to present the facts of the claim and get a decision on its merits. Like most pioneering tasks, this is a long process, and such cases often take years longer to come to trial than routine cases.

The lawyer who is seeking to create a brand-new cause of action while working on a contingent fee basis is as far out on the limb as he can get. It is much more comfortable to seek new horizons for the common law when you are paid a nice hourly fee for these heroic efforts. When you are working on a contingent fee basis, and you are up against a powerhouse law firm representing a wealthy client willing to spend liberally in order to get your case dismissed or drive you into the ground by attrition, then you are really in trouble. Such were the prospects we faced as Al Gans, Paul Rheingold, and I sat down to draft the complaint in the Nader case.

The Opposition

General Motors was represented in the Nader case by the law firm that Theodore Sorensen joined after leaving the White House staff, Paul Weiss Rifkind Wharton & Garrison, shortened to "Paul Weiss" in lawyer's parlance, even though both Paul and Weiss have been dead for years. Since GM has more than 200 lawyers ("house counsel") on its own corporate staff, and also uses dozens of the nation's largest law firms, its legal officials should know something about selecting lawyers for particular cases. In choosing the Paul Weiss firm for the Nader case, they brought into play one of the ultimate weapons in New York litigation. As *New York Magazine* put it:

> When Charles de Gaulle announced that he was stepping down as President of France, the joke went a year ago, the New York legal community expectantly awaited the announcement that he was joining the law firm of Paul Weiss Goldberg Rifkind Wharton & Garrison.
>
> And why not? Many firms have an outstanding and famous figure in their ranks. But only one can boast of having within the past 10 years a cast of partners that included Adlai E. Stevenson (Governor, U.S. Ambassador, Presidential candidate); Arthur J. Goldberg (U.S. Supreme Court Justice, U.N. Ambassador, Secretary of Labor); Ramsey Clark (U.S. Attorney General); Theo-

dore Sorensen (Presidential adviser); Lloyd K. Garrison (President of N.Y.C. Board of Education); Simon H. Rifkind (U.S. District Court Judge); and Edward N. Costikyan (leader of Tammany Hall).

To this list could be added names like Morris Abram, former president of the American Jewish Committee and of Brandeis University; Representative Elizabeth Holtzman; former Secretary of Labor Willard Wirtz; and former FCC Chairman Newton C. Minow.

Simon H. Rifkind is recognized as the sparkplug of Paul Weiss. Indeed, it did not become one of the nation's leading firms until Rifkind came in as a senior partner in 1950. To quote again from *New York Magazine:*

> Rifkind joined the firm after nine years' service as a judge on the U.S. District Court. Before that, he was a legislative assistant and law partner of Senator Robert F. Wagner, Sr. . . . Under the administrations of former Mayor Wagner, which began at the time Rifkind settled into his office, the slight and mustached Rifkind was one of the most influential men in the city, frequently consulted by his former partner's son. Reportedly, Rifkind helped select Costikyan as the successor to Carmine De Sapio.

Rifkind represented Mrs. Jacqueline Kennedy in her celebrated court battle against papparazzi photographer Ron Gallella and in her disputes with William Manchester, author of *Death of a President,* the study of the John Kennedy assassination. He represented Supreme Court Justice William O. Douglas when Douglas was threatened with impeachment by House minority leader Gerald Ford. He represented New York City in its struggle against insolvency. Under his direction, the Paul Weiss firm has handled many other famous cases, including defense of Spiro T. Agnew against the criminal charges that led to his resignation as Vice-President of the United States.

Paul Weiss's 110 lawyers outnumbered us by more than four to one. (By 1979, they had grown to 178 lawyers.) Size is not always an advantage; there are instances in which a smaller firm has outmaneuvered a larger one, but usually it is a case of the smaller firm's first team against the larger firm's second or third team. We had no such luck. We drew the first team: the captain himself, Simon H. Rifkind, assisted by Martin Kleinbard, one of his top litigation partners. As I contemplated this awesome opposition, it was no comfort to read in the *New York Law Journal* that in their spare time, the Paul Weiss firm softball team had won the 1966 pennant in the Central Park Lawyers League. Incidentally, the cellar team that year, with a record of no wins and seven losses, was Nixon Mudge Rose Guthrie Alexander and Mitchell.

A firm whose litigation power is backed by a client with a bottomless treasury can often cause enough delay and expense to overwhelm a weaker opponent, even if the opponent's cause is just. Although this may appear a bit unsportsmanlike, it is perfectly legitimate practice in the real world of litigation. A tragic example is the marathon litigation between Edwin Howard Armstrong, inventor of frequency modulation (FM) broadcasting, and alleged infringers of his patents, notably Radio Corporation of America (RCA). Although Armstrong was acknowledged as an inventive genius in the class of Edison and it was known that television broadcasting would have to be based upon his FM inventions, his suits against RCA and others in the 1940s dragged on for so many years that they broke his spirit and nearly wiped out his considerable fortune. All the suits eventually were decided or settled in his favor, but Mr. Armstrong did not live to enjoy any court victories. In 1954, while the suits were pending, he committed suicide by jumping out the window of his New York apartment.

The New York state courts are tailor-made for attrition tactics by a wealthy litigant against a weaker one. There are dozens of motions that can be made, such as motions to dismiss the complaint for failure to state a cause of action; motions to strike language from the pleadings (which consist of the plaintiff's complaint and the defendant's answer); motions for summary judgment (a final decision of the case by the judge, without a trial); and motions to compel production of carloads of records and other evidence. Litigants and witnesses may have to endure day after day of questioning in depositions taken in lawyer's offices before the case even gets close to trial, and they can be forced to produce their business and personal records for copying. Disputes arising from depositions may be the subject of further motions. Each of these motions puts a tremendous burden on the weaker party and his attorneys, since the motions are based on voluminous affidavits (containing detailed statements of facts under oath) and briefs (containing legal arguments and citations of pertinent court decisions) which must be analyzed and answered, lest the case be prejudiced or lost. It requires at least forty hours of lawyer's time just to read the affidavits, briefs, and authorities cited in the briefs in an average motion that is vigorously contested.

Motions are usually argued before a judge of the trial court, which is the lowest of three levels in the New York State court system, even though it is called the Supreme Court. But argument of a motion is just the beginning of the attrition process. Nearly every type of motion can be the basis for an appeal to the second level, the Appellate Division of the New York Supreme Court. Each of these appeals before trial (called interlocutory appeals) can hold up the case for six months to a year, even if it only goes as far as the Appellate Division.

In some instances it can go on from the Appellate Division to the third level, the Court of Appeals in Albany, the state's highest court. In this respect New York procedure is unique. In most other states and in the federal courts, after rulings on motions are made by the lower court judge, appeals are usually held in abeyance until the case has been tried, and after that, the trial verdict and all rulings on motions can be appealed; this minimizes the opportunity for attrition tactics. But in New York, a litigant can be bounced up and down on many inter-locutory appeals before the case ever comes to trial.

The Complaint

It was clear that we would have to do some pioneering, but as far as possible we wanted to keep the allegations of our complaint within the boundaries of recognized causes of action. The existing law would have to be stretched to fit the GM-Gillen activities, but it would afford us some basis for resisting the anticipated motion to dismiss the complaint for failure to state a cause of action. We searched through all of American and English tort law, seeking a recognized cause of action based on some legal duty owed to Nader but breached by GM and Gillen. The leading candidates were "defamation," "invasion of privacy," and "intentional infliction of mental distress."

We took a close look at defamation, which is slander if oral and libel if written. Whether oral or written, it requires proof that false statements were made. We had no evidence that any of the investigators had made any false statements about Nader to any of the persons they interviewed, other than to disguise their identities and the purpose of the investigation. The kinds of questions that they asked were not designed to enhance Ralph's reputation, but apparently they did not make any affirmative claims that there was anything wrong with Ralph's personal or professional life. Al Gans found a few cases in which plaintiffs had been allowed to sue for indirect slander based on insinuations contained in questions, but these cases required proof of "special damages," meaning actual financial harm caused by the questions. Since Ralph did not lose a job or any other source of income, we could not claim special damages. Also, there was emerging at that time a new principle that made it impossible for a "public figure" to win a defamation case, unless one could prove actual malice on the part of defendant. There was no doubt that Ralph came within the definition of a public figure. Therefore we decided that we could not successfully sue for any recognized form of defamation.

Al Gans was more encouraging about the law of invasion of privacy—that is, everywhere except in New York, the place where we wanted to sue GM. The late Dean William Prosser of the Hastings College of Law, University of California, a leading authority, has summarized the subject as follows in his highly respected textbook on torts:

> In 1890 there appeared in the Harvard Law Review a famous article, by Samuel D. Warren and Louis D. Brandeis, which reviewed a number of cases in which relief had been afforded on the basis of defamation, invasion of some property right, or breach of confidence or an implied contract, and concluded that they were in reality based upon a broader principle which was entitled to separate recognition. In support of their argument they contended that the growing excesses of the press made a remedy upon such a distinct ground essential to the protection of private individuals against the unjustifiable infliction of mental pain and distress.
>
>   *   *   *
>
> The first state really to come to grips with the doctrine thus advanced was New York. After cases in its lower courts had accepted the existence of the right of privacy proposed by Warren and Brandeis, it fell into the hostile hands of the Court of Appeals in *Roberson v. Rochester Folding-Box Company* (1902), where the defendant made use of a pulchritudinous young lady to advertise its flour without her consent. In a four-to-three decision, with a vigorous dissent, the court flatly denied the existence of any right to protection against such conduct, because of the lack of precedent, the purely mental character of the injury, the "vast amount of litigation" which might be expected to follow, the difficulty of drawing a distinction between public and private characters, and the fear of undue restriction of liberty of speech and freedom of the press.
>
> The immediate result of the *Roberson* decision was a storm of public disapproval, which led one of the concurring judges to take the unprecedented step of publishing a law review article in defense of the decision. In consequence, the next New York legislature enacted a statute (Sections 50–51 of the New York Civil Rights Law) making it both a misdemeanor and a tort to make use of the name, portrait or picture of any person for "advertising purposes or for the purpose of trade" without his written consent. This act remains the law of New York, where there have been upwards of a hundred decisions dealing with it.

Unfortunately for us, the New York statute described by Prosser was construed by the courts to be the exclusive protection of privacy. The only claims that New York courts will recognize as coming within this statute are *appropriations* of the name, portrait, or picture of the plaintiff for advertising or trade purposes without plaintiff's consent. GM had not appropriated anything from Nader, nor had they published any of the results of their investigation. They had *intruded* into his privacy, but the New York courts would not recognize this as an invasion of privacy under the statute. Indeed, New York was about the worst state in which to have your privacy invaded by intrusion, because the statute limited the remedy to cases of appropriation.

Fortunately, most other states did not follow New York's narrow view of privacy rights. Since most of the snooping into Ralph's private life had occurred in Connecticut and the District of Columbia, we studied their decisions, and found that neither of them limited privacy suits to appropriation. They left the door open for intrusion claims, but there were no clear precedents holding defendants liable for intrusion.

Here we were confronted with a classic "Choice of Law" problem. *Conflict of Laws* is a popular course in law schools. It seems to fascinate professors and students. Our fifty states and our separate federal court system, combined with the mobility of our population, create many situations that involve events in two or more states. Which law will the court apply? To lawyers who must deal with conflicts in real cases, they bring nightmares. We may be forced to prepare our entire case without knowing which law will apply until the very end.

In the Nader case, we were claiming that acts of harassment occurred in Connecticut, the District of Columbia, Iowa, Massachusetts, New Hampshire, Pennsylvania, and New York; the greatest in number and importance occurred in the District of Columbia and Connecticut. Because the law of privacy was different in each of those states and hazy in all of them, we had conflicts galore. We seriously considered filing separate suits in Connecticut and the District of Columbia as well as New York, to cover the possibility that the restrictive policy on privacy rights in New York might make its courts refuse to enforce Connecticut and District of Columbia law. We even drafted complaints for these separate suits, but in the end we decided against them and put all our eggs into one basket: New York. We felt that Ralph had carried the David and Goliath act far enough. One man taking on GM in three different courts would give GM too many chances to wreck the case by attrition. They could keep Ralph tied up in procedural aspects of this litigation for years, and wear him out along with his lawyers. I was admitted to practice in Connecticut and the District of Columbia as well as New York, but I did not see how I could cover three hot spots at once. Also, if we split up the claims, no single jury could be told the whole Nader–GM story. Each jury would pass its judgment based upon fragments instead of the overall picture of harassment.

We were confident that we could convince the New York courts to apply the Connecticut and District of Columbia law to such parts of the case as were based on the GM–Gillen activities in those states. We also felt that in New York we had the best chance of getting a large jury verdict and sustaining it in the appellate courts, because of New York's more liberal tradition. In the end, that was the most important factor in deciding where to sue. Despite the disadvantages of New York privacy law and the opportunity for GM to delay the trial by numerous appeals, the final goal was to collect a large sum of money. No matter how much easier the procedures might be in other states, they were not likely to produce the kind of verdict or settlement we were after. Furthermore, Ralph wanted to expand the law in order to discourage future corporate harassment and snooping. New York was the perfect place to do that, since it did not recognize any common-law right of privacy, and therefore we would have a chance to pioneer the concept of a *constitutional* right of privacy. If we could convince the New York courts that there was such a right under the federal Constitution, this would be a higher law than their own precedents, and they would have to change New York law to allow suits for intrusion.

Since Ralph was a public figure, he had relinquished some of his right to privacy. We would have to find a way around precedents such as *Samuel Cohen v. Julius Marx,* better known as *Canvasback Cohen v. Groucho Marx.* The concise opinion of the California intermediate appellate court that disposed of the case in 1949 tells the whole story:

> The essential allegations of plaintiff's complaint as amended were that: in 1933, he had entered the prize ring as a professional boxer under the name of "Canvasback Cohen"; that he continued this ring career, losing decisions, until about 1939, when he abandoned the prize ring as a career; that on January 12, 1949, defendant Groucho Marx broadcast over a program of the defendant American Broadcast Company on its program "You Bet Your Life," "I once managed a prize-fighter, Canvasback Cohen. I brought him out here, he got knocked out, and I made him walk back to Cleveland."
>
> The sole question presented for our determination is: Did plaintiff, by entering the prize ring, seeking publicity, and becoming widely known as a prize fighter under the name of "Canvasback Cohen" waive his right to privacy?
>
> *   *   *
>
> This question must be answered in the affirmative. A person who by his accomplishments, fame, or mode of life, or by adopting a profession or calling which gives the public a legitimate interest in his doings, affairs, or character, is said to become a public personage, and thereby relinquishes a part of his right of privacy.
>
> Applying the foregoing rule to the facts in the present case it is evident that when plaintiff sought publicity and the adulation of the public, he relinquished his right to privacy on matters

pertaining to his professional activity, and he could not at his will and whim draw himself like a snail into his shell and hold others liable for commenting upon the acts which had taken place when he had voluntarily exposed himself to the public eye. As to such acts he had waived his right of privacy and he could not at some subsequent period rescind his waiver.

In view of the foregoing rule and the facts as alleged in the amended complaint, the pleading did not state a cause of action and the trial judge properly sustained a demurrer thereto without leave to amend.

Note that Groucho *demurred* to Canvasback's complaint: he argued that even if everything in Canvasback's complaint was true, it did not spell out a cause of action against Groucho because there was no invasion of any legally protected right of Canvasback. Thus Canvasback Cohen kept his record intact: he was knocked out in the first round without ever laying a glove on his opponent, for he never got to try his case. A simple motion to dismiss made by Groucho's lawyers disposed of his claim, and Groucho never had to go to court to defend himself. We hoped to differentiate that case from ours by showing that *Cohen v. Marx* involved appropriation and publication, while ours involved intrusion.

Our agonizing choices did not end with the decision to sue in New York. We also had to consider *diversity of citizenship* because Ralph was a citizen of Connecticut, while the defendants in the suit were citizens of other states. This gave Ralph the right to file his case in the federal courts under the federal diversity of citizenship statute, a statute designed to protect litigants against favoritism in the state courts which might tilt the scales of justice toward the home team. Since all the defendants had offices in New York, the suit could have been filed in the U.S. District Court for the Southern District of New York, which is located in Manhattan. In diversity suits, the federal courts must apply the choice of law rules of the state in which they are sitting, so the same law applied to us whether we sued in state or federal court.

We pondered this choice for quite a while. The federal court held some advantages for us. For example, interlocutory appeals are not usually allowed in the federal courts, and therefore GM would be prevented from bouncing us up and down like a yoyo, which they could do through the New York state appellate process. But we finally decided against the federal court because it is very difficult for a federal judge sitting in a diversity case to change state law—it must be taken as it is. Since one of Ralph's main objectives was to broaden state law on invasion of privacy, we decided to take our chances in the New York state courts.

We still faced the problem of convincing the New York state

courts that Connecticut and the District of Columbia permitted suits for intrusion. There were only a handful of reported decisions on intrusion under their law, and none of them really covered the facts of the Nader case. When there is no decision directly covering the point at issue, common-law courts often will look to decisions of other states and even to English decisions. So we were forced to create a mosaic of privacy law from the few sparse threads that could be found anywhere in the entire common-law system.

By scraping together all of the several dozen reported privacy-intrusion decisions in the history of *all* of our state and federal courts, we built a foundation for claiming that the common law as a whole would allow suits for: intrusion on the plaintiff's physical solitude or seclusion, eavesdropping by wire-tapping and microphones, peering into the windows of a home, persistent and unwanted telephone calls, prying into plaintiff's bank account, and ostentatious or obtrusive surveillance, known as "rough shadowing." We had to build on the existing case law to fit the Washington surveillance of Nader into the category of rough shadowing, since the shadowing was intended to be unobtrusive, and the reported decisions limited this action to shadowing that was designed to embarass the plaintiff publicly. Prosser's text states that "on the public street or in any other public place, the plaintiff has no legal right to be alone; and it is no invasion of his privacy to do no more than follow him about and watch him there." Nevertheless we decided to include rough shadowing as the effect, if not the intent, of Gillen's work.

If we could interpret the Connecticut and District of Columbia common law to include types of intrusion ruled actionable by other states but never ruled on by those two jurisdictions; and if we could then convince the New York courts to apply this expanded concept of Connecticut and District of Columbia law to the Nader case, despite New York's own limitation of privacy to appropriation cases, we hoped to be in a position to oppose a demurrer successfully. At the outset, this seemed a formidable task, but we were confident that the unusual facts of the Nader-GM controversy would carry us a long way toward what would be, in the average case, a most difficult goal. Many times in the history of tort law, outrageous conduct has caused judges to go beyond strict precedent and enlarge the law to redress the wrong.

Our study of the damage awards in privacy cases showed that we would have to blaze a new trail there, too. Again we reviewed every known privacy case in American history, and found only a dozen that reported actual awards of damages. In a Montana case, $250 was awarded to a tenant whose landlord tried to evict him improperly by moving in with him. In California, a garbage collector who had been harassed out of business by a continuous campaign of malicious conduct extending throughout his whole area of operation had finally collected a mere $5,250 in damages. In Georgia, a woman's room was outrageously invaded while she was a guest in a hotel, and she collected $5,500. These three awards were the only ones we could find for intrusion in the entire jurisprudence of our country. The other awards we found dealt with appropriation, and they were equally paltry. In the seven reported cases in which awards for appropriation were made, the amounts ranged from a low of $300 in a New York case involving appropriation of a photograph to a high of $12,500 in another New York photo-appropriation case. In one New York case an entire motion picture had been appropriated, and the courts reduced a $7,000 jury verdict to a final recovery of $5,000.

Thus, the national high for invasion of privacy damages was $12,500, and the average recovery for the few plaintiffs who actually collected anything was less than $3,000 at the time we drafted the Nader complaint. Despite these low damages, we really had no choice but to proceed under the label of invasion of privacy. It was the only recognized cause of action that covered the GM–Gillen activities, and its damages were based upon intentional infliction of *mental* pain and distress. If we tried to fit into other tort categories, we would be faced with a requirement of showing special damages by way of actual economic loss, which did not exist in the Nader case.

There was one other tort category that we studied hopefully: "intentional infliction of mental distress." This tort is very close to invasion of privacy, but it can occur under circumstances which do not involve a legal invasion or intrusion. It is a relatively young tort, first gaining recognition during the 1930s. It is generally used where there is outrageous conduct which does not quite amount to assault, battery, false imprisonment, defamation, fraud, or breach of contract. The leading English case involved a practical joker who amused himself by falsely telling a woman that her husband was hospitalized with serious injuries. The woman suffered severe nervous shock, which incapacitated her for a long time and nearly drove her insane.

Intentional infliction of mental distress has also been recognized as a cause of action against collection agencies who use intimidating tactics, and against others who improperly use threats and bullying tactics which do not fit into other tort categories. However, its use is severely restricted by the requirement in many states that the mental distress be so severe as to manifest itself in physical illness. The courts are still somewhat reluctant to permit suits based entirely on allegations of mental distress. While the current trend is toward more liberality, at the time of the Nader complaint in 1966 there were very few cases in which substantial damages were awarded for intentional infliction of mental distress without proof of nonmental injuries as well.

The leading case in the District of Columbia required proof of non-mental damages. The only nonmental injury we could claim was that Ralph had lost about eight pounds while under the stress of the GM investigation. We decided to include in the complaint a cause of action based on intentional infliction of mental distress, but we regarded it merely as a backstop in case the causes of action for invasion of privacy were dismissed.

We decided to include four separate causes of action in the complaint. The first cause of action was for invasion of privacy, based upon allegations of harassment that took place in the District of Columbia, Connecticut, Iowa, Massachusetts, New Hampshire, and Pennsylvania, but specifically excluding acts that took place in New York. The second cause of action was also for invasion of privacy, but it was based solely on allegations of harassment that took place in New York. We decided to split up the invasion of privacy allegations into two separate causes of action because we knew that GM would attack the complaint by a motion to dismiss for failure to state a cause of action. If we had left all the privacy claims in one bundle, the court might have dismissed all of them because of the limitation of New York law to appropriation. Also, packaging the New York invasion of privacy as a separate cause of action made it more convenient for us to attempt to make new law by establishing a right to privacy under the federal constitution.

As a third cause of action, we alleged the same acts of harassment as in the first two causes of action for invasion of privacy, claiming that these acts also constituted intentional infliction of mental distress, the tort category that we would fall back on if the privacy claims were dismissed.

There was also a fourth cause of action, based on the tort of "improper interference with advantageous economic relations." Ralph was convinced that GM had used its advertising leverage to coerce newspapers, magazines, radio and television broadcasters into refusing to carry his writings and speeches, in order to suppress his criticism of GM products. This was an extremely difficult claim to prove, since we would need testimony from editorial personnel of newspapers and broadcasters that they had been pressured into censoring or deleting Nader material. At the time that lawyers draft a complaint, they are supposed to include all claims that may be made in the case, so that the opposition can prepare its defenses properly. For this reason, complaints often contain claims that are merely potential at the start of the suit. Many such claims cannot be supported by sufficient evidence and are later dropped from the case. We decided to include these allegations in the fourth cause of action, hoping that we might be able to back them up with concrete evidence. As it turned out, Ralph's increasing popularity as a writer and television personality made it unnecessary to pursue this claim.

The complaint named four defendants: General Motors Corporation; Vincent Gillen Associates, Inc., the corporate name of Gillen's detective agency; Vincent Gillen individually; and Fidelifacts, Inc., a nationwide network of private investigators of which Gillen's agency was a member. It appeared that Gillen had used Fidelifacts to handle some of the Nader investigation outside of New York City.

In the complaint we alleged that when GM learned of the imminent publication of *Unsafe At Any Speed* in 1965, GM "determined and decided to conduct a campaign of intimidating, maligning and otherwise severely injuring plaintiff, to suppress plaintiff's criticism of and prevent his disclosure of information about automotive safety, including the automotive products" of GM; and that GM hired Gillen and his associates to participate in this campaign. The complaint went on to charge six specific types of intrusion and harassment:

> (1) By interviewing under false pretenses many persons who knew plaintiff, and questioning them about, and casting aspersions upon plaintiff's political, social, economic, racial and religious views, tendencies and possible prejudices; his integrity; his sexual proclivities and inclinations; and his personal habits, such as use of intoxicants, narcotics and the like.
>
> (2) By surveillance, direct following, tailing and shadowing him on the streets and into buildings and other places; all of which was accomplished by unreasonable means for an unreasonable length of time and without any legitimate or justifiable purpose, and all of which constituted obtrusive surveillance of such an extreme degree as to be outrageous, oppressive and malicious.
>
> (3) Upon information and belief, by having plaintiff accosted by girls for purposes, inter alia, of entrapment into improper or illicit relationships, and extortion.
>
> (4) Upon information and belief, by making telephone calls to plaintiff of a threatening, obnoxious and harassing nature.
>
> (5) Upon information and belief, by the use of wiretapping, and of electronic or mechanical equipment used for eavesdropping, without consent, against plaintiff and persons with whom he was associated, all of which was as to communications in which plaintiff was a participant.
>
> (6) By conducting a continuing investigation of plaintiff in a manner which, with reasonable foreseeability, would and did violate plaintiff's right of privacy, subject him to harassment and intimidation, and intrude into and invade his seclusion, solitude and private affairs.

This was about as close as we could come to stating a cause of action for a recognized tort, based on the information we then had. We used the legal term "upon information and belief" for items 3, 4, and 5 because we had no proof that any of the defendants had committed those acts, even though Ralph was certain that the two women were sent by someone to entrap him, and that the telephone calls were intended to harass him. He also felt certain that wiretapping had been used on at least one occasion, since he had been put under surveillance at a legislative hearing in Albany, New York, and he had not mentioned his plans for that trip to anyone except during a telephone conversation.

I have found that in drafting the complaint and in preparing the case for trial, it's a good idea to look ahead to the instructions that the judge will give to the jury at the end of the case, particularly on the method of calculating damages. I learned this the hard way during my first jury trial. As the trial neared its end and the time came for the opposing attorneys to submit requested instructions to the judge, I realized for the first time that I had been barking up the wrong tree for a good part of the trial. If I had prepared my requested instructions before the trial, I would have known exactly how to direct all of the proof toward the proper elements of damage. From that time on, I made it a practice to learn the instructions that the judge is likely to give the jury at the very beginning of my work on the case—in fact, during the process of deciding whether to take on the case. Today this task is easier because there are books of "pattern jury instructions" in most states. The New York pattern instruction on damages for invasion of privacy is:

> If you find the plaintiff is entitled to recover, you will award him such amount as, in the exercise of your good judgment and common sense, you find is fair and just compensation for the *injury to his feelings and his mental anguish.*

With that instruction in mind, we alleged in the damage section of the complaint:

> That because of the foregoing wrongful acts and activities of all defendants, the plaintiff was made to suffer ridicule, embarrassment, vexation, humiliation, mental distress, loss of sleep, and injury to a property interest inherent and inextricably woven in plaintiff's personality. That said acts and activities interfered with plaintiff's right to personal health and well being and to be free from emotional distress and mental anguish, and caused plaintiff to be put in fear of the continuation of said wrongful acts and their extension to more violent means of intimidation and harassment, all from unidentified sources and, therefore, completely beyond the power of plaintiff to cope with.

In most states, a tort complaint must include a demand for a specific amount of damages. In the ordinary tort case, neither the lawyers nor the courts pay much attention to the damage claim that is inserted in the complaint. Generally, it is a rough guess at the very highest figure the plaintiff could possibly recover. There are procedural steps which follow the complaint, such as interrogatories and demands for particulars, that require the plaintiff to spell out the details of the damage claims. In the Nader case, we did not treat anything as routine, since we knew that every word in the complaint could form the basis for a motion or an attempt by GM to create unfavorable publicity for Ralph. Therefore, the decision on the amount of damages to sue for was an unusually difficult one. If we set the figure too low, we might be depriving Ralph of a higher judgment or settlement. If we asked for too much money, GM might try to hold the suit up to ridicule and damage Ralph's public image. There was no easy way out of this problem. Finally, we decided that we would claim $2 million as "compensatory damages," to compensate Ralph for the mental distress caused by GM's invasion of privacy.

We decided to add a claim for an additional $5 million for "punitive or exemplary damages." While the legal precedents at the time did not support punitive damages, we felt that it was best to include such a claim to cover the possibility that the law might be expanded before the Nader case came to trial. Punitive damages are not related to the damage actually suffered by the plaintiff. Rather, they are designed to inflict a penalty on the defendant to discourage future misconduct.

As it turned out, the press multiplied our $2 million by 3, because there were 3 counts on which we based our claim for compensatory damages. Our punitive damages claim for $5 million, the press multiplied by 4, because that claim had been based on 4 counts. By such arithmetic our case made the headlines as the "$26 Million Lawsuit." The most Ralph could have recovered at trial was $2 million, but we were stuck with this $26-million label throughout the litigation.

We started the suit by serving the complaint on the defendants on November 16, 1966, just two days before the first anniversary of the beginning of GM's investigation of Ralph Nader. In the process of drafting the complaint, we had to face up to the weak points of the case. We saw our major problems as: lack of precedent for substantial damages for invasion of privacy; lack of financial damage to Nader, causing us to rely entirely on mental distress; Ralph's status as a public figure, which narrowed his right to privacy; restrictive New York law which did not permit suit for invasion of privacy by intrusion; lack of evidence that Gillen's actions were ordered or authorized by General Motors, and probability that GM would claim that Gillen's harassments were unauthorized frolics, as in the Ribicoff hearings; and a Maginot Line of attorney-client privileges erected by GM's legal department in hiring Gillen through Washington attorney Danner, who in turn hired Gillen, who was a lawyer himself. If these claims of attorney-client privilege were upheld, we would not be able to get the evidence needed to establish the responsibility of GM for the actions of Gillen.

Normally a tort suit is brought because the plaintiff wants to collect damages from the defendant. This was one of Ralph's reasons for suing. He wanted to collect a whopping sum of money to be used for the advancement of automobile safety and other consumer activities. But there were two other objectives that were equally important to the rather unusual plaintiff we represented. Above all, he wanted to expose the true role of GM in the Gillen harassment, as opposed to the "frolic" tale which was put forth in Roche's apology to the Senate. He also wanted to expand the legal protection of the individual against corporate snooping and harassment.

We hoped that the complain we had fashioned would serve as a slingshot that would enable our David to accomplish all these objectives. We fired the slingshot on November 16, 1966, by serving the complaint on the defendants and thereby commencing the lawsuit. Then we awaited the reaction of the giant.

The Talking Detective

We knew that GM's huge public relations apparatus would go to work as soon as the complaint was served on them. Since Ralph was anxious to preserve his image by stating his motives for the suit, he distributed the following press statement at the time that we served the complaint:

> This action is brought to remedy a wrong inflicted upon an individual and the public interest in the freedom to speak out against consumer hazards. An individual's right to speak and act freely on such matters without being subjected to intimidation, harassment and invasion of privacy is a cardinal principle of an operating democracy. Especially is this true when human life is at stake.
>
> As has occurred in our nation's past, the courts will be asked to judge the facts and render justice, so that future advocates of safety in automobiles and other products will no longer need to perform acts of courage just to make statements of truth.
>
> Any money damages obtained as a result of the court's decision will be explicitly devoted to the cause of consumer safety for all.

The filing of the complaint made front page news throughout the country. Most papers carried GM's statement, which treated the suit fairly lightly. GM said that they had turned the case over to former Federal Judge Simon H. Rifkind, and that Judge Rifkind "advises that General Motors has no legal liability to Mr. Nader and that in due course the courts will vindicate our position."

Articles by Morton Mintz in *The Washington Post* and by Douglas Robinson in *The New York Times* picked up some of the language of the complaint. Robinson was able to get a statement from Vincent Gillen, who described the charges in the complaint as "a lot of nonsense" and said, "I'm not concerned about the lawsuit at all."

While Nader and General Motors were content with prepared statements, detective Gillen was giving out a different statement to each reporter who called him. In the *New York Daily News,* he was quoted as saying that "the $26 million damages being sought by Nader was a modest amount," adding that he was somewhat flattered to be sued for that amount of money. In *The Wall Street Journal,* he was quoted as denying the charges in Nader's complaint and terming some of the allegations "silly." In a radio interview, he was quoted as asking whether Nader wanted the $26 million paid "in cash or by check." Apparently Gillen was stung by some of the allegations in the complaint, for we had accused General Motors of deliberately selecting Gillen and his associates as "persons who were willing to intimidate, malign and inflict other injuries, in order to obtain the maximum effect" in its campaign of intimidation against Nader.

Most of the newspaper, radio, and television reports picked up the major allegations of the complaint, and while most of them branded it as a "$26 million lawsuit," they also quoted Ralph's statement about devoting the proceeds to consumer safety. GM was content to rely on its advice from Judge Rifkind that the suit was without merit. Only detective Gillen attempted to ridicule the suit, and this tactic gave us what turned out to be the major break in the case. On November 16, 1966, the day that the complaint was served, Gillen gave a telephone interview to Saul Friedman, a member of the Washington Staff of the *Detroit Free Press*. In his article on the lawsuit published in the *Detroit Press* on November 17th, Friedman wrote:

> Gillen said then he investigated Nader under the pretext of making a pre-employment check. He said he usually gets paid about $600 for such investigations, but in Nader's case GM paid him $6,700.
>
> When contacted by the Free Press, Gillen turned on a recorder to tape the telephone conversation.
>
> "He's got no case at all," he said. "It's ridiculous."
>
> Gillen acknowledged he investigated Nader, questioned

his friends and acquaintances and at times had him followed.

"He claims he was followed in all those places—Detroit—Philadelphia—I would refer him to a psychiatrist. He was followed, but not at the times he claims."

From the *Detroit Free Press* article and from the other loquacious interviews that Gillen was giving, it was obvious that he knew how to supply readable copy to the press. Ralph was disturbed about the publication of Gillen's statement that he needed a psychiatrist, since he was in the early stages of establishing his reputation and did not want to suffer any further smears. We talked it over and decided that we would file a separate lawsuit against Gillen, charging that his statement, "I would refer him to a psychiatrist," was defamatory and tended to hold Nader up to ridicule and scorn. We decided to sue for $100,000, hoping that this lawsuit would deter Gillen from further smears.

From the beginning of our work on the case, Gillen's position had fascinated me. GM had used him as the fall guy at the Ribicoff hearing and had been able to bring off the alibi that the harassment of Nader was an unauthorized frolic. This served GM well at the Ribicoff hearing, but after we filed our lawsuit, GM was faced with some tough questions about use of the unauthorized frolic defense. Suppose that GM provided defense counsel for Gillen and agreed to indemnify him by paying any damages assessed against him. If we were able to present these facts to the jury, GM's unauthorized frolic defense might be impaired. It might appear that GM was admitting that they had authorized Gillen's tactics, or that they were ratifying his frolic and thereby making themselves responsible for what he had done. On the other hand, if they cut him adrift and let him defend himself, they would be giving him a very strong incentive to come forward with whatever evidence he might have that GM had instructed him to go as far as he did. Ordinarily this type of situation does not pose a terrible dilemma because most agents who get involved in these situations are not "good for judgment' in that they usually don't have much in the way of assets. But Gillen had a very successful business as well as a fine home and other property which he could have lost if Nader won a suit against him. If we won a judgment against both General Motors and Gillen, we could collect from Gillen as well as General Motors. Therefore, we knew that if Gillen was not being indemnified and defended by General Motors, it would be in his best interests to produce evidence that he had followed GM's instructions in the Nader investigation.

I was especially interested in Gillen's status because it appeared that we had years of work ahead of us in the task of penetrating the screen of attorney-client privilege that GM had erected. The law gives

strong protection to the attorney-client relationship in order to encourage clients to confide completely in their attorneys without fear
that such confidences will ever be used as evidence in court. Under
New York law, the attorney-client privilege even extends to house
counsel, so that attorneys employed by a corporation cannot testify to
conversations or communications with officials of the corporation if
the corporation does not wish them to disclose this information. Therefore, we would have a difficult time forcing any of the GM staff lawyers
to testify about instructions or other communications between them
and other officials of General Motors. On top of that, since Danner had
been retained as an attorney by the legal department of General
Motors, and he in turn retained Gillen as an attorney, while Gillen
retained his own company, Vincent Gillen Associates, Inc., to do the
investigating, there were three layers of attorney-client privilege insulation. We could have claimed that Danner was acting as an agent
rather than as an attorney, and if successful, we might have forced him
to testify about his instructions from General Motors. However, we
might have needed several years of hearings and appeals on that point
alone, by which time Danner and other key witnesses might have
suffered lapses of memory.

The attorney-client privilege belongs to the client, so that General
Motors could prevent any of the three layers of attorneys from testifying on key points in the case if the claim of privilege was upheld. It is
possible for the client to waive this privilege, by publicly revealing
the contents of attorney-client communications outside of court. We
had hoped that the Gillen investigation report which was produced by
General Motors for the Ribicoff subcommittee would be available to us,
and we were prepared to claim that attorney-client privilege as to that
report was waived by GM's production of it for the Senate hearing.
However, GM's attorneys had done their homework. They succeeded
in keeping the Gillen investigation report out of the public record and
out of the public domain. When Nader tried to get a copy of it in the
spring of 1966, he was first advised that it had been returned to
Theodore Sorensen, and finally was told that it had been sent to the
National Archives, where it would not be available to Nader or to the
public. This maneuver would block any claim that GM had waived
attorney-client privilege. It also stymied our preparation of the case,
because we were lacking the names of many people whom Gillen had
interviewed, and any effort on our part to force any of the defendants
to produce a copy of the Gillen investigation report would have been
met by a claim of attorney-client privilege by General Motors.

I was happy that I did not have to face the decision that GM's
lawyers would have to make on Gillen's status. I would have loved to
have a long talk with Gillen, but talking to him was out of the ques-

tion, since he was an adverse party in the litigation and any attempt by me to convince him to come forward with evidence harmful to General Motors might have been branded as attempted collusion. Nevertheless I couldn't help but wonder which way GM would jump on Gillen's status. As it turned out, the answer was revealed to me in a dramatic and unexpected way.

When we drafted the complaint for the second action against Gillen alone for defamation (let's call it the *"Detroit Free Press* action" to distinguish it from the main action), we decided to bring it in the same court as the invasion of privacy suit: the Supreme Court of the State of New York for the County of New York. Under New York procedures, it is possible for the plaintiff's attorneys to serve a summons and complaint on the defendant and officially start the suit without filing any papers in court. The suit can be carried on without filing any papers until a motion or trial comes up in court. We decided to take advantage of this secrecy in order to keep General Motors from interfering with this separate suit against Gillen. We did not want to get bogged down in the expense and attrition of facing General Motors on a second front. Therefore, when we served the summons and complaint on November 19, we did not file it in court.

In order to show Gillen that Nader would not stand for Gillen making derogatory remarks about him in the press, we decided to start discovery immediately in the *Detroit Free Press* suit. All of our state and federal courts allow the parties in civil suits to conduct pretrial discovery (sometimes called disclosure), so that the important facts and contentions of the parties will be known to the opposing attorneys when they come to trial. This takes a lot of the guesswork and gamesmanship out of the trial procedure, and it helps to settle a large percentage of cases before they come to trial. When the opposing lawyers know the strengths and weaknesses of each other's cases, the stage is set for productive settlement discussions, and the expense and uncertainty of trial can often be avoided.

Through discovery procedures, lawyers can force their opponents to produce documents and physical objects for inspection and copying; they can address written questions (interrogatories) to opposing parties, which must be answered under oath; and they can take the depositions of parties and witnesses. Depositions usually are the most productive discovery tool, since they allow extensive questioning on any topics that may come up at the trial or that may lead to the discovery of evidence. Usually depositions are conducted in lawyers' offices, but they may be just as meaningful as testimony in court. The witness must take the oath, and a shorthand reporter takes down and transcribes the testimony, after which it is signed and sworn to by the witness. It was during the deposition of Alger Hiss (taken in the civil defamation case that Hiss brought against Whittaker Chambers) that the evidence leading to his indictment and conviction for perjury was uncovered. And the deposition of then U.S. Senator Edward W. Brooke, taken in his wife's divorce suit, revealed discrepancies in his statements about finances that contributed to his defeat in the 1978 Massachusetts senatorial election campaign.

Depositions of opposing parties can be set up simply by serving a written notice on their attorneys, fixing the time and place. The notice can also specify that relevant books, records, and other documents be produced at the deposition. I served a notice on Gillen's attorney calling for his deposition to be taken at my office on December 16, 1966, and requiring him to produce all relevant documents. Although attorneys can (and often do) make requests or motions to delay the taking of depositions and to oppose the production of documents, Gillen showed up at my office on December 16, with his attorney, Francis T. Maguire, who also happened to be his brother-in-law. The deposition was being taken only in the *Detroit Free Press* case, and therefore no attorneys or representatives from General Motors were present. Indeed, since no papers had been filed in court, neither GM nor its attorneys were aware that we had brought this suit against Gillen or that we were taking his deposition.

I found myself looking forward to meeting Gillen, in spite of his role as one of the villains of the Nader story. I have never been able to resist a character, and even before I met him I was certain that Mr. Gillen was a character. During the Ribicoff subcommittee hearing, he had busied himself by snapping photographs of the participants with a miniature camera that looked as if it had come out of a James Bond film. When his time came to testify, he was not content to identify himself in a sentence or two as the other witnesses had done. Instead, he launched into a long biographical reminiscense, recalling many of the highlights of his professional and personal life, caring not that senators, GM officials, and lawyers were squirming in their seats. He tried to put the subcommittee on the defensive by objecting to a statement that Senator Gaylord Nelson had inserted in the Congressional record, referring to the "seamy trade" of the private detective. To Gillen, Senator Nelson's remark was an insult "not only to me, but to the citizens of every state which licenses private investigators." Another Gillen classic was this exchange with Senator Robert Kennedy on the subject of investigations made under pretext:

> Senator KENNEDY: Let me just ask you a question. You are including the use of false names, including all of these personal questions in connection with Mr. Nader, on the basis that

it is a pre-employment investigation when in fact is was not?
Mr. Nader didn't authorize this.

Mr. GILLEN: When you conduct an investigation under a pretext, you have to carry it out completely, sir. You have to ask
all questions normally pertinent to that pretext. If you do anything less or inject extraneous matters, you run the risk of losing
the pretext.

Senator KENNEDY: But you were lying. What you mean was that
you were conducting an investigation under a lie and that you
had to carry the lie out completely.

Mr. GILLEN: Did you ever have that happen while you were the
Attorney General?

Senator KENNEDY: No, I did not, but I am asking you the
question.

*   *   *

Senator KENNEDY: But you see that your objective was to obtain
a good deal of information, and you were proceeding under a
false pretext.

Mr. GILLEN: Oh, Senator, come on, come on. For goodness
sake, where did I learn to do this? In the FBI.

Senator KENNEDY: Well maybe Mr. Hoover should come up and
testify. Did he teach you this?

Mr. GILLEN: He didn't teach the classes I was in, no sir. His
organization did, yes.

When Gillen materialized at the deposition, he did not disappoint me.
He reminded me immediately of Paul Douglas, the New York radio
sportscaster who had become a popular comic film star in the 1950s.
Gillen was about five foot eleven, looked to be about fifty years old,
and had greying hair. I remembered Frederick Condon's description
of Gillen based upon his "pre-employment interview" of Condon in
New Hampshire:

> Of medium build, but with a peculiar barrel-chested
> quality . . . I think his eyes were blue, and his hair was kinky-
> curly combed straight back neatly, and steel gray in color. He
> had a peculiar voice, probably baritone, and a hesitant way of
> speaking which I cannot put into words but which I would rec-
> ognize at once.

It was Gillen's gravelly voice and his comic-opera manner that reminded me most of Paul Douglas. Gillen's lawyer and brother-in-law,
Francis Maguire, was short, middle-aged, and dignified. He had been
a member of Thomas E. Dewey's crack young prosecuting team in the
New York of the 1930s. Yet there was something about him that
reminded me of a leprechaun.

To put Gillen at ease, I took the deposition alone, even though
we usually like to have more than one lawyer present at a deposition
in case the number-1 man misses a point. So there were just four of

us in my office: Gillen, Maguire, me, and the shorthand reporter. I thought that the best way to start was to give Gillen a chance to talk about himself, so I quickly got into a little ego massage:

> Q: I understand that in the course of your business as a private investigator, you have done work for a number of the largest corporations in the United States, is that correct? A: That's right.
> Q: I think you once mentioned that you had worked for about three quarters of the 500 largest corporations listed in Fortune Magazine, is that right? A: Yes, sir.
> Q: I understand that this is one of the largest investigative agencies of this kind in the world, is that correct? A: Yes.
> Q: Aside from those that furnish plant protection and uniformed guards? A: It is my understanding that I am the largest of this kind in the world, without any plant protection or uniformed guards, strictly surveillance or insurance information.
> Q: I take it that due to the highly sensitive nature of this work that you very often deal with people high up in the corporate hierachy when these corporations hire you, is that correct? A: Yes.

After a few preliminary questions about his first meeting with Danner, I asked him to produce all the records of his investigation which I had requested in the notice of deposition. However, his attorney, Francis Maguire, declined to produce the records at that point. He said that as I proceeded with the examination and as specific documents became relevant, they would be produced. I then went directly into his first meeting with Danner in Washington on January 13, 1966, at which time (as I had learned from his Senate testimony) he received his investigation instructions.

> Q: I understand that you discussed at that time the fact that you believed that the investigation that General Motors wanted could best be carried out by means of the pretext of a pre-employment check, is that correct? A: That is correct.
> Q: Did you at that time fully explain to Mr. Danner just what was involved in a pre-employment check? A: I explained as much as he needed. I knew that Danner had been an FBI agent for some 10 or 12 years, and during that period he had been in charge of at least three offices of the FBI as agent in charge, and he well knew all about the intricacies and the depth of a pre-employment investigation. I didn't have to educate him as to what was required.
>
>   *   *   *
>
> Q: So that in [Nader's] situation, it was necessary to delve deeply into his personal life, is that correct? A: Yes.
> Q: Now, as I remember too, this pre-employment check required you to really delve into all facets of his life, is that correct? A: Yes.

Q: Of course, this was absolutely clear to General Motors and Mr. Danner when they hired you to do this investigation, was it not? A: I had no doubt about it. I had no doubt as to what was clear to me and to him.

*   *   *

Q: Of course, this operation and the pretext of the pre-employment check, this was approved before you ever got the job, isn't that correct? A: Oh, yes.

Up to that point, I could not be sure that Gillen was going to be a helpful witness. He had made it clear that Danner and GM understood what a pre-employment investigation entailed, but he had said pretty much the same thing to the Ribicoff subcommittee. I decided to ease into Danner's instructions a little more. First I asked him how he went about setting his fees for the Nader job, and he produced the first exhibit, which was a letter dated January 19, 1966, from him to Danner, on his lawyer's letterhead, showing that he had set one scale of fees for regular investigation, and a different fee for surveillance, which obviously was contemplated before he took on the job. Then I asked him if there was any other correspondence with Danner in January, and he replied:

> Yes, he wrote me a letter dated February 28th complaining about the fact that we were not getting the kind of information which our client anticipated, and he raised the question of the possibility of justifying my fees.

I then asked for the letter to be produced. He handed me a one-page letter written by Danner on Danner's attorney letterhead addressed to Gillen as an attorney. Attached to Danner's letter was a three-page letter on plain white paper dated February 25, 1966, addressed "Dear Dick" and signed "Eileen." These four pages became Exhibit 2 of the deposition. I read them quickly, and I could hardly believe my eyes. This one exhibit was enough to destroy the GM defense that they had been investigating Ralph's connection with the Corvair litigation. It also proved that rather than GM being annoyed at Gillen because he was going too far in his investigation, just the opposite had happened. GM was angry because Gillen was not going far enough in his delving into Nader's personal life! Danner's letter to Gillen read as follows:

Re: Ralph Nader

Dear Vince:

I am attaching hereto a copy of a letter dated February 25, 1966, from our client. As you can gather from the letter and I certainly note from my telephonic conversations, these people are not too happy with the investigation, nor am I. It just does not seem to me that good investigative techniques are being used and too much time has been spent in detailing long-winded dissertations on the same subject, namely, that Nader is a brilliant fellow who went to Princeton and to Harvard and who wrote a book. As pointed out in the attached letter, there are many areas as yet uncovered which might divulge some very interesting information.

You know and I know from what we have learned to date about Nader that this fellow hasn't hit a lick of work in years, apparently lives by his wits and he just couldn't be that perfect. Frankly, I think we are going to have trouble justifying your bills unless information is unearthed that hits a little closer to home wherein Nader's background is concerned than we have come up with to date. I am also attaching hereto the copyright statement of Nader's book and the transcript of the Senate Hearing as mentioned in the client's letter.

I think it would be well to stop interviewing Nader's friends, get to digging into his bank accounts, stock transactions, sources of income, etc., or if you think this is impossible, let me know and we will see what the client wants done.

Sincerely yours
Dick

The Dear Dick letter, three pages long, was replete with complaints that Gillen was not digging up enough dirt on Nader:

> Dear Dick,
>
> I am still disappointed with the odds and ends we are receiving. It strikes me that the reporting is being duplicated by two or three people doing the same thing but not knowing of each other.
>
> It also strikes me that everyone is going overboard to impress us with what a great, charming intellectual this human being is—Eagle-Scout type.
>
> *   *   *
>
> Neither the report of the 14th nor the 17th mentions money. This was quoted on the telephone on the 14th and 23rd. Savings account, stock?

Eileen went on to complain to Dick that on February 14 she had requested a number of personal items about Nader to be checked and had not received any reply. She gave further detailed instructions listing items that should be checked out by the detectives. There was not one word in her letter or in Danner's letter about the Corvair litigation or any possible connection that Nader might have with it. The letter ended with this message:

> Well friend, have fun. I will be talking to you. Call if anything great appears.
>
> Sincerely,
Eileen

After a quick reading of the Dear Dick letter, I was convinced that
Gillen would not have produced it if GM was indemnifying him. I felt
a surge of excitement at the prospect that the pressures of litigation
were forcing him to become a star witness for us. But I still didn't
know how much helpful evidence he would disclose; so, instead of
questioning him in detail about the Dear Dick letter right away, I went
on to other questions which I hoped would disgorge all of the documents that he had brought along. I asked him about some other documents, and he then revealed that he had been instructed by members
of the legal department of GM to destroy some documents between
March 10, 1966 (the date on which Senator Ribicoff requested GM to
produce its records of the Nader investigation) and March 22, the
date of the Ribicoff hearing. So now we had evidence of an attempted
cover-up.

Despite his instructions, Gillen took the precaution of saving
extra copies of some important documents. I asked him to produce a
copy of the complete investigation report which had been given to the
Ribicoff subcommittee and which had later been sent to the National
Archives, out of our reach. He handed over the entire report, all 117
pages of it. The report summarized every interview and every step
taken by Gillen's investigators. Now at last we had the names and
addresses of all the potential witnesses who could testify to GM's
campaign against Nader. Not only did he produce the entire report,
but he testified that the first page, which contained a statement of the
purpose of the investigation, had been changed prior to its submission
to the Ribicoff subcommittee, in order to minimize the embarrassment
to GM.

I kept asking for copies of all correspondence with Danner and
GM officials regarding the Nader investigation, and he kept producing them. Among these gems was Exhibit 7, a copy of Gillen's six-
page letter to GM president James Roche dated April 5, 1966, outlining all the mistakes that Gillen found in GM's handling of the
Nader affair. As I read this letter, I wondered who had drawn the
distasteful assignment of delivering it to the austere Mr. Roche in his
GM executive suite.

GM chairman Frederick G. Donner was not left out of Gillen's
juicy correspondence. On May 27, 1966, Gillen wrote a four-page
letter to Donner which became Exhibit 8 in the Gillen deposition.
Again, I did not ask him any questions about the letter because I
wanted to keep moving forward to scoop up all available documents.
But I couldn't resist taking a peek at Gillen's letter to GM's chief
executive officer. I spotted a few gems:

> . . . if you will search the department files adequately, you may
> find a memorandum dated February 25th, written by a member

of the legal department, clearly indicating that our investigation was within the scope of our instructions from the legal staff.

*   *   *

I do not mind Mr. Roche's apology for *any* investigation. What I do find unpalatable is the continued implication that the apology was for the method, the surveillance, and the questioning in certain areas. These were all adopted with the concurrence or instructions of your Washington counsel and duly reported in plenty of time for corrective action by General Motors. I refuse to be the "fall guy."

The "memorandum dated February 25th" was the Dear Dick letter. Thus, Gillen's letter to GM chairman Donner corroborated his claim that everything he did for GM was carried out under their instructions.

Gillen produced several other interesting documents during the first session of the deposition. Exhibit 11 consisted of notes about his various trips to Detroit between March 11 and March 22 during the "cover-up." Exhibit 12 was a copy of Gillen's instructions to his staff and his correspondence about the scope and direction of the investigation. It was most important for what it did *not* say: it made no mention of the Corvair litigation or any possible connection between Nader and the Corvair plaintiffs' attorneys. Here was the very heart of the investigation, the master detective's instructions to his field agents, and it said nothing about the subject that GM claimed to be the central purpose of the investigation.

Gillen had brought twelve documents to the first session of the deposition. I wanted some time to read them and prepare to question Gillen about them, so we agreed to continue the deposition on December 21. Before adjourning, I tried to pin down the facts about the Detroit "cover-up" sessions, swinging cautiously from limb to limb:

Q: Just to refresh your recollection, the Congressional Record of March 10, 1966 states that [Senator Ribicoff] has invited Ralph Nader and the President of General Motors and the detective agency to appear before the Senate Subcommittee on Executive Reorganization, on March 22, 1966. The Congressional Record states that. So that when you met with Mr. Danner in Detroit on March 11, 1966 and when you met with General Motors' legal staff on March 12, 1966, in Detroit, all the General Motors people knew that they were going to appear before the Senate Committee and were going to be called on to produce the record of the Ralph Nader investigation; is that correct? A: I assume they did.
Q: Did they discuss the Senate hearing? A: Yes, that was the target date.
Q: In other words, one of the purposes of the meeting in Detroit was to prepare for the Senate hearing, is that correct? A: Yes.
Q: In fact, was that the main purpose of the meeting in Detroit on March 2th? A: That was my understanding.

The Gillen deposition stretched out over four more sessions during December 1966 and January 1967, all of them held in my office. Each time, I questioned Gillen in detail about documents that he had produced in the preceding session, and then went on to cover new ground that brought new documents into the picture. Gillen produced practically every document that was referred to in his testimony—hundreds of pages of business records, all of them relevant to the Nader investigation.

During the Ribicoff subcommittee hearing, Gillen testified that Danner had given him certain records of GM's past investigation of Nader during their meeting at Danner's office on January 13, 1966. However, those records were not produced at the Ribicoff hearing. I asked Gillen to produce them, and sure enough, he handed over copies of two seven-page documents. The first, our Exhibit 16, was a report by an investigator named William F. O'Neill, who made a brief investigation of Nader in and around his home town of Winsted in November of 1965. Again, this exhibit was most important for what it did *not* show. It gave very routine information of a type that one would expect in a retail credit report. It said nothing about anti-Semitism, drugs, homosexuality, or any of the highly personal items that were included in Gillen's investigation.

The next document, Exhibit 17, was another seven-page report, on plain white paper. It was a dossier containing all the useful information that GM had on Nader as of January 1966. Of course, all of the information in the dossier had been compiled by GM through persons other than Gillen, since it was handed to Gillen by Danner on January 13, before Gillen was given the job of investigating Nader. Putting Exhibit 16 (the O'Neill Connecticut investigation report) alongside Exhibit 17 (GM's dossier on Nader as of January 13, 1966) it was easy to see that the source of the embarrassing questions later asked by Gillen's agents was Exhibit 17, GM's own dossier, which was handed along from Eileen Murphy to Dick Danner to Vincent Gillen. On the front page was the smear, "Father is allegedly anti-Semitic and quite vocal about it." The dossier went on from there to catalogue the items that GM wanted investigated. They covered just about everything that could be put in the form of an embarrassing question—everything, that is, except the Corvair litigation, which was never mentioned. I question Gillen about the GM dossier (Exhibit 17):

> Q: Prior to January 13, 1966, you had no personal knowledge of Ralph Nader's background, is that correct? A: That is correct.
> Q: So any ideas that you got about looking into anti-Semitism and homosexuality and dope addiction came from your meeting with Mr. Danner on January 13th, is that correct? A: Yes.

Q: As far as documentation is concerned, all three of these sub-jects were first mentioned in Exhibit 17, which is the memoran-dum from Miss Eileen Murphy to Mr. Danner concerning Mr. Nader, is that right? A: If you are referring to those docu-ments which I obtained from Danner that day, that is correct. Q: In any event, prior to your receiving Exhibit 17 in Mr. Danner's office on January 13, 1966, you had no knowledge or information which would lead you to investigate anti-Semitism, homosexuality or dope addiction of Ralph Nader, is that right? A: That is right. Q: Did you or anybody in your organization or any of your representatives ever speak with or contact Mr. O'Neill, who is the author of Exhibit 17? A: Not in the past couple of years.

I was familiar with the Corvair products liability litigation and knew many of the plaintiffs' lawyers who were involved in it. The great majority of the cases had been filed in California, Michigan, Illinois, and Florida. After establishing that Gillen was a nationwide operator who was frequently hired by large corporations to do work in several areas of the country, I then tried to drive another nail into the coffin of the Corvair litigation defense:

Q: Danner and General Motors did not request or direct you to do any investigation in the States of California, Michigan, Illi-nois or Florida, is that right? A: Yes, they did not. Q: They did not give you any leads to any potential witnesses or people to be interviewed in the States of California, Michigan, Illinois or Florida, is that correct? A: That is correct. Q: Neither Danner nor General Motors ever told you where the Corvair products liability cases were pending, did they? A: Well, Danner in the first instance did say that they seemed to be concentrated among three or four lawyers, and I think he did mention those general areas of the country. Q: But you were not told to make any investigation in those areas concerning those lawyers directly, is that right? A: That is right. Q: You were not told any of the details about the Corvair liti-gation such as specific claims that were being made by the plaintiffs about the specific design elements of the Corvair that they thought were faulty, were you? A: No, he didn't tell me that. We did not get into details. Q: You were not given the names or addresses or descriptions of any known expert witnesses or known consultants who were working with the plaintiffs or the plaintiffs' attorneys in the Corvair cases, were you? A: No.

It was obvious to me that if GM's legal department had really thought that Nader was involved in the Corvair litigation, they could have found out (probably without cost) by simply calling the insurance lawyers who were defending GM in the four states where the cases

were pending. It would be difficult to imagine a method less likely to
ascertain Nader's connection with those cases than to engage a Washington lawyer to hire a New York investigator, telling neither of them
anything about the Corvair cases and giving them no instructions on
that subject.

On the last page of the seven-page GM dossier there were notes
in the handwriting of Eileen Murphy. There was an intriguing reference
to "IRS" that I wanted to know more about:

> Q: Now, the first thing I want to ask you about concerning
> Miss Murphy's notes is this. On Page 7 are the initials IRS; what
> did that refer to, what did the initials IRS stand for there?   A:
> Internal Revenue Service. Danner went down the line on this list
> with me. And I told him that I wasn't making any attempt to
> get any records out of the Internal Revenue Service, I just
> wouldn't do it.
> Q: There is no legal method of obtaining information about an
> individual from the Internal Revenue Service, is there? A: I
> don't know.
> Q: You refused to do it?   A: I refused to do it. I have many
> requests for individual Internal Revenue Service records, and I
> have absolutely refused to do it. And I wasn't going to do it for
> Danner or anybody else.

Gillen's testimony about his discussion of the seven-page GM
dossier with Danner brought me into a position to uncover the next
bonanza:

> Q: What was your discussion with Mr. Danner at that point?
> A: Among the things to cover, his possible use of dope or his
> associates, male and female. If he is sleeping with women, who
> are they. If he is not sleeping with women, maybe he is sleep-
> ing with boys. And, in fact, get anything on him that could get
> Nader out of their hair. This is quotes now. Shut him up.
> Q: Was it made clear to you by Mr. Danner that the purpose of
> this investigation was to "get anything you could get on Mr.
> Nader so as to shut him up and get him out of the hair of Gen-
> eral Motors?" A: Yes.
> Q: That was made clear to you by Mr. Danner on January 13,
> 1966, is that correct?   A: Yes. And it was also at the time
> that he discussed that when we found him we would put him
> under surveillance. I said, "Isn't he testifying? Maybe we can
> pick him up there." And he said, "Oh, let him shoot his mouth
> off all he wants to. If we find him testifying, sure, then you can
> start tailing him."

Now we had Danner giving the purpose of the GM investigation as the
search for something that would shut Ralph Nader up, and we had him
giving orders to put Nader under surveillance while he was serving

as a witness, contrary to Danner's assurances to Senator Ribicoff's sub-committee that they would not have put Ralph under surveillance if they had known he was going to be a Senate witness. I questioned Gillen further about their knowledge of Nader's status as a witness:

> Q: Mr. Danner instructed you to switch from full surveillance to spot surveillance by picking Nader up right after he testified before the Ribicoff Subcommittee, is that correct? A: No, to switch from full surveillance to spot surveillance thereafter and suggested that one time that I might pick him up would be after his testimony in some forthcoming hearing.
>
> Q: I understand, then, that Mr. Danner did not know the exact day on which Mr. Nader was going to testify for the Ribicoff Committee, but he did convey to you that he knew that Mr. Nader was going to testify before that Committee at some future date, is that correct? A: Yes.

To pin down Danner's knowledge of Nader's legislative activities, I showed Gillen an exhibit of my own:

> Q: Now, Mr. Danner gave you a copy of the book, *Unsafe At Any Speed,* at that first meeting? A: Yes.
>
> Q: I will show you this document and ask you if it is a correct copy of the dust jacket of that book, *Unsafe At Any Speed,* which Mr. Danner showed you at that time? A: It appears to be an exact copy of that which I received. I do not have my original dust jacket with me.
>
> Q: In any event, the book which he gave you was the original hard-covered edition with the dust jacket, which is a black cover with a red picture on the front, is that correct? A: Yes.
>
> Q: And it contained, particularly, this wording, as you recall, "Ralph Nader is an attorney who was an advisor to the Senate Subcommittee investigating automobile hazards," is that correct? A: Yes, sir.

Good old Exhibit 17, the GM dossier on Nader, also contained evidence that the GM bloodhounds knew of Nader's connection with the Ribicoff auto safety legislation. On the seventh page of Exhibit 17, in the handwriting of Eileen Murphy, there appeared this note:

> Mention the work with Ribicoff Committee—preparing questions for the hearings July '65 at which [GM Chairman Frederick Donner] appeared with J. Roche.

I was intrigued by Gillen's phrase, "This is quotes now." I had learned enough about Gillen to regard that statement as a sign that he might have recorded his conversation with Danner in the latter's office on January 13. Finally I asked him the question directly, and he said that he had in fact recorded the historic meeting with Danner. When I asked him to produce the tape, he said that he could not locate it, but that he did have an edited written transcript. I kept pressing for production of the tape, but it was apparent that either Gillen no longer had it or that there were some things on it that might embarrass him. When I read the edited transcript, I decided that it went about as far as any evidence could go to help our case, and so I did not press further for the tape. Here are some key excerpts from the edited transcript, "D" signifying Dick Danner, GM's attorney, giving instructions to "G," Vincent Gillen, soon to be commissioned as GM's investigator of Ralph Nader:

D: This is a new client . . . could be a very important one. They came to me and I'm anxious to do a good job because they have had trouble getting investigators . . . they want me to work with someone I trust . . . . . It concerns this fellow who wrote this book . . . . . . They have not found out much about him. His stuff there is pretty damaging to the auto industry . . . . What are his motives? Is he really interested in safety? Who are his backers, supporters? . . . . some left wing groups try to down all industry . . . . How does he support himself? Who is paying him, if anyone, for this stuff? How did he get all this confidential information from government reports or committees? . . . Was he put in there deliberately? . . .
G: Is he an engineer?
D: No evidence of it; he went to Harvard Law . . . . They made some half-baked investigation in Connecticut . . . . . He is not there and apparently is or has been in Washington . . . . I don't know where he is . . . . strange, but he doesn't show anywhere in any directory . . . . Here is what they gave me on him . . . . . You take this with you and a copy of the book and take over from here . . . .
G: This is dynamite. I remember reading a review of three books on this stuff in the New York Times recently . . . . This book got the biggest play.
D: Yes, that's why they are interested . . . . . apparently he's in his early 30's and unmarried . . . . . interesting angle there . . . . . They said "Who is he laying? If it's girls, who are they? If not girls, maybe boys, who?" . . They want to know.
G: Wow, this is dynamite that might blow, Dick, you know that.
D: Yes, he seems to be a bit of a nut or some kind of screwball . . . . . Well, they want to know, no matter what . . . They want to get something, somewhere, on this guy to get him out of their hair, and to shut him up. I know it is a tricky one . . . . . that's why I called you . . . . I told them how you handled . . . . . . and thought you could do this . . . . You're a lawyer, as I recall . . . . . How do you think you will approach this?
G: I have been trying to figure that out because you know we

will have to get close to him to get what they want . . . You know . . . . are they prepared for the worst? The subject is certain to learn of the investigation.

D: Yes . . . . that's why I told them I would know just how you plan to go about it and I want your ideas to see if they fit in with my ideas . . . .

G: I think the answer will be found in a thorough pre-employment investigation. We make hundreds of them every week . . . . .

D: That's a good idea . . . . about the safest . . . . I go along with that . . . Excellent . . . . . .

G: But, Dick, somebody must be in a position to say they authorized you to ask for it . . . If it blows . . . . . who will be there to say he is interested in hiring him? . . . A lot of organizations would be glad to have this fellow with his research and writing ability, from what I see in the book right now.

D: I'll take care of that.

G: You'd better give me an idea of who . . . because I may be forced to identify my client . . . suspicion is bound to be on the auto industry. I'm a lawyer . . . .

D: Why don't you be co-counsel with me and hire your organization to do the job?

G: I've done that. Good, but I believe as a private investigator in New York I would have to identify my client . . . I'm not sure as a lawyer I would, but I would just say that I am co-counsel with you . . . What is it here in DC?

D: I'm not sure, but I will take care of that and this idea will add an extra layer . . . so we'll be that much safer. Don't worry about it . . . Who will you use in Washington?

G. Dave Shatraw, an ex-agent, do you know him, he's retired now?

D: . . . . Good, if you can't readily determine who his supporters are, who he is dealing with, his sources of income, we may have to put a tail on him . . . Don't do it without my ok . . . . I think a tail will show who he is contacting . . . . His language in articles and the book is appearing in law suits in several parts of the country . . . . . . I'll tell you in the strictest confidence, to be revealed to no one, even in your own organization . . . . General Motors . . . . . If we handle this right, both of us will get a lot of business from them.

G: They must have membership in many organizations . . support them well . . . . Many of those groups could actually use a fellow with Nader's ability . . . . . It won't have to be directly connected with the automotive business, the further the better . . . That's the answer.

D: He's Syrian, or something, and maybe you will find an anti-Semitic angle which is mentioned in O'Neil's reports . . . . that will be interesting to Ribicoff . . . . . Here are other suggestions . . .

G: I'm not going to fool around with the Internal Revenue Service . . . . .

D: Well, you know a lot of people like to play investigator . . .

There is a lot of stuff listed there and I don't know just what it all means . . . Sniffing gave someone the idea that maybe he's on dope . . . . .
G: I know that Dr. Leary was experimenting with students at Harvard about that time . . . . . . He was kicked out of Harvard because of it . . . . . .
D: Some of those Harvard fellows are very liberal . . . hurt American industry cleverly . . . What they are really after is to get something that will shut him up and get him out of their hair. What gives him the expertise to write a book on safety? What is his knowledge of safety? Has he an engineering background? . . . . . . Where was he during Korean war . . . girls, who and if not, boys . . . . What are his motives? What lawyers is he dealing with? They found his name only once a year or so ago. . . . Some address in Washington . . . He's not in the phone book here now . . . It's strange . . . There's something somewhere, find it so they can shut him up.

Gillen also produced the tape of his recorded telephone conversation with Danner on March 10, 1966, the day after GM issued its press release in which it claimed that the Nader investigation was a routine operation to determine his connection with the Corvair litigation. The tape was played at the deposition and taken down word for word by the shorthand reporter, becoming our Exhibit 18. The most interesting item in that conversation was an admission by Danner that the statement in the GM press release (alleging that the purpose of the investigation was to determine Nader's connection with the Corvair litigation) was a pretext:

Mr. GILLEN: I thought their statement was very good. Now, did you get a page from me in this morning's mail?
Mr. DANNER: Yes.
Mr. GILLEN: Is that all right?
Mr. DANNER: Yes. Now you see, that was the pretext under which it was conducted.
Mr. GILLEN: Right.
Mr. DANNER: Their statement says this was a routine to determine what connections if any he may have had with attorneys prosecuting the Corvair cases.

The page that Gillen sent to Danner by mail was the new cover page for Exhibit 4, the 117-page Gillen investigation report, which Gillen testified that he had changed in order to minimize the embarrassment to GM. I traced the idea of changing the cover page back to Danner:

Q: On Page 2 of Exhibit 18, when you stated, "Now did you get a page from me in this morning's mail," you are referring to the changed first page of the Nader report, which is Exhibit 4 on this deposition, is that correct? A: Yes.

Q: Of course, the change in that first page was made at the request of Mr. Danner earlier that week, is that correct?   A: Yes.

Q: In other words, it was not your idea to voluntarily change that page; that instruction came specifically from Mr. Danner, is that correct?   A: Yes.

The March 10th telephone conversation between Gillen and Danner went on:

Mr. GILLEN: Well, I tell you, I on my own called this reporter back from Newsday—Newsweek, rather, and I put a little bug in his ear. I said, "You guys are missing—you're looking for a story. There is a story here at Winsted." I said, "Somebody jumped all over me for asking a question regarding his anti-Semitism," and I said, "That's all I'm going to say," and hung up.

Mr. DANNER: Yes.

Mr. GILLEN: Now, let him defend his mother and his brother and his father (laughing).

Mr. DANNER: Yes, that would be good for Ribicoff to know.

Mr. GILLEN: Yes. This may come out, and I want you to know I planted that seed, and that's the only place I found that you may be able to hurt him—if you get these Jewish writers on his neck up here.

I thought of the Jewish writers—Sidney Zion of the *New York Times,* Morton Mintz of the *Washington Post,* Saul Friedman of the *Detroit Free Press*—whose relentless bird–dogging of the Nader story had finally forced GM to admit that the investigation was theirs, and who kept on writing the story of the investigation and the litigation even though it involved the largest industrial corporation (and one of the largest advertisers) in the world. If it hadn't been for those particular Jewish writers, GM's role might never have been revealed, and Congress would probably not have passed the automobile design safety law in 1966.

The goodies continued to pour out of Gillen's attaché case. Exhibit 24 was a yellow pad containing twenty-eight pages of notes that Gillen had made in Detroit between March 11 and March 20 during the "cover-up" meeting with GM's legal staff. I took him through those twenty-eight pages of notes and pinned down many facts about his Detroit discussions concerning the documents that were supposed to be produced for the Ribicoff subcommittee. His rough handwritten notes in chronological sequence were the strongest possible corroboration of his story of that cover-up. He also produced many other notes, both handwritten and typewritten. From these notes it was apparent that Vincent Gillen was no fool. In fact, he was beginning to

look to me like the smartest of all the GM employees and agents who
had worked on the Nader investigation. He covered his tracks by making a record of just about anything that was said to him by anyone connected with GM.

In some of his answers, Gillen referred to other jobs that he had
done for GM prior to the Nader investigation. I wanted to compare the
methods used in those investigations with the circuitous route taken in
the Nader investigation:

> Q: Incidentally, the prior work that you did for General Motors,
> was that done directly for them or was it done through a sub-
> terfuge?   A: Everything I had done for them was done directly
> through them.
> Q: You directly billed General Motors for your work?   A: Yes.
> Q: You were paid directly by them, is that correct?   A: Yes.
> Q: Would you say you had done quite a few jobs for them be-
> fore? How many, about?   A: I'd say excluding those which
> were strictly pre-employment and credit checks of employees
> that there may have been over the past eight years perhaps
> twenty or so investigations. As to that, in one of my first inter-
> views in Detroit with Mr. Power, he mentioned that my previ-
> ous investigations for General Motors had been in personnel
> work. I remember very vividly asking him to repeat that. And I
> said, in effect, "Well, if you say so, I'll go along with that, that
> it could be so construed. I'll go along with what your records
> show." They were all handled through a man who I under-
> stand is in the personnel function.

He produced 26 reports of other jobs done for General Motors between
1959 and 1963. He did each of these jobs directly, using no subterfuges
or intermediaries. This was convincing evidence that the Nader investigation conducted through the screen of Danner was hardly a "routine
investigation," as claimed by GM at the Ribicoff hearing. He also produced his financial records of all 27 jobs done for General Motors,
which showed a total of $27,599.09 billed to GM, including $6,702.03
on the Nader case, which he had billed to Danner rather than to GM
directly. This showed the disproportionate cost of the Nader job.

Toward the end of the deposition, I tried to pull together the crucial facts that Gillen had revealed. First I took some precautions:

> Q: You never met me before this deposition, is that right?   A:
> That is correct.
> Q: You never met me outside of my office during the actual
> taking of this deposition?   A: That is correct.

Then I started to sum up:

> Q: Now, the real purpose of the investigation of Ralph Nader,
> as conveyed to you on January 13, 1966, at the first meeting with

Danner, was to get something on Nader which General Motors could use to discredit him so as to get him out of their hair, in Danner's words, and to shut him up, in Danner's words, is that correct? A: Yes.

Q: Those instructions were never countermanded by Danner or by General Motors, is that correct? A: Yes.

Q: There was no change of purpose ever conveyed to you after January 13 by either Danner or General Motors, is that correct? A: Yes.

Q: Therefore, everything that you did and everything that you directed others to do on the Ralph Nader matter was done pursuant to that purpose, which Danner stated to you on January 13, is that right? A: Yes.

Q: And everything of any consequence that you and your employees and correspondents did on the Ralph Nader matter was communicated to Danner in written reports which are contained in Exhibit 4 here, is that correct? A: Yes.

Q: At no time did either Danner or General Motors complain to you or indicate to you that your investigation had gone too far, is that correct? A: Yes. The fact is just the opposite—it had not gone far enough.

Q: Their only complaint was that you had not gone far enough in digging up material which General Motors could use to personally discredit or embarrass Nader, as expressed in Exhibit 2, is that right? A: Yes.

Q: Therefore, you did exactly the job that Danner and General Motors hired you to do, is that right? A: Yes.

Q: You did not at any time exceed the authority conveyed to you by Danner, did you? A: No.

Q: Did you ever violate or go beyond the instructions given to you by Danner? A: No.

Q: Did you ever go beyond any instructions or authority given to you by General Motors? A: No. In fact, I went over this whole thing on several occasions with Danner, both in Detroit and in Washington, and I pointed out to him that I had been out of the FBI for many years and he had been an agent in charge of several offices, and I asked him what we had done that we should not have done, and he said there was no complaint that he could find with what we had done, that it was fine excepting that our men should have been a little bit more astute in the surveillance in the Senate Office Building.

Q: That refers to being more astute in the sense of not being detected themselves, is that correct? A: Yes.

Q: Now, Danner told you that he had full authority from General Motors to hire you on January 13th, is that correct? A: Oh, yes.

Q: And he also indicated that he had authority to direct you to use the pre-employment pretext, is that right? A: He asked me how I would go about it, and we agreed that that would be the best way to approach it. So I assumed he had authority in as much as he agreed with it, and he is an experienced investigator.

Q: In addition to stating to you that he was authorized by

General Motors to retain you for this investigation, he also
turned over to you on January 13 the General Motors investigation file on Nader, Exhibits 16 and 17, up to that time, so that
you also knew from that, from delivery of those documents,
that Danner had authority which came from General Motors,
is that correct?   A: It was obvious, yes.

Finally, after 166 pages of Gillen testimony and hundreds of pages of
documentary evidence contained in the 69 marked exhibits, we adjourned the deposition subject to it being reopened if any other questions occurred after reading the voluminous documents. Gillen signed
and swore to his deposition on January 21, 1967. We reopened the deposition on March 13, 1967, to cover some miscellaneous questions
that arose out of the documents which I had not had a chance to study
completely.

When we completed the second session of the deposition on December 21, I asked the shorthand reporter to do a rush job of typing it
up. I had a special reason. Ralph Nader was coming through New York
on December 22 on his way to Winsted, going home for Christmas for
the first time since he became a national figure. I had been keeping him
posted on Gillen's deposition by telephone, and he was eager to read
the transcript and the exhibits himself. He stopped by the office and we
rode the New Haven Railroad together, since it went through my home
town on the way to Winsted. As the old train rattled through the evening
snow, Ralph read the deposition. I was treated to the sight of our client
smiling, then chuckling, then shaking up and down with laughter.

I'd been through a lot of discovery proceedings, but I'd never had
such a treasure chest opened in my lap. In a single deposition taken in
an entirely separate lawsuit within a few weeks of the start of the main
action for invasion of privacy, we had solved many of the problems of
the main action. We had learned from the horse's mouth what detective
Gillen's real instructions were, and we now had stacks of documents
originating from GM and Danner, showing clearly that GM had authorized, inspired, and approved the harassment of Ralph Nader. We
had broken through the barrier of attorney-client privilege which might
otherwise have prevented us from getting any of this evidence. We had
destroyed the Corvair defense through GM's own documents. If Gillen
had not had an incentive to bare his soul and avoid being the fall guy in
the lawsuit, we might never have gotten any of this evidence. It would
have taken us several years of hard work in the trial and appellate courts
just to get the right to question witnesses about GM's instructions and to
examine whatever documents GM saw fit to produce.

On the plaintiff's side, all of us were elated over this breakthrough. But after we calmed down, we faced a big question: how could
we use all the Gillen evidence in the invasion of privacy lawsuit against

GM, since at the moment it existed as evidence only in the *Detroit Free Press* defamation suit against Gillen?

A Request For Admissions

In an ordinary case, it would have been simple enough to schedule another deposition of Gillen in the privacy suit and ask him the same questions as were put to him in the *Detroit Free Press* suit. However, we knew that in the GM privacy case, we faced years of motions and appeals before we reached the deposition stage. Why should we waste all that time and money when we already had practically all the proof that we needed to win the case? We could avoid that delay if we could devise a way of getting Gillen's *Detroit Free Press* deposition testimony into the privacy case.

We finally decided to use a discovery device called a "notice to admit" (also known as a "request for admissions"). Under §3123 of the New York Civil Practice Law and Rules (as under the rules of most courts), each litigant is allowed to serve a written notice requesting other parties to admit or deny the truth of matters of fact or the authenticity of documents. Generally this device is used for basic facts or documents which are not likely to be contested, such as dates of birth or marriage, or the dimensions of a building, or the authenticity of a written contract. Admissions save the time and expense of bringing in witnesses to prove these basic items, but they are not often used to prove facts or theories that are controversial, because there is no strong compulsion for litigants to help their adversaries by admitting controversial matters. While the costs of proving facts at trial can be assessed against parties who refused to admit those facts in reply to a notice to admit, judges rarely use this power.

In the invasion of privacy case, while we knew that General Motors would not make any admissions, we felt that Gillen probably would. He had already admitted many facts in his deposition in the *Detroit Free Press* suit, and it was to his advantage to prove in the privacy action that he had been acting under the explicit instructions of GM rather than engaging in an unauthorized frolic. Therefore I went through the Gillen deposition and the transcript of the Ribicoff subcommittee hearing and put together a mosaic of facts that included all the important evidence. I tried to write it chronologically and in narrative form, as a story of the case that would be understood by the court, the press, and the public. We always had to keep in mind that Ralph was keenly concerned about the public-relations aspects of the case, and that we were up against a corporation whose total wealth was greater than all but five nations in the world. GM's public-relations machine had already succeeded in convincing Congress and a large segment of the public that GM had been victimized, along with Nader, by Gillen's unauthorized frolic. We now knew that this was false, and Ralph wanted to let the public know immediately, instead of dragging through years of attrition litigation, by which time the public might have forgotten the whole story. For our purposes, the notice to admit was the ideal instrument.

On January 25, 1967, just four days after Gillen signed his deposition, we served on the attorneys for General Motors and Gillen a notice to admit, which started off like this:

> SIRS:
> PLEASE TAKE NOTICE that the plaintiff hereby requests defendant GENERAL MOTORS CORPORATION, defendant VINCENT GILLEN, and defendant VINCENT GILLEN ASSOCIATES, INC., pursuant to the provisions of Section 3123 of the Civil Practice Law and Rules, and within twenty (20) days after service of this notice, to admit, for the purpose of this action only and subject to all pertinent objections to admissibility which may be interposed at the trial, the truth of the facts set forth in the annexed papers.

The notice to admit covered 29 long, typewritten legal pages single-spaced, and contained more than 300 separate requests. Here are some samples:

> 10. a) At said Washington meeting of January 13, 1966, between Danner and Gillen, Danner turned over to Gillen a copy of the written report made by William O'Neil to General Motors on or about November 21, 1965, which report contained no reference whatsoever to anti-Semitism, homosexuality, or dope addiction concerning Ralph Nader.
> b) At said Washington meeting, Danner turned over to Gillen a seven-page document on Ralph Nader, which had been prepared in the General Motors legal department for the purpose of guiding the investigation of Nader in accordance with General Motors' objectives.
> c) Said seven-page General Motors document suggested that the subject of anti-Semitism of Nader and his family be investigated . . .
> e) At said Washington meeting, Gillen was instructed by Danner to investigate Nader and Nader's family for anti-Semitism.

f) The direction to investigate Nader and his family for anti-Semitism originated in the General Motors legal department . . .

k) The investigation of Ralph Nader conducted by Gillen and his agents, subcontractors and employees, pursuant to the instructions received from Danner, acting for General Motors, included raising the subject of Ralph Nader's anti-Semitism with many of the persons interviewed.

l) In the entire investigation conducted by Gillen for General Motors, which encompassed the interviewing of more than 30 persons, and the checking of Nader's records back to the time of his childhood, not a single statement was made or found which indicated any anti-Semitism on the part of Ralph Nader.

*   *   *

25. In the investigation of Ralph Nader by General Motors, which was authorized by Aloysius F. Power, Vice President and General Counsel of General Motors, the following subterfuges were used:

a) General Motors went through the motions of hiring Danner as an attorney, with Danner to hire Gillen, even though General Motors had previously hired Gillen directly for more than twenty-five (25) investigations prior to the Ralph Nader investigation.

b) Communications between General Motors and Danner were conducted through Eileen Murphy, a law librarian in the office of the General Motors legal department in Detroit, Michigan, and Danner, with the written communications from the General Motors legal department being written on blank paper, the addressee being "Dear Dick" and the signature being "Eileen," with no further indentification of the addressee, the sender, or the subject of the investigation.

c) Danner went through the motions of retaining Vincent Gillen as an attorney, with Vincent Gillen then, in turn, going through the motions of hiring Vincent Gillen Associates, Inc., as an invesigator to work for Vincent Gillen, Attorney; this latter subterfuge was abandoned prior to the Ribicoff Subcommittee hearings of March 22, 1966, and Gillen's billings, which reflected the subterfuge use of him as an attorney were changed so that the billing ran from Vincent Gillen Associates, Inc., to Richard Danner.

*   *   *

31. a) The papers annexed hereto, marked Exhibit "2," constitute a true and correct copy of a three-page letter written on or about February 25, 1966, by Eileen Murphy, an employee of the General Motors' legal department in Detroit, Michigan, to Danner in Washington, D. C.

b) The name "Dick" on the first page of Exhibit "2" refers to Richard Danner.

c) The signature on the third page of Exhibit "2," "Eileen," refers to the aforementioned Eileen Murphy.

d) The original of Exhibit "2" was written on blank paper with no letterhead shown.

e) The original of Exhibit "2" was dictated or type-written by Eileen Murphy in the legal department of General Motors at Detroit, Michigan, on or about February 25, 1966.

f) The original of Exhibit "2" was dictated or written by Eileen Murphy, at a time when said Eileen Murphy had already received and read reports of the Gillen investigation of Ralph Nader, indicating that the questions of anti-Semitism, homosexuality and dope addiction had been raised by the investigators involved in interviews with witnesses.

g) The purpose of Exhibit "2" was to advise Danner that General Motors was not satisfied with the Gillen investigation of Ralph Nader, in that said investigation had not produced any material which could be used by General Motors to discredit Ralph Nader.

*   *   *

33. a) Between March 10, 1966, and March 22, 1966, employees of General Motors' legal department in Detroit requested Gillen to surrender a copy of Exhibit "2" which he had in his possession, so that said copy of Exhibit "2" would not be available to the Ribicoff Subcommittee.

b) Between March 10, 1966, and March 22, 1966, employees of the General Motors' legal department in Detroit collected other copies of Exhibit "2" for the purpose of destroying them, or withholding them from the Ribicoff Subcommittee.

34. a) During the entire investigation of Ralph Nader by Gillen, no complaint was ever made by Danner or by General Motors to Gillen, to the effect that Gillen's investigation was going too far or had gone too far.

b) During the entire investigation of Ralph Nader by Gillen, the only complaints made to Gillen by Danner or General Motors were to the effect that the investigation had not gone far enough in attempting to discredit Ralph Nader.

The defendants had to respond "admitted" or "denied" to each requested admission. All of the above statements (and hundreds more) were admitted under oath by Gillen. Both our notice to admit and Gillen's replies were filed in court and therefore became public documents which were available to the press and the public. It did not take long for the press to pick up the story. On Sunday, February 5, 1967, shortly after Gillen's replies were filed in court, the *Washington Post* ran a front page story, featuring a big picture of Gillen testifying into several microphones at the Ribicoff subcommittee hearing. It was written by Morton Mintz, who had first broken the story of the Gillen fiasco in the Senate Office Building. Mintz analyzed the requests for admissions and Gillen's replies in great detail, and thus gave the public the true story of the GM investigation of Nader for the first time. The front page headlines were:

DETECTIVE ADMITS GM INSTRUCTIONS TO MUZZLE
NADER—Auto Executives Lied at Hearing, Gillen Swears

The Sunday *New York Times* of February 5 also made the admissions a
front page story. Sidney Zion's long article quoted many of Gillen's
shocking admissions, and he included a telephone interview with Senator
Ribicoff.

While Gillen replied promptly to the request for admissions, General Motors was not so accommodating. As we expected, GM's attorneys
immediately filed a motion asking the court to strike out the notice to
admit. We knew that, even if the court denied that motion and ordered
GM to reply, GM would probably deny all the requests for admissions.
It was in their best interests to deny everything and put us to the task
of breaching the wall of attorney-client privilege that they had built
around the crucial evidence.

We were more concerned about another motion that GM made at
the same time. They asked the court to *consolidate* the two cases, so
that all future proceedings in the *Detroit Free Press* case would also involve GM. This was designed to prevent any further disclosures by Gillen when GM was not allowed to participate—and participation in this
instance meant shutting Gillen up for as long as possible. Their basis
for consolidating the two suits was that they involved common questions
of law and fact, namely, the investigation of Nader by GM and Gillen.
The existence of common questions of law or fact is the basic reason for
granting consolidation of two separate actions, which would then be
linked together for all purposes, including discovery and trial.

Along with their motion to consolidate the two suits, GM sought
a *protective order* under §3103(c) of the New York Civil Practice Law
and Rules, claiming in their motion papers:

> From what has been said it should be clear that the plaintiff
> has grossly abused the rules of practice, particularly the dis-
> covery rules, in instituting a private lawsuit to get discovery for
> use in the principal action without the knowledge or participa-
> tion of the real party in interest. Accordingly, this is an appro-
> priate case for the exercise of the Court's power to order "that
> the information be suppressed" as "improperly and irregularly
> obtained" [CPLR §3103(c).] Owing to his demonstrably im-
> proper conduct, plaintiff should be prevented from making any
> use of the deposition in the Nader-Gillen action and everything
> based thereon: the Notice to Admit and admissions in the
> Nader-GM action.

In their motion papers and in the argument of the motion before Justice
Saul Streit, GM's attorneys accused us of initiating a "sweetheart suit"
against Gillen. They claimed that there must have been collusion be-

tween us and Gillen or Gillen's attorneys in order to produce such damaging evidence without GM's knowledge. They called the *Detroit Free Press* action "a device for obtaining discovery for use in Action No. 1 (the privacy action) without notice to or participation by the defendant General Motors." The affidavit of Simon F. Rifkind, for General Motors, went on to say:

> The Nader-Gillen action is not a lawsuit in the well-understood sense of that word. It is an arrangement between Nader and Gillen to provide them with a vehicle for obtaining pretrial discovery against defendant GM for use in the Nader-GM lawsuit, without affording to GM its fundamental right to participate in any such discovery proceedings and protect its rights.

> We know, for example, that in the Nader-Gillen lawsuit, plaintiff—without notice to GM—took Gillen's deposition and then promptly turned around and used the information and documents obtained in that deposition to prepare over 300 requests to admit which were served on GM in the Nader-GM lawsuit.

*   *   *

> The Nader-Gillen action is not a lawsuit in the traditional sense. It is not an adversary proceeding—it is a joint venture designed to prejudice the rights of GM.

In reply, I stated that there had been no collusion or arrangement whatsoever between Nader and Gillen, and that Gillen's deposition had simply revealed the truth, which is the basic purpose of any deposition, or, for that matter, any lawsuit. I pointed out in my affidavit:

GENERAL MOTORS OBJECTS TO GILLEN TELLING THE TRUTH

> At no time has General Motors ever charged that any of the statements made by Mr. Gillen or his answers to the Requests for Admissions in Action No. 1 were in any way false. Apparently, they think it is most unsporting of Mr. Gillen to tell the truth after he had been hired as an agent for General Motors. General Motors fails to point out how they can possibly be prejudiced legally by the truthful testimony of Mr. Gillen, or any other witness.

I suggested that the motion by GM to suppress the admissions made by Gillen was "merely a continuation of attempted suppression of the truth by General Motors" as evidenced by Gillen's sworn statements that meetings had been held at GM headquarters in Detroit between March 10 and March 22, 1966, for the purpose of deciding "what to give to the Senate, what to suppress, and what to fabricate."

The motion was argued on March 23, 1967, before Justice Saul S. Streit, who was then the chief administrative judge of the Supreme Court for the County of New York. Simon H. Rifkind argued for GM, and I argued for Nader. Members of the press corps were present, and after the argument, the story of the Gillen revelations was played out again in the newspapers.

On April 3, Justice Streit handed down his decision. The key parts of it are as follows:

> The moving party, [General Motors], however, asserts that this second action is, in reality, a so-called "sweetheart" action and a device by the parties thereto for conducting pre-trial discovery proceedings, for use in the first action here, without notice to or participation by defendant General Motors.
>
> * * *
>
> It cannot be determined from the papers submitted on this motion whether, in fact, General Motors is a person who has an interest in the alleged libel action. A serious question of fact with respect thereto has been raised in the affidavits before the Court. Similarly, the Court cannot determine from these affidavits and the submitted pleadings alone whether the second action was instituted in good faith, as plaintiff asserts, or whether, in fact, it is merely a device intended to place General Motors at a disadvantage sufficient to warrant the relief it seeks under the protective provisions of CPLR 3103.
>
> Accordingly, these issues are referred to Hon. Seymour Bieber, Special Referee, to hear and report thereon, together with his rcommendations. Pending the referee's report, final disposition of this motion is held in abeyance.

This meant that our direct thrust to avoid years of attrition would be put to the test of a full-scale trial on the question of our good faith in bringing the *Detroit Free Press* libel action against Gillen. If GM could prove that the libel action was not instituted in good faith, then presumably Justice Streit would grant their motion to suppress the notice to admit and the Gillen deposition, moving us all the way back to square one.

Under New York practice, a special referee has virtually the same hearing powers as a trial judge. He can issue subpoenas for witnesses and documents, rule on the admissibility of evidence and all objections, and conduct a hearing on the matters referred to him as though it were a formal trial of those issues. After the hearing he makes a written report of his findings, which forms the basis of a final decision by the referring judge.

The Referee's Hearing

On the morning of April 25, 1967, the hearing opened before Referee Seymour Bieber in Room 250 of the New York County Court House.

Al Gans and I appeared for Ralph Nader; Martin Kleinbard and Allan Blumstein appeared for General Motors; and Francis T. Maguire appeared for Gillen. Martin Kleinbard opened his case by calling as his first witness Francis T. Maguire, the attorney for Gillen. Kleinbard had obtained a subpoena from the referee compelling Maguire to testify as a witness for GM, and he had included in the subpoena a long list of documents which Maguire was required to produce, including his entire file of the *Detroit Free Press* suit and his own personal diaries and office records of all telephone calls since November 1966, when the Nader suits were commenced.

From his questions, it became clear that Kleinbard's strategy was to show that Maguire had not been following the *Detroit Free Press* suit as though it were a serious case, but had been regarding it simply as a device by which Gillen could spill out information which was injurious to General Motors. Kleinbard introduced into evidence hundreds of pages of pleadings and other documents from the *Detroit Free Press* suit, which by this time was called "Action No. 2." First he would test Maguire's recollection of these papers without letting Maguire read them, and then he would attempt to show that Maguire did not recall details of these documents, as presumably he would know the details of a serious lawsuit. Kleinbard went about this task for the better part of two days. His direct examination of Maguire covered more than 200 pages of transcript. I attempted to sidetrack Kleinbard's strategy by objecting to this assault on Maguire's recollection, but I didn't have much luck.

> Q. by Mr. KLEINBARD: Were there further stipulations in Action No. 2 with respect to any other witnesses? A: I don't know of any at the moment here, Mr. Kleinbard.
> > Mr. SPEISER: Your Honor, in the interest of saving time, may I suggest that if Mr. Kleinbard has a public record, he should show it to Mr. Maguire instead of testing his recollection.
> > The REFEREE: I can't tell him how to try his case. He may want to affect this man's credibility, and I don't want to say anything.

In addition to the recollection tactic, Kleinbard was attempting to prove that there must have been collusion between Maguire and me in setting up the Gillen deposition. Through his subpoena, Kleinbard was able to forage through Maguire's diaries, office files, and all of his records pertaining to his conversations and communications with me in the preceding six months, going back to the start of the privacy suit. Kleinbard was not able to come up with any evidence supporting this contention, although it was not for lack of trying.

Q. by Mr. KLEINBARD: Do you recall being in Washington, D.C., last week? A: I do.

Q: Was Mr. Gillen also in Washington, D.C., last week? A: He was.

Q: Was Mr. Speiser in Washington last week? A: He was.

Q: And did you and Mr. Speiser see each other in Washington? A: I saw Mr. Speiser as my client was testifying, sitting among the spectators.

Q: And did you and Mr. Speiser and/or Mr. Gillen together, have any conversations? A: I don't think Mr. Gillen did. He probably said, "Hello" to him and I said "Hello."

*   *   *

Q: Did you meet with Mr. Speiser last evening, Mr. Maguire? A: No, sir—last evening?

Q: Yes. A: I was working in my office. I had to get a brief out.

> The REFEREE: Your answer is no.
> The WITNESS: That's right, no.

*   *   *

Q: Have you made your correspondence and files available to Mr. Speiser prior to the commencement of this hearing? A: No, sir.

Kleinbard tried every which way to show that there must have been many private discussions between Maguire and me that were not in Maguire's diaries or records. Finally I suggested to Kleinbard that he ask Maguire directly whether there was an agreement between us. Kleinbard replied that this was "an interesting suggestion, but I will take it up in my own way." However, since he had made Maguire GM's own witness and he correctly anticipated a negative answer from Maguire, Kleinbard never asked him directly whether there was any agreement between us as to any phase of this litigation.

After examining Maguire minutely for nearly two days, Kleinbard demanded that we produce the Gillen deposition. GM had first requested production of the Gillen deposition in the motion that they had made before Justice Streit, but the judge had referred the issues to Referee Bieber without ordering the Gillen deposition to be produced, and GM still had not seen it. Now Kleinbard was claiming that he couldn't possibly prove his case of collusion without having the deposition itself, because it would be the best evidence of how Gillen disclosed damaging evidence through cooperation with Nader rather than through the give-and-take of a contested lawsuit. But because GM's motion had asked for production of the Gillen deposition, I argued that to have it produced for the purpose of this referee's hearing would be granting GM indirectly the relief which they had not yet obtained directly from Justice Streit. After extended argument of this point, Referee Bieber finally ruled:

I think Mr. Speiser's point is well taken. You are seeking to get indirectly from me the relief that you may not get directly. If I give you the deposition, then this whole hearing is worthless, and so are the motions, and everything else. That is exactly what you want. You cannot get it this way if you are not entitled to it. That is why the Judge sent it here.

After this ruling, Kleinbard stated that he could not complete his questioning of Maguire or proceed with his case without having the Gillen deposition. He asked for an adjournment of the referee's hearing in order to make a new application to Justice Streit to have the Gillen deposition produced, so that he could question Maguire, Gillen, and possibly other witnesses as to how and why Gillen had disclosed so much evidence in his deposition. The Referee agreed to adjourn the hearing so that Kleinbard could make the application to Justice Streit. I thought that we were finished for the day, but just before the hearing adjourned, Kleinbard asked for permission to put on another GM witness. It was none other than former Federal Judge Simon H. Rifkind, the senior eminence of the Paul Weiss firm:

> Mr. KLEINBARD: I have Judge Rifkind here. And I will have him for five minutes.
> The REFEREE: Is there any objection to putting Judge Rifkind on before you examine Mr. Maguire?
> Mr. SPEISER: No.
> Mr. KLEINBARD: Judge Rifkind.
>
> *   *   *
>
> Q. by Mr. KLEINBARD: Are you the attorney for the defendant General Motors in *Nader v. General Motors*?   A: I am.
> Q: Approximately when were you retained in this action?   A: You would have to refresh my recollection, but it is some little while ago—from the very beginning. There was—I was not substituted for anybody.
> Q: Were you representing General Motors in the month of November, 1966, in this action?   A: I was.
> Q: *Nader v. General Motors*?   A: Yes.
> Q: During that month, did you have a conversation with the defendant Vincent Gillen?   A: I had a telephone call from Mr. Gillen, who told me that he was in the offices of Messrs. Cahill, Gordon, and so forth, and in the room of Doyle—Jerry Doyle, and that he was contemplating the retainer of Messrs. Cahill & Gordon and Mr. Doyle, but Mr. Doyle wanted to put some questions to me before he undertook such an assignment. He turned the telephone over to Mr. Doyle, whom I know, and whose voice I know, and he spoke to me.
> Q: Can you place the approximate date of that conversation?   A: November 25th.
> Q: Do you recall the substance of your conversation with Mr. Doyle?   A: Mr. Doyle—well, we passed the pleasantries of the day, usual amenities, he said he was sitting with Mr. Gillen,

who had invited him to represent him in the lawsuit, *Nader v. General Motors and Gillen,* and he said he was considering the acceptance of such an invitation on the part of Mr. Gillen, provided he was given to understand that General Motors would look after Mr. Gillen's obligations. This was the substance of that conversation.

Q: Did you have any further conversations with Mr. Doyle on behalf of Mr. Gillen during the next few days? A: I told Mr. Doyle I would make inquiry concerning any such assumption of responsibility on the part of General Motors. I thereafter had two more telephone conversations with Mr. Doyle, one on the 30th of November and one on December 1st. I am unable at this moment to pinpoint which conversation occurred in those two time periods. But, between those two dates.

Q: Could you give us the substance of what you learned from Mr. Doyle?

> The REFEREE: I will take the substance of what was said.
>
> The WITNESS: Mr. Doyle asked me again what I found out as to my client's disposition of the matter. I told Mr. Doyle that I understood that Mr. Gillen's request extended into three areas. First, he wanted General Motors to pay his fees—counsel fees. He wanted General Motors to pay for his time in testifying and working on this matter and so forth. And third, he wanted General Motors to indemnify him against any possible judgment to which he may be subjected. And, in one or the other of those conversations, I assume it was the last, I told Mr. Doyle that General Motors could not undertake those three assignments; that as to one of them—I am trying to recall now which one—they would not pay him for his services. That was absolute. As to the other two, they thought it was out of order to make any arrangements with him now. It would make it appear as if they were trying to buy his testimony. Consequently, they could not make any such agreement. When the whole thing was over, if the situation was such that the defendant—that General Motors felt a sense of moral or other responsibility which would warrant paying it, that would be an open question.
>
> Mr. KLEINBARD: I have no further questions.
>
> The WITNESS: Mr. Doyle, under those circumstances, said he would not undertake the retainer.

As this evidence unfolded, something clicked in my mind. I rummaged around in the pile of papers in front of me and fished out the complaint in the *Detroit Free Press* action. I turned to the last page and noted that it had been sworn to and notarized on December 2, 1966. Judge Rifkind had just testified that as late as December 1 he had still been talking to Gillen and his lawyers about the possibility of GM indemnifying him, paying his legal fees, and paying him for his working time on the case.

If Gillen was still talking to GM's lawyers as late as December 1, how could Nader's libel action possibly have been instituted in bad faith when the complaint was dated December 2?

I never thought that I would have the privilege of attempting to cross-examine Simon H. Rifkind, one of the nation's greatest lawyers. I was tempted to let his testimony stand without cross-examination, since I did not think that it had hurt us, and there was always the chance that he had a haymaker waiting for me on cross. But I decided to plunge in anyway.

> Q. by Mr. SPEISER: Mr. Rifkind, you stated that you had these three telephone conversations with Mr. Doyle, and you were not able to recollect exactly which took place on which dates and what the substance of each was on each particular date. Do you have any records in your office which would indicate the substance of these conversations, sir? A: I will tell you what I have. My secretary prepares every day—there is a printed list which says "Telephone calls"—on it are the list of persons I talked with. I looked at those. There was an entry on November 25th. I talked to Mr. Doyle on November 30th and December 1st. But, it does not give the conversation. This is kept by the girl at the telephone, and while I do not remember which of the last two conversation were—how they were spaced, the first I remember very vividly.
>
>> The REFEREE: Do you keep any diary entries?
>> The WITNESS: Some, but I have no diary entry other than the fact that I had a telephone conversation with Mr. Doyle.
>
> Q. by Mr. SPEISER: Do you have any memoranda or written papers of any kind relating to this entire transaction of the consideration you were giving to indemnifying Mr. Gillen? A: I have no further memoranda of my own with respect to this matter.
>
> Q: Do you know of any other papers relating to this matter? A: I know other persons in my office that had conversations with Mr. Gillen and the client. They were not my conversations. I am not in a position to testify.
>
> Q: At the next adjournment, will you be kind enough to produce all the records you and your office have relating to what you testified to with respect to Mr. Gillen? A: I have no records that I testified——
>
>> The REFEREE: Not yours personally, but office records.
>> The WITNESS: To these—there are no other office records with respect to these conversations.
>
> Q: Are there any office records or any records or papers, that you know of, which deal with this entire question of negotiations with Mr. Gillen concerning his indemnification?
>
>> Mr. KLEINBARD: I would object. The witness testified as to his conversations. He has no records with respect to his conversations.

The WITNESS: Other than those I told you about on the telephone.

Mr. KLEINBARD: Other than the telephone information. I don't think this is a general inquiry as to what he or anybody else——

The REFEREE: The testimony elicited to assume certain demands which you contend Mr. Gillen was making. If you have other papers which bear upon that, they are entitled to see it in view of that testimony. If you have them, produce them.

Mr. KLEINBARD: I will undertake to look for them.

These questions were designed to pin down the December 1 date, and to force the production of records which might show that representatives of GM were still negotiating with Gillen even after December 1.

I decided to try the same tactic on Judge Rifkind that Kleinbard had used on Maguire: asking him about the date of a legal paper without showing him the paper.

Q: Your motion to consolidate the two actions was then made on March 7, 1967, is that correct? A: Show me the paper.

Mr. KLEINBARD: I will so concede.

The WITNESS: I don't keep a mental diary.

Judge Rifkind was justifiably miffed at being asked to recall from memory the date of any particular legal paper out of hundreds that he dealt with. I looked quickly over at the Referee. The analogy to Kleinbard's pounding of Maguire's recollection was not lost on him. I also questioned Judge Rifkind about Richard Danner, the Washington lawyer who had been hired as go-between to hire Gillen:

Q: Have you been in touch with Mr. Danner at all? A: I never talked to the man in my life.

Q: Has anyone in your firm been in touch with him? A: I do not know.

Q: Do you have any records to indicate who has been?

This question was cut off by an objection and was not answered, but the testimony of Judge Rifkind was to be continued, and the Referee ordered that the Paul Weiss firm records of conversations with Gillen be produced when the hearing resumed, since Gillen was not their client and there was no attorney-client privilege involved.

I also wanted to follow up the question of conversations with Danner in the *Detroit Free Press* action, but he proved to be elusive. Even though he was a lawyer, we were unable to serve a subpoena on him for the taking of the deposition at his law office. We first sent a clerk out from our Washington office to serve him, but found we were sending a boy to do a man's job, since it proved impossible to penetrate his office defenses. Feeling the need for a professional touch, we turned the problem over to Don Madole, head of our Washington office. Don came up with a real pro: Hugh F. Duffy, who was reputed to be one of the world's greatest process servers. He prided himself on the fact that he had once served a subpoena on Jimmy Hoffa by dressing himself in black tie and tuxedo and piercing the screen of Hoffa's bodyguards (also wearing tuxedos) at a Teamsters Union function. But even the great Hugh Duffy was not up to the task of serving the eel-like Danner. First he tried Danner's suburban home, and found himself run off the premises by a pack of wild-eyed dogs. He then camped at Danner's law office, and managed to escape arrest for loitering and disturbing the peace only by ducking out of the door just before the police arrived, after having been lulled into accepting a hot cup of coffee from a secretary. I was interested in whether Danner had been conferring with any of the other GM lawyers in this litigation. Since he was billing himself as a GM lawyer, it would have been natural for him to discuss his proposed deposition with the Paul Weiss firm. I was most interested in the substance of those conversations, and I was prepared to press these questions and the request for all of the documents from the Paul Weiss firm when the referee's hearing resumed and Judge Rifkind returned as a witness.

At the end of Judge Rifkind's testimony, the hearing was adjourned to permit Kleinbard to renew his request to Justice Streit for production of the Gillen deposition. The next day, after we had read the stenographer's transcript (which was typed up overnight and delivered to us the next morning at expensive "daily copy" rates), Al Gans and I sat down to analyze our position. We decided that we had come through the first two days of testimony in pretty good shape. Maguire had stood up very well as a witness. He had nothing to hide, since there was no agreement of any kind between us, and Kleinbard had not even dared to ask him that question directly. Kleinbard had pounded away at him for two days and had come up with no proof of collusion or bad faith. But we felt that we had reached the high point of our case. Whether or not Justice Streit ordered the Gillen deposition turned over to GM, we knew that Kleinbard would call Gillen as his next witness, and we did not relish that prospect. Gillen was the kind of witness who was completely unpredictable, and we did not want an important part of the case to hang on what might pop out of his mouth during extended probing by an expert cross-examiner like Martin Kleinbard.

What could we do about this situation? We felt that we had some trading bait for Kleinbard. He knew that he couldn't possibly make out a case of collusion without having the Gillen deposition, because he was claiming that all of the injurious evidence came from that deposition. It was the very heart of his collusion claim. As he said during the referee's hearing, trying to prove his case without the Gillen deposition was like putting on a performance of Hamlet without the prince. We were not really afraid of producing the Gillen deposition, because it read like any other deposition—all the Gillen disclosures were made in answers to properly phrased questions. It was unusual only in that apparently the witness (an adverse party) was being completely candid and was willing (if not eager) to produce documentary evidence to back up his answers. Kleinbard needed the deposition badly, and he was not likely to get Justice Streit to order its production. We were in a position to consider trading it for something we wanted. After much soul-searching, Al Gans and I agreed that we should take a shot at making a deal with Kleinbard. We would let him have the Gillen deposition, and in exchange, the testimony portion of the Referee's hearing would be closed, and we would submit our final arguments to the Referee based upon the record as it then existed: the testimony of Maguire and Rifkind and all the exhibits that had been introduced, plus the Gillen deposition. Kleinbard thought it over for a few days, and finally he agreed.

We appeared before Referee Bieber again on May 8, at which time I handed over to Kleinbard a copy of the Gillen deposition with all of its exhibits. After the Gillen deposition was received in evidence, Referee Bieber formally closed the hearing. He ordered us to submit opening briefs by May 22 and reply briefs by May 29. This was done. GM's opening brief was 68 pages long, and its reply brief was 34 pages long. We submitted an opening brief of 21 pages and a reply brief of 32 pages. The reporter's transcript was 385 pages, and of course there were hundreds of pages of exhibits to go through. Despite this burden, Referee Bieber made his way through all these papers, and on June 28, 1967, he handed down his decision.

I was in Austria at the time, and when the phone rang in my hotel room and I heard Al Gans's happy voice, I knew that we had won. Referee Bieber found that "General Motors has failed to establish any collusive or other improper arrangement among Nader, Gillen, and their attorneys (or between any of them) with respect to the institution or maintenance of Action No. 2." In the course of his decision, he made the following findings:

> With regard to the referred issue of good faith (supra), General Motors, as noted, asserts that Action No. 2, in effect is a "private lawsuit between [Nader and Gillen] to inflict substantial damage on a third party [General Motors] in another lawsuit" (Gen. Motors Memo., pg. 66). Nothing in the record, however, in my opinion, warrants such conclusion. An analysis of the proof adduced before me, including the Gillen deposition which was made available to General Motors by Nader (pursuant to stipulation of counsel at the last hearing) and the voluminous documentary evidence adduced at the hearings (e.g., Deft. Ex. B, B–1) fails to establish any "joint venture" or collusive agreement between Nader and Gillen, or any effort by them

to defeat or prejudice General Motors' position in Action No. 1.

* * *

Moreover, the record adduced before me, in my opinion, clearly supports Nader's assertion that General Motors itself had furnished the true motivation for Gillen's obvious desire to testify at great length and to make full disclosure to plaintiff without any intervention or obstruction by General Motors. The precise testimony of General Motors' counsel at the hearings before me sets forth in detail the unsuccessful efforts by Gillen to obtain for himself financial indemnification by General Motors. These negotiations between them took place sometime between November 25 and December 1, 1966. I believe that the date of these negotiations are of great significance in eliminating the claimed collusion between Nader and Gillen in the institution of Action No. 2, for it now appears that the complaint in this second action was being drafted while Gillen was still looking toward a possible indemnification agreement with General Motors. Furthermore, the documentary proof establishes that Nader's complaint in Action No. 2 was actually verified on December 2, 1966 (Deft. Ex. H). Thus, these time factors, adduced by General Motors, itself, clearly conflict with and obviously rebut its contention that Action No. 2 was "contrived" between Nader and Gillen as a "sweetheart suit" intended to foster collusive action by them against the interests of General Motors.

GM had argued that collusion was apparent from the "breathtaking speed" of the *Detroit Free Press* suit; from Gillen's acquiescence "in almost every litigated step"; and from Gillen's failure to defend against the charges made by Nader. The Referee found that all of these allegations were

> based purely on suspicion, surmise and conjecture. The fact that Gillen volunteered information, gave long answers, and, indeed, was often unduly loquacious on his deposition, is not proof of collusion or bad faith.
>
> * * *
>
> Moreover, contrary to General Motors' argument that Action No. 2 was contrived between the parties as a "sweetheart suit" in order to permit collusive action by them against it, it is noteworthy that the record is barren of any meaningful proof of contact between Nader, Gillen or their attorneys (relating to Action No. 2) at any time prior to the actual institution of such lawsuit on December 9, 1966. The single established telephone conversation between counsel for Nader and Gillen on or shortly before this date related only to a statement by Nader's attorney that his client was ". . . somewhat sensitive about being told that he needed a psychiatrist, and that an action was going to be commenced because of the publication of the article making reference to the psychiatrist" (Stenographer's Minutes, pg. 44–45). Other than this one communication *prior* to suit,

there is no other credible evidence of any meeting or discussions in Action No. 2 (*after* this action was instituted) between the parties or their respective counsel except for those occasions on which Gillen's deposition was actually taken.

*   *   *

The record shows that counsel for General Motors examined Gillen's attorney at great length and in minute detail at two of the three hearings before me. At best, his testimony merely establishes that he has a poor memory for dates and details. Nothing elicited from Gillen's counsel, including the fact stressed by General Motors that certain pages of his personal diary were torn out, is inconsistent with his claim that only the convenience, time and best interests of his client motivated the expeditious manner in which Gillen's deposition was taken.

As to the Gillen deposition, the Referee found that it

clearly indicates that, other than obviously being aware of what Gillen had previously testified to at Senate Subcommittee hearings (e.g. Deft. Ex. A, pg. 8, 11, 33, 59) examining counsel had no advance knowledge of what would be elicited and produced, and that he attempted, as he claims, merely to ascertain all of the relevant facts and evidence which Gillen's replies to his questions suggested.

*   *   *

However, just as General Motors infers therefrom that this is proof of collusion or "bad faith," it is equally within the realm of similar speculation that Gillen, as his counsel urges, by that time, may have been motivated to make full disclosure in his deposition by General Motors' refusal to indemnify him financially (supra). This, however, does not establish any absence of good faith *on the part of Nader* in instituting or maintaining Action No. 2.

*   *   *

Furthermore, it is significant that at no time has General Motors alleged that Gillen's answers, even to purported "improper" questions, were untruthful.

We had guessed right and we had won the first round. We had kept GM from knocking out of the case the precious evidence that Gillen had dropped into our laps. We had overcome Judge Rifkind's argument that the Gillen deposition and all of its exhibits were "fruit of the poisoned tree" which should be banished from the case forever. Now we had a good chance to shortcut the long journey through the courts that GM had planned for us.

After the referee's report had been filed, it was up to us to make a motion before Justice Streit asking him to confirm the referee's findings. We filed such a motion on July 3, pointing out that the issues had been examined exhaustively by Referee Bieber, and that there was a 385 page transcript of testimony and hundreds of pages of exhibits to support his findings. GM, of course, opposed this motion and made a cross-motion asking Justice Streit to reject the referee's report and to grant them all the relief they had requested, including suppression of the Gillen deposition.

On July 28, 1967, Justice Streit entered an opinion confirming the report of the Special Referee and denying GM's motion to suppress the Gillen material. But GM had the right to appeal from Justice Streit's order, and they did this promptly on August 21, serving a notice of appeal to the Appellate Division of the Supreme Court for the First Department, which covers the New York City boroughs of Manhattan and the Bronx. To conduct this appeal, they had to print all of the proceedings before the Special Referee, which produced a bound volume of 639 pages, not including the Gillen deposition and its hundreds of pages of exhibits, which were also submitted to the Appellate Division. GM submitted an opening brief of 60 pages; we submitted an answering brief of 28 pages; Gillen submitted an answering brief of 27 pages; and GM submitted a reply brief of 20 pages.

The Appellate Division for the First Department is one of the world's busiest appellate courts, but the serene beauty of its building gives no hint of the court's heavy workload. In 1966, the Appellate Division Courthouse was officially designated as a New York City landmark, with this description:

> Distinguished for its classic beauty, this small marble courthouse represents, in a civic building, the epitome of collaboration between architect, sculptor, and mural painter. Classic Eclectic in design, but influenced by the Italian Renaissance architect Andrea Palladio, the three-story building with low basement expresses the best of Classical tradition in its columned porch (portico) and much fine sculpture, one of the building's chief distinctions.

It is located at 25th Street and Madison Avenue, on the same block as the famous Jerome mansion which housed the family of Winston Churchill's mother. The stained glass windows, paintings, and statues would fit in very well at the J. P. Morgan Library and Museum, which is a little further north on Madison Avenue. Fully one-third of the appropriation for the courthouse was spent on statuary and paintings, and that was back in 1899, when artworks were a lot cheaper.

There are seven regular justices, and usually two or three temporary justices, who sit in teams of five. Our case came on for argument on May 23, 1968. Judge Rifkind argued for General Motors and I argued for Nader before a court composed of Presiding Justice Bernard Botein, and Justices Stevens, Capozzoli, Rabin, and McNally. Vincent Gillen showed up in person and made a little speech to the court, stating that he was willing to submit to an acid test of his veracity. He offered to waive the privilege that all litigants enjoy against libel suits based on statements made during litigation. He was willing to repeat all the statements in his deposition, in or out of court, so that he could not be accused of hiding behind the litigation privilege against libel actions. He challenged Judge Rifkind to do the same on behalf of General Motors. I was enjoying this joust immensely, but Presiding Justice Botein told Gillen that his remarks were improper and that he had better sit down immediately.

After hearing argument for nearly an hour and asking many pointed questions, the judges reserved decision. On June 13, 1968, they handed down their decision, unanimously affirming Justice Streit's order, without writing an opinion. They also awarded us costs of the appeal, which would reimburse only our printing costs of $725.86, the first money that we had collected in this case since we started working on it two and a-half years earlier.

But this was not the end of the trail. GM had the right to request New York's highest court, the Court of Apeals, to hear a further appeal. They did not have the absolute right to appeal to the Court of Appeals, but had to seek its permission. They started the process of seeking leave to appeal to the Court of Appeals on July 18, 1968, with a 23-page motion addressed to the Appellate Division, which denied the motion on September 19. They then made a similar motion addressed to the Court of Appeals in Albany, which resulted in the filing of more than 100 pages of printed affidavits and briefs by the parties. Finally on December 11, the Court of Appeals denied leave for GM to carry the appeal any further.

Gillen had made his fateful disclosures in his written admissions on January 29, 1967. But it was not until December 11, 1968, more than 22 months later, that the final action of the Court of Appeals assured us that this crucial evidence would remain in the case.

To critics of our legal system, 22 months may seem an unreasonable amount of time for a procedural step that left the case still a long way from trial. To me, it illustrates the high quality of justice that is dispensed by our hard-pressed courts. During the long fight over the Gillen admissions, a dozen experienced lawyers worked on the facts and the law, putting in thousands of man-hours overall. Referee Bieber, Justice Streit, five Appellate Division justices, and seven Court of Appeals judges had to review a voluminous record, and then had to consider authorities cited by both sides (case decisions, statutes, textbooks, and law review articles). The history of each case decision had to be checked in *Shepard's Citations,* which lists all affirmances, reversals, and citations of the subject case by other courts—a process that often leads to reading dozens of other cases and authorities, to make sure that you have turned every stone and have not cited a decision that has lost its authority.

To measure this burden, I had one of the young lawyers in our firm time his reading of the papers that were before the appellate courts after Referee Bieber's hearing. He estimated a total reading time of 300 hours for the entire record, all the authorities cited in the briefs, and further authorities found through Shepardizing. That is just the reading time, without allowance for contemplation, discussion, or thrusts in new directions.

Litigation lawyers are criticized for piling up unnecessary paperwork which is costly to clients and the public. Yet, in the Nader case our side created as much paper as did GM, and all of it was necessary to support the all-out effort that our client needed and was entitled to expect of us. Since we were working on a contingent fee basis, it was disadvantageous for us to increase the paperwork, but there was no other way to present our case fully. And GM's lawyers, of course, had to reply in kind and had to exhaust all possible appeals on every important point in the case. This process may seem like an expensive luxury, but to the millions of Americans who must look to the courts for protection of life, liberty, and property it is a necessity.

In addition to their visible work on civil and criminal trials, the judges of the New York County Supreme Court handle at least 150 motions per day. Some are simple, but many are complex and require creative thought and research by the court, beyond mere reading of the papers submitted by the parties. The Appellate Division of the First Department decides more than 2,000 appeals a year, many of them far more complex than the appeal from Justice Streit's order (which encompassed 300 hours of reading material). Of course, the appellate judges cannot read all the material submitted, but they must consider all the arguments made by counsel based on that material.

The layman and the critic see only the few minutes spent in oral courtroom argument, and to them the 22-month process of ruling on the Gillen admissions seems inefficient. What they miss, which takes place mostly behind closed doors, is a remarkable intellectual performance— one of the few functions of government that actually works well. If we want it to work faster, we must devote more money to expanding the court system, which always lags behind its ever-increasing burden of civil and criminal cases. Delay is the price we must pay for painstaking and evenhanded resolution of serious controversies.

The hearing before Referee Bieber had become the central thrust of the litigation, and in the end it was to be the only hearing on the facts. If GM had been successful in suppressing Gillen's disclosures, we would have faced years of tough sledding trying to get the same information directly through discovery in the privacy action. But having won the referee's hearing, we now felt that we would not have to go through the attrition process, for which Nader had neither money nor time. We believed that with all the damaging Gillen disclosures in the case, and with the facts known to the press and the public, GM would not want to air them repeatedly, as would happen if the factual part of the case dragged on. There would be little point in GM trying to contest most of the facts that Gillen had already admitted, particularly those which sprung from GM's own documents such as the Dear Dick letter and the seven-page GM dossier with its vicious implications. We felt that we had pretty well wrapped up the factual phase of the case, but we knew that GM would not hesitate to put us through another obstacle course—the law. And that's exactly what they did.

General Motors Demurs

From the beginning of the case, we had anticipated that GM would attack the complaint. We knew that we were on pretty thin ice in alleging invasion of privacy, since this was a newly developing tort and there was no precedent for the Nader situation in the entire history of American law. So, it was no surprise to us that in the early spring of 1968, the Paul Weiss firm served upon us a motion to dismiss the first and second causes of action in Nader's complaint.

GM's motion to dismiss was filed after Justice Streit had denied GM's motion to throw out Gillen's evidence, but before Justice Streit's order had been passed upon by the Appellate Division. GM's appeal from Justice Streit's confirmation of the referee's report was argued on May 23, 1968, and was affirmed by the Appellate Division on June 13, 1968. While we were engaged in defending the hard-won victory on the factual side of the case, they hit us with the motion to dismiss for failure to state a cause of action, on March 15, 1968. GM was giving us the double team treatment, moving us from the lower courts to the appellate courts and back again on two fronts at once. Therefore we decided that I would stay with the Referee Streit appeal on the factual issues, and that Al Gans would play the principal role in fighting off the motion to dismiss in the lower and appellate courts. His superior knowledge of the law was not ignored in making this decision.

Knowing our adversaries' reputation for legal research, we were not surprised at the thoroughness of the job that they did on the motion to dismiss. The brief they delivered to us on March 15, 1968, was 52 pages long, and as usual it contained dozens of quotations from court decisions that could knock us right out of the case unless we could distinguish them from the Nader-GM situation.

Al Gans set about the task of answering the GM arguments. He was ably assisted by Paul Rheingold, and I put in a few ideas, although I was occupied with the GM appeal from the Referee Streit decision which was scheduled for argument on May 23. We submitted an opposing brief of 71 pages—we had topped Paul Weiss's page total for the first time. But our supremacy was shortlived. On the evening of Sunday, May 5 they served a 50-page reply brief on me at my home. Again it was loaded with dozens of potentially lethal citations, and we had just two working days before the motion was to be argued in court.

GM's motion to dismiss came on for argument before Justice Joseph A. Brust in Special Term, Part I of the Supreme Court for New York County on May 8, 1968. Under New York's rather antiquated procedure, the judge who happens to be sitting in "Special I" will decide motions in hundreds of cases that come before him in a given week, even though he has no prior knowledge of the cases and may never have anything further to do with them. In most other courts, each case is assigned to a single judge shortly after it is filed, and that judge handles the case right through the trial, ruling on all motions that are made along the way. By the time that it comes to trial, the judge usually has a good feel for the case, and his task is not impeded by rulings made by other judges who had the file in front of them only briefly. But New York County has never adopted this system, except for very complicated litigation like mass disaster cases, and so it was that half a dozen different judges who happened to be sitting in Special I at different times ruled on motions made in the Nader-GM case.

The argument of the critically important GM motion to dismiss was entrusted to Martin Kleinbard for General Motors and to Al Gans for our side. Each covered the ground that was presented in great detail in the briefs. Justice Brust reserved decision, as is almost always done after the argument of a motion to dismiss the complaint. On July 3, less than two months after the argument, Justice Brust filed his decision. We were elated to learn that he had upheld our complaint, ruling that both the first and second causes of action stated claims that would be recognized by the courts of New York. He held that under District of Columbia law, the first cause of action was a common-law action for invasion of privacy by intrusion. While there was no precedent in the District of Columbia squarely dealing with the type of conduct involved in the Nader case, Justice Brust looked at it the other way:

> No District of Columbia case has been cited to this court by the defendant which holds that there is no recognized cause of action for invasion of the right of privacy, by so-called intrusion, as compared to acts amounting to publication.

This meant that if Justice Brust was upheld by the appellate courts, we would be clear to go to trial on the first cause of action, which covered virtually everything that GM and Gillen had done to Nader. Instead of being restricted by New York's "publication only" version of privacy, we would be able to proceed under District of Columbia law, which, as interpreted by Justice Brust, would allow us to ask the jury for damages for all of the intrusions into Nader's life that we could prove.

But our biggest thrill came when we read Justice Brust's decision on the second cause of action. You will recall that we had purposely framed the second cause of action to cover GM's activities in New York, so that in case the restrictive New York law was applied to those activities, they would be separate from the first cause of action and would not prevent us from collecting damages for GM's activities in the District of Columbia. Ralph was determined to raise a constitutional question. If the federal constitution gave every citizen the right to be free from invasion of privacy, then New York's attempt to restrict such actions to publications, as in the Rochester Folding Box case, would be unconstitutional. It is not customary for trial court level judges to decide constitutional questions. In fact, even appellate courts (including the United States Supreme Court) usually avoid constitutional questions when they can decide a case on some other ground. But Justice Brust decided to break with tradition, and he bravely launched into constitutional waters:

> Much more serious problems are raised by the defendant's motion to dismiss the second cause of action. Defendant argues that any common law cause of action for invasion of privacy in New York is precluded by the line of cases commencing with the leading case (*Roberson v. Rochester Folding Box Co.*, 171 N. Y. 538) to the effect that any cause of action is limited by statute to commercial cases (Civil Rights Law, §§50, 51). Indeed, plaintiff Nader makes no claim here under these statutory sections, and explicitly asserts that he has a common law cause of action. His contention is two-pronged.
>
> Firstly, he argues, there is a common law right of privacy relating to intrusion which has not been passed on or at least has not yet been explicitly rejected by the courts. Secondly, and in the alternative, plaintiff argues, provisions of the Federal and New York constitutions will be violated if this court were to hold that plaintiff Nader cannot maintain his second cause of action. As to the former argument, it is apparently true that no reported New York case has ever involved an action based upon the highly unusual sort of conduct alleged against defendant in this case (and conceded to be so for the purposes of this motion). It is entirely possible that if our Court of Appeals were to be asked to pass upon the unprivileged wiretapping, the "use" of girls, the making of harassing telephone calls, the trailing by private detectives, and the other flagrant acts of investigation, that court might find some facet of the common law right of privacy to have been invaded. Nevertheless, it is

equally true that much of the language in the decided New York cases ban common law actions where plaintiffs have attempted to assert a violation of a right of privacy.

However, there is presented a constitutional right of plaintiff to privacy—a right to be left alone. The right of privacy stands on high ground, cognate to the values and concerns protected by constitutional guarantees (See: 4th, 5th, and 14th Amendments. Fed. Constit.; *Tehan v. United States ex rel. Shott,* 382 U.S. 406; *Griswold v. Connecticut,* 381 U.S. 479; *Shelly v. Kramer,* 334 U.S. 11; *Afro-American Publishing Co. v. Jaffe,* 366 F.2d 649.)

Under the circumstances, the court is constrained to allow the second cause of action to stand on constitutional grounds.

Accordingly, the motion is denied.

We had not only held our complaint together, but we had established a beachhead for a new principle of constitutional law: the right to be let alone, to be secure from intrusion into one's private life. As *U.S. Law Week* summarized the Brust decision:

It would appear, therefore, that at least until the New York Court of Appeals prohibits the use of a common law action as a remedy to enforce a constitutional right of privacy, unconstitutional invasions of a right of privacy are enforceable in a common law action in New York courts despite New York's limited privacy statute.

Back to the Appellate Division

Justice Brust filed his decision on July 3, 1968. Although GM had 30 days to file a notice of appeal, they filed it within two weeks. This moved the battleground back to the Appellate Division of the Supreme Court for the First Department, where we had just beaten off GM's attack on the Referee-Streit decision. Generally, it takes about six months to complete the appellate procedure, from the time of filing the notice of appeal to the time of oral argument. By working through the summer on the brief, Paul Weiss accelerated this schedule. They filed their 66-page printed brief on October 15, 1968. They repeated all the arguments that Justice Brust had rejected, and they threw in some new ones for good measure.

Although the acts complained of in the second cause of action occurred in New York, Nader was living in the District of Columbia at the time, and since invasion of privacy deals with injury to feelings and personal dignity, the residence of the plaintiff at the time of the invasion of privacy is the key to choice of law. Therefore, GM conceded in its brief that District of Columbia law should apply to the second cause of action as well as the first cause of action. If this concession was accepted by the appellate courts, it would take the constitutional question out of the case. There would be no need to decide whether New York's restrictive law of privacy violated the Fourth, Fifth, or Fourteenth Amendment, as held by Justice Brust, if the courts applied District of Columbia law to all the causes of action for invasion of privacy. This was a surprise to us, and we could only guess that GM felt that they had a better chance to throw us out completely under the vague District of Columbia law than they did by fighting the constitutional right-of-privacy battle.

GM's brief also hit hard on the point that they had been making from the beginning of the case: that there is no general right of privacy or right to be let alone, but only a right to sue for specific invasions of privacy described in statutes and court decisions. They claimed that Nader was suing for "harassment" rather than for invasion of privacy, and that his claims of harassment were covered by the third cause of action (infliction of emotional distress). Since GM was not moving to dismiss the third cause of action, they argued that there was no need to stretch invasion of privacy into a new tort covering harassment or intrusion.

Our brief, which consisted of 47 printed pages, was mainly the work of Al Gans, again assisted by Paul Rheingold. We still had no District of Columbia case squarely holding that GM's conduct in the Nader case gave rise to a cause of action for invasion of the right of privacy. Here's the way Al Gans handled that problem in the brief and on oral argument:

> GM correctly states that there is no District case exactly like the Nader-GM situation. But how often are our largest corporations caught in the act of invading privacy in this outrageous manner? Even less often would a plaintiff dare to bring suit on such charges. The fact that reported District cases deal mainly with publication does not mean that the District would constrict its protection of privacy by limiting redress only to "publications," thereby condoning intrusion—no matter how gross or shocking—as in this Nader case.
>
> The courts are not impotent to grant redress for injury resulting from conduct which universal opinion in a state of civilized society would unhesitatingly condemn as indecent and outrageous.

We filed our brief on November 21, 1968. GM had the right to file a reply brief, which of course they did. It was 20 pages long and was

filed on December 16, 1968. These printed briefs cost about $50 per
page. This may sound high, but appellate printing calls for special skills
and services. Appellate printers will pick up a typewritten draft at a lawyer's office and deliver a carefully checked 50-page printed proof the
same day. Many of them work day and night shifts, and they can print,
bind, and file a brief in court within hours of attorney approval. Paul
Weiss and other large litigation firms have enough manpower to do their
own proofreading, with one person reading aloud from the original and
another following the printed proof. We had to rely more on our printer,
but we had a secret weapon that even Paul Weiss could not match. Our
regular appellate printer, Meilin Press of New York, had in its employ
a veteran proofreader named Carrie, who almost never let a typographi-
cal error slip through. But Carrie was more than a proofreader. She had
read so many briefs in her long career that she knew the cases and authorities better than many lawyers. She would not hesitate to pencil in
the margin of a galley proof comments such as, "This case was overruled
by the later case of *Smith v. Brown*" or "You'd better read this case
again—it doesn't really help you on this point!" If Carrie liked the arguments in our briefs, we felt we had a better than even chance to convince the appellate judges.

GM's appeal came up for oral argument on January 8, 1969, in
the Appellate Division for the First Department. Al Gans and Martin
Kleinbard drew a bench composed of Justices Samuel W. Eager, Louis
J. Capozzoli, Owen McGivern, Emilio Nunez, and Aaron Steuer. Since
the presiding justice of the Appellate Division, Bernard Boetin, was not
a member of this panel, Justice Eager, the senior judge, was designated
as the "Justice Presiding." This panel was a good cross section of the
great ethnic variety that exists among New York judges.

We had to wait two months (until March 13, 1969) to learn that
we had won in the Appellate Division by the narrowest of margins, a
three-to-two decision. Justice Owen McGivern wrote the opinion for the
majority. Another of Tom Dewey's bright young assistant prosecuting
attorneys, he continued his public service as a member of the state legislature for twelve years, then as a trial judge in the City Court and Supreme Court for seventeen years, and finally was appointed to the Appellate Division in 1967. The combination of scholarship and wit that
made him a popular after-dinner speaker also showed up in his opinions.
He started the majority opinion in the Nader case with this lively description of the parties:

> The plaintiff, an author and a lecturer on automotive safety,
> by his activities has become a gadfly to the automobile manu-
> facturers. The defendant General Motors, learning of the im-
> minent publication of his book, *Unsafe At Any Speed,* author-
> ized other defendants to undertake a thorough unveiling of him.

The scrutiny and the surveillance of the plaintiff, carried on by the defendant's operatives, were characterized by such uninhibited gusto that the culmination was an apology tendered him before a Senatorial Investigating Committee.

On the first cause of action, he wrote:

> Treating these causes in seriatim, we uphold the First Cause of Action. Although it may be true that until the present there does not seem to be any District of Columbia precedent permitting a cause of action for invasion of the right of privacy, aside from the making public of facts pertaining to a subject's private life, the absence of an exact precedent is no bar to the relief.
>
>   *   *   *
>
> . . . these courts in the District of Columbia have never categorically held that unauthorized publications of private facts alone will give rise to a right of privacy action. Rather, they are replete with repetitious endorsements of the Restatement of Torts, Sec. 867, and Prosser on Torts, 635, 638, 642, indicating an ever burgeoning approach to this field of the law. Indeed, in view of the broad and sweeping language of these cases, we can do no other but hold that the District of Columbia cases not only give welcome to a classical common law action for invasion of privacy but also to the "sub-doctrines" of intrusion into one's seclusion or solitude as an actionable tort. And since we are not dealing with the laws of the Medes and the Persians, the lack of an exact precedent is no reason for turning the plaintiff out of court when receiving his action will further the bringing of the law into harmony with the known practices of our modern society.

On the second cause of action, Justice McGivern's opinion accepted the agreement of the parties that the District of Columbia law applied. He went further and held that District of Columbia law should apply in any event, since the injuries consisted of humiliation and outrage to plaintiff's feelings. He wrote:

> The plaintiff herein was a District resident, the principal obtrusions and impact of the activities occurred there, and all "the grouping of contacts" relate to the District. Thus, there is no need of passing on the Constitutional ground assigned by the Court at Special Term for sustaining the Second Cause of Action.

Thus, Justices McGivern, Capozzoli, and Nunez held that both causes of action for invasion of privacy were governed by District of Columbia law, which (they found) would permit actions for invasion of privacy by intrusion.

The dissenting opinion of Justice Steuer stressed the fact that all of the District of Columbia decisions in which recovery had been allowed for invasion of privacy had been publication cases. He reminded us that it was not easy to pioneer new causes of action:

> Furthermore, the practice of giving claims new names for the purpose of avoiding restrictions on the established forms is impermissible (*Morrison v. National Broadcasting Co.,* 19 N Y 2d 453). And this has been attempted, unsuccessfully, by labelling the action an invasion of privacy (*Gautier v. Pro-Football,* 304 N.Y. 354; see Hofstadter and Horowitz, The Right of Privacy 6). When the new name is also designed to create new rights of recovery, the utmost circumspection should be employed. Decision should not rest on the individual reaction of the judge or bench in question.
>
>   *   *   *
>
> Similar caveats that extensions of tort liability into unexplored areas should be left to the legislature, which can effectively limit the boundaries, are still issued and have a prominent place in our judicial philosophy.
>
>   *   *   *
>
> It would be hard to conceive of any field in the law where the recognition of a new ground of recovery could do greater mischief. Is it to be understood that an undefined phrase such as "to be let alone" can furnish any guide to actionable rights? The most mortifying instances of privacy invasion are occasioned by domestic accidents. Is the test to be the effect on the sensibilities of the plaintiff, or the turpitude of the defendant? In a field where individual predilection for privacy can vary from the morbid seclusion of the hermit to the extroverted conduct of the publicity seeker, is the right to be let alone to depend on the particular reaction of the individual judge to the practically limitless number of ways in which privacy can be invaded? These questions are to such a degree rhetorical that it is not contemplated that the District of Columbia courts will find any answers different from the quoted guides to decision.

Justices Steuer and Eager voted to dismiss the first and second causes of action, on the ground that there was no District of Columbia precedent allowing a suit for invasion of privacy based upon intrusion. But Justices McGivern, Capozzoli, and Nunez gave us the benefit of the doubt, and so we cleared the Appellate Division by the skin of our teeth. So close was the question that when GM moved for leave to take the question to the Court of Appeals, the Appellate Division granted their motion on May 13, 1969. This meant that the case would go to the state's highest court on the question of whether our complaint stated a cause of action for invasion of privacy.

The Court of Appeals Decides

Again GM filed a printed brief, 60 pages long, on September 3, 1969, together with an Appendix of 103 pages which reprinted all the prior legal decisions on the first two causes of action. They also filed a 31-page reply brief on October 17, 1969. Their briefs covered all the arguments they had made in the two lower courts, augmented by the scholarly dissenting opinion of Justice Steuer. In our 48-page printed brief, we repeated the arguments that we had made in the lower courts. We relied heavily on Dean Prosser and the *Restatement of Torts,* now joined by the Brust and McGivern opinions. But this time we had a little more to hang our hats on, thanks to another bizarre Washington incident that wound up in the civil courts.

In 1965, Washington newspaper columnist Drew Pearson and his then associate (later successor) Jack Anderson gained access to information about the activities of Senator Thomas J. Dodd (Dem., Conn.) through two former Dodd employees who entered the Senator's office without his authority or knowledge, removed numerous documents from his files, made copies of them and replaced the originals. Then they turned the copies over to Jack Anderson, who was aware of the entire caper. Pearson and Anderson published six newspaper articles exposing Dodd's questionable conduct as a senator, including alleged padding of expense accounts and improper relationships with lobbyists for foreign interests. These revelations brought about Dodd's censure by the Senate, which eventually ended his political career. When Pearson-Anderson published their articles about Dodd, he filed suit against them in the U.S. District Court for the District of Columbia, charging them with invasion of his privacy in two ways: first, by obtaining copies of documents that had been taken from Dodd's office by means of improper intrusion; and second, by publishing the information so obtained.

Since Pearson and Anderson did not deny that their information had been obtained from the purloined documents, Senator Dodd's lawyers made a motion for partial *summary judgment* on the issue of liability. When the crucial facts are undisputed, a trial may be avoided by moving for summary judgment. If the judge hearing the motion rules that the undisputed facts give rise to liability, then that issue can be decided on the motion papers, and the only issue left for trial is the amount of damages. The motion came on in January 1968 before District Court Judge Alexander Holtzoff, who ruled only on Senator Dodd's second claim of privacy invasion—publication of the six newspaper articles based on purloined documents. He held that the articles dealt with Dodd's activities as a senator, and therefore were matters of public interest which were not within the protected right of privacy. His opinion did not mention the claim based on intrusion.

Dodd took his case to the U.S. Court of Appeals for the District of Columbia, which agreed to review Judge Holtzoff's decision. There, Circuit Judges Wright, Tamm, and Robinson addressed themselves first to the claim of invasion of privacy by intrusion, before getting to the question of publication. In their February 1969 decision, which didn't do much for Senator Dodd, they presented us with the first statement by a District of Columbia court that recognized intrusion as a form of privacy invasion:

> "Intrusion" has not been either recognized or rejected as a tort in the District of Columbia. It has been recognized by a number of state courts, most recently by the New Hampshire Supreme Court in *Hamberger v. Eastman*. Hamberger found liable a defendant who eavesdropped upon the marital bedroom of plaintiffs by electronic means, holding that "the invasion of the plaintiffs' solitude or seclusion . . . was a violation of their right of privacy."
>
> We approve the extension of the tort of invasion of privacy to instances of intrusion, whether by physical trespass or not, into spheres from which an ordinary man in a plaintiff's position could reasonably expect that the particular defendant should be excluded. Just as the Fourth Amendment has expanded to protect citizens from government intrusions where intrusion is not reasonably expected, so should tort law protect citizens from other citizens. The protection should not turn exclusively on the question of whether the intrusion involves a technical trespass under the law of property. The common law, like the Fourth Amendment, should "protect people, not places."

But on the facts of the Dodd-Pearson case, the circuit court judges were not willing to hold the two columnists liable for merely receiving purloined documents, even though the court assumed that the actions of Dodd's former employees (who were not sued) constituted improper intrusion by them. They agreed with Judge Holtzoff's decision that publication of the six articles was not invasion of privacy since they dealt with matters of public interest. Therefore they affirmed Judge Holtzoff's decision which had denied Senator Dodd's motion for summary judgment on the issue of invasion of privacy.

Of course, we quoted the beautiful intrusion language of the Dodd-Pearson appellate decision in our Court of Appeals brief. GM's lawyers argued that the portion we quoted was *obiter dictum*—a passing remark that was not an essential part of the court's holding, and therefore of no value as a legal precedent.

The GM appeal was argued before the seven judges of the Court of Appeals in Albany on October 28, 1969, by Simon H. Rifkind for GM and by Al Gans for our side. In keeping with its upside-down approach to nomenclature, New York designates a member of its highest court, the Court of Appeals, as "Judge," whereas the judges of its lower court, naturally called the "Supreme Court," have the more majestic title of "Justice." On January 8, 1970, the Court of Appeals handed down its decision. It was not a complete victory for either side. We were thankful that it left Ralph with a chance to go to trial and to prove all of the facts alleged in the complaint. However, the first and second causes of action were not entirely intact. The majority opinion, written by Chief Judge Stanley H. Fuld, was joined in by three of the other six judges.

The Court of Appeals addressed itself only to "the reach of the tort of invasion of privacy as it exists under the law of the District of Columbia." Judge Fuld's opinion found that the District of Columbia was "the place which has the most significant relationship with the subject matter of the tort charged," and that under New York choice of law rules, the law of the place having the most significant relationship would be applied. He then found that the District of Columbia had broadened the scope of its common law action for invasion of privacy in the Dodd-Pearson case to include intrusion, thus ruling against GM's contention that the intrusion language in Dodd-Pearson was *obiter dictum*. Justice Brust's constitutional ruling under New York law was not mentioned, since the court held that District of Columbia law would apply to both causes of action.

Judge Fuld concluded that Nader had the right to sue for intrusion under the District of Columbia law. However, he went on to define intrusion rather narrowly:

> It should be emphasized that the mere gathering of information about a particular individual does not give rise to a cause of action under this theory. Privacy is invaded only if the information sought is of a confidential nature and the defendant's conduct was unreasonably intrusive . . . In order to sustain a cause of action for invasion of privacy, therefore, the plaintiff must show that the appellant's conduct was truly "intrusive" and that it was designed to elicit information which would not be available through normal inquiry or observation.

Judge Fuld then proceeded to throw out three of the strongest allegations in our first two causes of action: the allegations that were backed by the Gillen disclosures. He disallowed the claims based upon the interviewing of Nader's friends and associates, even if the questions cast aspersions on Nader's character. Judge Fuld felt that if the questions did disparage the plaintiff's character, the proper remedy was an action for defamation. We had considered suing for defamation, but we had no proof that any false statements were made by Gillen's investigators. To sue for disparaging questions, we would have to prove that they caused financial damage, but of course there was none. Judge Fuld also found that accosting by women with illicit proposals and making threatening and harassing telephone calls were not actionable invasions of privacy. He wrote:

> Neither of these activities, however offensive and disturbing, involve intrusion for the purpose of gathering information of a private and confidential nature.

Thus, Judge Fuld and the majority of the court took the view that only those allegations that fell precisely within the historical language of the District of Columbia court decisions would be actionable as invasions of privacy. Here we were hurt by the fact situation in the Dodd-Pearson case. A senator was seeking to collect damages from newsmen who had performed a public service by exposing the senator's misconduct, and the newsmen had not intruded into the privacy of the senator's office themselves. The appellate court that ruled against Senator Dodd had good reasons for stressing the nonprivate nature of the information gathered by Pearson and Anderson, but when that decision was applied to the Nader-GM case, it narrowed the protection of privacy considerably.

Judge Fuld held that two of the allegations in our complaint came within the protection of District of Columbia privacy law: wiretapping and obtrusive surveillance. He noted from our bill of particulars that we alleged that Nader was followed so closely that one of the detectives was able to see the denomination of the bills he was withdrawing from his bank account.

At the end of his opinion, Judge Fuld pointed out:

> We would but add that the allegations concerning the interviewing of third persons, the accosting by girls and the annoying and threatening telephone calls, though insufficient to support a cause of action for invasion of privacy, are pertinent to the plaintiff's third cause of action—in which those allegations are reiterated—charging the intentional infliction of emotional distress. However, as already noted, it will be necessary for the plaintiff to meet the additional requirements prescribed by the law of the District of Columbia for the maintenance of a cause of action under that theory.

The "additional requirements" he referred to were that we would have to prove these acts were intentional or at least reckless. Fortunately, we had the Dear Dick letter and the other Gillen disclosures to show that the harassment of Nader was intentional or at least reckless. Thus, the third cause of action turned out to be a lifesaver. It kept in the case much of the most damaging evidence: the grilling of more than 60 associates of Nader, the accosting by women, and the nocturnal telephone calls. However, we did not have any evidence that the harassing telephone calls or the use of the women were intentional or reckless, since Gillen denied any connection with them. Only by getting depositions from GM personnel and obtaining GM records could we hope to prove that GM had hired people other than Gillen to unleash the women and to make the harassing telephone calls.

Although all seven judges agreed that the first and second causes of action should not be dismissed, there were two separate opinions. Judges Scileppi, Bergan, and Gibson joined with Chief Judge Fuld in his opinion. Judge Charles D. Breitel wrote a separate concurring opinion, in which Judges Burke and Jasen joined, expressing disagreement with part of the majority opinion. Judge Breitel and his colleagues agreed that the first two causes of action were sufficient under District of Columbia law. They departed from their brethren by saying that the court should go no further in examining the pleadings, lest they inhibit the trial court from hearing evidence which might well be relevant, in light of the rapidly evolving scope of privacy protection. Judge Breitel wrote:

> The real issue in the volatile and developing law of privacy is whether a private person is entitled to be free of certain grave offensive intrusions unsupported by palpable social or economic excuse or justification.
>
> True, scholars, in trying to define the elusive concept of the right of privacy, have, as of the present, subdivided the common law right into separate classifications, most significantly distinguishing between unreasonable intrusion and unreasonable publicity [citing the Second Restatement of Torts and Prosser]. This does not mean, however, that the classifications are either frozen or exhausted, or that several of the classifications may not overlap.

Judge Breitel suggested that it was premature to rule at the pleadings stage that public surveillance, attempted entrapment by women, harassing telephone calls, and Gillen's extensive interviews, were not part of an overall plan or course of conduct which might be actionable as invasion of privacy. He wrote:

> It is not unimportant that plaintiff contends that a giant corporation had allegedly sought by surreptitious and unusual methods to silence an unusually effective critic. If there was such a plan, and only a trial would show that, it is unduly restrictive of the future trial to allocate the evidence beforehand based only

on a pleader's specification of overt acts on the bold assumption that they are not connected causally or do not bear on intent and motive.

Judge Breitel went on to say that the law of privacy was in an early stage of development in the District of Columbia and that there was "no justification, on the present record, for giving an illiberal and restrictive scope to a cause of action based on the right of privacy as that right is likely to be defined under the applicable law of another jurisdiction."

Judge Breitel later became a distinguished Chief Judge of the Court of Appeals. At the time of this writing (1979), it is likely that if the same issue came before the Court of Appeals, it would be decided in accordance with Judge Breitel's opinion rather than Judge Fuld's opinion, since all four of the majority judges are gone from the court. But we had to take the law as it was in 1970, and we came away from the Court of Appeals breathing a sigh of relief that we had kept all of our allegations in the case, even though we would have to rely on the backstop third cause of action for intentional or reckless infliction of emotional distress to get into evidence the smearing questions, the harassing telephone calls, and the accosting women.

The beachhead of constitutional law that had been established by Justice Brust's decision remained intact. Both the Appellate Division and the Court of Appeals found it unnecessary to review his holding on the constitutional point, because GM had taken that issue away from the appellate courts by conceding that District of Columbia law would govern the second cause of action. In the 4th Edition of his famous *Handbook on Torts,* Dean William Prosser said of Justice Brust's decision:

> But the most significant decision may be that of a trial court in New York, again involving intrusion in several forms, which held that the existence of the Constitutional privilege extended the liability beyond the cases of appropriation specified in the statute. While the appellate courts went out the back door by holding that the case was governed by the law of the District of Columbia, which recognized the liability for intrusion, and therefore did not reach the Constitutional question, the decision in the trial court was not overruled, and may still be followed.

GM's motion to dismiss was finally decided 21 months after it was filed on March 15, 1968. This was not an unusually long period of time for the decision of difficult and novel points of law in a case which had to take its turn on the calendars of three of the busiest courts in the world. It illustrates how a defendant with the power of General Motors can administer the yo-yo treatment to anyone bold enough to sue them. At the same time that the GM motion to dismiss was making its way up through the appellate courts, we were struggling with voluminous GM motions and appeals on other aspects of the case.

The Settlement

When the Court of Appeals denied GM's motion to dismiss on January 8, 1970, we had reached the point where it was sensible for General Motors to consider settlement. While the Court of Appeals decision had weakened our case somewhat, it had upheld our right to sue for invasion of privacy and for infliction of emotional distress. Thanks to the Gillen disclosures and the favorable decisions of Referee Bieber and Justice Streit, affirmed by the Appellate Division, we had compelling evidence to back up these charges—evidence that included GM's own documents, such as the Dear Dick letter. If the case went on from that point, the next step would have been depositions, with Ralph Nader to be deposed first, followed by the depositions of GM employees and agents, including Gillen and Danner. This discovery, and the various motions and appeals that could result from it, would probably have taken up several more years before the case ever got to trial, especially in view of GM's ability to use attorney-client privilege to prevent disclosure. This prospect might have discouraged an ordinary plaintiff, but GM had learned that Ralph Nader was not an ordinary plaintiff. Additional years of attrition would cost GM a lot of money in legal fees, but that would not get Nader out of their hair, and it would not prevent us from proving our case when it finally came to trial, even if we found no further evidence to supplement the Gillen disclosures. Thanks to the four-to-three Court of Appeals decision, we knew that all of Ralph's claims would be submitted to a jury, supported by (at least) the Gillen evidence.

There was another strong incentive for GM to settle. From the beginning of the suit, the public-relations battle had been going against them. Every major development in the case was covered by the press, and many of the articles repeated the sordid story of the Dear Dick letter and the other Gillen disclosures, which kept returning like bad pennies in Gillen's admissions, our bill of particulars, Referee Bieber's hearings, and numerous motions and appeals. For example, here is how Murray Kempton treated the case in his syndicated column of February 17, 1967:

> Comes now Gillen to tell his version of his assignment from
> GM . . . He occasionally takes the customary business precau-

tion of giving a false name; but one cannot, reading his testimony and Roche's, end up feeling that his standards of absolute candor under oath are inferior to those of the president of GM.

*   *   *

"Have fun, friend," had been the last line in the memo from GM's legal department setting forth his instructions. It seems to be a sad aspect of corporate management that it never turns out to be fun.

While the carefully worded Roche apology to Senator Ribicoff portrayed GM as a victim of Gillen's overzealousness rather than as the instigator of it, the later Gillen disclosures in the lawsuit wiped out that image and threw GM into the same boat as Gillen. The press and the public came to treat the Roche statement as an admission of responsibility for all of Gillen's activities, rather than as an apology for an inadvertent and unauthorized frolic. Thus, in his Appellate Division majority opinion, Justice McGivern wrote:

> The scrutiny and the surveillance of the plaintiff, carried on by the defendant's operatives, were characterized by such uninhibited gusto that the culmination was an apology tendered him before a Senatorial Investigating Committee.

*   *   *

> . . . the defendant General Motors has already conceded wrongdoing . . .

This turnabout has persisted through the years. On April 3, 1978, (twelve years after the Roche apology) Reginald Stuart wrote in *The New York Times:*

> In March 1966, James Roche, then GM's chairman, acknowledged in Washington hearings that the company's legal department had hired private detectives (without his knowledge) to spy on Mr. Nader's private life, apparently in hopes of smearing the reputation of Mr. Nader, an outspoken critic of the company. Such spying was wrong, Mr. Roche said.

From the personal standpoint of GM's top executives, there was little incentive to carry on the litigation after the Court of Appeals finally upheld Nader's right to maintain the action in 1970. James Roche had been moved up to chairman, and Edward Cole, whom Nader had first met at Warren, Michigan, in 1966, was now president. Aloysius M. Power had reached the age of 65 and had retired as general counsel in 1967. The new regime could dispose of the embarrassment of the Nader case without having been responsible for creating it.

In addition, a kind of reverse attrition process had begun to affect GM's cost position. Originally, in line with the accepted strategy in David-Goliath situations, the giant used its superior resources to stretch out the case and drag the impecunious plaintiff through endless court proceedings. But as we completed the third year of litigation, the calculator began to run against General Motors. We had weathered all of the major motions and appeals and had come through with our right to sue established and our supporting evidence much stronger than we had expected, thanks to the Gillen disclosures. GM could have continued the litigation for many more years, but they would have been on the defensive practically all the way. We would have been pounding on the doors of their inner sanctum, demanding documents and questioning their officers and employees. They could have used their litigation power to delay discovery, but the chances were that every time we hauled them into court to force disclosure, the press would have accused them of covering up the facts. And all of these maneuvers would be expensive, since they had hired one of the great litigation firms whose services commanded healthy fees. In addition to the Paul Weiss fees, the suit was costing GM money through the involvement of its own officers and legal department.

Serious settlement discussions began early in 1970. Ralph would have preferred to go on with the case, pressing for discovery of all details of GM's involvement, and then bringing all the facts to light in a public trial. However, as a lawyer he recognized the strength of the opposition and their ability to spend unlimited funds to block us, using attorney-client privilege at every turn. He knew that it could easily take another five or six years to complete the trial and the last appeal, by which time the public might have tired of the whole matter.

By 1970, Ralph Nader had branched out from automobile safety and was deeply involved in other public service projects. He had announced at the beginning of the GM suit that he would dedicate any recovery to the cause of consumer safety. His small staff was working almost on a volunteer basis, and he knew that he could accomplish much more if he had the money to hire more people. With this in mind, on August 13, 1970, Ralph agreed to settle the case for $425,000. Settlement negotiations are conducted in confidence, and most lawyers —myself included—believe that they should remain confidential forever, in order to free the negotiators from any inhibitions that might stall the settlement process. Therefore, I cannot tell you any details of the negotiations.

The $425,000 settlement, all paid as compensatory damages, was more than 30 times the size of the highest previous award for invasion of privacy, even in cases where there had been loss of income or destruction of a business. Looking back on the settlement in the light of the hyper-inflation of the late 1970s, it is still a healthy payment for compensatory damages to a plaintiff who suffered no financial loss. However, I have no doubt that if the same case came up in 1979, it would have a settlement value of $1 million or more. Inflation would add several hundred thousand dollars. Then there is the increased accountability of large corporations for the damage they inflict upon individuals—an accountability that was originated by Ralph Nader and the Nader-GM case itself, and then expanded in the post-Watergate era. Other factors are the growing public awareness of the seriousness of emotional injuries, and the increasing tendency of the courts to uphold larger damage awards for injuries.

Under the retainer agreement, our fee was supposed to be one third of the first $300,000, and thirty percent of the $125,000 balance, making a total of $137,000, plus return of our out-of-pocket expenses which came to about $10,000. Ralph would have received $277,500, and we would have been paid a total of $147,500. However, we agreed to reduce our fee so that Ralph would receive $300,000 net. In the end, we received a fee of $115,000 and reimbursement of our $10,000 in expenses. At $100 per hour (considered a modest rate for important New York litigation), our fee would have covered approximately 1,150 hours of work by senior attorneys such as Al Gans, Paul Rheingold, and me. We did not keep any time records because we had undertaken the case on a percentage fee basis. However, I know that the case took at least a full year of my time, and I estimate that lawyers in our firm spent more than 4,000 hours on it, which means that we were working for less than $30 an hour, a rate charged by young attorneys to fill out the simplest legal forms.

In October 1967 Ralph had announced the concept of a nonprofit law firm, the forerunner of the public interest law firm movement. What he did not say was that he was in the process of turning our firm into a nonprofit operation—but we loved every minute of it. It was a case that we would have enjoyed working on without any fee, if we could have afforded that luxury.

We did not escape with the entire $115,000 fee intact. At Ralph's request, we made a contribution of $10,000 to help launch a new aviation consumer organization, later named the Aviation Consumer Action Project.

The story of the settlement was headlined in newspapers throughout America, and it even made the front page of the London *Times* on August 14. The *Washington Post* story straddled the $26-million question:

> The suit which GM said demanded $26.2 million but Nader said was only $2 million with many overlapping claims, was filed more than three and a half years ago.

The *Los Angeles Times* headlines read:

GM SETTLES NADER SUIT FOR $425,000
$2 million case over privacy invasion ended

Taking note of the fact that the GM statement denied any wrongdoing, the *Standard-Star* of New Rochelle, N.Y., published on its editorial page a cartoon showing a GM executive taking cash out of the GM safe and handing it to Ralph Nader, with this caption: "Of course, we don't admit we invaded your privacy. But anyway, here's $425,000 to offset your embarrassment at becoming internationally famous." In his *New York Times* column for Sunday, August 16, Tom Wicker wrote:

> . . . take the Ralph Nader case. General Motors actually paid him $425,000 although the company insisted it had not turned loose any private eyes on Mr. Nader, had not invaded his privacy and didn't owe him a cent. It is not only reassuring to know that big business doesn't do that kind of thing, it is downright comforting to know that the reason GM paid off was to protect its good old American stockholders against the horrendous cost of proving it didn't owe the 425 G's. Now that's responsibility.

And on August 17, the following editorial appeared in the *New York Times:*

> The out-of-court settlement of Ralph Nader's suit against General Motors for invasion of privacy concludes this landmark case on a positive note. The New York Court of Appeals has affirmed that Mr. Nader had a cause of action, but litigation could have tied up talents and the courts for years. Instead, the proceeds of the $425,000 settlement will be used after expenses are deducted, for "continuous legal monitoring" of GM by Mr. Nader in safety, pollution and consumer relations.
>
> Today, Mr. Nader's book, *Unsafe At Any Speed: The Designed-in Dangers of the American Automobile,* is recognized as one of the most important investigatory studies of the last decade. But only five years ago its revelations caused GM to look into the personal life of the author instead of looking under its own hood.
>
> The settlement is significant in ways that go beyond Mr. Nader's own case. It gives added legal standing to the developing notion that an individual's private life must be safeguarded from intrusion and snooping by various institutions. And it provides further recognition to the problems of automobile-caused hazards without making these vital matters appear to be merely the concern of one bold consumer gadfly.

But it remained for Ralph himself to supply the final punch line, as quoted in *Newsweek* for August 24, 1970:

The $425,000 settlement will be General Motors' contribution to the consumer movement. They are going to be financing their own ombudsman.

A Balance Sheet

When we started the lawsuit, Ralph Nader's principal objectives were to destroy the unauthorized frolic defense by revealing the true GM role in the investigation; to strengthen legal protection of the individual against corporate snooping and harassment, even if this required us to make new constitutional law; and to collect enough money to fuel Ralph's consumer activities. We were able to accomplish all three objectives in relatively short time, compared to the many more years that would be required to complete GM depositions, try the case and weather all the appeals, with the final recovery allowed by the appellate courts not likely to exceed the $425,000 that was paid in settlement. As lawyers, we were delighted with the result, although Ralph, being a perfectionist who is in a constant state of rebellion against any injustice, could never have been satisfied with anything short of a public trial that revealed the activities of all GM employees and agents.

There were some intriguing questions that we had to leave unanswered in order to achieve Ralph's three main objectives within a reasonable time. We were convinced that there must have been other people besides Gillen investigating Nader on behalf of GM, but we were never able to develop any hard evidence to support our suspicions. Gillen steadfastly denied that his men had followed Ralph in Iowa during the attorney general's safety hearings, or in Philadelphia after the Mike Douglas show. He also insisted that he had nothing to do with the harassing telephone calls or the hiring of girls to accost Ralph. I found myself willing to believe Gillen, mainly because it appeared from his records that he had never billed GM for any such activities. If Gillen and his bloodhounds did not perform these services, who did?

The seven-page GM dossier on Nader that Eileen Murphy handed over to Dick Danner for the guidance of Gillen contained a great deal of information that could only have been obtained by intensive investigation. It went far beyond the very sketchy investigation report of O'Neill, who had in November of 1965 spent just a few days checking Ralph's Connecticut history. And as we have seen, that seven-page dossier was the source of Gillen's instructions to question Nader's associates about sex, anti-Semitism, narcotics, and the like.

My suspicions were aroused even further when I interviewed J. Donald Remmert, one of Gillen's investigators, who had trailed

Nader in Washington and had been ejected from the New Senate Office Building on February 11, 1966. He told me that on several occasions while he was watching Nader's rooming house, he noticed another car driving slowly around the neighborhood and then parking near the rooming house. Remmert's private detective instinct told him that somebody else had Ralph under surveillance.

One of Remmert's assignments was to go to the New Senate Office Building to read the transcript of Nader's February 10 testimony before the Ribicoff subcommittee. He told me that when he explained his mission to the receptionist at the subcommittee office, she informed him that four other investigators had reviewed the transcript the same day, February 16. And while Remmert was in the subcommittee office on February 16, still another private investigator arrived and asked to see the same transcript. I asked him if he knew who the man was. He said that he did not know the man but that he had to be a private investigator, for two reasons. First, the man was wearing "delicatessen shoes," meaning that he had the wardrobe and the appearance of a private eye. Second, Remmert noticed that when the other man was asked by the receptionist to show identification, he pulled out a card that all private investigators licensed in New York are required to carry.

There were further indications that Gillen's men were following a trail that had been scouted by others. Mary McDonald at Harvard told GM investigator O'Neill that three other investigators had recently been in touch with her about Nader. William Foulis, a witness interviewed by Gillen investigator Bernard Morley on February 11, 1966, mentioned that somebody else had been in to see him recently asking questions about Nader.

The 1970 settlement also left unanswered the question of how high up in GM management there was knowledge of Gillen's activities. In 1979, Detroit automotive journalist J. Patrick Wright published an intriguing book called *On a Clear Day You Can See General Motors,* which originated as a collaboration with John Z. DeLorean, a former high executive of GM. DeLorean had risen through the ranks to become General Manager of the Chevrolet division in 1969 (at age 44), and Group Executive in charge of the entire domestic vehicle business in 1972, at an annual salary of $650,000. He resigned in 1973 and started his own company to produce a newly designed sports car. Mr. Wright states that DeLorean withdrew his collaboration because "he feared that reprisals from GM would sink his attempts to launch a new car company." However, when the book was published by Mr. Wright in 1979, it was written as a first person narrative by DeLorean, who refused to repudiate it. Therefore, we can probably accept as Mr. DeLorean's words the following statement about the Nader-GM affair:

When Nader's book threatened the Corvair's sales and profits, he became an enemy of the system. Instead of trying to attack his credentials or the factual basis of his arguments, the company sought to attack him personally. This move failed, but, in the process, GM's blundering "made" Ralph Nader.

*   *   *

I find it difficult to believe that knowledge of these activities did not reach into the upper reaches of GM's management.

The DeLorean book also confirms the correctness of Nader's charges that the Corvair was unsafe as originally designed, and that high level GM executives were aware of this when they put the car on the market in 1959. DeLorean claims that he tried to persuade his colleagues to correct the Corvair's defects but he was unable to overcome the arguments of those who were more concerned with costs than with safety.

I had been looking forward to taking the depositions of GM's employees, such as Eileen Murphy, Aloysius F. Power, and Louis Bridenstine, to determine where they got the information in the seven-page dossier on Nader which was compiled before they hired Gillen. But the settlement in 1970 left that question unanswered, along with others, such as the role of Dick Danner, the Washington lawyer who collected a "legal" fee from GM for hiring Vincent Gillen, an investigator who had been hired directly by GM on dozens of past occasions. Our efforts to take Danner's deposition in the *Detroit Free Press* libel action against Gillen were thwarted by Danner's evasion of the subpoena which we had entrusted to ace process server Hugh Duffy.

Danner had a very interesting background. He was an ex-FBI man who had been a special agent in charge of the FBI office in Miami during World War II. In 1946 Danner resigned from the FBI and became city manager of Miami. In 1950, he was the campaign manager for George Smathers in the famous senatorial race against the incumbent, Claude Pepper. Smathers charged that Pepper was soft on communism, and the campaign included publication of photographs that purported to show a connection between Pepper and prominent communists. Some of these photographs were later revealed to have been composites or fakes, but they were very effective in helping Smathers to defeat Pepper in the Democratic primary and to bring Smathers to Washington as a senator from Florida. According to Claude Pepper, Danner played an important role in producing these photographs and other smears which helped Smathers to defeat Pepper.

Danner made news headlines long after the 1970 Nader settlement, in the fall of 1973, when it was disclosed that he had been working for the Howard Hughes organization in Las Vegas, and that he had delivered $100,000 in cash taken from the Silver Slipper gambling casino in Las Vegas to President Nixon's close friend, Florida banker

Bebe Rebozo. According to press reports, Danner claimed that the $100,000 was a campaign contribution.

Danner's involvement in the Watergate episode reminded me of how many striking parallels there were between Watergate and the Nader-GM case. Both cases had come to the surface because of the bungling of hired operatives in Washington office buildings—the hired burglars in the Watergate headquarters of the Democratic National Committee, and the hired investigators who trailed Nader into the New Senate Office Building. In both cases, double and triple layers of lawyers were used to create a shield of attorney-client privilege. Nader was propositioned by two attractive young women, which paralleled Gordon Liddy's plan to use attractive women to compromise men on the White House enemies list. Then there was the Runyonesque character, ex-New York policeman Tony Ulascewitz, and his "background investigations" of political figures and White House enemies in which he used the pre-employment pretext to delve into sex, drinking, social life, finances, and the most intimate personal details. Senator Lowell Weicker of Connecticut called this activity "dirt gathering." It was, of course, very similar to what Gillen was hired to do in the Nader case. In Watergate, the pre-employment pretext had been used to investigate Daniel Schorr, the CBS correspondent who had been an outspoken critic of the Nixon administration.

There were similar happenings in both cases after the bunglers were caught in the act and the question of ultimate responsibility was raised. The Watergate cover-up, which involved the destruction of documents and instructions to witnesses to conceal the truth, was brought to light by a turncoat witness, former White House counsel John Dean. A similar cover-up in which documents were destroyed and witnesses were told to conceal the truth was testified to by turncoat witness Vincent Gillen in the Nader case. Just as the White House attempted to brand Watergate as an unauthorized frolic by Liddy, so GM tried to portray the harassment of Nader as an unauthorized frolic by Gillen. The Nixon White House tapes were the key to breaking open the Watergate case, just as detective Gillen's tapes were so important to us in the Nader case. And there was the presence of Dick Danner in both cases—the bearer of $100,000 in Las Vegas casino money to Bebe Rebozo, and the "Dear Dick" of the Nader case.

The public reaction to both incidents was similar: surprise that high-level people would get caught in such a lowly caper, rather than shock that high-level people were actually stooping so low. This was the theme of an article in the British Sunday newspaper, *The Observer;* shortly after the Ribicoff subcommittee hearing of March 22, 1966, at which GM president Roche delivered his apology, Anthony Howard wrote:

> How long the sprawling power and the cozy shelter en-
> joyed by great corporate organizations will go on being the un-
> grasped nettle of American public life is anyone's guess. But if
> precedent is anything to go by, this week will have changed
> nothing. For there is a melancholy pattern to American business
> scandals: a contrite public relations statement is made, an ex-
> ecutive or two is sacked, and then life goes on as before . . .
> If there is a disease eating away at American business it is
> not wickedness or even greed; it is a blasé indifference—an in-
> difference that even the sight of General Motors having to pick
> itself up off the floor and dust its clothes off has probably done
> little to challenge.

This is an accurate assessment of the indifference to governmental
action such as the Senate hearing at which Roche delivered his apology.
But it was written before GM had to face a tougher test than a Senate
hearing—Ralph Nader's lawsuit. Even though our large corporations
can emerge from congressional investigations and actions of administrative agencies to operate pretty much as before, they are far less likely
to maintain "business as usual" if they have to face damage judgments in American courts. Just as Watergate showed that our criminal
law system can deal with crimes committed in the Oval Office of the
White House, so the Nader case demonstrated that our civil law system
can expose and deal with injustices done at the apex of American industry, in the Detroit headquarters of General Motors.

In both the Watergate and Nader cases, personal accountability
was the key factor. John Dean was personally accountable for his mis-
deeds, and it was his fear of punishment that caused him to make
revelations that exposed the sordid Watergate story. In the Nader case,
Vincent Gillen was personally accountable for his investigation of
Nader, and he had plenty to lose—a profitable business, his home, and
other property that he had worked all of his life to acquire. We sued
him personally, and a jury could have assessed heavy damages against
him alone if they believed that he had gone beyond GM's instructions.
It was this concern for his personal accountability that drove him
to reveal his true instructions from General Motors and thus break
the case wide open for us.

The Nader-GM incident and the litigation that followed have
caused some permanent changes. Few corporate executives or legal
advisers would seriously consider launching a Gillen-type investigation
against a critic today. And a beachhead has been established for a
constitutional right of privacy through the decision of Supreme Court
Justice Joseph Brust in the Nader case. However, further steps are
necessary to consolidate these gains. Corporate, government, and
political officials must be held personally accountable for outrageous
conduct. In the end, all outrages are committed by individuals, and the

law should be structured so that the injured individual stands on equal ground against the individual who used corporate or government machinery to inflict injuries—*one on one*. Ralph Nader faced Vincent Gillen one on one, and so justice was done. And because of the ongoing litigation revolution of the 1970s that the Nader-GM case helped to launch, officials of large corporations cannot escape responsibility for outrageous conduct as easily as before.

Individuals and small companies with grievances against large corporations have gained some power to recover damages. And these damages will not always be paid from vast corporate treasuries, as in the Nader case. Today such a case might give rise to a second lawsuit —one by the shareholders of the large corporation, to recover from the responsible corporate officials the settlement money that was paid to protect them from embarrassment, prosecution, or personal payment of damages. As the litigation revolution gathers momentum, it is moving in the direction of personal accountability—not fast enough to suit Ralph Nader, but on a scale broad enough to make corporate officials think at least twice before committing torts.

Professor Marshall S. Shapo of Northwestern University School of Law explains why he starts his torts course each year with the Nader-GM case:

> The case features an intuitively sympathetic situation with two well-known antagonists, and presents a cauldron of difficult issues for beginning students. It provides a stretching experience in distinguishing allegations from proof, stating issues, deriving rules and analyzing judicial conflict about the role of the court in an advancing area of legal doctrine. It raises essential questions concerning the role of tort law in protecting individual personality and dignity, gives an excellent opportunity to link questions concerning the quantum of damages to substantive law problems, and offers a nice springboard beyond the next two assignments into the intentional torts.

Those who deplore the "litigious society" seem to be under the impression that it is easy to right such wrongs or to collect a lot of money from big corporations in American courts. But you should know better, now that you have read the story of what we had to go through to collect damages for Ralph Nader. How many lawyers have a client like Ralph Nader fall into their laps? To take on a major corporation in a battle of this kind, you almost need a super-plaintiff who has a spotless character and personal life and is completely dedicated to the public good. Even this combination is probably not enough. You have to be lucky enough to catch the offenders redhanded, as Gillen's gumshoes were caught in the New Senate Office Building. For good measure, it would help to have an apology from the corporation's president on nationwide television and a turncoat private eye who was clever enough to preserve all the evidence for you.

In drawing up a balance sheet of the Nader-GM case, I place on the asset side its long-term effects on American litigation. It helped to speed up diffusion of litigation power, so that many individuals and small companies can wield power in the courts—power that once was reserved for corporate giants like General Motors. It furnished a winning model for David-Goliath confrontations, giving other individuals the inspiration to criticize, to challenge, to sue. But overshadowing all these gains was the single most important effect of the case, one that Ralph Nader's lawyers had nothing to do with: he used the settlement proceeds to build the world's first effective consumer movement, saving thousands of lives and changing American government, business, and society as no private individual had ever done before.

Ralph Nader's consumer revolution was underway long before the 1970 settlement of his lawsuit, but it was pretty much a one man show, with a little help from a few underpaid overworked cohorts. He used the fees from television and lecturing appearances to keep a tiny staff going under hectic operating conditions. In the summer they were augmented by student volunteers, known as Nader's Raiders. After nursing the National Traffic and Motor Vehicle Safety Act of 1966 through Congress, Ralph moved on to inspire and lobby for the Wholesome Meat Act of 1967, the Natural Gas Pipeline Safety Act of 1968, the Radiation Control for Health and Safety Act of 1968, the Coal Mine Health and Safety Act of 1969, and the comprehensive Occupational Safety and Health Act of 1970. His Raiders exposed serious problems at the Federal Trade Commission in 1968 and the Food & Drug Administration in 1969, and strong corrective action followed at both agencies. Thus Ralph packed into the years 1966–1970 enough major accomplishments to last most crusaders a lifetime. But not until he received the $300,000 net proceeds of the GM settlement did he have the funds to assure the continuity of his operations and to build the permanent staff needed to fight on so many consumer fronts.

Today, Ralph's activities are not limited to criticizing and lobbying. His Public Citizen organization includes the Litigation Group with a staff of full-time lawyers who have conducted many significant public-interest lawsuits; Congress Watch, the lobbying unit, with a staff of eleven; Critical Mass, which exposes and opposes dangerous energy projects; the Tax Reform Research Group, whose staff of eight lobbies for tax reform; the Health Research Group, which has exposed many health hazards; and Aviation Consumer Action Project, the only group that represents the airline passenger in regulatory and safety proceedings. There are other important Nader units outside the Public Citizen organization: Center for Study of Responsive Law; the Corporate Accountability Research Group; the Consumer Complaint Research Center; Clean Water Action Project; Freedom of Information Clearinghouse; and my favorite Nader creation, the Public Interest Research Group (PIRG), which has spawned hundreds of little PIRGs on college campuses, involving hundreds of thousands of students in consumer action projects ranging from lobbying to picketing and to the filing of public-interest lawsuits.

It would take a book at least as long as this one to catalogue what Ralph Nader's consumer movement has accomplished since its scope and momentum were augmented by the 1970 GM settlement. His influence is now worldwide—he is as much a hero in Japan and Australia as he is in Connecticut. There are periodic predictions that his movement will run out of gas or that he will lose his credibility by making a serious blunder, but there are no signs that this will happen. Even though many people don't like to be forced to take care of themselves, and some consider Ralph the "national scold," he always turns up as the most popular and most trusted American public figure when polls are conducted on such choices. In 1971, *Chicago Daily News* columnist Mike Royko asked his readers to indicate their preferences for the 1972 presidential election, giving them five choices: Senators Muskie, Kennedy, McGovern, and Humphrey—and Ralph Nader. The results of this poll were: Nader 1614, Muskie 148, Kennedy 42, McGovern 41, and Humphrey 11. A 1975 Louis Harris poll found that a cross section of American adults favored Ralph's activities by a majority of 76 percent to 8 percent. Even on the loaded question, "Nader is a troublemaker who is against the free-enterprise system," only 11 percent agreed. Perhaps the ultimate salute to Ralph came in the muted tones of this 1973 *Wall Street Journal* editorial:

> Mr. Rust [president of the U.S. Chamber of Commerce] is simply suggesting that the business community take a fresh look at Mr. Nader and be prepared to hear him out on the merits of his arguments and complaints, for he articulates "the dissatisfactions and the frustrations that are widespread among American consumers." This is wise counsel. Mr. Nader has proven himself an excellent diagnostician of the ills of the marketplace . . . But the more attentive American business is to his diagnostic skills, the less shrill he will have to be in getting his message across.

Knowing Ralph Nader, I am convinced that he would have gotten his consumer revolution under way somehow, even if Vincent Gillen's private eyes had not bungled their assignments in the New Senate Office Building on February 10, 1966; and that eventually he would have become the world's leading consumer activist even if he had not

been able to use $300,000 of GM's money for his public-service ac-
tivities. Yet I am equally certain that those two events, occurring when
they did, enabled Ralph to save many lives and to avoid much human
misery that would otherwise have been suffered. In the decade since
the GM settlement, more than 60 million cars and trucks have been
recalled for repair of safety defects. In the same period, coal miners and
their beneficiaries received more than $8 billion in compensation for
black lung disease, a benefit that did not exist before Nader helped to
get it enacted and enforced. In the end, these are the most important
entries in the balance sheet of *Nader v. General Motors.*

Comparative Law

Ralph Nader's lawsuit against General Motors ended when it reached
the point where both parties knew most of the facts that would be
brought out at the trial and their lawyers were in a position to assess
their positions accurately. It came to an undramatic finale, settled before trial, as happens in more than 90 percent of American lawsuits.
But what would have been its fate in the courts of other nations?

To answer that question, I requested colleagues who practice
law in other countries to study the facts of the Nader case and to comment on the probable treatment of such a suit in their respective nations. I asked the commentators to assume that Ralph Nader was a
local client coming to them for advice in 1979 on his potential claim
against a local company similar to General Motors, and to assume that
all the facts of the Nader-GM case occurred in their respective nations.
I solicited their opinions as to whether Ralph could state a cause of
action (and thus survive a motion to dismiss the complaint); what his
cause of action would be called; and the likely outcome in their courts
if the case went to trial.

I have divided their comments into two groups: the common-law
nations and the Roman ("civil") law nations. This is a somewhat arbitrary division, since nations that follow the common law or Roman
law traditions do not always have the same substantive law or procedures as other nations within the same grouping. However, it is the
simplest way to classify the world's major legal system for purposes of
comparison.

I did not seek comments on the treatment of the Nader-GM case
in the communist nations, since I cannot imagine how such a case
could arise there. Where both economic and political power are held
exclusively by the state, there can be neither a Ralph Nader nor a
General Motors, and the state may spy on its critics at will.

Apart from the United States, the common-law nations consist mainly of Great Britain and the present and former members of the British Commonwealth of Nations. Our commentators from England, Canada, and Israel give us a good sampling of common-law treatments of the Nader-GM case.

The Roman ("civil") law system which originated in 450 B.C., is the oldest and the most widely used. It is the dominant legal tradition in most of Western Europe, Asia, and Africa, and all of Latin America. Our commentators from France, Belgium, the Netherlands, West Germany, Spain, Portugal, Norway, Japan, and Mexico provide a panoramic view of Roman law treatment of such a case. The comments from the Western European nations are generally applicable to the legal systems of their present and former colonies throughout the world.

Three distinguished lawyers agreed to comment on the common law nations.

England: John D. Sheerin, senior litigation partner of the Bury St. Edmunds solicitors' firm of Greene & Greene. Mr. Sheerin has had extensive experience with American tort law as solicitor for several Bury St. Edmunds families that lost relatives in the 1974 Turkish Airlines DC-10 crash at Paris. He also served as a deputy circuit judge, and in 1979 was appointed Recorder of the Crown Courts for the South Eastern Circuit, a judicial post that he fills while continuing private law practice with Greene & Greene.

Canada: Kenneth E. Howie, Q. C., a member of the Toronto firm of Thomson Rogers, barristers and solicitors. Mr. Howie is lecturer on trial practice for the bar admission course of the Law Society of Upper Canada, and trial demonstrator at Osgoode Hall Law School. He is past president of the County of York Law Association and of the Medico-Legal Society of Toronto.

Israel: Paul H. Baris, a member of the Tel-Aviv and Jerusalem firm of Yigal Arnon & Co., advocates. Mr. Baris was born and educated in the United States and practiced law in New York from 1958 to 1973, when he emigrated to Israel and was admitted to the bar there. In addition to his law practice, Mr. Baris has been professor of law at Bar-Ilan University, Ramat Gan, Israel, since 1973.

We are equally fortunate in the calibre of our Roman law commentators.

France: Jean-Marc Gernigon, avocat à la Cour de Paris since 1945. Maître Gernigon is a former secretary of the Conference of the Paris Bar, and a former member of its Counseil de l'Ordre (regulating body). He is a chevalier of the Legion of Honor and an officer of the National Order of Merit. He is noted among French lawyers as an expert on aeronautical and tort law, and has represented many French citizens in civil suits brought in the United States.

Belgium: Roger O. Dalcq, a member of the Brussels firm of Janson, Baugniet et Associes, one of the largest law firms in Belgium. Maître Dalcq is also professor of comparative law, torts and insurance at the University of Louvain; author of a major two-volume treatise on torts, as well as numerous published articles; and is editor in chief of the *Revue Générale des Assurances et Responsabilités.* He is a former secretary of the Brussels Bar Association and a former member of its council.

Netherlands: Dr. A. F. X. Drilling, a member of the Amsterdam firm of Boekel, Van Empel & Drilling, Advocaten, one of the largest Dutch litigation law firms. Dr. Drilling has had extensive experience in tort litigation both in the Netherlands and in the United States, where he represented a large group of Dutch families that sued in New York for damages arising out of the 1977 Tenerife collision of KLM and Pan American jumbo jets.

West Germany: William Schurtman, a well known litigation specialist and a member of the New York international law firm of Walter Conston Schurtman & Gumpel, P. C., who prepared the West German comments in collaboration with his colleague Dr. Heinrich Senfft of the Hamburg, Germany, bar. Dr. Senfft is a senior partner of the Hamburg law firm of Senfft Rollenhagen Lagenbuch & Partner. He was a member of the Max Planck Institute for Foreign and International Law in Hamburg and also studied American law at the University of California at Berkeley. He is a specialist in German defamation and media law and also acts as a consultant on German law in New York.

Spain: William T. Washburn and Miguel Ortiz-Cañavate of the Madrid firm of Washburn & Ortiz-Cañavate. Mr. Washburn is a New York lawyer who has been a technical adviser in Madrid since 1953. Mr. Ortiz-Cañavate has been a member of the Madrid bar since 1955. Messrs. Washburn and Ortiz-Cañavate collaborated on the Spanish comments, as they did in writing the chapter on Spain in the 1965 publication, *International Cooperation in Litigation.* Their firm has specialized in assisting English-speaking companies and individuals with Spanish legal matters since 1955.

Portugal: Ronald Charles Wolf, a member of the New York bar since 1957. Mr. Wolf now practices in Lisbon, where he represents American citizens and corporations. He has also represented many Portuguese citizens who have filed civil suits in the United States. Mr. Wolf prepared the Portuguese comments in collaboration with Dr. Leal de Oliveira, Advogado, of the Lisbon bar, who has served as assistant attorney general and professor of law in the Institute of Professional Training of the Portuguese Ministry of Justice.

Norway: Mathias Dahl-Hansen, a member of the Oslo firm of Schjødt, Dahl-Hansen, Christiansen, Schjødt, Høeg Rasmussen Og

Waerenskjold, is a famous Norwegian advocate who escaped to England from Nazi-occupied Norway in 1941 and served as legal adviser to the Norwegian Shipping and Trade Mission in London until 1945. He returned to Norway in 1945 and was a special prosecutor in the trial of Quisling and his "ministers." He has served as an examiner at the Norwegian law examination, and is now senior partner of one of Norway's leading international law firms.

Japan: Francis Y. Sogi, a member of the bars of New York and Japan. Mr. Sogi is a member of the New York firm of Miller, Montgomery, Sogi, Brady & Taft; the Tokyo firm of Sogi, Shinmyo & Tsuchiya; and the Taiwan firm of Sogi & Lin. He is an expert on international law, and was assisted in his Japanese law comments by Michiko Ito Crampe, a member of the bars of New York and Japan who is associated with Miller, Montgomery, Sogi, Brady & Taft.

Mexico: Dr. José Luis Siqueiros, of the Mexico City law firm of Barrera, Siqueiros y Torres Landa, an expert on international law, who collaborated in the comments on Mexican law with Dr. Jorge Carpizo, Director of Institute de Investigaciones Juridicas of the National University of Mexico.

In the common law nations, our commentators reached similar conclusions despite differences in local law. Messrs. Sheerin, Howie, and Baris all believe that Nader could probably sue in tort; that he would have a fair chance of winning despite the lack of an exact precedent; but that his damages would be very small by American standards, and he would run the risk of having to pay GM's legal bills if he lost.

In England, John Sheerin feels that Nader's best bet would be a tort action for intimidation or for conspiracy to cause injury, since there is no action for invasion of privacy as such. While there is no English precedent for the Nader-GM situation, and the case would probably be tried without a jury, John feels that Nader would probably win. The damages would be very difficult to estimate, but probably would not exceed $10,000.

In Canada, Kenneth Howie reports that three provinces (Saskatchewan, British Columbia, and Manitoba) have passed statutes in the 1970s establishing remedies for invasion of privacy. In the other provinces, he feels, Nader would have to grope around for a remedy under the heading of conspiracy to cause injury or defamation. Jury trial is discretionary in Canadian civil suits. Howie is among the most optimistic of all our commentators. He feels that Nader would win the case, and would probably be awarded $20,000 to $25,000 (1979 Canadian dollars) in compensatory damages, with another $10,000 added if punitive damages were awarded.

In Israel, Paul Baris feels that Nader's right to sue would be a close question, largely because the Supreme Court of Israel held in 1957 that there was no actionable right of privacy there. A committee chaired by Justice Kahn of the Israel Supreme Court published a report in 1976 recommending adoption of a Protection of Privacy statute, but as of this writing (December 1979) it had not been submitted to the Israeli Knesset (legislature). Baris believes that Nader might be able to state a cause of action under present Israeli law by stretching the tort of defamation to fit his case, but the trial outcome would be difficult to predict. Israel does not have trial by jury, and Baris believes that Israeli judges tend to follow the model of the English courts on tort damages, so that Nader's recovery would be a very small one if he was lucky enough to win.

While contingent fees are permitted in Israel, they are prohibited in England and some of the Canadian provinces (including Ontario), as they are in most other common law nations. In England, Canada, and Israel, the losing party must pay the attorney's fees of the winning party. (In the United States, the "costs" assessed against the losing party usually consist of little more than court filing fees and do not include attorney's fees.) Nader probably could not qualify for legal aid in any of the three nations, so that he would have to pay his lawyers out of his own pocket. Therefore it is apparent that in England, Canada, or Israel, as in practically all of the other common law nations, Nader would have to assume great financial risks to get his day in court—risks that are out of proportion to the relatively low damages that he would recover if he won the suit.

In most of the nations following the Roman-law tradition, the outcome would be similar to that predicted for England, Canada, and Israel. However, in two nations (the Netherlands and Spain) our commentators report that the suit would face even greater difficulties. In the Netherlands, Dr. Drilling reports, while Dutch lower courts have rendered judgments in the past ten years allowing compensation for "nonmaterial damages" in tort cases, the Supreme Court has not yet done so. In any event, Dr. Drilling believes that the damages would be quite low in comparison to the costs. In Spain, Messrs. Washburn and Ortiz-Cañavate report that theoretically Nader would have a right to sue, but in practice the legal system of Spain, which has lagged behind its political system in the move toward democracy, is not ready to accommodate such actions. They feel that the long-term trend is in the direction of enforcement of individual rights, and that perhaps the 1980s will see such suits in Spanish courts.

In the seven remaining Roman law nations, our commentators report that Nader could state a cause of action (either for invasion of privacy or for general tort liability under the civil code); that he could sue for "moral" as well as material damages; that the trial would be conducted by from one to three judges, without a jury; that contingent fees are not permitted, except in Japan and Mexico; that if he lost the case, he could be called upon to pay the defendant's legal fees in France, West Germany, and Norway; that he would probably win the case (although the outcome would be doubtful in Belgium, Germany, and Japan); and that his probable damages would range from a low of $250 in Japan to a high of $40,000 in Norway. In many of the Roman law nations, the action could be brought in either the civil or criminal courts. For purposes of our comparisons, I have limited the discussion to the civil courts.

In France, Maître Gernigon reports that the civil action could be based on Article 1382 of the French Civil Code, which provides:

> Any act by which a person causes damage to another makes the person by whose fault the damage occurred liable to make reparation for such damage.

This simple sentence, unchanged since its appearance as part of the original Code Napoléon of 1804, is the basis for the entire body of French tort law. It matters not whether the instrument of damage is an oxcart, an automobile, or a prying detective. In addition, there are now specific provisions in the French Civil Code for protection of privacy. Although those code provisions have been used only to protect privacy against publication, Gernigon believes that they could be extended to protect privacy against harassment without publication. While there is no French decision involving harassment by detectives, Gernigon feels that Nader's damages would approximate those collected in the most serious French cases of harassment by publication—about $25,000 in 1979 U.S. dollars.

In Belgium, Maître Dalcq foresees a rougher road for Nader. While the Belgian Civil Code also provides for general liability under Section 1382, Dalcq feels that the case would not be easy to win, and that at most Nader would collect a few thousand dollars for moral damages. Our Mexican commentators, Dr. Siqueiros and Dr. Carpizo, believe that the outcome in their courts would be similar.

In West Germany, Mr. Schurtman and Dr. Senfft report that the action would be based on violation of privacy (Persoenlichkeitsver-letzung); that the outcome would be hard to predict; and that if Nader won he would be awarded only a very small fraction of the settlement that he received in the United States.

In Portugal, Mr. Wolf and Dr. Leal de Oliveira advise that the action would be based on a civil code provision protecting the right of privacy. They believe that Nader would win the case and receive about $20,000 in moral damages.

In Norway, Mr. Dahl-Hansen reports that the action could be

maintained for invasion of privacy and probably also for defamation, since he believes that the questions asked about Nader by GM's detectives would be considered extraordinary in Norway—that they "clearly tend to give the impression that something was suspected that would have to be cleared up before employment." He believes that Nader would win the case in Norway, and would be entitled to compensation for mental anguish under the Norwegian doctrine of "oppreisning," which literally means "raising up" and is a vindication of plaintiff's honor as well as a means of compensation. Since the Norwegian courts would be permitted to consider GM's financial position in fixing damages, Dahl-Hansen believes that Nader would receive a higher award than those made in past cases—probably between $20,000 and $40,000 in U.S. dollars. In his opinion, the results would be similar in the courts of Denmark and Sweden.

In Japan, Mr. Sogi believes that Nader would have roughly the same causes of action as he pleaded in New York—invasion of the right to enjoy a quiet life (seikatsu bōgai), and intentional infliction of emotional harm (seishinteki kutsū). He reports a 1971 Japanese case in which a detective interviewed the plaintiff's neighbors, asking questions which indicated that the plaintiff had committed a crime. The court found that the detective's conduct was illegal and that it damaged the plaintiff's social reputation. The detective was ordered to pay $250 damages to the plaintiff and $150 damages to plaintiff's wife for their emotional distress (isharyō). Mr. Sogi believes that Gillen's questioning of Nader's neighbors and associates would probably fall within the customary Japanese form of pre-employment investigation, and therefore would not justify recovery of damages for mental anguish (isharyō). Because of the difficulties of winning this case in Japan, and the very small potential damages, Mr. Sogi believes that it would be difficult to find a Japanese lawyer willing to undertake it on a contingent fee basis, although such fees are customary in Japanese tort cases.

Thus it is apparent that only in the United States could Ralph Nader have accomplished what he did in his lawsuit against General Motors. To understand why this is so, we must turn to the story of the lawyers who opened the way for Nader and others to enforce their legal rights against any wrongdoer, no matter how large or powerful.

Chapter 2

THE EARLY AMERICAN TORT LAWYER: COLONIAL TIMES TO 1950

As we saw in the preceding chapter, Ralph Nader would have had the right to sue General Motors for damages in other countries, but he would have been unlikely to recover enough money to make such a suit worthwhile outside the United States.

Why was Nader able to bring his lawsuit to a successful conclusion in the United States? Why was a law firm there willing to conduct his case against the largest industrial corporation in the world, even though Nader did not have the money to pay legal fees? Indeed, why were there thousands of American lawyers who would gladly have taken on his case and could have done the job as well as the lawyers he selected? The answers to these questions span the history of the American legal system and the development of three features that are unique to American tort litigation:

1. The right to *jury trial* in most civil cases.

2. The *contingent fee* (a percentage of the money the client receives upon winning the case, and no fee at all if the case is lost).

3. The *entrepreneur-lawyer* (an advocate who carries a client on his shoulders by providing and financing services that most individual clients cannot afford—services which can put an average individual on an equal litigation footing with a corporate giant).

Largely because of these three developments—which we might call the trinity of torts—our civil courts today are open to almost anyone who has a legitimate grievance. But that has not always been so. We started out with a civil legal system that was useful only to the rich and powerful—a copy of the harsh eighteenth-century English system. The way we achieved our present unique position can be viewed as a fascinating study in the evolution of law, but I see it more as a story about the changing of *lawyers*. I consider the period from Colonial times up to the middle of the twentieth century the Early American era. The great sea changes made by entrepreneur-lawyers started around 1950.

In the beginning, American tort law was very favorable to the claimant, but there were practically no claims. The old common law of England and American eighteenth-century law which had been adapted from it made everyone responsible for injuries inflicted on others, regardless of fault. But since the courts were dedicated to upholding property rights rather than personal rights, and because few lawyers in those days could supply the clout their clients needed to battle the establishment, there was very little tort litigation. Thus the reports of civil cases tried in the first century of American law are dominated by disputes over property rights. Even with a favorable law of absolute liability and the right to trial by jury, the absence of the entrepreneur-lawyer and the contingent fee shut the doors of the civil courts to all but the wealthy property owners and business enterprises.

Tort law was one of the earliest protections of English society. Since it existed before organized government and enforceable agreements, it antedates criminal and contract law and traces back to the blood feuds of primitive societies—private warfare between families, tribes, or clans, that could be terminated by payment of a fine (called a "composition") to the victim's family or clan. The injured person or his cohorts would capture the wrongdoer and engage him in trial by battle, which was replaced by jury trial in Anglo-Norman times. The loser of the early tort case would usually forfeit property, or his life, or both. By about 600 A.D., there were regular schedules of fines to be paid to the victims of various injuries, as in the Law of Ethelbert:

For each of the four front teeth, VI shillings;
for the tooth which stands next to them, IV shillings;

for that which stands next to that, III shillings;
and then afterwards, for each a shilling.

When trial by jury developed in the twelfth century, the jurors were permitted to make their own assessment of money damages for torts. In his *History of the English-Speaking Peoples,* Winston Churchill described the origin of the civil jury in the reign of King Henry II (1154–1189):

> A bait was needed with which to draw litigants to the royal courts; the King must offer them better justice than they could have at the hands of their lords. Henry accordingly threw open to litigants in the royal courts a startling new procedure— trial by jury.
>
> *   *   *
>
> The jury system has come to stand for all we mean by English justice, because so long as a case has to be scrutinised by twelve honest men, defendant and plaintiff alike have a safeguard from arbitrary perversion of the law.

America's founding fathers had an equally high opinion of the importance of trial by jury in civil cases. Just as the Sixth Amendment to the U.S. Constitution required trial by jury in criminal cases, the Seventh Amendment preserved the right of jury trial in all federal civil cases involving more than twenty dollars. The state constitutions contain similar provisions.

Before the Industrial Revolution (about 1760 to 1830 in England, and a little later in North America), America was a rural society where life moved slowly, dependent upon draft animals to power farm equipment and transport people. Even the early railroads were powered by horses. Most accidental injuries that gave rise to damage claims were caused by animals, and the potential compensation was not significant enough to generate much litigation, given the difficulties of mounting such lawsuits at that time. So the earliest American lawyers were little concerned with tort law, and negligence received only a few lines in Blackstone's *Commentaries,* the definitive reference work for American lawyers well into the nineteenth century. In England, there was no treatise on torts until 1859, and it was another twenty years before Thomas M. Cooley wrote the first American textbook on torts.

The momentum of the Industrial Revolution, and particularly the nineteenth-century growth of the railroads, brought tort law to life. Suddenly Americans by the hundreds of thousands were injured in accidents every year, most of them hurt or killed on the job. They had the right to sue for damages, but most of them had no lawyers and little or no money for legal fees. This gave rise to the contingent fee, which started in the mid-nineteenth century and was well established by

1880. It was then that American tort lawyers emerged as an identifiable species.

From the beginning, much of the bar looked down upon the tort lawyer. The practice of taking cases on contingent fees horrified many lawyers whose business arrangements were more rewarding and less speculative. Typical was the reaction of the leading nineteenth-century authority on torts, Thomas Cooley, who wrote in 1881 that contingent-fee lawyers were a contemptible lot, debasing the legal profession and creating "a feeling of antagonism between aggregated capital on the one side, and the community in general on the other." In one respect, Cooley was not far off the mark: the tort lawyer faced the challenge of becoming the champion of the "community in general" in the uneven nineteenth-century struggle against the legal interests of "aggregated capital."

Many early tort lawyers were poorly equipped for this formidable task, and were far from the heroic figures that one imagines in the role of "keeper of the poor man's key to the courthouse." In most instances they were picking up the dregs of the law practice that their better educated, better connected, more refined brethren of the bar did not care to handle. The cream of the legal profession was at the beck and call of the railroads and other tort defendants, from Abraham Lincoln (who served as general counsel of the Illinois Central Railroad) to Clarence Darrow (Chicago & North West Railway) to the young Edward Bennett Williams (who defended the District of Columbia's street railway in the 1940s). The industrial establishment found it cheaper to hire the best legal talent than to run the risk of paying adequate compensation to accident victims.

This, of course, was the temper of the times. As the American branch of the Industrial Revolution reached full bloom, everything was dedicated to its prosperity, and the captains of industry were able to manipulate all three branches of government to protect their enterprises from accident claims. So great was their control, and so overmatched were the early tort lawyers, that industry had little need for liability insurance until the twentieth century. Nothing that threatened to curb industrial progress could be tolerated, least of all the claims of those who had been maimed or widowed by it. As U.S. Supreme Court Justice Louis D. Brandeis described the age in which the American tort lawyer was born, the decisions of the courts were based upon

eighteenth century conceptions of the liberty of the individual and of the sacredness of private property. Early nineteenth century scientific half-truths, like "The survival of the fittest," which translated into practice meant "The devil take the hindmost," were erected by judicial sanction into a moral law.

While in private practice in Boston, Brandeis himself had been the first "attorney for the people"—a forerunner of Ralph Nader. He took on many worthy public causes—such as defending the earliest state wage and hour laws and opposing utility and railroad rate increases—and he contributed such legal services free of charge. But before he engaged in his public interest activities, he had taken the precaution of becoming one of the highest-paid lawyers in the nation. By 1890, at the age of 34, he was earning well over $50,000 a year, mostly by representing wealthy families and corporations. In those days, most American lawyers did not earn as much as $5,000 a year at any time during their careers.

One of Brandeis's greatest triumphs was the 1908 U.S. Supreme Court decision in *Muller v. Oregon*. Curt Muller owned the Grand Laundry in Portland, Oregon, and among others he employed Mrs. E. Gotcher. On September 4, 1905, Muller required Mrs. Gotcher to work more than 10 hours which violated a 1903 Oregon statute limiting the working time of women in factories and laundries to 10 hours a day. He was convicted and sentenced to pay a fine of $10. He appealed the conviction to the Oregon Supreme Court, and after it affirmed the lower court, he took his case all the way to the U.S. Supreme Court in 1908. His lawyers attacked the constitutionality of the Oregon statute, for in the thinking of those times, it was considered a violation of the Fourteenth Amendment for a state to interfere with the "freedom" of workers to contract for their services in any way they saw fit (or were forced to see fit). Three years earlier, in the 1905 case of *Lochner v. New York,* the Supreme Court had nullified a New York statute limiting the working time of bakery employees to 60 hours a week, on just such "freedom of contract" principles.

Louis Brandeis was invited to brief and argue the case for the State of Oregon, and his brief became a legend. His only chance to avoid the authority of the 1905 New York bakery decision was to show that the Oregon statute was a reasonable exercise of the state's police power, which could be used "for the protection of health, safety, morals, and the general welfare." He devoted only two pages to the constitutional issue, and more than 100 pages to sociological data. Nobody had ever filed such a brief in the Supreme Court. Noting that Brandeis's brief contained "a very copious collection" of "expressions of opinion from other than judicial sources," Mr. Justice Brewer included the following in his decision:

> In foreign legislation Mr. Brandeis calls attention to these statutes: Great Britain, 1844: Law 1901, Edw. VII, chap. 22. France, 1848: Act Nov. 2, 1892, and March 30, 1900. Switzerland, Canton of Glarus, 1848: Federal Law 1877, art. 2, §1.

Austria, 1855: Acts 1897, art. 96a, §§ 1–3. Holland, 1899: art. 5, § 1. Italy, June 19, 1902, art 7. Germany, Laws 1891.

Then follow extracts from over ninety reports of committees, bureaus of statistics, commissioners of hygiene, inspectors of factories, both in this country and in Europe, to the effect that long hours of labor are dangerous for women, primarily because of their special physical organization . . .

Perhaps the general scope and character of all these reports may be summed up in what an inspector for Hanover says: "The reason for the reduction of the working day to ten hours— (a) the physical organization of woman, (b) her maternal functions, (c) the rearing and education of the children, (d) the maintenance of the home—are all so important and so far-reaching that the need for such reduction need hardly be discussed."

The Supreme Court upheld the Oregon statute; Mr. Muller paid his $10 fine; an important blow was struck for humanitarian conditions of employment; and the law had a new instrument, the *Brandeis brief,* part of Louis Brandeis's concept of "the living law." Unfortunately, Louis Brandeis was not interested in representing tort plaintiffs, as were few of his talented contemporaries. Let us look at the position of the poorly represented tort victim at the time when our railroads and factories started to mow people down in large numbers.

The Obstacle Course

As industry and the railroads expanded, they left accident victims in their wake by the hundreds of thousands. The old tort law that made the injuring party absolutely liable was an inconvenience to the Industrial Revolution, so the early-nineteenth-century courts changed it, first in England, and then in the young United States. The new concept was: fault had to be proved before there could be any payment of damages.

This seemed fair enough. But the captains of industry knew that jurors in accident cases would probably be more sympathetic to injured people than to big business; so something had to be done to prevent juries from impeding industrial progress by compensating its victims too freely. The defense lawyers and the judges who were persuaded by these arguments were equal to the task. They erected an obstacle course designed to wear down or eliminate all but the hardiest accident claimants and their lawyers. Since most of the tort claimants in those days were workers injured on the job, they designed three ingenious obstacles to employer's liability: the fellow-servant rule, assumption of risk, and contributory negligence.

The fellow-servant rule (which originated in England in 1837 and was first adopted in the United States by a South Carolina court in 1841) absolved an employer from liability to an injured employee if the injury occurred as the result of the negligence of a co-employee. This made it practically impossible for workers to recover damages in the usual situation, where an injury on the job involved activities of co-workers. The late James A. Dooley, a pioneering tort lawyer who became a justice of the Supreme Court of Illinois, described the fellow-servant rule in his treatise, *Modern Tort Law* as follows:

> The rule found ready acceptance in a society committed to industrial expansion at the expense of the working class, and was justified by the American courts on various theories. One such theory was that the negligence of a fellow servant was a risk assumed by the servant as an incident of his employment. Another theory, frequently indulged in by the courts, was that application of the rule would tend to encourage the servant not only to be more careful in his own behalf but to be more observant of the conduct of his fellow employees and thus reduce the number of accidents. The arguments advanced for adopting and perpetuating this harsh doctrine conveniently overlooked the fact that the employee has no control over the conduct of a fellow servant, and is seldom, if ever, in a position to guard himself against it. Although never admitted by the early common law courts, the underlying reason for the rule was an overriding desire to relieve infantile industry from the financial burden of industrial accidents.

Francis Hutcheson Hare, a pioneer tort lawyer in Alabama, recalls an early case in which the fellow-servant rule reached the limits of dehumanization: a coal miner whose hip was broken when a company mule kicked him was met with the defense that the mule was a fellow servant. Mercifully, the judge disallowed this defense.

Almost as harsh was the doctrine of contributory negligence. This prevented any plaintiff (whether a worker or not) from recovering if he was negligent in the slightest degree—even if the defendant was 99 percent responsible for the accident. It originated in an English case decided in 1809, but was not used much in the United States until the expansion of the railroads after 1850 brought many crossing accidents into the courts. Like the fellow-servant rule and assumption of risk, the contributory negligence rule enabled judges to take cases away from juries by declaring that the plaintiff was barred from recovery as a matter of law. In order to have an employer's liability case submitted to the jury, injured workers had to produce evidence that the accident was caused by negligence of the employer; that neither they nor any other employees were negligent in the slightest degree; and that the accident was not caused by any known hazard or risk that the workers assumed when they took the job. Since there was a good chance that the worker would be fired for making a claim, only those seriously injured or disabled for life were well advised to sue.

Even the fortunate plaintiffs who made their way through the obstacle course to the jury were not home free. Because the defendants were represented by the most skillful and influential lawyers, and because the plaintiff's lawyers were often poorly prepared and unimpressive, many jurors were afraid to vote for the plaintiffs. Who were they, the little people of the community, to challenge the establishment? The powerful defense counsel and the authoritative figure of the judge warned the jurors that they could not indulge their natural sympathies. They were sworn to decide the case strictly on the evidence presented in court by opposing counsel, and often the contrast between the two lawyers was so great that jurors did not dare to strike a blow against the establishment. Often they would hold for the defendant, or award only minimal damages.

When jurors brought in verdicts that came close to compensating plaintiffs for their disabilities and expenses, judges often took it upon themselves to reduce these verdicts by *remittitur,* the device of ordering a new trial unless the plaintiff agreed to accept a much lower sum. One judge who placed a valuation of $2,286 on the loss of a leg by a 30-year-old working man, rationalized his action this way:

> The plaintiff's disability is for life, but for life only.

Politics played an important part in keeping the tracks clear for expansion of the railroads without incurring the expense of compensating their victims. In the nineteenth century, the railroads were able to manipulate many state legislatures. Some states empowered railroads to issue their own paper money for labor and materials; others loaned the railroads large percentages of their starting capital. By 1861, more than 31 million acres of land had been given to railroads by state legislatures. Clarence Darrow told the story of the closing speech by the presiding officer of the Pennsylvania State Senate: "The Senate will now stand adjourned—that is, if the Pennsylvania Railroad has no further business to transact."

This control came in handy when a legislative problem arose concerning the ultimate personal injury suit: the action for wrongful death. In one of the great foul-ups of the common law, an English judge, Lord Ellenborough, decided in the 1808 case of *Baker v. Bolton* that, while passengers injured in a stage coach accident could sue the coach line, families of those passengers who were killed could not, since the right of action expired at the death of the passenger. This monstrosity was accepted by the American courts and was applied to all types of fatal accidents. Its harshness was relieved by the enactment of statutes giving families of accident victims the right to sue for the losses caused by their deaths. The first was an 1846 English statute, Lord Campbell's Act, which set the pattern for similar statutes in each of the United States.

Thus, the law of fatal accidents became a creature of statute rather than a part of the common law. This gave each of our state legislatures a crack at setting up a special obstacle course for wrongful death cases, which were of special interest to the railroads because the railroads were the principal instrument of accidental death. The railroad lobbies were so strong that they did not bother to construct anything as subtle as the fellow-servant rule. Instead, they simply put their own price tag on human life by limiting the amount that could be recovered in any wrongful-death case, regardless of the actual losses sustained by any particular family. In the nineteenth-century wrongful-death statutes, each state adopted its own limitation, and the price tag was usually about $5,000. Many states (including Massachusetts and Illinois) were to keep these arbitrary ceilings in effect well into the second half of the twentieth century.

The upper segment of the bar that represented the defendants also had the leverage to select judges who could be relied upon to run interference for the Industrial Revolution. Indeed, most of the judges— especially those sitting in the influential appellate courts—came from the upper segment of the bar. Thus, the basic philosophy of the judges who shaped the law was the final obstacle in the path of the early American tort lawyers and their unfortunate clients. As late as 1922, a federal judge wrote in an appellate court decision:

> It should be remembered that of the three fundamental principles which underlie government, and for which government exists, protection of life, liberty, and property, the chief of these is property.

The quotation is from a 1922 decision of the District of Columbia Court of Appeals holding a federal minimum wage law unconstitutional, which was affirmed by the U.S. Supreme Court in 1923 on the ground that the law interfered with "freedom of contract."

Using today's welfare state standards, it would be easy to condemn such judges as barbarians. But they were expressing the mainstream American laissez-faire philosophy of their time, that all we had to do was to keep the climate right for industrial expansion, and all other problems would be taken care of. Writing of this period, legal historian Professor Bernard Schwartz found that American law was shaped by the philosophy of the English writers Charles Darwin and Herbert Spencer. "Survival of the fittest" was the law of society as well as nature, which meant that the courts should keep their hands off business and allow "freedom of contract" to determine the rights of injured persons. As Professor Schwartz observed:

> Laissez-faire became the touchstone in all branches of the law, including those governing the relationships between private individuals. Spencerean doctrine dominated contracts, property, torts, and the other private law subjects. . . . The prosperity and growth of the country appeared to demonstrate the potential in an environment free of legal controls; the frontier experience had been a veritable proving ground for Darwinist arguments.

A Brandeis brief could have marshaled facts and arguments that might have convinced the courts (and perhaps industry itself) that the human victims of industrialization could be cared for at trifling cost without impeding progress. But there was no Brandeis representing tort victims.

SS Eastland, General Slocum, Titanic

The helplessness of earlier tort lawyers is vividly illustrated by the case of the SS *Eastland*, which was in the courts for nearly 21 years, from 1915 to 1936. Part of the story was re-created in a 1977 television documentary produced in England by the ATV Network, with Glenn Ford as the narrator.

> GLENN FORD: July 24th, 1915 in Chicago. The beginning of a summer weekend with the kids home from school and beautiful Lake Michigan beckoning the holiday makers. The 9,000 staff and families of the Western Electric Company were eagerly boarding the four ships tied up at Clarke Street, en route to their annual picnic. The favorite was the *Eastland*, a tall, sleek, three-decker known for her speed but also as the temperamental ship of the lakes. There were fully 2,500 vacationers aboard when Captain Peterson noticed her listing to starboard. His orders were to fill the port ballast tanks, but not too much. There was precious little ballast anyway, and the *Eastland* had a bad

reputation for keeping her trim. Jack Billows was working on the excursion steamer directly behind the *Eastland*.

JACK BILLOWS: I was on the ship the *Theodore Roosevelt* over there, past the bridge, past the river. The *Eastland* was about right here ready to go out. As she pulled away from the dock, she just keeled over on this side and covered half the river.

GLENN FORD: The mass of happy humanity was transformed into a screaming chaos of desperate bodies. Many died instantly, crushed in the wreckage. Some slowly trapped and suffocated, others drowned, sucked down into the depths of the Chicago River.

JACK BILLOWS: We started rescue. We really couldn't use the lifeboat for doing it. We just floated in it and grabbed anything we saw floating or if it was a body we grabbed—alive or dead—we grabbed it. We couldn't use the oars and everything was floating around. You could have walked across the river on what was floating. Children being held by their dead mothers or dead children and dead mothers together. That was the most tragic thing. Kissing the rosary. You could see they were frozen stiff. They couldn't do anything.

GLENN FORD: In all, the official toll was 815, but in the confusion it is more likely that 1,100 people perished.

JACK BILLOWS: They set the figure below to save their neck for overloading the ship.

GLENN FORD: The cartoonists captured the outrage of a nation while the headlines told their own harassing stories. So why did the *Eastland* capsize? Was the legal limit of 2,500 passengers in fact far too many? Were there in any case more than this number? As she was preparing to leave, did the pilot tug take the strain too early and pull her over, or had the basic design made her top-heavy anyway? Was the water level in the river dangerously low, or had too much ballast water been pumped out, making her dependent on her land line to hold her up? All these questions had to be answered, and as the casualties mounted, wholesale arrests were ordered. The court convened in the outraged atmosphere of 1915 was still sitting twenty years later. Finally the case was thrown out in August 1935. No blame was apportioned and none of the bereaved or those maimed by the *Eastland* received a penny in compensation. We shall officially never know who was to blame.

The Chicago newspapers of the time told many pitiful stories of the disaster. One reporter wrote:

> Above all the cataclysmic scene there was a great and dreadful wailing sound as the cries and pleas of the drowning blended in a terrible symphony with the moans and apprehensive shrieks of those who stood helplessly on the dock or watched in disbelief and torment from the other excursion vessels.

The newspapers revealed that the *Eastland* was badly overloaded and defectively designed. Two years before the 1915 sinking, a naval architect had warned the Chicago harbormaster that the *Eastland* was likely to tip over when heavily loaded, but the warning was ignored. When she began to list, her sixty crew members, aware of the danger, jumped onto the dock, leaving the thousands of passengers to save themselves or drown.

The public was incensed at this needless tragedy, and prosecutors moved swiftly to start criminal proceedings. A federal grand jury indicted three officers of the company that owned the *Eastland,* the manager of the company that chartered it for the excursion, the captain and chief engineer of the vessel, and two government steamship inspectors. But with Clarence Darrow defending, the indictments were dismissed on February 19, 1916, when U.S. District Judge Clarence W. Sessions ruled that the government had failed to make out a criminal case.

The claims of property owners were looked after promptly. On September 22, 1915, just five weeks after the disaster, U.S. District Judge Kennesaw Mountain Landis (later to become the first commissioner of baseball) signed an order directing that the wreckage of the *Eastland* be sold to satisfy the claims of salvage operators and property owners, and it was sold at auction on December 21, 1915, for $46,000. Shortly thereafter, the entire amount was paid out to the salvage and property claimants.

There remained the damage claims of the families of those who had perished in the disaster. Although the first claim was filed in the Chicago federal court on November 18, 1915, the case did not come to trial until 1933. In the words of the appellate court that reviewed the trial court decision in 1935:

> There is no showing in the record why the disposition of the case was not pushed by the parties for a period of ten or twelve years.

On December 21, 1933, the trial court decided that the accident was caused by the negligence of the engineer in charge of operation of the water ballast tanks, "in that they were improperly handled and the water therein not properly distributed so as to give her stability." Nevertheless, the court found that the plaintiffs had failed to prove that the ship was "unseaworthy," and therefore they were turned out of court without a penny of damages.

Glenn Ford's narration tells us that the case was finally thrown out in August 1935. That was the date of the decision of the U.S. Court of Appeals for the Seventh Circuit, which reviewed and affirmed the holding of the trial court. However, that was not quite the end of the line. The plaintiffs made one last effort to get the U.S. Supreme Court to review the case. Because neither the plaintiffs nor their attorneys were able to pay the cost of printing the trial transcript and appellate brief as required by Supreme Court rules, they asked the high court for permission to proceed *in forma pauperis* (in the manner of a pauper), a special dispensation provided for those too poor to comply with the rules. On January 20, 1936, the Supreme Court denied this request and refused to hear the case. Thus ended the litigation more than twenty years after the *Eastland* capsized.

That terse Supreme Court order stating, "Motion for leave to proceed further herein *in forma pauperis* is denied," tells the story of the uneven struggle. The combined resources of more than 800 families were not sufficient to muster a legal effort capable of bringing the case to trial in a reasonable time with a reasonable chance of winning—despite public indignation and despite the strong evidence of negligence.

The *Eastland* was an extreme case, but many other accident claims of that era ended with similar results. In 1904, the *General Slocum,* another excursion boat, caught fire in the East River of New York while carrying 1,500 picnickers. Although the burning boat was only 300 yards from the shore of Manhattan, the captain headed her toward the more distant North Brother Island, ignoring the stiff winds which fanned the flames that were sweeping the old wooden ship. The crew were inexperienced and had never held a fire drill. They tried to use the fire hose, but it had not been touched for 13 years, and it burst the moment that the water was turned on.

When the burning ship finally beached at North Brother Island, most of the crew abandoned her, leaving the 1,500 passengers (mostly women and children) to save themselves. Many donned life preservers and jumped into the water, but most of the ancient life preservers were rotten. They went to pieces or failed to furnish any support, and hundreds of passengers drowned. Hundreds more were trapped and consumed by the flames. In all, 1,021 passengers died. The captain and the entire crew escaped.

Captain William Van Schaick was prosecuted under a federal statute for misconduct, negligence, and inattention to duty while acting as master of a ship. He was found guilty and sentenced to ten years in prison. Among the government attorneys who participated in the criminal prosecution were Henry L. Stimson and Felix Frankfurter. But in the civil litigation, the bereaved families had to rely on their own lawyers, and no such legal clout was available to them. While they had the satisfaction of seeing Captain Van Schaick go to prison, they were not able to recover any damages from the owners of the *General Slocum.*

The mid-Atlantic sinking of the British White Star liner *Titanic* on April 14, 1912, which lost 1,517 of the 2,207 people aboard, has become the world's most famous maritime disaster. For our purposes, it is important to note that the attorneys representing the families of deceased passengers in the United States were able to recover a total of only

$97,772 for all of the deaths involved in the litigation. Under an 1851 federal statute that is still in effect, the liability of shipowners may be limited to the value of the ship *after the accident,* plus the amount paid on that voyage for freight and passenger transportation. When a ship sinks at sea and this limitation is applied, there is usually little money available to pay passenger claims. In the case of the *Titanic,* the value of the 14 lifeboats recovered and the amount paid on its fatal voyage for freight and passengers came to a total of $97,772. If that sum had been divided among the families of the 1,517 people who died, each decedent's family would have received only $64.45. These included eleven young widows who had spent their honeymoons aboard the *Titanic,* only to say their final farewells to their husbands, who went down with the ship.

The 1851 limitation was based on the maritime law of medieval Europe, which was designed to encourage and protect shipbuilding and sailing ventures at a time when neither insurance nor corporate business organizations existed. This limitation does not apply when the ship is unseaworthy or when there is negligence by the crew that is within the knowledge or "privity" (participation) of the owners. In the *Titanic* disaster, the iceberg made a 300-foot gash in her hull, cutting her like a can opener; but this did not injure a single passenger. All of those who had boarded lifeboats were rescued. The 1,517 people who remained aboard and went to the bottom as the band played "Nearer My God to Thee" died only because there were not enough lifeboats. This shortage was known to the owners. J. Bruce Ismay, chief executive officer of the White Star Line, was aboard the *Titanic* for her maiden voyage, and he managed to slip into one of the last lifeboats. Ismay acted like some sort of super-captain, giving the chief engineer orders concerning the speed of the ship without consulting the captain. He also was notified, hours before the disaster, of the ice warnings received from other ships, but he ignored them because he did not want to delay the festivities and press coverage that were awaiting the *Titanic* in New York. Yet the courts held that whatever negligence caused the deaths of the passengers was not within the knowledge or privity of the shipowners.

The 1851 limitation of liability statute which applied to the *Titanic* also applied to the *Eastland* and *General Slocum* cases. Although the limitation for loss of life or bodily injury was increased in 1935 to a total of $60 per ton of the ship's weight, this is still woefully inadequate for the real damages of a maritime disaster if the plaintiffs cannot break through this limitation by proving knowledge or privity on the part of the owners. It would be difficult to find a lawyer who believes that any shipowner today could successfully defend charges of knowledge or privity in such cases of outrageous negligence and unseaworthiness as those of the *Titanic,* the *Eastland,* and the *General Slocum.* Today's tort lawyers have brought maritime law into the twentieth century by breaking through the privity barrier in cases not nearly as shocking as the three we have considered.

The Iroquois Theater and Triangle Shirtwaist Fires

When Chicago's Iroquois Theater was rushed to completion for the 1903 Christmas season, it was hailed as a model of elegance and safety. Its first attraction was the London musical hit "Mr. Blue Beard," starring the famous comedian Eddie Foy. The printed program mentioned at the top of the front page that the theater was "ABSOLUTELY FIRE-PROOF." Chicagoans were delighted with their new showplace, but they did not know that many shortcuts had been taken in order to open it in time for the holiday business. There were no fire alarm boxes, no useful fire extinguishers, no exit signs, no plans or training for fire or emergency evacuation, and no water available to the firehoses.

On December 30, 1903, just five weeks after it opened, the management crowded 1,900 people into the theater designed for a maximum of 1,600. As the second act started, part of the curtain brushed against a hot carbon lamp, igniting the curtain and quickly spreading flames to the scenery and the stage. Eddie Foy rushed to the stage from his dressing room when he heard the first cries of "Fire!" Most of the orchestra patrons were calmly filing toward the exit doors, but panic was swelling in the crowded balconies, where, unknown to the theatergoers, the management had sealed off the balcony seats by locking two heavy iron gates. Eleven of the theater's exits were also locked and bolted.

Foy tried to calm the crowd. He yelled to the orchestra director, "Play! Start an overture—anything! But play!" He shouted directions to the stage manager to lower the asbestos curtain—but it would not go down. Finally, his costume smoking, unable to help and in frustration, he fell to his knees on the stage. As he looked up at the balconies, "They were in a mad, animal-like stampede—their screams, groans and snarls, the scuffle of thousands of feet and bodies grinding against bodies merging into a crescendo that was half-wail, half-roar—the most dreadful sound that ever assailed human ears."

Foy survived the fire, but the theater was gutted in 15 minutes, and 602 theater patrons, mostly women and children, died in the flames and the stampedes. The coroner's jury found that the locking of the exits and the iron gates in the balconies had cost hundreds of lives, and that the theater owners and builders had violated many city laws and ordinances which required fireproofing of scenery and stage woodwork, fire alarm boxes, fire hoses, flues, fire extinguishers, and a working asbestos curtain.

As in the later *Eastland* disaster, public indignation ran high against the businessmen and public officials responsible for the carnage. But in the end they all escaped criminal punishment, and after more than five years of inconclusive litigation, a few dozen of the civil suits were settled for payment of $750 per death. Many other families received no compensation at all. So ended the worst theater fire in American history.

The 1911 fire at the Triangle Shirtwaist factory in New York City that claimed the lives of 145 employees has become a legend. It happened on a sunny Saturday afternoon when the employees were about to finish their six-day work week, for which they were paid about five dollars and had to endure sweatshop conditions. Isaac Harris and Max Blanck, the owners of Triangle Shirtwaist, had designed the work space so that the employees would have to file through a narrow corridor and exit through a single door, where they could be searched for stolen merchandise. It later transpired that the total value of items pilfered from the Triangle factory before the fire was less than twenty-five dollars.

Triangle was located in the Asch Building on the corner of Washington Place and Greene Street, now the site of New York University. Although such buildings were required to have three complete staircases, the Asch Building had only one staircase that went all the way from the roof to the street. A second staircase ran from the street to the top floor, but had no exit to the roof. A third "staircase" was a single fire escape that ended at the second floor, too high to permit safe exit under emergency conditions.

The Triangle factory was spread over the eighth, ninth, and tenth floors of the ten-story building. Just before closing time on March 25, 1911, a bundle of oil-soaked rags caught fire in the cutting department on the eighth floor. Most of the employees were on their way out or preparing to leave when the fire started. Production manager Samuel Bernstein attempted to put the fire out with the eighth floor fire hose, but it was rotted and not properly hooked up to a water source, so it proved to be useless.

The flames spread rapidly throughout the eighth, ninth, and tenth floors. Although the fire department was notified a minute after the fire started and responded quickly, there was little that the firemen could do, for their hoses and ladders could reach no higher than the sixth floor.

Panic set in among the trapped workers, most of them young Jewish or Italian women. All was over in less than twenty minutes, but in that time 145 employees had died a horrible death. Some were burned to death. Some were crushed to death in elevator shafts or in their vain attempts to open doors that allegedly had been locked to make certain the employees filed past the security guard who searched them for stolen goods. Horrible death scenes were viewed from the street by hundreds of spectators, who stood by helplessly as employees, trapped by the flames, jumped to their certain death on the pavement below. This is how Bill Shephard, a United Press reporter on the street below, described the scene to his editor over the telephone: "Thud–dead! thud–dead! thud–dead! I call them that because the sound and the thought of death came to me each time at the same instant." Shephard saw 62 bodies smash into the pavement, and he did not see them all. He went on to write this heartbreaking story:

> A young man helped a girl to the window sill on the ninth floor. Then he held her out deliberately, away from the building, and let her drop. He held out a second girl the same way and let her drop. He held out a third girl, who did not resist. They were all as unresisting as if he were helping them into a streetcar instead of into eternity. He saw that a terrible death awaited them in the flames and his was only a terrible chivalry. He brought around another girl to the window. I saw her put her arms around him and kiss him. Then he held her into space—and dropped her. Quick as a flash, he was on the window sill himself. His coat fluttered upwards—the air filled his trouser legs as he came down. I could see he wore tan shoes. Together they went into eternity. We found later that in the room in which he stood, many girls were burning to death. He chose the easiest way and was brave enough to help the girl he loved to an easier death.
>
> *   *   *
>
> The floods of water from the firemen's hoses that ran into the gutter were actually red with blood. I looked upon the heap of dead bodies, and I remembered that these girls were the shirt-waist makers. I remembered their great strike of last year, in which the same girls had demanded more sanitary conditions and more safety precautions in the shops. These dead bodies were the answer.

Locking the doors of a factory during working hours was a violation of the criminal law. Triangle owners Harris and Blanck were indicted for locking the door on the Washington Place side of the building and thereby causing the deaths of the employees who were consumed by flames during their vain efforts to get that door open. Harris and Blanck retained as defense counsel Max D. Steuer, then the outstanding trial lawyer in New York—if not in the entire nation.

In addition to the criminal charges against Harris and Blanck, many civil suits were filed on behalf of injured and deceased employees against their employer and also against the owner of the Asch Building. The International Ladies Garment Workers Union (which gained great strength in the aftermath of the disaster) advised its members to bring such suits, and the Italian consul in New York gave the same advice to the Italian families.

Public outrage was so great that on December 6, 1911, more than 300 women attacked Harris and Blanck when they appeared at the Criminal Court Building for their trial. The district attorney brought in dozens of witnesses who testified that the Washington Place exit door was locked. Many witnesses, including firemen, testified that at least 20 employees died at that door. However, Judge Thomas T. C. Crain instructed the jury that in order to reach a guilty verdict, they had to find that Harris and Blanck knew that the door was locked. Apparently the jurors believed Steuer's contention that the Washington Place door was locked accidentally by employees who had escaped through the door themselves. His brilliant defense brought Harris and Blanck an acquittal.

The normally pro-business *New York Tribune* reacted sharply to the verdict:

> The monstrous conclusion of the law is that the slaughter was no one's fault, that it couldn't be helped, or perhaps even that, in the fine legal phrase which is big enough to cover a multitude of defects of justice, it was "an act of God!" This conclusion is revolting to the moral sense of the community.

Despite the continuing public outcry, the courts seemed to be powerless to do anything about the disaster. Max Steuer also defended the Triangle Shirtwaist Company in the civil actions. The first case to come to trial was a suit by Anna Gulla, an injured employee who sought $2,000 in damages. The plaintiff's attorneys had access to the extensive evidence of the employer's negligence that had been presented publicly by the district attorney in the 1911 criminal trial of Harris and Blanck, which had lasted nearly four weeks and had produced dozens of witnesses, including surviving employees and firemen. Many newspapers and other publications, as well as labor organizations and public agencies, had investigated the fire and published their findings. Yet when Anna Gulla's lawsuit came to trial on February 26, 1914, her attorneys presented their entire case in one day. Once again Steuer was able to save Harris and Blanck from judgment. The trial ended on its second day with the jury unable to agree on a verdict, and that effectively terminated the efforts of the bereaved families and the surviving injured employees to get compensation from the Triangle Shirtwaist Company.

Less than two weeks later, the remaining civil suits that had been brought against the owner of the Asch Building were settled for $75 each. Each of the 23 claims were death cases, so that the value of the lives of the Triangle Shirtwaist employees was fixed at $75 each through those settlements. The *New York World* tried to explain this travesty:

> The claimants have been tired out. Their money and their patience has been exhausted. So far as personal guilt is concerned, the men whose methods made everything ready for the tragedy have gone free. So far as financial liability is concerned, the whole affair is in the hands of an insurance company and stricken families are not well equipped to carry on expensive litigations with corporations.

That statement of a leading New York newspaper summed up the plight of plaintiffs seeking compensation through our tort law system in 1914. If the hundreds of stricken families of Triangle Shirtwaist were "not well equipped to carry on expensive litigations with corporations" despite the strength of their numbers and the outrage of the public, despite assistance from the press and the district attorney, then we can well imagine the plight of an individual plaintiff injured in a routine accident that did not take place before the horrified eyes of the press and the public.

The basic law applicable to the five cases we have just examined is the same today as it was then. Then as now, such defendants had a legal duty to use reasonable care for the safety of persons who became their passengers or occupants. That duty was not enforced by the courts in any of those five cases. Yet, if any such disasters occurred today, under virtually the same basic provisions of tort law, defendants would be forced to pay millions of dollars in damages and, indeed, would be lucky to survive as business enterprises. Why the change? Today's stricken families are not much better equipped to carry on expensive litigation against insurers or large corporations than they were in 1914. Then as now, there were contingent fees and the right to jury trial. All five of the disasters we have studied occurred during the "Progressive Era"—the time just before World War I when America became an urban nation and turned away from concentration of economic power. Labor power was rising and suffrage was expanding, but there was no parallel movement in tort litigation. It is true that our economic philosophy has changed from the laissez-faire of 1914 to the welfare state of today. But the welfare state does not nourish individual tort suits; it attempts to provide compensation through broad social legislative schemes. Nations that are much more advanced welfare states than the United States, such as Great Britain, have not developed anything approaching the 1980 American tort compensation system. Why, then, would the same duty that was ignored in 1914 be enforced in our courts today?

The answer is the change in the *enforcers:* the lawyers who represent the claimants and thus assume the responsibility for enforcing their rights to compensation. We must ask why, in the Progressive Era of Teddy Roosevelt and Woodrow Wilson, there was a Max Steuer to represent Harris and Blanck and Triangle Shirtwaist, but there was no equivalent champion for the legion of their victims.

Where Were the Plaintiffs' Steuers?

Max D. Steuer arrived in the United States in 1877 at the age of 6, the son of a poor Jewish tailor. He helped to support his family as a newsboy and paid for his education by working in a tailor shop. When he graduated with honors from Columbia Law School in 1893, he hoped to find employment with one of the prominent New York law firms, but he was turned down by all that he approached. So he began as a struggling individual practitioner and picked up clients as best he could.

From this difficult start, he built one of the greatest trial practices ever enjoyed by an American lawyer. During his 47 years at the bar, he came to represent many prominent people and corporations, and was often called in by other lawyers (including some of those who had snubbed him for employment) to try difficult civil and criminal cases. His famous criminal cases included the successful defenses of Charles E. Mitchell, president of the National City Bank of New York (now Citibank) on income tax evasion charges; Harry M. Daugherty, Warren Harding's Attorney General, on charges of defrauding the federal government in the administration of German property seized by the Alien Property Custodian during World War I; and sports promoter Tex Rickard, on charges of statutory rape. Other famous clients of his were singer Rudy Vallee, chain store owner S. S. Kresge, film magnate Alexander Pantages, actress Lillian Gish, and publisher William Randolph Hearst.

Once established, Steuer demanded and got a sizeable advance retainer in every case he agreed to take on. Even during the Depression years, he was charging $1,500 a day for court appearances, over and above his initial retainer. Since he was swamped by wealthy clients eager to pay for his services and willing to advance whatever investigation and preparation expenses he considered necessary, there was no need for him to work on a contingent basis. Instead, he became a defender of the establishment, and it paid him very well. He was also prominent in New York Democratic politics, serving as a member of the unofficial board of strategy that made important decisions for the Tammany Hall organization. By the time of his death in 1940, he was one of the few remaining lawyers whose trials always drew a crowd.

Such a man would seem destined to become a plaintiff's tort lawyer, especially in his early days when he lacked clients, reputation, and money. But in his early years at the bar, tort practice was a dirty business on both sides, and many lawyers considered it unworthy of their talents.

American tort practice began in the second half of the nineteenth century, which coincided with the high point of laissez-faire, a philosophy that was little concerned with social justice. A nation preoccupied with industrial expansion was not going to spend much time grieving over accident victims whose claims might inconvenience or delay the march of true progress. In the name of free enterprise, railroads and industry were permitted to deal brutally with injury claims. They had notorious claims departments, staffed by men who drew their moral standards from the pirates and highwaymen of earlier days. With this background, early tort litigation could not help but turn into a perjury contest.

As soon as a serious accident had occurred, the defendant's "investigators" would sweep into action, often buying up witnesses, creating their own eyewitnesses where there were none, falsifying records, and sometimes inducing severely injured victims to sign away their rights for a few dollars in cash laid on a hospital bed. It was not necessary for defendants to hire lawyers for this work. They could hire "investigators" and "claims adjusters" at lower rates. By the time the railroad defense lawyers (such as Abraham Lincoln and Clarence Darrow) came to court, the case had usually been wrapped up for them by the swift and effective work of their clients' claims departments.

This practice bred its own antidote. The early plaintiffs' lawyers were faced with the problem of overcoming the handiwork of the claims department if they were to have any chance to win the case. The plaintiffs had no claims department; so the dirty work had to be done by their lawyers, who had no one else to buy up their own witnesses or create evidence. Some plaintiff's lawyers became pretty good at this game, which had started at a time when law practice was being deprofessionalized in most states. Following the American Revolution, there was wide distrust of all things English, including their legal system and the privileged position of lawyers. Indeed, the whole idea of an organized, responsible, self-governing profession seemed undemocratic to American leaders of that era. They felt that all callings should be considered businesses, and that anyone should be eligible to participate. In his 1833 book *The Pioneers,* James Fenimore Cooper, who was an exponent of frontier democracy, described a hardy pioneer society that was inherently law-abiding and therefore had no need for professional lawyers. Indeed, between 1836 and 1870, popular distrust of professionals and the individualistic spirit of Jefferson and Jackson resulted in opening the practice of law in most states to all citizens, residents, or voters, without any special requirements of education or skill.

Given the conditions of the nineteenth century, it is not surprising that most able lawyers disdained accident practice as a mug's game unworthy of their professional skills. Instead, it attracted the lawyers who could not afford to be choosey about the type of cases they handled. In the big cities, these tended to be immigrants or the sons of recent immigrants who taught themselves the little that was needed to pass the bar examination (which was generally required before 1836 and after 1870). In the biography of his father, New York Supreme Court Justice Aron Steuer noted that these early tort lawyers usually were not vicious people, but—

> Put into a profession by the sweat and sacrifice of their families, they lacked both the skill to make a living at the law and the character to abandon it for a livelihood more suitable to their talents.

In urban centers, many of the early tort cases involved claims of pedestrians injured by streetcars that were operated by street railway companies. Most of them had claims departments modeled on those of the intercity and transcontinental railroads. The street railway investigators would usually get to the witnesses first and were adept at finding an ample number who, for a few dollars in cash, would testify to whatever version of the accident the investigators specified. The most enterprising of the plaintiff's attorneys would have their own "investigators," who also knew how to buy the desired testimony. As a result, it was not uncommon for the trial of a street railway accident case to start with the testimony of witnesses who lived on the first, second, third, and fourth floors of an apartment house overlooking the accident scene. The witnesses for the plaintiff (whose case was presented first) would testify how they were looking through their windows at the time of the accident and observed that the motorman was going very fast and was looking off to the side at the moment the streetcar ran over the plaintiff. When the street railway put on its defense, it would produce witnesses who lived on the first, second, third, and fourth floors of the same building (or one across the street with an equally good view of the accident). They would testify that, as they looked through their windows, the motorman was proceeding slowly and was looking straight down the tracks, but he was unable to stop in time because the plaintiff carelessly darted in front of the streetcar at the last moment.

That was tort law as it was practiced by the strongest plaintiff's lawyers—those who had the money and the determination to take on the street railways at their own game. At least they were trying to provide legal services for their clients by bringing their cases to trial, and they did it in the one way that offered them any chance to win: by fighting fire with fire. There was, however, an even lower rung to this ladder: the plaintiff's lawyers who took on such cases with no intention of ever bringing them to trial, but in hopes of promoting a small nuisance settlement (often no more than twenty-five or fifty dollars). They would commence the action (often by serving only a summons or a very short standardized complaint) and would then attempt to settle the case (often as part of a wholesale batch of claims). If no settlement could be made, they would drop the case, even if it had merit. They settled many serious cases for small amounts and made their profit on volume, quick turnover, and the low overhead that went with their lack of any truly professional services. Many a badly injured plaintiff was sold out by his lawyer in that way.

This type of practice also lent itself to ambulance chasing—the solicitation of clients by lawyers or their paid intermediaries. This happened predominantly in the ghettos and ethnic neighborhoods of big cities, where few residents read and spoke English and even fewer had their own attorneys. It was easy for enterprising bilingual intermediaries to contact accident victims, sign them up to contingent retainer agreements, and feed them to lawyers. Often, the more advanced plaintiff's attorneys who hired their own investigators would also use these investigators to procure cases, especially when they were bilingual.

If these conditions were not enough to discourage the better lawyers from entering tort practice, there was one final hurdle: the contingent fee. This was at the very heart of the system, since the plaintiffs could hardly ever afford to hire a lawyer on any other basis. Apart from the economic drawbacks of contingent fees in those days when the tort system was rigged in favor of defendants, many lawyers abhorred them because they saw themselves as successors to the tradition of the English barrister. This had developed from the feudal concept of advocates as champions who were carrying out a duty based on kinship or nobility rather than commercial considerations.

The earliest English and European advocates were not paid at all, and in later years when advocacy became a lifetime vocation, it was considered unprofessional for the payment to be contingent upon the outcome of the case. The Roman emperor Justinian disallowed contingent fees, and in his *Digest* he likened them to the "morals of a pirate." They were not permitted in New York until 1848, and as late as 1857 the Supreme Court of Michigan held that a contingent fee was *malum per se* —an evil in itself. Taking cases on contingent percentage fees was and is considered unprofessional in England and in most nations of the world. According to their traditional theory, lawyers who want to maintain professional standing and detachment should not go into business with their clients.

By 1928, conditions in New York accident practice had so deteriorated that a broad investigation was ordered by the Appellate Division of the Supreme Court, First Department (covering the boroughs of Manhattan and the Bronx). New York Supreme Court Justice Isidor Wasservogel was assigned to make a searching inquiry into abuses on both sides. With a staff of 22 lawyers, he held public and private hearings for six months, questioning 1,100 witnesses and producing a record of 10,780 pages of sworn testimony. The investigation was aimed mainly at the pervasive ambulance chasing by laymen who had developed sophisticated methods of learning about the occurrence of accidents from police, newspaper, and hospital sources. The chasers would rush to the accident scene, or to the hospital, and use high-pressure sales tactics in persuading the injured to sign retainer agreements in which the attorney's name was often not specified. Then the chasers would peddle these retainers to lawyers, often to the highest bidder.

The 1928 Wasservogel investigation report exposed this practice, marshaled the evidence against the worst offenders, and brought that type of ambulance chasing to an end in New York. But there were other abuses revealed in Justice Wasservogel's report. Thousands of accident cases each year fell into the hands of attorneys who had no facilities for bringing the cases to trial or rendering any professional services. Each of these attorneys took on hundreds of cases for the sole purpose of settling them without doing any work. To the defendant, each case had a nuisance value, even if it was only fifty dollars or seventy-five. In the 1920s, 500 or more of such cases added up to a very good annual income for the lawyer, who took such cases on a fifty-fifty basis—a contingent fee of one-half the amount collected. One attorney who testified before Justice Wasservogel had been admitted to the bar for only four years, and in that time he had handled more than 3,000 such cases.

Such lawyers relied on threatening letters to the defendants, or at most the filing of a summons and complaint, as their ultimate weapon. If they could not settle the case at that point, they would discontinue the action and thereby forfeit the client's right to recover damages. Most often they would sell out their clients for cheap settlements, disposing of dozens of cases at a time with the same defendant.

The Wasservogel report also described activities on the defendants' side:

> The evidence before me shows that casualty companies, transportation companies and other corporate defendants have engaged in practices equally reprehensible. Frequently the insur-

ance adjuster races with the "ambulance chaser" to the bedside of the injured person to obtain a release from him while he is overwrought and in pressing need of money. If a release cannot be obtained, the injured person is asked to sign a statement of the circumstances of the accident, or is plied with questions. The oral or written statements thus extracted do not present a fair or complete picture. Nevertheless, they are used against the plaintiffs at trials with exaggerated and harmful effect.

* * *

It should be made clear to attorneys for corporate defendants that they will not be allowed to evade their responsibilities as members of the bar by deliberate and disingenuous blindness concerning the operations of the claim departments of their companies, usually located in the same building and in intimate association with the legal departments.

The abuses reported by Justice Wasservogel were practiced by a small group of attorneys, of whom 74 were singled out for disciplinary action. This helped to curtail many of the worst practices that Justice Wasservogel brought to public light, but it did not enhance the standing of the tort lawyer. Given this history, it is little wonder that only lawyers of the least skill, education, influence, and opportunity were attracted to the plaintiff's side of tort cases in the nineteenth century and the early part of the twentieth.

The Wasservogel Report gives us a picture of New York City negligence practice in 1928, and it probably reflected similar situations in most of our large cities at that time. Some of the abuses reported by Wasservogel were indigenous to urban areas teeming with recent immigrants, where semiliterate accident victims existed in wholesale lots. In the smaller towns, the situation was somewhat different.

The small-town lawyers were truly general practitioners in the early tort days, and many took on all types of cases that came their way, including the representation of accident victims on contingent fees. Many did a good job for their clients, considering the difficulties of overcoming the investigation tactics of organized defendants. Often the small-town general practitioner would have a good rapport with jurors, and sometimes that would help to win a case for a plaintiff. At that point, the superior clout of the defendants came into play at a different level. Defense lawyers were often able to get trial or appellate judges to reduce the amount awarded, or to set the verdict aside entirely, on grounds that it was contrary to some provision of law or contrary to the weight of the evidence. The judges were selected by the establishment, and the great majority of them followed the establishment's laissez-faire philosophy. The lawyers for individual plaintiffs were not strong enough to overcome the superior leverage of corporate defendants and the eminent lawyers that they regularly retained. Francis Hutcheson Hare, a leading Alabama plaintiff's tort lawyer who began practice in 1927, wrote of that era in his memoirs:

> When the young lawyer graduated he was met with the proposition that defense counsel had almost a monopoly on prestige. The smartest law graduates went with the big corporate law firms and the plaintiffs were represented by lawyers who relied largely upon the sympathy or prejudice of the jury. The defense attorney mousetrapped the plaintiff in the pleadings or reversed him on refused written charges, and, if he got a good-sized verdict without other error, the supreme court would reduce it as excessive. The role of the advocate declined to the point where the plaintiff was compared to the jackal and no lion was needed to oppose him—or at most an old, mangy lion or a young cub, not a Martin Littleton or a John W. Davis.
>
> "The simple truth," [said Supreme Court Justice Felix Frankfurter] "was that the leading lawyers of the United States had been engaged mainly in supporting the claims of corporations, while the people and their interests had been represented generally by men of very meager legal ability."

Even in those early days, there were some skillful, honest, hard-working, professional advocates in big cities and in small towns who did represent plaintiffs in tort cases. But the deck was stacked against them, because they were arrayed against the highly organized laissez-faire establishment that was able to manipulate the legal system against the plaintiff. Not even the fifty-percent fees customary in those days would yield lawyers enough money to help change the system. That, as we shall see, came later, when the fees were actually lower.

The Beginnings of the Entrepreneur-Lawyer

Despite the sordid revelations of the 1928 Wasservogel investigation, there was—even then—a small group of entrepreneur-lawyers who were providing professional services to tort victims. They had their genesis in the rise of organized labor and in the development of an American version of the English solicitor-barrister relationship.

As the labor movement gathered strength in the 1890s, accident compensation improved, at least for injured workers. Apart from safety legislation which helped to prevent some accidents, the obstacle course of the employer's liability lawsuit was replaced by new workmen's compensation statutes (now called worker's compensation) that gave injured employees the right to make claims against their employers without going to court. These statutes established worker's compensation boards or commissions to decide such claims, and they eliminated the question of fault. All the employees had to prove was that they had been injured in connection with their work. The old defenses of contributory negligence, assumption of risk, and the fellow servant rule went out the window. Industry battled the early worker's compensation statutes in the courts, charging that they were unconstitutional interferences with freedom of contract and due process of law. The first New York statute was held unconstitutional in 1911, but the state constitution was amended in 1913, and in 1915 the new statute was upheld by New York's highest court. Most states adopted valid statutes by the early 1920s, although Mississippi did not get around to doing so until 1948.

Injured workers paid a price for eliminating the old restrictive rules. Medical expenses were covered, but the other benefits payable under the worker's compensation acts were quite limited, based upon a percentage of wages lost and a schedule setting forth the number of weeks of compensation that could be collected, depending upon the seriousness of the injury. Those plaintiffs who had been lucky enough to win an employer's liability action and hang on to the amount awarded by the jury all the way through the court proceedings were, at least theoretically, able to collect more money than the meager amounts provided in the worker's compensation schedules. But labor was happy to trade the workers' slim chances under the old employer's liability actions for the assurance of collecting some compensation in every case. Gradually, the benefits have been increased, but they still vary widely from state to state. In 1979, the maximum weekly benefit for total disability ranged from a low of $87.50 in Arkansas to a high of $607.85 in Alaska, with New York at $215, and most states at less than $200.

The labor movement was also responsible for two federal statutes that helped to change tort litigation. In 1908, Congress passed the Federal Employers Liability Act (FELA), which was a magna carta for injured railroad workers. Unlike the worker's compensation statutes, the FELA did not take away the common law rights of railroad workers to recover the full amount of their damages. But it did sweep away the common law booby traps of the fellow servant rule and assumption of risk, and it substituted a more humane standard of "comparative negligence" for the old contributory negligence rule. In the 1920 Jones Act, Congress put maritime workers in the same position as railroad workers.

These two federal statutes were a great boon to injured railroad and maritime workers. They also gave rise to the first group of American tort lawyers who could face their legal adversaries with any semblance of equality. Often, the lawyers who handled railroad and maritime injury cases would also represent the workers' unions, and thus would have a source of steady income from noncontingent fees. They were able to handle a great many cases arising out of similar conditions, which created economies of scale and all the other benefits of specialization which their adversaries had long enjoyed in representing the defendants. At last there were some tort lawyers who could afford to become specialists. Almost immediately, their specialization and professionalism paid off for their clients. While lawyers who represented plaintiffs injured in nonindustrial accidents were still taking 50-percent contingent fees in many cases, the union lawyers who represented railroad and maritime workers were reducing their fees to 33⅓ percent, or even less in serious injury cases.

These specialists began to win cases more consistently and to raise the level of damages to amounts approaching the real harm done to their clients. They had the money and the personnel to do the research that helped them to convince judges of the merits of their legal position. They had the resources to investigate and prepare thoroughly (often with help from union officials), and this enabled them to settle cases favorably or to convince juries on the facts. Moreover, their connection with the rising labor movement gave them enough political clout to have some influence in the selection of judges.

With the advent of the mass produced automobile in the 1920s, the focus of tort law shifted to auto accidents and the liability insurance companies that wrote coverage for motorists. This helped the development of tort lawyers, but the public was not nearly as well served in auto accident cases as were railroad and maritime workers whose lawyers were truly professional specialists. Right through the first half of the twentieth century, most plaintiffs in accident cases were represented by lawyers who were outmanned and outgunned by defense lawyers.

Most of the leading lawyers were still shunning the plaintiff's side of tort cases. Until the late 1940s, young trial lawyers with great potential—such as Edward Bennett Williams, who began practice in 1944—were still likely to be representing the railroads and insurance companies. The giants of the profession—such as Wendell Willkie, Thomas E. Dewey, John W. Davis, Herbert Brownell, and William P. Rogers, who attained cabinet rank or became candidates for President of the United States—mixed their public careers with the legal defense of business and finance. There were some exceptions, such as Louis Nizer, who could and would try any interesting case, even if the fee was contingent; but their leverage came from lucrative corporate practices rather than specialization in tort cases.

By the 1920s, the controversy surrounding the contingent fee and the need to counteract the handiwork of defendants' investigation departments had discouraged many good lawyers from handling accident cases. In addition to those "dirty business" aspects, there was another strong deterrent: calendar congestion. The courts, which were staffed to handle litigation volume based on nineteenth-century experience, were getting crowded with negligence cases. Much of this backup was caused by the emergence of the automobile age, but some was also due to questionable claims of the type described in the 1928 Wasservogel report. Lawyers in the crowded metropolitan areas had to sit around courthouses waiting for the availability of judges and courtrooms. Specialists were geared to this, but for the general practitioner it represented loss of valuable office time that could not be charged to any client. Also, the cases that went to trial were getting more scientific and specialized, particularly in medical testimony.

As the automobile began to make its imprint on American society, it brought with it injuries of a severity and subtlety that had not been seen before in our courts. Those who aspired to be tort specialists soon realized that they had to become knowledgeable in medicine, and many of them studied medicine at least informally. Some even sat through autopsies to learn all they could about anatomy. Some who had doctors as relatives or friends tried to learn from them. On the defense side, the insurance companies and other regular defendants had their own staff doctors as well as staff lawyers who were experienced in the trial of medical issues. To put themselves on an equal footing with defense doctors and lawyers, the lawyers for the plaintiff had to educate themselves extensively for each case—if they handled only a few negligence cases—or they had to become specialists.

Out of these conditions a new practice arose: the referral of tort cases from general practice lawyers to plaintiff's tort specialists. This practice has been compared to the English solicitor-barrister relationship. The English system is based upon the centuries-old monopoly of the barristers in the trial of all but petty civil and criminal cases. The barristers are in court regularly and have specialized training in court proceedings. Solicitors are generally business lawyers who are trained for paper work and counselling rather than for trial advocacy. Even so, there are many English solicitors who specialize in accident cases today. Solicitors do all the pretrial preparation work, including discovery and interviewing of witnesses. Barristers never meet witnesses until they appear in court. Thus the analogy between the English and the American system is not completely accurate, but both are based upon the practical consideration that one group of lawyers in each country has the advantage of continuous presence in the courtroom; it is thereby in a position to do a more efficient job for the clients of the other group of lawyers who deal with their clients primarily in their offices. However, English solicitors and barristers were never called upon to become entrepreneurs in the sense that American tort specialists were, since contingent fees are prohibited in Great Britain.

The development of referrals did much to professionalize plaintiff's tort practice. Being consulted by their own peers in the general practice firms gave the tort specialists unaccustomed prestige, and this began to attract better lawyers to tort practice. Whether their firms were large or small, general practice lawyers in New York and other urban centers could not handle occasional injury claims for personal clients without either investing inordinate time in self-education or putting the client's compensation at high risk. In practice, it was much sounder to refer these cases to specialists.

Plaintiff's lawyers who could rely on a steady stream of referral work from the general practice lawyers could now begin to professionalize their practices. They could take on staffs of legal assistants who would help with legal research and the increasing burden of paper work. More of their cases required interrogatories and depositions as well as expensive investigation and preparation of legal, factual, and medical issues. It was a far cry from the earlier street railway cases, in which the main task of the plaintiff's lawyer was to find eyewitnesses to counteract the devastating testimony that would be produced by the railway investigators.

The American solicitor-barrister relationship involves a sharing of fees between the referring attorney and the specialist. Since this practice is sometimes questioned by persons who do not understand its purposes, some explanation is in order here. Unlike the medical profession, the legal code of ethics has never prohibited sharing of fees, provided it is based upon a sharing of services and responsibilities. Referring lawyers take great responsibility in referring a case to a particular specialist, since they are turning over their most precious possession—their personal client—to another lawyer. If the specialist does not do a good job, the judgment of the referring lawyer will be questioned, and he may lose a lifetime client relationship. Also, there is much preliminary work to be done by the referring lawyer to decide whether a claim is worth pursuing. Once the case gets under way, the meticulous lawyer will monitor the work of the specialist and keep the client advised. Most tort cases are settled before trial, and the referring lawyer plays an important role in helping the client to appraise settlement offers. Since plaintiff's tort lawyers were widely distrusted in earlier days, and some were known to be engaging in high volume wholesaling, it was important for the referring lawyers to satisfy themselves that the settlement offer was the best that could be obtained under the circumstances. It would then be their job to convince the client to settle the case, or to refuse the offer if it was not satisfactory.

One might expect that the sharing of responsibility, services, and fees between the referring lawyer and specialist might have increased the overall fee, but it had the opposite effect. It was the non-professional volume operators who were consistently charging 50 percent fees and then selling out their clients in many cases. The real professionals—the advocates who had the personnel, facilities, and skills to properly prepare the cases and bring them to trial—were getting the bulk of their cases from general practice lawyers. The referring attorneys who fixed the overall fee were dealing with their own clients in a long term relationship, and so had a stronger incentive to keep the fees down than the lawyer involved in a one time representation. Referring attorneys had greater bargaining power than one-time clients, since they were a source of continuing business for the specialists. Therefore, when the American solicitor-barrister relationship started to develop, it actually brought the fees down. In most serious cases, the overall fees do not exceed 33⅓ percent for the combined services of the referring lawyer and the specialist, even though the services rendered are much more extensive and professional than they were in the old days of the 50 percent fees.

The pioneer entrepreneur-lawyers of the 1920s had to finance accident cases themselves. Calendar delays could range from three to five years, during which the specialists had to carry their own overhead expenses, including salaries of all of those who worked on the case. In addition they would have to lay out their own money for court filing fees and the expenses of investigation and preparation. As a rule, they also laid out their own money to pay the physicians who came to court to testify for their clients. These expenses added up to fairly large totals for one lawyer to carry in the dollars of the 1920s and 1930s, especially when compared to the relatively small sums that could be recovered by settlement or trial in those days. While this was a strain on the pioneering specialists, it did not approach the amount of cash outlay per case that is commonplace today, even if the amounts are adjusted for inflation. But it was a start on the road toward balancing the scales of justice in tort cases. It got the cases prepared to the point where the specialist could produce the expert testimony (usually a physician) and had an even chance to win a worthy case.

This was what had been missing from the Triangle Shirtwaist case in 1914, when Max Steuer had experts on construction and fireproofing at his disposal, but the plaintiff's attorneys could only muster evidence that lasted a little over one day. Investigation, scientific education of the trial lawyer, and expert testimony were always available to the defendants in those days, but rarely could the plaintiffs or their attorneys afford them on the same scale. In this way defense attorneys were usually able to overwhelm the few plaintiff's lawyers who could bring such cases to trial.

With the emergence of the railroad and maritime lawyers and the referral specialists, the picture started to change. The plaintiffs were not always pushovers at trial. In fact, some plaintiff's specialists became so adept in the preparation and trial of automobile cases that most defendants settled their cases before trial, rather than chancing a large jury verdict. In this way the defendants, who were for the most part well organized casualty insurance companies, could keep their total payments down to the desired level by forcing the weaker lawyers to settle cheaply or lose their cases at trial, and by pursuing a settlement strategy that kept the stronger lawyers from raising the overall damage levels and making too much new liability law in the appellate courts.

As the tort specialists in big cities became more adept and more professional, some people still called them "ambulance chasers," even though most of them had enough cases referred to them by their professional peers to keep them busy without soliciting cases from strangers. This professional evolution was recognized by Isidore Wasservogel, the same Supreme Court Justice who had reported the shocking condition of New York negligence practice in 1928. Twenty-seven years later, in 1955, Justice Wasservogel was again called upon by the Appellate Division for the First Department to make an inquiry into negligence practice; this time, to consider whether it was appropriate to limit the fees paid by plaintiffs in negligence cases. In the course of deciding that such limitation was not necessary or appropriate, Justice Wasservogel summarized the changes that had taken place between his 1928 and 1955 investigations. He pointed out that there was no longer any stigma attached to the representation of plaintiffs in negligence cases:

> With respect to this, I desire to state that I have the highest personal regard and esteem for the professional integrity and ability of those members of the bar whose legal activities are primarily concerned with the trial of negligence actions. The public should understand that the proposed rule and hearings before me relative to such proposal were not due to a recurrence of conditions which existed in 1928, when I conducted the "ambulance chasing" investigation. There is no evidence before me which indicates that similar activities are engaged in today by members of the legal profession to any degree which would warrant another investigation of this kind. On the contrary, I am certain that the publicized results of the prior investigation, the enactment of applicable canons of ethics and general supervision of attorneys by their bar associations, have practically eliminated these former undesirable practices.

Justice Wasservogel also commented on the increased effort and expense required in 1955 negligence practice:

Economic conditions and the cost of litigation, however, are entirely different today from what they were 27 years ago. The practitioner, in recent years, in addition to being saddled with rising costs of office rents, clerical help and other items of overhead, also has had to cope with increased court costs, filing fees, lengthy examinations before trial [depositions] which are generally required in all negligence actions regardless of the nature of the injury or the amount of the probable recovery, discovery and inspection, classification and pretrial hearings and delays which are time-consuming and costly to the attorney.

Justice Wasservogel found that most tort lawyers were performing intricate professional services for which they needed to set fees adequate to assure continuation of their entrepreneurial functions and to cover the heavy costs of losing cases.

Despite the development of tort specialists in the 1920s and 1930s, some general practice lawyers and firms handled their own tort cases on contingent fees. Outside of New York and other large metropolitan centers, many of the larger general practice firms have always handled their own plaintiff's tort cases on contingent fees. The strength and professionalism of these firms did much to improve the plaintiff's position and to develop tort law in an evenhanded way. In some areas, the best insurance defense lawyer was also the best plaintiffs' lawyer—indeed, sometimes a law firm that represented many insurance companies was the *only* one in the area equipped to take the case all the way through the courts for plaintiffs. In the days before World War II, many such firms took on plaintiffs' claims that did not involve any of their insurance clients on the defense side. Often they made important contributions to tort law on behalf of individual clients, and sometimes they blazed trails that helped future plaintiffs. But because of their insurance affiliations, they could not become all-out crusaders for the rights of plaintiffs. It took a later, nationwide movement to balance the scales in the uneven contest in which individual plaintiffs were arrayed against the organized forces of the insurance, transportation, and industrial giants who operated throughout the United States, either as separate entities or through associations.

While professionalism was slowly making its way into accident cases, it was the exception rather than the rule. If you walked into a courthouse prior to World War II in search of an interesting tort trial that would illustrate full use of scientific litigation techniques by highly skilled advocates, you were not likely to find it in the form of a negligence case being tried by a contingent fee lawyer. You were more likely to encounter that where one property owner or corporation was suing another, with both sides represented by highly skilled counsel who were paid by the hour regardless of the outcome.

One such lawsuit was *Hahn v. Duveen,* a slander case that

came to trial on March 8, 1929, in the Supreme Court of the State of New York for New York County, the same court in which *Nader v. General Motors* was heard. Sir Joseph Duveen, later Lord Duveen, was the most spectacular and successful art dealer in history. He dealt with most of the world's wealthiest collectors, buying and selling many of the world's most expensive art works. He literally made the American art market for nearly fifty years. His clients included J. P. Morgan, William Randolph Hearst, Henry Ford, Andrew Mellon, H. E. Huntington, and Henry Frick. The works that he sold them, such as Gainsborough's "Blue Boy" and Rembrandt's "Aristotle Contemplating the Bust of Homer," were the beginnings of the great art collections in America.

Throughout his career, Duveen used litigation to help establish his mystique and his authority. In June 1920, Mrs. Harry J. Hahn of Junction City, Kansas, put up for sale "La Belle Ferroniere," a painting by Leonardo da Vinci. This created a stir in the art world, since works by the creator of the "Mona Lisa" rarely came on the market. At the time Mrs. Hahn was negotiating the sale of her painting to the Kansas City Art Institute for $250,000, a *New York World* reporter telephoned Duveen for his comments. Duveen said:

> The Hahn picture is a copy, hundreds of which have been made. The real "La Belle Ferroniere" is in the Louvre.

Duveen's remarks were widely published, and his influence was so great that the Kansas City Art Institute purchase was cancelled and the painting became unsalable. Mrs. Hahn brought suit against Duveen in 1920, charging that his remarks were untrue, that they constituted a slander of her painting (technically, a case of "slander of title"), and that this had caused her damages of $500,000.

The story of the 1929 *Hahn v. Duveen* trial is best told in the words of S. N. Behrman in his 1952 book *Duveen,* based on a series of articles that Behrman wrote for *The New Yorker* magazine:

> The resulting trial, although it didn't take place until nine years later, was a sensation—a heresy case with a picture as defendant. First, there was a preliminary hearing at the Louvre, where the Louvre Leonardo was placed side by side with Mrs. Hahn's Leonardo and peered at by experts. . . . The trial itself took place in New York, and lasted twenty-eight days. A journalist of the time said that the Hahn Leonardo trial was "a lowbrow and highbrow circus—the smartest show in town." Duveen marshalled a gallery of experts for his defence—including [Bernard] Berenson—such as had never before been rounded up for an art suit.

*   *   *

This was one lawsuit Duveen did not enjoy; the opposition was too formidable. The jury turned in a mixed verdict—nine to three in favor of Mrs. Hahn. Justice Black ordered another trial, but Duveen avoided this by settling with Mrs. Hahn out of court for sixty thousand dollars. What the whole thing cost him, in time and money, cannot be computed, but the sum was certainly vast.

*   *   *

During the suit, Duveen's associates couldn't understand why he should deny the authenticity of a picture with which he had nothing to do, and thus involve himself in expensive litigation, but his recklessness in expressing his opinions about other people's stuff was not without value. Duveen looked upon himself as the Pontifex Maximus of the art world; he was tolerant of an associate who customarily called him Josephus Rex. His lawsuits, even those he lost, helped to establish his pre-eminence as a monopolist not only of merchandise but of opinions.

Duveen could well afford this showcase trial, even though his trial lawyers were George W. Whiteside and Louis J. Levy of Chadbourne Stanchfield & Levy, one of New York's leading firms. Mrs. Hahn was represented by another leading firm, Frueauff Robinson & Sloan. Duveen was wise to settle for $60,000, since a second trial and ensuing appeals would probably have cost him that much in legal fees. He had achieved a narrow escape when the jury disagreed 9 to 3, since a 10 to 2 verdict would have been sufficient to award Mrs. Hahn $500,000.

The Hahn-Duveen trial was a battle of depositions and experts. Most of the knowledgeable witnesses were located in Europe, and their depositions were taken there. Some testified in person at the trial. The jury was bombarded with expert testimony, photographs, and even X-ray negatives. Fifty years later, a sightseer in the same courthouse might see another jury trial, with high powered counsel and expert witnesses on both sides, contesting complicated issues through depositions, X-rays, photographs and documents, with hundreds of thousands (if not millions) of dollars in the balance. But it would probably not be a slander case or a suit involving art or other property. It would be a tort case involving personal injuries or death. Today the rich property owners would avoid trial and would settle their differences outside of court; a Duveen would not be likely to risk his reputation or his fortune in litigation.

What happened in those fifty years to change the cast of characters? There was not much change in the twenty years following the 1929 Duveen trial. There still were very few strong law firms specializing in plaintiff's tort cases. Insurance companies and other regular defendants were still retaining the most prestigious litigation firms, and were maintaining their leverage over the trial courts, the appellate courts, and the legislatures. Plaintiff's lawyers were not organized; they had very little influence in the state legislatures or in the bar associations; and they had no authors of legal treatises who were capable of opening the minds of judges to the plight of tort plaintiffs.

Those who had become specialists were entrepreneurs in a small way. They could support their own small organizations while waiting out the delays of litigation, and they could do a good job on the uncomplicated cases that came their way. But the real entrepreneur-lawyers who could put their clients on even terms with corporate opponents in accident litigation had not developed yet.

The age of the entrepreneur tort lawyer began shortly after I graduated from law school in 1948. The concurrence of these two events was purely coincidental, since I had no interest in becoming a tort lawyer, much less an entrepreneur-lawyer. However, I became involved in the great changes wrought by entrepreneur-lawyers that started about 1950. Since there is no other history of this movement to draw upon, and I am one (of thousands) who has participated in it, I must ask your indulgence at this point. I believe that the revolution which ended the age of the early American tort lawyer was a lawyer-made revolution; that its history is best told as the story of the lawyers involved; and that if I am to provide you with any useful historical insight, I must relate some personal experiences—particularly my fortuitous involvement with some of the giants who created the revolution of the entrepreneur-lawyer. I promise to limit personal reminiscences to those that are historically relevant.

Since my involvement in the development of the entrepreneur-lawyer has been mostly in aviation cases, the rest of this book emphasizes aviation. Tracing the history of the entrepreneur-lawyer through aviation cases is appropriate, since aviation itself is an American invention of the twentieth century, and I happened to be starting practice when the serious litigation of aviation accidents began (around 1950). Aviation cases mirror the changes that occur in other tort cases, since all are basically personal injury or wrongful death claims. I shall try to keep you informed of major parallel developments in other types of tort cases during the course of my eyewitness account of the aviation scene.

An Unlikely Tort Lawyer

I had started my studies at Columbia Law School in the summer of 1942, and had left to go into pilot training with what was then the U.S. Army Air Force. Before returning to Columbia in the fall of 1946, I put in some time as an aerial crop duster in Florida and Cuba, and I also worked as a broker in the sale of second-hand and surplus aircraft. When I completed law school in June of 1948, I had not shaken off the flying bug, and I hoped to find a legal position that would allow me to use my flying experience. I applied to several New York law firms that represented airlines, but found no opening.

Like most of my fellow Columbia graduates, I thought only of landing with a firm that represented corporations. There seemed little future in representing individuals. Apart from Bill Kunstler, I can't remember anyone even mentioning this idea. I was happy to find a job with a small Wall Street law firm that represented, among others, a major league baseball team, a financial newspaper, several stockbrokers, and a large department store. I had hoped to be assigned to one of the more glamorous clients, but being at the bottom of the ladder, naturally, I got the least interesting jobs. One of my chores was to defend the department store in the Small Claims Court, where ordinary people could have their day in court against any defendant without the complications of an ordinary lawsuit. At that time the New York City Small Claims Court was limited to claims below $100. (By 1979 its jurisdiction was up to $1,000.) While individuals do not need lawyers in Small Claims Court, the corporations that are sued there (or in any other court) must be represented by a lawyer. In case after case I was confronted by irate housewives who sought to return merchandise (sometimes after using it for a couple of years). Turned down by the store's adjustment bureau, they were forced to go to law, and they came to Small Claims Court in large numbers. I became known as the department store defense lawyer. On several occasions I was cornered in a corridor of the courthouse and berated by disgruntled customers of the department store, who accused me and the store owners of living off the fat of the land while they struggled to keep their families together. They looked upon me as the embodiment of the store owners' greed. I could not summon the courage to tell them that this champion of the privileged classes was being paid $60 a week.

During my first year with the Wall Street law firm, a piece of luck brought me the opportunity to combine law and aviation. A friend and classmate at Columbia, Jesse Silberstein, had taken a job with the Palestine Economic Corporation (PEC), which served as business agent for the emerging state of Israel. The PEC had been asked to locate an American who was familiar with aerial crop dusting and could serve as consultant to the man who was organizing the first aerial crop dusting service in Israel. They needed someone who was familiar with the procurement of crop dusting aircraft, pilots, chemicals, and other equipment. They would prefer that he be located in New York. It would also be handy if he were familiar with the legal intricacies of exporting aircraft. And of course it would not hurt if he were Jewish. As far as I have been able to determine, I was the only person on the face of the earth who met all of those requirements, besides being a friend of Jesse Silberstein, who had been asked to locate such a consultant. Through that chain of circumstances I came to meet Wim Van Leer, a Dutch pilot who was then organizing Chim Avir, the Israeli crop dusting service.

Wim Van Leer turned out to be the son of Sir Bernard Van Leer, who had built one of the most successful manufacturing enterprises in Europe, Van Leer Metal Products, only to lose it to the Nazis when they occupied Holland. The business was restored to the family after World War II, but Wim was more interested in Palestine, later to become Israel. He and his family were instrumental in supplying some badly needed military equipment (including airplanes) to the Israeli forces in the 1948 war of liberation. After serving with the fledgling Israeli Air Force himself, Wim decided to make his home in Israel. He saw that the new state needed to increase agricultural production immediately, and he was determined to use his aviation and organizational skills to bring this about.

Wim and I hit it off very well, and my first real client became a lifelong close friend. I helped him to obtain airplanes, pilots, and chemicals for Chim Avir. In my nine months with the Wall Street firm, I had found the practice of corporate law less exciting than the prospect of getting back into aviation, and so, with the encouragement of Wim Van Leer, I decided to leave and set up my own practice. This was a bold move for a lawyer with only one client, especially when that client was not a big airline or even a small airline, but Chim Avir, owner of three used Piper Cubs and an unwritten franchise to dust crops in places where not many pilots (even crop dusters) wanted to fly. Yet, the modest fees that I charged Chim Avir enabled me to open a law office of sorts in those pre-inflation days of 1950.

I set up shop in the heart of the downtown financial district at 25 Broad Street as the only crop dusting lawyer in New York—if not in the whole world. While I was ecstatic at the turn of events that enabled me to become a practicing aviation lawyer, I did not get carried away with the financial prospects. I rented a small private room in a suite that included nine other single practitioners who were sharing the rental, telephone, and receptionist charges. The cost was $90 a month, a healthy sum to me then, but I quickly brought my overhead back to zero by arranging to perform ten hours of work per month for one of the more affluent lawyers in the suite, and by getting a sub-tenant who used the office only to receive mail and telephone messages. Since I had no secretary or other employees, my profit margin was well over ninety percent of gross fees. Sometimes I think that I reached the peak of financial leverage right at that point.

Shortly after I began individual practice, I discovered another field that few people had ever heard of: aviation negligence law. A lawyer friend of mine who worked for a firm that specialized in automobile accident cases told me about a case in which his firm was representing a passenger who had been injured in the crash of an American Airlines DC–6 at Love Field, Dallas, Texas, in 1949. The case involved fuel management, piloting, and navigation of a four-engine airliner, and he remembered that I had been a four-engine pilot. He told me that they were having a lot of difficulty with the case, since it was their first experience with an airline crash. Finally he arranged for me to help his firm in the investigation and preparation of the case. Soon I discovered that the airlines and their insurers were being defended by Haight Gardner Poor & Havens, a large admiralty law firm that often represented Lloyd's of London. Haight Gardner had a staff of pilot-lawyers, some of them prewar fliers, and others who had finished law school after flying in World War II. I also found that Haight Gardner and two similar firms (Bigham Englar Jones & Houston, and Mendes & Mount) seemed to have a monopoly of the pilot-lawyers who were active in New York aviation negligence cases. All three were insurance defense firms. No pilot-lawyer had come along to represent the plaintiffs in such cases.

The Love Field Case opened my eyes to a field of law practice which was then just beginning in the United States. To understand its development, you must know a bit about the history of airline service.

Like the Wright brothers' first successful powered flight in 1903, the first scheduled airline service was also an American achievement. On January 1, 1914, the St. Petersburg-Tampa Airboat Line started operations with a Benoist flying boat that covered the 18 miles between St. Petersburg and Tampa, Florida, in 23 minutes and made two round-trip passenger flights daily. The Benoist, which had room for only one passenger and the pilot, looked like the original Wright brothers air-plane with a canoe slung under the wings. While the Florida service was operated safely and pretty much on schedule, it was more of a novelty than a necessity, and it closed down after the winter of 1914. For the next ten years, there was practically no significant scheduled airline service in the United States. Before World War I, there were few aircraft capable of sustaining reliable scheduled service, and there were none that could carry enough passengers to make the service economically feasible. The war accelerated aircraft development, and after 1918 airlines began to spring up all over Europe; but the U.S. did not follow suit, for reasons best explained by British aviation historian R. E. G. Davies:

> When the war ended, Europe hastened to find work for a vast armada of aircraft whose military usefulness was finished. France and Britain, with that ideal proving ground for transport aeroplanes, the London–Paris cross-Channel route, founded airlines immediately, while Germany, denied the right to build any military aircraft whatever, concentrated on civil types as the means of preserving its aircraft industry. In the United States, on the other hand, the social and geographic conditions were unfavourable; there were few situations involving a water crossing, and the densest inter-city routes were already served by efficient railways, often providing excellent service under the stimulus of competition.

Civil aviation development in the United States up to 1926 was practically limited to the air mail service operated by the U.S. Post Office (1917–1927), but in the mid-1920s there were four events which brought the United States into the forefront of scheduled passenger service. First, the Contract Air Mail Act of 1925 (known as the Kelly Act) transferred the air mail service from the Post Office to private operators through a system of competitive bidding. Of the original twelve successful bidders under the Kelly Act, ten survived to become the foundation stones of today's major trunk airlines. Then the Air Commerce Act of 1926 set up the first framework for federal regulation of aviation operations. At the same time came the first airliner that could carry a reasonable number of passengers with some semblance of comfort and reliability: the Ford Tri-Motor. The first one flew in 1926, and a few are still flying as this is written 53 years later. Henry Ford's pride was a high-wing monoplane with a corrugated aluminum skin which resembled the washboards of that era. Cruising at about 120 miles per hour, it carried two pilots and twelve to seventeen passengers in its final versions and was powered by three Pratt & Whitney 420 horsepower Wasp engines—one in the nose, and one mounted under each wing. As the "Tin Goose," it was to become one of legendary airplanes of all time. In all, 198 were built, and they dominated U.S. airline service from 1927 to 1933, when faster, quieter, more efficient, twin-engine low-wing monoplanes such as the Boeing 247 and the Douglas DC–1 began to appear.

The final event that opened the door to U.S. airline development was Charles Lindbergh's epic solo flight from New York to Paris in May of 1927. We think of it as a heroic individual achievement, but it was also of great importance commercially. It demonstrated the airplane's great potential and attracted the business and financial interest that was sorely needed. Lindbergh followed it up with many other flights that demonstrated the reliability of airplanes and laid the groundwork for new passenger routes.

Putting these four elements together, commercial airlines in the United States, which had been third in the carriage of passengers in 1928 (behind Germany and Canada), moved far ahead of all other nations in 1929.

In contrast to America's slow start, some European nations had jumped into passenger service soon after the 1918 armistice. They started out with converted World War I bombers, such as the British Vickers Vimy and the French Farman Goliath. Both of these were huge, fabric-covered, wooden twin-engine biplanes that had two pilots and carried ten passengers in a closed but noisy cabin. Although it was feasible then to close in the pilots' cockpit, it was thought that they needed the feeling of the wind on their faces to fly properly, and so they were left out in the cold air.

The First Major Airline Crash

One of the first British aircraft manufactured for airline service was the De Havilland D.H.34, a single-engine fabric-covered biplane with an open pilot cockpit and a closed cabin that seated nine passengers. The D.H.34 cruised at 105 miles per hour and was the mainstay of Imperial Airways' cross-Channel services during the early 1920s. The first Imperial Airways crash involving passenger fatalities occurred on December 24, 1924. A D.H.34 scheduled to fly from London's Croydon Airport to Le Bourget, Paris, experienced engine trouble shortly after takeoff. The pilot tried to turn back to attempt an emergency landing at Croydon, but the aircraft stalled and dove to the ground from an altitude of about 200 feet. It burst into flames on impact, killing the pilot and all seven passengers.

The task of proving fault on the part of Imperial Airways in the first case of its kind to arise in England fell to one of her ablest barristers, Gilbert Beyfus. He was called to the Bar at the Inner Temple

in 1908, and in his active career of more than 50 years, he was to win
many famous cases. These included a five-year battle against the unfair
attempt by American auto magnate Walter P. Chrysler to take over
the British Chrysler company; a libel action against the Duchess of
Argyll; and dramatic courtroom successes for Jaime Ortiz-Patino, heir
to the great Bolivian tin fortune; cabinet minister Aneurin Bevan;
and Liberace, the American entertainer. Most judges and barristers
considered him one of the best British advocates of the twentieth century, especially in cases where complicated fact situations had to be
simplified for jury presentation. He was also famous for his escapes
from prisoner of war camps in Germany during World War I, although he seems to have been equally adept at getting himself re-
captured.

In the 1924 Croydon D.H.34 accident, the airline's records
showed that the plane's engine had been experiencing serious troubles
for the preceding six days. Imperial Airways Captain W.G.R. Hinchcliffe had been flying it for most of the week prior to the crash. He
testified that the engine was "very rough" on his December 18th flight
from Croydon to Amsterdam; that after takeoff on the return flight
from Amsterdam he had experienced severe loss of oil pressure (a
sign of serious engine trouble), so he decided to abort the trip and
returned to Amsterdam; and that the mechanic who checked the engine
at Amsterdam told him that he found specks of white metal in the oil
filter, which might indicate bearing trouble. Captain Hinchcliffe had
experienced various other troubles with the engine before he finally
returned the airplane to Croydon on the morning of December 24th. He
was concerned enough about the engine to report its troubles directly
to Major Brackley, superintendent of the airline, and to two mechanics.
He also wrote up a special report on the engine troubles and mentioned them to Captain Stewart, who was to take the plane on the
fatal Paris flight that afternoon. Gilbert Beyfus questioned Captain
Hinchcliffe:

> Q: Would you yourself have flown this machine at 12 o'clock to
> Paris with a load within 30 pounds of the maximum permissible
> load?   A: I personally would not. I should have wanted 200
> pounds to 300 pounds less load.
> Q: Has [the traffic manager] ever threatened to report a pilot for
> refusing to take a full load?   A: Yes, I personally have been re-
> ported by him for refusing to take a full load off Ostend aero-
> drome.

Captain Hinchcliffe had also reported the engine trouble to the airline's mechanical superintendent at Croydon, who was cross-examined
by Beyfus:

Q: Did Captain Hinchcliffe speak to you that day about the difficulties he had experienced with the engine? A: Yes, and I told him, "Very well, Hinchcliffe, she will go through our usual routine, and if defective, we shall change her."

Q: Do you mean to say that when special defects were reported to you, all you said was, "She will go through our usual routine"?

A: There were no special defects.

Q: Did you do anything at all? A: I, personally, did not.

Another important witness was Major J.P.C. Cooper, Inspector of Accidents for the British Air Ministry, who supervised the government accident investigation. He testified that when Captain Stewart experienced engine trouble shortly after takeoff, he could not make an emergency landing straight ahead because there were buildings in his path. His only choice was to turn back, which resulted in the stall and crash. Beyfus elicited key points from Major Cooper:

Q: As I understand it, this aeroplane only arrived at 10:30 that morning, and the report was that the engine was very rough?

A: Yes.

Q: Assuming the pilot had made a special report about having engine trouble, do you think an ordinary routine examination carried out in half an hour was sufficient? A: No, I do not.

Q: I suggest to you that if the machine had been flown for half an hour's test flight, it would have been discovered what was wrong? A: It probably would, yes.

Q: But of course the objection is that the passengers would not have been able to go up? A: I cannot express an opinion on that.

It was also shown that Captain Stewart used 700 yards for his take-off run (just about all the runway that there was at Croydon) instead of the normal 400 yards. All of this evidence gave Gilbert Beyfus the basis for accusing Imperial Airways of "gross and culpable negligence" in his final speech, a charge that he did not make lightly. But Beyfus lost the case, and the families he represented recovered no damages, although the facts that he brought out forced Imperial Airways to grant its pilots the right to decide what loads they would carry.

Beyfus considered this the worst defeat of his career. It was this kind of experience with the difficulties of airline crash cases that laid the groundwork for limited liability of European airlines, in exchange for certainty of recovery without having to assume the heavy costs and risks of European tort litigation. If the best of the English barristers couldn't win the Croydon case with the Imperial Airways pilots on his side, how could the passengers' families ever expect to recover any damages in such litigation?

The European nations sponsored a conference at Paris in 1925 to draft a treaty governing air carrier liability for passenger injuries and death on international flights. Historically, European legal systems permitted domestic and international rail and ship carriers to limit their liability to small sums, simply by printing notices to that effect in their tickets. Given that background, plus the need of fledgling air carriers to fix limits of liability in order to obtain insurance coverage, and the grim outlook for passenger liability claims as in the Croydon D.H.34 crash, the final result was not surprising. The Paris conference of 1925 was followed by one at Warsaw in 1929, at which the Convention for the Unification of Certain Rules Relating to International Transportation by Air, popularly known as the Warsaw Convention, was adopted by 23 nations, most of them European. The Warsaw Convention made carriers automatically liable for injuries and deaths of passengers unless the carriers could sustain the burden of proving that they took "all necessary measures to avoid damage." In exchange for this concession, which was an important one for European passengers of the 1920s and the 1930s in view of the difficulty of proving fault and overcoming ticket limitations, the liability of carriers was limited to 125,000 gold francs (the American equivalent of $8,291) for each passenger.

Eventually more than 100 nations adhered to the Warsaw Convention. It applies only to international transportation, but many of the nations adhering to it, including the European nations that sponsored it, adopted their own national legislation which makes the terms of the Convention applicable to their domestic flights as well. By various amendments and agreements, the limitation has been raised to $20,000 or $75,000, depending upon carriers and itineraries.

Early American Aviation Tort Law

The United States chose to go a different route. Although we adhered to the Warsaw Convention in 1934 and it became part of the law of the land governing international flights, we made aviation accident claims arising out of domestic crashes a part of our common law of torts. We did not have the tradition of limited carrier liability, since our Supreme Court had ruled in the nineteenth century that railroads could not limit their liability by printing such conditions in their tickets. There was no great policy debate leading up to the application of our common law of torts to aviation accidents. There was very little aviation accident litigation before the late 1940s, and by that time airplane crashes had become part of the common law by osmosis.

American aviation tort law begins with the case of *Guille v. Swan,* decided by the New York Supreme Court in January 1822. The facts are described in the court's opinion:

> The facts were that Guille ascended in a balloon in the vicinity of Swan's garden, and descended into his garden. When he descended, his body was hanging out of the car of the balloon in a very perilous situation, and he called to a person at work in Swan's field to help him, in a voice audible to the pursuing crowd. After the balloon descended, it dragged along over potatoes and radishes about thirty feet, when Guille was taken out. The balloon was carried to a barn at the farther end of the premises. When the balloon descended, more than 200 persons broke into Swan's garden through the fences and came on his premises, beating down his vegetables and flowers. The damage done by Guille with his balloon was about $15, but the crowd did much more. The plaintiff's damages, in all, amounted to $90.
>
> It was contended before the Justice that Guille was answerable only for the damage done by himself, and not for the damage done by the crowd. The Justice was of the opinion, and so instructed the jury, that the defendant was answerable for all the damage done to the plaintiff. The jury, accordingly, found a verdict for him, for $90, on which judgment was given, and for costs.

The Supreme Court ruled that it was foreseeable to Guille that his aeronautical activities would naturally draw a crowd of people around him, "either from curiosity, or for the purpose of rescuing him from a perilous situation." Since he had put himself in a position to invite the help of the crowd, he was responsible for the trampling of vegetables done by the crowd as well as the damage that he did himself. For an 1822 court, this was a very liberal construction of damage rules, based upon the common sense bedrock of foreseeability. As we shall see, 150 years after the *Guille* decision, plaintiff's tort lawyers were still struggling to apply the same standard of foreseeability to protection of human life and limb that the 1822 court extended to Mr. Swan's potatoes and radishes.

A later ballooning case is described in the first American book on aviation law, the *Textbook of Aerial Laws* by Henry Woodhouse, published in 1920. It involved two American balloonists, A. Holland Forbes and Augustus Post, who represented the Aero Club of America in the international balloon races held in Berlin in 1909. They had difficulties with their balloon which resulted in an explosion at an altitude of 3,000 feet, from where they dropped down rapidly and de scended through the roof of a private home. Woodhouse concludes his report of this case as follows:

> Messrs. Forbes and Post were saved from the great shock of the basket striking the roof of the house, which made a hole in the roof, and they were dragged down by the basket. They found themselves in a lady's boudoir but the lady was not at home. Two days later she wrote to them inviting them to call while she was at home!

Prior to the late 1940s, American aviation accident litigation was dominated by arguments over the wording of life insurance policies. During the early days of aviation, many life insurers excluded payment of double indemnity for accidental death where the policyholder was "participating in aeronautics." There was often a dispute as to whether merely riding as a passenger made one a participant in aeronautics, and the courts took many different positions on this issue.

Passenger claims against operators were rarely litigated before the 1940s, for several reasons. Most of the aviators who caused injuries or deaths were barnstormers and sightseeing pilots who carried no liability insurance and had few assets that were not heavily mortgaged. Even the early airlines were not heavily insured and were often close to insolvency. The pre-World War II lawyers who customarily handled accident claims were not geared for cases as complex and difficult as air carrier accidents. As a result, when a major airline had an accident, it was relatively simple for its insurers to settle cases involving the deaths of breadwinners for $10,000 or less. They were aided by the fact that many states still had the limitations on death damages that emanated from the nineteenth-century railroad control of state legislatures. Many such limitations were as low as $10,000 well into the 1940s.

Actions against aircraft manufacturers were almost unheard of, since it was necessary for plaintiffs to prove negligence in the design or manufacturing process, a task that would have required their lawyers to learn all the details of designing and manufacturing an airplane, after which the claims would still be subject to the defense that the plane was designed and manufactured according to the existing "state of the art." There were few products liability suits brought against *any* manufacturers prior to the 1940s, and aviation manufacturers were among the least likely to be sued successfully.

If you were to read all of the reported aviation cases in the United States through the end of 1945, you would find that only one lawyer in the whole country represented plaintiffs in more than one aviation accident case. He was Arnold W. Knauth of the New York City firm of Lloyd Decker Williams & Knauth, a well known admiralty lawyer whose principal practice was defending claims for Lloyd's of London underwriters. In the 1930s, he had applied his knowledge of admiralty law to the new field of aviation law, particularly in cases involving crashes of flying boats on the high seas. Although primarily an insurance lawyer, he appeared for plaintiffs in about half a dozen prewar cases. In the few other aviation accident cases that came to trial before 1946, the plaintiffs were represented by lawyers whose firms received their main income (and supporting services, such as investigation) from insurance carriers and therefore had the resources to cope with complicated cases. Thus, when Arthur V. Conklin, a young executive of W. T. Grant Stores, was killed in an airline crash near Newark Airport in 1930, his widow retained the prominent New York insurance defense firm of Evans Hunt & Rees to bring suit against the airline.

Conklin was a passenger on a Fairchild 71 operated by Canadian Colonial Airways on scheduled mail and passenger service between Montreal, Albany, N.Y., and Newark, N.J. (This airline became Colonial Airlines in 1942, and was absorbed by Eastern Air Lines in 1956.) The Fairchild 71—a stately, high-wing, fabric-covered monoplane powered by a single Pratt & Whitney 420 horsepower engine— was not equipped with radio, and there were no electronic navigation aids in 1930. When fog rolled in over Newark Airport, the pilot groped his way through the low clouds, hoping to sight a landmark that would guide him in to the field. But, about five miles from the airport, he had the misfortune to collide with one of the highest obstacles in his path: a 150-foot tower owned by the Public Service Corporation and supporting four power lines that carried 132,000 volts of electricity. The plane burst into flames, and the pilot and his three passengers were killed.

This was a typical airline accident of the 1930s. To win a wrongful death action for the widow of an airline passenger, the plaintiff's lawyer had to overcome the following advantages the defendant had: unlimited access to expert testimony; ability to explain complicated aeronautical terms or to take refuge in them, hiding behind the mystique that surrounded the romantic pioneer aviators; and the tendency of jurors to believe that anyone who went up in an airplane assumed whatever risks were encountered. The Fairchild pilot had voluntarily descended so low that he hit the power line, but it was customary in those days for airline pilots to do their own weather reconaissance, and Canadian Colonial would be able to produce their own glamorous pilots (in uniform) and others of national renown, who would testify in court that the airline was not at fault.

Since Arthur Conklin had been flying on business for W. T. Grant, his widow was entitled to about $20 per week in worker's compensation benefits. The insurance carrier who wrote W. T. Grant's compensation coverage would be entitled to recover from Canadian Colonial the full amount payable to Mrs. Conklin, if it could be proved that the airline had negligently caused Arthur Conklin's death. This "subrogation" claim of the compensation insurance carrier was a blessing for Mrs. Conklin. The carrier took a strong interest in the case and recommended that Mrs. Conklin retain the Evans firm to sue the airline. The insurer's investigation staff would interview all prospective witnesses, and the insurer itself had enough clout to line up prominent aviators as expert witnesses for trial. The Evans firm rarely handled the plaintiff's side of accident cases, but they did a lot of legal work for the insurance carrier, and they agreed to represent Mrs. Conklin on a contingent fee basis, provided the insurance carrier took care of the investigation and procurement of expert witnesses.

In this way, Mrs. Conklin was raised to a level of litigation power approaching that of the airline when the case came to trial in September 1933. As trial witnesses, her lawyers were able to call: the U.S. Weather Bureau observers from Newark, Albany, and New York City; the managers of Newark and Albany airports; eyewitnesses to the flaming crash; and three superb expert witnesses. The first was Homer Berry, pilot of the personal airplane of *Chicago Tribune* publisher Colonel Robert R. McCormick. He was followed by Colonel Clarence Chamberlain, who at that time was second only to Lindbergh in status as a pilot. The final plaintiff's expert was a leading woman pilot, Ruth Nichols—an attractive, articulate, convincing witness who was a Wellesley graduate and was listed in the Social Register. All three of these experts testified that pilots should not descend below the height of known obstacles to explore in the fog; that they should know the height of all obstacles along their route; and that they should divert to another airport instead of doing what the Canadian Colonial pilot did.

The airline lawyers put on a strong case, calling as witnesses a phalanx of attractive airline employees who testified that the airline and all its personnel had complied with all applicable regulations and customs on the fatal flight. Then came their experts: aviation pioneer Charles S. (Casey) Jones and around-the-world record-breaking pilot Clyde Pangborn. Both of them testified that fog was an Act of God which could not be anticipated by the most careful pilot, and that decisions about landing in marginal weather had to be left to the judgment of the airline pilot.

The result was a $75,000 verdict for the plaintiff, the first in favor of a passenger against an airline in the New York courts, and probably the highest amount ever awarded in a wrongful death case up to that time (although it was later reduced to $50,000 by the Appellate Division). I am certain that had Mrs. Conklin not been assisted by the worker's compensation carrier, she would have lost the case on the prestige of Casey Jones and Clyde Pangborn alone. Without Clarence Chamberlain and Ruth Nichols to offset them, Mrs. Conklin's lawyers would have had little hope of overcoming the aviation mystique.

I confirmed this opinion in 1979 when I interviewed the senior partner of the Evans firm, Walter G. (Butch) Evans, who at the age of 93 was still erect, slender, quick of mind and speech, and hard at work reviewing a dozen files in his office. Butch agreed that there was no plaintiff's lawyer in New York who could have put on such a case in 1933 (or at anytime prior to the late 1940s), and that his own firm would not have taken the case on a contingent fee if the insurance carrier had not undertaken to make a complete investigation to educate the trial lawyers on the technicalities of the case and to arrange for the testimony of the three expert witnesses.

The Conklin case was a rare excursion into plaintiff's practice for the Evans firm. Butch always preferred the security of insurance defense practice, and he made no attempt to use the Conklin verdict as a building block for an aviation tort practice. He looked upon it as just another service to an insurance client, since winning the case against Canadian Colonial had resulted in compensating the insurance carrier for the weekly $20 benefit it was obligated to pay to Mrs. Conklin.

A Self-Taught Specialist

I was not aware of this aviation litigation history when I plunged into the job of investigating the 1949 American Airlines DC–6 Love Field crash. In fact, I didn't have the slightest idea how to go about such a task. By trial and error, I managed to get the job done to the satisfaction of the plaintiff's attorney who had hired me, which is not saying much, since he also had never handled such a case. He had filed the suit in the state court, but American Airlines removed it to the federal court because of diversity of citizenship. Using the federal discovery procedure for the first time, I arranged for the production of important airline documents and took depositions of some key witnesses, including the surviving crew members. The case was settled on the eve of trial for a sum that the plaintiff and his lawyers were very happy with. In the process of doing the job, I learned that there was a need for such services among New York plaintiff's lawyers. Other cases arising out of the 1949 Love Field crash were pending in New York, and also quite a few arising out of crashes going all the way back to 1943, in which the plaintiff's lawyers had made little progress toward proving the liability of the airlines. Most of these cases were in the hands of general practice lawyers and automobile accident specialists who had no aviation expertise and were therefore at a disadvantage against the experienced admiralty-aviation defense firms. I began to see the possibilities of developing a specialized practice.

With the exception of the few lawyers who represented injured maritime and railroad workers, most plaintiff's tort lawyers were not used to working in the federal courts in those days. The leading automobile accident lawyers practiced largely in the state courts. When they were retained in an airline accident case, they would usually file suit in the state court, where they were familiar with the practice rules and comfortable with the type of juror that normally sat there. However, since most airline cases involved diversity of citizenship between the plaintiffs and the airline corporations, the airlines usually could (and did) remove these cases to the federal courts. There the plaintiff's lawyers would be faced with unfamiliar rules and (at least in the New York federal courts) with upper middle class jurors who were inclined to favor business interests. Also, the federal courts required unanimous verdicts by all twelve jurors, while the New York state courts required only 10 to 2 verdicts in civil cases.

Airline cases were much more complicated and expensive than the cases negligence lawyers were accustomed to handling in the 1940s. The products liability revolution had not yet begun, and even the most successful plaintiff's negligence specialists who had four or five other lawyers working for them were not staffed to handle complicated cases. Many of them were doing well financially by trying and settling automobile cases and other relatively simple suits (such as premises liability) that did not involve extensive scientific investigation, expert testimony, or paperwork.

When an airline accident occurred, often the family lawyer would call in the negligence specialist to whom he customarily referred automobile cases. Airline insurers did not offer settlements that approached the true financial losses, since they were aware of their tactical advantages in this type of litigation. Even when a deceased passenger had an annual income of $15,000 to $25,000, a life expectancy of 20 years or more, and a wife and young children to be supported, settlement offers rarely exceeded $40,000 in the 1940s and early 1950s unless the plaintiff appeared able to bring the case to trial with some promise of success. Each case had to be tried separately from others that arose out of the same accident, and each plaintiff had to prove the airline's liability before any damages would be assessed.

For most lawyers accustomed to automobile cases, there was actually too much potential evidence available in aviation cases; they were not staffed either to digest or to use so much scientific information. The Civil Aeronautics Board (which investigated aircraft accidents until that function was taken over in 1967 by the National Transportation Safety Board) held public hearings and made transcripts of testimony and copies of exhibits available. These transcripts often ran to more than four hundred pages, and the exhibits added another thousand or so pages of technical information, such as diagrams of airline equipment, pictures of wreckage, complicated flight charts, and maintenance manuals. Lawyers who were used to spending only a few days preparing for trial in automobile cases now faced the prospect of studying the government file for months, just to understand the significance of all these strange documents. Then, after being reasonably certain of which evidence was helpful to the plaintiff, the lawyer had to get that evidence into the case by deposing witnesses who were often hostile and could take refuge in the complicated terminology of aviation.

The Civil Aeronautics Board issued a public report giving the probable cause of each accident; but since the government did not want to take sides in civil litigation, a federal statute provided that this report could not be used in court. So even for the best plaintiff's lawyers it was a struggle to get ready for an aviation trial. The result in many aviation cases that went to trial in the early postwar years was that the plaintiffs either lost the case entirely or had to settle for much less than they would have recovered after an automobile accident.

Some plaintiff's lawyers tried to overcome these difficulties by relying on the doctrine of *res ipsa loquitur*—the thing speaks for itself. This may be used when the defendant has exclusive control of the instrument that caused the injury, and when the accident is one that would not ordinarily occur unless the defendant had been negligent. Since airplanes normally do not fall out of the sky unless someone is at fault, the law allows a plaintiff to submit such a case to a jury by simply showing the circumstances surrounding the accident. In relying on *res ipsa loquitur,* one hopes the jury will infer that the airplane crashed because of negligence on the airline's part. But reliance on *res ipsa loquitur* did not prove fruitful for plaintiff's attorneys. A study published in the 1951 *Virginia Law Review* showed that a total of 24 airline cases had been submitted to juries on a *res ipsa loquitur* basis. Of these, 22 had resulted in defendant's verdicts, meaning that the families of injured or deceased passengers got nothing. The airlines usually came forward with positive evidence of the great care they took in training, maintenance, and flight operations. This evidence was presented by articulate, highly qualified pilots and engineers who often appeared in uniform. Since *res ipsa* cases do not pinpoint any act of negligence, jurors were unwilling to infer fault on the part of intrepid airmen or other clean-cut airline employees in the absence of specific proof. Take the case of Earl Carroll, the famous impresario of Earl

Carroll's Vanities who was killed in the crash of a United Airlines DC–6 at Mt. Carmel, Pennsylvania, in 1948. His case was tried under *res ipsa loquitur,* but a Pennsylvania jury decided that the airline was not liable.

In countless other cases, plaintiff's lawyers were forced to settle death claims for fractions of their potential value because the risk of losing was considerable, and the defense attorneys sensed that the economic burden on the plaintiff's side was too great to bring the case on for trial. There were some early attempts at cooperation between attorneys for various plaintiffs involved in the same accident, but they did not meet with great success because there was always the problem of who would take on the very heavy work load. Even among groups of plaintiff's attorneys, there were no aviation specialists who could approach the case in the same way as the admiralty-aviation defense firms hired by the airline insurers on an hourly fee basis.

There were exceptions, of course. There were plaintiff's lawyers who took the time to educate themselves sufficiently to try an aviation case. Some spent months or even years preparing a single case or a small number of cases. But in the usual situation, this simply was not destined to happen, and the defense lawyers were well aware of this. Even if they lost the case against one such heroic plaintiff's lawyer, they would have a fresh start against all of the other plaintiff's attorneys, who would each have to prove liability before getting a crack at damages. Even when a complete record of the first trial was available, it was not easy for the second plaintiff's lawyer to follow in the footsteps of the winner. The airlines had so many technical data and witnesses at their command that they could rewrite the script for the second trial.

My work for one of the victims of the 1949 American Airlines Love Field crash brought me to the attention of lawyers who represented the families of other passengers on that flight. It also brought me into contact with the small group of leading New York plaintiff's attorneys to whom most aviation cases (and other complicated tort suits) got referred in the late 1940s. Most of them were happy to find someone with an aviation background who was willing to undertake the liability phase of airline accident cases on a contingent fee basis. The plaintiff's lawyers themselves had been retained on contingent fees, so they were not in a position to pay me on an hourly basis. I, in turn, was thrilled to be working on large cases with leading trial lawyers so early in my career. I took on every case that was offered to me, with little regard for the economics of working as a contingent-fee subcontractor to contingent-fee lawyers.

Since airline cases took so much time, I had to decide at that point whether to devote my career to a contingent-fee practice. It seemed likely that I would in time make a comfortable living in business law practice, but the action of which I was getting a taste in these early aviation cases seemed more exciting. Also, while there were thousands of good business lawyers in New York, nobody else was doing what had become my job. I was needed by the widows and children who were the victims of these accidents, even though I rarely met them, and most of them were only names to me. More important to my ego, my expertise was needed by the most independent and self-reliant group of lawyers anywhere: the leading plaintiff's negligence lawyers of New York. Thus my ego won out over my sense of financial security, and I decided to specialize in aviation accident cases. As far as I have been able to determine, I was the first pilot-lawyer to become a specialist on the plaintiff's side of aviation cases.

I had no trouble keeping busy with airline cases, since I had walked into a waiting backlog of suits arising out of accidents that happened as far back as 1943. I found myself in court or getting ready to go to court much of the time during those early years. The cases took a long time to bring to trial then—often three to four years—and frequently I was not certain that I would survive until pay day. In most cases I was working for leading plaintiff's specialists or established general practice lawyers who were able to pay the litigation expenses, such as travel, investigation, deposition transcripts, expert witness fees, and copying of voluminous documents. Occasionally, though, I was retained by some less successful lawyer who had a fairly large damage case but could not afford to lay out the money needed to prepare it properly. In those situations I had to scrape up the money myself, and thus I had my first taste of being an entrepreneur-lawyer even before I could afford to hire a regular secretary.

My role in those early cases depended on the law firm that I was working with. The most capable tort specialists needed me only to investigate and prepare the liability phase of the case, taking the necessary depositions and discovery steps, and assisting them at the trial through whispered suggestions or scribbled notes. Others had me conduct parts of the liability trial, such as the questioning of each side's expert witnesses. Some engaged me to handle the entire liability case; others turned the client and the entire case (liability and damages, trials and appeals) over to me.

I believed that my chance discovery of the aviation accident field might lead to a successful practice as a specialist; but that would require some staying power, since the income from airline cases was spasmodic and unpredictable. My fees as a crop-dusting consultant were helpful, but never enough to support a practice or a family. I wanted to spend most of my time on the challenging airline cases at the top level of tort practice, but the more airline cases I handled, the closer I moved toward financial disaster, since each case was a long-term investment for me. Along with the glamorous airline cases, I therefore took on whatever work came my way. Predictably, most of that work consisted of the bread-and-butter negligence cases that find their way into the offices of young lawyers.

I should have sensed that my career was pointing toward wrongful death cases. One of my first negligence cases involved the partial collapse of the ceiling in a run-down New York apartment. The falling plaster had landed in the lap of my client, the young woman who occupied the apartment, and had caused her minor bruises and contusions. In addition, a chunk of the ceiling had fallen directly on the cage of her pet canary and had killed the canary on impact. I approached this case eagerly because the liability of the landlord seemed clear, and it looked like a claim that could be settled quickly to the plaintiff's satisfaction. I soon got into settlement negotiations with the adjuster who handled such minor claims for the landlord's insurer. I demanded $500, but after several conferences I could not budge him past $200. Finally I said, "Jack, I think you're overlooking an important item of damage here. In addition to the bodily injuries that my client suffered, there is also the death of the canary to deal with." The adjuster was ready for me on that one, and he replied, "I have already considered the value of the canary and the cage in the offer, and the case is still not worth more than $200." But cases like this were my means of livelihood, and I was not ready to give up so easily. Having noticed that the adjuster had a southern accent, I quickly replied, "There's an important fact that I don't think you're aware of: this was a canary who whistled 'Dixie.'" That story was worth another $100, so we settled the case for $300, and I closed the file on my first wrongful death claim.

Another early client of mine was a young man employed as a bagel stringer. Until I came to represent him, I was unaware that there was such an occupation. The practice of bagel bakers, I learned, was to deliver their hardy merchandise to bakery shops in groups of one dozen to the string, and the bagel stringer's job consisted of putting the string through their twelve holes and tying up the string. My bagel stringer client had been injured in an automobile accident and had lost a few weeks pay. As I came to the point of my checklist where I had to ask him what his weekly salary was, I chuckled smugly to myself. After all, it was nice to be a lawyer, otherwise I, too, might be out somewhere stringing bagels and probably starving to death. When I asked him how much he was paid for stringing bagels and he told me, "Sixty-five dollars a week," my smugness left me. That was more than I had earned any week during my nine months of salaried law practice, and it was more than I was netting then as an independent consulting counsel on Broad Street.

From those small cases I learned little except the art of survival, but in the airline cases I was getting a valuable legal education. I had been lucky enough to attend Columbia University Law School in New York. However, like most first-rate law schools, it taught students practically nothing about the real world of clients, litigation strategy, and money needed to finance litigation. I learned this from some old masters by actually working with them and their staffs—in their offices, out on the road, and through every phase of major accident cases. I observed how their organizations were put together and functioned, how they analyzed and reacted to real life litigation situations, and sometimes I even sat in with them while they were interviewing clients on new cases.

When I started working on airline cases, I knew something about airplanes and was able to put my Air Force experience as a radar test pilot to good use. But I knew very little about litigation, and at that time no helpful training courses were available. There was a constant need to blend what I knew about aviation with the old masters' practical litigation savvy. Of all the masters that I was privileged to work with, four deserve special mention here: Billy Hyman, Harry Gair, Mel Belli, and Perry Nichols. Their achievements illustrate the dramatic transition that started around 1950, even though all of them began practice long before then.

Battling Billy Hyman

The first master I worked with closely was William A. Hyman, known to his intimates as Battling Billy. Billy battled not only the opposition: he was in a constant state of combat with all around him, including his employees, his clients, and anyone else he could find to fight with. He was a man who would rather fight than eat.

I first met Billy Hyman in 1951, when he was 58 years old and at the peak of his powers. He was short and slender, about five feet five inches tall, with a full head of wavy white hair and a waxed grey mustache. He spoke with a trace of Virginia accent acquired in his college days at Washington and Lee University, where he had graduated in 1912 at the age of 19. He went on to get his law degree at Columbia in 1915 at age 22.

His offices were in the Aetna Insurance Building at 111 Fulton Street, in the heart of the insurance district of downtown Manhattan. He had half a dozen lawyers working for him, a large staff for a negligence firm at that time. The backbone of his law practice was his position as subrogation counsel for the Aetna Insurance Companies. He handled cases in which Aetna had paid insurance claims and then had been subrogated—put in the place of the policyholder. For example, if Aetna paid a policyholder for water damage to business inventory and the water damage was due to the negligence of someone other than the policyholder (such as a roofing contractor), Aetna could elect to sue the roofing contractor to recover the amount it had paid out. Aetna's subrogation claims added up to large sums every year, and they gave Billy Hyman's practice a foundation that few other plaintiff's lawyers enjoyed. He was free to take on any other cases that did not conflict with his subrogation work for Aetna.

By 1951 he had many outstanding achievements behind him. He had been appointed special deputy attorney general of New York State to investigate official corruption. He had handled some famous lawsuits, such as the Horace Dodge divorce case in the 1930s, and a landmark subrogation case which he won for Aetna in the U.S. Supreme Court, opening the way for all insurance companies to sue the U.S. government on subrogation claims. He had a strong following of general practice lawyers who referred negligence cases to him, and he was one of the few plaintiff's lawyers with adequate staff and facilities for handling complicated state and federal court cases. In 1950 his peers had elected him president of the Brooklyn-Manhattan Trial Counsel Association. At that time, he was one of the few New York plaintiff's attorneys active in the American Bar Association and a member of its standing committee on aeronautical law. He was also prominent in political circles and served as financial chairman of the Democratic National Committee in the Harry Truman days.

Billy telephoned me, asking me to come to his office because he had several cases arising out of the 1949 American Airlines Love Field crash and wanted to discuss the possibility of retaining me. The chance of working with him thrilled me, for he was likely to be called in on any major airline crash that involved suit in New York.

His impressive modern offices in the Aetna Building were a sharp contrast to the dingy quarters then occupied by most plaintiff's tort lawyers in the drafty old buildings around New York's City Hall. When I arrived for our appointment, I was armed with copies of the depositions I had taken in the other Love Field cases, plus a DC–6 flight manual and a lot of other technical data, which I was prepared to display in an effort to impress him with my usefulness. Our meeting lasted more than two hours, but I never got my briefcase open. In fact, I barely got my mouth open. Billy proceeded to dazzle me with a long exposition of his own vast experience in aviation cases. It began with the way he had represented the family of Notre Dame football coach Knute Rockne, who was killed in the 1931 crash of a TWA Fokker

F–X–A trimotor at Bazaar, Kansas—a crash that ended the use of the wooden-winged Fokkers by U.S. airlines. Billy said that there had been a clause in Rockne's life insurance policy to exclude payment of the customary double indemnity for accidental death when it occurred while the policyholder was "participating in aeronautics." During the 1930s and 1940s many courts construed this clause to bar double indemnity claims by families of airline passengers, but Billy said he had been able to collect the entire double indemnity for Rockne's beneficiaries.

He then proceeded to tear other plaintiff's negligence lawyers apart, mentioning how cheap they were and how ill-equipped for complicated litigation in the federal courts, such as he was accustomed to handling every day. This diatribe was interrupted by numerous phone calls and by the appearance of several of his staff lawyers and secretaries, who were all harangued unmercifully. He chewed out one lawyer for handling an inquiry on the telephone, insisting that the telephone was unreliable, and that the lawyer would have to go to see the witness and get the information from him face to face. He conducted several other major battles on the telephone, darting about his office like a bantam rooster, and each time returning to the one-sided interview with me. After two hours of this I was almost limp in my seat, frustrated at being unable to get a word in edgewise or demonstrate my aviation expertise. Finally he almost knocked me over by saying, "Well, young man, I don't have any more time. I've got to be in court in fifteen minutes. But I'm very impressed with your knowledge of this field, and I think we can work something out. Call me next week and we'll talk about putting you to work on the Love Field cases."

I was delighted to get the chance to work on the Love Field DC–6 cases, but meeting Billy Hyman face to face had shaken me up. He was a man whose status I hoped to attain some day in the distant future. He was called in on the big aviation cases, but his practice seemed to have turned him into a madman. He had a severe facial twitch that caused him to grimace every few minutes, and as he mentioned to me during his babbling conversation, he also had a spastic colon. Moreover, his relationship with everyone who came into contact with him—whether on his side or on the opposition—was outright combat. I began to wonder whether I wanted to climb the ladder toward those big cases if this was the price one had to pay.

After recovering from the shock of our initial meeting, I reminded myself how important it was to work with Billy. Up to that time, I had been working on aviation cases for smaller plaintiff's law firms that did not have the time or the staff to direct me. It had been left up to me to figure out a theory of liability and a method of proving it through discovery and organization of trial evidence. I had been

learning how to do this by trial and error, since there were no books
on the subject and very few enlightening articles or lectures. But when
I worked with Billy, he did not leave me alone. We had long discussions
on every proposed theory of liability. He insisted on questioning every
witness himself, both during depositions and during trial, and he ordered me to write out a list of questions to be asked of each witness,
each question backed up by a reference to a document or some other
source, so that the witness could be confronted if he did not give the
kind of answer we wanted.

Billy Hyman believed in the conspiracy theory of history. He automatically assumed that there was an evil plot behind every move that
anyone made, and he expected every witness to lie in answer to every
question. Through him, I got a liberal education in the roughhouse
school of litigation, one that helped me to cope with complicated aviation cases and would have been useful even if I had been forced to earn
my living on either side in the railway negligence cases of the nineteenth
century.

Soon after my first meeting with Billy, I delivered to him the depositions I had taken from American Airlines personnel in the other Love
Field cases that I had worked on. I also made up a summary of the liability case, citing the pages of these depositions and the exhibits that
supported my theories. The lawyers for American Airlines were willing
to let these depositions be used in Billy Hyman's cases, since I could
readily duplicate them by simply asking the same witnesses the same
questions. I suggested this to Billy as a way of saving money, and I was
very proud of my handiwork, thinking that I had touched on all the important liability points.

After Billy had read the depositions and my liability summary, he
called me to his office for a meeting. He announced that the depositions
were entirely inadequate for his purposes; that he was going to question
each witness himself, and possibly some other witnesses that I had not
deposed; and that I was to get to work immediately on a comprehensive
outline of proposed questions for the new depositions. This was a blow
to my ego, but I wrote it off to Billy's eccentricity and plunged into outlining new depositions. Then I found that there were a lot of points that
had not been covered clearly or completely, and that a lot of questions
had been left open. Under Billy's relentless prodding I went over the
same material repeatedly, and finally we produced a history of the Love
Field DC-6 crash that was about twice as detailed as the CAB investigation and my previous depositions combined. We deposed the witnesses
again, in Texas and in New York, with Billy doing most of the questioning. Some days he would let me ask a few preliminary questions, but
he would soon take over and cover the same ground again in his own
words.

Only after the entire case was redone in this way would Billy discuss settlement. He had the largest group of Love Field cases, and he settled all of them at good figures just before they were scheduled for trial. He believed that early settlement negotiations were a waste of time, since the defendant's lawyers would not offer adequate amounts until they were under the gun of a trial date with a well prepared adversary.

At the same time as the Love Field cases, I worked with Billy on cases arising out of the Air France Lockheed Constellation crash in the Azores Islands in October 1949, killing all aboard. Among the unfortunate passengers was the popular Frenchman Marcel Cerdan, who was then middleweight boxing champion of the world, leader of a class that included Tony Zale, Rocky Graziano, Jack La Motta, and Sugar Ray Robinson. In this case we faced some staggering hurdles. The only investigations of the accident were conducted by the governments of Portugal (since the Azores were its possessions) and France (the owner of Air France). Unlike our CAB accident investigations, these had not been public hearings, and there were no documents or statements of witnesses available to the public. The French government promised to issue a report, but at the time that we were working on the case, they had released nothing to the public, and there seemed to be no way of forcing them to give out any information until it was too late to be of use to us.

On top of that, the accident involved international transportation, so the claims of passengers were covered by the Warsaw Convention, the international treaty which limited damages to $8,291, regardless of the actual damage incurred. In order to recover actual damages, we would have to prove that the accident was caused by the airline's *wilful misconduct,* a burden much greater than proving ordinary negligence. Indeed, in the 1940s, the New York courts construed wilful misconduct as something akin to criminal intent.

The French cases were settled in France for $8,291 or less. We represented the families of the American passengers, who had received a letter from Air France shortly after the accident advising them that the Warsaw Convention limited their claims to $8,291, but that Air France would deduct the cost of sending the bodies back to the United States, so that their compensation would be reduced to about $7,000 per family. That letter enraged Billy Hyman and gave him the momentum he needed to function properly in this case. Ordinarily, most passengers' families accepted the Warsaw Convention limitations in those days and settled for $8,291 (or less) without attempting to prove wilful misconduct. But Billy convinced these American families that he could do the job, and they authorized him to reject the settlement offers and try to break through the Warsaw limitations.

This time some of Billy Hyman's anger rubbed off on me. I couldn't believe that the officials of Air France could be so insensitive, but this was my first experience with the European attitude toward accident compensation. I was charged up by Billy Hyman's fury, and I was also enervated by the great challenges of the case. With the French government sitting on all the evidence in protection of Air France, we didn't have a shred of proof in our file that would support a claim of ordinary negligence. How could we possibly undertake to go beyond negligence and prove wilful misconduct?

It was the first time I had undertaken an aviation case without benefit of a government accident investigation file as a starting point. While we had no access to any information unearthed by either the French or Portuguese governments, we knew that Air France had full access and had participated in all the government investigations. Here the great power of modern discovery came into play. We couldn't force the French or Portuguese governments to release any information, nor could the U.S. State Department or the congressional representatives of the bereaved families. But once the families filed suit, they were entitled as litigants to discover and copy all the relevant information that our adversaries had in their files. If Air France disobeyed a court order to produce this information, the judge could enter judgment for the plaintiffs for the full amount of their damages.

I decided to make the federal discovery rules take the place of a public accident investigation. I would try to cover all the subjects that our Civil Aeronautics Board would have included if this had been an investigation of a domestic airline crash. I spent weeks constructing a detailed outline of information that we would need about every aspect of the crash: the airplane itself and all of its systems and history; the crew and its qualifications and training; the flight plan and the route from Paris to the Azores; the weather conditions; the navigation and traffic control facilities enroute and in the Azores; the radio messages and communications relating to the flight; the statements of all witnesses from Paris to the Azores who had anything to do with this flight or who observed or heard any parts of it; the wreckage of the aircraft, including all photographs and studies made of it; the investigation of the accident by the French and Portuguese governments; and so on. I then turned this outline into a series of questions within the framework of Federal Rule 33, which allows parties to propound written interrogatories to each other. I wound up with 1,522 questions, many of which also required production of documents. For example:

Interrogatory 110

(a) Does the defendant have any documents, memoranda, or writings now in its possession or control relating to radio and navigation facilities, or their functioning, or their use by aircraft in the Azores on October 28, 1949 [date of the accident]?

(b) Did the defendant have any such documents in its possession or control on October 28, 1949?

(c) If the answer to (a) or (b) is yes, annex copies thereof.

Normally, production of documents must be sought by a motion under Rule 34 specifying the documents and showing good cause for their production. But I attempted to combine Rules 33 and 34 in the interrogatories, hoping that the judge would go along with this as an economy measure which would help both sides to organize the liability phase of the case. As expected, the defense attorneys made a motion under Rule 33 objecting to the interrogatories. They asked that the entire set of interrogatories be stricken out because they were unduly burdensome and were meant to harass Air France. They also objected separately to each of the 1,522 interrogatories for one reason or another, claiming that the questions were irrelevant or vexatious, or would require compilation of voluminous data.

Air France's objections to the interrogatories came on for hearing before Judge Walter Bruchhausen in the U.S. District Court for the Eastern District of New York, sitting in Brooklyn. The late Judge Bruchhausen was not noted for liberality toward plaintiffs in accident cases, and I was fearful that my privately concocted substitute for the CAB investigation might be thrown out the window into the streets of Brooklyn. This would have been particularly distressing because, not having a secretary and being unable to get any paperwork done in the bedlam of Billy Hyman's office, I had spent an entire weekend typing up the 1,522 interrogatories myself. However, the judge was struck by the plight of the plaintiffs who had no access to liability information, which was all under the control of Air France, due to its relationship with the French government. The judge issued a ruling that said in part:

> As a general practice, the production of documents should be separately sought under the proper rule and not by way of interrogatories. However, in a case such as this, where the number of interrogatories is necessarily voluminous, this Court will utilize the cumulative effect of the rules, and good cause having been shown, will grant full relief. . . . This Court is convinced, however, that no harassment is involved in these interrogatories.

Judge Bruchhausen then proceeded to sustain objections to nine of the interrogatories, but he overruled the objections to all of the others, so that we defeated Air France by a score of 1,513 to 9.

Judge Bruchhausen ordered Air France to answer the remaining

1,513 interrogatories under oath within 90 days and to annex copies of all the documents that we requested. This was a severe blow to the airline. Interrogatories addressed to a corporation that is a party to litigation can be very effective. They search the knowledge and records of the entire corporation and its employees, not just those of a chosen spokesman or witness. If they are carefully framed with follow-up questions that anticipate either positive or negative answers, they can produce a lot of useful information. Air France's New York attorney told me that there was no comparable procedure in France, and that he was having great difficulty in getting his clients to understand and comply with Judge Bruchhausen's order. Finally I had to prepare a motion to strike out the answer of Air France (which would have resulted in the court imposing liability for willful misconduct upon them). At this point they came forward with the answers to the interrogatories and the documents. Their answers and the documents ran into thousands of pages. We had succeeded in duplicating (if not exceeding) the scope of a CAB aircraft accident investigation, using the American rules of discovery to force a foreign, government-controlled airline to produce its entire accident file and to submit it to us under oath.

Ordinarily it is not feasible to prepare an entire case through interrogatories, because the answers are drafted by attorneys who take care to avoid damaging admissions. The most one can usually hope for is the names of witnesses and lists of documents that may lead to useful deposition testimony. But in this case, we had to get more mileage out of the interrogatories, for we had neither the time nor the power to examine the foreign witnesses in the way that a government investigating agency could. I therefore tried to tie all the questions to documents, so that, in addition to the lawyers' answers, we would get the written records of what the key witnesses had actually said or done. It took us the better part of a year to make Air France produce all the documents called for in the interrogatories, but when we had them translated and analyzed them, we found that we had the makings of a liability case. Even so, there were still quite a few gaps in our liability proof, and to close them we needed to take some depositions.

We decided there were four key Air France officials who had the knowledge that would help us to prove our case. All four were stationed in France. So we served on the attorneys for Air France a notice of deposing those four witnesses in New York, and we also served Air France with a subpoena for documents to be produced at the depositions. As expected, the attorneys for Air France made a motion to vacate our notice of taking depositions and to quash the subpoena for the documents. These motions came on before Judge Clarence Galston (not before Judge Bruchhausen, because it was not yet customary in New York federal courts to assign cases to a single judge before trial.) Billy Hyman and his chief assistant, Harold Hayman, argued the motion before Judge Glaston and won an important victory. The judge ordered Air France to produce the four officials and have their depositions taken in New York. He found that "in view of the fact that defendant is an airline and can carry its employees at no charge, this request is not unreasonable."

Judge Galston also upheld our subpoena. The first item of the subpoena was very important. It called for Air France to produce all of their "regulations and rules in regard to drinking by air crew members." Billy Hyman had been at work again, probing for the secret behind this accident. Without telling me, he had hired investigators in Paris who reported to him that the famous French singer, Edith Piaf, had been at the airport to see off her friend Marcel Cerdan and had thrown a bon voyage champagne party which had included some members of the flight crew. Hyman believed that he would be able to produce witnesses who saw the pilots drinking champagne shortly before takeoff from Paris, in violation of flight safety regulations. The champagne might help to explain why the Air France crew crashed while attempting to land at San Miguel, an island 56 miles north of Santa Maria, the intended destination. Of the two islands, only Santa Maria had an airport. All of the evidence indicated that the crew thought that they had arrived at Santa Maria. After receiving landing clearance from the Santa Maria tower, they reported that they had the field in sight and were descending for a landing. Apparently they crashed into the mountains of San Miguel when they thought that they were nearing their final approach to Santa Maria airport, 56 miles away.

Shortly after Judge Galston had upheld the subpoena and ordered the Air France officials to come to the United States to be deposed, the defense capitulated and the American passenger cases were settled for amounts substantially in excess of the $8,291 ceiling of the Warsaw Convention. To my knowledge, these were the first cases involving a foreign air carrier to be settled above the Warsaw limits. Major credit must go to the old-fashioned tactics of Billy Hyman, who never stopped searching for embarrassing items like champagne bottles, no matter what kind of case he was dealing with.

Even in the early 1950s, there were few plaintiff's lawyers who could have afforded to take on this kind of a suit. The whole liability case had to be discovered from scratch. The thousands of pages of documents that Air France produced in answer to our interrogatories were mostly in French and had to be translated at our expense. It was a case whose preparation required an investment of tens of thousands of dollars without any certainty of return beyond the few thousand dollars in fees payable under the Warsaw Convention limitation of $8,291. The chances of breaking through the Convention by proving wilful misconduct were slim, and there were abundant opportunities for the airline to wear down the plaintiffs by attrition. But Billy Hyman (whose major assets were his basic distrust of everyone and his insatiable appetite for infighting) was equal to the challenge, and I enjoyed being along for the ride.

I learned a lot from working with Billy. I also learned to like this feisty, cantankerous little man who always questioned everything I said or did. From him I learned to take nothing for granted in litigation, but fortunately I never adopted Billy's cynical attitude toward the whole human race. In fact, I'm not quite sure that he really felt that way; he could be very considerate, even downright charming, as long as it did not interfere with the ferocious facade he felt it necessary to maintain in litigation. He was very kind to me when we were not working on a case, but I never did get a decent meal out of our relationship. He would always insist upon eating at the Fulton Street Cafeteria, and I usually wound up paying my own check. Maybe he thought that was good training for me.

One of the last major cases I worked on with Billy was the 1957 Northeast Airlines Rikers Island crash. Northeast Airlines had just been awarded a new route from New York to Miami. In their rush to cash in on the winter tourist business in Florida, they had leased a Douglas DC-6A cargo aircraft from the Flying Tiger line and had hastily converted it to passenger service. Because they did not have adequate facilities at La Guardia Field, they had to remove the snow from the airplane in a nose hangar (which would accommodate the nose of the airplane but not its tail). Northeast flight 823 departed from La Guardia Airport on February 1, 1957, a snowy day, at 6:01 P.M. Less than a minute later, it crash-landed one mile north of La Guardia Field on Rikers Island, site of a New York City prison. With the help of prisoners and guards, 81 of the 101 persons aboard survived the crash, although some were badly burned. Because of their heroic rescue efforts, 57 inmates of Rikers Island Penitentiary were released immediately or had their sentences reduced, and 44 prison employees received special commendation from New York Mayor Robert F. Wagner.

I was retained to handle the liability phase of the case on behalf of most of the passengers whose lawyers filed suit in New York. This was one of my easier jobs because the liability of Northeast Airlines was quite clear. It was obvious that they were not equipped or trained for this operation, and that they had sent their pilot off to an almost certain crash. The plane's tail section, which had remained out in the cold air because Northeast did not have a suitable hangar available, had not been properly cleared of snow and ice. There was abundant evidence that Northeast should not have commenced New York-to-Florida flights until the spring or summer of 1957.

Most of the other cases were settled within a year or so of the accident. But Billy Hyman would not settle any of his until he had run down every possible conspiracy. He insisted that I go ahead with detailed discovery. By this time he was letting me question witnesses. However, he always insisted upon being present so that he could chew me out in the presence of our opponents for asking stupid questions and leaving out the most important points. The captain had survived the crash, and when I questioned him, Billy was right there with me, although he was then past 65 and getting pretty deaf. Our opponent was John Martin, one of New York's leading defense lawyers, who was the partner in charge of aviation cases at Bigham Englar Jones & Houston. Billy issued instructions to me in a stage whisper that was loud enough to be heard by John Martin and anyone else within fifty feet. I had gotten all of the useful information that could be obtained from the captain, when Billy broke in. "You didn't ask him anything about his record in high school!" Wearily I asked the captain about his high school career, and found that it had been uneventful. But Billy was not satisfied. He was not going to close out his claims and take good settlements in a clear liability case, as the other plaintiff's lawyers had done. He had to find something extra, something more sinister than the obvious negligence in snow removal.

Billy's nose for dirty politics told him that there was something strange about the way in which Northeast Airlines had been awarded the route to Miami. Prior to 1957 it had been a small, folksy airline, flying little old DC-3s between Boston and other points in New England. The Civil Aeronautics Board hearing examiner who considered applications for a new route to compete with Eastern and National had selected Delta Airlines as the third carrier. But the CAB overruled its examiner and awarded the route to Northeast on August 10, 1956, by a vote of 3 to 2. That was the same year in which it was reported that Howard Hughes had loaned $225,000 to Donald Nixon, brother of Richard M. Nixon, then the Vice-President. The majority stockholder of Northeast Airlines was Atlas Corporation, and Howard Hughes was one of the principal stockholders of Atlas Corporation. To Billy Hyman, there was enough of a connection between Hughes and Nixon to make the route award smell bad. He also suspected that Sherman Adams, former governor of New Hampshire and then assistant to President Eisenhower, had something to do with pressuring the CAB to reverse its examiner and pick Northeast instead of the much better qualified Delta Airlines for the Miami route. So Billy started digging into the political background of the route award through his connections in Washington. About the time that he started making plans to depose witnesses who had been involved in the route award, the offers in his cases were increased enough to compel settlement. Content with the conclusion that his delving into the route award had produced higher settlements for his clients, he happily closed his files on the Rikers Island disaster. And I was relieved that I would not have to spend the next few years trying to prove that the Miami route award had been the result of behind-the-scenes payoffs at the highest levels of American government.

Billy's fighting spirit was not confined to lawsuits. In the early post-war years, the nation's airlines used their required tariff filings to gain some extra leverage in accident cases. In one of the complicated tariff documents that they filed with the Civil Aeronautics Board, they had tucked away a provision that anyone claiming damages because of injury or death incurred in the course of an airline flight would have to send the airline a written notice of claim within 60 days after the accident. This notice was patterned after similar requirements in many states when claiming for injuries due to some action or inaction by state or local government. It provides the opportunity to investigate an accident while the facts are still fresh in situations where, without notice, the defendant might not be aware of a potential claim. But that is hardly the case with airline crashes. The airlines are the first to know of an accident and are fully involved in the ensuing investigation. It might have been legitimate in cases where passengers were claiming injuries from in-flight turbulence, where it would enable the airline to interview crew members and other witnesses before the trail became too cold. But it was used time and again by the airline insurers in cases arising out of major crashes. Even in cases of serious injury or death, where the claimants would still be involved in the tragic aftermath of the accident 60 days later, the airlines would plead that lawsuits should be dismissed because no written notice of claim had been sent to the airline within 60 days. You can imagine how this went over when they tried it on Billy Hyman.

Without a moment's delay, Billy launched a campaign to expose the presumed corruption in the CAB that allowed such a tariff to be filed. He started administrative proceedings before the CAB to prohibit airlines from filing this kind of information in the tariff, on the grounds that it was not called for by the tariff, that it was simply a self-serving, defensive device which was deceptive and unfair to the traveling public. In 1952, the CAB held a public hearing in New York at which Billy Hyman was a principal witness. He asked me to help him prepare his testimony, but as usual I barely got a word in, since he was primed to argue the case himself. Following this New York hearing, the CAB decided in 1953 that the notice-of-claim provision was inappropriate for tariffs, and it was prohibited. While I never knew of a case in which the courts had dismissed an injury or death suit for failure to give the notice of claim, the presence of that defense was a source of uneasiness for many plaintiff's lawyers. I have no doubt that many cases were settled for lesser amounts than they would have been ordinarily because the bereaved family had not notified the airline of their claim within 60 days.

Thanks largely to Billy Hyman, the present generation of bereaved claimants has been spared this burden.

Billy Hyman devoted most of his life to the law. He had no children. He and his wife lived in a midtown Manhattan apartment, and his wife was the business manager of his office. He shared the attitude of many New York lawyers who were born in the nineteenth century that litigation was a deadly game, always to be played to the hilt, and that nothing was ever to be taken at face value. While he was old-fashioned in some ways, he had great imagination and was often ahead of his time. He became interested in the newly emerging law of outer space, and wrote a book that was published in 1966 under the title, *The Magna Carta of Space*. (Billy was not given to understatement.) In 1966, he died at the age of 72. Every now and then I get the feeling that he is up in the sky looking over my shoulder, telling me not to interview witnesses by telephone, and exhorting me to keep searching for the intrigue that must be behind every case.

Gentleman Harry Gair

Harry Gair was born in 1894, just one year after Billy Hyman. Their law careers paralleled each other, but it would have been difficult to find two men who were less alike in outlook and temperament.

Harry Gair came up the hard way. He never attended high school; instead, he worked in piece-goods textile factories until he landed a job reading to a blind lawyer, Benjamin Berinstein. He absorbed most of what he was reading and decided to make the law his career, but had no way of getting a formal education, so he went to work for an insurance company as an investigator. He kept on reading law, and in a few years this unusual investigator was actually writing briefs for Reed Jenkins Dimock & Finnegan, the law firm that defended his insurance employer. Soon he was going to court with the lawyers and helping them to win cases. Finally in 1919, at the age of 25, Harry had read enough law on his own to pass the bar exam, having never spent a day in any institution of learning higher than grammar school. In 1923, after working for an older lawyer, he opened his first office in the Bush Terminal Building at 130 West 42nd Street and started one of New York's legendary law practices.

Harry was about five foot six, of medium build, and there was nothing remarkable about him physically. He was a quiet, unassuming man, rather plain looking except for neatly parted long black hair and a suntan that he managed to maintain throughout the year. His voice was raspy, with a nasal tone, and he seldom rose to great eloquence in delivery. It was the content of what he said, both in and out of the court-room, that revealed one of the greatest legal minds in American history. Harry was totally dedicated to law practice, just as Billy Hyman was. But he did not see it as a rough-and-tumble barroom brawl. To him it was the ultimate intellectual challenge—a great game on the order of Sherlock Holmes's detective practice.

For me, 1951 was a watershed year. That's when I started working with Billy Hyman, and as a bonus I also worked on my first case for Harry Gair. He had been called in to try four personal injury cases aris-ing out of the crash at Michigan City, Indiana, of an American Airlines Douglas DC-3 on December 28, 1946. Another lawyer had handled those cases while they were pending in the federal court in Manhattan for more than four years, but nothing had been done to prepare them for trial.

By 1951, at the age of 57, Harry Gair was in his prime and was considered the leading plaintiff's tort lawyer in New York—if not in the entire nation. I met him in his modest office at 84 William Street, an old building in the insurance district near the New York court houses. His firm was known as Gair & Gair, the other Gair being his wife, Harriet. At that time Gair & Gair had eight lawyers, one of the largest staffs among plaintiff's firms in New York. His leading associate was Ben Siff, a great appellate lawyer whose knowledge of New York negligence law has probably never been matched. One of the sparkplugs of this firm was Herman Brand, a bundle of energy and legal know-how, who was Gair's best right-hand man in court. It was with the team of Harry Gair, Ben Siff, and Herman Brand that I started to work on the Michi-gan City cases.

Until one had the opportunity to work on a case with Gair, it was hard to explain his great success. Then it became apparent that he had uncanny powers of total concentration on the facts and the law involved in the case at hand. It is difficult to describe this unusual talent in a lawyer. Justice Aron Steuer sought to explain it in writing about his father, the great trial lawyer Max Steuer. After listing some qualities that his father shared with quite a few other lawyers—such as a good memory and a capacity for hard work—Aron Steuer put his finger on the exceptional one:

> Beyond all this there was an especial attribute. This fac-ulty is very simple to state, though it is not so easy to convey the complete idea. It is the ability at all times, but especially during the trial, to keep the entire case within mental range.

Almost every lawyer has had the experience of formulating some of his best arguments after it was too late to present them, but this never happened to Max Steuer or Harry Gair. I often wonder what would have happened if Harry had been around to try the Triangle Shirtwaist Factory damage claims against Steuer. Having worked with Harry, I must admit some prejudice; but I cannot imagine any way in which he could have lost that case—even in 1914. Probably Steuer would have been wise enough to recommend that his clients settle before trial for adequate compensation.

Together with Harry's total concentration came a great power of analysis. Often I would come to his office to discuss a problem encountered in the liability phase of a complicated aviation case. I would be stumbling over a piece of evidence that did not seem to fit into our trial plan. Harry would drop his small frame into his huge black leather chair, and in a minute or two, instead of struggling to focus a pocket flashlight on the problem, it would be like standing in Yankee Stadium at night while somebody turned all the floodlights on. He illuminated all sides of the problem, and then it was apparent that there was no real obstacle, or that there was an easy way around it.

Some lawyers called him a great mechanic: a man who knew all of the parts of the litigation system and was able to make them all work at once. I don't think this description does him justice, although it is perfectly accurate. I think he was more like a great architect. He would plan every phase of the case in advance. You could not possibly give him too much material to read. If there was a textbook or an article or a speech or a yellowed newspaper clipping about the subject at hand, he wanted to read it himself. He didn't merely want to hear about it or see a summary of it. He wanted to read it and reflect on it and decide if he could fit it into his trial plan.

His effect on juries seemed remarkable to outsiders. But watching the faces of the jurors as this undemonstrative little man spoke to them in his raspy voice, I could tell what they were thinking. He was flooding their minds with illumination. He was taking complicated problems, such as the workings of aircraft engines, cockpit instruments, electronic beams, and making them seem simple. Harry helped jurors to discover the truth for themselves, instead of trying to sell it to them or to stuff it down their throats. Leading them on an exploration of the facts, he let them share the excitement of discovery. Thus he managed to make the strongest possible case for his clients without ever taking a chance of having the jurors doubt anything that he said.

Harry was also a great organizer. When he went into the courtroom he had a separate accordion file for each witness, neatly broken down into compartments for each subject to be covered. He prepared back-up briefs in advance to support the admissibility of all the important evidence that might be objected to. These briefs he would hand up to the judge as he made his responses to the objections. No lawyer could ever have been more thoroughly prepared for trial than Harry Gair.

During every aviation trial, he ordered daily copy from the court reporters. This was expensive, since it required the reporters to work in relays. Every half hour one reporter would leave the courtroom and dictate the preceding half hour's testimony so that it could be typed immediately. Each night, that day's testimony would be delivered to Harry's apartment, where he would devour it, often with Ben Siff and me reading along. He would store the important testimony in his mind and use it to build the case day by day. By the end of the trial, he had circled all the key questions and answers in the transcript. When he read those passages to the jurors in his summation, it was clear to them that he was arguing the case *on the evidence.*

He was a master of cross-examination, but he rarely attacked a witness. Rather, he would draw the witness into an amiable discussion aimed at taking the sting out of unfavorable testimony. Very often he got opposing witnesses to go along with his version of a case, especially physicians, who soon learned that Gair's encyclopedic knowledge of medical literature would make them look foolish if they adhered to statements that were harmful to his clients.

The Michigan City cases were a challenge for both of us. One case arising out of the same accident had previously been tried by Jay Leo Rothschild, another outstanding New York trial lawyer. It had resulted in a compromise verdict—for less money than the defense lawyers had been willing to pay in settlement—because of jurors' doubts about liability. This had emboldened the airline's insurers to hold back on any substantial settlement offers in our cases, especially during the years when nothing had been done on the cases. We were taking over a case that was nearly five years old, and the defendant had control of practically all the witnesses and evidence. I spent a few hours discussing with Harry Gair the ideas that I had about proving liability in the case. He completely reversed some of my theories and vastly improved others that were left in our plan. Then he left me on my own to take the depositions and get the documents produced that we would need for trial. This I did in a few months time, consulting with him and with Ben Siff from time to time about questions that arose during the preparation process.

Harry represented four passengers injured in the Michigan City crash. He could have tried all four cases together by moving to consolidate them. He chose to try them separately, feeling that it might cheapen the individual verdicts if he asked one jury to fix damages for four plaintiffs. Also, it was a difficult liability case, and even the Civil Aeronautics Board had not come up with a complete explanation of the crash. He wanted to learn all that he could about the strengths and weaknesses of the case before trying the two most serious injury claims. Therefore he started off with one of the passengers who had made a good recovery from his injuries. He tried that one on liability and damages, and won it. Then a few months later he went on to try the cases of a husband and wife who were more seriously injured. He won that, even though he had to try liability all over again, in addition to damages. Finally the fourth case was settled just before it was scheduled for trial. We had been ready with our briefcases full of exhibits and transcripts of the prior trials, and the defense lawyers knew that Harry would try the case five or six times if he felt that he would get more money for his clients that way, regardless of what it cost him in effort or expenses.

If you read Harry Gair's summations in the Michigan City trials, you would not find them remarkable for rhetoric or force. That was exactly the effect he wanted. He was like Joe DiMaggio playing center field for the New York Yankees. DiMaggio was one of the greatest outfielders of all time, yet it is difficult to remember any sensational catches he made. But he was always right where the ball was, waiting for it to fall into his glove. And so it was with Harry Gair: the thing you remembered about him was that he won almost every time. And he was always the soft-spoken gentleman who left his opponents with the feeling that they had done their best with a hopeless case.

From the time of the Michigan City trials until his death in 1975 at the age of 81, I had the privilege of working with Harry Gair on many aviation cases. Among the most memorable were those arising out of the American Airlines Convair crash and the National Airlines DC–6 crash, both of which occurred in 1952 near Newark Airport, resulting in the airport being closed down for extensive modifications; the 1959 crash of an American Airlines Lockheed Electra at La Guardia Field; and the United Airlines-TWA mid-air collision over Staten Island, N. Y. in 1960. He really didn't need me, but it was typical of him that he would never pass up a chance to strengthen his case or to increase his chances of winning. He could master any kind of lawsuit, and he thrived on the challenge of complicated cases involving the collapse of buildings at the New York World's Fair of 1939; malfunctions of complicated scientific instruments and machinery; and all types of medical-legal problems. But he often told me that he enjoyed the aviation cases more than any others.

One of the most valuable things I learned from Harry was when and how to settle a case. He was not only a peerless trial lawyer, he also was a great settler. The two do not necessarily go hand in hand, although the strongest trial lawyer will usually generate the highest settlement offers—provided the defense lawyers are convinced that he is prepared to do his usual top-flight job. There are some excellent trial lawyers who are not always good at settlement because their egos sometimes get in the way of their client's best interests. A trial lawyer with a busy practice can afford to take a chance at hitting the jackpot: if he loses one case he can make up for it in his next trial. But the client for whom he has lost the case will never get a second chance. Harry always kept that in mind, despite his complete mastery of each case. He never let overconfidence or ego get in the way of a good settlement. Many of his best settlements came after he had made his opening statement and had impressed the judge, the jury, and the defense lawyers with the strength of his case and the jury appeal of his clients. He probably could have operated with a smaller staff and made more profit if he had settled more cases before going into the courtroom, but that was not Harry Gair's style.

Considering Gair's many courtroom victories during six decades of great progress for plaintiffs, it may seem surprising that his cases rarely broke new ground in the law, even though he had the ultimate appellate advocate in Ben Siff. But he and Ben were able to make nearly all of their cases appear to fall within the boundaries of existing law, no matter how novel the fact situation might be. Sometimes I would suggest untested theories to Harry, who would usually find a way to accomplish the same result without risking innovation. He pictured himself at the trial as swinging from limb to limb like a monkey, and he would want to know where that next limb was before he let go of the first one.

Judges loved to try Harry's cases. They knew he would be thoroughly prepared, and that any time he did anything unusual, he would present them with supporting citations. They were confident that when they accepted his and Ben Siff's legal arguments, they would not look bad in the appellate courts. Even defense lawyers enjoyed trying cases against him, although they knew that they were probably going to get their ears pinned back. But Harry never tried to show them up. His object was to make them look good in settling the case at a high figure. After a strong opening statement and a display of his leading witnesses, he would often convince the defense lawyers (who would then convince their clients) that they were getting a bargain by settling with Harry at what might otherwise seem to be a very high figure.

In his later years Harry took on a young protegé, Robert Conason, whom he groomed as his successor. Harry's thorough preparation extended even to his own departure, for when he died in 1975, Bob Conason was already established as an outstanding trial lawyer in his own right and in the gentlemanly style of Harry Gair. The firm carries on as Gair Gair & Conason, with Harry's widow, Harriet, as the senior partner. Harriet serves as a Town Justice in Putnam Valley, New York, one day a week and devotes the rest of her time to the law firm.

As the old guard passed, Ben Siff left the firm to establish his own practice in the Woolworth Building as an appellate consultant to the New York bar. He briefed and argued dozens of important appeals with great success until his death in 1975. His practice is now carried on by his partner, Tom Newman. Herman Brand also left the Gair firm in Harry's later years. He spent some happy years with our firm and then left to establish his own successful practice in Manhattan.

Among the other illustrious alumni of the Gair firm is Charles Kramer, who set out on his own after a short apprenticeship with Harry, and became New York's leading medical malpractice specialist. He continues to hold that lofty position in his fifth decade of trial practice.

To Billy Hyman, the battle was everything. To Harry Gair, it was the result that counted, although he enjoyed the battle as much as anyone did. Harry reached a pinnacle of prestige that had never been attained by a tort lawyer. In climbing to his lofty position, he carried the rest of us up several notches in public acceptance and self-esteem. Often I think back to the excitement that this quiet man stirred in all who worked with him, in his office during the days of preparation; in the courtroom during the trial; in Gasner's restaurant near the Manhattan court houses, where he could hardly get through a meal as lawyers and judges buzzed around him; in his apartment at night as he fashioned the day's testimony into weapons for tomorrow. That excitement kept me from sleeping for hours after I went home, as I imagined how he would use those weapons in the morning. It was exciting just to be around him for one simple reason: he was the greatest.

Billy Hyman and Harry Gair started practicing in the era of the Early American tort lawyer and lifted themselves up by force of will to become leading entrepreneur-lawyers. In the next two chapters you will meet two lawyers whose main practice started after World War II, who built on the foundation that the Hymans and the Gairs had provided.

Chapter 3

DISASTER AT THE GRAND CANYON

O n June 30, 1956, two airliners departed from Los Angeles International Airport within a few minutes of each other on cross-country flights. TWA Flight 2, a Lockheed 1049A Constellation, took off from Los Angeles at 9:01 A.M., bound for Kansas City, Missouri. United Air Lines Flight 718, a Douglas DC-7, took off from Los Angeles at 9:04 A.M., scheduled to fly to Chicago. According to their flight plans, both planes were scheduled to fly through the area of the Painted Desert and the Grand Canyon in Arizona, an area that was not then on the civil airways and was therefore considered "uncontrolled airspace." This meant that both airlines would have to rely on the eyes of their pilots for collision avoidance, because air traffic controllers of the Civil Aeronautics Administration (CAA) did not provide traffic separation off the airways. Both flights were governed by the Visual Flight Rules (VFR), which have "see and be seen" as their basic principle. Both airlines could have chosen routes which would have kept them on airways all the way across the continent, and thereby each could have flown in a separate block of airspace provided by the CAA. But the transcontinental airlines often chose the route over the Grand Canyon because it was shorter and more scenic than the airways route.

Even though they were operating under VFR in the Grand Canyon area, the planes were required to give periodic position reports to the CAA Air Route Traffic Control Centers (ARTC); they were scheduled to return to the airways later, so ARTC had to follow their general progress in order to anticipate the time of their return to the airways. After they left the area of the Los Angeles ARTC, the planes had to report their positions to the Salt Lake City ARTC. At 9:58 A.M. Pacific Standard Time, the United flight reported to Salt Lake ARTC that it would be over the Painted Desert (the next reporting position) at 10:31 A.M. at an altitude of 21,000 feet. One minute later, at 9:59 A.M., the TWA flight sent exactly the same report to Salt Lake City ARTC: they, too, would reach the Painted Desert at 10:31 A.M. at an altitude of 21,000 feet. Salt Lake City ARTC was in radio contact with both of the airplanes, but the flight crews could not hear each other's transmissions, and ARTC did not advise either plane that the other would get to the Painted Desert at the same time and altitude. At 10:31 A.M. and in clear weather the two airliners collided near the Painted Desert and fell into the Grand Canyon, killing a total of 128 persons in what was then the world's worst air disaster. The time was fixed by the chilling radio message received from the United flight exactly at 10:31 A.M.: "Salt Lake, United 718—ahhh—we're going in!"

I was first retained by the lawyer for the family of a New Hampshire businessman who had been killed in the accident. I filed suit for his family in the federal court in Manhattan, suing both TWA and United. This proved to be the first Grand Canyon suit filed, and it was soon followed by dozens of others. However, only two more cases were filed in New York, since most of the passengers had come from other cities, principally Los Angeles, Kansas City, and Chicago, and their families were scattered all over the country. In 1956 there was no method of centralizing this kind of litigation. Each family lawyer or negligence specialist would be inclined to file suit in his own local court, either state or federal, depending on where he thought he would get the best result. Therefore, the Grand Canyon suits were filed in a dozen different courts across the country.

The two airlines had no problem in coordinating their defense. They were insured by two major insurance groups which had leading New York admiralty-aviation firms as their general counsel: Haight Gardner Poor & Havens for United, and Bigham Englar Jones & Houston for TWA. These New York firms were defending the suit that I had filed in the New York federal court, and they were in a position to coordinate the entire defense effort with the law firms who were defending TWA and United in other cities. Thus the dispersion of the litigation did not hurt the defendants; in fact, it had always helped them, since it divided the plaintiffs and made it difficult for them to centralize their efforts and to gain strength from numbers.

There I was, with a single case in New York. How could I possibly take on the work and expense of proving liability? At first blush, it seemed that proving liability should be easy; you don't get two big airliners colliding in mid-air under VFR conditions without somebody being negligent. An Air Route Traffic controller whom we shall call Benson received identical position messages from the two airplanes. All he did was to post these messages on his flight progress strip board, without attempting to warn either airliner of the other's position report. Both airlines were blaming ARTC for allowing the planes to continue on a collision course without advising them of the traffic conflict. If this were an ordinary negligence case, we would sue all three defendants (the two airlines and the federal government) and let them fight it out among themselves. Usually plaintiffs are better off when there are two or more defendants accusing each other of fault—the jury may well decide to let all three of them share the damages. But one of our prospective defendants was the United States of America, which through its Civil Aeronautics Administration (later to be replaced by the Federal Aviation Agency) operated the Air Route Traffic Control Centers. That gave us a big problem.

Prior to 1946, it had not been possible to sue the government for negligence at all. The old maxim, "The king can do no wrong," insulated the United States from liability. Anyone injured by the negligence of a federal employee would receive nothing, unless Congress passed a special private bill awarding compensation. This applied even to routine accidents, such as a postal truck going through a red light and running down a pedestrian. As the federal government expanded, Congress was inundated with private compensation legislation. It was a messy situation in which politics governed the amount and timing of payment, if any. Recognizing that this judicial function should be removed from politics, Congress passed the Federal Tort Claims Act in 1946, giving its consent for the United States to be sued. But there were some conditions attached to that consent. All claims had to be brought in United States District Courts, and the cases were to be tried by federal judges without a jury. Also, the United States was not to be liable for failure to carry out a "discretionary function."

Thirty years of litigation since the Tort Claims Act was passed have failed to develop a complete definition of "discretionary function." The term means basically that where the government has to act in its governing capacity and make decisions to provide a finite amount of service to a very large number of people, it cannot be sued for its decision to help a certain person or class and not another. So suits cannot be brought against the government, for instance, for failing to provide social security benefits to people below the age of 65; or for the decision of an administrative agency which causes financial damages; or for a wrong decision of the President or Secretary of State to emphasize good relations with China rather than the Soviet Union. But where there is a nondiscretionary act which the decision-maker has a *duty* to perform, the government can be sued for this official's failure to do it properly. Thus, if the federal government had not undertaken the duty of giving traffic separation or traffic advice off the federal airways, the U.S.A.

could not be sued for failure to provide it to the two planes that collided over the Grand Canyon.

My experience as a pilot and my research into the history of air traffic control convinced me that since the Painted Desert and Grand Canyon areas were "off airways," there was no duty on the part of the Salt Lake City ARTC to advise either airliner of the report received from the other. However, the regulations governing ARTC duties in 1956 were a hodgepodge of aviation jargon and legalese. It was difficult even for lawyers to determine exactly what these duties were, and there was one regulation that seemed to support the airlines' position. It applied to "flight assistance service," which was to be given to airlines both on and off airways, and it said:

> In cases where air carrier aircraft are proceeding into an actual or potentially hazardous condition, the company should be advised. In cases where company personnel are not readily available or when delay would add to the hazard, the information should be transmitted to the pilot.

The CAA claimed that this referred only to hazardous *weather* conditions and not to traffic problems, but there was no regulation or publication that spelled out such a limitation.

Normally we would have sued the U.S.A. and let their experts fight that question out with the airlines' experts in front of the jury. But here we faced an insidious problem—a legal Catch 22. A jury would be impanelled to hear the claims against TWA and the United Airlines. At the same time, the judge would hear all the evidence against the United States. Since the Tort Claims Act required a nonjury trial of the claims against the government, the judge would decide its liability, but not until the jury had made its decision on the liability of the airlines. Thus, three of the parties to the case—the plaintiff and the two airline defendants—would be presenting evidence of negligence of the government, and the jury would hear all of it. Although the plaintiffs would also be presenting evidence of negligence of the airlines, the jurors might decide that the accident was really caused by the failure of the controller at Salt Lake City to warn the two airlines about the identical messages he had received from them. The judge might decide later that the controller had no duty to give such a warning, but in the meantime the jurors might be misled into thinking that the judge was probably going to hold the government liable, and so they might decide in favor of the airlines without realizing that plaintiffs would receive no compensation.

In 1956, most of the people on jury panels had done little or no flying (even as passengers) and were inclined to believe that it was risky. Airline lawyers could introduce enough confusing evidence to convince many jurors that the airlines were forced to rely on the government for air traffic separation and advice, and that they could not fly their aircraft anywhere without getting some kind of government clearance or traffic direction. I was therefore greatly concerned that by suing the U.S.A. we might be walking into a deadly trap. The airline lawyers perceived this immediately. In their answer to our complaint, they pleaded the affirmative defense that the accident was caused by the negligence of the CAA.

Faced with these legal problems and with the practical problem of how to do an effective job for a single client, I decided that I would try to get the plaintiffs' lawyers together. Each of us had a common interest in the liability phase of the case. On damages, Arizona's wrongful-death statute was automatically applicable in 1956, since Arizona was the place of the accident. That, however, raised a lot of problems, for there were only a handful of Arizona decisions construing this statute. The plaintiffs needed to make common cause. But how to contact the other plaintiffs' lawyers and convince them that we should try to organize a joint effort?

A unique bar association provided the solution. The National Association of Claimants' Compensation Attorneys (NACCA) had been founded in 1946 by a group of worker's compensation attorneys who saw the need for a specialists' national bar association. For the first few years its membership consisted mainly of worker's compensation specialists, but in the 1950s it expanded to take in all types of plaintiff's lawyers. In 1955 the president of NACCA, a courtly Beverly Hills trial lawyer named Ben Cohen—who was a dead ringer for film star Adolphe Menjou, except that Ben was better looking and a nattier dresser—appointed me chairman of NACCA's newly formed Aviation Law section, a position that I was to hold for the first ten years of its existence. That section helped to establish communications among plaintiff's lawyers throughout the country in aviation negligence cases, through educational seminars and the pooling of information about specific cases. Through the Aviation Law section of NACCA we assembled a group of Grand Canyon plaintiff's lawyers who knew each other and were eager to cooperate—leading tort lawyers such as Craig Spangenberg of Cleveland, Jim McArdle and Dennis Harrington of Pittsburgh, Jim Dooley of Chicago, Jim Markle of Detroit, Everett Hullverson and Orville Richardson of St. Louis, Bill de Parcq of Minneapolis, John McGeehan of Newark, Irving Green of Beverly Hills, and Melvin M. Belli of San Francisco, Hollywood, Rome, and points east and west.

After several organizational meetings, it was decided that my firm would investigate and prepare the liability phase for all cases in the group. Our contingent fee would be paid by each plaintiff's attorney out of his own contingent fee. In addition, each plaintiff's lawyer was to pay

$250 per case into a joint expense fund, so that we would have the money to do the extensive discovery job that was required. Although the group had its genesis in NACCA and consisted of NACCA members originally, we were soon joined by non-NACCA lawyers (including some large general practice firms in New York, Chicago, and Los Angeles) who saw the need for a joint effort. In the end the group included 68 cases, the majority of those that were litigated.

Preparing for Trial

Our first task was to prove that a collision had occurred. It is hard to believe, but the airline lawyers, determined to put us to the proof of every fact they were not forced to admit, denied that there had been a collision. There were no eye witnesses, and since the two aircraft had fallen into the Grand Canyon at wreckage sites about 8 miles apart, it was an expensive job to assemble evidence of collision. The CAB had issued a report concluding that there had been a collision, but a federal statute prohibited use of the CAB report in litigation.

Our first discovery thrust was a motion for production of the aircraft wreckage. Most of the wreckage was still at the bottom of Grand Canyon, but the government investigators had recovered portions of the left wing of the United airplane and the tail section of the TWA plane, which they brought out of the Canyon with the help of helicopters and a team of Swiss mountain climbers. These key pieces enabled the government investigators to determine the angle and other details of the collision. They had assembled these pieces of wreckage on the floor of a hangar at Washington National Airport, and had then taken photographs and made laboratory tests from which they concluded that the left wing of the United aircraft had hit the tail of the TWA aircraft from behind. After the government investigation was completed, the wreckage was turned over to the respective airlines that owned it. Our discovery motion was granted, and the airlines were ordered to produce the wreckage for our inspection at Washington National Airport.

The wreckage was produced on the appointed day. But instead of neatly tagged pieces that we could assemble on the hangar floor as the Civil Aeronautics Board had done, the airlines produced assorted jagged metal parts that gave no clue to their identity or position. Fortunately, we had the CAB committee report, which included photographs of all the recovered wreckage. From these we were able to puzzle out the reconstruction, but it was slow work. Two and a half days later, we had completed the reassembly on the hangar floor, and our expert, Sam

Tour, was ready to go to work. Sam was a metallurgist whom we had brought down from New York with his cameras and spectrographic analysis equipment. We hoped that he would be able to determine the fact and angle of collision from the paint of the United Airlines wingtip that had lodged on the TWA tail and from other markings on the wreckage, as the CAB had done. But at that point, before Sam could do anything, the airline attorneys announced that we had had enough time for discovery, and that they were shutting down the operation.

After the hangar door was shut in our faces, we went back to the federal court in Manhattan and sought out an order requiring the defendants to continue the discovery. We laid out all the facts for the judge, and he granted our motion. When we finally got Sam Tour back into the hangar, he took his photographs, made his spectrographic analysis, and was then in a position to testify to his conclusions as an expert. We took his deposition for all of the cases in our group, so that each plaintiff would be able to prove that there had been a collision.

The defense lawyers tried to discredit Sam on his deposition because he was not an aeronautical engineer. At that time, it was almost impossible to find qualified aeronautical engineers to testify against any branch of the aviation industry. But Sam was an experienced expert witness who was not about to be downgraded. When a defense lawyer asked him whether he had ever made an analysis of a mid-air collision before, his answer was:

> No, but a piece of metal is a piece of metal, whether it is on an airplane or on a stove.

With Sam Tour's deposition behind us, we turned to the defense contention that the collision was caused by Salt Lake City controller Benson when he failed to notify the two airlines of the identical position reports. I have changed Benson's name because newspaper stories in 1956 unfairly accused him of causing the deaths of 128 people by failing to perform his duties, a charge that was thrown in the faces of Benson's young children by their Salt Lake City schoolmates.

The first step in dealing with this defense was to confer with the CAA officials in Washington who were responsible for air traffic services. They assured me that all of the airlines knew very well that there was no traffic information given off the airways, and that the airlines had no basis for relying on any such warning. The airways, which were designed as federal highways in the sky, had many visual and aural navigation facilities, such as marker beacons and radio beams, that were designed to pinpoint the position of aircraft. Along the airways, traffic controllers could use these reliable position fixes to provide traffic separation and advice. But in the vast airspace off the airways, there was no means of determining position accurately enough for the requirements of traffic control. The CAA officials in Washington explained to me that in the early days of traffic control they had attempted to give some traffic information off the airways, but found that this did more harm than good. They had succeeded only in creating confusion, because neither they nor the pilots they attempted to warn could determine the relative positions of two aircraft in the wilderness of the unmarked airspace.

The two Grand Canyon airliners had selected off-airways routes, but they were converging on "Painted Desert," so there remained the question of why the CAA did not warn them of their simultaneous approach to what appeared to be a fixed navigation point. The answer was that "Painted Desert," as used in air navigation, was not a fixed point, but was actually the 321° radial of the Winslow omnidirectional radio range station, a "line of position" 175 miles long. Therefore, there was no way to determine whether these two aircraft would be passing within 175 miles of each other. Benson's training and instructions told him simply to record the two messages and do nothing about issuing any warnings, since the airlines knew that they had to keep their own traffic lookout off the airways.

However, the CAA Flight Assistance Service (FAS) manual seemed to indicate that even if the airlines were not expecting the routine traffic services they received on the airways, they had a right to expect warnings of any potentially hazardous conditions known to the CAA, whether on or off the airways, as part of an emergency Flight Assistance Service which the CAA had undertaken to furnish to all aircraft. And would not the convergence of two high speed airliners at the same time, altitude, and line of position be a "potentially hazardous condition" that Benson could have warned them of by a flick of his microphone button?

CAA officials and attorneys assured me that the potentially hazardous condition referred to in the FAS manual related only to weather hazards or information about airports and navigation equipment; that the phrase never was related to traffic hazards; and that the airlines understood this and never expected traffic information off airways through Flight Assistance Service or any other service of the CAA. It would have made my job much simpler if the CAA officials who wrote the FAS manual had spelled this out clearly, for the ambiguous phrase "potentially hazardous condition" was to become the central battleground of the Grand Canyon litigation in courts across the nation during the next four years.

I decided that we should start out by suing only the two airlines. I tended to believe the CAA officials who branded the potentially-hazardous-condition defense as a concoction of the airlines, but there was no need to commit the plaintiffs at that point. We would have two years from June 30, 1956 (date of the accident), for filing suit against the U.S.A. In that time we could probe the airlines' defenses fully through discovery, and if they produced any evidence showing assumption of off-airways emergency traffic warning duties by the CAA, then we would bring the government into the suit and let the three defendants fight it out. But there was no point in suing the government in the absence of CAA assumption of such a duty. Under the Federal Tort Claims Act, the government was only responsible for performing duties that it had actually assumed; it would not be legally responsible for failing to assume duties, or for failing to perform functions it had not assumed. Naturally, the CAA attorneys wanted to convince the plaintiffs' attorneys that they should not sue the U.S.A. They were therefore most cooperative in providing us with witnesses and documents that would prove the CAA had never assumed such a warning duty. One might suppose that government agencies always cooperated in that way, but I found that the CAA's desire not to be brought into the suit produced more tangible assistance than they had ever given me before.

They produced a prize witness in Charles Carmody, who had spent his entire working life in air traffic control, starting with the Army Air Corps and switching to the CAA in 1938. He had served as the operations chief for the entire air traffic control system, and in 1957 he was appointed assistant director of air traffic control. Carmody had written many of the manuals and directives that were involved in the Grand Canyon case.

We took Carmody's deposition at CAA headquarters in Washington. I appeared for the plaintiffs. Arrayed against me were the New York lawyers who represented the airlines: Paul Pennoyer of Bigham Englar Jones & Houston for TWA; David Corbin and Maurice Noyer of Haight Gardner Poor & Havens for United. These New York lawyers were in charge of the overall defense for the airlines. By that time it had become clear that the first Grand Canyon cases would come to trial in Los Angeles, since those suits were on a faster moving trial calendar than the suits in New York and other states. For this reason, the Los Angeles lawyers who would defend the airlines there joined us at the Carmody deposition: Elber Tilson for TWA, and Forest (Red) Betts for United. Each was the senior partner of a prominent, large Los Angeles firm.

I had known and worked against the New York airline lawyers since the beginning of my practice. Paul Pennoyer, a lanky World War II Navy pilot, had moved rapidly to the forefront of New York airline defense lawyers. Dave Corbin, a shorter, pudgier man in his late forties, son of the famous Yale professor Arthur L. Corbin who wrote the monumental *Corbin on Contracts,* was the senior aviation lawyer in Haight Gardner. His trial experience went all the way back to the case of

American Airways vs. Ford Motor Co., in which he helped the airline to recover the value of a Ford Trimotor that had crashed in 1931. Since he was not a pilot, he was assisted by Morrie Noyer, a young Pan American pilot with an engineering degree, later to become a senior aviation partner in Haight Gardner. The two California lawyers were new to me, and I was immediately struck by their contrasting styles. Both men were in their 60s. Elber Tilson was a small, silver-haired man who spoke softly and smiled often, a kindly family lawyer right out of Hollywood central casting. No juror could ever dislike him. Red Betts, on the other hand, was stocky, surly, blustery, red-faced, red-freckled, red-haired, and very quick-tempered. He looked like a cowboy in a Gene Autry film—the one with the foghorn voice who leads the unruly mob that threatens the local sheriff. He even used a red cowboy bandana as a handkerchief.

While Tilson and Betts had different styles, both had winning records in aviation cases, even those involving passenger claims against scheduled airlines. Tilson had successfully defended the Martin and Osa Johnson cases. The Johnsons were explorers and photographers, world-famous for their films, books, and photos of Africa and the South Seas. They were traveling on a Boeing 247D operated by Western Air Express (now Western Airlines) in January of 1937 en route from Salt Lake City to Las Vegas to Burbank, when it crashed in the San Gabriel mountains near Burbank, killing Martin Johnson and seriously injuring his wife. That case involved some of the same routes and navigation facilities as the later Grand Canyon accident. It was tried before a jury in Los Angeles; the verdict was for the defendant, and the Johnsons got nothing. More recently, Tilson had achieved defendant's verdicts for Transocean Air Lines in three passenger death cases arising out of a 1953 Transocean Douglas DC-4 crash shortly after takeoff from Wake Island on a flight that was scheduled to go on to Honolulu and Oakland.

Betts had an equally impressive trial record. Among his important triumphs was the defense of Western Air Lines in death cases arising out of its 1942 Douglas DC-3 crash in Utah on a flight bound from Salt Lake City to Los Angeles. Betts tried the case twice against Bill De-Parcq, one of the leading plaintiff's lawyers of the day who had been brought all the way from Minneapolis to Salt Lake City for the trials. Both times the jurors decided in favor of the airline. Both trials were filled with acrimonious outbursts and the trading of insults by counsel, noted by the appellate courts in each case. But the verdicts stood the test of appeal, and the families of the deceased passengers received no compensation.

I had been warned that Red Betts was accustomed to objecting to any question that could possibly hurt his case, and that he would do his best to irritate, confuse, and disconcert me and the witness. There is no judge present at depositions, and objections are reserved for the trial, except for objections to the form of a question, which must be raised at the time to give the questioner a chance to rephrase what might be a faulty question. There is no legal reason for filling a deposition record with buckshot objections, but Betts used them as a strategic weapon. I took extra care to outline my questions for Carmody minutely, so that Betts's fireworks would not distract me from covering the important points. When the deposition got under way in a stuffy conference room at CAA headquarters on September 3, 1957, Betts did not disappoint me. Here is one of his shorter objections:

> Mr. BETTS: We object upon the ground that it is uncertain, ambiguous, compound, complex, incomprehensible, unintelligible, incompetent, irrelevant, and immaterial.

Then for a change of pace, he used this one:

> Mr. BETTS: We object upon the ground that it calls for this man to be an all-seeing eye, the omnipotent one, and the question is incompetent because it patently can't be answered by him or anybody else.

Betts's tactics made the examination of any witness a tortuous process in which the interruptions would cause the witness and the other lawyers to forget the question and lose their train of thought. Here is a typical excerpt from the Carmody deposition:

> Q. by Mr. SPEISER: Was any such traffic advisory service maintained or supplied by the CAA outside of control areas and control zones as of June 30, 1956?
>> Mr. BETTS: We object on the ground that it is incompetent, irrelevant and immaterial to ask this man for an answer to a question concerning which no proper foundation exists, it assumes that he knows all of these things that go on at all of the various centers and by all of the various controllers, and further than that, that it is an opinion on his part, a conclusion, and is incompetent, irrelevant and immaterial, and that the answer would invade the province of the Court as to the law and the interpretation of the rules and regulations and of the jury to determine the facts with reference thereto.
>> MR. SPEISER: You may answer.
>> THE WITNESS: May I have the question? (The question was read by the reporter.)
> A: No.

That represents an entire page of testimony, all to get one "no" answer —and I have spared you Betts's second speech, in which he repeats his objection in the form of a motion to strike out the answer.

I must confess that with all his bluster, there was some substance to Betts's objections, and this had me worried right through to the end of the Grand Canyon case. As a rule, you cannot ask questions that call for legal conclusions. The judge decides questions of law, and he does this by consulting lawbooks, not by listening to the testimony of witnesses. However, we were facing a unique and troubling question: what was the meaning of "potentially hazardous condition" in the CAA Flight Assistance Service manual? Ultimately that was a question of law to be decided by the trial judge. But how could the judge decide that question without knowing what the man who wrote those words meant by them? I knew that in cases where the meaning or purpose of government regulations is not clear, the courts will look to the interpretation placed upon those regulations by the agency that enforces them. I determined to plough ahead and ask Carmody a slew of questions calling for legal conclusions, all of them designed to be read by the judge who would one day be called upon to decide the legal meaning of "potentially hazardous condition."

Betts knew what I was up to, and he did his best to make Carmody and the government lawyers shy away from answering those questions. But they were as determined as Betts was, and in the end we came away from the Carmody deposition with a complete history of air traffic control service in the United States, backed up by more than 800 pages of certified government records, all attesting to lack of CAA duty to give any traffic information off airways in 1956. Here (without the objections) are some of the key questions:

Q: by Mr. SPEISER: Now during the time that these airplanes were flying east of Red Airway 15 toward the Painted Desert line of position, what method of traffic separation was in effect for them?   A: The CAA Air Traffic Control facilities provided no traffic separation for them, and the only means available to the pilot was pilot vigilance.

Q: Is there any other term for pilot vigilance?   A: Yes, the phrase I used yesterday, the see-and-be-seen rule.

Q: Will you identify Exhibit 18, please?   A: Exhibit 18 appears to be a photostatic copy of the manual, Standard Procedures for Flight Assistance Service, in effect as of June 30, 1956.

Q: Who wrote that manual, Mr. Carmody?   A: Actually I wrote parts of it myself, but the manual was written either by myself or by my staff.

Q: Was it all compiled under your supervision?   A: Yes.

Q: Does the CAA Flight Assistance Service Manual (Exhibit 18) make reference to potentially hazardous conditions?   A: There is a reference to potentially hazardous conditions in Paragraph 2.32 on Page 3 of that manual.

Q: What does that "potentially hazardous condition" mean?   A: This phrase in this paragraph refers to those conditions which

I described earlier as being provided to a pilot under in-flight service and includes meteorological or weather conditions of a hazardous nature, such as tornadoes, other types of storms, severe icing conditions, turbulence, and it includes situations wherein the failure of a radio navigational aid might impair the navigation of the flight over some later portion of his route which the controller wanted to make sure the pilot was aware of. Q: This term, "potentially hazardous condition," which you wrote in this manual and which you had sent on as instructions to the field personnel, did it have anything whatsoever to do with traffic? A: No, it did not.

Q: As of June 30, 1956, did the CAA ARTC have available the necessary procedures, facilities, and personnel for keeping advised of potentially hazardous *traffic* conditions in areas outside of control zones and control areas? A: No, they did not.

Q: Now, have you examined the official records which we have in evidence here (Plaintiffs' Exhibits 6, 7, 8) for Los Angeles, Salt Lake City, and Albuquerque air route traffic control centers with regard to their contacts with these flights? A: Yes, I have.

Q: I will ask you to state whether all of those contacts were handled in accordance with the applicable CAA procedures at that time. A: Yes.

The airline lawyers did not ask any questions calling for legal conclusions. Most of their questions were designed to show collusion between Carmody and me, but on redirect examination he testified that he had spent as much time conferring with the airline lawyers prior to the deposition as he had with me.

There remained more than a dozen other witnesses to be deposed: Salt Lake City ARTC controller Benson, his supervisor, other CAA officials, and the chief pilots and other employees of both airlines, through whom I hoped to prove that the airlines had never expected to receive any traffic warnings off airways. I took their depositions in New York, Kansas City, Salt Lake City, and Los Angeles, with the same team of airline lawyers in opposition. At one of the final depositions in Los Angeles, more than a dozen airline lawyers were present, for the airline insurers were holding a national strategy meeting there to which they had invited all the principal defense lawyers from the various cities where suits were pending. In that deposition, the foghorn voice of Red Betts was joined by prominent defense lawyers from New York, Philadelphia, Pittsburgh, Chicago, Kansas City, and points west, each of them noting objections in the distinctive jargon of his local practice rules.

Finally, after nearly two years of work and a total of over 5,000 pages of discovery, I thought that we had done everything possible to get ready for the first trial, which was scheduled to begin in Los Angeles in October of 1958. There remained the final decision on the strategy of suing only the two airlines. I was convinced that the CAA had not undertaken the duty to warn, and that the airlines did not expect such warning, but this was a decision that had to be made by each plaintiff's lawyer for his own clients. We took advantage of the NACCA convention to hold a strategy session with the leading plaintiff's trial lawyers who were part of the Grand Canyon group. In a villa at the Americana Hotel in Miami Beach, Florida, the evidence was reviewed by a group that included Melvin Belli, Jim Dooley, Craig Spangenberg, Jim Markle, Bill De Parcq, Jim McArdle, Moe Levine, and Dennis Harrington. The decision was unanimous: we would proceed only against the airlines, and we would do our best to get the airlines' defense thrown out of the case on the grounds that, as a matter of law, there could be no CAA negligence without assumption of the duty to warn. We committed the fate of 68 plaintiffs to that strategy, knowing that if the airlines proved that the CAA had assumed such a duty, our clients (or possibly their new lawyers) would have a lot of embarrassing questions to put to us.

Thus the stage was set for the first Grand Canyon trial in Los Angeles in October of 1958. Elber Tilson of Los Angeles and Paul Pennoyer of New York appeared for TWA; for United, it was Red Betts of Los Angeles and Dave Corbin of New York. The trial lawyers for the plaintiffs were Irving H. Green and Melvin M. Belli, with me as associate counsel. Green represented the widow and children of a Los Angeles passenger, and Belli represented the orphaned children of a husband and wife from Ventura, California. These three death cases had been consolidated for trial.

I had met both Green and Belli at NACCA conventions before the trial. I knew that both of them were outstanding trial lawyers, but I had no idea of the adventure that awaited me in Los Angeles.

Mel Belli was 51 years old when we started the Grand Canyon trial in 1958. He was just under six feet tall, broad shouldered and husky, his luxuriant silver hair set off by black horn-rimmed glasses. He was and is the personification of Hollywood's vision of the trial lawyer: handsome, impressive, sure of himself, and equipped with the greatest courtroom voice that I have ever heard. It is a soft voice, but not syrupy. He can control it to convey nuances of expression from doubt to outrage without seeming to get excited. He can move people with that voice, and his brain is quick enough to supply him with the right words. Although he rarely uses notes, I have never heard him stumble over a word or speak a nonsentence. I had never worked with him before, and in common with most other lawyers, I had mixed feelings about him. He had received enormous publicity, notably in a 1954 *Life Magazine* article that crowned him as "The King of Torts." Though his boyish pranks and obvious egotism rubbed a lot of people the wrong way, he seemed to know what he was talking about, and he was creating great public interest in tort cases. I looked forward to learning more about him, but I was most concerned about winning the first Grand Canyon trial and surviving the ordeal of working with such an unconventional genius.

Irving Green was then in his early fifties, a distinguished looking man of medium height and build with piercing grey eyes and thinning white hair. He had moved from Minnesota to Beverly Hills, where he had established himself as a one-man law firm with a remarkable record of success in jury trials. Although his high-pitched voice was not as soothing as Belli's, he was just as capable of capturing the attention and the favor of jurors as Belli.

This was the first time Green and Belli had worked together in a trial, and for each of them this would be his first trial of a major airline case. Each would have preferred to try his case without the other, but once the consolidation of their cases had been ordered, they resolved to put their egos aside and make the best of it. I was to serve as the catalyst and peacemaker, but there was very little friction after the trial got under way.

Belli, Green, and I met in Los Angeles about a week before the trial was to begin, to work out our trial strategy. Mel and I were staying at the Town House Hotel on Wilshire Boulevard (now known as the Sheraton Town House). Mel had some strange housekeeping habits. He informed me that he started out each day with a steam bath, and since the hotel did not have a sauna at that time, he made his own steam by running the hot water in his bathtub and sink at full force. In the morning the floor of his hotel room was covered with wet towels which he had used in the steam bath, and strewn among them were the bones of a fish he had eaten for dinner the night before, as well as a melon rind or two. It was in this atmosphere that we sat down to prepare for trial of the first Grand Canyon case. I was a little dismayed at his personal idiosyncrasies, but when we started preparing for trial, my anxiety disappeared in the excitement of working with a great legal mind.

A few days before the trial opened, Mel, Irving, and I went to court for a pretrial hearing. Belli was wearing bright red trousers and Congress gaiters, high black shoes that looked like old western cowboy boots and had been made to order for him by Peal's of London. Irving Green took him aside and made some suggestions about how Mel should dress for the trial. "Mel," he asked, "are you going to wear those boots all through this trial?" I happened to look down at Irving's feet at that moment and noticed that he was wearing open-toed sandals. I decided to stay out of the discussion.

Irving and Mel straightened out their differences during that week before the trial, and we worked out a division of labor. Each would present his own clients' damage claims, of course; and on liability, they divided up the witnesses, documents, and depositions so that each had a fair share. I began to sense the advantage of having two topflight trial lawyers in our corner, for their styles complemented each other, and there was always the chance that one would make a point that eluded the other. Both men used the week before the trial to become intimately acquainted with the trunkful of potential trial evidence that I had brought with me. The most highly technical part of the case was the airlines' defense that the accident was caused by CAA negligence, and it was decided that I would handle our presentation on that point.

The cases we were trying had been filed in the Superior Court for the County of Los Angeles. Because they involved diversity of citizenship (suits by California citizens against Delaware corporations), the airlines could have removed these cases to the federal court, but did not do so. There were other Grand Canyon cases pending in the Los Angeles federal court, and the airlines' strategy was to keep the plaintiffs dispersed in various state and federal courts across the nation. This strategy had worked well for the airlines in the past, since the costs and risks of separate trials for each plaintiff usually enabled the airlines' insurers to settle claims cheaply, or to win many of those that came to trial. This case involved something new: plaintiffs from all sections of the country had pooled their resources and unified their liability preparation in the hope of overcoming the defendants' natural advantages. Now all these maneuvers were to be put to the ultimate test of a jury trial, which assumed national importance for that reason. Also, the total damages claimed by all the Grand Canyon plaintiffs made this the largest tort litigation ever submitted to American juries up to that time.

These large stakes went on the line in an unlikely and uncomfortable setting: a tiny state courtroom in the Mexican section of Los Angeles. The first Grand Canyon trial started on October 10, 1958, just before the magnificent new Los Angeles County Courthouse was opened. The claims directors of the two leading aviation insurance groups and interested lawyers from distant parts were in the audience as Superior Court Judge Jesse J. Frampton had the first 12 prospective jurors sworn. Judge Frampton was a veteran who quickly sensed that his mettle would be tested in this trailblazing case which involved Irving Green and Melvin Belli on one side, and the volatile Red Betts on the other. During pretrial conferences in the Judge's chambers it was obvious that Betts hated Belli and wanted to drive him out of the courthouse. Belli was amused at this, and knowing Betts's quick temper, he took every opportunity to irritate his red-faced adversary.

Picking the Jury

The rules governing jury selection vary from court to court. In many
federal courts, the *voir dire* (questioning of prospective jurors) is
handled by the judge, who usually asks a few perfunctory questions
designed to identify jurors who clearly should be disqualified, such as
those related to or employed by any of the parties. In most state courts,
this prelude to the trial is handled by opposing lawyers. Most experienced trial lawyers feel that the *voir dire* questioning of jurors is one
of the critical parts of any lawsuit. It gives the lawyers a chance to
educate the jurors and to create a favorable first impression. It is also
the only time during the trial that the jurors are allowed to speak, and
therefore it is an opportunity for the lawyers to get some idea of how
jurors react to their presentations.

Judge Frampton, aware of the national importance of this first
Grand Canyon trial, gave all the lawyers wide latitude on the *voir dire*.
As a result, the jury selection which usually takes less than two hours
in a routine tort case stretched over three days of court time.

Belli and Green used the *voir dire* as a conditioning process. They
opened the minds of the jurors to the issues in the case, and they tried
to get from each prospective juror a public commitment to fairness in
dealing with the plaintiffs' claims.

> Q. by Mr. GREEN: Mrs. Watson, have you ever sat on a jury
> before?   A: Yes.
> Q: Have you sat on any cases involving either personal injury
> or death to anyone?   A: Well, I sat on a poison case. There
> was no death involved.
> Q: Was that a poison case in criminal court?   A: Yes.
> Q: I see. That's a case where someone was being charged with a
> crime?   A: Yes.
> Q: Did you ever sit on what we call a civil case?   A: No.
> Q: Mrs. Watson, there is a difference in the rules of evidence in
> a criminal case and a civil case that you may or may not have
> been instructed about. In a criminal case, before you can find
> someone guilty, the proof must be beyond any reasonable doubt.
> His Honor, Judge Frampton, will instruct you that in civil cases,
> all that is required of a plaintiff is proof by what is called a
> preponderance of the evidence; that is, evidence that weighs a
> little more in favor of one party than the other. Do you believe
> that if you were selected to serve on this civil case that you could
> apply that rule rather than the rule that you were instructed on
> in the criminal case?   A: Yes.
> Q: All right. Now, Mrs. Watson, in this case the plaintiff, Mrs.
> Nesbitt, is the widow of Andrew Jackson Nesbitt who met his

death while riding as a passenger in a TWA plane when a collision occurred between that plane and a United Airlines plane over Grand Canyon National Park in Arizona. Now, the Court will instruct you that a passenger on an airline, a common carrier of this kind, is entitled to be accorded the highest degree of care consistent with the operation of an airline, which is a little different rule than an automobile accident case. Do you believe that you can apply that rule of law in this case if so instructed by the Court? A: I think so.

Q: Do you feel that if the law gives Mrs. Nesbitt the right to bring such an action that you could try this case and, after the Court has instructed you on the rules concerning negligence and the rules concerning damages, you could put a price tag—which is somewhat revolting, in one sense, putting a price tag on the death of a man, a father and husband—but could you put such a price tag on the life of this man in accordance with the evidence and return a verdict in such an amount that you feel that the Arizona law says is fair and just under the circumstances? A: Yes.

Q: You wouldn't start out a trial having any reluctance whatever to do that? A: No.

Q: And if you found from the evidence that the verdict should be in the sum of $500,000, the amount we are suing for in this case, would you hesitate at all to return a verdict for $500,000 if that is what you felt was justified by the evidence? A: If that is what I felt was justified by the evidence.

Q: In other words, what I am getting at is that even though $500,000 seems like a lot of money to you or to other people, nevertheless, if that is the damages that were suffered, would you award such damages, based upon the evidence? A: Yes.

Q. by Mr. BELLI: On behalf of these three children, I filed a complaint here asking for $1,000,000 damages for the supreme personal injury, wrongful death, and I want you, if you will, to tell me if you have ever sat down and given any thought to monetary dollar damages in a wrongful death case. Have you ever given any thought to what that should be? A: Not especially, no.

Q: You have never had occasion to be called upon to face this rather formidable task of sitting in judgment as to what a wrongful death should be appraised at, once we prove that there has been negligence in this lawsuit, have you? A: No.

Q: As you sit there now, I mentioned the sum of $1,000,000. We have lost a father and have lost a mother in this case, and I tell you too that the father, William Harkness, was a trial lawyer, just like Mr. Betts and Mr. Tilson and like I am. He was from Oklahoma. He was a member of the Oklahoma Bar and the California Bar, and they had just moved out here. He was about forty-two at the time of his death and the mother was forty. I give you those bald facts to give you this rather wound-up question. Do you think that when I give you those facts and those figures that there is anything that would cause you to say at the outset that you couldn't consider this claim for $1,000,000 for the remnants of this family, when I put that to you? A: No.

Q: You don't think that this is too much or too little just at the outset, do you? You would wait until you heard the evidence; then if you heard it was too much or too little you would make up your determination on that, is that right? A: Yes.

Q: If this were a claim for the loss of an airliner or a house or the death of a racehorse or something like that, you would use the same yardstick to measure damages, wouldn't you? A: Yes.

Q: Is there any feeling that you may have as you sit there that an airline couldn't be guilty of negligence; that with all of their care, with all of their maintenance, with all of their advertising, with all of their public relations, that they just couldn't be responsible for one of these accidents? A: No.

Q: Would you wait and hear what we prove from that witness stand here? A: Yes.

Each prospective juror was questioned individually in this way, and each had to respond on the record, in the presence of the other jurors. Belli and Green took as much as half an hour to question some jurors, to make sure that there was no prejudice or quirk hidden in their minds. The defense lawyers also questioned painstakingly.

Q. by Mr. Tilson: Now, Mrs. Craft, do you have any idea that damages for a death occurring in an airplane accident should be any greater than for the death of a person, say, killed in an elevator accident? A: Well, no, I don't.

Q: I mean do you start with any feeling that damages are awarded or assessed by reason of the manner in which the accident happened, rather than based on the damages that were suffered? A: I wouldn't see any difference.

Q: You don't start off at this time with any feeling that because these lawsuits have been brought and have gotten here to court that these plaintiffs necessarily should receive some money damage, do you? A: No, I do not.

Q: And I take it that before you would ever get around to considering the question of damages at all, you would want to know all of the facts of the case and then be in a position to determine in your own mind what happened and whether or not anyone was at fault, wouldn't you? A: Yes, I certainly would.

Q: Now, do you start off with any feeling that because Mr. Belli and Mr. Green have mentioned $500,000 and $1,000,000 that that makes either one or both of these cases of any such value? A: No, I don't.

Q: Do you understand that in the event you were to award any damages, that you would arrive at a figure by law or the method that the Court would advise you was applicable to this case? A: Yes, I would.

Q: You feel you can give the two airlines in this case the same fair and impartial consideration as if they were two individuals being sued here? A: Yes.

Q: Do you have any quarrel with airlines as such? A: No.

Q. by Mr. BETTS: Now, if selected as a juror in this case, will you, to the level best of your ability, when the matter is finally submitted to you, attempt to determine what the true facts were and what the preponderance of the evidence is with your fellow jurors and determine the issue of liability before you are influenced by any matter of damages? Would you try to do that, Mr. Pearson, if the Court so instructs you?   A: Yes, sir.

Q: You wouldn't be influenced, because of any matter of sympathy in this case, Mr. Pearson, to hark back and say, "Well, I feel sorry for those children. Maybe we ought to give them something"? You wouldn't administer justice that way, would you?   A: No.

Q: Now, we, in the first place, have denied that United Airlines was negligent. You understand that, don't you?   A: Yes.

Q: And to the extent that the Court may advise you that the burden of proving the issue of negligence against us lies with the plaintiffs, you will follow that instruction, won't you?   A: Yes, I will.

Q: You won't attempt to guess or conjecture at any point in this matter without having factual elements to satisfy your mind, will you?   A: No, I won't.

Q: And if you find that the United States of America or one of its agencies was the sole cause of this accident, would you have any hesitancy in releasing the airlines of liability?   A: No.

Although the lawyers put the same questions over and over again to each new panelist, the three days of *voir dire* were not boring. All the lawyers in the courtroom zeroed in on the face of each juror to catch nuances and reactions to each question put to these ordinary people who had been plucked out of their homes and were about to be given the power to decide the future of a widow and five children. While many of the answers were "yes" or "no," there were some notable exceptions. Judge Frampton asked some routine questions of each juror before turning the questioning over to the lawyers. On the second day, he asked a Mrs. Gaither:

Q: Have you or anyone in your immediate family had any accidents which have resulted in personal injuries or death to any person?   A: What do you mean, automobile or plane or something like that?

Q: Any means of accident, yes.   A: I had a cousin that was killed by her husband about two years ago. That was an accident; killed by a gun, but not by a car.

Q: A gunshot wound?   A: Yes.

Q: A hunting accident?   A: No. He thought she was a burglar and he shot her.

The same Mrs. Gaither had been employed as a secretary in Howard Hughes's office from 1943 to 1946. Since Howard Hughes held a large interest in TWA, we were not anxious to have her sit on the jury. Irving Green questioned her skillfully, trying to get her to disqualify herself:

> Q: Did you work personally for Howard Hughes?   A: No. I was just one of the workers in the office. I don't think he even knew me. I knew him, but he didn't know me personally.
>
> Q: Well, do you think you would identify yourself so much with him that you would feel that you were sort of trying a case against yourself in any way if you sat on this case?   A: Well, I don't know just how to answer that exactly. I know this: the job I had with Hughes Aircraft and Hughes Productions was a very nice job and I liked it very much, and I don't know whether you would want me sitting on here or not.
>
> Q: I will put it to you one other way, Mrs. Gaither, to help you decide for yourself and help us. If you were a party to this lawsuit and you wanted to get 12 jurors that were just, fair, who had open minds, who would listen to the evidence and decide the case without prejudgment, would you be satisfied to have 12 people of your frame of mind sit on that case?   A: No, I would not want them sitting on the case.
>
> Q: Because you would feel that they would have some prejudice of some kind?   A: Yes, I would.

It was important to us that Mrs. Gaither be excused *for cause,* because that avoided the use of one of our precious peremptory challenges— the powers that are given to each party to strike a limited number of jurors for any reason whatsoever. Each side was given 12 peremptory challenges in this trial, but we wanted to save them for people who looked as though they would be against us or might not award full damages. Trial lawyers have built up a mystique about the selection of jurors, based on supposed ethnic and sociological factors which label prospective jurors as plaintiff-minded or defendant-prone. These guidelines are not always reliable, but few trial lawyers would be willing to give up their peremptory challenges and take pot luck on jurors. There is no limit to challenges for cause, and Irving's questioning of Mrs. Gaither brought out enough prejudice for the judge to excuse her for cause.

As the *voir dire* went into its third day, each side used its peremptory challenges carefully. The airlines used one to get rid of an attractive, well-dressed wife of a retail shoe merchant who lived in Beverly Hills (smelled too much like big money); then we excused an auditor for the telephone company (penny-pinching and institution-oriented?) So it went until we had exhausted an entire panel of 36 jurors, and the judge had to send for and swear in another panel of 36. Finally we agreed on 12 jurors, and went on to pick two alternates who would step in if any of the jurors became incapacitated during the long trial.

Of the 12 jurors, 8 were women. Except for one dentist's wife, all of the jurors were from homes in which the breadwinner had a routine job, such as carpenter, printing press operator, department store salesperson, house painter, letter carrier. Most were middle-aged and looked conservative but considerate—the kind of jury that Norman Rockwell might have painted for the cover of the *Saturday Evening Post.*

Presenting the Evidence

Our pretrial study of the evidence convinced us that we had to keep the case as simple as possible. Complications always favored the airlines, for jurors might throw up their hands and decide that it was beyond their powers to condemn the highly skilled airline personnel on points that were contested on technical grounds. There was a simple way of presenting the Grand Canyon case. Both airlines had chosen to take the shorter and more scenic route over the Grand Canyon instead of the longer route along the federal airways. They had assumed the burden of flying in clear (VFR) weather so that they could avoid collision by seeing and being seen. If there were high clouds over the Grand Canyon area, they had no business flying there, assuming that they were warned in advance of cloud buildups. If there were no high clouds, like there was no excuse for their failure to see and be seen. Flying too close to clouds or to other aircraft was a violation of the Civil Air Regulations, and the airlines could have no excuse for such violations unless the jurors believed that they were relying upon the CAA to warn them of any potentially hazardous traffic conditions. We were prepared to deal with that defense. Our first job was to present our affirmative case as simply and effectively as possible, considering that we had no witnesses of our own and had to drag the evidence out of the mouths of airline employees.

I had taken the depositions of all of the important witnesses, and so we could have opened the case by reading their testimony to the jury. But Mel and Irving thought that we would have a better chance of capturing the jurors' attention and creating initial momentum in our favor by calling live witnesses, even though most of them were TWA or United employees. Fortunately, some of them lived in the Los Angeles area and could be subpoenaed to court for live testimony.

We decided to start off with live testimony of the TWA dispatcher who was in charge of the fatal flight. The dispatcher is always a good lead-off witness because he is involved in the planning of the flight and is supposed to follow it all the way to its destination. According to the Civil Air Regulations (now called the Federal Aviation Regulations) he is required to maintain "joint operational control" of the flight with the captain. I knew that the airlines paid only lip service to this regulation, since the captains were not inclined to share operational control with low-salaried ground employees who had little training and flight experience compared to that of the captains.

Belli and Green questioned the TWA dispatcher for two days, taking him through the history of his flight and setting the stage for the rest of the trial. First Mel had him describe his duties.

> Q. by Mr. BELLI: First, let's get your duties delineated here. As a dispatcher, you are supposed to monitor the flight from Los Angeles all the way to the point where the next dispatcher takes over; isn't that right?   A: Yes, sir.
> Q: You are supposed to have joint control of that flight; right? A: Are you referring to joint control with the captain of the flight?
> Q: Yes, you and the captain, you and the captain.   A: That is true.
> Q: In other words, the man on the ground has as much to say about that flight, except in an emergency, as does the captain; right?   A: That is true.
> Q: In other words, if the captain wants to change course, if he wants to go off the airways, or if he wants to change from IFR to visual, you would have to check with him and approve, too, wouldn't you?   A: Generally, the approval is done by silence. However, if we dispatchers observe any captain on any flight taking actions which we think would be unsafe, we should advise him, yes, sir. That is part of our duties.

Then Belli read into the record a portion of the TWA Domestic Flight Operations Policy and Procedural Manual, which we had obtained through an order for pretrial discovery and inspection. It contained strong language about the duty of dispatchers, and Mel questioned the witness on these duties:

> Q: Are you familiar with those TWA regulations that we have now offered as to your duties—"most careful attention to weather; close watch over all phases of flight operation"—do you recall that as being one of your duties as a dispatcher? A: That is true.
> Q: Fair enough. And on page 04.05.01, "Captain and dispatcher have responsibility for determining suitability of weather, field, traffic conditions and airway facilities." Are those also your duties?   A: That is true, yes, sir.

We knew from the TWA dispatcher's deposition that he denied any knowledge of thunderstorm activity in the Grand Canyon area. These thunderstorms were a key point in the case, because they were accompanied by buildups of cumulo-nimbus clouds to more than 25,000 feet—well above the 21,000 foot altitude that both planes were flying at and higher than their maximum operating altitude, so that they could not have flown above those clouds, even if they had wished to do so. We sought to prove that both airlines received warnings of thunderstorms and high clouds from weather reports, forecasts, and pilot observations. This became a central controversy at the trial, with both airlines trying to convince the jury that the weather information was so technical and fragmentary that it was impossible to tell what the cloud conditions were or would be over the Grand Canyon. If we let them get away with it, then they could argue to the jury that there was a sudden unanticipated buildup of high clouds—an act of God—that robbed the pilots of the visibility they needed to see each other and avoid collision. We knew that several TWA and United captains were prepared to testify that visibility from Constellation and DC–7 cockpits was limited and that the crews of these two aircraft would have great difficulty seeing each other if confronted with a sudden emergency in the form of unanticipated cloud buildups. Given those facts, jurors of the 1950s might be reluctant to hold the airlines responsible.

We tried to knock out this act-of-God defense in the first round, in the direct testimony of the TWA dispatcher. He had admitted that he was jointly responsible for determining suitability of weather conditions over the whole route, including the Grand Canyon area. Belli now zeroed in on the weather reports and forecasts for that area. There was no regular weather reporting station at the Grand Canyon. The two closest stations then giving regular reports were Flagstaff and Winslow, Arizona. Belli questioned the TWA dispatcher on the Flagstaff weather.

> Q. by Mr. BELLI: I could ask you this question, What was the weather report at the Flagstaff station? But it is a fact, is it not, that the weather was so bad that the thunderstorms actually knocked out the Flagstaff station from June 29th until after the accident on the 30th?   A: I don't have any information on that.
> Q: Don't you know that as a matter of fact?   A: I don't know that information.
> Q: Well, then, being jointly responsible in monitoring this flight, being jointly responsible with the pilot for the weather, you couldn't have gotten any weather over Flagstaff or in this entire area in here [indicating Grand Canyon area on map] before dispatching that flight, could you?   A: We could have got considerable reports that would be representative of the weather in that area. They wouldn't have to be in any one particular spot. For example, we get reports north and south of that route that

the pilot is going to take, and we can get a very good idea of what the weather will be along the route from—not necessarily the reports over the route which he is flying, but the reports all around the whole area.

Q: What would it mean to you if you were told on that day before and during the whole day of June 30th that the thundershowers and storms were so bad at Flagstaff that that station was knocked out? Flagstaff being here and the Grand Canyon being up north about what—about 50 miles? Would that have been of any significance to you? A: Well, it would confirm the fact that we had forecasts of scattered thundershowers on the airways and also in the whole general area, particularly in the eastern end of the route.

Q: How about in the Grand Canyon area? A: There were forecasts for isolated or scattered showers in the whole area.

Q: In the whole area? A: Right.

Q: How about thunderclouds or cumulo-nimbus clouds? A: The cumulo-nimbus or thundershowers practically are synonymous terms.

Q: That's the big cauliflower-shaped things? A: Yes, the cumulo-nimbus is a high type cloud with what we normally think of as rain and thunder.

Q: You don't go in those, do you, at any time? A: Never.

Q: Never. And they run up to 40,000 feet, 50,000 feet, don't they? A: Yes, many times they run up forty, fifty thousand or even higher.

Q: And the ceiling of the Connie is 25,000 feet; is that correct? A: Well, from a practical operating point, where we have our power charts and information for operating the engines, it is 25,000 feet. The airplane will fly higher than that, of course, but the power charts we have extend up as high as 25,000 feet.

Q: You don't go over 25,000? A: No, sir, not as a matter of general practice.

Q: You certainly wouldn't fly above a cumulo-nimbus, would you? A: Not at that time of the year. In the wintertime it is possible to do that because sometimes they are lower and it is possible.

Q: But on this day, June 30, you would have to fly around the cumulo-nimbus? A: Yes, the pilot would do that.

Q: Where he could be VFR off the airways, see and be seen? A: Yes, I would think that would be a correct procedure, to stay away from the area of turbulence.

With Flagstaff out of action, Winslow became the reporting station closest to the Grand Canyon, and its weather conditions became that much more important to the fate of TWA Flight 2. We had put into evidence the records of the TWA radio operator at Las Vegas, who had spoken to the TWA crew as they headed toward the Grand Canyon and had given them a special report that the barometric pressure at Winslow was falling rapidly. Belli questioned the TWA dispatcher about this message, but he denied that he had received the Winslow pressure

report even though the flight crew had acknowledged receipt. Mel
bored in to get these important facts across to the jury:

> Q: Now, what you really got from Las Vegas was, "Flight 2
> called Las Vegas and reported he was over Lake Mojave at 9:55,
> a thousand feet on top at 21,000, estimating the 321 radial at
> Winslow at 10:31 Pacific Standard Time. Next check point
> Farmington. Las Vegas radio repeated back and gave Flight 2
> a Winslow barometric pressure of 30.11 and advised Winslow's
> barometric pressure was falling rapidly. Flight 2 repeated this
> information back." Is it your testimony that as dispatcher you
> got part of this message but not the other part until after the ac-
> cident?   A: I received the position report, the first part of the
> message; I received all that; and I did not receive the altimeter
> setting which is given to the pilots flying in different areas as a
> means of keeping a correct reading on their altimeters which
> register the height above sea level in the airplane.
>
> Q: May I ask you, sir, with reference to these last two sentences
> about barometric pressure falling rapidly, do you know whether
> your Las Vegas radio operator ever sent that message on into
> Los Angeles?   A: That message was not transmitted to Los
> Angeles. I never received that.
>
> Q: Well, then, you never did get the information that the baro-
> metric pressure was falling rapidly at Winslow, is that correct?
> A: That message is—the part about the altimeter setting and
> the barometric pressure falling rapidly was not transmitted to
> Los Angeles, correct. That is right.
>
> Q: Now, just to be certain on this, so we won't have to come
> back to it, you never got the information contained in the last
> two sentences, "Winslow barometric pressure at 30.11" and
> "Advise Winslow barometric pressure falling rapidly"? You
> never got that from Las Vegas radio until after the accident had
> happened?   A: That is correct. I didn't receive it from Las
> Vegas radio, no.

So the crucial report of conditions at Winslow was never sent to the
dispatcher, even though under company and CAA regulations he had
joint responsibility for determining that the flight could proceed in the
Winslow-Grand Canyon area without running into thunderstorms and
high clouds. Now Mel moved in for the clincher: proof that "barometric pressure falling rapidly" was a warning of thunderstorm activity
and the buildup of high cumulo-nimbus clouds. But when Mel asked
the question, the TWA dispatcher claimed that "pressure falling
rapidly" was not a weather warning but a comment relating to "altimeter setting." The altimeters then in use were actually barometric
pressure gauges that had to be adjusted to the barometric pressure at
the destination airport in order to give the pilot a proper reading of his
height over the field on arrival. But every pilot knows that altimeter
settings are given in inches of mercury such as 29.98, or the 30.11

that was actually given in the Winslow report before the warning of a pressure drop. The pilot turns a little wheel on the altimeter to the proper mercury setting, just as one would set a digital alarm clock or the odometer on an automobile. But it was so important for TWA to minimize the Winslow weather warning that its dispatcher was attempting to pass it off as an altimeter setting. Belli fought with the witness and the opposing lawyers over this point as the dispatcher's first day on the stand drew to a close.

While we were driving back to the hotel, I asked Mel whether he would consider confronting the TWA dispatcher with an altimeter. If he handed the altimeter to the witness and asked him to make an altimeter setting of "pressure falling rapidly," the jurors would see that there was no way to do so, and the act-of-God defense would be demolished. Mel liked the idea, so I called an instrument dealer and arranged to buy a secondhand altimeter of the type used by the airlines.

The next morning, Mel resumed his questioning of the TWA dispatcher:

> Q: Well, is it your statement that this weather report of the barometer dropping from the Las Vegas station was for the benefit of the pilot to make an appropriate adjustment for his reading on the altimeter? Is that what you are trying to say here?
> A: I believe that to be a fair statement. Yes, sir.

Mel then walked slowly over to the counsel table and took our altimeter out of his brief case. He moved it around in his hands, toyed with it, looked at its face for a moment, and then turned back toward the dispatcher. I kept my eyes glued on the dispatcher's face as Mel pulled out the altimeter. He looked as though Belli was about to hand him a dead skunk. But to my dismay, Mel didn't give the altimeter to the witness; he just kept rolling it around in his hands, and then asked:

> Q: And is that the only reason, if that is the reason, why that report was given to him?   A: I wouldn't say it is the only reason, no.
> Q: What is the other reason, sir?   A: I think the main reason would be so the pilot would be alert to a change in pressures in the area he is flying in.

By this time I was almost bursting with impatience—why didn't Mel shove the altimeter in the dispatcher's face, instead of continuing to let him give weaseling answers? Suddenly Mel walked briskly toward the witness stand and started to extend his right hand—the one with the altimeter in it—toward the witness as he asked again:

Q: And what is the other reason?

Very quickly, as if to ward off the unwanted object in Belli's hand, the dispatcher blurted:

A: The other reason could very well be that there is a thunderstorm in the area.

Having breached the defense, Belli stepped in to finish it off with the help of the now cooperative witness:

Q: Is it not true that a rapid fall of pressure indicates that thunderstorms and cumulo-nimbus clouds are rapidly approaching?
A: That is one of the reasons for a drop in pressure, yes.
Q: And isn't that one of the reasons why you are advised when there is a rapid drop in pressure?   A: I believe so, yes.

The TWA dispatcher seemed to have been relieved of a great weight. As a loyal company man he had gone along with the act-of-God defense, but when he saw the altimeter he would go no further. I now appreciated the wisdom of Belli's gentle approach. The dispatcher was Mr. Average Man on the witness stand, probably much like the jurors or their husbands. In fact, the husband of one juror was a truck dispatcher. There was no point in demolishing him as I probably would have tried to do in my enthusiasm over the altimeter confrontation. In the end he told the truth; the jurors knew that the airlines had been warned about the thunderstorms; and he was allowed to leave the stand with his dignity intact. Belli did it so smoothly that he seemed to have everyone in the courtroom, including the witness and the jurors, reaching out to find the truth.

Belli's willingness to use the altimeter was characteristic of his style. I don't think that Harry Gair would ever have used the altimeter, even if it had been demonstrated that there was no way to set it for "pressure falling rapidly." Gair was supercautious about any mechanical gadget or technical exhibit. He preferred to carry the witness along in a controlled word pattern that could not boomerang. If he handed a little black box up to a witness, the trial would suddenly be out of his control, and the black box might somehow be turned against him. Belli was more daring in the use of demonstrative evidence.

Now that the jurors knew that there were high thunderclouds building up in the Grand Canyon area, Belli questioned the TWA dispatcher on what the pilots should have done:

Q: What happens when the clouds go up to a ceiling higher than his plane can fly; does he have to land or turn around and go to the nearest airway? A: Well, ordinarily, if the clouds are so high and so extensive that the pilot can't go over them or around them, he will alter his flight plan and proceed in visual conditions to an airway until he can get an IFR clearance where he can fly in the clouds.

Q: Because if he went into that cloud or in that weather, he wouldn't know who was in there, isn't that right? A: That is true.

Q: You have to depend on your seeing someone else or they seeing you, isn't that right? A: That is correct, sir.

Q: And that is called "see and be seen"? A: I have heard that expression; yes, sir. I know about that.

Q: And you know what that means? A: Yes, sir.

It took the better part of four trial days to wring all of this testimony out of the TWA dispatcher, but it was worth it. The jurors now knew that these airliners had given up the safety of the airways to take a chance on dodging known thunderstorm activity over the Grand Canyon; and they could not have been strongly impressed with TWA's safety compliance after hearing how little their dispatcher knew about the fatal flight.

The next witness we called was the United dispatcher, who had been sitting in the courtroom during much of the testimony of his TWA counterpart. He did his best to duck the hard questions, but in the end his story came out much like that of the TWA dispatcher. Irving Green did most of the questioning, and then Mel Belli cut through the complicated weather evidence to punch home the central points of our case.

Q. by Mr. BELLI: When you dispatched your plane over the Grand Canyon, what kind of weather did you expect to have it encounter? A: When I dispatched Flight 718, the weather that I anticipated over the route he planned to fly was a probable generally overcast to broken clouds in the Grand Canyon-Durango area with occasional buildups, thunderstorm activity, if you call it that, with considerably more activity in the Great Plains, Missouri-Kansas area.

Q: How high did you expect those thunderclouds to be? A: That would be a matter of conjecture. The weather bureau forecast some thirty to forty thousand feet. I had no reason to forecast otherwise.

Q: In answer to Mr. Green's question, I think you stated that the normal operating ceiling of your plane was 25,000. In emergencies, would your plane go to forty and fifty thousand with passengers aboard? A: I don't believe it would be possible; no, sir.

Q: Now, what kind of weather did your plane encounter over Grand Canyon? A: I have no report.

Q: You don't know? A: I was not advised.

We hoped that the jurors were starting to get the impression that the dispatchers and the flight crews of both airlines had been playing Russian Roulette in the thunderclouds over the Grand Canyon. But we still faced the problem of overcoming the reluctance of jurors to accept the idea that the impressive and highly trained airline technicians would ever act that way. When Red Betts questioned the United dispatcher, the first thing he went into was the witness's training and qualifications. He had graduated from the University of Michigan with an engineering degree, and then attended the Boeing School of Aeronautics before taking his first job with United in 1935. Betts made a detailed review of his military service, starting in 1941 as an air operations officer, with special training at the Pentagon for high-level duties. This is the sort of testimony that airlines can produce almost at random from employees who happened to have been on duty at the time of a crash.

Q. by Mr. BETTS: And where did you go? A: From there I went to North Africa, where after about two weeks processing I became the Air Operations Officer of the Twelfth Air Force Service Command in Algiers.

Q: Again this is the head of the dispatching service? A: In this particular field I was probably closer to the loads, inasmuch as I was the final say-so as to what would be delivered from where to where. However, the knowledge of dispatching was very valuable in this case.

Q: All right, go ahead. A: I established the first scheduled air transport in North Africa from Casablanca to Tripoli in this particular job and ran it for about four months, when the Mediterranean Air Transport Service was established and I went again into the ferrying of aircraft, in addition to which we had a couple dozen C-47s which we operated in the rear area, which at that time was in Algiers. From there I went to the Mediterranean Air Transport Service Headquarters where I was Deputy-Operations for a period of about a year, in which, this being commanded by a brigadier general, I was out of the actual dispatching phase but was more in the control and supervision of all phases of the actual operation. For four months after that, I was the Deputy Director for the senior American officer in the Air Forces Subcommission of the Allied Commission in Control. The Subcommission was commanded by an Air Vice-Marshall, who is equivalent to an American Major General, and I was a deputy to him. We were responsible for the administration and operation of the Italian Air Force. I returned to the States after a little over three years overseas and spent about nine months in the propeller laboratory at Wright Field as deputy chief of the laboratory. I got out of the service in the fall of '46 and went back to United Airlines at San Francisco for six months' indoctrination, because I had been gone about five years, and worked as an assistant dispatcher in San Francisco until I

moved to Los Angeles in the spring of '47. I have been dispatch-
ing in Los Angeles since that time.
Q: Now, have you severed your connection with the United
States Air Force? A: No, sir. I am a full colonel in the Air
Force Reserve. I have a mobilization assignment in the Pentagon.

To further buttress our claim that these planes should have stayed on
the airways, we were able to find two airline captains who had decided to stick to the airways because of the thunderstorms over the
Grand Canyon. The first was an American Airlines captain who had
left Los Angeles at 9:06 A.M. on June 30, just a few minutes after the
TWA and United flights took off from the same runway. He had discussed the weather data with the American Airlines dispatcher and
meteorologist and had decided to stay on the airways all the way to
Chicago, although he would have flown over the Grand Canyon if
there had been no weather problems. Although he was not employed
by either of the airlines we were suing, he was obviously unhappy
about being subpoenaed to give testimony that would raise questions
about the judgment of his dead colleagues, one of whom (the United
captain) had been a friend of his. When Irving Green put crucial
questions to him, he took the position that weather forecasting was so
complicated that he could not explain it to the jury. But Irving handled
him skillfully and finally produced an unanticipated trump card for
our side.

Q. by Mr. GREEN: Now, when you had this weather briefing
before your trip, did you make a determination as to whether or
not VFR conditions would exist if you took the flight over the
Grand Canyon? A: Well, I couldn't say definitely if it would
be VFR or not. In other words, there was some doubt perhaps
in my own mind, being cloud layers over there, whether or not I
might have to go down to an airway or something like that. The
reason I took the airway is merely to have an ace in the hole, so
to speak, to fall back on if I could not maintain VFR conditions.
Q: If you couldn't maintain VFR conditions, you would have
to go back to an airway anyhow, wouldn't you? A: That's the
customary procedure in our airline at that time and still is.

Mel Belli could not resist the image of the ace in the hole, the card
that had been taken away from the unlucky passengers whose families
we represented.

Q. by Mr. BELLI: Captain, I want to ask you about just one
thing, about the ace in the hole. What did you mean, that if you
stayed on the airways you would have an ace in the hole?
A: Actually to be able to—it requires a long explanation, Judge.
Q: You would be surprised now. The jury has heard a lot here.
    Mr. TILSON: I don't think it needs any comment. You
    are entitled to ask him a question.

Mr. BELLI: And he is entitled to answer.

Mr. TILSON: That's right.

Mr. BELLI: All right.

The WITNESS: May I go into a lengthy explanation? If we are off airways, let's put it that way, and we are maintaining VFR on top, and we run into cloud conditions that we cannot top —in other words, if we have to go on instruments—then we have to stay VFR by backtracking or proceeding in another direction to an airway, and once on airways we can get clearance and have traffic separation on actual instrument conditions. Does that satisfy you?

Mr. BELLI: Yes, that's all I've got.

Mr. GREEN: That's all. Thank you.

The second pilot who spurned the Grand Canyon route was potentially even more useful to us, since he was a TWA captain. However, he had been flying in the other direction, from Chicago to Los Angeles, and he passed by the Grand Canyon area about three hours after the collision, so that his testimony about weather conditions referred to a later time period. Nevertheless, Belli made some strong points with him.

Q. by Mr. BELLI: And because of the thunderstorms and the probable low ceilings, you decided not to go over the Canyon, didn't you? A: That's right.

Q: And that was because of the weather over the Canyon? A: In the afternoon when I would be there.

Q: When in the vicinity of Bryce Canyon—that would be up here [indicating on map]—you looked south. Now, south would be down toward Grand Canyon, wouldn't it? A: That's right.

Q: And in that direction you saw some extremely large thunderheads that extended up about 45,000 feet? A: Probably.

Our final liability witness was another TWA captain who had been a member of the committee designated by the airline pilots union to help investigate the accident. He had been on the team that recovered parts of the wreckage from the floor of the Canyon, and he had signed a report which confirmed our conclusion that the left wing of the United DC–7 had hit the rear section (empennage) of the TWA Constellation, thus making United the overtaking plane. Under the Civil Air Regulations, the plane being overtaken has the right of way, and United had the duty to see TWA ahead of it and turn away to avoid the collision. Since our clients' relatives were TWA passengers, that airline owed them the highest degree of care, whereas United owed them only the duty of ordinary care. Therefore, it was to our advantage to show that United as the overtaking plane was more clearly negligent than TWA. We hoped that this would cause the jurors to hold both airlines liable, since it required two planes flying off airways in questionable weather to cause the accident. Juries sometimes

will award higher damages against two defendants than against one, on
the theory that two can better afford to shoulder the burden than one.

Again we had a reluctant witness on the stand, who probably
deplored the fact that he lived in Los Angeles and could be subpoenaed to the trial. Mel Belli was struggling through repeated objections to his questions and useless answers to those that survived the
objections. As the courtroom clock moved toward the 4 P.M. adjournment time, he had established little other than that this TWA
captain had been in the Grand Canyon, had read the committee report
(although he didn't remember signing it), and had little knowledge
about the important wing and tail fragments. Finally Judge Frampton
became impatient with the time wasted on jockeying without yielding
evidence, and he decided to question the witness himself. This seemed
to unsettle the witness, who was apparently not prepared to deal with
questions from the judge. After the first series of the judge's questions,
the witness said, "I want to apologize if I have offended you, your
Honor." Belli then zeroed in on the evidence that showed the sequence of collision.

> Q. by Mr. BELLI: When you went down in the Canyon you
> examined the wreckage to determine what paint marks there were
> on the pieces of wreckage; right?
>> Mr. BETTS: We object to it upon the ground that it is
>> incompetent, irrelevant, and immaterial whether they did
>> or did not, your Honor.
>> The COURT: Overruled. Did you make such a determina-
>> tion while you were down there?
> The WITNESS: Yes, sir.
> Q. by Mr. BELLI: And the purpose of your going down was to
> get these pieces of wreckage so that they could be brought back
> and reassembled to determine what part of what plane touched
> what part of the other plane; isn't that correct? A: Yes, sir.
> The COURT: All right. Now, what, if anything, did you see on
> any parts of the TWA plane to indicate that it came in contact
> with anything else?
> The WITNESS: Just forward of the empennage there were some
> slight discolorations and forward—
> The COURT: What did those discolorations appear to you to be?
> The WITNESS: Colors from the wing tip of the DC–7.
> Q. by Mr. BELLI: Did you notice a cut in the L–1049 fuselage
> belly aft of the rear cargo door on the left side of the center
> line? A: Yes, sir. I did observe them.
> Q. And did you observe that these marks also had paint on
> them? A: Yes, sir.
> Q: And did you match that paint up with a DC–7 propeller?
> A: Yes.

Finally Mel gave the beleaguered TWA captain an easy one:

Q: When one plane is overtaking another plane, there is no way for the forward plane to see the plane in the rear, is there?
A: No.

That completed our liability case. The evidence on damages was all under our control and therefore went in with less difficulty, although Betts and Tilson kept up their barrage of objections at every opportunity. In the Harkness case, the main problem was to establish the earning power of the 42-year-old lawyer who had given up his promising Oklahoma practice to move his family to southern California because two of his three children had asthma. He had been earning about $10,000 per year during his last two years in Oklahoma, but in his first 18 months in California he had netted only about $7,000.

Bill Harkness had been a small-town general practitioner who lacked institutional clients such as banks and insurance companies. He had to look to the occasional contingent fee in a tort case to make his practice successful. Mel Belli had a special feeling for this case of a brother lawyer in the same field of practice. He produced two star witnesses to the ability and earning power of Bill Harkness. Both of them were highly respected appellate judges whom Harkness had practiced before when they were trial court judges—one in Oklahoma and one in California. The first to be called to the stand by Mel was Ben T. Williams, a Justice of the Supreme Court of Oklahoma who had been the local judge in the town where Harkness first practiced. Mel had compiled a list of cases that Harkness had handled in Judge Williams's local court. He had the judge go through the list of cases and recollect how Harkness had performed in each one. Justice Williams was a folksy Will Rogers type who lent some colorful Oklahoma touches to his description of these small town lawsuits:

> Well, here is one case, *Nell Gatling versus Dan W. Gatling*. Mr. Harkness represented the husband, Mr. Gatling. Mr. Gatling had, well, some property. The wife was trying to discover his property. I remember a considerable hearing about it. I remember this case for one reason, particularly, because, out campaigning one day, I went into a beer joint in Lindsay and Mr. Gatling happened to be sitting there with a woman other than his wife, and they scuttled out of the place. He later died and the case was dismissed.

After having the judge recollect dozens of cases that made up Harkness's practice, Belli then asked:

> Q: Justice, before you tell us about any more of those cases, let me ask you a couple of general questions about the man's reputation. Could you tell us what kind of a working lawyer he was,

from your observations of him, as to whether he was prepared, versed in the law, scholarly, or what? A: He was hard-working, he was scholarly, he would work in his office till midnight preparing trial briefs and bring those up at the beginning of court and lay a trial brief on the Court's bench so you could know what the points were that would be presented.

Q: All right. How about the man's personality, as to whether he was pleasant or affable, how would you characterize him, both in and out of the courtroom? A: He was affable. He was a man that stood better than six feet tall. He was sandy-headed and he had a pleasant grin and a pleasant personality.

Q: Well, as a Supreme Court Justice of Oklahoma, would you be able to tell the ladies and gentlemen of the jury, at the time that Bill Harkness left Oklahoma in 1954, where you would rank him as to his ability as a lawyer, as a trial man, among the lawyers that you knew in Oklahoma? A: I would rate him among the higher ten percent in ability.

Red Betts was not awed by the task of cross-examining a Supreme Court Justice. He asked:

Q: Do you consider the type of practice that you have testified to here to be representative of that type of practice which is possessed by the 10 percent of the best lawyers in Oklahoma? A: Yes, sir, because half of the 10 percent of the best lawyers in Oklahoma will take any kind of a case that is honest that they can get.

Q: All right. Then on that basis you think this cross-section of the divorces and people charged with liquor violations and the other matters that you have described here, personal injury cases, represents a cross-section of the practice of the top 10 percent of the lawyers of Oklahoma? Is that your testimony, Judge? A: For a young lawyer beginning as of the time these cases were tried in our community, yes, sir.

Betts then read into the record Bill Harkness's annual earnings from the beginning of his practice to 1953, which ranged from a low of $1,200 to a high of $11,000, and he asked:

Q: Now, Judge, would you say that that would represent the earning capacity of the top 10 percent of the lawyers in Oklahoma? A: No, sir. That wasn't the intendment of any answer I gave yesterday. I said he was amongst the top 10 percent in ability and capability and hard-working character.

Then Belli called a second judge, Walter J. Fourt, a Justice of the District Court of Appeal, the intermediate appellate court for the Los Angeles area, just one step below the California Supreme Court. Justice Fourt had been a Superior Court (trial level) judge when Harkness started his California practice in 1954. Under Belli's questioning he brought Harkness's career up to date for the jury:

Q: On the occasions that you saw him in court and observed his activity about his professional pursuits and duties, could you give the ladies and gentlemen of the jury any concept of his prowess as a lawyer? A: Yes. I would say that as he appeared to me he was, in the vernacular, a good lawyer. He presented his matters well, and it is my recollection that in the matters in which he represented the clients that he was successful.

Q: O.K. Fair enough. Now, you had practiced in Ventura before you went on the bench, didn't you, Justice? A: Yes, I did, sir.

Q: And you practiced there for a number of years? A: Yes, sir.

Q: Justice, would you have an opinion personally as to your rating of Bill Harkness at the time of his death amongst those lawyers: the top, the middle, the bottom, or what? A: Yes, I would have an opinion.

Q: Would you state it for us, please? A: Yes. I would say that he was substantially well among the top of what I would call those immediately below the top lawyers in the county. In other words, at the top of the medium-class lawyers in Ventura County. I would say that the list of top lawyers in Ventura County, that is, such as I would classify as top lawyers, was extremely limited.

Q: Taking into consideration the knowledge that a trial judge must have of the fees being paid in his community in order to fix attorney's fees in some probate matters, divorce matters, and other matters where a guardian has been appointed, could you tell us about what the lawyers who would be in the class or bracket in which you classified William Harkness are earning presently in Ventura? A: Well, if I must answer the question that I know positively, I would have to say, no. If the question were, do I have a good estimate as to what they earn or should earn, I would have to say, yes. In other words, I have not seen the income tax returns and I have not seen the books and records of the various lawyers there, but I've got a good estimate as to what they make.

Q: Could you give us your estimate on that, your Honor? A: Yes, I would think it would be in the neighborhood of $25,000 annually.

That gave Mel the solid foundation he needed to ask for large damages. $25,000 a year times 30 years of life expectancy comes to $750,000 gross. The jurors would have to make some adjustments of the $750,000 figure when they computed damages, but the evidence now included the key figure Mel needed to project Bill Harkness's future income, which had been cut off at Grand Canyon in 1956. Tilson and Betts sought to minimize the impressive testimony of this distinguished judge. Tilson pointed out that 36 percent of lawyers then earned less than $10,000 a year, and less than 10 percent of lawyers earned more than $20,000 a year, but Justice Fourt stood by his testimony that Harkness would have been able to make $25,000 a year practicing law in Ventura at that time. He repeated that statement for Betts and added, "My answer is, without any hesitancy, that I think he could do it without any great trouble."

The next three witnesses were the Harkness children: a 14-year-old son and two daughters aged 11 and 8. They painted a picture of close family life and the deceased parents' dedication to the welfare of the children. Mel brought it out in a warm but businesslike manner so that no juror would think he had put the children on the stand to play on the jury's sympathies. He questioned the son:

Q: Now, let me ask you a few questions about your dad, Billy. You were the janitor in the office, were you, the associate lawyer? What did you do?   A: I cleaned up after they left. I mean, I swept and kept the lawn mowed and everything like that.

Q: Did you go down regularly to the office?   A: Every night.

Q: Did you get an honorarium or salary for that?   A: Yeah, I got about three dollars a week.

Q: Three dollars a week. Did you go with your dad on trips or on cases that he went on when he went out of town?   A: Yeah, I used to go on trips with him. I mean, we would go to San Francisco or Santa Barbara or Bakersfield, and places like that.

Q: He would take you with him?   A: Uh-huh.

Q: How about cases he had out of town, back in Oklahoma and here, too?   A: Yes, I went with him most every place.

Q: You were pretty young then, weren't you?   A: Yeah, I was about—well, I was about 12 years old when we moved out here.

Q: Did you have the evening meal together—would your dad come home from the office for supper?   A: Yes.

Q: Then he would go back to the office?   A: Yeah, then he would go back at night.

Q: And the family would all eat together; is that right?   A: Yes.

Q: Now, did your father help you save, establish a bank account, or get you buying a bond, yourself?   A: Yes, he saved bonds for me. I mean I saved my money from working, and then we put it in bonds together. He would match it. Once in a while, on my birthdays, he would give me a $25 bond or something.

Q: What did you have?   A: I had about $200 worth of bonds saved up.

Q: How about your school work; did your dad work with you in your school work?   A: Yeah, he helped me a lot. I mean, I probably wouldn't have got good grades if he didn't help me.

Q: Did he help the other children, too?   A: Yes.

Then Mel called two witnesses who were school officials in the California town where Mrs. Harkness taught the first grade during 1955 and 1956. Her salary was $4,780 the first year, and she was raised about $300 the second year. She was scheduled to work her way up to $7,100 over a ten-year period, according to the school officials. Mel questioned the school principal:

> Q: Could you tell the ladies and gentlemen of the jury something about Mrs. Harkness as a teacher. Was she a good teacher? A: Well, yes, I considered her a superior teacher. I think she was the kind of a person that liked children, and I believe she was really dedicated to her work, and she got wonderful results with youngsters. She got along well with the teachers. The parents liked her, and in fact, she was really a great loss to the school.
> Q: Could you tell us something about her disposition, as to whether she was even-tempered or— A: Yes, I think she was quite even-tempered. I think anyone who has to work with first graders has to be even-tempered to do a good job.

Irving Green started the other damage case by calling Mrs. Nora Nesbitt, the widow of Andrew Jackson Nesbitt. She was 32 and her husband had been 30 when he was killed. They had two sons aged 10 and 8. Irving questioned the widow.

> Q: Now, what kind of a man was your late husband so far as his showing his interest in his family was concerned? A: Well, he was very conscientious about getting ahead and having a future for the children, an education, and so forth.
> Q: Did he work every day that he was able to? A: Yes; sometimes seven days a week.
> Q: Was he in good health? A: Yes.
> Q: Did he evidence any interest in promotion or getting ahead in the world? A: Oh, very much so, yes.
> Q: Did he talk about his plans with you from time to time? A: Well, about his wishes, yes, what he would like to do, and he was working for them. Whether he would be able to do it or not would be another question.

Mr. Nesbitt had been in military service during the first four years of the marriage (1946–1950). Then he went to work as a gasoline service station attendant and quickly became a station manager. From 1950 to 1955 he earned $4,000 to $6,000 per year working in or managing service stations. Then in December 1955 came his big break. He was able to start his own business by leasing the service station that he had been managing. His former employers thought enough of him to finance his acquisition of the business. During the first six months of operating the business on his own (which ended on June 30, 1956, the date of his death) the station showed a net operating profit of $6,478. Green established these figures through Mr. Nesbitt's accountant. He also called as a witness a man who worked for Nesbitt at the service station. Green questioned him:

Q: Did you have an opportunity to observe the kind of a workman he was in the filling-station business? A: Yes, sir.
Q: Did you observe how he got acquainted with customers, for instance? A: Yes, sir.
Q: How was that? A: Very good.
Q: Did he learn to know the customers by name? A: Very definitely.
Q: Did he get to know their cars when they were brought in? A: Yes, sir.
Q: Did he during the time that you saw him devote his complete time to his business? A: Very definitely.
Q: Did he ever do any drinking on the job or anything of that kind? A: No, sir.
Q: Did he ever take time off that wasn't explainable? A: No, sir.
Q: Did he know how to take care of the details of a filling station, such as what kind of gasoline to order and how much and what kind of oil and greasing work and all the things that were necessary? A: Yes, sir.
Q: While you were working with him, did you ever discuss his family with him? A: Oh, yes. They came in several times. I mean he had two boys and he was always planning their future, wanted them to go to college.
Q: He told you that? A: Yes, sir.

Then Green called to the stand Nesbitt's former employer, who had made the decision to lease the station to Nesbitt. Green brought out:

Q: And what were your conclusions about his aptitude for running the station? A: Well, he was a very dependable and reliable, conscientious man, and was very capable as far as handling the operation; very good with customers.
Q: He was good with the customers? A: Yes.
Q: Is that important in running a filling station? A: Very important.
Q: By this time, were you well acquainted with his aptitude and abilities? A: Yes, very definitely.
Q: And what was your impression of him? A: Well, he was a very capable man, and it was one of our larger units, and we decided to put our key man or our best man into the location because it was the first station we had built in that particular section of town, the San Fernando Valley.

Irving finished his damage case by calling Nesbitt's two sons aged 10 and 8 as witnesses. The older son testified to the help his father had

given him in school work, and to the fishing and camping trips they
had taken together:

> Q: And on the fishing trips did you catch any fish?   A: Yes.
> Q: Who would catch the most fish, you or your dad?   A: He
> caught the biggest ones.
> Q: Would your dad talk to you and give you advice about things,
> about what to do and how to do things?
> A: Yes.
> Q: Did he give you some spending money once in a while?
> A: Yes.
> Q: Did he let you work and earn some money once in a while?
> A: Yes.

The younger son, A. J., Jr., spoke in a voice that was barely audible.
Everyone in the courtroom strained to catch his words as Irving
gently asked him:

> Q: How old are you, A. J.?   A: Eight.
> Q: What do the initials A. J. stand for, do you know?   A: An-
> drew Jackson.
> Q: But you like to be called A. J.; is that right? Speak up, please.
> Don't just nod your head.   A: Yes.
> Q: And do you know who Andrew Jackson was?   A: Yes.
> Q: Who was he?   A: My dad.
> Q: And do you remember your dad?   A: Yes.

As Irving asked the last question there were tears in his eyes and a
catch in his throat. It was a gripping moment and entirely unrehearsed.
Irving had expected the boy to say that Andrew Jackson was a president of the United States, but his answer was one that would stay in
the minds of the jurors (and all those in the courtroom) long after the
trial was over.

On this note the plaintiffs rested their cases, and it became the
turn of the defendants to present their evidence. Some defense lawyers
think that in cases involving serious injuries or death, it is best for
them to present a short case, leaving the plaintiffs with the burden of
bringing in all the evidence, and avoiding controversial or unsympa-
thetic defense witnesses who might give skillfull plaintiff's lawyers the
chance to make points on cross-examination. This strategy may be wise
in some types of cases, but it has never been considered sound in airline accident trials. The airlines have so many impressive officers and
employees and they take such elaborate safety precautions (as required by government regulations) that they present defense lawyers
with a golden opportunity to parade effective witnesses before the jury.

Tilson and Betts did not overlook this opportunity. They dug into
the deep well of operations and safety personnel, both executives and

ordinary workers, who would impress any jury with their qualifications and their dedication to passenger safety. They called to the stand meteorologists, dispatchers, dispatch supervisors, radio operators, check pilots, flight supervisors, operations directors, training directors, personnel directors, so that the jurors must have wondered how either airline could ever have an accident with these All-American stars on the scene. These witnesses testified to elaborate training, coordination, and safety systems that each airline used, and they stressed the qualifications and training of the two flight crews who had collided over the Grand Canyon. Tilson questioned TWA's director of flight operations personnel about Captain Gandy.

> Q. by Mr. TILSON: Can you tell us what his total flying time was that was logged? A: At the time of his death he had in excess of 14,900 hours.
> Q: Do you know whether or not Captain Gandy had flown in the military service? A: Yes, sir. He was trained as a naval aviator and served four years of active duty, and during World War II he returned to active service and was on active naval service for three years. He came back to TWA with the rank of Lt. Commander in the United States Naval Reserve.

The jurors were told that he had passed rigid flight tests and physical examinations every six months, and that he was a family man, leaving a widow and three children.

For United Airlines, the training and qualifications witness was even more impressive. Betts questioned him.

> Q. by Mr. BETTS: Do you have any official rank in the United States Air Force? A: Yes, sir.
> Q: What is it? A: Brigadier General.
> Q: Will you tell us, please, what your present occupation is? A: I am the Director of Training, Flight Operations, for United Airlines.
> Q: What was the date of Captain Shirley's last en route proficiency check, General? A: That was on February 24, 1956.
> Q: And the date of his last pilot instrument proficiency check? A: January 17, 1956.
> Q: Have you ever flown with Captain Shirley? A: On many occasions; yes, sir.
> Q: What was your official relationship with Captain Shirley as his flight manager? Is that the right term, flight manager? A: Yes, sir. I gave him en-route checks. That is, I checked his proficiency and knowledge of route and equipment in flying on United Airlines routes.

The General gave Captain Shirley and the rest of the United crew the highest ratings for proficiency and knowledge of the DC–7 and the

route from Los Angeles to Chicago. So it went through weeks of testimony, records, manuals, all designed to convince the jurors that if they
brought in a verdict for the plaintiffs, they would be condemning the
cream of American airmanship on unfounded and unproven charges of
negligence. Both defense lawyers piled up evidence showing the complexity and uncertainty of weather forecasting over the Grand Canyon.
Our simple case, based on the failure to see and be seen and on the
clear warnings about high thunderclouds that would make visual collision avoidance dangerous if not impossible, was buried under a mountain of details of airline operations. Betts also produced a United
captain who had flown east from Los Angeles over the Grand Canyon
route about an hour before the crash. He had flown at 21,000 feet,
just as the fatal flights did, and he testified that the weather had been
good, with unlimited visibility at 21,000 feet over the Grand Canyon
area.

Both airlines presented evidence in support of their defense that
the failure of Salt Lake City ARTC controller Benson to warn of the
collision hazard was the cause of the accident. Tilson called to the
stand the TWA radio operator at Las Vegas who handled the last
communications between the TWA flight and Salt Lake City ARTC.

> Q. by Mr. TILSON: Did you ever, before the 30th of June,
> 1956, receive traffic information from the ARTC Center at Salt
> Lake concerning east-bound flights?   A: Yes, I did.
> Q: Did you receive any traffic information from Salt Lake City
> concerning flights which were off airways or Grand Canyon
> flights, so to speak?   A: Yes, I did.
> Mr. TILSON: That's all.
> The COURT: Was this information in turn transmitted by you to
> the pilots of the planes?
> The WITNESS: Yes, sir.

This led up to the testimony of the key witness, ARTC controller Benson, the hapless man who received both position reports but did nothing about them. His testimony had been taken by deposition in Salt
Lake City. At the trial both Tilson and Betts offered parts of his testimony, along with blowups they had made of the flight progress strips
on which he had recorded the identical time and altitude over Painted
Desert for both flights. Belli and Green objected to this testimony, but
the judge allowed it in, including these admissions:

> Q. by Mr. TILSON: You were the one that had the conversation
> with both TWA and United?   A: Yes, sir.
> Q: Did you have any further conversation with anyone con-
> cerning either TWA flight 2 or United Air Lines flight 718 on
> that day?   A: No, sir.

Q: Did you then at that time, which would be approximately 10:14 Pacific Time, know of the estimate of TWA 2 at Painted Desert at 10:31 and of the United estimate (when it was over Needles) of Painted Desert at 10:31? A: Yes, I had received the position reports that were placed as indicated on the progress strips contained in sector D–3X.

Q: Regardless of who may have placed them on the progress strips, were you personally aware of those estimates at that time as controller? A: Yes.

Q. by Mr. BETTS: After you received the information that both TWA flight 2 and United 718 had estimated that they would arrive at Painted Desert at 10:31 Pacific Standard Time, what if any steps did you take to notify either TWA or United concerning the progress of the two flights? A: None.

On cross-examination, I tried to overcome the effects of Benson's failure to warn the flights of the identical Painted Desert estimates.

Q. by Mr. SPEISER: Mr. Benson, was all of your aeronautical experience brought out in the questioning by the airline lawyers? A: No, sir.

Q: Were you at one time a pilot in the Navy? A: Yes, sir.

Q: What years did that cover? A: Principally the war years, 1942 to 1947.

Q: What rank did you hold in the Navy when you were discharged or released from duty? A: Lieutenant.

Q: You have been promoted from the position of controller to senior controller since the date of this accident, have you not? A: Yes, sir.

Q: When did that promotion take place, approximately? A: Approximately eighteen months ago, a year and a half ago I imagine.

Q: That would be about the beginning of 1957? A: Yes, sir, thereabouts.

Q: How did your duties as senior controller differ from the duties as controller that you had before? A: The duties of the senior controller as compared to the controller is that he is in a supervisory capacity generally over the controllers.

Q: In other words, you have a number of controllers working under your supervision, is that correct? A: Generally, yes, depending on the assignment for the particular day.

Q: Mr. Benson, do you recall that when you first came to work for the CAA there was a time when the air route traffic control centers attempted to give airplanes some traffic information when they were outside controlled airspace? A: I am aware of it. However, at my location at this time we were not concerned with that particular function.

Q: Do you recall that this service was discontinued and abandoned in 1948 at the time that Section 2.18 of the Flight Assistance Service manual was changed? A: If the new manual omitted that particular section, then it was discontinued as of the new manual.

Q: Mr. Benson, in order to give traffic information to airplanes, you must know what altitude they are flying at; is that correct? A: Yes, sir.

Q: You must also know what course or direction they are flying in, is that correct? A: Yes.

Q: In order to give traffic information to any two airplanes, you must know their relative positions, is that correct? A: Yes.

Q: In order to give this information, you must also know the location of other traffic, is that correct? A: If involved, yes, sir.

Q: Now, these four things that are required in order to give traffic information, that is, altitude, course, relative positions, and other traffic, as I understand it, you have this information only for planes which are operating within controlled airspace, is that correct?

      Mr. BETTS: We object to that upon the grounds it is incompetent, irrelevant, and immaterial; it calls for this witness's opinion with reference to a matter which is a matter of law to be determined by the Court.

      The COURT: Overruled. You may answer.

A: Yes.

Q: Now, with regard to the information which is necessary for you to give traffic advice or traffic information (altitude, course, relative positions, and the location of other traffic), do you have that information for planes operating in uncontrolled airspace? A: No, sir. The only positive information that we may rely on is that information when aircraft are flying on controlled airways.

From that point on, Betts objected to every question that I asked Benson, but Judge Frampton overruled each objection, and Benson's answers went into evidence.

Q. by Mr. SPEISER: Now, getting down to these two specific airplanes, that is, TWA flight 2 and United Flight 718, on June 30, 1956, after these planes passed east of Red Airway 15 and as they proceeded towards the Painted Desert line of position, both of them were in uncontrolled airspace, is that correct? A: Yes.

Q: Now, as to this term "uncontrolled airspace," is that familiar to you? A: Yes, in that it represents any area that is not a control area.

Q: Is that a term that you use in your work in air route traffic control? A: Generally that area is referred to as uncontrolled airspace or out-of-control area.

Q: Is it also known as "off airways"? Is that another expression for it? A: Off airways, yes, sir.

Q: Tell us, then, after these planes passed east of Red Airway 15, as they proceeded towards the Painted Desert line of position, what kind of airspace were they in? A: Uncontrolled airspace, off airways.

Q: Now, at that time, when these planes were flying between the eastern boundary of Red 15 and the Painted Desert line of position, did you know at what altitude these airplanes were flying?   A: In that area? No.

Q: Did you know what changes of altitude they might make to take advantage of favorable winds or weather conditions?   A: No.

Q: Did you have any control of the altitudes at which either of these planes would fly in this airspace?   A: No.

Q: Now, in this airspace between Red 15 and the Painted Desert line of position, could these planes make any changes of altitude that they wanted so far as air route traffic control was concerned?   A: I would say they could.

Q: In this area between Red 15 and the Painted Desert line of position, did you know the course that either plane was flying?   A: No, sir.

Q: Did you know what changes of course or detours they might make for sightseeing purposes or to avoid bad weather or other traffic?   A: I would have no knowledge.

Q: Did you have any control over the courses that these planes would fly in this uncontrolled airspace that you have mentioned? A: No, sir.

Q: I take it, then, that they could make any changes in course that they wanted to so far as air route traffic control was concerned, is that correct?   A: Yes, sir.

Q: Again, in this area that you have described as uncontrolled airspace between Red 15 and the Painted Desert line of position, did you know the relative positions of these two planes as to each other?   A: No.

Q: Did you know out in this area whether TWA would be on the right or left of United at any given point?   A: I would have no knowledge.

Q: Did you know whether United would be on the right or left of TWA in this airspace?   A: There again, I would have no knowledge.

Q: Do you have any control over the relative positions of these two planes in that airspace that you have mentioned? A: No, sir.

Q: Again, in this area between Red 15 and the Painted Desert line of position, did you know what other traffic was in that area at that time?   A: No. The only knowledge I would have would be of aircraft under similar conditions under IFR flight plans.

Q: Did you know or do you know at this time whether there was any other traffic in that area at that time?   A: No, sir.

Q: There was no traffic in that area at all which was under your control, was there?   A: No.

Q: Again limiting ourselves to the airspace between the eastern boundary of Red 15 and the Painted Desert line of position, which all my questions referred to, in that airspace and based upon the information available to you on your flight strips, Exhibit A, and on any other information available to you at Salt Lake air route traffic control center that day, was there any way that you could tell whether either or both of these planes would create a collision hazard?   A: I would say that would be speculation on my part.

Now the defendants had completed their cases, and it was time for us to press our motion to dismiss the defense based on CAA negligence. We had raised this point several times during the trial, but Judge Frampton said that he wanted to hear all the evidence before ruling. As the trial progressed, the judge seemed to be leaning toward a ruling that the airlines were entitled to present their defense to the jury. He knew that both planes had been flying in uncontrolled airspace, but Betts argued that all airspace, including the Grand Canyon area, was "advisory airspace" in the sense that the CAA's flight advisory service was supposed to be given to all flights in the United States, whether or not they were flying on airways. Clearly, part of this advisory service was warning of any "potentially hazardous condition," but we argued that this phrase applied only to weather conditions and not to traffic. Now that testimony was completed, both sides had to prepare final jury arguments, and each was entitled to know how the judge would instruct the jury about this difficult point on which the entire Grand Canyon litigation turned.

It was my job to argue for dismissal of the "CAA duty" defense. To help Judge Frampton, I prepared a memorandum of law outlining all of our arguments. I had been working on it as the trial went along, and it went through several drafts. When the time came to present the finished memorandum to the judge, it became a ploy in the private war that Red Betts and Mel Belli were waging against one another throughout the trial.

The day before we were scheduled to present the CAA duty memorandum, Mel and I were reading over the final draft while lunching in a restaurant. Mel was eating a piece of chocolate layer cake, and he dropped a piece of chocolate icing on one page of the memorandum, smudging it badly. I said, "I've got another copy here, Mel. Give me back that messy one and I'll give you a clean one." But Belli suddenly lit up and said, "No—don't bother. I've got a better idea for this copy." He ordered another huge portion of chocolate layer cake, and then he took the icing and spread it over every page of the memorandum so that when he had finished it was more brown than white. I didn't understand what he was up to, and so I asked, "Mel, is the memorandum that bad?" He replied, "No, no, it's fine, but I want our friend Mr. Betts to have this copy!"

We were going to hand the memorandum up to the judge the next morning, and before doing that we had to supply a copy to each defense lawyer. I couldn't believe that Mel was actually going to serve that copy on Red Betts, but sure enough, Mel personally handed the brown and white copy to Betts before he gave the original to the judge.

Betts was the most aptly named "Red" that I have ever met. When he was completely relaxed, his face and hair were almost beet red. When excited, his color turned closer to purple. Out of the corner of my left eye I peeked over at him as he thumbed through the memorandum. I could see the purple coming up from the back of his neck. I expected him to jump to his feet and ask that Belli be held in contempt of court. But he never said a word. I'm sure that he could not possibly read that important memorandum through the chocolate icing. I am equally convinced that he thought Belli had used that copy of the memorandum as toilet tissue. Betts must have searched his vast store of legal experience for the proper form of objection. As a former Stanford football halfback, did he start to charge "unsportsmanlike conduct"? Had he finally run out of objections, or was his foghorn voice for once paralyzed by exasperation? In the end, since I had slipped a clean copy to Betts's colleague Dave Corbin, Betts must have decided that he would suffer the indignity in silence.

Mel's clowning was not limited to the courtroom. I could write half a book about his leisure-time antics, but he himself has written several books covering that subject, so I will confine the discussion here to a representative example. During the trial Mel was frequently visited at his hotel by Mickey Cohen, the notorious Los Angeles hoodlum. Mickey was then free of the jailhouse, but he had some criminal law problems and he was trying to convince Mel to represent him. Mel was willing to be wooed, and the two went out to fashionable restaurants and night spots several times during the trial. Mel invited me to come along, but I always told him that I was busy getting ready for the next day's courtroom work. I also tried to discourage Mel from being seen in public with Mickey Cohen. I was not trying to be snobbish. I simply thought that it might hurt our case if Mel's picture appeared in the paper with Mickey Cohen. On our jury of twelve people, we had eight middle-aged women, most of whom looked conservative enough to be Daughters of the American Revolution. Also, there was a lot of gang warfare buzzing around Cohen, and I did not want to wind up with a bomb in my shrimp cocktail, even if Mickey was picking up the tab. But one night during the trial Mel trapped me. I was climbing into an automobile to join Mel for dinner before I realized that he had Mickey and Mickey's current girl friend in the car with him. It was too late for excuses, and so I decided to make the best of the evening.

Mel had not forgotten my reluctance to join the Cohen party. As a special treat, he arranged for me to sit in the back of the car, next to Mickey Cohen's English bulldog, who was addressed as "Mickey Junior." I don't mind English bulldogs as a breed, but this one was something special. Mickey had the dog trained to go into a growling, drooling tantrum at the mere mention of the names of law enforcement officials. As we drove along the Sunset Strip, Mickey was showing off his dog-training prowess. He said to the dog, "Junior: J. Edgar Hoover!" At that point, the four-legged Mickey started growling, drooling, and foaming at the mouth, mostly in my direction. It occurred to me that he might have Junior trained to tear apart J. Edgar Hoover and any other lawman who came within his range. Mickey and Mel were convulsed with laughter as I cringed in the corner, completely intimidated by the English bulldog. Mickey and Mel ran through the names of most of the top echelon of the Los Angeles Police Department before they finally broke up the act when we arrived at Dino's Lodge for dinner.

This was my first (and last) dinner with a famous racketeer. I was not prepared for the bowing and scraping that would precede our entry into the restaurant, then one of the most popular in Hollywood. We had the best table in the house and the best service. On the way back to our hotel I managed to slip into the front seat so that Mel Belli could have exclusive jurisdiction over Mickey Cohen's bulldog.

"Potentially Hazardous Conditions"

Now we were down to the end of the trial, and I was preparing to argue our motion to dismiss the airlines' defense of CAA negligence. In order to sustain this defense, the airlines would have to prove that the CAA's failure to warn was the *sole* proximate cause of the accident. It is no defense to claim that someone else was partially at fault—you are still responsible if you played *any* part in causing damage. The airlines undertook that burden, claiming that they relied on the CAA for warnings of any potentially hazardous traffic conditions and that the collision occurred solely because controller Benson failed to warn the two flights of their converging courses at the same time and altitude.

Before the argument, Judge Frampton read the Carmody deposition. His testimony that there was no traffic information expected or given off airways impressed the judge, but I sensed that he was not going to throw out the defense on the basis of Carmody's word alone. I understood and even shared Judge Frampton's reaction: If the CAA did not give traffic information off airways, then why, in the thousands of pages of government manuals, instructions, and directives, was there not a clear statement of this by the CAA? Why did it have to depend on interpretation by Carmody?

At the start of the argument, the judge indicated his thinking. He had already drafted a jury instruction that left the defense in the case.

> The COURT: In going over the situation, I drew, very roughly, this memorandum for an instruction: "If it becomes known to an ARTC controller that an aircraft is proceeding into an actual or potentially hazardous condition, it then becomes his duty to advise the company or, where personnel are not readily available, or when delay would add to the hazard, then to transmit such information to the pilot of the aircraft involved."

That was bad news, but I had put nearly two years of work into preparing for this argument, and at last I had the chance to put it all together.

> Mr. SPEISER: I would like to start off with what the Congress has said about this particular accident and about the duties of the CAA. Our position is that this "potentially hazardous condition" in the Flight Assistance Manual, which the defendants rely upon, has nothing whatsoever to do with traffic; that is, it relates only to hazardous conditions of weather and of airways aids being out.
>
> Now, here is what the Congress said, and I have given your Honor a copy of this report. The Congressional Committee at page 5 says: "At present two methods are used to prevent collisions between aircraft during en route flights." Then it goes on to explain just what those two methods are. The first method, of course, is the IFR clearance on airways at an assigned altitude during which you are given the standard separation, that is, the block of air space. The second method that they describe is "See and be seen," and those are the only two methods of avoiding a collision.
>
> Now, the defendants here are claiming that there was a *third* method of avoiding a collision, that is, receiving advisory service from the CAA off the airways. Everything in the Congressional report and the testimony which I will quote from shows that this third method did not exist and has not existed since 1948.
>
> Now, the Congress goes on further to say, at page 6, "Witnesses told the subcommittees that both aircraft involved in the Grand Canyon accident were operating off airways in what is known as uncontrolled air space. Such air space is outside the jurisdiction of CAA traffic controls. Pilots operating in uncontrolled air space are on their own under the 'see and be seen' system."
>
> Now, obviously, Congress would not say that these planes were on their own if they had any right to expect any informa-

tion, advisory, or any kind of a duty from the CAA. In the Congressional hearings from which this report arises, the question was asked whether there should have been a duty imposed on [Benson], legal or moral or otherwise, and I am quoting now from page 231 of the testimony before Congress. At that time, Mr. Pyle, who was the head of the CAA, the Administrator of Civil Aeronautics, was being questioned by Congressman Williams, and Mr. Williams asked this question:

"Before Mr. Pyle leaves, I would like to get back to one question that we intended to query the CAA about, and that is the question of whether there should have been a moral responsibility placed on the shoulders of the CAA controllers to have notified both of those planes in the Grand Canyon area of the presence of each other." And Mr. Pyle goes on to answer that question, saying, at page 232: "Now, I think what we are really discussing is the effectiveness of what our people can do with the information they have at hand," and he goes on to explain why the CAA has never imposed even a moral obligation upon the controllers to do this, because it would be more dangerous to try to give such a service than to leave the planes on their own.

And Mr. Pyle explains again, at 233, bringing it right down to this accident: "I think it is a matter of effectiveness, and I don't believe that in this case the controller could have been very effective in notifying the airplanes, because bear in mind where this accident took place," and he indicates on the map. "If the TWA man had been looking out the window, in accordance with the information, he would have been looking for the airplane down here. But there is where the airplane was, so right there you have the giving of false information, and fragmentary information of this kind might be worse than no information, and the answer, I think, to the question is how can we effectively give them proper information. The only way we can do it is to get the facilities and the communications, navigation aids, and the radar to do this job. Until we do that, I think we are playing with fire."

Now, here is the Administrator of Civil Aeronautics telling the Congress why this service was *not* given legally, morally, or any other way, and so I think it is clear from the findings of Congress, of which the Court can take judicial notice, that the service was not given at that time and at any time since 1948.

Then I traced the history of the aviation statutes and regulations pertaining to traffic services, which I had portrayed on a large cardboard chart:

Now, getting down to the history of it, I have prepared this chart for the Court, which goes back to 1946.
The COURT: I have looked at that.
Mr. SPEISER: As we can see from this chart, traffic information service for off-airways flights existed up until 1948, and at that time it was completely discontinued. However, during the time

that the traffic information service existed, this "potentially hazardous condition" also was in the Flight Assistance Manual, and
nobody thought that it had anything to do with traffic in any
way. Nobody claimed that. As a matter of fact, it would have
been ridiculous to transfer a traffic responsibility from the Army,
Navy, and CAA to the CAA and the Weather Bureau. The CAA
and the Weather Bureau are the parties to this flight assistance
service, whereas the traffic service is given by the Army, Navy,
and CAA. The CAA has about 10,000 employees engaged in traffic control work, and the military has about 5,000 in this country, and they share that work. I submit that it would be ridiculous
to assume that they would take a traffic service away from the
Army and Navy and give it to the Weather Bureau, but that is
what is actually being claimed here by these defendants.

So in 1948 we not only have a discontinuance of the service but we have a direction to the controllers like Benson: *"Don't
give the service. It is dangerous. It is more dangerous to try to
give it than not to give it."* And I submit that these controllers
like Benson were put into a position where they had less of a
duty than that of a bystander. If some bystander had walked into
the Salt Lake Center that day and had seen these flight strips,
he might think, "Well, maybe we better try to tell these people
something," but Benson had been told and warned, and all those
controllers had been told and directed by the CAA, *not* to give
this service because it was dangerous.

Now, we have some further interpretations of this service
and the duties of the CAA by the CAA itself, and I point out to
the Court that the construction by an administrative agency of
its own regulations, of the regulations that it operates under, are
entitled to controlling weight in this court as against any other
way that Mr. Betts or anyone else may try to construe it, unless
they are clearly erroneous on their face, and we will submit—
The COURT: That is true as a matter of law.
Mr. SPEISER: Yes, sir. I will submit some further interpretations
by the CAA of what they consider to be their duties under the
various regulations. And, of course, they have never construed
this "potentially hazardous condition" to relate to traffic in any
way.

I ran through several other CAA publications relating to Flight Assistance Service. While none of them stated flatly that "potentially
hazardous condition" excluded traffic, they did describe the Flight
Assistance Service solely in terms of weather and airways aid hazards.
Then I went on to the Carmody deposition:

I submit further that we took the deposition in this case of
the man who wrote the Flight Assistance Manual, Mr. Carmody,
who was the head of the CAA air traffic service, and we asked
him directly whether "potentially hazardous condition" in his
work had any relation to traffic, and he said no, and the defendants didn't cross-examine him on it. They subpoenaed all the
records of the CAA and all of these circular letters going back

for ten or fifteen years, and they found nothing to support them. And I submit that the airlines cannot contradict Mr. Carmody's interpretation, which is the interpretation of the administrative agency, by just coming in here and picking a phrase like "potentially hazardous condition" completely out of context and saying that it relates to traffic. That cannot overcome the controlling weight which this Court must give to the administrative agency's own interpretation.

Then, of course, in the airline manuals, which run into thousands of pages, they describe all of the services which the pilots can rely on and how they are to use them. There isn't one word in any of those manuals relating to any Flight Assistance service having any relation to traffic whatsoever.

Judge Frampton listened attentively, and at one point he paid me a great compliment by calling me "an expert in aeronautical law." But as the first day's argument ended, I had the distinct feeling that the compliment was intended to prepare me for the letdown of an adverse ruling. Judge Frampton was carrying a heavy burden. Technically, he was trying only three cases out of 128, but all of us knew that this trial was the pacemaker for all the other claims. The plaintiffs and the airlines had thrown everything into this trial, each side trying to shape the course of the litigation for the immediate claims and those that remained to be tried. It would take a lot of courage for a trial-level judge to dismiss the main defense of the airlines. Unlike the jury's decision on the facts, the judge's dismissal as a matter of law would be a precedent for all the other Grand Canyon cases.

We were dealing here with a mixed question of fact and law. Whether the CAA had the duty to warn of traffic off airways should have been purely a question of law. But because the CAA had not written out its regulations clearly, it was left open to the airlines to claim that they understood the regulations to provide for such service and that they relied on it to avoid a collision. The airlines' reliance on such warning service could be considered a question of fact, particularly since they had produced some testimony that there was such reliance. Under those conditions, even if the judge did not believe the testimony, he could not throw out the defense as a matter of law. Unless we had a piece of paper created by the airlines admitting that there was no such service off airways, we would be in the realm of conflicting oral testimony, which would have to be resolved by the jury.

I was discouraged at the apparent failure of two years' work, but I decided to take one last shot at finding another argument—just one more stone to put on the scale that might tip Judge Frampton toward our position. I went to the Los Angeles County library that evening and read through the Civil Air Regulations again, trying to find something I might have missed. I found nothing helpful. As I was about to leave, I decided to take a look at a book called *1957 U.S. and Canadian*

Aviation Reports, for I remembered that it contained the CAB investigation report on the Grand Canyon accident. CAB accident investigation reports cannot be used in court because Congress felt that bringing them into civil litigation would inhibit the safety functions of the CAB and would make the government investigation a battlefield for litigation lawyers. Thus I was really clutching at a straw as I picked up *1957 U.S. and Canadian Aviation Reports.* Immediately above the reprinted CAB report was a headnote—a short summary of the main points in the full report. While the CAB report itself covered 32 pages, the headnote, written by the pubication's editorial staff, ran only a couple of paragraphs. I had probably seen it before without really absorbing it, but now my eyes were riveted on the headnote's last sentence:

> ATC does not offer advisory service to aircraft operating off-airways and outside controlled areas.

The editorial board of U.S. and Canadian Aviation Reports was composed almost entirely of airline and government lawyers, and prominent on its list of editors was David L. Corbin, the United defense lawyer who was masterminding most of the argument against me. I felt like shouting "Eureka!" Here, at last, we had a piece of paper proving that the airlines could not have been relying on CAA traffic warnings off airways. It was an admission made indirectly, by one of the airlines' lawyers. But together with all our other evidence, it might be enough to tip the scales. I borrowed the book from the law library and presented it to Judge Frampton the next day. With a little more confidence, I began my final argument:

> In order to find that there was a legal duty on the part of the CAA to give advisory service off the airways, I submit that the Court would have to find that the CAA went beyond the duties set forth in the Civil Aeronautics Act, which relate only to the civil airways; the Court would have to find that Congress was wrong in stating that there were only two means of avoiding a collision, and that Congress was wrong in saying that these planes were on their own outside of CAA jurisdiction when they are off the airways: and you would have to find that the CAA was wrong in interpreting its own regulations; and you would have to overcome the controlling weight that is to be given to their interpretation; and you would also have to find that the CAA imposed a duty on its controllers to give traffic information off the airways, *without mentioning it* in the ANC Traffic Manual—which is the manual given to each controller telling him what to do about traffic—and *without mentioning it* in any training manual or telling them how to do it, and despite the fact that the very same duty and service was cancelled in writing by deleting it from the Traffic Manual due to inherent dangers.

The defendants ask you to believe that this service was set up without a word being said. They ask you to believe that the CAA controllers were to imply that the "potentially hazardous condition" in this Weather Bureau-CAA Manual now took the place of a service which the controllers were told not to give because it was dangerous. That is what they ask you to believe and that is what you would have to find if you ruled that there was any duty on the part of the CAA to give traffic advisory service. And our position is corroborated by the headnote here in the U.S. Aviation Reports. They extract the legal principles which are involved in a particular accident, and one of the legal principles stated here is: "ATC does not offer advisory service to aircraft operating off-airways and outside controlled areas."

The judge carefully studied the blue-bound *1957 U.S. and Canadian Aviation Reports*. Now it was time for the defendants to counter my arguments. Judge Frampton turned to them and said:

Gentlemen, I would like to have your authorities now which impose a duty as a matter of law on the CAA to give traffic information.

Tilson took up the challenge and listed a number of items, but they all applied to flights on the airways. Judge Frampton was not taken in.

The COURT: Well, all right. *Off airways,* now what is your authority for the duty imposed by law on the CAA to give notice of the proximity of another plane?
Mr. TILSON: Well—
The COURT: Well, it must be here someplace now. My question is, where is it?
Mr. TILSON: Well, of course, we go back again to the Flight Assistance Service Manual, to the duty of these controllers. They assumed a duty there. They did have us on the board. They did know where we were, and those things weren't done merely because they had nothing else to do.

Red Betts then picked up the argument:

The testimony of Benson was that when that plane reached the time when it naturally would have passed out of his area, he took the control slip off the board. Up to that time, this plane was under the control of Benson, because if it were not under the control of Benson there would be no purpose, under the Civil Aeronautics laws, for him to have any control card on his sector "D".
I want your Honor to remember that no flight may fly from Los Angeles Airport even to Burbank or Long Beach, IFR, without getting an approval from the CAA Air Route Traffic Control, and they may not fly from Los Angeles to Denver or to Chicago or Kansas City or New York on an IFR plan without getting

ARTC consent, without having it approved, and the record shows that on this morning these planes did not attempt to get off here until the government had approved the route.

Now, the definition of the duties of the air route traffic controller as set forth on page 32 of the Civil Aeronautics Administration Federal Airways Manual of Operation, in effect on June 30, 1956, includes the following statement: "A continual alert is also maintained to determine the necessity for administering flight assistance and emergency services." There is no limitation in the definition of the words "actual or potentially hazardous condition," so under our law those words would have to be given their normal interpretation, their usual interpretation. What do they mean? We haven't attempted to indicate to the Court what they mean because it seems to us apparent. As your Honor said when we came in here the first time: How can it be said that a person can sit by and see these two planes coming together without saying that they are going into an actual or potentially hazardous condition? There is no limitation on those words as used in the section, and it is clear that none was intended.

Flight assistance service is a service provided to what? to whom? "To all classes of pilots, for the purpose of assisting them in the conduct of safe flight from the standpoint of known and anticipated conditions." Now, that covers everything, and it doesn't say on or off airways.

I am going to come back a minute to the purposes of air control and to some of the history that Mr. Speiser talked about yesterday. What does "potentially hazardous condition" indicate? Does it indicate that there is just some little proposition of weather that might be up ahead of them? It means that a danger exists because of the planes that are up there, or for some reason not plainly visible to the pilot.

Judge Frampton then turned to me and said:

Let me pick up here now, and let's go back over here to the plaintiffs' side. The CAA had the right to refuse to release these planes from the International Airport on the flight plan as shown and designated on the plans filed, did they not?

Mr. SPEISER: Only in so far as they intersected airways. In other words, they had the right to refuse to allow them to fly on Red 15—

The COURT: They had the right to refuse to let them fly, didn't they?

Mr. SPEISER: No; only if there was a traffic conflict on an airway.

The COURT: And once they approved the flight plan, then they had the right to demand that these planes fly on the routes designated in the plans?

Mr. SPEISER: No, sir; only on airways. Let me read what it says in the ANC Manual: "Clearances authorize flights within control zones and control areas only. No responsibility for separation of aircraft outside of these areas is accepted."

The COURT: Let me pursue this inquiry a little further. Well, they were flying on these airway routes and you say that they could have taken off of these routes at any time without consent of the ARTC?

Mr. SPEISER: Yes, sir.

The COURT: They could have changed altitudes without their consent?

Mr. SPEISER: Yes, once they are off the airways. Restricting ourselves to the law, the only way that the CAA gives any permission for anything is in the form of a clearance, and the ANC Manual which covers clearance says very simply that clearances authorize flight within control zones and control areas only and no responsibility for separation of aircraft outside of these areas is accepted.

Mr. BETTS: Will you tell us what section that is?

Mr. SPEISER: 2.1300 of the ANC Manual, and I will also read from part 60: "Air Traffic Clearance: Authorization by air traffic control for the purpose of preventing collision between known aircraft for an aircraft to proceed under specified traffic conditions within a control zone or control area." In other words, that is what a clearance means and that is the only permission they give.

Mr. TILSON: If the CAA didn't assume an element of control, then why in the world were they even interested in the speed of the respective planes, the estimated time of arrival at given points, and so forth?

Mr. SPEISER: The answer to Mr. Tilson's question as to why the CAA took these reports off the airways is that they have to keep getting estimates every so often of the speed and the position of the planes so when they come back on airways the CAA will have a rough idea of where and when they are going to intersect the airway, because they have to reserve that space on the airway in advance.

Mr. BETTS: I have been listening to Mr. Speiser on air law, and, with no disrespect to him at all, I have been trying air cases since before he started practicing law.

The COURT: Let's get away from personalities.

Betts got back to his legal argument. A few minutes later, Judge Frampton announced his decision.

The COURT: Well, I am satisfied, as a matter of law, that while these planes were flying off airways that there was no duty on the part of the controller there at Salt Lake City or any other controller to furnish them separation. That is the way I am going to instruct the jury. As to the duty to warn: under these circumstances it didn't exist. And therefore the warning, or the failure to warn, was not, as a matter of law, the sole proximate cause of this accident.

Mr. BETTS: Well—

The COURT: All right, gentlemen, that's it.

Flushed with success, we immediately moved to strike out defendants' exhibit A–13, the page of the CAA Flight Assistance Manual with the deadly "potentially hazardous condition" language that had been admitted into evidence during the trial. With the CAA warning defense dismissed, this exhibit was no longer relevant to any issue before the jury, and Judge Frampton granted our motion to strike it out. Thus the piece of paper bearing the ambiguous bureaucratic instructions that had haunted us for more than two years silently faded out of the case.

With that ruling, court adjourned for the day. It was lunchtime, and time to celebrate. We decided on the nearby restaurant at the old Union Station, the picturesque railroad terminal which many films of the 1930s used as a backdrop for the budding starlet's entry to the wonders of Hollywood.

As we looked back on the trial we marvelled at the way things had fallen into place for us. The dismissal of the CAA warning defense had come at the worst possible time for the airline lawyers. They had stressed CAA responsibility in their opening statements and throughout the trial. Now, as we neared final argument, the main foundation of their case had been demolished. But it was not over yet. We still had the burden of proving that the accident was caused by negligence of the airlines. Both defendants had produced testimony of the strong qualifications and experience of their captains, and the jurors would not easily presume that these men had been negligent. There was still the danger that our jurors, most of whom had never flown, would decide to blame the inherent hazards of flight rather than some heroic airmen of the type that had been paraded before them.

We had little time to celebrate, for the day following our lunch at the Union Station was to be devoted to argument of proposed jury instructions. It is possible to win every battle during a trial and then lose valuable ground (if not the entire case) by failing to give proper attention to jury instructions. This is particularly true when you are up against large firms who try to wear you down with paperwork and manpower. Hard-won points of evidence and law can be meaningless unless you translate them into instructions that convince jurors of your side of the case; and thousands of trial court verdicts have been reversed on appeal because of erroneous jury instructions.

Judge Frampton excused the jurors on Friday, November 14, and we spent the entire day carving out the jury instructions. As anticipated, the defendants submitted dozens of requested instructions which would have blunted the force of our case, and we submitted those that we thought put our case in the strongest light without risking reversal on appeal. At the end of the day we had what seemed to us to be a fair set of instructions. That left the weekend to prepare for final jury arguments.

The Jury Decides

Judge Frampton knew that it was impossible to sum up the key points of a six-week trial in an hour or two. Therefore he gave both sides the widest latitude, and the final jury arguments stretched over four days. Belli skillfully summarized the liability evidence:

> I don't criticize any dead pilot. He is the one that rides up front there, and he is the one that gets it first; and of course he is going to be as careful as he can. But, ladies and gentlemen of the jury, as you go back through this evidence, wasn't this a situation that they had been building up to for a long time through their sloppy manner in sending these planes out? And on that day, the combination of these various things—the inattentiveness of the dispatcher, his not doing his duty, disregarding the weather, not knowing what the weather was over the Canyon, not being told that the barometer was falling rapidly, and all of these various things, the combination piling up, Flagstaff knocked off the air, thunderclouds or storms off the airways, they didn't have the forecast from Grand Canyon—all of these things piled up and all combined on that one day, the 30th of June, 1956, when TWA flew through there in a place where it shouldn't have been. United came behind it, closing like that [indicating].
>
> If they were in clear weather, VFR, and if they could see each other, then it was their duty to *see and be seen*. That was the testimony of every witness here on that witness stand. If it was IFR, if they were flying in clouds or in thunderstorms, then they were violating their own company rules off the airways. So either way that you take it, it makes no difference. If they were in clear weather, they had to see each other and be seen.
>
> Ladies and gentlemen, the American Airlines captain told you that the reason that he stayed on airways on that day was so that he wouldn't run into the trouble that United and TWA ran into. These accidents don't happen every day, thank God, but if all of them follow the rules, not only the pilot but the dispatcher, the weathermen, all of them, so that this sloppy combination doesn't build up like it did on this day—if they follow these rules, you can sit in the plane and relax knowing that no accident will happen.
>
> The defendants started in with this lawsuit telling you they were going to show that it was the government's fault, the government's responsibility. That has taken us most of this time, to do what? To resolve that as a matter of law that *alleged* defense is out of this lawsuit. His Honor is going to instruct you at the end of this case—you will hear his Honor's instruction, and if there is any question about it, have it reread to you—that the government had no responsibility in this case, flying directly in the face of the defense that was set up for you in this lawsuit.
>
> I submit to you, ladies and gentlemen, that that leaves the

defendants with nothing. And it is nothing that I gloat over. It is something that is as clear as day and night. There is no defense to this lawsuit.

On damages, Belli did some simple arithmetic to establish a base figure for the earnings lost through the deaths of Mr. and Mrs. Harkness. The law required the jurors to render separate verdicts for the death of the husband and the death of the wife. One might suppose that the death of the mother of three young children would be at least as great a loss as the death of their father; but at the time the Arizona law did not permit consideration of any factors other than earning capacity. Therefore, Mel put the two deaths together in his argument. He took the $25,000 earning potential of the lawyer-husband, added $3,000 per year for the teacher-wife, and multiplied the $28,000 total by 30 years, their joint life expectancy, to reach a total of $840,000. There were adjustments to be made for personal living expenses and taxes that would reduce the $840,000 figure, but there were others that would offset the reductions, and so Belli argued in round figures that the financial loss to the three orphaned children was close to $1 million:

> We are asking for a value there worth probably the value, not quite, of one of these airplanes. They have a means of determining value of an airplane if it is destroyed by fire. If something had happened to that airplane and someone was responsible, it would be paid dollar for dollar. If there were a race horse being taken from Hollywood Park down to Hialeah, or someplace, a horse that was valued at $500,000, if that horse had a broken leg and that horse had to be shot, that horse would be paid dollar for dollar, $500,000. I am giving you a dollar value of a human being and his wife, an outstanding trial lawyer in Oklahoma and an outstanding trial lawyer out here in Ventura, California, and I have given to you, to the best of my humble ability, under the Arizona law, the things that you must as fair-minded jurors consider when fixing a price tag on human life, as it were, and it comes to less than an airplane. It comes to less than an airplane because this is the worth, the $840,000, and when you consider the capital gains and the other investments that a lawyer hopes to be able to come by, it would be over a million dollars. An airplane is valued by one standard. Human life is valued by this standard [pointing to figures on blackboard] and this, ladies and gentlemen, is what these children are entitled to in this lawsuit.

Irving Green's final argument on liability was similar to Mel's, but he hit the key points in his own style:

> You could find that the very fact that both airlines failed to exercise care in choosing off-airways routes, not knowing what

the weather conditions were—so as to throw that ace in the hole away—that was negligence. And that was negligence not only of the pilots, it was negligence of the company in permitting that kind of an operation to exist. It was negligent of the dispatcher in not insisting on seeing where they are going and why, as well as negligence on the part of this crew and the captain in selecting that route.

Please consider this rule of United Airlines, which I think is most significant: "When flying in VFR weather conditions, regardless of the type flight plan or air traffic clearance, it is the direct responsibility of the pilot to avoid collision with other aircraft." And the Court will instruct you on another section of the law: "No aircraft dispatcher shall release a flight unless he is thoroughly familiar with existing and anticipated weather conditions along the route to be flown."

Green went on to cover the damage phase of the Nesbitt case:

The Court will tell you that your damages should be fair and just, and that's all we are asking. Under the decisions of the Arizona courts, you can take into consideration these factors: What kind of a man was Andrew Jackson Nesbitt? What kind of a family did he have? What was his station in life? What was he trying to do? What was his incentive to take care of his family, and what was his incentive to create an estate to give security and protection to his family?

Now, what does the evidence show? It isn't easy after a man is dead to reconstruct these things for you, but we have done a fair job of it, I think. We have shown you that this fellow, after he got out of the military service, went to work as a filling station attendant. Now, one thing about America, outside of our great heritage of freedom, we also have the heritage of the opportunity that there is for us in this country. I don't know how many of you on that side of this jury box bar had opportunities and what advantage you took of them. I know at least about one person on this side of the bar, what he started from and the opportunities he got to go ahead. But if your life is cut off just about the time when everything you have worked for is starting to go, that's when it may be difficult to prove. But you people here have the right to take all of those factors into consideration in determining what this man would have made of himself.

He starts out as a filling station attendant, and in six weeks on his first job, he is promoted to manager of the station. Well, that's a pretty good sign of what kind of a man he is. You don't get to be manager unless your boss thinks that you are little better than someone else that is working for him. They have to put a lot of trust and confidence in him.

So isn't it fair to assume that if he could make thirteen thousand dollars per year the first year, that he would make seventeen to twenty thousand per year when the thing got rolling? The man was willing to work. He worked the first shift until 3 o'clock, when the other help came on, and then he continued to work until 7 or 8 o'clock at night.

Using the base figure of $20,000 per year for Nesbitt's 41-year life
expectancy, Green made various adjustments for taxes, living expenses,
and interest. Finally he told the jurors that they could bring in any
sum up to the $500,000 that he had sued for, and concluded:

> I give you this figure not to try to tell you folks what to do;
> that is strictly your function. I am giving you these figures and my
> opinion only to give you a guide that I, as an officer of this court,
> as a lawyer, even as an advocate for a client, know what under
> the circumstances and the law would be a fair verdict that we
> won't have to be afraid to take before any court of appeals or
> anything else. And I say to you that if you will bring in a verdict
> for these people in the sum of $350,000 you will be doing the fair
> and just thing determined by the law.

Betts made the first defense argument. He stressed the plaintiffs'
burden of proving their charges by a preponderance of the evidence
and without forcing the jurors to use speculation or conjecture—always
a strong argument when it is beyond the power of plaintiff to present
most of the details in court. Then he went on to the presumption that
the dead pilots were exercising due care:

> You have a rule of automobile traffic that says that you
> shall see the traffic that is on the highway. Now, may I digress
> for just a minute to go to that proposition and suggest to you
> that the colloquialism of see-and-be-seen is an anomaly, and one
> that does not fit together with itself. You have the same duty,
> driving an automobile, but there is no duty on your part to hang
> your head out the window and yell at somebody that you are go-
> ing to meet at the crossing and say, "Do you see me? If you
> don't, look at me."
> Now, they will probably pick that up and say, "Well, these
> people either didn't look or didn't see." But you have to remem-
> ber in this case that there is the presumption of the Law that Mr.
> Shirley and Mr. Harms, as well as the TWA pilots, exercised
> reasonable care. If they say, "Did he look?" the Law says, "He
> did." If they say, "Did he see?" the Law says, "He did." If they
> say, "All right, is he negligent," the Law says, "No, he wasn't
> negligent." The presumption is a form of evidence, and it is the
> only evidence that you have before you as to how this accident
> occurred. There isn't a person in this room, probably no person
> in the world, that can accurately tell how this accident happened.
> Do you think that those men wanted to die, any more than
> they wanted the passengers on that plane to die? Do you think
> that it is within the realm of reasonable argument to say, "We
> are not blaming Chaptain Shirley; we are not blaming copilot
> Harms; but we are blaming United Airlines"?
> Now, at 6080 feet per nautical mile, 300 miles an hour, you
> are traveling 1,824,000 feet per hour. That reduces itself to the
> phenomenal figure of 30,400 feet per minute, or 507 feet per
> second.

So that on the "iffy" basis that the plaintiffs put to you—
and I don't know how you are going to conclude that they have
proven that there was clear visibility or that there wasn't clear
visibility, unless you just guess at it—but at 507 feet a second, it
would be less than four seconds to travel 2,000 feet. Now, at
that speed, who is there to say, who has been brought here before you to say that you can turn an airplane travelling at that
speed. Just go back and consider the difficulty you have in turning an automobile at 60 miles an hour. You have to slow down to
make any turn. And if you are going at 60 miles an hour, how
much space would you have to have for your automobile to
turn? And for all that appears in this record, these two crews
could have been flying entirely within the law and discharging
every obligation that they owed and have come upon each other
in visual conditions under circumstances where there wouldn't
have been a thing in God's world they could have done to have
avoided the accident. For all that appears in this record, that is
true.

Now, you may say, "Well, so what happened?" Well, that's
what I say: what happened? As to the United Airlines, they are
required to prove what happened. They are required to tell you
what happened and to prove it by a preponderance of the evidence beyond the point of speculation and to prove it against the
presumption of ordinary care. You may say, "Well, what is this
ordinary care?" I say to you that it is a presumption which the
Law gives to us. It is a witness on our behalf. It is a witness that
has all of the integrity that the Law has given it since the development of the English law from the time of the Magna Carta.

And that is what I say we have here. They are going to say
that we were obligated to look. Yes, and Mr. Presumption says
we *did* look. They say, "But you looked carelessly and how do
you know?" Mr. Presumption says, "How do you know? I say
that they looked carefully. I say it and the Law says it for me."
And then they say, "Well, you didn't see." And Mr. Presumption
says, "Yes, but the reason they didn't see was that the circumstances were such that they had no control over their inability to
see."

We are entitled to the presumption, by virtue of the death
of the members of the crew, that they used that degree of care
required of them and commensurate with the operation of this
flight. But, you see, that applies only to the members of the crew.
It doesn't apply to the dispatcher or to the weather men, and
therein lies the story of this whole lawsuit as it has been presented to you.

Counsel know that the presumption in so far as members of
the crew are concerned prohibits them from claiming they have
established a preponderance of the evidence that any members
of the crew were negligent; so they decide, "Well, here, we can't
establish a case in that manner, so we have to select somebody
else to show that he was negligent in some way so as to cause this
accident."

Tilson continued the defense argument. While Betts brazened it out to the end, arguing that there was no liability, Tilson hedged a bit. If the jury found one or both airlines liable, Tilson wanted to be sure that the damages were kept to a minimum:

> The law is applicable here by reason of the deaths, not by reason of the manner in which the deaths occurred. And so the damages, if any, would be exactly the same as if any one of these three people had been killed while crossing the street or while riding in an automobile, or in any other fashion.
>
> But you see, there again, plaintiffs take the position, "Well, now, here we are in a very advantageous position. We not only have one airline here that we are suing; we have got two of them, and as a consequence, we will sell this jury on the idea that here they will double or triple the damages."

Then he focused on the damage evidence, arguing that we had relied strictly on future claims, ignoring the modest incomes that both families had actually been living on. It was an effective one-two punch: the tough Red Betts arguing that the plaintiffs were not entitled to any money, and the fatherly Elber Tilson asking that the jurors be fair to the airlines if they felt that some award was justified.

The last argument was concluded at 10:30 a.m. on Thursday, November 20. Judge Frampton then began his instructions with the old standbys that are used in all civil cases:

> You must weigh and consider this case without regard to sympathy, prejudice, or passion for or against any party to the action. You are to decide this case solely upon the evidence that has been received by the Court, and the inferences that you may reasonably draw therefrom, and such presumptions as the law deduces therefrom, as noted in my instructions, and in accordance with the law as I state it to you.

He went on to explain negligence, proximate cause, the burden of proof, and the measure of damages, using mostly standard forms of instructions. Then he went on to those he had tailored specially for this case:

> There is a presumption of law that the deceased crewmen of the defendant airlines exercised that degree of skill and care which was commensurate with their duties and that they were not guilty of negligence. Such presumption exists because the deceased crewmen are not available to testify. This presumption is also a form of evidence which the jury is required to consider along with the other evidence, and unless it is overcome by contrary evidence, would require a finding in favor of the presumption that the deceased crewmen were not guilty of negligence.
>
> If you find from the evidence that the aircraft here in-

volved were, at the time of the accident, flying under visual flight rule conditions, then it was the duty of the pilots in charge of the respective aircraft to use the degree of care required of them to keep a proper lookout for other aircraft.

Then he read to the jury twelve sections of the Civil Air Regulations, covering responsibilities of dispatchers and pilots as to weather data and route selection, and the duty of pilots to see and be seen. Finally he said the words that we had practically memorized by that time:

> At the time of the accident here under consideration, both planes were being operated off civil airways, and in that portion of the air space outside of a controlled area or controlled zone. There was no duty imposed by law upon the Civil Aeronautics Administration or its agents or employees to warn an aircraft flying off civil airways of the proximity of other aircraft or to furnish traffic separation.

He concluded his instructions at 11:24 A.M., and the jurors retired to consider their verdict. We knew that it would take them some time, but we hoped they would decide by the end of the day. At 4:31 P.M. they returned to the courtroom, and the foreman informed the judge that they would not be able to reach a verdict that day. Judge Frampton excused the jury and ordered them to resume their deliberations at 9:30 the next morning.

It was Friday, November 21, the second day of our jury vigil, 43 days after jury selection had begun. The morning wore on slowly, as it does always when a jury is out. Now we speculated that the jurors would prolong their deliberations to get a free lunch. Lunchtime passed; still no word from the jury room. Then at 4 P.M., just as we were beginning to feel that the jurors were hopelessly deadlocked, they returned to the courtroom. Judge Frampton took the bench.

> The COURT: In the case on trial, let the record show the jurors are present and in the box. The alternate jurors are in the courtroom, and all of the parties are represented. Have you reached verdicts in this case, ladies and gentlemen?
>
> The FOREMAN: We have.
>
> The COURT: Will you pass them to the Court, please, through the bailiff.
>
> Read the verdict, Mr. Clerk.
>
> The CLERK: In the cause of Harkness against Trans World Airlines and others, "We, the jury in the above entitled action, find for the plaintiff, the Estate of William W. Harkness, Sr., deceased, and assess damages at $200,000, and for the plaintiff, the Estate of Mildred Harkness, deceased, and assess damages at $20,000, and against the defendants Trans World Airlines, In-

corporated, and United Airlines, Incorporated, as to each
amount."
Ladies and gentlemen of the jury, is that your verdict in the case
of Harkness against TWA?

The JURY: It is.

The CLERK: Shall I poll the jury?

The COURT: Well, let's read the other one.

The CLERK: In the cause of Nora Nesbitt against Trans World
Airlines and others, "We the jury in the above entitled action,
find for the plaintiff, the Estate of Andrew Jackson Nesbitt, deceased, and against the defendants, Trans World Airlines, Inc.,
and United Airlines, Inc., and we assess damages in the sum of
$100,000. This 21st day of November, 1958."

Ladies and gentlemen of the jury, is that your verdict in the case
of Nesbitt vs. Trans World Airlines and others?

The FOREMAN: It is.

The Clerk then polled the jury. There were nine "yes" answers and
three "no" answers, meaning that we had won the case by the narrowest
of margins allowed by California law.

There were audible gasps in the courtroom when the verdicts were
announced. While these figures seem low today, in 1958 they were
considered very high—more than twice as much as the defendants were
offering in settlement at any time, and probably as high as any verdicts
achieved for families with comparable income up to that time. A
total award of $320,000 by one jury was extraordinary in 1958, even
though the deaths of three human beings were involved.

Aftermath

I had left New York in the sunshine of late September. When I returned it was nearly Thanksgiving time, and there was two months of
mail and work to catch up on. But my work on the Grand Canyon case
was not finished. Shortly after the $320,000 jury verdict on Novem-
ber 21, 1958, Betts and Tilson asked Judge Frampton to set these
awards aside as excessive and to order a new trial. Both sides submitted briefs, with Belli and Green seeking to justify the awards on the
basis of the evidence of future earning power, even though there had
been only a handful of wrongful-death verdicts above $75,000 up to
that time. On January 19, 1959, Judge Frampton announced his decision. In the Nesbitt case, he would order a new trial unless the
plaintiff agreed to reduce the award from $100,000 to $75,000; in the
William Harkness case, plaintiff would have to agree to a reduction

from $200,000 to $150,000 to avoid a new trial; and in the Mildred Harkness case, he would allow the $20,000 verdict to stand.

Trial judges do not actually have the power to rewrite the jury's verdict, but they do so indirectly through "remittitur"; they order a new trial unless the plaintiff agrees voluntarily to "remit" part of the jury's verdict. This is an important power which I feel is needed to correct the occasional jury verdict that exceeds reasonable compensation. However, it has been used traditionally in accident cases to keep jury verdicts within predetermined limits regardless of the evidence of real loss. For example, in the William Harkness case, the only evidence of future earning power was that the 42-year-old lawyer was capable of earning $25,000 per year in 1958—and that evidence came from a respected California appellate judge who knew Harkness. Although the jury could consider his past earnings ($11,000) as some indication of his probable future income, they were not restricted to a verdict based upon maximum earnings of $11,000 for the last 30 years of his life. They could have selected any figure between $11,000 and $25,000 and multiplied it by the 30-year life expectancy. The jurors were instructed that this gross earnings figure would have to be adjusted for various factors, but the adjustments largely cancel each other out, so that any verdict between $330,000 and $750,000 would have been supported by uncontroverted evidence in this case. The jury had been conservative enough in awarding $200,000. Yet, Judge Frampton, an eminently fair and scholarly judge, felt compelled to reduce it by a quarter, to keep it within the traditional limits of accident awards.

Even when reduced by a quarter, the final amounts were far beyond the expectations of plaintiffs in 1958 death cases. Our clients eagerly accepted the reduced amounts rather than endure the delay and expense of a second trial. Even if they won the case again, it was doubtful that Judge Frampton or any other judge would allow any larger verdict to stand.

I was angry at the reduction because I felt that we were being pushed around. I wondered what the result would have been if we had represented the owner of a valuable painting that had been destroyed through proven negligence. If we had produced expert testimony on the value of the painting (as we had done to establish the earning power of the dead airline passengers) and the jury had found as a fact that the testimony about value was correct, would the judge have reduced the jury's assessment of the painting's value simply because a large sum of money was involved?

Here we were past the middle of the twentieth century, and one of the most liberal courts in America was still protecting property rights down to the last dollar but arbitrarily restricting compensation of widows and orphans. In my short career as a Wall Street lawyer I had represented property interests, and I had not been pushed around in that way. I swallowed my disappointment, but it taught me that we still had a long way to go to balance the scales of justice. Plaintiff's tort lawyers were still outsiders, as we were in Los Angeles. We could not match the clout of the entrenched defense firms and insurance carriers in the bar associations, courts, and legislatures. Even when prestigious business lawyers represented individuals, they had difficulty with the built-in prejudices of the system. Louis Nizer is as great a trial lawyer as New York has ever produced, and he is highly influential in legal and government circles. In 1961 he wrote:

> Appellate Courts have, on a number of occasions, reduced verdicts in negligence cases I have tried on the ground that they were excessive. The law suspects that a large verdict may be the result of passion or sympathy. I have always felt that while an award may be disproportionate in comparison with those for similar injuries in other cases, they were not too high in any other sense. They reflected a jury's feelings, based on sensitive understanding of the ordeal through which the injured person had passed and, in case of permanent injuries, will continue to suffer every second of every day for long years to come. When nature's psychological blocks against such full comprehension have been overcome, the injured victim should not be deprived of adequate damages by invidious comparison with less fortunate victims.

After our 1958 Los Angeles trial, the majority of the 128 passenger death cases remained unsettled, but the defendants started making more reasonable settlement offers, and over the next two years most of the remaining cases were settled. However, in 1959 and 1960, half a dozen more cases did have to be tried both on liability and damages in various courts around the country before the last one was settled. In those trials, the plaintiffs did not have to struggle with the defense of CAA negligence. We presented Judge Frampton's ruling to other judges and got that defense thrown out of the case before trial. A large group of Grand Canyon cases was pending before federal judge Albert A. Ridge in the U.S. District Court in Kansas City, Missouri. On October 6, 1959, Judge Ridge entered a pretrial order that stated:

> Mr. Carmody, in his deposition, *supra*, relates the intendment of CAA in the publication of those regulations.
> The Court must accept the administrative "intent and purpose" of promulgation by CAA of Exhibit 7 and 8 to be as stated by Mr. Carmody, and, in its interpretation thereof, rule that the same does not impose on ARTC personnel a positive duty to afford defendant "advisory service" or "protection" as it here claims, as a matter of positive law.
> In light of the foregoing, the Court declares the law to be:

That neither "Standard Procedures for Flight Assistance Service," (Ex. 7) nor the ANC Manual, (Ex. 8) afforded "advisory
service protection" to defendant's Flight 718, as a matter of positive law. No other rule, regulation or manual here cited by defendant and published by CAB or CAA imposed upon ARTC
personnel a positive duty to "warn" or grant "protection" to
defendant's flight as contended by defendant, as a matter of positive law. It is so ordered.

All of the passengers' families were compensated, and even the families
of the deceased crew members were able to recover damages against the
other airline. Had they not been able to do so, each of the crew members would have been limited to worker's compensation benefits, which
were far below the amounts that they collected as tort damages in the
lawsuits against the opposing airline.

The Grand Canyon case had important effects on aviation negligence litigation. It was the first mid-air collision of airliners; the first
case to explore the air traffic control service in depth; and the first that
involved a coast-to-coast series of trials, in which plaintiffs had successfully prosecuted a large group of cases on an equal footing with
the airline defendants. The Grand Canyon litigation broke the pattern
of isolation and dispersion that had been maintained so carefully by the
airline insurers in the past. The insurers did not welcome this development, and they were determined to make every step of the case expensive and time consuming, knowing that lawyers working on contingent
fees would find it difficult to keep pace with the powerful defense firms
that were brought in against us all over the country. They made Grand
Canyon an all-out battleground, particularly the first trial in Los
Angeles. But by proving our staying power and establishing our ability
to take the necessary thousands of pages of depositions and discovery
and put them together into a successful trial effort, we changed the
face of aviation litigation and started to swing the balance of litigation
power toward the middle, away from the advantageous position the
airlines and the insurers had enjoyed up to that point. At a cost of only
$250 per case for expenses, we had centralized a nationwide effort that
was successful in meeting the heavy demands of this litigation. Without
that grouping of cases and coordination of efforts, it would have been
extremely difficult for any of the plaintiffs to underwrite the analysis
and expert testimony of Sam Tour, or the two-year nationwide deposition program that was needed to overcome the defense claim that the
CAA was at fault, or the two years of trials that followed the
depositions.

I believe that Grand Canyon was a milestone in establishing
aviation negligence law as a recognized specialty. Up to that point, the
defense of aviation cases had largely been handled by admiralty firms

with established aviation departments. On the plaintiff's side, efforts had been fragmented and in the hands of general negligence trial lawyers; but Grand Canyon established a precedent for the use of pilot-lawyers who could balance their counterparts on the defense side.

Grand Canyon still remains the case with the most trials on liability in different courts. It probably cost the airline insurers much more in legal fees and expenses than they had ever spent before, and in the end, the settlements and judgments that they paid were much higher than they had expected. This gave me a great deal of satisfaction at the time, since I felt partially responsible for bringing the plaintiffs closer to equal litigation power with the defendants. But my satisfaction was blunted when I faced up to the fact that in the end our clients had been shortchanged—not as badly as the victims of the *Titanic,* the *Eastland,* or the Triangle Shirtwaist fire, but shortchanged nevertheless. As I write these words in 1979, I feel certain that none of the Grand Canyon families who received six-figure payments twenty years ago have any money remaining from those funds now, even though many of these payments were supposed to cover loss of support extending into the 1980s. We could not be blamed for failing to anticipate the hyperinflation of the 1970s, but even if we had, we could not have convinced the courts to allow jurors to consider inflation in their award of damages. There was a long way to go before we could think of ourselves as equalizers.

The Grand Canyon collision was an important milestone in aviation history, for it led directly to the establishment of the Federal Aviation Administration (FAA) in 1958. The Congressional investigation of the Grand Canyon accident documented the need for such a new agency with broader powers and much larger appropriations for air traffic control equipment and personnel. The old Civil Aeronautics Administration (CAA) had been a part of the Department of Commerce, but because of the need for better traffic control facilities and closer supervision of aviation as we moved into the jet age, Congress appropriated the funds necessary to establish the FAA as an independent agency. Under the direction of Charles Carmody, the FAA introduced radar and automation into air traffic control.

The Grand Canyon collision could not happen in the same way today. We have moved from the CAA to the FAA; from pistons to jets; and from see-and-be-seen to radar. The Painted Desert and the Grand Canyon are now on the airways, and all airline flights are provided with traffic separation from takeoff to landing throughout the United States. When a mid-air collision occurs today, you can be sure that the United States of America will be sued as well as the aircraft operators, since the government now has the duty to furnish the kind of traffic services that Betts and Tilson wrongly claimed it had in 1958.

The Importance of Melvin Belli

Before we leave Grand Canyon, I must pause to record some thoughts about the principal actor in the case, Melvin M. Belli.

It was only after I had returned to New York from the 1958 Los Angeles Grand Canyon trial that I collected my thoughts about the importance of Mel Belli. I had to recover from my seven weeks of exposure to his boyish clowning tactics and his courtroom brinkmanship, which obscured his real significance. Now that I had been through a trial with him, I realized that this man was the central thrust of a revolution. Without question, I would rank Melvin Belli as the most influential lawyer in the entire history of American tort law.

From 1950 to the present (1979), he has devoted himself to an unprecedented educational campaign of teaching judges, lawyers, and the public new methods of evaluating and presenting tort cases. He wrote law review articles and multi-volume textbooks; he barnstormed and crusaded throughout the country, appearing before bar associations, law students, and the television public; and through all this he continued to try cases and argue appeals at a breakneck pace in all parts of the nation.

His most influential article, "The Adequate Award," was published in the California Law Review in 1951. Belli's main point was that tort awards had not risen proportionately to the increased cost of living. Trial and appellate judges reviewing jury verdicts had taken an extremely narrow viewpoint, usually looking backwards to older decisions that had been set up as barriers to adequate compensation. Thus, if the highest award granted for the loss of a leg was $25,000 in a particular state, even if it had been awarded in 1910, the courts of the 1940s and 1950s would raise that old award to the lofty status of a legal precedent, without bothering to make any adjustments for the decreased value of the dollar. The article cited many shortchanging remittitur decisions, such as an 1896 Indiana case holding that a verdict of $1,100 was adequate for the loss of a leg by a seven-year-old girl, and a 1911 Arkansas case in which a verdict of $10,000 was ordered reduced to $5,000 for a plaintiff who had lost both his legs.

Then Belli proceeded to document the decreased value of the dollar, using common items such as the cost of a four-room house, the rental charge for a secretary's office, the hourly wages of carpenters, and the quarterly tuition fees at Stanford University. Many of these figures had multiplied by five to ten times in the first half of the twentieth century but, as Belli pointed out, the unofficial ceilings imposed by courts on jury verdicts for personal injuries and death had not increased by anything approaching the difference in the purchasing power of the dollar.

In his 1951 article, Belli mentioned that a jury in Santa Clara County had very recently awarded $100,000 in a wrongful death case, the first time that six figures had ever been reached in a California death case. He also demonstrated through analysis of hundreds of cases that there was a sound barrier in the vicinity of $50,000, after which most state and federal judges got their knives ready to perform surgery on jury verdicts. In place of this arbitrary limitation, Belli suggested that for reviewing jury damage verdicts, modern judges should use the criteria established by Chancellor James Kent, the first great New York judge. In an 1812 New York decision, Kent wrote:

> The damages, therefore, must be so excessive as to strike mankind, at first blush, as being beyond all measure unreasonable and outrageous, and such as manifestly show the jury to have been actuated by passion, partiality, prejudice, or corruption. In short, the damages must be flagrantly outrageous and extravagant, or the court cannot undertake to draw the line, for they have no standard by which to ascertain the excess.

Belli also cited dozens of cases in which plaintiffs had collected amounts exceeding $50,000. These data, which had not been published anywhere, he had obtained from plaintiff's lawyers in various states, and they included cases settled before trial. In order to avoid raising the general level of verdicts, insurance companies and railroads had long made a practice of settling their severest cases before trial when they involved strong liability and heartbreaking injuries. Settling a handful of such cases for comparatively generous amounts was much cheaper for them than allowing juries to pass on them and thereby running the risk that judges would start to back away from outmoded precedents in ruling on the excessiveness of awards. Belli's unique data on settlements were more significant than the old shortchanging cases that one could find in the law books. Here was a register of the true value of serious injury cases in the marketplace which trial and appellate judges should take into account when deciding on excessiveness, rather than adhering to precedents dating back to the era of the *Titanic* and the Triangle Shirtwaist fire.

Belli's eye-opening article was quoted by many formerly backward courts to justify the affirmance of much higher awards than had been allowed to stand before Mel wrote "The Adequate Award." Included among them were the supreme courts of Mississippi, Arizona, and Oregon, which in the 1950s had been classified as "low verdict areas" using nineteenth-century yardsticks to measure twentieth-century damages. Looking back on the Grand Canyon verdicts, I felt Judge Frampton might well have reduced our Los Angeles jury award of $320,000 by 50 percent rather than the actual 25 percent if Mel had not written "The Adequate Award" and his 1954 textbook, *Modern Trials.*

Mel was original and dramatic in devising new methods of presenting evidence. He had started out as a criminal lawyer, working closely with Father George O'Meara, the Catholic chaplain at San Quentin Prison, who brought the young Melvin Belli into many cases that seemed hopeless. Then, when he started trying civil cases, he began to wonder why plaintiff's lawyers in such cases used so little tangible evidence. As Belli wrote in his 1976 *My Life on Trial:*

> I had learned a valuable lesson, one taught by Captain Kidd [Belli's law school instructor] but only half realized: that jurors learn through all their senses, and if you can tell them and show them, too, let them see and feel and even taste or smell the evidence, then you will reach the jury. "A good trial attorney," said Captain Kidd, "is a good teacher. He doesn't overestimate the jury's knowledge, either. He has to show them." A lot of lawyers knew this, of course, and some of those who did were even using the knowledge in court. But for some reason, they only saw it as a tool in criminal trials—when someone was accused of breaking a law, murder or robbery or rape. The D.A. would bring in the lethal weapon, the autopsy picture, even the aborted fetus, the blood-spattered scene of the crime. All would be admitted, no matter how grisly. But they weren't using demonstrative evidence nearly enough in civil cases. (It would be years before I could get a picture of the deceased admitted in a civil case.)

Melvin Belli developed a system of trial by blackboard, because he is essentially a teacher. First he would educate himself in medicine, science, economics, trying to learn every aspect of the case so that he could confidently teach it to the judge and jury. He used the blackboard like a high-school or college instructor, printing key words and figures in chalk to make a more lasting impression than his spoken word. He also had a skeleton named Elmer, whose component parts he used in courtroom anatomy lectures that helped jurors to understand and evaluate serious injuries.

Much of his six-volume work, *Modern Trials,* first published in 1954, was devoted to demonstrative evidence. Mel asked trial lawyers all over the country to send him pictures and stories about models, maps, movies, slides, blow-ups, and any other type of demonstrative evidence that they had used in civil cases. He used these contributions and his own experiences to give lawyers their first definitive textbook on the art and science of presenting tort cases.

As he wrote, lectured, and traveled around the country, Mel put the blame on plaintiff's lawyers for failing to pick up the gauntlet that he had thrown down to them: the challenge of using "The Adequate Award," demonstrative evidence, and trial-by-blackboard to lift their local courts out of the nineteenth century. As he wrote in *Modern Trials:*

> That too low a standard had been put upon man's life, his mind, his members, his family, has been almost entirely the fault of the plaintiff's trial lawyer himself in failing, in the so-called low verdict centers, properly to educate juries, trial judges, and appellate judges. Adequate preparation and adequate use of demonstrative evidence has produced adequate awards. Plaintiffs' lawyers first had to convince themselves before convincing judges and juries that there was no justification for law putting the lowest price upon man himself, when the things he creates for his own use and pleasure were being marked at much higher values.

It was this challenge, plus Mel's charisma and his own record of success in the trial and appellate courts, that convinced many plaintiff's lawyers to try his methods of education, first teaching themselves and then educating judges and jurors.

Until Belli came along, many injured persons had their compensation fixed by an unofficial formula of five to ten times the special damages (medical expenses, loss of earnings, and other actual out-of-pocket expenses) without regard to such items as physical and emotional suffering, loss of enjoyment of life, and loss of potential earning capacity. While this formula was never spelled out in court decisions, it was often used by insurance adjusters, defense lawyers, and even judges in making the final evaluation of damages in a tort case. Belli mounted the first effective nationwide campaign against this arbitrary standard by substituting methods that were both scientific and humanistic.

The common law has developed largely from ideas that have been written down and passed from generation to generation in books. The importance of well researched and well documented books and law review articles like *Modern Trials* and "The Adequate Award" is that eventually their ideas will be picked up by judges whose minds are open, and they will help to expand and modernize the law. Before World War II, there were practically no such authoritative texts or law review articles that fair-minded judges could use as the basis for bringing tort law into the twentieth century. Thus the only textbook on torts published during the first century of American independence—and the most influential up to World War II—was Thomas M. Cooley's *Treatise on the Law of Torts.* In his first edition (1880) Cooley commented on an English wrongful death case in which the court had set aside an award of 75 English pounds as *excessive* for the deceased man's father, who was old and infirm (and therefore needed the support of his 21-year-old working son). Cooley thought that this decision had been a bit unfair:

> This seems a very strict application of the law. An American court would probably not disturb a verdict, unless the excess appeared more manifest.

But Cooley went on to set his own value on human life:

> Thus, if the deceased is a common laboring man, and it is not shown that he could bring to the assistance of the family other resources than his daily earnings, an award of five thousand dollars is clearly excessive. . . . Many of the statutes fix a maximum of recovery, five thousand dollars being a common limitation.

Perhaps such comments were to be expected in an 1880 textbook which drew upon the primitive first century of American law. But shockingly, the same comments were repeated *verbatim* in Cooley's second edition (1888), his third edition (1906), and his fourth edition (1932). In the formative period of American tort law, when the courts were struggling with the difficult problem of appropriate compensation for wrongful death, all they had before them was the action of the many state legislatures that arbitrarily limited damages, and Cooley's equally barbaric evaluation. Until the 1941 publication of William L. Prosser's monumental work on torts there was no authoritative expression of a twentieth century view of damages for wrongful death. But Dean Prosser's writings did not bring sweeping or rapid changes. That did not happen until Melvin Belli's revolution was well under way.

When I came to appreciate the importance of Mel Belli—the legal statesman disguised as a clown—the idea dawned on me that there was a great need for a definitive textbook on wrongful death cases. None had been written since 1913, and Prosser's treatment of the subject covered barely a dozen pages. Belli's writing concentrated on personal injury cases. I decided that I would somehow find the time to write a new book on wrongful death. Finally in 1965 it was published as *Recovery for Wrongful Death,* and over the years it has been cited and quoted frequently by the U.S. Supreme Court and many other appellate courts. I don't think that I would have attempted it without the example of Belli's acceptance as a legal authority.

Belli had the drive to package his courtroom victories, his books and law review articles, his blowups and blackboards, and Elmer the skeleton into a traveling circus of legal seminars which were unlike anything that had ever been seen in law practice before. From 1951 through 1956 he conducted a five-year cross-country crusade, lecturing in 44 states, most often under the auspices of NACCA (National Association of Claimants' Compensation Attorneys), which was then emerging as a nationwide force in tort law. NACCA had been founded in 1946 by Samuel B. Horovitz, a prominent Boston worker's compensation lawyer. Until 1949, it concentrated on worker's compensation issues, and its membership was limited to "lawyers helping injured workers." But all that changed in 1949, when Sam Horovitz discovered Melvin Belli and sold him on the future of NACCA.

Mel became president of NACCA in 1951, and during his presidency, it outgrew its base in worker's compensation and reached out to plaintiff's tort lawyers all over the country. Here were hundreds of outstanding lawyers who had never taken much interest in the activities of state, local, or national bar associations because they felt like outsiders. The American Bar Association had started in the 1870s as a semisocial organization that convened at Saratoga Springs, New York, during the summer racing season without any thought of representing the entire bar of the United States. To a lesser degree this was true of state bars, and even of some local bar associations. Most seasoned plaintiff's tort lawyers considered bar association activities as a waste of their time, since these associations were dominated by establishment lawyers. Lawyers who represented railroads, insurance companies, and large business corporations comprised the majority on their governing boards, which took positions on legislation, changes of law, and the selection of judges that favored business and financial interests. Now at last, somebody had come up with an equalizer: a bar association dedicated to the interests of plaintiffs and plaintiff's lawyers. Belli was the natural choice for heading a nationwide drive to breathe some life into NACCA, and this he did on a grand scale.

As Belli traveled around the country preaching adequate awards and demonstrative evidence, he often made side trips to try cases. In 1954, for example, he interrupted a lecture tour to spend four weeks on trying a case in Montana. In a county where the highest previous award had been $30,000, he achieved a jury verdict of $183,000 for a man who had lost his leg and suffered other serious injuries in a gas explosion.

Building on the wide acceptance of his 1951 California Law Review article, Mel used the NACCA Law Journal and his *Modern Trials* textbook to promote the continued collection and publication of verdicts and settlements exceeding $50,000. Thanks to him, we now have a continuous record of the progress made toward equality in tort litigation.

He also created and directed the "Belli Seminar," which became a one- or two-day feature of NACCA conventions starting in 1951. Each seminar was an exciting experience for the audience and the participants. Lawyers young and old, from all parts of the country and with different accents, stood up there to attest to the changes that were starting to take place in tort law. The very process of collecting these lawyers and having them relate their experiences, with Mel orchestrating and darting in with his own lively comments, gave us the feeling that an irresistable wave was building up, a wave strong enough to sweep away the obstacles that had confronted tort plaintiffs for centuries. It was thrilling to be a part of this process, especially for the older lawyers who had so long despaired of serving any useful function in bar associations. Belli was the apostle and the deliverer. He was the man who brought it all together. While his personality, sense of humor, and scholarship dominated the seminar, he was very gracious about it. He would allow anyone to speak on any topic, and gradually the seminar spilled over into a second day, sometimes running from eight o'clock in the morning until after midnight, with the house packed at all times.

During the Grand Canyon trial, Red Betts sneeringly referred to Mel's teaching as the "Belli College of Law." It *was* a college for thousands of lawyers to whom Mel Belli's revolution brought the inspiration, the knowledge, and the confidence to seek adequate damages in tens of thousands of cases. They knew that their arguments for fair compensation rested on the solid bedrock of Belli's legal and sociological research, not on the gimmickry which the press was apt to stress in writing about Mel.

Other tort lawyers have been just as good as Belli, if not better, in the courtroom. Some have been greater students of the law and better writers. A few have even been better public speakers. But nobody ever combined all those talents with the zeal to put himself on the line by publishing, lecturing, teaching, crusading, and fomenting a revolution, in addition to winning cases and building a successful law firm. In the process, he inspired many other lawyers to perform beyond their ordinary potential and to contribute their services to this revolution free of charge.

I wish that I could end the Belli story on that note. But the tremendous drive which made him the most important tort lawyer carried with it the seeds of controversy. Mel always had an overriding penchant for publicity, no matter whether it was good or bad. Newspaper and television reporters flocked around him because he always gave them much more sensational statements than other lawyers would dare to utter. To fit in with his flamboyant image, he bought an old building on Montgomery Street in 1959. It had been a saloon during the San Francisco Gold Rush, and in the house next door, Bret Harte had written "The Luck of Roaring Camp." Belli had his building restored to the decor of the Barbary Coast in the nineteenth century. His personal office is on the ground floor, visible to tourists and pedestrians on the street. It features a huge fireplace, mahogany bookshelves from floor to ceiling, a solid mahogany bar across the width of the room, and high, white ceilings trimmed with gold and interspersed with golden cherubs and the Belli coat of arms. The Belli Building has become a regular stop on the Gray Line tour of San Francisco. In the front window, on display to anyone passing by, is a photograph of seven Mexican bandits, complete with rifles and cartridge belts, right out of the annals of Pancho Villa. The inscription under this photograph which Belli had printed in old-English lettering reads, "Adjusters of the Holy Grail Insurance Company." He also installed a roof flagpole on which he runs up the Jolly Roger whenever he wins a case. It was this buccaneer image which Belli relished for himself that became an embarrassment to the more conventional tort lawyers.

The Belli Seminars got wilder as the publicity increased. At one of them, Mel was scheduled to put on a demonstration of a physical examination. This is an important matter to tort lawyers, since all plaintiffs must submit to physical examinations by doctors chosen by the defendants, and the plaintiff's lawyer is normally present when such an examination is conducted. As his model for the demonstration, Belli had chosen a local stripteaser, who appeared in the briefest of costumes. This was cheered at the time, but of course it made television and newspaper headlines, and as far as the media were concerned this was the high spot of the lawyers' convention. To tort lawyers who were trying to impress the public with the importance of their mission, this kind of clowning was a serious indignity, and it resulted in the discontinuance of NACCA's sponsorship of the Belli Seminar.

Mel then shifted the Belli Seminar to the annual American Bar Association convention. There he fell into disfavor when he presented a Professor Julian O'Brian of Harvard as a speaker on tax problems. Professor O'Brian turned out to be the notorious mobster Mickey Cohen —this time appearing without his dog. Neither the ABA nor Harvard were amused, and after that Belli had to put on his seminar independently.

Belli's worst moments came when he took on the defense of Jack Ruby, the man who was photographed on nationwide television while fatally shooting Lee Harvey Oswald, the assassin of President John F. Kennedy. As Mel put it:

> In 1963, I had reached a pinnacle in the law. Then, all of a sudden, I was plunged into a whirlpool of hatred from which I have never completely emerged. My crime was daring to defend Jack Ruby, killer of the man still officially designated as the assassin of President John F. Kennedy. In the public's mind, I might just as well have been defending Lee Harvey Oswald.

Mel feels that his judgment was vindicated by the subsequent appellate reversal of Ruby's conviction, but after the Ruby trial, Belli was no longer the knight that lawyers young and old sought to emulate.

Mel appeared on many television talk shows, and hosted one of his own in California for several years. In 1973, during an interview on the Merv Griffin show, Mel made disparaging remarks about a federal judge who had set aside a verdict that he had won in a malpractice action in the U.S. District Court for the District of Columbia. His public attack on the judge earned him a rebuke by the entire panel of judges of the District of Columbia federal court, including that of Chief Judge John J. Sirica.

These and other excesses, all linked to publicity, caused many of Mel's old friends and followers to abandon him. I think that most of them still had a soft spot in their hearts for Mel, and many secretly envied this trial lawyer who had a drunken parrot named John Silver, who participated in orgies with his good friend Errol Flynn, and had his own segment on *Sixty Minutes*. But plaintiff's tort lawyers were still the underdogs, and few of them had the time or inclination to defend Belli's public hijinks. Besides, Belli's revolution created enough momentum to carry on without him as the central figure.

The Grand Canyon litigation started a long and enjoyable relationship between Mel and our firm. We never knew what kind of a case he would involve us in next, because his worldwide reputation and publicity often brought him calls from lawyers and clients who had claims to be litigated in New York. Once it was the case of Ferdinand Waldo (Fred) Demara, who wanted to halt the filming of his life story because he claimed that he had been bilked into signing away his rights. The only problem with the case was that it turned on a question of credibility, and our only witness was Fred Demara, who called himself the "world's greatest imposter." He had served as a Trappist monk, as assistant warden of a Texas prison, as a surgeon in the Canadian Navy, and as a lecturer to brain surgeons, despite his lack of all recognized qualifications for any of these jobs. With Mel's help, we managed to work out a settlement for Fred, who later became an investigator in Mel's San Francisco office. Another time it was the wrongful death case of the late John S. Knight, publisher of Knight newspapers—an unlikely case for Belli to be retained in, since he had successfully sued Knight and his *Miami Herald* for libel.

Mel Belli was and is important to every person who has suffered a serious injury since the 1950s. Without the life work of this one man, millions of injured persons would have much smaller chances of recovering adequate compensation. And many lawyers would still be struggling to eke out a living from unrewarding law practices shackled by nineteenth-century concepts designed to protect property rights.

*   *   *

Now let's look at another case that arose about the same time as
Grand Canyon. It also involved a collision of airplanes, but fortunately
nobody was killed. A man was seriously injured, and so we will be
looking at the most common of tort cases: the negligence action for
personal injuries. And another giant of tort practice comes into this
story—Perry Nichols of Florida.

Chapter 4

PERSONAL INJURIES

Collision at Page Field

A few months before the 1956 Grand Canyon collision, two smaller aircraft collided on the ground at Page Field, the municipal airport of Fort Myers, Florida. The accident did not make headlines around the world as had Grand Canyon, but the case that grew out of it made a more lasting impact on American tort law than all of the Grand Canyon litigation.

On December 8, 1955, at 9:15 A.M. a twin-engine executive Beechcraft model 18 came in for a landing at Page Field. As the eight-passenger Beechcraft touched down and rolled on the landing runway, it was struck from the side by a Stearman (a World War II surplus training aircraft) being operated by a cropduster. The cropduster was attempting to take off at the time he struck the Beechcraft. There was no control tower at Page Field, but the Beechcraft, as the landing aircraft, clearly had the right of way under the air traffic rules, since the plane seeking to take off can always wait a few seconds. Also, the cropduster had started his takeoff from the intersection of two runways, instead of taxiing to the takeoff end of the runway, as required by a normal takeoff pattern. The collision occurred right at the intersection, which was about halfway down the Beechcraft's landing runway.

There were several passengers aboard the Beechcraft, but only one was injured: a carpenter who had flown from Miami to Fort Myers to estimate construction costs for a land developer, the man who owned the Beechcraft. This unfortunate carpenter had been sitting at the very spot where the cropduster's propeller penetrated the Beechcraft cabin. His right arm was struck by the propeller and nearly severed. Thirteen operations saved the arm, but it was practically useless to him in his trade.

I was retained by the carpenter to determine whether he had any chance of recovering damages. This was an open-and-shut case against the cropduster, since he had no right to start a takeoff from the runway intersection and, in any case, had to yield the right of way to the landing Beechcraft. But like most cropdusters of that day, he had no liability insurance and very little in the way of tangible assets. If we were to recover any money for the injured carpenter, it would have to come from the owner of the Beechcraft, who was both solvent and well insured. Thus we faced one of the classic struggles of the tort lawyer: the need to prove liability of a solvent defendant when another impecunious defendant was principally at fault. If this concept strikes you as unfair, consider three points: (1) if the solvent defendant is not made to pay, you and the other taxpayers will ultimately pay the bills; (2) the solvent defendant pays only in situations where his negligence is a cause of the accident; (3) one of the main purposes of tort law is to deter wrongdoing, and a money judgment is a deterrent only to solvent defendants.

Choosing a Florida Law Firm

Since all the parties were Florida residents, the carpenter's lawsuit had to be brought in the Florida state courts. This meant that I had to choose a Florida law firm to try the case. While there were several excellent Florida plaintiff's firms—particularly in the Miami area, where the carpenter and Beechcraft owner lived—there was, in my mind, only one choice for this case: the Perry Nichols firm.

Perry Nichols came closer than anyone else to building the all-star team of tort lawyers; in fact, he actually had one going for more than 10 years. Perry is a tall, husky former football player from Texas who looks like Fred MacMurray and talks like Lyndon Johnson, with an added touch of cornpone. But there was no cornpone in his approach to building a law firm. It was all science, business management, and professional skill. When Perry graduated from Florida's Stetson Law School in 1937, he first worked as an insurance adjuster and then took a job with Charlie Moorhead, a Miami attorney who defended tort claims for insurance companies. Perry learned tort practice from the defense side and at a time when Florida was a typical low-verdict state —a place where most of the good trial lawyers represented railroads or insurance companies, where the plaintiffs in tort cases were the underdogs, and the lawyers who represented them were not part of the establishment. Perry saw this situation as an opportunity to create a new kind of law firm which would use what he had observed in defense practice to put the plaintiffs on an equal footing with their adversaries. He launched this ambitious project in 1943.

Perry knew that he would have to overcome the defendants' clout in many areas—the courts, the legislature, the bar associations, and public relations. He became a lobbyist for the Hialeah racetrack, which put him in touch with those who controlled legislative power. As his first partner, he took on Billy Gaither, another trial lawyer trained on the defense side and also a skillful political campaign manager and fund raiser. Gaither helped to make political campaigns successful for long-time U.S. Senator George Smathers and Florida governor LeRoy Collins, among others. Nichols and Gaither were largely responsible for passage of an amendment to the Florida constitution that requires one circuit court (trial level) judge for each population unit of 50,000 people. This resulted in a flood of new judicial appointments to be made by the governor. Perry Nichols became a member of the Florida Judicial Council, and he and Billy Gaither were consulted on judicial appointments, along with other Florida lawyers. Nichols and Gaither also helped to gain passage of legislation raising judges' salaries from their low levels of the 1940s, to make the new judgeships attractive to successful lawyers. In addition, Perry and Billy built political bases within their state and local bar associations, which were often consulted on the qualifications of prospective judges and the need for legislation revising the common law. Perry was ultimately elected president of the Dade County Bar Association.

Having set the public stage for a revolution in Florida tort practice by remaking the trial court benches through his own political clout, Perry then turned to the internal structure of his own law firm. Perry recruited another leading defense lawyer, Clint Green, as the third member of the firm. By 1950, the firm of Nichols Gaither & Green had become the leading plaintiff's tort lawyers in Florida, and their practice was growing faster than any other in the state. Along with all the people of Florida, Perry's firm benefitted from the requirement of one trial judge for every 50,000 people. It kept court calendars up to date, so that lawyers could try or settle most of their cases within a year from the date of accident. This helped the lawyers' cash flow, and it also created the need for more lawyers, since new cases had to be processed quickly. For his own firm, Perry reached into the defense bar again for reinforcements: Walter Beckham and Bill Frates from prominent Miami defense firms in 1950, with the firm's name changing to Nichols Gaither Green Frates & Beckham; then Bill Colson from the firm that defended the Miami Transit Company; then two young assistant state attorneys general, Murray Sams and J. B. Spence; then Larry Hastings, a young doctor-lawyer who had been employed by the U.S. Public Health Service.

By 1952 the firm had outgrown its quarters in Miami's Shoreland

Arcade Building. Perry sighted in on the Pan American Bank Building, which was then under construction in downtown Miami. He wanted a brand-new building, so that he could take an entire floor and design it from scratch to fit his own concept of the modern tort firm. This he did, and when the Nichols firm moved into the Pan American Bank Building in 1952, they had a law office that was unique in all the world. The space was designed to reflect the structure of the firm, which had been organized into operating divisions. Each division consisted of a partner trial lawyer, an associate lawyer who worked with the same partner regularly, a full-time investigator who worked only for that division, and one or two secretaries. Each division kept its own files and functioned almost as an independent law firm, except that some important services were performed centrally for all divisions. There was a central photography department, with two full-time professional photographers and their own developing laboratory. There was the medical department under doctor-lawyer Larry Hastings, complete with a uniformed nurse, and equipped to give clients thorough physical examinations to determine the extent of injuries. There was a legal and appellate division headed by Sam Daniels, a brilliant legal scholar who had been clerk to U.S. Supreme Court Justice Hugo Black. Sam did most of the heavy legal research and writing for trial memoranda, appellate briefs, and in-house consultation on legal problems.

In addition to his genius for organization, Perry Nichols was one of the first to use demonstrative evidence in tort cases. He was one of the first plaintiff's lawyers in the south to have an office skeleton, parts of which he would take to court to educate jurors and dramatize injuries. He used aerial photographs, blowups, models—anything that would increase the jurors' knowledge and understanding. Mel Belli featured Perry on his seminars and in his writings as a prime example of the modern tort lawyer using up-to-date techniques and achieving adequate awards. In Mel's famous 1951 California Law Review article "The Adequate Award," he cited a $260,000 personal injury verdict obtained by Perry Nichols as the largest rendered anywhere in the world up to that time.

By the mid-1950s Perry Nichols was known throughout the nation as a powerhouse in the Florida courts and a leading innovator. But I did not choose him on reputation alone, for I had worked with him once before and could look back to the results. The earlier case involved the crash of a photographic airplane in the Dominican Republic. The airplane was operated by Compania Dominicana de Aviacion (CDA), an airline owned by General Rafael Trujillo, the brutal Dominican dictator. The plane was being used to film a television program designed to publicize a Dominican shipyard that was also owned largely by General Trujillo. A young American cameraman from New York was being flown over the shipyard to photograph it, when the airplane crashed and the cameraman was killed.

The cameraman's family retained Moe Levine, one of New York's leading negligence trial lawyers who was a colorful character, given to smoking huge Cuban cigars. Moe was a very warmhearted man who had a deep understanding of human nature. He was noted for his masterful summations in accident cases; some have been reproduced on tape and studied by tort lawyers throughout the country. I had handled some aviation cases for Moe in the past, and he decided to turn the Dominican case over to me.

I discovered that CDA's occasional cargo flights between Ciudad Trujillo and Miami International Airport were its only operations in the U.S. This meant that suit would have to be brought in Florida, since I was neither brave nor foolish enough to challenge the dictator in his own courts. In fact, filing suit against Trujillo even in Florida was not to be undertaken lightly, since we would have to go to the Dominican Republic for investigation and discovery. I decided to bring in a suitable counterforce: the Nichols firm.

One of my first tasks was to research the Dominican Republic wrongful death law, since at that time all of our courts automatically applied *lex loci delicti* (the law of the place of the wrong) in tort cases. This was an unhappy situation for us. Trujillo had such a tight grip, he could have forced his legislature to pass any wrongful death law he desired—even a retroactive one prohibiting suits against CDA, maybe including jail sentences for the plaintiffs' lawyers, just for good measure. It was difficult to find any court decisions construing the Dominican wrongful death law, so instead, I turned to the search for an expert on Dominican law. I found the ideal man on the faculty of Columbia Law School: Professor Jesus Galindez, a Dominican lawyer who had been legal advisor to Trujillo. We agreed to meet at my office, which then occupied one room at 545 Fifth Avenue. He was a tall, thin, bald-headed man who appeared to be in his late forties and spoke English well, with a slight Spanish accent. He told me that the Dominican wrongful death law was very favorable to plaintiffs, at least on paper, since it was based upon the Napoleonic Code, which permitted awards of compensatory and "moral" damages (for grief and mental anguish) suffered by surviving relatives. In practice, little or no money damages were awarded in Dominican courts, especially against CDA and other businesses in which General Trujillo had an interest. However, the Florida courts would apply the *wording* of the Dominican law, and would leave the measure of damages to Florida jurors, so that Trujillo's nullification of the law in his own courts would have no effect on our right to damages in Florida.

Since foreign law is a question of fact that must be proved by the party seeking to recover under it, we needed an affidavit from Professor Galindez attesting that the Dominican law gave us the right to recover damages, and eventually we would need him to testify on this point at the Florida trial. I had been told that he was a refugee from Trujillo's persecution, and I hesitated to ask him to make his collaboration with us public. But there was no choice, since we could not find another expert of equal qualifications, and it was essential that our expert supply an affidavit and testify in court. I was delighted when he readily agreed to sign the affidavit and to testify. He explained that he had nothing to lose because he was already *persona non grata* with the Trujillo regime.

Three days later I read in the New York newspapers that Professor Jesus Galindez was missing and apparently had been kidnapped while entering the subway near Columbia University. The newspapers recounted his career as a foe of Trujillo and his connection with exiled anti-Trujillo forces. They speculated that he had been abducted by agents of Trujillo, and that he was not likely to be seen alive again.

CDA was insured by the American International Group (AIG) whose offices are in New York. Their New York-based general counsel, Frank Sterritte, had telephoned me after we filed suit in Miami, to see if the case could be settled. Frank was an aggressive insurance lawyer who resembled Bennett Cerf in appearance, but he was not nearly as affable, especially in dealing with accident claims. He told me that he did not see any fault on the part of CDA; that we would never be able to get anyone in the Dominican Republic to testify to any negligence on the part of Trujillo's airline; and that we would probably not even be able to find an expert lawyer qualified to give an opinion on Dominican law. Despite all these obstacles, out of the goodness of his heart, he was willing to settle the case for its true value: the nuisance and expense of hiring a Miami law firm to defend the case, which he calculated at "a few thousand dollars." I told him that we were not interested in that kind of a settlement, since we were confident that we could win the case in Miami, and as for an expert lawyer, I had landed Professor Jesus Galindez that very day.

When I learned of Galindez's disappearance, I telephoned Sterritte and said, "Frank, I know that you have a reputation for being a hard fighter, and you told me that you were going to defend this case to the hilt. I'm used to pretty stiff opposition, but I've never had an opposing lawyer kidnap my expert witness before!" Frank forgot himself for a moment and laughed at my joke, but then he was back at me again, painting the plaintiff's position as more desperate than ever. Finally I told him that a little setback like a kidnapped expert witness was not going to hold us up for long, because we had a weapon that was as strong in the Florida courts as Trujillo was in his home town: the Nichols firm. Frank laughed again, this time his defense lawyer's laugh, and asked, "Who the hell are they?" I suggested that he check with the Miami lawyers whom he had hired to defend the case; they would be able to tell him who Perry Nichols was.

A few weeks after that telephone conversation, the case was settled for an amount that was very satisfactory to the cameraman's family. Several years later, Frank Sterritte called us in to work with him in representing the widow of an executive of his company who had been killed in a plane crash, and thus Frank became our colleague. He told me then that he had taken my advice about checking out the Nichols firm with his Miami counsel, and the report he received had shaken him up so much that he decided right then to depart from his "no pay" attitude and settle the case as quickly as he could.

The story did not end happily for Professor Galindez. He was never seen again after his disappearance. Investigations by the New York police, the FBI, and a Congressional committee turned up evidence that Galindez had been kidnapped and had presumably either been flown to the Dominican Republic for execution or been thrown into the boiler of a Dominican ship in New York harbor.

Looking back on that experience, I felt if the Nichols firm could make Frank Sterritte and General Trujillo capitulate merely by appearing for the plaintiff, they had to be my choice for the Page Field collision case. But this time there was no capitulation. The Beechcraft's insurers and their attorneys were convinced that the collision was entirely the fault of the cropduster, and they weren't about to pay out any money on a case in which their pilot had made a perfect landing, only to be struck by a reckless cropduster who was taking off from the middle of the runway, where the Beechcraft pilot had no chance to see him.

Preparing for Trial

Although the Nichols firm was perfectly capable of handling the case alone, it was agreed that I would help wherever I could, since I had been brought in as an aviation specialist. I undertook the initial investigation and continued to collaborate with Clint Green and Walter Beckham, the two Nichols partners to whom the case had been assigned.

As we started to map out our strategy, we concentrated on one provision of tort law that was helpful to us. Even if the cropduster was 99 percent to blame, the injured passenger whom we represented could recover his full damages against the owner of the Beechcraft if we could prove that *some* negligence of the Beechcraft pilot, however slight, had contributed to causing the accident. I found some records in the Civil

Aeronautics Administration (CAA) accident investigation files in Washington to indicate that both pilots were at fault. Within two hours after the accident, J. T. Watson, a CAA investigator, had questioned the Beechcraft pilot about his approach pattern. According to Watson's report in the CAA files, the Beechcraft pilot had replied that he had made a fairly straight approach to the field, turning only slightly to line up with the landing runway before starting his final descent. The air traffic rules required the Beechcraft pilot to fly parallel to the landing runway in the opposite direction from the landing heading (known as the "downwind leg"); then to turn perpendicular to the landing runway (known as the "base leg"); and then turn to the landing heading, maintaining an altitude of at least 500 feet during all these turns before starting the descent from 500 feet for landing. This U-shaped pattern serves two purposes: it enables the pilot of the landing aircraft to fly close to the landing runway for some time so that he can observe other aircraft on the field, and it enables other aircraft on the field (such as the Stearman cropduster) to notice that a landing will soon be made.

CAA investigator Watson was very meticulous in his questioning of the Beechcraft pilot. Watson drew a diagram which illustrated the Beechcraft pilot's description of his approach pattern, and asked him to verify that it was accurate. The pilot made a slight correction, but described only a straight-in approach to the landing runway, without the downwind and base-leg portions of the U-pattern. Such an approach would have deprived the cropduster pilot of the opportunity of observing the Beechcraft in the air because the straight-in approach would put the Beechcraft too low to be seen over the hangars that obscured the cropduster's view of the final approach path. It would also have made it impossible for the Beechcraft pilot to see the cropduster taxiing from the gas pump to the runway intersection from which he started his takeoff. According to Watson's report of what the Beechcraft pilot had said two hours after the accident, it was a case of concurrent negligence—violations of traffic rules by *both* pilots—and that would make both defendants liable to our client, provided we could convince the jury. If the cropduster had no money, the entire judgment could be collected from the Beechcraft owner, whose insurance company would have to pay it.

During the discovery phase of the case, our concurrent-negligence theory started to slip away. On his deposition, the Beechcraft pilot swore that he had completed the entire traffic pattern at the prescribed altitude, so that the cropduster pilot could have seen him if he had been looking. The Beechcraft owner produced half a dozen more witnesses who backed up the pilot's claim that he had flown the entire traffic pattern. Worst of all, there was a statement signed by our own client, the injured carpenter, that also supported the pilot's claim of a complete traffic pattern. Our client had signed this statement at the request of the Beechcraft owner's lawyer before consulting a lawyer of his own. He did not realize that it might hurt his chances of recovering damages. He thought that he was just doing a favor for the pilot, "keeping the CAA off his back."

At that point, we had no eye-witness evidence that the Beechcraft pilot did not fly a proper pattern, since all the witnesses who observed the approach said it was proper. I suggested to Clint Green, who was concentrating on the liability phase of the case, that we call CAA investigator Watson as a witness and establish through him that the Beechcraft pilot had admitted his failure to fly the required pattern. This admission against the interest of the Beechcraft owner would be enough evidence to put the issue of concurrent negligence to the jury. Somehow we had to make the admission work, because it was all that we had.

Clint Green informed me that under Florida law, accident investigation reports are confidential and investigating officers cannot testify about any statements made to them by parties to the accident. There was also a provision of the Civil Aeronautics Act that prohibited the use of any federal aviation accident investigation report in civil litigation. However, I knew from experience that the CAA interpreted that restriction to apply only to opinions or conclusions about the cause of an accident. The CAA did not want its investigators to be put in the position of helping one side or the other to win civil cases by giving their opinions on the causes of accidents, but they usually would permit their investigators to testify about *facts* learned during investigations. Often it was hard to fix the line between fact and opinion, but I felt that the CAA would consider it a fact that the Beechcraft pilot had told Watson that he had made a straight-in approach. We were not asking Watson whether it was his opinion that the Beechcraft had actually made a straight-in approach; we were only asking him to testify that the Beechcraft pilot had described a straight-in approach when questioned two hours after the accident.

The Trial Begins

The case came on for trial in the Circuit Court for Dade County at Miami in January of 1958, a little more than two years after the accident. With Florida's fast-moving calendars it could have been tried sooner, but our client had to go through 13 operations on his injured right arm, and Walter Beckham (who was presenting the damage phase) wanted to know the final extent of damage to the arm before trying the case, since we could not come back for a second trial if the damages were underestimated the first time. It was the most challenging kind of case a tort lawyer can face, because the 43-year-old client's entire future was at stake. His doctors told us that he could never work as a carpenter again, and he lacked training for any other kind of work. In the past he had been self-sufficient and the supporter of his family; now his principal asset was the lawsuit.

In such cases the tort lawyer's burden is greatest when a substantial settlement offer is made before trial. Suppose that the Beechcraft's insurers had offered $40,000 or $50,000 to settle the case. That would not replace our client's lost future wages, but it would help some, and would be a lot better than nothing. With the slim evidence we had against the Beechcraft pilot, would we have dared to advise the plaintiff to reject such a settlement offer, knowing that the jury might well hold the uninsured cropduster solely to blame? Indeed, there was a chance that the CAA would order Watson not to testify, or that the judge would exclude his testimony about the traffic pattern. If that happened, the case against the Beechcraft owner might be dismissed since there was no other evidence of a straight-in approach. This would leave us with a large but uncollectible judgment against the cropduster. Fortunately, we were not put in this position. The Beechcraft insurers thought so little of our chances of winning against them that they decided not to offer anything but "nuisance value" to settle the case. We then got ready for trial knowing that it was all or nothing, depending on the jury. That is less of a burden than agonizing all through the trial about a substantial settlement offer.

William Clinton Green was then, at 50, the oldest and most experienced trial lawyer in the Nichols firm. He was a short, trim man with wavy white hair, a deep tan, and the look of a distinguished banker. He had a soft but clear voice and spoke in a drawl that he could control, depending on the audience. As he opened the trial, he had his mind firmly fixed on the principal problem of the case. We were suing the Beechcraft owner and the cropduster, and he had to convince the jury that they should find both of them liable. He could not tell them that the cropduster was uninsured—he was not allowed to refer to either defendant's financial condition. That tightrope he would have to walk all through the trial. In his opening speech to the all-male jury of six, he described the evidence that would be presented against both pilots: the improper approach pattern flown by the Beechcraft pilot, and the improper takeoff by the cropduster. He told the jurors:

> Our contention is that *both* of these pilots were in error.
> They didn't intend to hurt anybody, but they were in error. It
> took the doings of *both* of them to bring this about. In other

words, if either one of them could have caused the accident separately, but if one was ten percent to blame, and the other was
ninety percent to blame, they are *both* held responsible under the
law, because you men don't have to figure out those percentages.
The law says they are both liable. It is the same as an auto accident. If you are driving your car too fast and another fellow runs
the stop sign, you are *both* to blame.

Clint Green then proceeded to keep faith with the jury by presenting
evidence to support those contentions. He and Walter had organized the
trial evidence beautifully. There were 79 exhibits for the plaintiff, including many blowups of aerial photographs of the airport and traffic
pattern area, which were placed in evidence through the testimony of the
photographer. Every time a witness made a statement about the position
of either aircraft, Clint asked the witness to mark the position on one
of his charts or photos, so that the jury could grasp the significance of
the testimony.

The Key Witness

The trial came to a climax on the second morning, when Clint called
CAA investigator J. T. Watson as a witness for the plaintiff. Clint had
arranged for a subpoena to be served on Watson at his office in St.
Petersburg, requiring him to testify at the trial and to bring his investigation file with him. I had helped Clint to prepare a memorandum of law
supporting our position that Watson could testify to what the Beechcraft pilot had told him, without violating the federal statute restricting the use of accident reports. As Clint zeroed in and asked Watson
what the pilot had told him just two hours after the accident, the
Beechcraft owner's lawyer objected. The jurors were sent out of the
courtroom as the lawyers argued before the judge. The defense lawyers
contended that Watson's diagram and his version of the pilot's statement were part of a federal aviation accident report, no part of which
could be used in civil litigation according to the federal statute. Clint
argued that the statute prohibited only opinion testimony, and that he
was not going to ask Watson his opinion of anything. Clint submitted
citations of five cases decided in the 1950s, in which government aviation accident investigators had been permitted to give factual testimony. There was no objection from Watson or any other CAA official
to the giving of this testimony under subpoena. Judge John W. Prunty
finally ruled:

It will be the ruling of the Court that the objection to the last question will be overruled. The witness may be permitted to answer that question, or any other questions concerning statements that were made to him personally from witnesses in the course of his investigation.

The jurors were then brought back into the courtroom, and Clint resumed his questioning of Watson, who testified that he interviewed the Beechcraft pilot within two hours of the crash and drew a diagram of the approach pattern that the pilot had described. The diagram was then received in evidence as Plaintiff's Exhibit No. 38. It told the whole story Clint wanted to get across to the jury: that the straight-in landing approach portrayed in Watson's diagram made it impossible for the Beechcraft pilot either to see the cropduster moving toward takeoff or to be seen by the cropduster. It was truly a picture worth a thousand words, a graphic demonstration of complete disregard for the routines prescribed in order to prevent collisions at airports without traffic control towers. To pin it down, Clint asked Watson a final question.

Q. by Mr. GREEN: Now, he never did at any time describe to you a complete traffic pattern on the approach to this runway, did he?   A: No, he did not.

The trial went on through the testimony of 15 more witnesses, including both pilots and five eyewitnesses who had been aboard the Beechcraft or awaiting its arrival at the airport. These eyewitnesses, all of whom had business or family connections with the Beechcraft owner, supported the Beechcraft pilot's claim that he flew the proper traffic pattern. The Beechcraft pilot testified that CAA investigator Watson had misunderstood his description of the traffic pattern, which he had given while still under the immediate stress of the collision. As the trial neared its end, the lawyers for the Beechcraft's insurers were still confident of victory, for they did not increase their settlement offer beyond "nuisance value."

In his cross-examination of the Beechcraft pilot, Clint Green established that he had flown into Page Field at least 15 times before the accident, and was aware that it was used regularly by cropdusters. Having once been a Florida cropduster, I advised Clint that all commercial pilots flying into airports like Page Field would know that cropdusters were notorious for taking off in a hurry from almost anywhere on the field, since they had just a few hours in the morning to spread their dust while the wind was calm and there was enough dew on the plants to make the dust stick. Every minute on the ground during morning hours would cost the cropdusters money, and they would do everything possible to take off quickly. Thus, the action of this cropduster in moving quickly from the loading area to the nearest runway intersection for an immediate takeoff would not be a surprise to commercial pilots using Page Field. It was another strong reason for carefully adhering to the prescribed traffic pattern, instead of coming straight in and making it impossible to see and be seen.

In those days cropdusting was performed mostly by small operators who used World War II surplus equipment such as the Stearman, a single-engine biplane trainer that looked like a World War I fighter plane. I have always been an antique airplane buff, and the Stearman was one of my favorites, since I had flown it both in military service and as a cropduster. Clint Green had commissioned models of the Beechcraft and the Stearman for the trial, and he took the Stearman model in his hands as he questioned the Beechcraft pilot:

> Q: And you knew that their principal business in flying was cropdusting, didn't you?   A: Yes, that company.
> Q: And they had three of these old crates like this?   A: Yes.

As a Stearman lover, I thought that Clint had gone too far in describing them as "old crates," but it was part of his strategy for letting the jury know that our client would not be able to collect any damages from a company whose main assets were three (now two) old Stearmans.

Damages and Final Arguments

Walter Beckham took over for presentation of damages, calling as witnesses three doctors and two carpenters (one a union official) who testified to the plaintiff's inability to continue his career and the financial losses that his disability would cause him in future years. Walter was then 37, a tall, slender man who projected integrity and sincerity to an unusual degree. Somehow he could manage to be quiet spoken and forceful at the same time. It would be easy to imagine him speaking from the pulpit instead of the counsel table. His appearance and speech, including his Southern drawl, reminds one of Ramsey Clark. In this case, the defense lawyers paid Walter the supreme compliment: they did not call a single witness to challenge his damage proof. They knew that they would only make matters worse by subjecting their own doctors and carpenters to Walter's cross-examination.

It was time for final argument. In Florida, the plaintiff makes the first argument, followed by the defendants, and then the plaintiff is allowed the final word in rebuttal. (In some other states, such as New York, the defendant makes his argument first, and then the plaintiff makes his entire argument at the end of the case.) Clint and Walter asked for two hours total argument time, but Judge Prunty limited them to a total of one hour. That was a short time in which to summarize the testimony of 18 witnesses, the contents of 79 exhibits, and damage calculations that covered 30 years of the plaintiff's life. Fortunately, Clint and Walter had ordered daily copy from the court stenographer, and they were able to organize their final arguments so that they reflected exactly what the jury had seen and heard during the trial.

Clint Green took the opening argument on liability, and in his clear, methodical way he brought the case into sharp focus for the jurors. He reminded them that both pilots had been in a hurry: the Beechcraft's takeoff had been delayed by fog, so its owner was late for an appointment in Fort Myers; and the cropduster had lots of dust to put out while the morning dew was still on the ground. He told the jurors:

> I would say that the thing that set this up on both parts was haste. They got a little too much behind schedule and were hurrying a little too fast to be as careful as they should have been.

Clint went on to explain the legal responsibilities that followed from the hasty actions of both pilots. Then he tied them together in a neat package for the jury, so that they would not be tempted to bring in a verdict against the cropduster alone:

> We sued both of the parties involved in this case, as we told you at the outset, because we felt they were both responsible. We did some investigation, of course, before we sued them. You see the results in Court today of that investigation.
>
> Under the law we can sue both of them. We don't have to prove that they were equally guilty. The law says that both are held liable; a verdict is entered against all of the parties, and then the adjustment of that comes after your decision comes in.
>
> I have tried to analyze this case, not to determine the degree of guilt, but to determine the guilt of *both* pilots. As I see it, it took both of them to make this thing possible. *If either one of them had done what he should have done,* the accident wouldn't have happened.

He then contrasted the Beechcraft and the cropduster from the standpoint of duty to the plaintiff:

> The Beechcraft pilot was carrying a human cargo. Carrying passengers, he has got to maneuver the ship so as not to injure them.
>
> Now, they have a human cargo there and a fast ship. Certainly, compared to the duster it is a fast ship—a twin-engine monoplane with a cruising speed of 165 miles an hour—and he is a full-time pilot. So, I ask you to keep in mind these circumstances: human cargo, a fast ship, a full-time pilot, and his duty to the passenger.

He stressed the full-time professionalism of the Beechcraft pilot because the cropduster pilot was a part-time flier whose regular job was sales clerk in a hardware store. Then he reviewed the specific charges of negligence by the professional pilot in disregarding the required approach pattern:

> He took a shortcut. He didn't make any pattern. You heard the CAA investigator, the first man on the witness stand, tell you what the Beechcraft pilot told him. He came *straight in* from Alva, made a slight correction, and landed on Runway 22.
>
> Why do you circle the field? *To see and be seen,* to declare your intention to land—to show that you are not just some fellow looking around or taking pictures or touristing or something like that.
>
> So the fact is that he used the blind runway and he should have used the circular pattern, but what actually happened is that he violated the whole landing pattern by making a straight-in approach.

Back to his balancing act, Clint reminded the jurors that he was delivering both defendants to them in one package for judgment:

> Now, let's see what the cropduster did—and you know, it matches out. When I got this accident figured out, I was amazed to see that it was just tit for tat. Every time you put something in the scale against one defendant, you stick something in the scale against the other.
>
> This is not a complicated case. The cropduster didn't taxi to the end of the runway. Why *should* he make a taxi pattern? To *see*—to get out where he can see other aircraft—and to declare his intention to take off.
>
> One violated the landing pattern, and one violated the takeoff pattern. One came in too low, and the other took off too short. That is the case, gentlemen.
>
> It is an amazing thing, but every time you hurl a charge against one, you find that you have a countercharge against the other. I have never seen a case where the fault was so evenly balanced. Even if the law required us to prove equal fault, we have proven it.

Complicated fact situations and conflicting testimony usually favor the defendant, since the plaintiff has the burden of proving his allegations

of negligence without forcing the jury to indulge in speculation or conjecture. Every defendant is entitled to such a jury instruction in a
tort case, and no defendant is required to prove his freedom from
fault. During the trial Clint had to deal with many complicated fact
issues arising from the inherent complexity and unfamiliar terminology
of aviation. But in his summation, Clint had simplified the liability
issues and had tried to seal off every possible escape route by establishing a balancing rhythm. Even though the wild cropduster had been
negligent, the plaintiff would not have been injured if the Beechcraft
business pilot had not also been negligent at the very same time and
place.

Now it was Walter Beckham's turn to open on damages. He reviewed the testimony of the plaintiff and his three physicians relating
to injuries and disability, and he reminded the jurors that the only way
they could do justice in this case was to award whatever damages the
law allows for those injuries:

> Now, if we could come here, gentlemen, and ask for ab-
> stract justice, if we could ask you for complete justice between
> these parties, we would not be here asking you for money. We
> would be asking you to put this man back where he was before
> this accident, when he had a good right arm, when he was asking
> no help or favors from anybody, when he was supporting himself
> in the way that all of us support ourselves—by the sweat of our
> own brow—and that is what this man had done.
>
> But we can't do that. We don't have it within our power,
> nor do you gentlemen have it within your power, to give back
> the physical ability that he has lost; and in place of that, the law
> says that he is entitled to be compensated.

Walter then produced a large white cardboard chart, about two and
one-half feet wide and three feet high, on which he had written out in
heavy black ink all the details of the damages claimed. It was the
Belli and Nichols blackboard teaching technique carried out to its most
effective development: a scoreboard that the jurors could check against
their own recollections of the trial evidence. Walter had divided the
chart into two sections: damages suffered up to the date of the trial,
and future damages, all of which would have to be fixed by this one
jury if they found for the plaintiff. The chart was designed to dovetail
with Walter's review of the damage evidence. It looked like this:

1. DAMAGES TO DATE OF TRIAL

Medical Expense
[Here Walter listed 15 separate items, including four hospital bills, seven
doctor's bills, two nurse's bills, and costs of drugs and medicine.]

Total medical expenses: . . . . $ 9,244

Pain and Suffering
12/8/55–1/30/58, 783 days
at $15 per day   11,745

Physical Disability and Inability
to Lead a Normal Life
12/8/55–1/30/58, 783 days
at $5 per day   3,915

Loss of Earnings
111 weeks at $125   13,875
                                                   ——————

        Total Damages to Date: $ 38,779

2. FUTURE DAMAGES

                        10,220 days   28 years
Medical Expense   500

Pain and Suffering
10,220 days at $1 per day   10,220

Physical Disability and Inability
to Lead a Normal Life
10,220 days at $3 per day   30,660

Loss of Earning Capacity
To age 70 (27 years)   162,000
                                                  ———————
        Total Future Damages: $203,380
                                                           ————————
        Total of All Damages: $242,159
                                                           ————————

Pointing to the chart, Walter said to the jury:

> Now, I will ask you to listen to the Court's charge, and I
> think you will find that the Court will charge you that the plaintiff
> is entitled to be compensated for *every* item of damages which
> we have listed on this chart; that under the law of this state, if he
> is entitled to recover, he is entitled to recover for *each one* of
> these elements.

Thus the chart was not a gimmick but a graphic guide to the legal items
of damage that the jurors were sworn to consider and decide. On each
item in the chart, the jurors had before them the claims of the plaintiff,
based upon the evidence in the case as shown in the daily trial transcript, which Walter then reviewed for them. He went through each of
the medical bills and reminded the jury of the 13 operations needed to
repair nerve damage and save the plaintiff's arm, limited though its usefulness was. Then he went on to the second item on the chart: pain and
suffering. He recounted the bone grafts, skin grafts, and the excruciat-

ing pain of the injury and its long aftermath, all of which was supported by uncontradicted testimony. But how to translate pain and
suffering into money? Walter Beckham did it this way:

> Now, gentlemen, pain and suffering, that is an intangible
> unless *you* are suffering, and then it is the most tangible thing
> in the world.
>
> I don't know how to talk about pain and suffering except
> one day at a time, because that is the way we suffer. You can't
> say, "Well, I am sick of it. Give it to me all in one day and let
> me have it over with." That isn't the way you have pain.
>
> Pain, gentlemen, is something none of us like. We don't like
> to look at it. When we are in the presence of severe pain we
> cringe. The idea that most of us have of hell is a place of
> terrible pain. Pain is something repugnant to the human mind.
> It is hard for us to think about pain and to realize pain unless we
> are experiencing it, because we like to shut it out of our minds,
> it is so unpleasant.
>
> But when we experience pain, we experience it every day
> and every night, one day at a time and one night at a time.
>
> Do you think that twenty dollars a day for that period of
> time up to the present would be unreasonable? I don't. I don't,
> considering the thirteen operations and all that this man has gone
> through. Dr. Russell said he has been in that cast about three-
> fourths of the time, in one kind of a cast or another; forty days
> with his arm tied to his stomach.

Walter now returned to his chart, where he had written $11,475 for
the 783 days of pain and suffering from the date of the accident up to
the last day of the trial, at $15 per day:

> It is 783 days, and you can make it anything you want. If
> you think it is worth fifty dollars a day, that is your prerogative.
> If you think it is worth a nickel a day or whatever you think it is,
> *he is entitled to be compensated for it.*
>
> Gentlemen, at fifteen dollars a day, that would come to
> $11,745. Now, the only reason it comes to $11,745 is that it is
> 783 days. It is still just fifteen dollars a day. That is less than a
> thousand dollars for each one of the thirteen operations that he
> had. These were major surgical procedures.

The 75 percent disability that the plaintiff suffered to his right arm
was especially serious in this case because he was a carpenter, and
because a prior accident had left him with some disability in his left
hand. As Walter told the jury:

> Gentlemen, let me tell you one other thing in the law: that
> is that these defendants took the plaintiff as they found him
> when they hurt him. They didn't cause the prior injury to his
> left hand, but it is much more serious for a man who has a dis-
> ability in his left hand to lose the use of his right arm than if he

didn't have the left hand problem. You can take that into consideration, because they take him in the condition that they found him at the time that they hurt him.

We are not claiming any compensation for injury to his left hand. These defendants had nothing to do with that, but that *is* a factor that you gentlemen should take into consideration in evaluating the injury to his right arm.

The pre-existing left hand condition was important to the next item on Walter's chart: physical disability and inability to lead a normal life:

He is entitled to be compensated for his physical disability and inability to lead a normal life. Listen to what the Judge tells you about *personal inconvenience*. Gentlemen, there are twenty-four hours in a day. We work eight, we sleep eight. For what? Because under our form of government we have a right to the pursuit of happiness.

We believe in the pursuit of happiness, and we have over the years been able to reduce our workweek. We have eliminated sweatshops. We have eliminated a man having to work sixteen and eighteen hours a day, except in emergencies. Why? Because a man wants to be able to do the things that *he wants* to do, his pleasures, his recreations, being with his family, doing things around the house, in the other eight hours.

That is one-third of our time, gentlemen, that we like to spend doing what we want to do, and that is what we are talking about here: physical disability and inability to lead a normal life. Up to the present time that is 783 days. During that time he was three-fourths of the time in a cast, with absolutely no use of the right arm. He was forty days with the arm tied into him here [indicating stomach] in a flap.

He was in the hospital on eleven different occasions, confined much of that time in bed. Think of the helplessness, the bother of being in the hospital, the bother of not being able to go where you please and do what you please, and to be where you want to be and to use your arm and to do things around the house and to have pleasure in living.

He can't cut his own meat. He can't eat with his right hand. He can't write with his right hand. He can't shave with his right hand. He can't comb his hair. He can't get his right hand up to his head. That is the testimony. That is not what I am saying, gentlemen. That is what you heard from the witness stand and that is what we are talking about here.

Do you think five dollars a day is unreasonable for that? Well, if you do, you give him what you think he is entitled to. I think it is worth *ten* dollars a day, but assuming five dollars a day, that would be $3,915.

Then Walter got to the largest item of damages, loss of earnings:

Now, gentlemen, it doesn't seem like we make much money. When I go home and the first of the month comes

around and I see the bills, it doesn't seem like we are making
any progress except backwards; but when you sit down and
think about it and you consider how much money you make in a
week and you consider that over a period of time, it is amazing
how much money a man makes in his lifetime.

Right here [indicating chart] we are talking about lost
earnings only up to the present time. Now, the uncontradicted
testimony in this case is that he was making a hundred and
twenty-five dollars a week. There is no evidence to the contrary—none whatsoever.

He had a good job, and if he didn't continue in that job,
then Mr. Stewart, the business representative for the carpenter's
union, told you that he was a well-qualified journeyman carpenter
and all he had to do was come back and go to his union, and
they could place him in any one of a number of jobs at $3.05 an
hour. Mr. Stewart said he should do even better than that, because he was qualified to be a foreman and supervisor, and in
his opinion should average a hundred and twenty-five to a hundred and fifty dollars a week.

Take it at a hundred and twenty-five dollars a week, which
is what he was making, and he hasn't been able to work at all up
to the present time. He has *lost*—and this is money for food, for
clothing, for shelter, for everything that he needs to support
himself—he has *lost* a hundred and twenty-five dollars a week.
It has been a hundred and eleven weeks. Gentlemen, it is a little
over two years, and that is $13,875. That is money he has
actually lost out of his pocket that he would have been able to
make if he had been able to work.

Now, that totals $38,779 in damages, up to the present
time.

Walter moved on to the last half of his chart, where he had calculated future damages. He had put into evidence life expectancy tables
which showed that the plaintiff, at age 43, could expect to live another
28.8 years, to age 71. On the chart, Walter rounded that down to 28
years, which came to a total of 10,220 days. He explained that this was
the plaintiff's one day in court. He could not come back each year and
ask another jury to award him damages for what he had suffered in
the past. This jury, on this day, had to fix damages for his entire lifetime.

On future medical expenses, the surgeon testified that there was
only one more operation that might help the plaintiff, a tendon transplant which he planned to perform in a few months. The total cost of
that operation would be $500, and that is what Walter entered in his
chart for future medical expenses. On future pain and suffering,
Walter reviewed the medical testimony that indicated less pain than
in the past, but some soreness and discomfort in the damaged arm and
the parts of the body from which skin and bone were taken for grafts.
Walter said:

> Well, do you think that a couple of dollars a day for that
> would be unreasonable? Well, whatever you think is what you
> should give him. If you give him a dollar a day—if you just
> give him a dollar a day—that would be $10,220 [indicating chart]
> because he is going to be living through 10,220 days and nights.
> That is fifty cents a day and fifty cents a night.

On future physical disability and inability to lead a normal life, Walter
reviewed the testimony showing 75 percent disability of the right arm,
and again went through the list of basic functions that the plaintiff
would not be able to perform normally in the future. Again he stressed
the devastating impact of the right-arm injury to a man who already
had a disability in his left hand. Then he went back to his chart:

> Well, do you think that five dollars a day for loss of use
> of your right arm, or loss of 75 percent of it, would be unrea-
> sonable? I don't think that would be unreasonable. But if you
> gave him just three dollars a day, at three dollars a day it would
> be $30,660 [indicating chart] because it is 10,220 days.

Moving into the homestretch, Walter came to the largest of all items
of damage, the future loss of earning capacity from the end of the trial
to the end of the plaintiff's working life:

> Now what is going to happen to this man? Who is going to
> take care of him? This injury was not his fault—nobody says it
> was his fault. He wasn't asking anybody for any help, and if he
> hadn't suffered this tragedy in his life he wouldn't be here ask-
> ing for damages.
> You don't have to leave your common sense out. You can
> also take into account that as a man gets older he may not work
> quite as hard and not quite as steady as he does in his prime,
> but I say to you gentlemen that it is not unusual for a good finish
> carpenter to be still working at age 75. You think about it in your
> experience: a good finish carpenter, a cabinet-type man who
> can do doors and cabinets—light carpentry work that takes
> skill but is not heavy work. Certainly a good finish carpenter
> can work until he reaches age 70, and that is 27 years [indi-
> cating chart.]
> The uncontradicted testimony is that he was making
> $8,600 a year. If we give him four weeks off each year, and
> multiply his $125 a week by 48 weeks, that is $6,000 a year;
> and that is the testimony, that is the evidence, that he has lost
> $6,000 a year, and he has lost it for 27 years.
> Now, gentlemen, that is $162,000 [indicating chart.] You
> make a lot of money in your lifetime. That man was making a
> good living.
> All of these damages on the chart add up to $242,159. I
> have tried conscientiously to be conservative in the figures that
> I have used here, but this is a tremendous injury. Gentlemen,

that is a lot of money, but I say to you that it is also a lot of injury and there is a lot that has been lost in the life of this man.

That ended the opening arguments for the plaintiff. The defense attorneys took their turns, but did not argue damages. They used all their time to argue that their clients had not been negligent and were not responsible for any damages.

Clint Green had the final word. He punched holes in the liability arguments made by the defense lawyers and from the trial transcript he read to the jury the testimony of CAA investigator Watson that contained the Beechcraft pilot's admission that he had not flown the required traffic pattern. Then as a final stroke, to make certain that the jurors did not reward him with an uncollectible judgment, he called the jurors' attention to the fact that when the medical bills and other damage documents were being put into evidence, the lawyer for the cropduster had not bothered to look at them, whereas the lawyers for the Beechcraft owner had gone over each one carefully:

> Now I want to point out one interesting thing. Sometimes a straw shows which way the wind blows. Did you notice that every time we offered a bill or a hospital record in evidence, who grabbed it and started auditing the bill? Well, the subconscious mind works in strange ways—the fellow who really expects to pay the check is the one that is going to check the totals.

When Clint finished his brief closing speech, Judge Prunty immediately started his charge to the jury. There were no surprises, since both sides had submitted written requests to charge, and the judge had heard argument and ruled upon all the requests in advance. He gave standard instructions on the plaintiff's burden of proving negligence and proximate cause by a preponderance of the evidence. At Walter Beckham's request he also gave these special instructions:

> One of the responsibilities of the pilot of an airplane is to keep a proper lookout. A person is charged with seeing what he should have seen or what he might have seen by the exercise of reasonable and ordinary care. His failure, if any, to have seen that which he should have seen upon looking constitutes as great negligence under the law as though he had not looked at all.
>
> You are instructed that where a person is damaged either in person or in property by the joint or concurrent negligence of two or more persons proximately causing the injuries, he does not have to show that one was more or less negligent than the other.
>
> In this case, the plaintiff is proceeding against all of the defendants on the theory that they are joint tort feasors; that is, that they are jointly guilty of negligence, and upon the

theory that their negligence combined or concurred to cause his injury.

Consequently, if you find that the injury to the plaintiff was caused by the concurring negligence of both of the operators of the aircraft involved, then all of the defendants would be liable to the plaintiff.

At the request of the attorneys for the Beechcraft owner, he charged:

You are instructed that the owner and pilot of an aircraft are not liable for any injuries a passenger in their aircraft may receive if the injuries to the passenger are a result of the sole negligence of another aircraft.

He then instructed on the items of damages they should consider, which were exactly the items that Walter Beckham had listed on his chart. This was not a coincidence. Because of careful preparation of requests to charge, both sides knew in advance of the final argument the exact language that the judge would use in his instructions.

The jury retired from the courtroom at 12:15 P.M. to start their deliberations. The 829-page record of the trial ends this way:

At 4:02 o'clock P.M. the jury returned to the courtroom, and the following proceedings were had:
The COURT: Gentlemen of the jury, have you reached a verdict?
The FOREMAN: We have, your honor.
The COURT: Give it to the clerk, please. All right. Gentlemen, I see there is no date on this. Is there any objection to my filling in today's date? All right, read the verdict, Mr. Clerk.
The CLERK (reading): "We, the Jury, find in favor of the plaintiff against all defendants. We assess the damages of the plaintiff in the sum of $198,339. So say we all. (Signed) G. E. Michael, Foreman."

Aftermath

Naturally, the plaintiff and his lawyers were elated at the verdict. Clint Green and Walter Beckham had steered through a minefield of problems almost perfectly. But the problems were not gone—they now moved to another stage. The attorneys for the Beechcraft owner immediately exercised their right to appeal to the District Court of Appeal, Florida's intermediate appellate court. The appeal involved two questions that had never been ruled upon by Florida's appellate courts. The first question was whether the plaintiff had the right to use the diagram drawn by CAA investigator Watson and to question him about admissions made by the Beechcraft pilot. Both were parts of government accident investigation reports that seemed to come within the federal statute barring their use in damage suits. The second question was whether the trial judge had acted properly in allowing Walter Beckham to use his chart with the itemized damages, and especially the "per diem" amounts, such as the $15 per day for pain and suffering. While the per diem argument had never been considered directly by the Florida appellate courts, there had been a 1957 District Court of Appeal decision which upheld a trial judge's *refusal* to allow the use of a blackboard or chart during summation.

The law on per diem arguments was in its formative stages in most states in 1958. Several states had allowed both the chart and the per diem argument, but the New Jersey Supreme Court went the other way in a famous 1958 case, *Botta v. Brunner*. Because our case involved policy questions that would affect the trial of all types of damage suits in Florida, the District Court of Appeal did not reach a decision until April 9, 1959, more than a year after the jury's verdict.

The three-judge appellate court ruled unanimously that CAA investigator Watson's testimony was properly allowed, since it came under the exception to the federal statute (as interpreted by the federal courts) which permitted testimony about facts rather than opinions or conclusions. The three judges also agreed that the trial court properly allowed Walter Beckham to use his charts and his per diem arguments. They reviewed all the arguments for and against allowing their use, and concluded:

> In so holding we give due regard to the proposition that "pain and suffering have no market price." But the very absence of a fixed rule or standard for any monetary admeasurement of pain and suffering as an element of damages supplies a reason why counsel for the parties should be allotted, on this item of damages, their entitled latitude in argument—to comment on the evidence, its nature and effect, and to note all proper inferences which reasonably may spring from the evidence adduced.

They held that all the items in Walter's chart were supported by evidence and they refused to set aside or reduce the jury's award of $198,339. Thus the case of the crippled carpenter against the bustling Beechcraft and the careless cropduster finally came to an end with payment of the jury verdict in full, plus interest from the date of the verdict.

That was not really the end of the case, however. The 1959 appellate decision came at a time when the use of blackboards, damage charts, and per diem arguments was being considered by many states. The issues in the carpenter's case were so clearly drawn, and the appellate court opinion so well written and definitive, that it became a landmark decision. It has been cited as authority in many Florida cases since 1959, and appellate courts in 31 other states have also cited it— an unusual record for an intermediate appellate court decision. It has helped judges and jurors everywhere to evaluate damages scientifically and humanely.

The jury verdict and the triumph in the appellate court were tributes to the thorough professionalism of the Nichols firm, at a time when it was approaching the peak of its power. The verdict of $198,339 was probably the nation's highest award up to that time for an arm injury. Indeed, there had been only a handful of higher verdicts for *any* type of injury in the preinflation age of the $125-per-week carpenter. It was not gained by mesmerizing the jury but by itemizing the damages in a scientific and businesslike way. Yet, if the case had arisen ten years earlier no lawyer in Florida (or in most other states) would have had much hope of winning it against the Beechcraft owner. At best, it might have been settled for a small fraction of the actual loss; for no plaintiff's lawyer then would have been confident enough to advise his client to turn down an offer of $10,000 to $15,000 in such a case. The injured carpenter got the full measure of 1958 justice because in Clint Green, Walter Beckham, and the Perry Nichols firm, he had lawyers who applied the accumulated knowledge of the whole plaintiff's bar to the problems of his case, and he had champions strong enough to make new law for his case on both liability and damages in the trial and the appellate courts of Florida. The organization working for him was far beyond his economic power to hire, and its members laid out thousands of dollars of their own money to make sure that his case would be won. He paid them nothing until he collected his damages in 1959.

To celebrate the victory, Clint Green, a boating fanatic, invited me out on his cabin cruiser, the *Green Star,* but I begged off. I have never been much of a boatman, and my enthusiasm was dampened further by recollections of a miserable day spent in trying to help Clint and the U.S. Coast Guard free the *Green Star* from a sandbar in Biscayne Bay when I accepted an earlier invitation. Clint was a much better navigator in the courtroom than on the seas. I was to have the double good fortune to work with Clint and Walter Beckham on other aviation cases and yet to avoid setting foot on the *Green Star* again.

The Nichols firm had everything going for it as the 1950s ended. Murray Sams and Dr. Larry Hastings had left it earlier in order to build their own powerhouse firms in Miami; but those who remained constituted the strongest force of tort lawyers ever assembled. There were the old standbys Perry Nichols, Billy Gaither, Clint Green, Bill Frates, Walter Beckham, Bill Colson, J. B. Spence, and Sam Daniels, who were later augmented by other bright stars, such as Bill Hicks, Peter Fay, Aaron Podhurst, Alan Schwartz, Bill Wagner, Ray Ferrero, Bobby Orseck, Buddy Payne, Gerald Wetherington, and Phil Hubbert. Every one of these lawyers achieved distinction in his own right, and most of them did so before turning 40. To their competitors and opponents in the Miami area they must have seemed to be everywhere at once. They moved into prominent positions in bar associations, political and community organizations, service clubs, and churches. They served on school boards and civic committees. They paid highly qualified speakers to address their weekly firm luncheons on public relations, medicine, and other disciplines that could be useful to the scientific tort lawyer.

This rising firm soon outgrew its floor in the Pan American Bank Building, and Perry brought another dream into reality: a Nichols law firm building. They had it designed and built to their specifications: a distinctive, circular, white stone and concrete structure, five stories high. To some it looked like the coil that was mounted on top of the 1930s model Frigidaire kitchen refrigerators. Miami cabdrivers called it the Roundhouse, and that name caught on with members of the firm. It was located at 1111 Brickell Avenue, just a few blocks from downtown Miami, on a large lot that went all the way down to Biscayne Bay. It was a building worthy of the headquarters of a multinational corporation, or a bank, or a television station (which it became eventually). Its central courtyard looked out on fountains, ponds, and gardens—a Taj Mahal of torts.

They moved into the Roundhouse in 1959, when Perry was 44 years old. The NACCA convention was held in Miami that summer, and the Nichols firm hosted a huge cocktail party, using chartered buses to carry hundreds of tort lawyers and their wives from the convention hotel to their new building. It was a memorable evening. Most of us were accustomed to working in musty old office buildings, our horizons limited by the everyday drudgery of functioning as cogs in the machinery of justice. But the new Nichols building was like a vision of Camelot to us. It was a symbol of the tort lawyers' dream come true—a one-firm fulfillment of the nationwide crusade of NACCA. Within a few years, Perry Nichols and his group of outstanding young men (most of whom looked and sounded like missionaries or Junior Chamber of Commerce presidents) had turned Florida around completely, from a low-verdict backwater of the Deep South to the best state in the nation for bringing a tort suit. And the building in which they practiced their skills dramatized their heroic achievements.

The Roundhouse made their operation more efficient and more spectacular than ever. Branch offices were established in Fort Lauderdale, Tampa, and Orlando. They still had the division system, with centralized medical analysis, legal research, and photography departments. Now they added a new wrinkle: an "interviewing attorney" who did nothing but interview prospective clients. It is difficult to describe this firm without making it seem like an assembly line, but the warmth, enthusiasm, and teamwork they brought to their practice made it anything but impersonal. The centralized interviewing technique was another Perry Nichols management idea that freed busy trial lawyers from detail.

The move to the Roundhouse seemed to herald even greater accomplishments, but instead it proved to be the beginning of the end of the tort lawyers' Camelot. Throwing together so many superstars in such a hurry, there was bound to be some reaction. It was practically impossible for so many strong-willed advocates to agree on all important policies. First Clint Green left to join Dr. Larry Hastings, and then Bill Frates set up his own firm with Peter Fay and former judge Robert Floyd. Gradually, the momentum that had brought the Nichols firm together began to work against it, and in 1967, under its final name of Nichols Gaither Beckham Colson Spence and Hicks, it was dissolved. To their great credit, they took the firm apart as professionally as they had put it together. They made orderly arrangements for carrying on their clients' cases without interruption, and the strong personal friendships that partners had formed, some of them bordering on brotherhood, survived the breakup of their dream firm. The Florida bar, enriched by the life of the Nichols firm, now gained a cluster of great new firms in place of the old one.

Perry Nichols formed a new partnership with his son Richard, practicing as Nichols & Nichols in Miami until 1975, when the firm moved its offices to Coral Gables.

Walter Beckham, who is at once a gifted teacher and an outstanding trial lawyer, decided to go back to teaching at the University of Miami Law School, where he had been a faculty member in the late 1940s before entering law practice. He joined the new firm of Podhurst Orseck & Parks as counsel, which allowed him to handle some cases while serving as Professor of Trial Advocacy and Torts at Miami. Aaron Podhurst had worked in Walter's division in the Roundhouse, and he soon established his new firm as a leader in aviation cases and other major tort litigation. Bobby Orseck had been a mainstay of the legal and appellate division of the Nichols firm, having previously served as clerk for a judge of the New York Court of Appeals. He died tragically in Israel in 1978 while attempting to rescue a young swimmer who had called for help.

Bill Colson, a dynamic spellbinder who was responsible for many of the important courtroom victories of the Nichols firm and served as president of NACCA after Perry Nichols, formed a new partnership with Bill Hicks, a more subdued but equally distinguished trial lawyer who was one of the first to specialize in products liability cases. Colson & Hicks quickly became one of Florida's leading tort firms.

J. B. Spence formed Spence Payne & Masington, another strong tort firm which includes Buddy Payne of the Nichols firm. Billy Gaither had planned to team up with J. B. Spence, but he died suddenly before the new Spence firm got underway.

In its glory years, the Nichols firm had about 18 lawyers working in the Roundhouse, although they increased their staff to as many as 26 lawyers in the mid-1960s when they diversified into labor law. The new firms that resulted from the breakup of the Nichols firm for the most part have stayed in the size range of three to seven lawyers, with the exception of the Frates firm, which diversified into general trial practice and grew to 26 lawyers in 1979.

Four of the younger Nichols lawyers went on to become judges. Peter Fay, who first left to join Bill Frates's new firm, then served as U. S. District Judge in Miami and was later elevated to the U. S. Court of Appeals for the Fifth Circuit, just one step below the U. S. Supreme Court. Alan Schwartz and Phillip Hubbert became judges of the District Court of Appeals, Florida's intermediate appellate court; and Gerald Wetherington became a Circuit Court (trial level) judge.

Recently I visited Walter Beckham and we talked about the old Nichols firm. He gives full credit to Perry Nichols for having the imagination and drive to put together that unique organization. Walter said:

> Perry was unselfish. He would share the limelight and the profits. He made real partners of all of us, not just echoes. He surrounded himself with people who could help. He never held anyone back. He was anxious for the youngest men in the firm to try the heaviest cases that they possibly could, just as quickly as they could.
>
> And when it came to a crunch, Perry reverted to his old football role as a fullback. When he made up his mind to accomplish something, he would just say that he was going to run over right guard on this play and go for ten yards. And then he would just put his head down and go get his ten yards, even if four men were hanging around his neck all the way. He would just go out and do it.

The breakup of the Nichols firm was a shock to plaintiffs' lawyers throughout the nation who thought that the Florida all-star team was invincible. It lent credence to the rule of thumb that the optimum practical size of a plaintiff's tort firm was five to eight lawyers, and that if you got more than one or two really high-powered tort lawyers under one roof, they were bound to split apart eventually.

Personal Injuries Today

The Page Field collision case was a landmark of the 1950s tort revolution, and it helped many other plaintiffs to obtain more adequate compensation for personal injuries, but to today's young tort lawyers it smacks of the horse and buggy era. Hyperinflation has made the $125-per-week loss of earnings for a skilled carpenter look ridiculously low, to say nothing of the $500 total cost of tendon transplant surgery. Inflation alone would more than double the probable award in such a case today. But it was not only inflation that changed personal injury awards so dramatically. The main reason for this change is that the revolution started by Belli, Nichols, and NACCA (now ATLA) has produced thousands of tort lawyers who know more about the effects of personal injuries than their predecessors and are better equipped to present these cases.

Through ATLA (and many other bar organizations and publishers that have followed in its footsteps) it is possible for any lawyer to obtain books, articles, photographs, videotapes, and audio cassettes that demonstrate the wide range of personal injury damages and the most successful methods of presenting them in court. Soon after a lawyer in Oklahoma makes a breakthrough in compensation for the psychological effects of burn injuries, colleagues throughout the nation learn what this lawyer did and how it was accomplished.

As the tort revolution continues, the real measure of devastation wrought to mind and body by serious personal injuries is coming to be appreciated by lawyers, judges, jurors, and insurance companies. This revelation is unfolding at a time when judges and jurors have come to realize that they can use the power of the state, through damage awards, to compensate fully, to deter wrongdoing, and to equalize the positions of the great and the small.

There are hundreds of examples to show these great changes in personal injury awards and as I worked on this chapter and struggled to select an appropriate illustration, a new instance to illustrate this took place right in my own office.

It was a steaming August day in 1979. All of the sensible lawyers were sitting around swimming pools, but I was at my desk in the Pan Am Building, reviewing the file in one of the most distressing cases our firm has ever handled. A 15-year-old boy from Connecticut had been a passenger in an automobile operated by the summer camp that he was attending. The auto left the road and turned over, which threw the boy out and injured his head so severely that he was never again able to see, speak, eat, or function like a normal human being.

The case was referred to us by Arthur Schatz of the old-line Hartford, Connecticut, firm of Schatz & Schatz, Ribicoff & Kotkin. Arthur, who is a leading authority on forensic sciences and medical jurisprudence, would have handled the case himself, but the camp was located in New York and could not be sued in Connecticut. As I looked through the heartbreaking papers and photographs in the file, my depression was relieved only by the prospect of seeing my good friend Arthur again. He is one of those sparkling, irrepressible spirits in whose presence it is impossible to be gloomy. He was coming to our office that day to take part in the meeting which we had scheduled to discuss settlement with the defense attorneys.

As the meeting got under way, we turned off the lights in our conference room and switched on our videotape playback machine. Instead of presenting the defense lawyers with oral arguments in support of our settlement demand, we played a one-hour color videotape that told the story of the case more eloquently than any lawyer possibly could.

The videotape was directed, produced, and narrated by Fred Heller, a young lawyer in our firm who has developed some expertise in the making of such tapes. He has produced several tapes illustrating the dangerous propensities of machinery (such as paper cutters that have cut off workers' hands) as well as the "Day in the Life of . . ." tapes that are often used today to record the daily regimen of seriously injured plaintiffs. In order to assure maximum utility of such tapes as trial evidence, it is advisable to keep a computerized log of all footage so that editing and splicing can be accounted for. There are now several organizations that make a specialty of working with lawyers to produce evidentiary videotapes. The tape of the 15-year-old Connecticut boy cost us over $10,000. We were about to learn whether it was a good investment.

The tape opened with scenes of the injured boy in his hospital bed shortly after the accident. He looked like a human skeleton huddled in the fetal position. As Fred Heller narrated the history of the accident and the subsequent medical treatment, the camera cut to more recent pictures of the boy, now taller, heavier, and sitting up with his eyes open, but still unable to communicate. Doctors, nurses, therapists, and the boy's parents told their stories as the tape ran on. Then it was time for the key witness, Dr. Lawrence I. Kaplan.

Larry Kaplan is a renowned New York neurologist and psychiatrist whose expertise is sought by lawyers for plaintiffs and defendants in many serious cases, so much so that it takes months to get an appointment with him. We had brought him into the case for a special purpose. Through depositions, we had quickly established clear liability, and the defense attorneys recognized this as a catastrophic injury case. They were prepared to make a very substantial settlement offer, probably around a million dollars, to cover the obvious need for the boy's medical care for the rest of his life expectancy. Under New York law, the cost of care was the major element of damages. The parents could not recover any damages for the devastating emotional impact of this tragedy upon them, nor could there be any award for the boy's own suffering and deprivation of normal life unless we could prove that he was consciously aware of his condition.

To the naked eye, it seemed that the boy was oblivious of his surroundings and incapable of comprehending his condition. It appeared so even to the doctors who were treating him. But as we studied the many hours of tapes that we had taken at the hospital, and as we zeroed in on the closeups, we saw small signs of what might be a flicker of understanding behind the blank stare in the boy's brown eyes. It was then that we called in Larry Kaplan, for he is one of the few doctors who could make such a determination that would stand up in court.

The camera moved to a shot of Dr. Kaplan in the hospital's solarium, explaining the boy's injuries with the help of a multicolored model of the brain. He showed and explained the remarkable Computerized Axial Tomograph (CAT) scans of the boy's brain that pinpointed the areas of injury. (Before CAT scans were available, exploratory surgery or dangerous tests were required to produce the same information.) Dr. Kaplan explained graphically that the boy had suffered contusions and swelling of the brain that resulted in paralysis of both arms and both legs (quadriplegia), loss of sight and loss of speech; and that these conditions were not curable by surgery or any other known method. Despite these horrible effects of the accident, the boy was able to breathe normally and was in good medical condition apart from his brain injuries. He was not unconscious or in a coma. He was intermittently awake, as evidenced by roving movements of his eyeballs.

Then the camera moved to the boy's hospital bed, where Dr. Kaplan examined him and made various tests, which he explained in clear layman's language. Dr. Kaplan then narrated his findings: in his opinion, the boy was awake and was *aware of his condition* despite his inability to communicate.

Then came the final scene. The boy's mother took his hand and stroked his face, repeatedly saying to him, "Speak to me, darling—come on, speak to me, please!" She continued her stroking and pleading for more than five minutes. The tape showed a closeup view of the boy's face—now he was trying to speak, but could not make a sound. Then suddenly there came from the boy's mouth a groan that lasted a few seconds, then another groan, then a continuous groaning for nearly a minute. If you watched that scene you would not doubt that he was trying to respond to his mother. Nor would you ever forget the sound of his groaning.

As the videotape ran out and we turned up the lights in the conference room, we could feel the effects on the defense attorneys. Despite their professional detachment, they were visibly shaken. They were thoroughly convinced that we could prove in court that the boy was suffering the living hell of knowing his condition and being unable to communicate. We never had to play the tape in court. Soon after its one showing to the defense lawyers, the case ended in a multimillion dollar settlement before trial.

Chapter 5

PRODUCTS LIABILITY

THE ALOUETTE II

The worldwide search for oil in the oceans has led to use of helicopters as commuting vehicles for oil companies. Drilling crews live on offshore platforms and are rotated back to land at frequent intervals. Officials of the oil companies shuttle back and forth between land offices and offshore platforms, and supplies are often ferried to the platforms by helicopter. For the most part, this transportation service is conducted by independent helicopter operators—not the airlines, but smaller companies devoted solely to helicopter transportation. Two major operators dominate this business worldwide. In the United States (principally in the Gulf of Mexico) the dominant company is Petroleum Helicopters, Inc., (PHI) of Lafayette, Louisiana, founded by pilot Robert L. Suggs in 1949 with one helicopter and now (1979) operating more than 250 helicopters. In European waters, the principal company is Bristow Helicopters Ltd., of England.

On November 30, 1959, PHI suffered an accident in the Gulf of Mexico which was to result in a landmark case tried in the U.S. District Court for the Southern District of New York by Chuck Krause of our firm. On that day George Stubbs, a PHI helicopter pilot, was ferrying two Gulf Oil employees to an oil platform off the Louisiana coast. Stubbs was flying an Alouette II helicopter manufactured by Sud-Aviation of France. The Alouette II was fairly new to the PHI operation at that time. It was the first French aircraft of any kind and the first turbine-powered helicopter in the world to receive American certification, which the FAA granted on January 14, 1958. The particular helicopter that Stubbs was flying, N519, had been sold to Republic Aviation Corporation in 1959 by Sud-Aviation. Republic was a large aircraft manufacturer, best known for the famous P–47

Thunderbolt fighter of World War II. Republic had entered into a contract to become the American distributor for the Alouette II, and they used N519 as a demonstrator until they leased it to PHI in August 1959.

When he was a few miles out over the Gulf of Mexico, Stubbs suddenly encountered difficulty in controlling the helicopter. He reported to the PHI operations base by radio that he was having trouble and was making a 180 degree turn to return to shore. But shortly after his last radio transmission, Stubbs lost control of the helicopter and it crashed into the Gulf, killing him and his two passengers.

Even though it involved an aircraft of foreign manufacture, this was a domestic accident, and its investigation fell under the jurisdiction of the Civil Aeronautics Board, Bureau of Safety (replaced by the National Transportation Safety Board in 1967). The CAB promptly dispatched investigators to Louisiana. The wreckage was recovered, and it was quickly established that an in-flight structural failure had occurred in the rear portion of the helicopter known as the tail boom. Helicopters are propelled by overhead rotors which would cause the craft to spin in the direction opposite from that of the rotors unless this spinning tendency is counteracted. To offset this "torque," a tail rotor is installed at the back of the helicopter, at the end of a section of metal tubing called the tail boom. On the Alouette II, the tail boom resembles a small oil derrick laid on its side. It is triangular in shape, with two steel tubes (called "longerons") at the top and one steel tube at the bottom, each tube about fifteen feet long and about one inch in diameter. Mounted about two-thirds of the way back on the tail boom, there is a horizontal stabilizer, designed to stabilize the helicopter during flight. It resembles a small straight wing. The stabilizer is mounted in two steel brackets which are welded to the upper right and upper left longerons respectively.

The CAB investigators concluded that a structural failure had occurred in the upper right longeron at the point where the horizontal stabilizer bracket was welded to it. Thus, the main cause of the accident became clear within a few weeks after the wreckage was recovered. But the question remained: why did this structural failure occur? As far as the families of the helicopter's occupants were concerned, the final answer did not come until eight years later.

The Louisiana lawyers retained by the three bereaved families to recover damages naturally looked first to PHI, the operator of the helicopter. The relatives of the dead pilot were entitled to worker's compensation benefits, which they received in due course; but that was their sole remedy against PHI. The families of the two passengers sued PHI in Louisiana, and they engaged us to file actions in New York against Sud-Aviation (manufacturer of the helicopter) and Republic

Aircraft Corporation (the owner and lessor). There were some thorny jurisdictional and legal problems that had to be cleared up before the case could be brought to trial. As we saw in the Nader-GM case, the presence of novel legal questions usually slows down the litigation process. Since the accident had occurred more than one marine league (three nautical miles) from shore, it was technically an admiralty case, and had to be prosecuted under the Death on the High Seas Act, a federal statute governing fatal accidents that occur at sea. Aviation lawyers have to become admiralty lawyers from time to time, since major airline accidents sometimes occur on the high seas and thus are subject to admiralty law. There had been few admiralty cases involving helicopters prior to this one, and none involving suits against a foreign aircraft manufacturer.

PHI carried a special form of insurance known as "admitted liability" coverage. PHI knew that they would be transporting employees of oil companies every day, and in the event of an accident they did not wish to get into litigation with employees of their regular customers. Therefore they took out admitted liability insurance, which is something like the trip insurance that airline passengers can buy at airports, except that this coverage is paid for by the operator. It provided that there would be automatic payment of up to $75,000 in damages per passenger regardless of fault whenever PHI had an accident while carrying business customers. If the passengers' families wanted to collect this insurance, they would have to give up the right to sue PHI in court. It was not clear whether they would also have to give up the right to sue the manufacturer in a case where a product defect might be responsible. That was one of the problems that we had to clear up before the case came to trial.

Eventually, the families of the two passengers accepted the admitted liability insurance payment from PHI and dismissed the suits against PHI in Louisiana. Their lawyers then instructed us to proceed with the claims against Sud-Aviation and Republic in New York. If we were successful, the amount they received through PHI's admitted liability insurance would be subtracted from any judgment rendered against the manufacturers. In other words, the manufacturers would get credit for the amount paid by PHI. But this still left a substantial amount of damages for which the passengers' families had not been compensated, and the worker's compensation benefits paid to the pilot's family covered only a fraction of their real loss. Thus there was sufficient financial incentive for the three families to undertake the novel task of suing a foreign helicopter manufacturer for an accident that occurred on the high seas.

Our investigation convinced us that the accident was caused by a faulty welding job at the Sud-Aviation factory, in that the weld that

had joined the upper right longeron to the stabilizer bracket was defective because of insufficient "root penetration," which left the weld
metal in a weak and dangerous condition. The defendants were equally
convinced that the weld was not defective, and that the structural failure resulted from a previous accident which PHI had experienced a
few months before the fatal crash, plus the failure of PHI to perform
required inspections which would have revealed the dangerous conditions leading to the structural failure.

Products Liability Law

The Alouette case arose at a time of transition in the law of product
liability. From the nineteenth century onward, a person injured by a
defective product could sue the manufacturer in American courts, *provided* the injured person had bought the product directly from the
manufacturer. The purchaser could sue for negligence (if he could
prove it) or for breach of implied warranty of merchantability and fitness—an easier claim than negligence because it required only proof
of a defect that caused the injury, without getting into the question of
how the defect came about. But if the plaintiff had bought it from a
dealer, or was injured by a product that he did not buy, then he could
not sue at all—not even for negligence—because he had no "privity of
contract" with the manufacturer. The only exceptions were for inherently hazardous products, such as poisons and explosives.

By the early twentieth century, marketing had changed. Fewer
people bought products directly from manufacturers, and the courts
were starting to weigh the need for consumer protection against the privity rule, which had been designed to foster the industrial revolution.
The first breach in the wall of privity was engineered by the great New
York Court of Appeals judge, Benjamin Cardozo, in the famous 1916
case, *MacPherson v. Buick Motor Co.,* in which the plaintiff was allowed to sue the auto manufacturer for negligence even though he had
bought the car from a dealer. But privity still barred the way to suits
for breach of implied warranty unless the product was purchased directly from the manufacturer. This meant that the plaintiff had to
prove negligence—a difficult and expensive undertaking, requiring
evidence of what went wrong during the manufacturing process and
what the state of the art was at the time. As a result, there were few
suits against manufacturers even after Cardozo's landmark *MacPherson*
decision. Individual plaintiffs and their attorneys simply were not
equipped to prove negligence at the factory level in those days, espe-

cially in cases involving complicated products such as autos, machinery, and aircraft.

The few complicated products liability claims tried before World War II were mostly brought by corporate plaintiffs who could draw on their own scientific expertise and had the resources to pay their lawyers on an hourly basis. Thus the first successful aviation products liability suit in New York was brought by American Airlines against the Ford Motor Company to recover damages for loss of a Ford Trimotor that had occurred on August 9, 1931, shortly after takeoff from the airport at Cincinnati, Ohio. The events leading up to that crash bear a startling resemblance to those surrounding the loss of another American Airlines three-engine airliner, the 1979 O'Hare Airport (Chicago) DC–10 disaster. In the 1931 accident, two eyewitnesses saw a propeller blade fall from the airplane to the ground just before the crash. Loss of the blade caused severe vibration in the affected engine, which soon tore loose from its mount and fell to the ground. At the same time, its remaining propeller blade cut through the aileron control cables, rendering the ailerons useless. The pilot could do little but shut down the remaining two engines to reduce the risk of fire. Now out of control, the Trimotor flipped over and fell to the ground. All occupants were killed and the aircraft was a total loss.

This Ford Trimotor had been sent to the Ford factory in May of 1931 for extensive modifications designed to bring its cruising speed up to that of the latest Ford models, about 122 miles per hour. This required new engines and propellers, which were installed by Ford pursuant to a written contract. The plane was returned to American on June 17, 1931, and operated by American from then until the fatal crash of August 9th. American's investigation convinced them that the propeller blade failed because of a fatigue crack in the hub, which propagated from tool marks on the inner surface of the hub. The airline's engineers concluded that the tool marks should have been discovered upon reasonable inspection of the type that Ford personnel were supposed to make during the factory modification; that Ford knew that such tool marks were a source of danger; and that Ford either concealed the existence of those tool marks from American or simply failed to detect them on inspection. American's lawyers decided that they had a good cause of action against Ford for breach of the modification contract, which required inspection of the propellers.

American brought suit against Ford in New York, claiming as damages the value of the airplane, which was about $30,000 in 1931. (Ford Trimotors, which were high winged, slab sided, noisy, but reliable, cost between $40,000 and $50,000 new at the factory in the 1930s.) American was represented by Haight Griffin Deming & Gardner (now Haight Gardner Poor & Havens), a large New York firm noted

then for admiralty and insurance defense work. The case was tried in
February 1939 without a jury before Justice Aron Steuer, son of Max D.
Steuer. It was a highly technical trial, with American calling 20 witnesses and putting over 100 exhibits into evidence, including many
metal fragments from the failed propeller blade.

Justice Steuer decided in favor of American Airlines and fixed
damages at $30,000, the value of the Ford Trimotor on the date of
crash. Since the claim was for breach of the modification contract,
American was able to collect interest from the date of the breach. This
added $13,489 to the judgment, making a total recovery of $43,489.
If the plaintiff had been an injured passenger instead of an airline, no
interest would have been allowed—another example of how the courts
give stronger protection to property rights than to personal rights.

The American-Ford case is the closest that can be found to an
aviation products liability claim before the late 1940s. It is doubtful
that any plaintiff's tort specialist could have handled such a complicated case at that time. Even with the staff of American Airlines at
their disposal, it took the Haight firm more than eight years from the
date of the accident to bring the case to trial.

By the late 1950s, consumers of food were allowed to sue manufacturers for breach of warranty even without privity, but most people
who were injured by nonfood products were still restricted to negligence actions until the New Jersey Supreme Court dealt a mortal blow
to the privity rule in the 1960 case of *Henningsen v. Bloomfield Motors,
Inc.,* by allowing a plaintiff who had been injured by a defective Ply-
mouth auto bought from a dealer to sue the manufacturer for breach
of implied warranty as well as negligence. This was a giant step forward, but the use of warranty (a contractual concept) as a device to
circumvent an outmoded tort rule brought some complications, such
as applicability of notice and disclaimer requirements of contract and
sales law that were not designed for personal injury claims.

The California Supreme Court went New Jersey one better in 1963
by allowing William Greenman to sue Yuba Power Products, Inc.,
(the manufacturer of a power tool that Greenman's wife had bought for
him from a dealer) for "strict liability in tort," thus creating a new tort
category for product liability actions which extricated them from the
intricacies of contract and sales law. Strict liability, like breach of implied warranty, meant that manufacturers and sellers would be liable
for injuries caused by defective products, even if negligence could not
be proved. The *Greenman* decision was written by Justice Roger Traynor, one of America's most respected judges who authored over 140
opinions on tort law during his 30 years on the California Supreme
Court. It was based on views that he had expressed nearly 20 years
earlier, in the 1944 case of *Escola v. Coca Cola* (argued for the

plaintiff by Melvin M. Belli). Justice Traynor's statement in *Escola,* that strict tort liability should attach to defective products which cause injuries, was only a concurring opinion in which the other justices did not join. But in the 1963 *Greenman* case, the entire California Supreme Court joined with its distinguished chief justice in creating strict tort liability, adopting his 1944 reasoning:

> Public policy demands that responsibility be fixed wherever it will most effectively reduce the hazards to life and health inherent in defective products that reach the market. It is evident that the manufacturer can anticipate some hazards and guard against others, as the public cannot. Those who suffer injury from defective products are unprepared to meet its consequences. The cost of an injury and the loss of time or health may be an overwhelming misfortune to the person injured, and a needless one, for the risk of injury can be insured by the manufacturer and distributed among the public as a cost of doing business.

Some states continued to label the new remedy "breach of warranty," while others preferred to follow California and call it "strict tort liability," thus eliminating the excess baggage of warranty-sales-contract law.

As strict tort liability developed in the 1960s, it was based upon the dangerous nature of the product involved, and so its applicability to each product category had to be determined by the courts. A few months after the 1963 California *Greenman* power tool decision, the New York Court of Appeals handed down a similar decision in *Goldberg v. Kollsman Instrument Corp. and Lockheed Aircraft Corp.,* permitting a client of ours to sue an aircraft manufacturer for breach of implied warranty (which the court equated to "strict tort liability") after her daughter had been killed in the crash of an American Airlines Lockheed Electra near New York's La Guardia Airport. *Goldberg* was the first appellate decision to extend the new rule to airplane passengers.

When the Alouette II crash occurred in 1959, none of these landmark cases had been decided. By the time that it came to trial in 1967, the strict liability doctrine was well on its way toward acceptance throughout the country, but there had been no appellate decisions applying it to admiralty cases. We had managed to convince a New York federal district court judge that it should be extended to admiralty in a 1960 case involving an aircraft accident on the high seas, but in 1962 a Delaware federal district court judge refused to follow that decision and ruled that breach of implied warranty was not a "wrongful act, neglect or default" within the meaning of the Death on the High Seas Act, thus requiring the plaintiff to prove negligence.

In the Alouette case we had sued both for negligence and breach of implied warranty, and we decided to try to prove both at the trial. If the trial judge ruled that breach of warranty or strict tort liability was applicable and we won on that theory without proving negligence, the appellate court might reverse the trial judge's ruling, and we would be out of luck. Proving negligence meant taking on the defendants in a battle of expert testimony about welding techniques, metallurgy, and the state of the art of helicopter manufacturing, instead of resting on the simpler strict liability theory that the admitted structural failure had been caused by a defective part whose origin we were not concerned with. But in those early days of the movement toward strict product liability, we could not afford to risk everything on an appellate ruling upholding a new legal theory.

The Trial

Since the case came under admiralty law, it had to be tried by a federal judge without a jury. It came on for trial before U.S. District Judge Thomas F. Croake in the federal courthouse in Manhattan's Foley Square on December 11, 1967. Our trial counsel was Charles F. (Chuck) Krause, who had been in practice for six years and was in his ninth year with our firm, since he had begun working for us as a clerk in his freshman year at law school. Chuck is a tall, muscular, handsome ex-football star whose service as a Marine Corps jet pilot during the Korean War included aircraft carrier duty. Emerging with the rank of captain after four years of flying with the Marine Corps, he went on to Rutgers Law School, where he became a member of the law review. He kept up his flying proficiency by joining a Marine reserve squadron. Although he had tried several aviation cases and had participated in the trials and appeals of many others, the Alouette II was to be the first major aviation case that he would try on his own.

Opposing Chuck Krause were two formidable trial lawyers. Sud-Aviation's American lawyers are Coudert Brothers, one of the nation's outstanding large general practice firms with special capabilities in international law. They assigned this case to Bill Rand, a leading trial lawyer who had once been special counsel to Governor Nelson A. Rockefeller and later became a New York Supreme Court Justice before returning to the Coudert firm. Republic Aviation's lawyers were Mendes & Mount, the principal New York claims attorneys for Lloyds of London, and they sent in their senior aviation partner, Matt Corrigan.

Chuck Krause opened the case by putting Joseph R. Bolen, a supervisory pilot for PHI, on the stand. Bolen described PHI's helicopter operations and his own functions. He testified that he was at the main operations base at Leeville, Louisiana, when pilot Stubbs called in on the radio to report his control problem. Bolen went on to describe the dramatic last minutes of the fatal flight.

Q. by Mr. KRAUSE: Had you ever heard George Stubbs's voice on the radio before?   A: Yes, I had, many times.

Q: Did you recognize his voice?   A: Yes, sir, I did.

Q: And can you describe his voice for us, as you heard it on this occasion?   A: Well, in the initial contact, the best that I can recall is that there was no undue concern. He just made a contact with the base and stated that he thought he had a pitch change failure, and he was making a 180-degree turn back to the base.

Q: You heard this come across the radio, is that correct?   A: Yes.

Q: Then what occurred?   A: Walter Smith [the radio operator] acknowledged the transmission, and I, being next to the microphone, took the microphone, and made myself known to George, that I was on the air there for any further transmission that he may have.

Q: Then would you tell us what occurred.   A: To the best of my recollection he told me that he had completed the 180-degree turn, he was headed back. And I asked him if he was able to maintain directional control. And he said that he was able to maintain directional control, and he was coming back toward the beach.

Q: Mr. Bolen, please tell us the rest of the conversation that you had with Mr. Stubbs.   A: He asked me if I thought that he should fly it on in to the base. To the best of my recollection I answered him, "George, that's up to you. You can land it at the beach or you can bring it on in; it depends on how things are going when you get a little closer in."

Q: Is Leeville, the base where you were, some distance in from the shoreline?   A: Yes.

Q: About how many miles?   A: Seven or eight miles.

Q: When you just referred to the "beach," are you referring to some point down on the shoreline?   A: Yes.

Q: Go ahead. After you relayed that information to him, what occurred then?   A: He made some remark about, did I think he should land it from a hover or land it with forward speed. And again, to the best of my recollection, I answered him, "George, that would be up to you; you're feeling this thing, you know how—what treatment you would have to give it for the landing at the time, when it comes time to make this landing."

And then there was a moment of silence when everything was going along, we didn't have anything more to speak of. Then I heard the high-pitched scream that to me said "Mayday." It was high, a very high-pitched scream; and I knew that something drastic had happened.

Q: Did you hear anything more over the radio after that?
A: I heard nothing more after that.
Q: Can you tell me approximately how long it was from the
time you first heard Mr. Stubbs' voice on the radio to the time
you heard this high-pitched scream? How much time elapsed?
A: To the best of my recollection, roughly three minutes.

From the extensive pretrial discovery, Chuck knew that the defendants
were going to blame the tail failure on damage that allegedly occurred
in a "tail dipping" incident about three months before the crash. He
decided to anticipate the defense by bringing out the facts about that
incident through the testimony of Bolen:

Q: Mr. Bolen, are you familiar with a tail dipping incident in-
volving this helicopter on August 19, 1959?   A: Yes.
Q: Were you present when that took place?   A: No.
Q: From whom did you gather information concerning that incident?   A: From George Stubbs and Jack Hyde, the two individuals that were in the aircraft during the tail dipping incident.
Q: What did Mr. Stubbs tell you concerning this incident?   A:
To the best of my recollection Mr. Stubbs and Mr. Hyde related to me an incident where the tail rotor struck the water.
Now, they felt the tail rotor strike the water. To what degree I
can't say at this time. A tail rotor striking the water has happened with helicopters as long as there have been helicopters,
when you are practicing autorotations [landings without power].
They told me that they got out and looked at the thing and felt
that it was safe enough to fly back to their base, which they did.
Q: Mr. Bolen, from your knowledge as a pilot qualified to fly the
Alouette II helicopter, is it possible to touch the *horizontal
stabilizer* in the water in a tail dipping incident without actually
crashing the aircraft?   A: In my opinion, no.
Q: In your opinion, also as one qualified to fly the Alouette II
helicopter, would a tail dipping incident place stress upon a horizontal stabilizer bracket?   A: There is no way I can foresee it
placing a strain on the horizontal stabilizer bracket.

Krause felt that he had done his best to minimize the tail dipping incident. The tail of the Alouette II is a very large section of the aircraft, and the dipping had not involved the horizontal stabilizer, which
was the part of the tail that later failed and caused the fatal crash.
But on cross-examination Bill Rand banged away at the tail dipping
incident.

Q. by Mr. RAND: Mr. Bolen, when you read this report for August 19th which reads, "Aircraft grounded due to damaged tail
rotor blades and tail rotor long shaft, Jack Hyde," did you feel
that that report was a sufficient report of the tail dipping incident?   A: I wouldn't feel that it was, no.
Q: Well, did you take any steps to see that a more complete

report was made out? A: I didn't feel it was necessary, since all the corrective actions had already been taken, other than to talk to Jack and tell him the next time he had anything to write in there to be a little more verbose in his explanation of what happened.

Q: Do you have any knowledge of the cost of repairs to the aircraft as a result of this incident? A: No, I don't.

Q: Can you tell us what the purpose of having pilots make reports on these forms was? A: Well, so it would show what was wrong with the helicopter and what needed to be repaired.

Q: And to some extent the purpose of these reports was to help the mechanics and the people that were in charge of repairing the helicopter to understand what repairs might be necessary, is that right? A: That is correct.

Q: Did you take any steps to see that the mechanics were informed that the tail had been dipped in the water in this incident? A: In this particular instance I knew that the pilot had talked to the mechanic immediately upon coming back to Leeville and that the mechanics that changed all the parts probably knew more about it than I did.

Q: And how did you know that? A: Johnny Howren was down there and he is the mechanic that did the work.

Q: So that since this report showed that a mechanic had done work on the aircraft, you knew that Mr. Hyde had reported to the mechanic the former circumstances under which the damage occurred? A: Not only from that, but from talking to Mr. Hyde I knew that, and I knew—

Q: Because Mr. Hyde told you he had informed the mechanic, is that how you knew? A: Yes. Mr. Stubbs was with him, too. I talked to George Stubbs also.

Q: Did you ever see any other written report of this tail dipping incident, other than this notation that it was grounded due to a damaged tail rotor? A: I don't recall. Not that I can remember.

Q: Was there any requirement that reports be made when the damage to a helicopter in an accident exceeds a certain amount, in monetary terms? A: To the best of my recollection, if it was a case that involved an insurance claim I am sure that there would have to be something to substantiate the claim. In the case of an operational thing such as this, I believe that Petroleum Helicopters bore the cost of the replacement, and I don't think that there would be anything that would be required by law or anything like that.

Q: Did you ever discuss with Mr. Howren, the mechanic, whether he had done the repairs that would have been required had the log book shown that the tail had been dipped in the ocean? A: I don't recall.

Q: Do you know as a pilot that it is a serious matter to put the tail rotor of a helicopter into the ocean while the rotor is moving at its usual speeds? A: Yes.

Q: Have you been instructed that it can create stresses and strains in a helicopter similar to a violent contact with the ground? A: Stresses and strains in a helicopter?

Q: In the frame of the helicopter. A: Not such as striking the ground, I wouldn't say so, no. I think that could be qualified quite a lot.

Q: Have you received instructions as to what the effect of a dipping of a moving tail rotor in the ocean would be? A: Well, I can say this, that I have had considerable experience in observing helicopters that have struck water, and I have seen helicopters that have struck land. I know that there can be considerable damage to a tail rotor blade and to the hub, tail, rotor drive shaft, as would happen with a good strike with the tail rotor blade, either on land or water. Now, this doesn't mean that you are going to have stresses and strains throughout the fuselage of the helicopter. It is mostly the moving parts that we have always been concerned with in all types of helicopters when the tail rotor strikes.

Q: Have you ever received any instructions as to what the effect on the frame of the helicopter would be if the helicopter were flown with a damaged tail rotor? A: There again I would have to answer that it would depend on the amount of damage to the tail rotor. As I stated from personal experience, I have flown helicopters with a damaged tail rotor with no ill effect to the frame of the helicopter. You didn't even feel it in the helicopter. The only way you could see it was on a visual examination of the tail rotor blades. There again, if you strike the tail rotor hard enough or you have a lot of damage to it, certainly there could be vibrations set up, assuming that the tail rotor was struck hard enough. The incident that we are referring to in August was not considered a hard strike. This is a strike that would happen on any helicopter in the course of normal training, and it does happen; it happens every day to our helicopters, in training helicopters.

Q: Would you say that it is a frequent occurrence in PHI's operations that a helicopter's tail goes into the ocean? A: It is a common occurrence in any helicopter operation where you have pilots in training. This does happen.

Q: Would you say that it occurred during the summer and fall of 1959 on almost a daily basis with the Petroleum Helicopter's operations? A: Absolutely not.

Q: About how often would you say that tail dipping incidents occurred? A: With the Alouette, this was about the only tail rotor dipping incident that I can remember.

Q: And how about the other helicopters that Petroleum Helicopters was operating during 1959? A: We had Bell helicopters that were assigned to just dual instruction or for recurrent training of our pilots. At various times we may have experienced one or two strikes in a year. But it did happen. And it does happen, and will continue to happen.

Rand's effective cross-examination had prevented the plaintiffs from writing off the tail dipping incident as a matter of no consequence. Since PHI was not a defendant, our clients would lose the case if the judge decided that the crash was caused by negligence of PHI.

Chuck Krause next called Richard (Johnny) Howren, the PHI mechanic, who testified about the tail dipping.

Q. by Mr. KRAUSE: Would you refer to the engineering log of N519 for August 19th and tell me if you performed the pre-flight inspection on that helicopter on that date. A: On August 19th I signed for a daily and preflight inspection.

Q: Your signature appears on that page, is that correct? A: It does.

Q: Did you see George Stubbs or Jack Hyde on that day? A: I did.

Q: Did you see them prior to the time they flew the helicopter? A: I did.

Q: Did you see the helicopter N519 in flight at any time during that day? A: I did.

Q: Tell us what you saw. A: They were practicing autorotations [landings without power] into a lake east of the heliport.

Q: How far away was this lake from the landing pad at Leeville? A: Three-quarters of a mile to a mile.

Q: Could you see the water from where you were, from the pad? A: Yes.

Q: Did you see the helicopter on the lake at all on that day? A: I did.

Q: Would you tell us what you observed? A: The helicopter was on the water, with the engine shut off, it wasn't running, and the two pilots had gotten out of the helicopter and appeared to be looking around.

Q: Then what did you observe? A: They returned to their seats in the helicopter and took off and made a slow flight over to the heliport and landed the helicopter and turned it off.

Q: Could you tell us approximately how long that flight took to bring it to the pad? A: Two to three minutes.

Q: Then what happened at that time, after they landed? A: After they landed and got out of the helicopter we asked them what had happened. They said they had dipped the tail rotor in the water.

Q: Then what did you do? A: Proceeded to inspect the tail rotor blades to see how much damage may have been done.

Q: Did you in fact inspect the tail rotor blades? A: I did inspect the tail rotor blades.

Q: Would you tell us what you observed? A: One tail rotor blade had a deformed area, in the first six inches of the blade was a dent and a raised area of the blade. It was a very slight dent. It wasn't real noticeable.

Q: Did you inspect the other blade? A: I did inspect the other blade.

Q: Did you observe any damage to that blade? A: I did not observe any damage that was visible to the other blade.

Q: Mr. Howren, you indicated that you inspected the tail rotor blades. Did you inspect any other portion of the helicopter at this time—and I am referring to the time after Mr. Stubbs and Mr. Hyde had returned and you started your inspection? A:

We gave it a visual inspection to see if there were any other parts damaged and what we may need from Lafayette in case anything else may have been damaged prior to telephoning Lafayette for any parts we may need. So I gave the helicopter an inspection to determine if anything else needed to be changed at this time.

Q: What portions did you inspect at this time?   A: The drive system of the helicopter.

Q: When you say "drive"—   A: The tail rotor drive system of the helicopter.

Q: What is the tail rotor drive system? Could you describe that for us?   A: You have the tail rotor long shaft, tail rotor gear box, tail rotor blades, and tail rotor hub assembly.

Q: Did you make the inspection of those parts at that time? A: I did make an inspection of the parts at this time.

Q: Would you tell us what you observed with regard to those parts?   A: I did not find any other damage at this time.

Chuck took Howren through all parts of the helicopter that he had inspected after the tail dipping incident, and Howren testified that the only part damaged was the one tail rotor blade. Nevertheless, he had replaced a lot of parts in addition to the tail rotor blade, and the defense attorneys banged away at him for hours, trying to get him to admit that the damage had been extensive enough to start the deterioration that caused the structural failure during the fatal November flight. They took him through the entire maintenance history of the helicopter as shown in its logbook, and they confronted him with the PHI maintenance manual inspection requirements. But Howren, who had only a high school education and had never testified as a witness previously, stood up well on cross-examination.

Q. by Mr. RAND: Mr. Howren, after that tail dipping accident you changed the tail rotor drive system, the tail rotor gear box, and the tail rotor blades on the helicopter, isn't that right? You replaced them?   A: As I indicated in my entry in the log book, yes.

Q: Do you know approximately what a tail rotor long drive costs? That is the shaft that runs fore and aft through the tail, is it not?   A: Yes. I don't know the cost of it now, no.

Q: Can you give us an approximation?   A: $700, and I am guessing.

Q: How about the tail rotor gear box, do you know what that costs, approximately?   A: I would imagine a couple of thousand.

Q: A couple of thousand?   A: Yes.

Q: And how about the tail rotor blade, a pair of them?   A: A pair of them, $700.

Q: Can you estimate approximately how many hours it would take to replace those three parts, hours of mechanic's time, that is?   A: Eight hours, eight man-hours.

Q: Now can you tell us why it was advisable to replace the drive shaft, although you observed no visual damage to the drive shaft? A: Only through instructions from the maintenance supervisor and as a precautionary measure.

Q: Will you tell us what those precautionary reasons were? A: So that they could be returned to Lafayette and inspected and probably returned to service if there was nothing wrong with them.

Q: Did you feel that they might be damaged? A: There is always that possibility.

Q: Did you feel that the damage might have been caused by some unusual strain or stress as a result of this tail dipping accident? A: It is possible.

Q: Well, Mr. Howren, anything is possible. I am asking you how you felt when you replaced those parts. A: The way I felt—

Q: What your belief was. A: My belief was that there was nothing wrong with them at this time.

Bill Rand had done his homework, and he demonstrated that PHI had failed to make an inspection that was required at the time that the helicopter had been flown 600 hours. Its total time was 622 hours at the time of the crash, and one of the items that should have been performed at the 600 hour inspection (22 flying hours prior to the crash) was to check the tail boom for cracks, an intensive inspection with a magnifying glass. If Rand could prove that the tail dipping incident had caused cracks that could have been detected during the 600 hour inspection, or if he could prove that the type of crack that caused the crash (regardless of its source) could have been detected then, he would put a big hole in our case. He laid the groundwork for this potentially decisive defense by proving that the required 600 hour check had not been performed. He would have to establish later through his own expert witnesses that the fatal crack could have been found during the 600 hour inspection.

Chuck went on to the next witness, Bruce G. Hoch, an air safety investigator for the Bureau of Safety, Civil Aeronautics Board, which was at that time the agency responsible for aircraft accident investigation. Mr. Hoch testified by deposition that he had taken custody of the wreckage at the PHI hanger shortly after the accident; had examined the break in the upper right longeron at the point where the stabilizer support bracket was welded to the longeron; had sawed off that part of the tail boom, and had sent it to the engineering division of the CAB Bureau of Safety in Washington, from where it was sent on to the National Bureau of Standards for closer examination by a metallurgist named William L. Holshouser. Chuck Krause next read from the deposition of Holshouser which had been taken at the Bureau of Standards in Washington. First Chuck read Holshouser's testimony about his education and experience, which showed that he had been employed as a metallurgist by the Bureau of Standards since 1939, and had published a number of papers on metal fatigue and service failures in metals. The projects assigned to him showed that he was regarded as one of the government's leading authorities on failures in metals. Then Chuck read the key parts of his testimony:

Q: Do you have an opinion as to the cause of fracture of the longeron which you examined from N519? A: Well, my opinion can only be stated in terms of a probable cause contributing to the failure. The actual failure would be caused by the stresses to which the part was subjected. However, in my opinion the presence of the weld in the area where the fracture occurred was a contributing factor.

Q: In what way was the presence of the weld a contributing factor? A: In my opinion, the portion of the tubing adjacent to the weld was more brittle than it would have been if the weld had not been present, and this portion of the tubing is not able to withstand the amount of deformation that it would have been required to withstand under the loads that would be imposed upon it.

Q: And what brought about this brittleness? A: I think the welding, and the fact that the part was not heat-treated after that.

Q: In what way did the welding bring about this brittleness? A: I don't have any information regarding the exact type of microstructure that was found in the tubing, and I have nothing in the report to refresh my memory on that point. It is generally true in welds in steel aircraft tubing that if the steel is brittle, it is caused by the heat of the welding changing the structure of the metal from a tempered martensitic structure to a structure of untempered martensite; this and the presence of stress concentrations in the vicinity of the weld can cause a brittle fracture to occur.

Q: Referring to the third paragraph of your report, in the weld of the stabilizer bracket to the longeron of N519, the upper right longeron, was there incomplete root penetration as observed by you? A: Yes.

Q: What was this incomplete root penetration which you observed? A: That was failure of the weld metal to fuse properly with the tubing metal and the bracket metal near the junction of the two parts.

Q: Now, did this incomplete root penetration contribute to the brittleness of the tubing? A: No, I don't believe incomplete root penetration in itself would contribute to the brittleness of the metal.

Q: What would be the effect of incomplete root penetration? A: It would increase the amount of stress concentration that is normally present under any loads that are transmitted between the bracket and the tubing.

Q: Would this be stress concentration points on the tubing itself? A: Yes. It would create stress concentration where the weld metal was joined to the tubing near the root of the weld.

Q: What would be the effect of increasing the stress concentration on the tube? A: It would, in effect, reduce the load that could be transmitted between the tube and the bracket.

Q: Previously you stated that the welding of this part to which we have been referring may have contributed to the cause of the fracture, that is, the transverse fracture of the tubing. Do you have an opinion as to whether the welding did contribute to the cause of this fracture? A: Yes, in my opinion, the weld did contribute to the cause of the fracture.

Q: Now, at the conclusion of your report, Plaintiffs' Exhibit 12, you stated that improved welding technique and heat treatment after welding would increase the resistance of the assembly to the type of failure that occurred. What is the improved welding technique to which you refer? A: Well, increased root penetration, so that the weld would fuse the parts together right up to the root of the weld.

Q: Would this increase the strength of the entire unit, the longeron and the bracket? A: Yes, I think it would.

Q: Was the welding technique employed in this case a contributing cause of the fracture in your opinion? A: Yes, I believe it was a contributing factor.

This testimony was extremely valuable to the plaintiffs, since it supported our theory that the longeron fracture was a type more likely to have been caused by faulty welding than by a tail dipping or other rough handling by PHI. However, we could not rely solely on Holshouser's testimony, since the defendants had objected to his expressing any opinion on the grounds that his report was part of the CAB accident investigation and therefore was subject to the statutory prohibition of opinion evidence. It was not clear from the precedents whether the statute prohibited opinions by CAB and FAA employees only, or whether it also extended to other government experts called in by those agencies. Holshouser was employed by the National Bureau of Standards, whose employees are not prohibited from giving opinion evidence in civil litigation. Judge Croake reserved decision on the defendants' motions to strike out Holshouser's opinion testimony.

It was important for Judge Croake to hear Holshouser's testimony, but we could not be certain that he would admit any of it (other than factual observations) into evidence. Chuck Krause had hired Isaac (Ike) Stewart, a consulting engineer, and he called Ike as a live witness at the trial. Here we were under a severe handicap because Ike Stewart had never seen the failed longeron parts or any other parts of the wrecked helicopter. By the time that we were called in on the case, the parts had been returned to PHI by the government investigators, and then, after PHI sent them to a private consultant's laboratory, they disappeared—as we shall see.

All that Chuck could show Ike Stewart were photographs of the failed parts. Chuck had to walk a tightrope between the possibly objectionable opinion testimony of Holshouser, who had examined the failed parts, and the admissible opinions of Ike Stewart, who had seen only the photographs. Ike had been an engineering officer in the Army Air Force during World War II, and had gone on to complete his chemical engineering studies before taking a job with New York Testing Laboratories. There he had risen to being in charge of their metallurgical laboratory and had then become their chief engineer. He had left to establish his own practice in accident and material failure evaluation. Although he held only a bachelor of science degree from the Newark College of Engineering (night school division) and had little experience with helicopters, we had used him in other cases, and we knew that he was usually able to make his opinions stand up in court. At that time it was practically impossible to find an aeronautical engineer experienced in the metallurgy of helicopters who would testify against a helicopter manufacturer, and so we had to make do with Ike Stewart.

First, Chuck had Ike Stewart draw a cross-section sketch of an aircraft structural tubing. Then he had Ike add to the sketch two pieces of metal welded to the tubing. The first weld, marked "1", showed complete root penetration. The second weld, sketched in red and marked "2", illustrated incomplete root penetration. Using this sketch, Chuck went right to the heart of our case in his questioning of Ike Stewart.

Q. by Mr. KRAUSE: Mr. Stewart, could you describe for us, with regard to welding technique, what is meant by root penetration? A: Yes. In welding, root penetration means the actual penetration of the weld-fused area to the root of the weldment. In other words, to maintain a good, solid weld, it is necessary that the fusion extend all the way into the root which, as I described earlier, was the point of junction of the two elements being fused together, sir.
Q: What does Number 2 show, the drawing that you have before you, the fillet marked Number 2? A: The fillet, which I have marked as Number 2, is one in which in the application of the weld penetration did not extend down to the point of the root, which is encircled in green. It bridged the area so that the actual weldment is not within the root area of the weld. That's in contrast to Number 1, where the root is within the actual fused welded area.
Q: Sir, is that incomplete root penetration, the drawing with the Number 2? A: Yes, sir.
Q: Is there a difference between incomplete root penetration and insufficient root penetration? A: Both terms are indicative of the same type of condition. The element of incompleteness is an element of insufficiency. In the design of a weld, the weld is designed to sustain the necessary loads and that is based upon a good-penetration solid weld. If the weld, as fabricated

for the same loading conditions, is insufficient or incomplete, then it is insufficient for the function which the two have been designed to originally take care of.

Q: All right, sir. Would you explain for us how loads that are applied to these two metal members that had been joined, first of all with regard to Drawing Number 1, how those loads would be transmitted through the weld area? A: If we refer to Drawing Number 1, which I indicated was a proper form fillet weld, and if we take as our first example a load that is pulling upward toward the top of the page, which I will represent with an arrow—

Q: Why don't you use this blue? You are drawing an arrow above the metal perpendicular on the Number 1 drawing? A: Right. And, of course, the resistance to that pull is exerted through the tube in a downward direction, and it is a typical example of a particular type of loading.

Q: All right. A: The load transfer occurs right straight through in line with and through the weld metal.

Q: All right. A: Represented by the red, and I can then draw a line through it like this.

Q: All right, sir. Fine. A: That is on a weld of good root penetration, where you get the transfer that you desire.

In contrast to that, we again use the same loading quantity, namely, a vertical load in that respect, and down below we note the circumstance now develops where directly below this vertical member there is no weld metal because of the fact that root penetration was not accomplished at the time of welding. So the stress that is within the piece itself at this point has to be transferred through the weld metal over to another location, namely, where the weld metal now contacts the tube.

So we have already now established an offset situation. It so turns out that if we take note of the heat-affected zone that this weld had produced, we now find that our heavy stresses are being introduced through that heat-affected zone, which as I described on the earlier drawing is on this exact location.

Secondly, you also set up a bending stress just by the use of ordinary linear stress, and these develop into additional defective loading conditions due to the insufficiency or the lack of root penetration in this type of a weld.

Q: All right, sir. Where, then, would the stress be placed on the horizontal piece of metal that you have drawn? A: Well, it would be placed at the point that I have drawn here.

Q: All right. A: So that if we were to put the heat-affected zone in you would note it goes right through the heat-affected zone, whereas, in the case of the unit on Number 1, the heat-affected zone area of the most detrimental location would be away from the area of actual stress transfer.

Ike Stewart's drawing showing the difference between a proper weld and one with insufficient root penetration was admitted into evidence by Judge Croake. Then Chuck moved to Plaintiffs' Exhibits 11 and 12a, the photographs that had been taken by Holshouser at the Bureau of Standards—the only evidence that would enable Ike Stewart to reach the conclusion that there had been insufficient root penetration in the Alouette's weld.

> Q. by Mr. KRAUSE: Mr. Stewart, have I briefly shown you the photograph [showing fracture in weld] that has been marked Plaintiffs' Exhibit 12–A? A: Yes, you have, sir.
>
> Q: Mr. Stewart, did you examine that photograph? A: Yes, I did, sir.
>
> Q: Did I also show you the photograph that has been marked Plaintiffs' Exhibit 11 [showing fracture in longeron] and also the report of Mr. Holshouser, which is marked Plaintiffs' Exhibit 12? A: I have seen all of those, sir, yes.
>
> Q: Mr. Stewart, can you tell me what type of fracture is indicated by reference to the face of that, the fracture on the longeron? A: This photograph indicates a brittle type of fracture along the fracture face of the longeron itself.
>
> Q: In the area that you are referring to, sir, would you describe that for us, please. A: It extends from approximately one inch or so from the right-hand end of the longeron shown here completely through to the other side, sir.
>
> Q: Is that area that you are referring to, the area just above the ink mark, the ink that runs along that area on that photograph, if you can see that? A: Yes, except that the ink mark extends a little further to the right, as I see it, by reflection of the actual area that I see this embrittled type fracture, sir.
>
> Q: What did you observe on the face of that fracture to lead you to that conclusion? A: Well, there is a chevron-type indication, and the coarse grain structure that I can see in this area.
>
> Q: Did you use anything to assist you in looking at that fractured face? A: Yes, sir.
>
> Q: Other than your naked eye? A: I did.
>
> Q: By reference to that photograph, sir, do you see the area which you have described as the root of the weld? A: I see it here, sir, yes.
>
> Q: Would you describe the root of the weld for us, please. A: In this view at the very center underneath an arrow there is an area where there is good and complete root penetration over a very small distance, measuring on the photograph approximately slightly over a quarter of an inch. That is a tack weld that was applied to retain the tube and bracket together for ultimate final welding. But on the extensions of that joint beyond that point going both ways we can actually see the edge, the rear edge of the bracket itself, and it shows no weld metal or root penetration to that location.

Thus Ike Stewart put his finger on the manufacturing defect that in his opinion had caused the structural failure and the fatal crash. Feeling that Ike's testimony had made a prima facie case for the plaintiffs,

Chuck Krause turned him over to the defendants for cross-examination. Chuck had spent hours in the office preparing Ike for cross by questioning his conclusions from every conceivable angle. The trial lawyer who accepts his expert's opinions without educating himself enough to test them often suffers unpleasant surprises at the trial.

Bill Rand attacked Ike Stewart on cross-examination, starting with his lack of experience with helicopters and taking him through hours of questioning on many details of the welding and construction process that he knew little about. But he stood by his opinion that incomplete root penetration in the weld would cause normal stresses originating in the horizontal stabilizer to be sidetracked through the weld metal to a weaker and more brittle part of the weld area, rather than being passed directly through the root of the weld. On the other hand, he testified, if the welding had been done properly with adequate root penetration, the two pieces would be fused and would transmit stress safely without placing undue strain on the weaker weld area. Ike's testimony supplied the weld that we needed to fuse our evidence into a prima facie case of negligence and breach of warranty. After Ike stood by his conclusions despite painstaking cross-examination, Chuck Krause rested the plaintiffs' case.

The first witness that Bill Rand called for Sud-Aviation was Everett Chapman, the nation's leading aviation litigation consultant, who had previously testified as an expert witness for the defense in at least 30 aviation trials, many of them won by defendants. Chapman was a distinguished-looking, white-haired man in his sixties, very positive (if not imperious) in his style of testifying. All you had to do was to ask him a general question and he would deliver a lecture which he did not expect to be challenged. He had the qualifications to back up his aggressive style, including a bachelor of science degree in electrical engineering and a master's degree in mathematics and physics from the University of Michigan. His experience with metals went back to the 1920s. During the 1930s he served as president of Lukenweld, a division of the Lukens Steel Company which built welded steel machinery and components. Here is a small portion of the qualifications that he stated in answer to Bill Rand's preliminary questions:

> Around 1940, Lukenweld had grown from a small company employing six welders in one corner of the open hearth to a two-plant thing where I was in charge of 2,000 welders. And during the war years we made our production sort of focused in on the submarine engines and 5-inch gun mounts, destroyer drives, gears and gear cases and that sort of thing.
>
> In 1943 I resigned from Lukens to start my own consulting business and, well, I had had as clients—I was on General Motors diesel problems for five years. I did some work for

American Locomotive Company on a retainer basis. I was employed by the Engineering Research Corporation at Riverdale, Maryland, who made small airplanes.

After my resignation I was also retained by the Navy Department to sort of troubleshoot battle damage, namely: how to get some of this stuff back to port, No. 1; and No. 2, there was a diagnostic activity with it, to see how we could improve naval machinery against depth charges and impacts and bumps which seemed to produce rather curious failures.

I was consultant with General Barnes, United States Army Ordnance, design and manufacture of antiaircraft gun mounts.

*　　*　　*

I have specialized most of my life in steel and metallurgy, arc welding and gas welding of all sorts, including flash welding. I built and operated for the Navy Department a flash welder at Coatesville, Pennsylvania, that was capable of welding 8-inch rounds together in 90 seconds. We were after some more crankshafts because the early days of the war we needed more destroyer escorts.

I hold 42 patents in the field of design construction and processes. I have maintained a laboratory fairly well equipped metallurgically: microscopes, hardness testers, and I have a sideline business in which we make optical instruments for the measurement of stresses and strains and evaluation of stress concentrations which have been sold all over the world.

During the 30s one of my major activities, when we first started Lukenweld, was to find out what was wrong with welding that in those days was suspect, and sometimes it busted and sometimes it did not, and we studied—well, I had a pretty good-sized research department. We studied the contours of various kinds of welds, the metallurgy, the complicated metallurgy that can go on around a weld. We thoroughly wrung out the subject of residual stresses, and I published some papers summarizing our results.

I also wrote some articles on welded steel diesel-engine construction, and welded structures in general. The American Welding Society published some of them; the Journal of the American Society of Mechanical Engineers and the Society of Naval Architects also published some.

In this case, he was first retained by Petroleum Helicopters to examine the failed parts when they were at the Bureau of Standards. Thus, in addition to his more impressive education and experience in metallurgy and welding, he had an advantage over Ike Stewart in that he had actually examined the failed Alouette parts. Rand questioned him about his visit to the Bureau of Standards shortly after the accident.

Q. by Mr. RAND: I show you Plaintiffs' Exhibit 11 and ask you if the pieces that you saw when you visited Mr. Holshouser, roughly, when assembled, constituted the piece that is pictured in that photograph? A: Yes, that is correct.

Q: Did you make any detailed examination of the pieces at the time you visited Mr. Holshouser? A: At the time I was at the Bureau of Standards Mr. Holshouser had separated one side of this bracket. He had it mounted up in a vise, and he had a Bausch & Lomb binocular microscope, and he allowed me the use of the microscope for as long as I wanted. I stared at these things for, oh, probably an hour and a half, an hour. It was a visual examination and nothing else.

Q: Did you look particularly at any welds in the course of that visual examination? A: Yes. My main interest was in the back side of the fillet weld which was on the left side of the bracket in the upper right longeron. I looked at the fracture that appears in one of these photographs and examined the weld for back penetration, things like that.

Q: Can you identify on either Plaintiffs' 11 or 12–A the fracture you referred to? A: Yes, the fracture I was specifically interested in is the one shown on 12–A, and that is the bit that was held, mounted for me in a microscope with the fracture face in a horizontal plane so that the microscope would be used in its normal position, looking down into it.

Q: At the time you made this examination, did you know what was the interest of Petroleum Helicopters with respect to that weld? A: Well, the question that was put up to me is, what happened, what kind of a failure did we have here? I am never assigned to find an answer, I am assigned to take a look and tell them what I saw.

Q: But did you know whether they would profit by the evidence that the weld was a good weld or whether it would be against their interest that there be evidence that the weld was a good weld? A: No.

Thus Bill Rand established the fact that when Everett Chapman first examined the failed parts, he was not working for Sud-Aviation but had actually been retained by PHI, the operator of the Alouette, whose financial interests would be served by a finding that the failure was caused by a manufacturing defect rather than by the tail dipping incident, rough handling, or improper maintenance. It was only after PHI got out of the case that Sud-Aviation hired Chapman as an expert, and therefore it could hardly be claimed that he was biased in favor of Sud-Aviation at the time that he examined the failed parts. Rand continued his questioning of Chapman:

Q: Did there come a time when you made a more detailed examination of the parts? A: Yes.

Q: Can you tell us approximately when that occurred? A: As near as I can reconstruct my diary, I received the parts at my laboratory on August 12, 1960. They were sent to me from Petroleum Helicopters, Lafayette, Louisiana.

Q: What did you do with them in August when you received the parts? A: Well, I got them under my own microscope.

Again, I had been puzzled down at the Bureau of Standards as to the nature of this fracture, whether it was impact or fatigue, and I was specifically looking for fatigue. I couldn't make up my mind about that, so I looked and looked and went on back and looked some more; and with regard to the little metalographical mount that Holshouser had prepared, it was a slice through the companion weld on the forward end of this same bracket. I examined the microstructure that was shown on Holshouser's original polish.

Here was veteran metallurgist Chapman (the man who once had 2,000 welders working under him and was consulted by the likes of General Motors, the U.S. Army and the Navy) saying that he could not determine the nature of the fracture after looking at it for hours through a microscope. Then, the implication was, how could Ike Stewart, the Newark night school graduate, determine the nature of the fracture by simply looking at some 8″ × 10″ black-and-white photographs? Rand continued to bang away at the very extensive microscopic examination that apparently was necessary to reach any conclusion about what caused the structural failure:

Q: Could you tell anything about the granular structure of the metal? A: Yes.

Q: What was your conclusion based on that? A: Well, that the metal had not been severely damaged by the welding heat. I have seen it a hundred times in normal welds where the heat distribution has been leveled out and where the quench ingredients are not too brief.

Q: What would you have seen under the microscope if the metal had been seriously damaged by the weld? A: You would see—again, the worst thing you could do alongside of the weld is to have the wrong paraffin content and to apply sufficiently sharp heat gradient so that the thing quenches into the diamond-hard region. Under the microscope that looks like little 60-degree needles. They are little things that look so, and there would be a bunch of them over here this way, but they are all characterized by a 60-degree sort of an arrow, and they call it Martensite, and it's very hard.

Q: Did you see any such needles when you looked under this microscope? A: No Martensite.

Q: You say you examined it visually through the binocular microscope? A: Yes.

Q: Did you examine it in any other way? A: No.

Q: What did you see as a result of your examination through the microscope? A: Well, I saw a fracture face that suggested, by characteristic markings, a fast fracture. I could not find these conchoidal shell marks which are characteristic of fatigue. I was interested specifically in finding fatigue, if I could, because it meant that there was something wrong with the structure from the time it started to fly. But the fracture I saw is a fast one and did not take many cycles of operation if it took more than one to execute.

The other thing I was looking for is some evidence of an old crack, that is, something that had started and gotten dirty or got some oil in it or something, and then the final fresh fracture face propagating from it. The fracture face is nice, bright and shiny. It wasn't as bright and shiny when I got it, but the photograph shows it better, through about 120 degrees on the lower half of this curved piece. Up near the ends of this arc there were some suggestions that a crack had been in existence. But there is nothing about that fracture that I could make any definitive statement about.

Q: Could you tell where the fracture originated, the point of origin? A: No, sir.

Q: Turning to the weld itself, did you examine the weld? A: I looked at it as best as possible, looking at it from the back side. There is nothing wrong with the front side. It was a beautiful weld on the front.

Q: Did you form an opinion as to whether the way in which the weld had been made had contributed as a cause to the fracture in August 1960? A: I concluded that it had nothing—that the basic construction of the weld was not a governing factor in the failure.

As Chapman testified, Chuck Krause made extensive notes. He knew that this case was getting down to a battle of experts in which Sud-Aviation had the upper hand. An aircraft manufacturer can always produce impressive experts and can spring at the trial facts and opinions which no plaintiff's expert can completely anticipate. The plaintiff's lawyer must steep himself in the science involved, so that he can joust with defendant's experts without getting cut off by technical jargon and pettifogging.

Bill Rand made capital of his advantages as he continued through the high point of his case, the direct examination of Everett Chapman. After drawing from Chapman the opinion that the weld did not cause the failure, he brought out the fact that all of Chapman's work in examining the parts was done while Chapman was under retainer from PHI. Chapman testified that while he was in the process of studying the wreckage and reaching these conclusions, he was notified by PHI that they had closed their file on the case because their insurance company had paid certain benefits to the claimants, and that Chapman was not to do any further work. Sometime after that, the parts which had been shipped to him apparently were taken off to the garbage dump by mistake. The disappearance of this vital evidence clearly was not engineered by Sud-Aviation, Republic, or any of their lawyers, because they had no contact at all with Chapman until after he had lost or disposed of the parts. During the entire time that the parts were in his possession, he had been working solely for PHI. (This problem of preserving potential evidence occurs often in product liability cases, as we shall see later in this chapter.)

Having taken Chapman through the testimony designed to destroy the plaintiffs' claim that the failure was caused by a bad weld, Bill Rand then questioned Chapman about the tail dipping incident, in an effort to provide the court with an alternative theory: that the tail dipping incident would have caused stresses leading to cracks in the weld area of the longeron.

> Q: Incidentally, do you have an opinion as to what form of stress caused the fracture in the longeron that you observed?
> A: Yes.
> Q: What would that be? A: Well, a longitudinal force applied along the upper right-hand longeron in a very, very small period of time, so short as to constitute a hammer-blow impact, very, very suddenly applied blow.
> Q: Did that force by itself cause the tube to fracture? A: That is my opinion with reference to the start of the damage at 430 hours or 432 hours or whenever the tail dipping incident occurred.
>
> *   *   *
>
> Q: With the assumptions that I have asked you to make, I ask you whether you have an opinion as to the cause of the fracture of the longeron? A: Yes, I do.
> Q: Would you tell us what that opinion is. A: It is my opinion that at the time of the tail dipping the upper right longeron was subjected to an impact blow putting the entire longeron in tension, and that small cracks were formed at the ends of the bracket ears, and that subsequent operation resulted in a deterioration of a portion of the tube circumference to the point where it was not able to withstand flight loads at approximately 622 hours—is it?
> Q: That is correct. A: —and that the gradual deterioration of the longeron had progressed far enough so that an impact break occurred at 622 hours.
> Q: Can you tell us when you first formed this opinion. A: Well, it would be in October, 1960.
> Q: That was at a time before you had been contacted by either Sud-Aviation or Republic Aviation? A: That is correct.

Since the Alouette II was the first French aircraft of any kind to receive American certification, and since Sud-Aviation is a prominent manufacturer with many multimillion-dollar aircraft (such as the Caravelle and Concorde) on the market, they spared no expense in defending the integrity of the Alouette II. After hiring Chapman as a consultant, they flew him over to the Sud-Aviation factory in France to help prepare for his trial testimony. Since the failed parts were no longer available, he had the Sud-Aviation factory make up a lifesize replica of the upper right longeron section and bracket which were involved in the failure, and he brought this replica to court, where it was put into evidence as Sud Exhibit J. Chapman used it extensively in his testimony to demonstrate to the judge the searching studies that he had made. Bill Rand took him back to the quality of the weld, this time using the replica to explain his conclusions.

Q. by Mr. RAND: Mr. Chapman, on Friday we were talking about a weld near a fracture in a longeron on pieces that you had examined. Can you tell me as a result of your examination whether you have any opinion as to the welding technique that was used in creating that weld? You understand, the weld I am referring to is the weld that is nearest to the fracture. A: Well, the welding technique was excellent.

Q: Did you notice any other welds that had been performed on that aircraft? A: Yes.

Q: Which other ones did you examine at about the same time? A: The two welds that support the one we have been talking about, and I had a section of the tail boom sent along with the parts and the welding. I must have examined probably fifteen of these welds, and the welding technique was excellent. It was very sophisticated and, as far as I am concerned, it was right out of Tiffany.

Q: In saying that, are you taking into account also the root-penetration of the welds as far as you could see them? A: Yes.

Q: Did you have occasion to visit the Sud-Aviation factory in France? A: Yes, I did.

Q: Do you remember what town that is in? A: Marianne.

Q: Which part of France is that? A: It is Southern France. It is about 15 miles from Marseilles.

Q: While you were there, did you have them manufacture for you a part similar to the part that you had seen in your laboratory some years earlier? A: I did.

Q: Is this the piece that was manufactured in the Sud factory while you were there [handing]? A: Yes. I scratched "Ch" on it when I was at the Sud plant.

Q: Does that generally set forth the appearance of the horizontal stabilizer support bracket and the longeron and the welds that attach the bracket to the longeron as you saw the pieces in your laboratory? A: That's correct.

Q: Can you, on Exhibit J [the replica made at the French factory] Mr. Chapman, point out to us approximately where the fracture in the longeron occurred in the parts you examined? A: Yes. I asked them to put some tubes of the same gauge—they were welding Alouette booms while I was there—I asked if they wouldn't put a tube in the bracket in the welding fixture and weld it up and let me have it. So this is a portion of the right upper longeron. This tubular member.

This is the bracket that supports the right side of the stabilizer. And the fractures that we have been discussing with a crack started at the point I have my pencil, which is just above

the ears on the little bracket. There were two cracks emanating
from that point in the pieces that I saw. One of them went down,
downward and rearward at about 45 degrees, as I recall it, and
went around the tube and back up and met the other ear on this
side. The second crack emanating from the same point encircled
the tube going around at right angles to the axis of the tube.
So that we have a two-crack formation, one right around the
tube and one coming off at 45 degrees.

Chuck Krause had been studying the replica carefully during Chapman's
testimony. He knew that the whole case hinged on his ability to discredit Chapman. If the judge accepted Chapman's conclusions, there
was virtually no chance of winning the case. When Bill Rand finished
his direct examination of Chapman, Chuck rose to cross-examine. He
picked up the replica of the failed part and pointed to the weld as he
asked Chapman:

> Q. by Mr. KRAUSE: Are you satisfied that this is a weld that
> would be on the upper right longeron of an Alouette?   A: That
> is what they [the Sud-Aviation factory in France] made for me.
> Q: Did you ask them to make it for you?   A: Yes.

Chuck was convinced that the replica was one of the *left* longeron
(which had not failed). Yet Chapman had testified positively that it was
the *right* longeron. The difference could be ascertained from the manner in which the horizontal bracket stabilizer was positioned on the
longeron. Chuck pointed to the bracket as he questioned Chapman:

> Q: This bracket is offset on here a little bit, isn't it?   A: Yes.
> Q: Can you tell me why?   A: The longerons taper inward as
> you go to the rear, and the stabilizer support bracket wants to
> stay at right angles to the center line of the fuselage, so there
> is a slight offset there to preserve that degree of alignment.
> Q: Would you take another look at that and tell me if you
> still feel that is the upper right longeron?

Chapman studied the replica carefully. Chuck thought that he could see
some of the color drain from Chapman's face as he hesitated. Finally he
answered, and for the first time the ring of authority and condescension
was not in his voice. He quavered a bit as he replied:

> A: No, this is the left-hand, left longeron.
> Q: Contrary to what you previously said?   A: Yes.
> Q: That is the left longeron; is that right?   A: Yes.
> Q: That is all.   A: This was not made—the welds in the
> righthand side are—it looks like this.
> Q: But that is not from the upper right longeron, that you are
> positive of now; is that right?   A: It is upper left.

The fact that Chapman did not know the left longeron from the right would have to create some doubt about all of his testimony, but it was important to discredit his conclusions on root penetration and other technical details as well. Chuck had noticed that during his direct testimony, Chapman had mentioned various degrees of root penetration without referring to any notes. Chuck took up the questioning on that point right after he had forced Chapman to admit that he didn't know the right from the left.

> Q. by Mr. KRAUSE: You indicated on Friday, I believe, that you thought the root penetration was how much? I believe 10 to 20 percent.   A: Something like that.
> Q: Then a little while later I believe you said it was not more than 30 percent, do you recall that?   A: Well—
> Q: Do you recall that?   A: Yes, I recall it.
> Q: All right. Mr. Chapman, you were asked the same question by Mr. Rand, on your deposition back in 1964, and you said, "Well, it was 50 percent"; do you remember that?   A: Yes.
> Q: What is it: 10, 20, 30, or 50?   A: It's anywheres from 0 percent to 100 percent.

Chuck then pounded away at half a dozen other measurements, opinions, and conclusions that Chapman had testified to, and in each instance he was able to cast grave doubt on the accuracy of Chapman's testimony. Chuck noticed that Judge Croake was taking a lot of notes during this cross-examination, especially when Chuck was able to confront Chapman with discrepancies between his trial testimony and his 1964 deposition. Chapman did his best to fight off these attacks on his credibility, and at one point he admonished Chuck, "You ought to listen to me." By the end of his testimony, he was back to his aggressive lecturing style.

After Everett Chapman left the stand, Bill Rand called two Sud-Aviation engineers from France, who testified to the welding and inspection techniques used at the Sud-Aviation factory. Sud-Aviation then rested its case, and it was Matt Corrigan's turn to put on his defense of Republic Aviation. We had sued Republic because they had assembled the helicopter after it was shipped to the United States and had operated it as a demonstrator for 437 of its total of 622 hours before it was leased to PHI. Since Sud-Aviation and Republic Aviation had all the aces up their sleeves and could produce surprise defenses at the trial, it would have been very risky for us to proceed without having Republic Aviation as a defendant. There could well have been testimony from Sud-Aviation employees or experts pointing to omissions or mistakes in the assembly procedure or inspections during the time that Republic operated the helicopter, which covered most of its service life. In that event, Sud-Aviation would have been blaming an absent culprit, and our clients would have been left holding the bag. Therefore it was our duty to sue Republic and to force disclosure of all the facts so that fault could be properly assessed.

Matt Corrigan did an excellent job of keeping a low profile throughout the trial. He questioned witnesses only on points that related directly to the possible liability of Republic. When it came time for him to put on his defense, he called as a witness William Cobey, Jr., an aeronautical engineer who had been director of helicopter engineering and assistant general manager of the helicopter division of Republic Aviation. He was the most highly qualified helicopter specialist to testify at the trial. He had inspected N519 when it was first assembled in the United States, and testified that it was in good condition, correctly assembled and properly maintained by Republic. He testified that the tail dipping incident, in his opinion, involved forces that were transmitted to the tail boom, and that the parts replaced after the tail dipping incident made a substantial change in the helicopter. He went to Louisiana after the accident and participated in the investigation as an observer. He saw the tail boom and examined the failed parts. Corrigan's final questions put Cobey directly in line with the testimony of Chapman.

> Q. by Mr. CORRIGAN: Did you observe the welding of the attachment of the bracket? A: Yes, I did.
> Q: What were your observations with respect to the welding? A: I made a purely visual observation without the benefit of a magnifying glass, but I detected nothing unusual about the welding.

On cross-examination, Chuck Krause drew from Cobey the admission that when the new helicopter arrived at the Republic factory, the welds were not inspected by Republic—this was done at the Sud-Aviation factory in France. Chuck then spent half an hour fencing with Cobey about Cobey's opinion that the tail dipping incident involved the transmission of serious stress to the tail boom. He could not get satisfactory answers to most of his questions, but he did weaken Cobey's testimony by making him evade any measurement of the loads which would have been transmitted to the tail. In real life it is rarely possible to demolish a witness in Perry Mason style. When dealing with technical testimony, often the best that the cross-examiner can do is to cast doubt upon the opinions of the expert by attacking the individual components that led up to his conclusions.

Cobey was the last witness, closing out seven days of testimony. The entire trial was devoted to liability, damages being deferred to a later date. Since there was no jury, there was no time devoted to juror selection, opening statements, or summations. The seven days of concentrated liability evidence were the equivalent of about three weeks' jury trial on liability and damages in ordinary negligence cases. It produced a 1,052-page record testimony plus several hundred pages of exhibits which Judge Croake had to study along with the extensive briefs submitted by all the parties. On page 1,052 the record ended with this final statement by the judge:

> This was a well tried case, and I wish you all a Merry Christmas and a Happy New Year.

Since daily copy was made of the testimony, we had the entire trial transcript and the exhibits to work with in submitting our final brief. The issues in the case were clear. The plaintiffs were claiming that the weld at which the failure occurred was an improper and unsafe one, in that the root penetration was insufficient to fuse the two pieces of metal into a unit strong enough to withstand normal flight loads over an extended operating period. The defendants, on the other hand, claimed that the weld was perfectly proper and that the cause of the failure was probably the tail dipping incident, coupled with the failure of PHI to make the 600-hour inspection which would have detected the serious effects of the tail dipping incident on the tail boom some 22 flying hours prior to the crash. Both sides had relied on expert testimony. Now the decision was in the hands of Judge Croake. Since he had several novel questions of law to decide as well as the facts of the case, and he was carrying a heavy load of other civil and criminal cases while mulling over this decision, it did not come until May 31, 1968.

The Decision

Judge Croake's written decision reviewed all the important facts and contentions of the parties. He rejected the main conclusions reached by Sud-Aviation's expert (Everett Chapman) and Republic's expert (William Cobey, Jr.), and found that Ike Stewart's testimony for the plaintiffs, citing insufficient root penetration of the weld, presented "the most viable theory" of how the structural failure occurred. He accepted Stewart's version and rejected all of the defendants' other theories, including the tail dipping incident and the failure of PHI to properly conduct the 600-hour inspection. He held Sud-Aviation liable both for negligence and breach of implied warranties of fitness and merchantability. He found no negligence or breach of warranty on the part of Republic, and so he let them out.

Judge Croake listed several reasons why he rejected Chapman's conclusions. He pointed out some important inconsistencies in Chapman's overall testimony, and he found that Chapman's attempt to blame the tail dipping incident had some vital pieces missing. He noted that there was no testimony adequate to explain how dipping the tail rotor in the water would result in the impact and the tension described by Chapman and defendants' other witnesses. Judge Croake commented:

> We think the nature and extent of any force ultimately exerted upon the upper right longeron as a result of the tail dipping incident is not a matter that can be assumed or left to conjecture. The attempts of Cobey to supply adequate proof in this area simply were not persuasive. In the course of a direct confrontation on cross-examination, Cobey was at worst evasive and at best unable to communicate how and to what extent the tail dipping would have affected the failed longeron.

Thus, Chuck Krause's fencing match with Cobey had the desired effect.

While Judge Croake did not mention the fact that Chapman had brought in a model of the wrong longeron, Chuck felt that the revelation of this error led to very careful scrutiny of all of Chapman's conclusions by the judge. Judge Croake concluded his analysis of the tail dipping incident by noting:

> Most of the evidence points to this tail dipping as having been relatively mild. If the tail dipping was the source of the failed longeron in this instance, it would seem possible to produce evidence that tail strikes are causally associated with structural failure. No such evidence was introduced.

The judge rejected the 600-hour inspection theory because the defendants had failed to prove that the tail dipping incident caused damage that would have been detected on such an inspection. He also found that there was no compelling evidence of rough handling or improper maintenance by PHI sufficient to cause the failure, and he rejected the defendants' claim that pilot Stubbs was negligent in heading back to shore instead of landing on the water immediately after he experienced control difficulties.

Of course we were elated with Judge Croake's decision, especially with his holding that the plaintiffs could recover for breach of warranty as well as negligence. This was the first time that claims of a pilot and passengers against an aircraft manufacturer were tried and won on the warranty theory. The *Goldberg* case which we won in the New York Court of Appeals had established the legal right of airplane passengers to sue for breach of warranty, but it had gone up on appeal at the motion stage and was settled before it ever came to trial on its merits.

The warranty holding was important because it was clear that Sud-

Aviation would appeal Judge Croake's decision. The appellate court might find that there was insufficient evidence of what occurred at the factory to support the negligence claim. Indeed, that was the thinnest part of our case because of the difficulty of countering Sud's evidence of the high quality of their welding technique and the state of the art of helicopter manufacturing in 1959. But even if the appellate court found our proof of negligence deficient, the plaintiffs would win the case on breach of warranty because Judge Croake had accepted Ike Stewart's testimony that the structural failure was caused by a defective weld. Thus our position in the appellate court was much stronger than if Judge Croake had found for us solely on the negligence claim—provided that the appellate court agreed that the new warranty principle applied to admiralty cases.

We had hoped that Judge Croake would order a trial on damages immediately after his liability decision, but Bill Rand convinced him that his rulings on the law (particularly on breach of warranty) involved novel and controversial questions which should be reviewed by the appellate court immediately. The U.S. Court of Appeals for the Second Circuit agreed to review Judge Croake's decision on liability before damages were tried, even though the normal procedure in the federal courts is to try all issues before any appeals are heard.

Chuck Krause argued the appeal against Bill Rand on March 5, 1969, before a Second Circuit bench consisting of Chief Judge Lumbard, Circuit Judge Smith, and District Judge McLean. Their decision was handed down on July 2, 1969. They unanimously affirmed Judge Croake's decision in all respects, holding that there was sufficient evidence to support his findings of liability both for negligence and breach of warranty. Thus they became the first appellate court to uphold the right to sue for breach of warranty without privity in an admiralty case. They noted that Judge Croake's factual determinations were made after a full trial which obviously turned on the credibility of the witnesses, and concluded:

> In this respect, the district court [Judge Croake] indicated that Sud's expert Chapman was inconsistent and that Cobey was evasive. The appearance and demeanor of the other witnesses undoubtedly also played a part in the court's evaluation of the testimony.

That ended the liability phase of the case. Soon after the Second Circuit's affirmance, we were able to work out satisfactory six-figure settlements for each of the three families, and so the damage issues were never tried. Thus the Alouette II story had a satisfactory ending for the bereaved families. We considered ourselves very fortunate to win a complicated product liability case in which the defective product was not available. Trying such a case was something like putting on a performance of Hamlet without the prince. But, as we shall see, it happens that way all too often.

PRESERVING THE EVIDENCE

When a person is injured or killed in an accident, probably the last thing in the minds of relatives is the preservation of evidence which may be needed in a subsequent lawsuit. While the family is preoccupied at the hospital or the cemetery, evidence that may be vital to their claims is being removed from the scene of the accident and sometimes altered or destroyed. This is a major reason why victims of serious accidents should immediately engage an attorney. At the time of the accident it is impossible to tell whether it will be difficult or easy to prove liability or even to identify all the prospective defendants. Often, there is an open-and-shut liability case against the operator, but the operator may have little or no insurance, so the plaintiff's lawyer will later be forced to pursue a products liability claim in order to collect any significant damages.

There is a derisive term, the "deep pocket theory," which has been applied to this hunt for a solvent defendant, but it is the duty of the plaintiff's lawyer to seek out all defendants who may have contributed in any way to the happening of the accident, since the law makes all such defendants liable for damages. It may be professional malpractice on the part of a plaintiff's attorney to assume that one defendant who is obviously at fault will be able to pay all of the damages, and to let evidence disappear which might establish fault of other defendants whose financial resources may be needed to make the plaintiff whole.

Experienced tort lawyers realize that they must take immediate steps to preserve evidence, particularly in a potential products liability case when the plaintiff was not the owner of the product. Even where the plaintiff was the owner, sometimes investigating authorities take custody of the defective product and in the process may destroy evidence. For example, in aviation accidents, the National Transportation Safety Board immediately takes custody of the aircraft wreckage. The NTSB does not have extensive facilities for making teardown inspections and tests, and so they must rely upon the expedient of sending components back to the original manufacturer for testing to determine if there was any malfunction or defect. This is supposed to be done under strict security, and there are government accident investigators present at the teardown and testing, but they cannot keep the components under constant guard. Thus the manufacturer, a prospective defendant, gains private access to evidence which may be used against him, and has an opportunity to disassemble it and to make various tests. It is possible that a manufacturer seeking to vindicate his own product or to avoid liability, can so handle this evidence as to make it useless to the plaintiff, or even to conduct tests in such a way as to make it falsely appear that the product was not at fault.

To the tort lawyer, this seems like the equivalent of turning the foxes loose in the hen house. Experienced plaintiff's attorneys will seek court orders (sometimes even before litigation has been commenced) directing that the wreckage be kept intact by whoever has custody of it until such time as the plaintiffs can have it inspected, tested, and photographed. This is particularly true of "general aviation" accidents, which unlike air carrier accidents, are not investigated by teams of top-flight government experts. However, even in major airline crashes, it is important to take steps to preserve the wreckage. You will recall our experience in the Grand Canyon case back in 1956, when we had to spend three days reassembling the wreckage of the two airliners on the floor of a hangar in Washington National Airport so that our expert could examine and photograph the parts. Often it is unsafe to rely on government photos and reports, for the government investigators may be pursuing a different theory of causation than the one finally selected by the plaintiff's lawyer. In the Alouette case, we were very fortunate that Mr. Holshouser of the Bureau of Standards observed the insufficient root penetration of the weld; that his photos showed it clearly enough to enable Ike Stewart to testify to that conclusion at the trial; and that the trial judge accepted that evidence. Often the plaintiff is not that lucky.

Insurance officials sometimes try to lull accident victims or their families by stating that there is no liability problem in the case and that they want to settle quickly without litigation. Therefore, they say, there is no need to hire a lawyer because this will only make it more expensive and will result in a lower net recovery for the plaintiff. But at that point the plaintiffs do not have the slightest idea of what is a reasonable settlement, and they should realize that insurance officials are under duty to their employers to make the smallest possible payments on all claims, regardless of how meritorious they may be or how serious the damages are. It is impossible for the plaintiff's family to know at that point whether they will need liability evidence because they may not want to settle at a figure that the insurance officials deem "reasonable" and will then have to pursue their remedies in court. If they have allowed the evidence to disappear because they did not hire a lawyer in time to preserve it, they will be dealing a mortal blow to their hopes for recovery of adequate compensation. Thousands of plaintiffs have lost their cases simply because the evidence that they needed disappeared before they retained attorneys.

We faced such a threat in a case that was referred to us by Melvin Belli. On May 17, 1956, a U.S. Air Force B-25 bomber took off from Lowry Air Force Base at Denver, Colorado, carrying a crew of five. Shortly after takeoff, one of the pilots reported an overspeeding propeller, an emergency condition which required an immediate forced landing. The pilot attempted to turn back to the airport, but the plane crashed in this attempt. Four of the occupants were killed instantly (two of them being decapitated). The lone survivor (whom we shall call Jim North) was an Air Force captain aboard as an observer. Captain North was a giant of a man who had played on a championship football team in the Rose Bowl during his college career. Although he lost both his legs and his spinal cord was severed, his life was saved because he was rushed to one of the nation's best medical facilities, the nearby Fitzsimmons General Hospital. He was flat on his back in the hospital for more than a year. When he finally emerged from the hospital, he was in a wheelchair, paralyzed from the waist down for life. He went back to his native California with his wife to try to pick up the pieces of his life. He was receiving free medical care and therapy and he also collected a monthly Air Force pension check, but since he was injured while on active duty, he could not sue the U.S. government to recover adequate compensation for his injuries and loss of future earning power. Eventually he was advised to seek legal advice, and through mutual friends he met Mel Belli.

Captain North was not able to tell Belli the exact cause of the accident, but he remembered that the pilot had radioed the control tower to say he had an overspeeding propeller and was attempting to return to the base. He recalled that when the right propeller overspeeded, the pilot attempted to feather it (shut it down so that it would not create any drag), but was unsuccessful and had to attempt to turn back to the field with the propeller still overspeeding. The only possible lawsuit was one against the manufacturer of the propeller, since an overspeeding condition means that the propeller went beyond its design limits, indicating that there might have been negligence in its design or manufacture. The propeller had been manufactured by United Aircraft Corporation, which had its factory and headquarters in the east. Therefore, when Mel Belli sized this up as a possible products liability case, he decided to refer it to us because United Aircraft Corporation could be sued in the New York courts. By that time it was nearly two years after the accident, and all of the propeller components and the rest of the aircraft wreckage had been disposed of by the Air Force. In fact, all of that vital evidence had been thrown out while Captain North was confined to his hospital bed, unable to even think about a products liability claim.

We accepted the referral from Mel Belli, and since I was the only one in the firm old enough to have flown a B-25, I decided to investigate the case myself. Captain North had requested a copy of the Air Force accident report, but the Air Force refused, telling him that it was against their regulations. They told him that the original report was kept at the office of the Inspector General of the Air Force at Norton Air Force Base, San Bernardino, California, and that if he came out there he would be permitted to read the report, although no copies would be given to him. I decided to go out to Norton Air Force Base with him to see if I could also look at the report. In June of 1958, we drove from Los Angeles to San Bernardino, and I wheeled him into the office of the Inspector General of the Air Force. I tried my best to look like a medical assistant, but apparently the Inspector General had no difficulty in guessing that I was a lawyer. I had to wait outside while the Inspector General sent for the accident investigation file and permitted the captain to look at it. I had suggested that he take a long time to read through the file and make mental notes (the only kind permitted) of important details such as the names of witnesses who testified about examination of the propeller parts, and descriptions of the propeller photographs taken after the accident, which I assumed would be in the investigation file.

Since Captain North was a highly intelligent engineer, he was able to recall many details of the accident investigation file which he dictated into a tape recorder as soon as we left the Inspector General's office. From what he had seen in the file, it looked like we had the makings of a products liability claim against the propeller manufacturer. This was before the days of breach of warranty and strict tort liability, but I felt that we had a chance to establish negligence in the design of the propeller, particularly since it was a type that had experienced quite a few incidents of overspeeding on other aircraft in the past.

Between that sunny day at San Bernardino in June of 1958 and the time when we actually got our hands on the photographs of the wrecked propeller parts and the statements of witnesses, more than five years were to elapse. Our first move was to start an action against United Aircraft Corporation in the federal court in New York. We obtained discovery of all of the records and photographs in their files, but they insisted that they had never received a copy of the Air Force report and that they did not have any significant photographs or data of their own, since this was a military accident whose investigation was under the sole jurisdiction of the Air Force. We then asked the Air Force to let us inspect and copy their file. We tried every possible way of making this request, including the intervention of senators and congressmen who took an interest in the case. However, we were turned down cold by the Air Force.

Their position was that they needed the cooperation of civilian contractors in making accident investigations; that they would not get such cooperation if the information disclosed by civilians could be used as evidence in future lawsuits; and that it would create a serious safety problem if their accident investigations were hampered by the obligation to disclose any such information. I pointed out to them in numerous letters that they had the power of life and death over civilian contractors, for United Aircraft Corporation and other major contractors would not dare to refuse cooperation in safety investigations for fear of losing multibillion-dollar government contracts. Although the Air Force officers I dealt with, from the Inspector General on down, were very sympathetic to the plight of Captain North, they felt that they could not bend the regulations in this case, and they finally refused to give us any information, even though they knew that this would make it impossible for us to proceed with the case—for the only possible sources of proof were the photographs and witness statements that sat in the Air Force file at San Bernardino.

When all of these efforts failed, we decided to take an unprecedented step. We filed a separate lawsuit in the U.S. District Court for the District of Columbia against the Secretary of the Air Force, for the sole purpose of forcing him to permit us to copy the evidence that we needed. We served a subpoena on the Secretary of the Air Force, calling upon him to produce the entire Air Force file. The government attorneys who appeared for the Secretary of the Air Force asked the District of Columbia to quash the subpoena on the grounds that it was against Air Force regulations and would impede their safety program. There was no claim made that national security was involved, since the B-25 was an ancient aircraft first designed and flown in the 1930s and used by General Jimmy Doolittle on the first American air raid on Tokyo in 1942. Anybody who wanted a B-25 could buy one as war surplus, complete with operating and maintenance manuals.

The District Court judge denied the Air Force's motion to quash the subpoena, pointing out that "no claim of privilege has been asserted or is being decided." After years of attempting to get access to the Air Force file, we felt that victory was in sight; but we were wrong. Five days after the District judge refused to quash the subpoena, the Secretary of the Air Force filed a formal claim of executive privilege. This meant that the motion to quash the subpoena had to be heard again, and this time it posed the thorniest of legal questions, one that our courts have carefully avoided since the earliest days of the republic. It is the same problem that arose during the Watergate scandal, when President Nixon refused to produce the tapes of his White House conversations on the grounds of executive privilege. The courts handle such cases like hot potatoes, because there is always this question lurking in the background: Suppose that the court turns down the claim of executive privilege and orders the executive department to do something—who is going to force the executive department (which controls the military forces) to carry out the court's order?

Faced with the Air Force's claim of executive privilege, the District Court reversed itself and quashed the subpoena. We were still without any evidence of the propeller overspeeding, even though our client had seen that evidence with his own eyes in the Air Force files.

We appealed to the U.S. Court of Appeals for the District of Columbia Circuit, and the case came on before Circuit Judges Washington, Danaher, and Burger (later to become Chief Justice of the Supreme Court). The circuit court wisely sought to avoid a confrontation on executive privilege by trying something that I had never seen an appellate court undertake before. They attempted to settle the controversy by reasoning with the lawyers for the Air Force, and they succeeded in convincing the government attorneys that they should produce the parts of the file that we needed to prove our case, including 34 photographs of the wreckage. The Air Force also agreed to produce a number of witnesses for deposition and to permit those witnesses to refresh their recollections from the Air Force records. All this material came under the heading, "Factual Findings of the Air Force Mechanics Who Examined the Wreckage." The court was careful to distinguish those factual findings from matters of opinion, which they held were privileged. Thus the circuit court made a Solomon-like decision which gave us the evidence that we needed and still kept intact the Air Force policy of protecting civilian witnesses who were asked to give their opinions and conclusions as to the cause of military accidents.

The information that we finally obtained from the Air Force files put us in a position to go forward, and on the eve of trial we were able to settle the case. The Air Force and other military services later set up new procedures under which they prepare a special litigation report which they now make available routinely to members of the public. It does not contain all of the information in the military service's files, but generally it gives enough information to determine the cause of the accident, and it includes photographs of failed parts which may form the basis for products liability claims.

DETERRENCE

In less than 20 years after the 1960 New Jersey decision in *Heningsen* and the 1963 California *Greenman* decision, there has been a revolution in products liability law. As Dean William L. Prosser put it in his famous textbook on torts:

> What followed [*Heningsen*] was the most rapid and alto-gether spectacular overturn of an established rule in the entire history of the law of torts. There was a deluge of cases in other jurisdictions following the lead of New Jersey, finding an implied warranty of safety as to a wide assortment of products.

This revolution was expedited by Dean Prosser, who started to chronicle the assault on the citadel of privity soon after he read Justice Traynor's 1944 concurring opinion in *Escola v. Coca Cola*. Prosser was also the reporter for the Restatement of Torts, and his influence was a key factor in getting the strict liability doctrine written into Section 402A of the Second Torts Restatement, which is given great weight by appellate judges throughout the nation.

While the ground-breaking was done by Dean Prosser and Justice Traynor, it remained for the entrepreneur-lawyer to fashion the concept of strict products liability into a real weapon for the consumer. Relief from the requirement of proving negligence did not make products liability cases simple or inexpensive. If the strict liability doctrine had been handed to the weak and disorganized plaintiff's tort bar of 1950, there would have been no products liability revolution. Under strict liability, the plaintiff is still required to prove the existence of a defect which made the product unreasonably dangerous and caused the accident. The Alouette trial excerpts gave you some idea of the homework that Chuck Krause had to do in order to take on a major manufacturer in court. Just ahead are some examples of how this task was handled by other entrepreneur-lawyers in the late 1970s, when the products liability revolution reached its peak.

There are several reasons for the products liability revolution other than the availability of the entrepreneur-lawyer and the plaintiff's indispensable allies, the contingent fee and trial by jury. NACCA, now called ATLA (the Association of Trial Lawyers of America) came into full flower as an education and information source for the scientific tort lawyer in the 1960s. ATLA established a products liability exchange which enabled lawyers throughout the country to obtain information about suits based on defective products—a sort of rogue's gallery of products liability defendants. As Ralph Nader's consumer movement gathered steam, Americans began to realize that many of our best-known products are unsafe, have always been unsafe, and never should have been sold to the public without safety modifications.

Prior to 1960, there had never been much financial incentive for manufacturers to make their products safe. Whole industries made unsafe products (such as football helmets and automobiles) because it was cheaper to do so. They competed with each other mostly through styling and marketing techniques rather than by trying to make safer products than their competitors. They made good profits by selling unsafe products. Today, even with government recall programs in effect for automobiles and other products, the main deterrent to manufacturers is the prospect of damage suits. Although the newspapers tell us that millions of automobiles are being recalled, many owners don't bother to bring the cars in for servicing. But most people who are seriously injured now have ready access to lawyers who are able to take on manufacturers in court. Because of the threat of products liability suits, many large companies now employ specialists or consultants who practice a new profession: risk management and loss prevention.

The idea of responsibility for defective products is not a new one. In the eighteenth century B.C., Hammurabi's Code provided that if a house collapsed and killed the occupant, the builder would be executed. Our law doesn't go that far today, but it has been developed to the point where a manufacturer who has an unsafe product on the market had better make it safe, or else it will be litigated off the market. At first, liability insurance will cover the damages, but after a few big judgments, the insurance companies will either cancel the coverage or make the premiums so high that it will no longer be profitable to make an unsafe product.

In all the history of litigation, it would be difficult to find a triumph of justice that equals the scope of the products liability revolution. Millions of people have been and will be spared serious injuries or death because of the deterrent effect of litigation on manufacturers. But the reaction of the well organized manufacturers was predictable. Facing their customers on an equal footing in court was not to their liking, so they turned to the legislative lobbying game that has served them so well.

In the 1970s, they were able to engineer the creation of a Federal Inter-Agency Task Force on Products Liability. After eighteen months of research, the Task Force came to the conclusion in 1978 that there was really no products liability crisis, and that the manufacturers who were making reasonable efforts to produce safe products had no difficulty in obtaining insurance at reasonable rates. But manufacturers continue to lobby for legislation restricting products liability claims, blaming runaway juries and greedy contingent-fee lawyers for skyrocketing insurance costs. Their arguments ignore the fact that increases in insurance rates reflect the absence of the right to make effective claims in the past. Shockingly dangerous products were sold by the millions because the public was practically without redress prior to the products liability revolution.

If manufacturers and insurers took the money they spend on lobbying for restrictions on product liability suits and devoted it to product safety research instead, they would accomplish three things. First, they would protect the public and avoid millions of serious injuries and deaths that occur because of defects in their products. Second, they would reduce their insurance costs to a minimum by reducing the safety hazard, since insurance costs are now directly proportionate to the dangers of the product. Third, they would improve their customer relations without spending additional billions on advertising and public-relations fees.

The products liability revolution is Adam Smith's free enterprise capitalism in its purest form, with the market weeding out the weaker products (through the legal system). If a manufacturer is not able to produce a safe product, then he should not be allowed to continue in business at the risk and expense of the consumer. If one cannot make a product safe, then a substitute can and must be found.

Many of our largest businesses use the courts without hesitation when *they* suffer financial losses due to product defects. Airlines and their insurers usually bring products liability suits against manufacturers when they lose a DC–10 or a Boeing 747. These huge property claims (which run to $50 million or more per airplane today) are not mentioned when attacks are made on the products liability revolution. Only when proportionate protection for life and limb is sought do we hear the outcry that such claims are clogging the courts and are threatening the very basis of the free enterprise system.

Critics of the tort litigation system used to claim that it was not a deterrent because cheap liability insurance paid for the damages. This argument faded away when damages began to approach reality, and we learned that neither business nor its insurers really want a deterrent system. Instead they want government regulation to restrict the free market. The marketplace is the courthouse, where the price of maiming and killing people is now being set at a high level, after centuries of bargain rates.

I believe that the deterrent effect of tort litigation is its most important public interest feature. Contingent fees, which make the deterrent credible and available to everyone, and the jury system, which allows the public to fix the price of maiming and killing its members, help to make this a self-regulating free market system which does not need any further government intervention. Manufacturers and other defendants can protest high insurance costs, but in the end they will have to make their products safe or take them off the market.

To take one product group as an example, factory machinery caused thousands of amputations a year in the 1970s. But machine manufacturers began to have difficulty getting insurance coverage because the products liability revolution created the industry's first strong deterrent: large verdicts that made it more expensive to sell dangerous machines than to make them safe. The National Safety Council took notice of the reasons for improved machine safety in the 1970s:

> Most machine manufacturers make point-of-operation and power transmission guarding "standard equipment" on all stock type machines, meaning the machine cannot be purchased without guards. This highly desirable state of affairs has in the main resulted from legal actions and legislation holding the manufacturer liable for accidents arising from unsafe design or manufacturing of his machines.

One would think that things would be different in the aviation industry, which had to be safety-conscious from its inception to overcome the public's fear of leaving the ground. There is extensive government regulation of virtually every phase of aviation, particularly safety. You would not expect that the highly motivated professionals who manage the airlines and fly the giant jets would need any further incentive to make their operations as safe as possible. But even in that field, the value of the tort deterrent is demonstrable. Consider the case of Captain Eddie Rickenbacker and the De Havilland Comet.

Eddie Rickenbacker could easily qualify for the title of Mr. American Aviation. He was America's leading fighter ace in World War I, and he went on to develop Eastern Air Lines as one of the nation's leading air carriers. He pioneered many advances in military and commercial aviation safety. In the early 1950s he was invited over to England for a preview of the first commercial jet airliner, the four-engine De Havilland Comet. He described this experience in his autobiography:

> We climbed to about four thousand feet and flew around over England. It was an amazingly smooth and comfortable ride. I visited in the cockpit, then strolled back toward the tail. Halfway down the aisle, I suddenly stopped short. I couldn't believe what I was seeing. The sides of the plane seemed to be moving in and out like an accordion. I pushed my finger up against the side. I could feel it.
>
> It scared the living daylights out of me. Sooner or later that metal would fatigue and crack. At forty thousand feet, the pressurized cabin would explode like a toy balloon.
>
> As casually as I could, I went back to the cockpit, tapped our host on the shoulder and said quietly: "I think we've seen everything we want to see. And we have an appointment, and we're about thirty minutes late now. So we'd like to go back, but please don't hurry on our account. Take your time going down."
>
> How I maintained my composure, I'll never know. I swore to myself, and later to my fellow Eastern executives, that never again would we all fly together in that type of plane. We could have lost the entire top management in one accident.

> On the ground, I talked to De Havilland's engineers, even
> the directors of the company. They refused to believe me. Three
> Comets crashed before the cause was determined. The fuselage
> had exploded, just as I feared it would. The Comet crashes
> were a great blow to British prestige. From my personal experi-
> ence with the plane, I was able to warn American manufac-
> turers about this accordion weakness, and steps were taken to
> prevent it.

Captain Eddie performed a public service by warning American manufacturers, but as a member of the exclusive club of aviation insiders, he
was inhibited from making a public statement critical of an aviation
manufacturer. A public announcement with Rickenbacker's prestige
behind it could have forced De Havilland to reveal the results of its
own tests or to allow impartial observers aboard to observe the weak-
ness that Captain Eddie had spotted. This could have saved the lives
of hundreds of people who died in the three Comet crashes. At the
very least, if he had spoken out after the first crash, he could have
saved the lives of those who were killed in the second and third
crashes. And if the Comet accidents had been subjected to American
tort litigation, it is very likely that discovery and depositions by the
plaintiffs' attorneys following the first crash would have uncovered
correspondence with Rickenbacker and other evidence that could have
forced De Havilland to ground the Comet until modifications made it
safe to fly.

I am convinced that the American tort litigation system is a
major reason why American aircraft are usually more safely designed
and constructed than those in other nations. Even though other nations have government regulators and manufacturing experts who are
equally knowledgeable and dedicated to aviation safety, they are not
pushed to the limits of their safety performance as American manufacturers are by the litigation system. The knowledge that they will
have to face intensive questioning for weeks at a time, covering every
piece of paper that they signed or handled in connection with the design of an airplane, has a sobering effect on the personnel of manufacturers, airlines, and government agencies. By this time, after a
quarter century of litigation involving the design and operation of
practically every major commercial airplane designed in the United
States, these officials are conditioned to the fact that they will be held
accountable if something goes wrong. No matter how skilled and
meticulous the staff may be, there is always room for more to be done
on safety if the pressure is applied by an outside force that cannot be
controlled or swept aside when something goes wrong. The American
tort system also causes the insurers who pay the bills to bring more
pressure on manufacturers and operators to maintain safety. This was

confirmed by John V. Brennan, president of United States Aviation Underwriters, Inc., one of the world's largest aviation insurance groups, who wrote:

> . . . products liability litigation has a positive effect on aviation safety. Aircraft manufacturers recognize the need to concern themselves with adequate warning and safe design of their products. This awareness is the result of a very aggressive legal profession using our courts to shed light on products liability injuries, as well as insurance underwriters increasing premiums in accordance with rising claims activity. It took many years of controversy and extensive litigation before there was an acknowledgment on the part of all concerned that the age of consumerism had arrived and that the safety of the product user was of paramount importance. . . . In conclusion, we have a legal system which in its own way has encouraged the growth of the biggest and safest and most efficient aviation environment in the world.

If the litigation process results in the insurer requiring one extra inspector in an aircraft factory, or one extra hour of training for a pilot, it pays for itself in the long run by the saving of lives. And this super-safety factor in aviation does not lead to excessive insurance rates. Indeed, just the opposite has occurred. Because of the intense pressure for safety, the annual accident rate of American-built aircraft and American airlines is usually the best in the world.

It is no coincidence that the United States is the world leader in aviation safety and at the same time the only major nation that permits judges and juries to award damages which approach the amount of harm actually done. Indeed, airline passengers throughout the world benefit from American litigation, since most of the world's airlines use some American-made equipment. When the jumbo jets were introduced in the 1970s, there was fear that insurance rates would skyrocket because of the concentrated risks involved in carrying 300 or more passengers in one airplane. But the result was just the opposite. There is aggressive competition among insurers all over the world to get into the business of insuring aviation risks. This resulted in driving insurance rates down throughout the 1970s. In 1978, reductions of more than 30 percent were obtained by some international air carriers because of the increased competition and the profitability of aviation insurance at lower and lower rates.

The products liability cases, such as the Alouette II, that were brought to trial in the 1960s paved the way for the cleansing of our environment and for reducing the industrial exploitation of life and limb by transmitting the message best understood by American business: the money judgment for damages.

We have spent billions to establish and staff government agencies

which can, at best, administer slaps on the wrists of giant corporations many years after they have exploited the public by keeping defective products on the market until they are obsolete. Trying to get a
dangerous product off the market through government regulation is
like punching a giant sponge. Many of the regulators are looking for
the first opportunity to jump to better-paying private jobs shielding
industry from regulation. Only the threats of large money judgments
and loss of cheap insurance coverage have brought safety progress in
most American industries. In my opinion, the products liability revolution is the best example of the deterrent effect of American tort litigation. Let's look at a few cases in point.

The Mohawk 600

On September 11, 1977, a prominent Austin, Texas, insurance defense lawyer, whom we shall call Frank Ramsey, was hunting with his
son, whom we'll call Tom, and two Texas district court judges. Young
Tom had been in a deer blind waiting for a deer that never materialized.
His rifle, a Remington Mohawk 600, which had been a present from his
grandfather, was set on safety. At one point, he thought he saw a deer,
and pressed down on the trigger. Realizing that the safety was on, he
moved it part way off, only to discover that the target had vanished. He
then moved the safety to the "on" position and heard the horn of his
father's car honk to tell him that the party was ready to leave. Leaving
the safety on, Tom walked back to the car and got in, with one of the
judges holding the door for him. His father was sitting in the front
seat, and as Tom got in, Frank asked him if the gun was loaded. Because the gun was in fact loaded, and good gun-handling practice calls
for weapons to be carried unloaded in vehicles, Tom followed the
usual procedure for unloading the rifle.

The Mohawk 600 is so designed that it cannot be unloaded with
the safety in the "on" position. It must be switched to the "off" position first. Tom pushed the safety to the "off" position as he sat in the
back of the car, and as he did so the gun discharged, firing the bullet
in the chamber into his father's back, through his spine, and into a
kidney. Tom screamed, "My God, I've shot my father!"

The judges saved Frank Ramsey's life by getting him quickly to
the nearest town, breaking into a locked hospital emergency room to
use the telephone, and getting a medical evacuation helicopter to the
scene. The bullet left Ramsey paralyzed from the tenth thoracic
vertebra down, and minus a kidney, in addition to other internal dam-

age. He lay near death for more than a month. It also left his 14-year-old son paralyzed with grief and guilt over the fact that he had been holding the weapon when it fired. He was convinced that he had been responsible for his father's injuries. Initially, it seemed that the trial lawyer's career was at an end and that young Tom would bear the scars of the disaster permanently. Most people who heard about the accident assumed that it happened because of faulty gun-handling on Tom's part.

At this point one of the legendary figures of modern tort law enters the story. Joseph Dahl Jamail, then 52 years old, and like Ralph Nader the son of a Lebanese immigrant, had established a reputation for fabulous results in large tort cases in Houston, where it takes some doing to attract attention in matters of big money. A dark, wiry, scrappy, fast-talking trial lawyer who radiates excitement, Joe Jamail had behind him more than two dozen seven-figure verdicts and settlements. The last time I visited Joe in his sumptuous Houston office on the thirty-third floor of One Allen Center, he took me into the recreation room where he and his associates relax over coffee or stronger beverages. One wall of that room was covered with cork board, on which he has pinned up clippings from newspapers and legal publications about his major victories. Joe had referred a case to us, the claim of a Texas woman who had been injured in a plane crash in New York, so the suit had to be brought in New York. We had been able to settle this case before trial for $1,225,000, which we thought was a great result. I looked through the dozens of clippings on Joe's cork board, hoping to find one of the write-ups of the case that he had sent to us. But since the recovery was only a little over a million dollars, that case did not make Joe's cork board.

At the time of the Remington Mohawk 600 incident, Frank Ramsey was defending an automobile accident case in which Joe Jamail represented the plaintiff, a young woman who had suffered brain damage. One of Frank Ramsey's partners called Joe to advise him that Ramsey would no longer be defending the case. He also made an unusual request. He and other friends and relatives of the Ramsey family were terribly concerned about the mental condition of young Tom Ramsey. The law partner knew that Joe Jamail was very adept at analyzing accidents and finding highly qualified experts in complicated cases. Ramsey's partner asked Joe if he would help the family by consulting a firearms expert who would be willing to examine the rifle to determine if there had been any malfunction—a finding that would help to ease young Tom Ramsey's mind. At the time that this request was made, the Ramsey family was not thinking about suing the gun manufacturer; they simply wanted to do anything they could to ease the emotional trauma of young Tom.

Although Joe Jamail had been in many pitched courtroom battles with Ramsey's firm—including one which he characterizes as "a blood-bath"—he readily agreed to try to help. Ramsey's partner brought the Mohawk 600 rifle to Joe Jamail in Houston. Joe knew just the right man to consult as an expert—a highly qualified weapons expert whose identity Joe Jamail still guards to this day. Joe called the expert on the telephone and started to describe the accident to him. Halfway through the conversation, the expert stopped Joe and said, "You don't have to say any more. I know what happened, and the gun you're talking about is a Remington Mohawk 600, isn't it?"

"Immediately," says Joe, "all the adrenaline started flowing and I knew I was onto something." Jamail took the gun to the expert, who lived a long way from Houston. The expert explained that with a round in the chamber and pressure on the trigger, a later movement of the safety to the half-safety position would cause a small part called the sear to drop down slightly from its original position in the trigger housing, exposing the firing pin. Moving the safety back to the full safety position would not move the sear back up in certain guns, and any later movement of the safety into the "fire" position would cause the safety mechanism to act as a second trigger, firing the weapon in whatever direction it was pointed. All of this could happen at any time after the trigger had once been squeezed, even months after the user's memory of whether the gun was loaded had completely faded.

The expert's analysis convinced Joe Jamail that, in addition to no fault being attributable to Tom Ramsey, there probably was a strong products liability claim against the manufacturer, the Remington Arms Co., which is a subsidiary of the Du Pont Company. Remington had employed a design that would not permit the user to unload the gun in the "safe" position (which would have eliminated the danger completely), and had allowed a number of the guns to get through quality control with the metal tolerances off enough for the sear to drop when the safety was used. Avoiding or remedying either of those two defects would have produced a weapon that, while not foolproof, would have been forgiving of a momentary oversight that could be expected in normal use. Numerous other manufacturers have taken care to see that their products forgive foreseeable minor deviations from prescribed procedures, so why not Remington? Perhaps they had not known about the problem. Joe Jamail intended to find out.

First, though, there was young Tom Ramsey to think about. After some further precision testing by mechanical engineers, Joe took the gun back to Austin for a meeting with two of Frank Ramsey's partners and with Mrs. Ramsey, but initially without Tom. Jamail demonstrated the defect as the expert had. Then he slipped a cartridge from which the powder had been removed into the chamber and called Tom into the room. Tom hated to touch or even see the gun again, but Joe prevailed on him to take it and demonstrate exactly what he had done. When he got to the "safety on" stage, the firing pin struck the back of the powderless cartridge and the muted report showed everyone present that, had a regular round been in the rifle, it would have fired again. Tom was greatly relieved, and Mrs. Ramsey and the law partners were galvanized into action. They asked Joe to sue Remington on Frank Ramsey's behalf, and Mrs. Ramsey passed the word on to Frank, who was still in intensive care, barely able to talk because of throat tubes. The lawsuit was filed against Remington and the dealer who sold the gun, claiming $7 million compensatory damages and unspecified punitive damages.

Joe Jamail's first move was to find out whether Remington had had any knowledge of the defect prior to the Ramsey accident. Joe's investigation included study of all of the periodical literature on guns published since the Mohawk 600 went into production, to see if there were any published accounts of other accidents. Joe compiled a thick package of indexed and summarized information showing a history of problems since the 1960s. This lead to an interview with a Remington dealer in the Texas back country who had talked to Remington representatives about the defect years before. The dealer told Jamail that Remington instructed him simply to replace any defective gun with a new one, for which Remington would reimburse him, because "we don't want to have a recall." For business reasons, the dealer would talk to Jamail only off the record, but his statement convinced Joe that Remington had known about the defects for years. At that point, Jamail amended the complaint to sue several Remington officers and directors personally because of their failure to take action when they must have known there was a grave danger.

Once the action was filed, the presiding judge of the court in Austin wanted to assign it to a judge who had not tried any cases with Frank Ramsey, to avoid any appearance of partiality. That was hard to do, because Ramsey had tried cases before all of the local judges who presided at civil trials. As a solution a criminal court judge, Thomas Blackwell, was chosen. Since he was a retired U.S. Army general, he knew something about weapons.

Remington's attorneys made a motion to force Joe to produce the weapon so that it could be examined by their own experts—a routine step, but one which posed a problem here. If the weapon were altered the slightest bit it would not perform for the jury as it had in the accident. Joe opposed the motion, and suggested as an alternative that any examination be conducted in open court in Austin, with the judge present and a court reporter and videotape camera recording all of the proceedings. While such a procedure is common in criminal practice for dealing with crucial physical evidence, it is not at all common in civil litigation, and the defense argued that it was "unheard of." The judge (a criminal judge, you will recall) said that, unheard of or not, he would allow it, and the gun went into a bank vault at the plaintiff's expense until Remington could get their experts together.

On the day of the examination, the judge, reporter, camera operator, lawyers, and experts from both sides were present, and the Remington crew looked the gun over for several hours, admonished by Jamail not to remove the trigger housing or safety for any purpose. Jamail's own expert was looking over the shoulders of the defense experts to be sure that they made no "repairs" on the gun while they handled it.

At the conclusion of the examination, the Remington experts stated on camera that the gun was free of any defects. Unknown to them, Jamail's partner Gus Kolius slipped a blank cartridge into the chamber after the Remington experts were finished. Gus said, "Would the Remington people or the defense lawyers like to see the gun malfunction? I'd be happy to demonstrate it." He then put the rifle through its paces, and as he pushed the safety forward, the blank fired as it had with Tom Ramsey, scattering the assembled lawyers and experts. The judge, maintaining admirable composure, asked, "Is everybody happy?"

The Remington lawyers had been offering $1 million to settle the case. After the gun fired in the courtroom demonstration, they asked permission to visit Ramsey and see his physical condition firsthand. He had been in bed, paralyzed, for nearly a year, and had suffered terribly, especially from the bedsores which are the special curse of the paralysis victim. Nevertheless, being a defense lawyer, he had performed his own defense-oriented evaluation of the case and thought that the million-dollar offer was appropriate. After the defendants had taken a look at him, they raised their offer to $2.5 million, but still clung to their insistence that the weapon was not defective, reminding Jamail that Tom Ramsey's exclamation that he had shot his father was evidence of fault on his part. Jamail angrily broke off negotiations and served subpoenas for the depositions of three Remington quality control workers, an executive vice president, and a public relations official. Remington had ten days to get ready for these depositions (to be held in New York) and only three months before trial was scheduled to begin.

Joe sent Gus Kolius ahead to New York to prepare for the depositions, with instructions not to discuss settlement. Evidently concerned about what would develop from the depositions of the company officials, Remington decided over the course of those ten days to raise their offer to $5 million, and asked Kolius to relay the offer by phone to Jamail. When Gus called, Joe told him to turn down the offer, but Gus was reluctant, and he handed the telephone over to the insurance official who was trying to negotiate the settlement. Joe reiterated that the suit was for $7 million and that he would not settle for $5 million. The insurance official told him flatly "I will not pay you $7 million." Joe then said, "Well, if you say yes before you hang up that phone, you can settle for $6.8 million and save $200,000, but if we finish without agreeing, I'll amend my complaint to ask for more money!" After a pause of perhaps ten seconds, the insurance official (an Englishman) said, "Gov'nor, you've just settled your lawsuit!"

The $6.8 million settlement was paid at the Austin courthouse on October 23, 1978, with reporters from newspapers and the wire services in attendance. They asked Jamail what he thought the company should do now about the Mohawk 600, and he reiterated a point that he had tried to impress on Remington during their settlement negotiations: "If they had any decency, they'd recall the damn thing!"

With the money paid, the Remington attorneys asked Jamail if they could have the rifle. Joe said, "No, no, my friends. You purchased Frank Ramsey's cause of action, not a rifle. I have the rifle now, and you can bid on it if you want it." It still belonged to Tom Ramsey, but of course he never wanted to see it again; so Joe arranged for its repurchase for the original price of $278.00 plus a letter from Remington Arms to Tom stating that the weapon was the entire problem and that he was in no way responsible for his father's injuries. Then, and only then, did Jamail turn over the rifle to Remington.

The contrast between Joe Jamail's dramatic settlement of the Mohawk 600 case and Chuck Krause's long struggle with the Alouette II illustrates the importance of preserving the *corpus delicti* of the products liability case: the failed product. Joe was able to work wonders through his possession of the defective rifle, while Chuck was barely able to make out a prima facie case with government photographs of the defective weld.

Frank Ramsey recovered sufficiently to return to his law practice on a part-time basis—in a wheelchair. Tom Ramsey is doing well in high school, and plays baseball and football. He has recovered emotionally from his wrenching experience, and if anything, the incident drew the Ramsey family even closer together.

On October 24, 1978, the day after the settlement press conference in which Joe Jamail urged recall of the Mohawk 600, Remington capitulated. They announced a nationwide recall program affecting 200,000 firearms, and published notices in newspapers and magazines, similar to this one that appeared in the January 1979 issue of *Field and Stream:*

IMPORTANT MESSAGE TO OWNERS
OF REMINGTTON MODEL 600 AND 660 RIFLES,
MOHAWK 600 RIFLES, AND XP-100 PISTOLS

Under certain unusual circumstances, the safety selector and trigger of these firearms could be manipulated in a way that could result in accidental discharge.

The installation of a new trigger assembly will remedy this situation. Remington is, therefore, recalling all Remington Model 600 and 660 rifles, and all Mohawk Model 600 rifles—except those with a serial number starting with an "A."

Also included in the recall are any XP-100 pistols with a serial number below 7507984, except those with the prefix "A" or "B" before the number.

Remington recommends that prior to any further usage of guns included in the recall, they be inspected—and modified if necessary. To obtain the name and address of the nearest Remington Recommended Gunsmith (who will perform the inspection and modification service free of charge), phone one of the following numbers . . .

Joe Jamail says of his role in the Mohawk 600 case, "After I talked to the expert, it was about as easy as rolling out of bed. It didn't take a lot of genius." But the fact is that before he arrived on the scene, no one in government, in the firearms industry, the insurance industry, the sports press, or the trial bar had put together the evidence on the dangers of the Mohawk 600. Without the genius of Joe Jamail, the Mohawk 600 might have continued its devastation of life and limb. Joe actually litigated an unsafe rifle off the market, and he did this by using the equalizing power of the entrepreneur-lawyer to impose the actual costs of making a dangerous and defective product on the manufacturer. Joe's successful battle against the Mohawk 600 is an excellent example of the deterrent effect of tort litigation; for the tort law process worked far more effectively to protect the public than did government regulation or the forces of the marketplace.

Products liability suits are an ideal instrument of deterrence because defective products have the built-in capacity to inflict repeated and continuing injuries. There is some deterrent power in suits against negligent automobile drivers, but the availability of liability insurance at low rates has diminished the deterrent effect. In the Mohawk 600 case, liability insurance paid for all of the $6.8 million settlement except for a small deductible. However, it does not take much imagination to picture what went on during the New York conference between Remington and the representatives of its insurers during the last minute negotiations with Joe Jamail. It is not likely that the insurers would have continued coverage of the Mohawk 600 unless Remington had agreed to recall and modify the dangerous rifles. Ultimately, it was the threat of cancelled insurance or skyrocketing premiums that caused Remington to act in the public interest and announce the recall. Thus, the economics of the Mohawk 600 situation worked in favor of deterrence. The rifles cost less than $300 each, and installation of the new trigger assembly under the recall program was not a major expense compared to the probable exposure to other multimillion-dollar damage claims.

Sometimes the economics of deterrence are a bit more complicated. When the defendant is one of our industrial giants who have (as Professor John Kenneth Galbraith has taught us) put themselves beyond the control of government and market forces, the protection of the public calls for even more heroic measures than those taken by Joe Jamail in the Mohawk 600 situation. A case in point is the Ford Pinto.

The Ford Pinto

Richard Grimshaw was riding as a passenger in a Ford Pinto on a southern California freeway one day in 1972, when the carburetor malfunctioned and caused the car to stall. As it sat stopped on the freeway, it was hit from behind by a van at a speed calculated by various witnesses at from 30 to more than 50 miles per hour. Unknown to Grimshaw or to Lily Gray, the 52-year-old mother of two who was driving the car, the Pinto was highly susceptible to fire when hit from the rear. The car had been designed with the fuel tank placed behind the rear axle, just aft of the differential (the cluster of gears that transforms the rotary action of the engine and drive shaft into the forward-rolling action of the rear wheels). The axle's size and strength made it a virtually immovable object, so that when the fuel tank was shoved against it by the irresistible force of another car hitting the rear of the Pinto, the fuel tank was likely to rupture. Tests showed that in the seconds following the rear impact, the axle would act like a can opener, splitting the fuel tank and spraying its contents into the passenger compartment through gaps left when the sides buckled; a spark or heat would cause the gasoline to ignite and explode; and the side doors of the car would jam shut, trapping the occupants inside the vehicle until they could be extricated by emergency workers or passersby—often a process that would take many minutes. Because of the very considerable physical forces which are generated in automobile accidents even at modest speeds, the passengers and drivers are often unable to help themselves. In many cases, the occupants suffered fatal burns before they could be rescued. If they escape with serious burn injuries, their lot will not be a happy one. For a number of hours immediately following the accident, burn victims are frequently so traumatized that they do not suffer or feel pain, but the treatment for serious burns is excruciatingly painful, highly specialized, and often not successful. In fact, a California hospital made news recently by offering an alternative to victims of severe burns: no treatment. Where the burns were so bad that doctors believed the victim would not recover, the hospital offered to withhold all survival-oriented treatment of conscious and rational patients to spare them days of torture and to allow them to die with dignity.

Mrs. Gray died of her burns in the 1972 California freeway collision, but 13-year-old Richard Grimshaw was taken from the wreckage alive with severe burns over more than 80 percent of his body. He lost his left ear, his nose, and several fingers, but after heroic medical treatment he beat the odds and survived, although he required 60 operations and would remain horribly scarred for life.

Grimshaw and the relatives of Mrs. Gray retained southern California lawyers Arthur Hews and Mark Robinson, Jr., to recover damages. Hews and Robinson soon found themselves in a history-making struggle against the Ford Motor Company, for they quickly determined that there was a potential products liability claim based on negligent design of the fuel tank by Ford. Working in cooperation with Francis Hare, Jr., of Birmingham, Alabama, who represented other Pinto victims in the South, Hews and Robinson uncovered an amazing story.

Their first big breakthrough was to obtain the services of Harley Copp, who had been with Ford for thirty years as an executive in charge of engineering and production of automobiles. He had risen to the rank of vice-president with a salary of $150,000 a year, but he was forced to retire in 1976 because he was rocking the boat on the issue of safety. Copp was able to confirm for Hews, Robinson, and Hare what they had been piecing together through their own laborious discovery: that Ford executives knew all about the firetrap they had created in the Pinto, but they determined to plow ahead, put it into production, and kept it in service despite their knowledge of its deadliness in even the lightest of rear-end collisions. Copp told the plaintiffs' lawyers that Ford was committed to producing the Pinto as a 2,000-pound car for a price of $2,000, and that everything else, including the safety of its occupants, was sacrificed to meet that goal.

With the help of Copp and through their own massive discovery efforts, the lawyers were able to force Ford to produce documentary evidence which spelled out the grisly story. Ford had made many tests of the Pinto, going back as far as 1968, which showed that rear-end collisions as light as at 20 miles per hour resulted in massive fuel tank leakage and subsequent fires, condemning occupants of the Pinto as surely as if they had been subjected to napalm attack. Ford's commitment to the 2,000-pound automobile at $2,000 prevented the Pinto from complying with Federal Motor Vehicle Safety Standard No. 301 (Fuel System Integrity) which was being proposed by the National Highway Traffic Safety Administration (NHTSA) in 1973. This government safety standard would have required the Pinto's fuel tank to withstand a rear end collision at 30 miles per hour. The plaintiffs' lawyers discovered a Ford document known as the "Fuel System Integrity Program—Financial Review" and dated April 21, 1971, in which Ford engineers concluded that in order to comply with proposed Federal Standard No. 301, a "flak suit" and/or a bladder within the fuel tank would have to be used. Since Ford engineers found that about $100 million would be saved by delaying the 30 mph standard until 1976, Ford executives recommended that nothing be done to make the fuel tank safe at that time (1971), thus giving Ford five years in which to produce and sell Pinto firetraps. But the most amazing document of all —possibly the most remarkable document ever produced in an American lawsuit—was yet to come.

On September 19, 1973, J. C. Eckhold, director of the Automotive Safety Office of Ford, sent to Dr. James B. Gregory, administrator of the National Highway Traffic Safety Administration, a letter and attachments which constituted Ford's petition for reconsideration of Federal Standard No. 301. The purpose of the Ford petition was to convince the NHTSA that the costs associated with making automobile fuel tanks strong enough to withstand a 30 mph rear-end impact without incinerating its occupants outweighed the benefits of such a program. Attached to Ford's petition to the NHTSA was an eight-page document entitled "Fatalities Associated with Crash Induced Fuel Leakage and Fires" by E. S. Grush and C. S. Saunby, Ford employees. In Table 3 of the Grush-Saunby study, the "benefits" of compliance with the proposed federal fuel tank safety standards by the entire U.S. automotive industry were calculated at $49.5 million per year. This was based upon an estimate of 180 burn deaths per year, which the Ford engineers estimated would cost the auto manufacturers or their insurers $200,000 each; 180 serious burn injuries, at an estimated cost of $67,000 per injury; and 2100 burned vehicles, with estimated average cost of $700 per vehicle. Multiplied out, if these deaths, injuries, and burned vehicles were avoided by the new federal fuel tank standards, there would be a total benefit or saving of $49.5 million per year. On the other hand, the costs to the automotive industry were estimated at $11 per car or truck which, multiplied by 12.5 million cars and light trucks produced each year, would cost a total of $137 million.

On this basis, Ford argued its case to avoid the imposition of the fuel tank safety standard which would have added $11 to the cost of each car manufactured. The Grush-Saunby study concluded that the benefits (avoidance of 180 serious burn cases and 180 flaming deaths per year) were not "cost effective." Thus, in the jargon of the bureaucrat and the corporate memo writer, the lives of helpless occupants of the Pinto firetrap were disposed of as not being worth the extra cost of $11 per car. This remarkable document was signed by Ernest S. Grush and Carol S. Saunby, both of whom placed under their signatures the title, Impact Factors.

Since Ford already had cheap liability insurance that covered the projected cost of $200,000 in death cases, $67,000 in injury cases, and $700 in property damage cases, this was an instance in which the deterrent effect of tort litigation was blunted by the ability of one of our corporate giants to insulate itself from the normal economic forces of the marketplace. When they had assembled their evidence, Arthur Hews and Mark Robinson, Jr., agreed that this was the clearest case for punitive damages they had ever seen, and they decided to make an all-out effort to recover punitive damages (in addition to compensatory damages) for Richard Grimshaw.

Punitive damages have always been controversial. The basic theory of damages in tort cases is that a defendant who wrongfully injured the plaintiff should compensate the plaintiff fully by restoring him to the equivalent of his position prior to the injury, insofar as money damages can accomplish this. Punitive damages have an entirely different objective. They are not related to injuries suffered or the need for compensation. They are designed to punish the defendant for particularly malicious and antisocial conduct, so as to deter that defendant from repeating the offense and to serve as an example to others who might engage in similar conduct. They afford juries of ordinary people the opportunity to strike back, even at the most powerful groups in our society, in those extraordinary cases in which there is clear proof of intentional, willful, wanton, or highly reckless conduct which represents a grave danger to the community. Because punitive damages are potentially the most destructive weapon in the arsenal of the civil courts, judges have always placed a heavy burden on plaintiffs to justify such awards.

Critics of punitive damages argue that private litigants should not be allowed to collect such awards, since they have a separate right to collect full compensation. Even in situations where the defendant's conduct cries out for punishment, the question arises as to why that punishment should create a windfall for the plaintiff who also gets fully compensated for his injuries. But proponents of punitive damages argue that the injured plaintiff is the only person who is in a position to seek punitive damages. No other members of society have any standing to sue, and in most instances there is no basis for such a suit by the attorney general or any other public official on behalf of the state. Only by furnishing the injured plaintiff and his attorneys with the incentives of damages and legal fees can punitive damages be made an effective deterrent under our present system. While this is not always as pure a form of justice as compensatory damages, it is the best solution that the common law has developed through centuries of experience in deterrence.

In the Pinto case, Ford's own Grush-Saunby study supplied the arithmetic which showed that mere compensatory damages were no deterrent to putting a deathtrap on the road. The range of average compensatory damages ($67,000 to $200,000) was well within Ford's existing liability insurance coverage and would not make the slightest impact on Ford's profits. If the NHTSA or any other state or federal agencies were given the power to seek fines against the Ford Motor Company for such conduct, the fines would have to be fixed at a ridiculously low level in order to overcome the strong lobby of the automotive industry. They would probably be a few thousand dollars per incident, and even at that low level, the state might be forced to prove its case beyond a reasonable doubt, as in criminal cases.

Ford and other corporate giants have made a science of stalling government regulations for years on end. There was only one way to teach Ford the lesson that the American people would not permit them to treat the face of a teenage boy or the life of a 52-year-old mother as "cost-benefit" statistics. That was to use the common law remedy of punitive damages in a tort action, leaving it to the jurors of Orange County, California, to fix a suitable punishment. The twelve jurors finally selected to sit in the *Grimshaw-Gray* case that started in the Superior Court for Orange County at Santa Anna, California, in September of 1977 had practically no power to punish or control the Ford Motor Company through the ballot box or participation in the work of government regulatory agencies. But through the judicial system, they had the power to hold Ford to the moral and legal standards which they could set through their verdict as a civil jury.

The case of *Grimshaw, et al., v. Ford Motor Company* was a marathon effort for Arthur Hews and Mark Robinson, Jr. The trial lasted six months. Hews and Robinson spent more than a quarter of a million dollars to get the case ready for trial. They presented an overwhelming case for punitive damages, including films of Ford crash tests which showed that at speeds as slow as 20 mph, the Pinto gas tank would rupture with almost explosive force after a rear-end collision. Former Ford engineer Harley Copp's trial testimony made it clear that Ford executives knew exactly what they were doing when they decided to delay the federal safety standard on fuel tank integrity.

Q. by Mr. HEWS: In your opinion, would an over-the-axle fuel-tank location on any vehicle withstand a 50 mph moving barrier test without fuel tank puncture?   A: Any?
Q: On any automobile that's on the road.   A: I believe it is.

*   *   *

Q: In your opinion, how many of the survivable, of the 700 to 2500 people who died from fire would have lived if the fuel tank had been located over the axle? A: 95 percent.

Q: Why is it so safe over the axle? A: That's a good place to hide. It's one of the most rigid, well-protected areas in a motor car.

Q: Of your own knowledge, was this known to Ford in 1970? A: Certainly.

Q: Of your own knowledge, did Ford Motor Company know in 1970 that an over-the-axle location would prevent the death of the survivable people who would otherwise have lived? A: Yes.

Q: Do you know of your own knowledge why the industry and Ford Motor Company have not placed—did not place the gas tank over the axle in 1970? A: Yes.

Q: Why is that? A: Cost.

*   *   *

Q: What was the cost of mounting a fuel tank over the axle to the Ford Motor Company? A: For a fully protected tank with a metal barrier around it so it is completely between the wheel houses with metal coming up and forming an enclosure, the cost of that design was $9.95.

*   *   *

Q: Do you know why the Pinto did not have more crush space? A: Because it was part of the style and an additional overhang would have cost more.

During Arthur Hews's questioning of Harley Copp, he brought out the fact that Copp had been in conflict with Henry Ford II, Chairman of Ford Motor Company, regarding Ralph Nader's automobile safety crusade. Copp quoted Henry Ford as saying, "This safety stuff is all a bunch of politics—it's going to go away. We are going to handle it in Detroit."

Copp also testified that the engineers designing the Pinto were fully aware of the dangers of placing the gas tank behind the rear axle. He explained that the engineers are given a style which has a fixed width and a fixed rear overhang. They have to squeeze the spare tire, the muffler, the fuel tank, and other components within the dimensions given to them by the styling experts. In order to overcome this priority given to styling, the automobile manufacturer would have to have a management that encourages its engineers to raise red flags about any safety problems, that can be overcome by spending a few dollars. But Copp said that the corporate management of Ford gave priority to styling over safety. He made it clear that the goal of selling the Pinto for $2,000 as a 2,000-pound car had to be met, come hell, high water, or safety problems.

Presented with these shocking facts, the *Grimshaw* jurors deliberated for eight hours and then handed up a landmark verdict. On February 6, 1978, they awarded young Grimshaw $2.8 million in compensatory damages, and the family of the deceased Lily Gray some $659,680. But they also decided to punish Ford's callous disregard for human life.

Judge Leonard Goldstein had instructed the jury that it could award punitive damages only if it found that Ford had intentionally caused the injuries or had willfully disregarded the safety of Pinto occupants. The jury concluded that Ford was guilty of willful disregard of safety. The plaintiffs' lawyers asked them to punish Ford by taking away the $100 million that Ford had saved by evading the proposed 30 mph federal fuel tank safety standard. But a majority of the jurors came to the conclusion that awarding the exact amount of Ford's savings would only put Ford back where it had been when it decided not to make the tanks safe, and that being left in the same position did not constitute "punishment." Reasoning that punishment implies being left in a worse position than before, they decided to charge Ford an extra $25 million, and they awarded $125 million in punitive damages, over and above the $3,459,000 total compensatory damages. Critics of the jury system should note that the seemingly breathtaking figure of $125 million was not pulled out of a hat and was not the result of blind passion or prejudice. It was based upon Ford's own financial projections.

This verdict was particularly significant because Orange County is considered to be one of the most conservative areas in California, in jury verdicts as well as in political matters. The community that produced Richard Nixon and his brand of politics also provided a jury of working class people (including a Western Electric employee who drives his own Pinto, a retired policeman, and a telephone company dispatcher) who did not hesitate to bring in the highest personal injury award in American history when the outrageous conduct of Ford was displayed before them. The foreman of the jury, retired policeman Andrew Quinn, was quoted in the Wall Street Journal:

> We came up with this high amount so that Ford won't design cars this way again. The Pinto is a lousy and unsafe product. The jury wanted a punishment severe enough to sting Ford.

After the trial, Ford made a motion to set aside the punitive damages award. The trial judge refused to set it aside, but he used his remittitur power to reduce the punitive damages to $3.5 million, leaving the compensatory damage award intact. The plaintiffs' attorneys agreed to accept the remittitur to $3.5 million but Ford refused, offering instead to pay a total of $3.5 million in both compensatory and punitive damages, which would have been only a little more than half of the combined total of $3.5 million in punitive damages and $3.459 million in compensatory damages sustained by the trial judge. Therefore the case went on to the intermediate appellate court, with Ford insisting that no punitive damages be allowed, and the plaintiffs' lawyers arguing for restoration of the full amount of $125 million originally assessed by the jury. There the matter stood at the end of 1979.

Regardless of the final outcome of the *Grimshaw* case in the appellate courts, the trial has left its mark on American history. As a direct result of the evidence disclosed at the *Grimshaw* trial, the National Highway Traffic Safety Administration undertook an intensive investigation of the Pinto and announced that public hearings would be held in mid-June of 1978, four months after the jury verdict in the *Grimshaw* case. The CBS television show *60 Minutes* scheduled a segment on the Pinto for June 11, 1978, including interviews with Grimshaw, Hews, and Harley Copp, featuring documents and films which had first been shown publicly at the *Grimshaw* trial. Ralph Nader brought all of his leverage to bear against the Pinto. Faced with all of this pressure, Ford finally saw the light and on June 9, 1978 announced recall of all 1.5 million automobiles that it had previously kept on the road with dangerous fuel tanks.

So it was that a very small group of entrepreneur-lawyers, spending their own money and investing thousands of hours of their own time, accomplished what legislatures and regulatory agencies had not been able to do. They brought the mighty Ford Motor Company to its knees and they redesigned the Pinto fuel tank through a lawsuit.

Some people were shocked by the jury verdict in the *Grimshaw* case. They see it as a symptom of Ralph Nader's headlong drive for a "risk-free society," and they argue that it is impossible to make every product so safe that it will withstand any impact. A few years ago, people like Richard Grimshaw and the relatives of Lily Gray would have had to look to the insurance policy of the owner of the van that struck them from the rear. Often there is only $10,000 worth of insurance coverage, and sometimes there is none at all. Very rarely is there enough insurance to pay for the type of injuries suffered by Grimshaw and the Gray family. Critics of the Grimshaw decision say that it is part of the "deep pocket" syndrome which is making us a nation of greedy, litigation-mad individuals. But any lawyer who has ever been involved in a products liability suit will tell you that we are a long way from attempting to create a risk-free society. No plaintiff's lawyer has ever gotten a case to the jury by claiming that the defendant failed to make a risk-free product. It is only when manufacturers refuse to remedy a product's likely or obvious defects which can be cured at relatively low cost that a prima facie case of strict products liability arises. One of the leading cases on "crashworthiness," decided by the U.S. Court of Appeals for the Eighth Circuit in 1968, defined the circumstances that would make automobile manufacturers liable for injuries caused by impact:

> The sole function of an automobile is not just to provide a means of transportation, it is to provide a means of safe transportation or as safe as is reasonably possible under the present state of the art.
>
> We do agree that under the present state of the art an automobile manufacturer is under no duty to design an accident-proof or fool-proof vehicle or even one that floats on water, but such manufacturer is under a duty to use reasonable care in the design of its vehicle to avoid subjecting the user to an unreasonable risk of injury in the event of a collision. Collisions with or without fault of the user are clearly foreseeable by the manufacturer and are statistically inevitable.

You may also be uneasy about the power of juries to award punitive damages against large businesses, with the amount to be based upon the defendant's wealth and the degree of culpability. (The wealth standard is necessary because a sum that would be a terrible punishment for you and me would be no deterrent at all to enterprises the size of Ford.) Rest assured that the courts are very careful to limit the award of punitive damages to cases of outrageous conduct which needs to be deterred and that the jury awards are very carefully scrutinized. The *Grimshaw* award was reduced from $125 million to $3.5 million even though there was ample testimony that Ford had profited by more than $100 million through its callous behavior. The reduced award of $3.5 million is equal to about one day of Ford's after-tax profits in 1979.

Some critics of punitive damages argue that it is unfair to punish shareholders for sins of the management. However, until we have a satisfactory method of deterring management from irresponsible behavior, punitive damages are the only remedy. Actually, the shareholders profit from the marketing of unsafe products (such as the Ford Pinto), and so it is only fair that those profits be forfeited as a deterrent to future disregard of public safety. I do not know of any company that has ever been put out of business by an award of punitive damages. There are some products that have been taken off the market because of awards or threatened awards of punitive damages, thus saving thousands of lives and avoiding millions of injuries. For that we can thank the entrepreneur-lawyers, without whom additional millions of people would still be expendable as part of the corporate cost-benefit analysis procedure.

The fact that such products as the Ford Pinto, the Chevrolet Corvair, and the Mohawk 600 were kept on the market by executives who knew of their dangers makes one wonder about the basic morality of American business management. Yet the top executives of our large manufacturing enterprises are leading contributors to the nation's welfare, through their military service and their support of education, religion, and good works. Where can we look for executives of higher moral character? Some insight into this dilemma was provided by John DeLorean, former $650,000 per year vice-president of General Motors, in the 1979 book, *On a Clear Day You Can See General Motors*. DeLorean devoted an entire chapter to "How Moral Men Make Immoral Decisions." He said:

> It seemed to me, and still does, that the system of American business often produces wrong, immoral and irresponsible decisions, even though the personal morality of the people running the businesses is often above reproach. The system has a different morality as a group than the people do as individuals, which permits it to willfully produce ineffective or dangerous products, deal dictatorially and often unfairly with suppliers, pay bribes for business, abrogate the rights of employees by demanding blind loyalty to management or tamper with the democratic process of government through illegal political contributions.
>
> * * *
>
> The impersonal process of business decision-making is reinforced by a sort of mob psychology that results from group management and the support of a specific system of management. *Watergate* certainly proved what can happen when blind devotion to a system or a process of thought moves unchecked. Members of the Nixon Administration never raised any real questions about the morality of the break-in and the coverup. The only concern was for the expedient method to save the system. So too in business. Too often the only questions asked are: What is the expedient thing to do to save the system? How can we increase profits per share?
>
> * * *
>
> There wasn't a man in top GM management who had anything to do with the Corvair who would purposely build a car that he knew would hurt or kill people. But, as part of a management team pushing for increased sales and profits, each gave his individual approval in a group to decisions which produced the car in the face of the serious doubts that were raised about its safety, and then later sought to squelch information which might prove the car's deficiencies.

Obviously, neither compensatory damages (covered by relatively cheap insurance premiums) nor government regulations (which exist by the thousands) are going to break down the "mob psychology" described by DeLorean. Often it will require the threat of punitive damages, and individual accountability, to bring such executives back to the moral standards that society requires of those who are entrusted with the lives and health of others.

You may wonder why Richard Grimshaw was awarded the entire amount of punitive damages, while the relatives of the deceased Lily Gray were awarded only compensatory damages of $659,680. The answer lies in one of the great anomalies of Anglo-American law: the notion that wrongful death cases should be treated differently from personal injury cases. It started with an historic error in the English courts. In the 1808 case of *Baker v. Bolton,* Lord Ellenborough held that no damages could be awarded under English law for an accident resulting in death. In England this barbaric decision was quickly reversed by statute—Lord Campbell's Act, which gave surviving relatives the right to sue for the damage they sustained because of the fatal accident. The nineteenth-century American courts followed *Baker v. Bolton,* though state legislatures soon passed counterparts of Lord Campbell's Act. This illogical separation of wrongful death cases from personal injury cases has been a disaster; for while damages in personal injury suits have been shaped by society's changing concepts of compensation, wrongful death cases have been tied to the rigid wording of statutes that cannot be amended rapidly enough to keep in step with the needs of the day. One of the most ludicrous side effects of *Baker v. Bolton* is that many courts have refused to allow punitive damages in wrongful death cases unless the applicable state statute specifically provides for them. Many of our states do have specific provisions, and other states have construed the general wording of the wrongful death statute to permit punitive damages in appropriate cases. But in California and many other states, the law permits punitive damages for hangnails but prohibits them for homicide.

There are Ford Pinto cases pending in American courts now (1979) in which all of the occupants of the Pinto were killed, unlike the *Grimshaw* situation in which there was one survivor and one fatality. In one of those cases where all of the occupants died, a New York court courageously ruled that punitive damages would be allowed despite the absence of specific authority for them in the New York wrongful death statute. This case, *Robert v. Ford Motor Company,* started to make its way up through the New York courts late in 1979. The Association of Trial Lawyers of America (ATLA) decided to file an *amicus curiae* brief in support of the right to punitive damages in wrongful death cases, and they designated me as the attorney to present ATLA's arguments.

In the *amicus curiae* brief, I pointed out that the relatives of the two Pinto occupants killed in the New York case were claiming punitive damages in order to remedy a wrong that had been inflicted upon society. They were suing as representatives of society, and the fact that their loss was a total one should not disqualify them from seeking to deter Ford and other manufacturers from selling dangerous products in New York state. Punitive damages are allowed in property damage cases, so that the owner of a Pinto damaged by a rear-end-collision fire who escaped without any injury at all would be able to sue Ford for punitive damages. So would the occupants of Pintos who suffered any kind of bodily injuries, no matter how minor. But the surviving children of a New York couple who were incinerated in their own Pinto would not be allowed to claim punitive damages because of the ancient case of *Baker v. Bolton,* which has long been discredited in the American courts.

Often it takes a spectacular case to publicize legal anachronisms and to put them to rest. Let us hope that the ill-fated Fort Pinto brings about the interrment of *Baker v. Bolton.*

Thalidomide

The shortcomings of legal systems that have no entrepreneur-lawyers, contingent fees, or jury trials in personal injury cases were dramatized in the pitiful story of the thalidomide children. The grim details will be found in *Suffer the Children: The Story of Thalidomide* (Viking Press, 1979), a book written by the Insight Team of the *Sunday Times* of London. Eight thousand children throughout the world were affected by their mothers' taking of the tranquilizer thalidomide during pregnancy and were born with various defects, some of them without arms or legs. The book tells the shocking story of the German manufacturer Chemie Grünenthal and its English licensee, Distillers Co., who put thalidomide on the market as a wonder tranquilizing pill, which they claimed to be nontoxic, without side effects, and safe for pregnant women—despite their lack of proper research and testing—and then kept on the market after clear evidence of its disastrous side effects had appeared in the form of horribly deformed babies.

The *Sunday Times* team followed the lawsuits filed by the parents of thalidomide babies in European courts, and they give detailed descriptions of the English litigation against Distillers Co., a corporate giant whose best-known products were Johnnie Walker scotch whiskey and Gordon's gin. The authors conclude that the English legal system was utterly incapable of dealing equitably with these suits, which they describe as "a contest between unequal parties." They find that cases of this type are almost impossible to win in England "for the individual not backed by a trade union or institution."

The individuals who sued Distillers were faced with ruinous expenses (including Distillers' legal fees) in the event that they lost, and English law was not flexible enough to give them much chance of winning. In 1972, because of the great difficulties they faced in this litigation, many of the plaintiffs were forced to consider a settlement offer that averaged only 7,500 English pounds per thalidomide child. As a result of heroic efforts by *Sunday Times* editor Harry Evans and the Insight Team led by Bruce Page and Elaine Potter, the parents were persuaded to turn these offers down and fight for something more than nominal compensation. But the limitations of the English legal system made it necessary to conduct their fight outside the courts—in the press, in Parliament, and finally in the marketplace. Because of Britain's strict rules against press comment on pending court cases, Harry Evans had to take the *Sunday Times* to the brink of contempt of court to inform the British public about the thalidomide children's plight. Jack Ashley, a Labor member of Parliament, took up the fight and condemned Distillers on the floor of the House of Commons in these words:

> For the 370 children, the sword of Damocles has been replaced by the jagged edge of a broken whisky bottle.

Rupert Murdoch, the newspaper and magazine publisher, took some risks by starting an English boycott of Distillers' liquor products anonymously. Other groups (including the clergy and Distillers' own shareholders) denounced Distillers publicly for stonewalling their helpless victims through the property-oriented English courts. Finally Ralph Nader got into the act. When his efforts to convince Distillers to pay compensation according to American standards fell upon deaf ears, he joined with English thalidomide parent David Mason to organize a worldwide boycott of Distillers' liquor products. This threat made headlines in Britain, and the price of Distillers' shares fell by $26 million the next day. In the following nine days, its shares fell a total of $80 million—much more than the difference between Distillers' settlement offer and the total sum demanded by the parents. Finally Distillers had received a message that it understood. The thalidomide war ended at that point in 1973, with Distillers paying an average settlement of about 54,000 pounds per child, more than seven times the amount of the average settlement that the parents had nearly been forced to accept a year earlier.

The Insight Team noted that the few thalidomide babies in America had been compensated at much higher levels than their English and European counterparts, and through routine court proceedings without any need for heroic intervention by public-spirited journalists, legislators, or amateur boycotters. For this, the authors of *Suffer the Children* gave credit to the strict products liability doctrine and the contingency fee system "that does a lot to redress the imbalance between the private citizen and public corporation." They could have added the right to jury trial and the entrepreneur-lawyer, two American elements which help to equalize the struggle between the injured individual and the huge business firm that controls its own market. *Suffer the Children* compares the European thalidomide litigation with the American litigation arising out of the anti-cholesterol drug MER/29, in which our firm (led by Paul Rheingold) was national lead counsel. The MER/29 cases, starting in 1962, set a pattern for lawyer cooperation in pharmaceutical litigation (based partly on experience in airline disasters such as the Grand Canyon case) that has been followed successfully in cases involving other major product defects. They also produced the first punitive damage awards in nationwide product liability litigation.

The American products liability revolution has had some effects in other nations; but for the most part, consumers and others injured by defective products outside of the United States have very little chance of recovering adequate damages for serious injuries or death. While the laws of most nations permit such suits, the absence of entrepreneur-lawyers, contingent fees, and jury trials has the same effect on products liability claims as on tort claims in general, as we saw in the Nader-GM story.

In the late 1970s, the European Economic Community (EEC) and the Council of Europe drafted legislation adopting a modified version of the American strict products liability doctrine. This legislation was still in the discussion stage at the end of 1979, and prospects for enactment in the member countries were thought to be several years off. While it is a step in the right direction, this proposal is accompanied by the customary European provision for limitation of the amount of damages that can be recovered. Experience with the Warsaw Convention in aviation and with other limited liability schemes makes it clear that they remove the deterrent effect of tort litigation and eventually become protectors of dangerous products and activities by making it cheaper to kill and to maim than to assume full responsibility. But even if the European nations did not limit the amount of damages, their lack of entrepreneur-lawyers, contingent fees, and jury trials, added to their requirement that unsuccessful plaintiffs pay the legal fees of the defendants, are enough to tip the scales against most plaintiffs, as we saw in the thalidomide case.

In recent years, I have seen direct evidence of this wide difference between the United States and the rest of the world in the use of products liability litigation as a deterrent. Several American law firms who represent foreign manufacturers considering opening factories in the United States have consulted with us on behalf of their clients. These foreign manufacturers had heard about the products liability revolution, and before starting American operations they wanted to be sure that they would not be put out of business by products liability suits. They had done practically nothing in their own nations to avoid products liability suits or to warn consumers about any dangers of their products. There was no incentive for them to do this at home, but they knew that it would be a different story in the United States, and so they directed their American lawyers to get some specialists' advice on how they could live with American products liability law.

We advised them that they should take every step possible to instruct their American customers on the proper use of their products, and to warn them about any uses or situations which posed the danger of injury. In one instance, we convinced a foreign manufacturer to produce a fifteen-minute color videotape program demonstrating the proper use of their machinery and warning specifically against situations that might make the machinery dangerous to workers and others who come in contact with it. From these personal experiences we know that the American products liability revolution is responsible for avoiding thousands of injuries and deaths. Let us hope that it spreads to the rest of the world and that some credit is given to the American legal system and the entrepreneur-lawyers who made this revolution an effective force for safety.

The Ultimate Deterrent: Taking On the Gun Lobby

While America has led the world in the drive toward product safety, there is one American product on which we have the most shameful record in the world. That product is the handgun, which accounts for thousands of deaths and serious injuries each year. I am not talking about defective guns that injure their owners—I mean the guns that function as their owners intend to use them: as instruments of deliberate harm. There are, of course, laws against shooting people with guns. But it is obvious that these laws are not furnishing a deterrent sufficient to keep America from becoming a shooting gallery, with all of our citizens serving as targets for an army of illegal gun users.

While there has been some legislation aimed at curbing the traffic in handguns, the gun lobby is too powerful to permit effective regulation. In fact, some promising political careers (such as that of former Maryland Senator Joseph Tydings) have been smashed merely by taking a stand in favor of handgun controls. Congress institutionalized this lobby by establishing a program in 1903 which permits the United States Army to sell surplus firearms, at cost, exclusively to members of the National Rifle Association, which is the most powerful element in the gun lobby. NRA members can save more than $100 on the purchase of each surplus Army rifle—but only NRA members are eligible for this subsidy, which creates an important membership benefit that helps the NRA to collect more money to devote to lobbying against gun controls.

I believe that it is about time that manufacturers of handguns were brought into the products liability revolution. They are at least partially responsible for the wounding and killing of victims, since they seem to devote little effort to minimizing the chances of their guns falling into the hands of people who are likely to use them criminally. I propose that the progress made in the products liability revolution be used to furnish the handgun manufacturers with an incentive for taking reasonable steps to keep their products out of the hands of criminals and others who cannot demonstrate the likelihood that they will use handguns only for proper and legal purposes.

The main defect in handguns is not the way that they are made: it is the way that they are distributed. Strict products liability has been extended to the entire chain of distribution, so that all those who play any part in bringing a dangerous product into the stream of commerce are strictly liable in tort. This includes distributors, wholesalers, importers, dealers, retailers, trade associations, and others who have nothing to do with manufacturing the product but are involved in its distribution. Therefore the basic element that we need to help control handguns—the strict liability of the distributor—is already in existence. But we need to go back one step farther and make handgun manufacturers control the distribution of their lethal products by requiring the manufacturers to pay the full cost of their operations in human terms.

If handgun manufacturers could be sued directly by gunshot victims (or by their next of kin in fatal shootings) in cases where the gun was bought by an obviously irresponsible person, and where it could be shown that the manufacturer did not take reasonable steps to prevent the distribution of his guns to such persons, I have no doubt that handguns would become far less accessible to criminals than they are today. Furthermore, the victims of illegal shootings would be compensated, at first through liability insurance and later (when the liability insurers refuse to cover those manufacturers who are not taking reasonable steps to restrict distribution) by the gun manufacturers themselves. Some efforts are being made now to compensate victims of crime from tax funds, but this puts an added strain on already overburdened public treasuries, and the compensations are pitifully small for those who have been victimized by such attacks.

If the victims could sue the gun manufacturers, you would see lots of verdicts and settlements such as Joe Jamail achieved in the Mohawk 600 case. It is foreseeable to a gun manufacturer that his product will be used to maim or kill people, just as it is foreseeable to the automobile manufacturer that his product will become involved in collisions. If the automobile must be crashworthy, then surely handgun distribution should minimize the access of criminals to its lethal product.

Foreseeability is the basis of modern tort liability. The products liability revolution has demonstrated that civil juries can force entire industries and chains of distribution to reform their practices in order to protect the public. It was natural that this would occur first in cases involving products intended for peaceful use, such as automobiles and aircraft. It no longer makes sense to limit responsibility to manufacturers whose intentions were good in the first place. The gun manufacturers, aided by the gun lobby, have prevented the criminal law and administrative regulation from protecting the public. It is time for the public to take the power into its own hands to remedy this situation, as they did in the case of the Ford Pinto, and as they would have done in the case of the Mohawk 600 rifle if Remington had been foolhardy enough to go to trial against Joe Jamail.

American industry is particularly ingenious in finding new methods of distribution. Practically all the items now offered in our retail shops are marked with a series of thin and thick colored lines. They are machine-readable codes that allow the shopkeeper to control inventory and to create other useful distribution records. No government agency ever required the use of these codes, but they have come into almost universal use because of the economic incentive to business. I see no reason why handgun manufacturers cannot be given an equally strong incentive to distribute their lethal products in ways that minimize the risk to innocent targets.

Today, gun manufacturers have very little incentive to restrict distribution. But a few million-dollar judgments against handgun manufacturers, accompanied by skyrocketing of insurance rates or the threat of complete loss of insurance coverage, will soon bring forth improved methods of distribution. Suddenly there will be hundreds of experts working on methods of restricting the distribution of handguns.

Although there is no court decision holding handgun manufacturers liable in the manner which I have suggested, I believe that all of the prerequisites for it exist. It would take only one case to become the catalyst which puts all the elements together into a new use of strict tort liability for the public good. I hope that such a case is now in preparation in somebody's law office. Several years ago, we were retained by a social worker who was blinded by a gunshot while sitting at his office desk, and we decided to sue the gun manufacturer as well as the agency that failed to give him proper protection. However, we were not able to obtain sufficient evidence of the identity of the gun or the manner in which the assailant obtained it. Let us hope that some plaintiff's lawyer has the ideal case which will bring the deterrent effect of the products liability revolution into the firearms field, to do the job that the gun lobby has kept Congress from doing.

A bill introduced in 1979 by Congressman Peter Rodino (D, N.J.), chairman of the House Judiciary Committee, would accomplish some of these purposes by requiring all handgun importers, manufacturers, and dealers to control and limit the transfer and sale of handguns. The bill recognizes that the widespread illegal use of handguns

> requires an increased obligation on the transferor of handguns and on law enforcement agencies to assure that there is no sale or transfer of a handgun to a person not authorized to possess it.

Congressman Ted Weiss (D, N.Y.), a cosponsor of the bill, said in his seconding speech:

> During the past decade, the body count in our country has steadily increased as bill after bill to control handguns has been proposed, debated, and ultimately defeated by a powerful and unrepresentative special interest lobby. With one American dying every hour of every day as a result of handgun violence, there can no longer be any plausible excuse for delay in this area.

If the Rodino bill should meet the fate of its predecessors, there is no reason why our entrepreneur-lawyers and our civil courts cannot do the job through the one branch of our government that cannot be controlled by an unrepresentative special interest lobby.

Chapter 6

GOVERNMENT LIABILITY

THE ROBERTO CLEMENTE CASE

I started writing this chapter in October 1979, just about the time that the Baltimore Orioles and the Pittsburgh Pirates began their series to decide the baseball championship of the world. In the great media avalanche that preceded the World Series, there was talk about the overhanging shadow of a dead baseball player. There was much comment about the "We are family" attitude of the Pittsburgh team, and how they had dedicated this World Series to the late Roberto Clemente. Following the second game, the *New York Times* reported:

> After tying the World Series at one game apiece, the Pittsburgh Pirates flew home tonight with a dramatic reminder of their links to the late Roberto Clemente, who dominated their 1971 victory over the Baltimore Orioles.
> "I have him in my heart," said Manny Sanguillen, the 35-year-old catcher, a few minutes after he had helped beat the Orioles with a two-out pinch-hit single in the ninth inning. "Anything we do we're going to do for him."

When the 1979 series ended, the floodlights and television cameras were on the beaming face of Wilbur Stargell, the remarkable man who replaced Roberto Clemente as the inspirational leader of the Pittsburgh team. President Jimmy Carter struggled to make his way into the crowded locker room of the world champion Pirates, who had just completed an extraordinary comeback to defeat the Baltimore Orioles in the seventh game after being down by three games to one. In his moment of glory, after being named the most valuable player in the series for his three home runs and record-breaking seven extra-base hits, Stargell said:

> 1971 was Roberto Clemente's moment of glory. He started something with his winning, driving attitude. Whatever contribution I've made has been merely an extension of what he started.

Stargell himself was known as a public-spirited man who gave much of his time to the drive to eradicate sickle cell anemia, among many other charitable and socially important activities.

Who was this man Roberto Clemente, who dominated the thoughts of his old teammates and the public eight years after his last great moment as a baseball player, and nearly seven years after his death? Obviously he was something more than a great athlete. Perhaps his special qualities were best summarized by José Torres, former world's light heavyweight boxing champion and special representative of the governor of Puerto Rico in the United States:

> In his own life, Roberto Clemente embodied the struggle of a people. And although many of us Latin athletes felt that our struggle was more than personal, Clemente instinctively transmitted this important message to all. For he was a natural hero.

On the baseball field, he was a great all-around player, one of the few who excelled at batting, fielding, base running, and the giving of effort beyond the call of duty that is known in sports jargon as "hustling." There are many photographs showing Clemente crashing into brick walls, climbing eight-foot fences, and diving on his face in pursuit of baseballs. His hustling took a toll on his body and he suffered from many ailments, including recurrent bouts with malaria and blood clots that required surgery. He overcame these problems and became one of the handful of players in the history of major league baseball who amassed a total of three thousand hits. He won the Golden Glove Award (for being the best fielder at his position) in each of the last twelve years of his career. He hit safely in all fourteen World Series games in which he appeared. His hitting, fielding, and base running in the 1971 World Series were the sensation of the sports world. He batted .414 and was directly responsible for driving in the winning runs in two of the series games, including the final one that clinched the championship. Clemente was past 37 at the time, an age when most major league baseball players have been retired for several years. The year 1971 was one of thirteen in which Clemente batted over .300, the dividing line between average hitters and the best in the game.

Clemente had come from a very poor family. When he boosted himself into the glamour and high salary of the baseball superstar, he remained a dedicated family man, spending most of his spare time with his wife and three young boys in his native Puerto Rico. However, Roberto did not have much spare time because he devoted himself to charitable causes when he was not playing baseball. He made radio and television commercials in Puerto Rico and he endorsed various products throughout Latin America, donating his fees for that to charities. In 1970, the Pittsburgh fans made him a gift of $6,000 on "Roberto Clemente Night," and he promptly turned the money over to the Children's Hospital of Pittsburgh. But the cause closest to his heart was his dream of constructing a "Sports City" for young Puerto Ricans, where they could learn the skills which might make some of them professionals and would help all of them to get more enjoyment out of life. He dedicated himself to raising funds for Sports City, and he obtained commitments from other Puerto Rican athletes to donate their services.

I met Roberto in October of 1971 when he and his beautiful wife Vera were guests of honor at a luncheon at Mamma Leone's restaurant in New York. He had come to receive the sports car that was awarded annually by *Sport Magazine* to the most valuable player in the World Series. He and his wife seemed to be unreal people, sculptured out of bronze instead of ordinary flesh and blood like those surrounding them. Even in a business suit he conveyed power and intensity. He spoke with great sincerity and strength, even though his English was imperfect. It was supposed to be a carefree occasion, with lavish food and drink supplied by *Sport Magazine*. Hundreds of New York's leading freeloaders (including me) were assembled, expecting no more than to escape the strains of the city for a pleasant luncheon. When Roberto accepted the award, we braced for the routine sports speech, giving thanks to all those who had made him a great baseball player. Instead, he said little about himself and spoke mostly about the poor boys of Puerto Rico whom he was trying to help through his Sports City project. He choked up with tears as he told of their poverty and their need for a chance to achieve some dignity.

He had a special quality that reminded one of the Brazilian soccer player Pelé, except that Roberto seemed more intense. If you tried to write such a character into a soap opera, he would probably seem corny. But in person Roberto Clemente was a man for all seasons.

The Mercy Flight

On December 23, 1972, a major earthquake struck the Republic of Nicaragua, devastating the capital city of Managua and causing widespread privation. It made thousands of people homeless, and there was a great need for emergency supplies of food, clothing, and medicine. Earlier that year, Roberto Clemente had led a group of Puerto Rican baseball players on a barnstorming tour of Nicaragua. That was enough to ignite a feeling of brotherhood in him. Despite the fact that the Christmas season was at hand and he was looking forward to spending the holidays with his family, he took it upon himself to mobilize the nonaffluent people of Puerto Rico in his effort to help the stricken people of Nicaragua.

Through the newspapers, radio, and television, he exhorted his people to draw upon their own slim resources for donations of food, clothing, medical supplies, and money, which he undertook to collect and transport to Nicaragua. He organized this program entirely on his own, without the help of any government agency in Puerto Rico or the United States. He arranged special events, including a marathon run at the baseball stadium, which drew thousands of people and helped to collect money for the emergency effort. He worked right through Christmas and sent three large airplane loads of emergency supplies to Nicaragua within a few days. For this purpose, he chartered a cargo airplane for three round-trip flights between San Juan and Managua. When the last of the three flights was ready to leave on December 30, there was more cargo than could be loaded aboard the airplane. In fact, Roberto's relief efforts had been so successful that the emergency supplies left over were enough for a fourth planeload. While Roberto was at San Juan International Airport on December 30 to supervise the loading for the third flight, he was approached by one Arthur S. Rivera, who introduced himself as the president of American Air Express Company.

Rivera said that his company had a DC-7 aircraft at the airport ready to go, and that he would transport the remaining cargo of emergency supplies to Nicaragua for $4,000. Clemente agreed to those terms. He was eager to get the fourth planeload underway, and he wanted to go along as a passenger on the flight. He had heard some disquieting rumors that there had been profiteering and inequitable distribution of the first two planeloads. These reports incensed Roberto, so he decided to accompany the fourth planeload in order to make certain that the relief supplies got into the right hands.

Clemente knew nothing about Arthur Rivera. Being unsophisticated in commercial aviation, Clemente must have assumed that anybody operating a large four-engine airliner would have to meet the licensing and safety requirements of the Federal Aviation Administration (FAA). He raised no questions about Rivera's qualifications, equipment, or personnel at he took his place on board the DC-7 bound for Managua the next day (December 31, 1972). It is doubtful that he would have entrusted his cargo of supplies—let alone his life—to Rivera's DC-7 if he had known anything about Arthur Rivera.

Rivera was a Caribbean tramp airplane operator, such as one might expect to find in a Graham Greene novel. He had picked up a pilot's license and some knowledge of aviation by working at odd jobs around the San Juan International Airport. His ambition was to head up his own airline. In the 1960s, he managed to scrape up the money to buy an old Douglas DC-3 in Miami. Then he flew it over to San Juan and started his own air service. He would carry any cargo and passengers he could get his hands on, even though he never attempted to comply with the FAA regulations governing revenue flights with that class of aircraft—full flight crews, maintenance personnel, dispatchers, training, emergency procedures, and dozens of other detailed requirements. For Rivera, it was enough that he had one airplane and one pilot—himself. The rules of the FAA meant nothing to him. After he had disregarded repeated warnings from the FAA Flight Standards District Office (FSDO) at San Juan, they finally were forced to take action against him in 1970 for 66 violations of Part 121 of the Federal Aviation Regulations, which governs the operation of "large aircraft" such as the DC-3. The FAA issued an emergency order revoking his pilot's license, finding that he was an "extremely independent and headstrong person who would not take advice," and that "his aviation knowledge and experience was relatively limited." During the proceedings to revoke his license, Rivera attacked FAA personnel verbally and in writing. He accused them of accepting bribes from competitors to put him out of business. He wrote an hysterical threatening letter to the FAA administrator in Washington and sent a two-page telegram to President Nixon. He even threatened one FAA inspector with physical violence.

The 1970 suspension seemed to cool Rivera down. He leased his DC-3 out to another operator and stayed out of trouble with the FAA until his suspension expired on July 20, 1971. But Arthur Rivera's career as an airline operator was not over. In fact, he had even bigger ideas. Leaving his twin-engine DC-3 days behind him, he went over to Miami and purchased a used DC-7 on July 12, 1972. Miami International Airport has a section known as "cockroach corner," an elephant's graveyard of once-proud airliners, such as the DC-6, the DC-7, and the Lockheed Constellation. Some of these are flown by legitimate operators who offer low-cost air transportation that is not available through the larger airlines. But there are also some irresponsible operators whose flights are a menace to those whom they carry and to the people on the ground who are unlucky enough to be in their path.

Rivera was even less qualified to operate the four-engine DC-7 than the smaller twin-engine DC-3. In September of 1972 he convinced a qualified pilot to ferry his newly purchased DC-7 from Miami to San Juan, with himself aboard as copilot. Although he was not qualified to act as copilot on a DC-7, he was able to make the ferry flight because it was not carrying any passengers or cargo for hire. When he arrived in San Juan on the ferry flight, the plane's No. 3 propeller was feathered, indicating an engine malfunction or failure which required that it be shut down. Rivera's DC-7 remained at San Juan Airport and was not flown again until December 31, 1972, when he persuaded Roberto Clemente to let him take the last load of supplies to Nicaragua.

Rivera's DC-7 was decorated to his taste. It was painted a distinctive greyish-white color with a large red-orange lightning bolt painted down the side. It looked like a macho airplane that was ready to fly. But there was little about the airplane that was in proper condition other than the paint job.

Having no personnel for his fledgling airline, Rivera decided to teach himself how to operate the DC-7. The first step was learning how to taxi the airplane around the airport. On December 2, 1972, Rivera was taxiing the DC-7 around San Juan International Airport for practice. In the course of this self-instruction, Rivera ran the DC-7 into a water-filled ditch, and the propellers of the two inboard engines, Nos. 2 and 3, struck hard objects on the ground while still turning. Under FAA regulations, such an accident involving sudden engine stoppage required that the aircraft be test flown before it could be used to carry passengers or cargo for hire, but no test flight was made. The FAA Flight Standards District Office at San Juan Airport initiated an investigation of Rivera's taxi accident. The FAA inspectors advised Rivera to change the No. 2 and 3 engines or to get them repaired before he flew the aircraft again. But all he did was to replace the damaged propellers.

To Roberto Clemente and his friends on the relief committee, Rivera's DC-7 looked fit and ready to fly to Nicaragua. After he made the handshake deal with Clemente on December 30, Rivera made frantic efforts to locate a qualified DC-7 pilot. He found one in Jerry Hill, an itinerant pilot who was described by the FAA as one "who seemed to have seen better days." He was on furlough from Airlift International, and there was a case pending against him for 13 violations of Federal Aviation Regulations incurred the preceding year. Although the FAA regulations required a complete flight crew consisting of a qualified pilot, a copilot, and a flight engineer, Jerry Hill was to be the only qualified crew member of this flight. To make things worse, Hill would not even have the required amount of rest between flights. He had flown another plane from San Juan to Miami on December 30 after Rivera hired him for the Managua flight, and he did not arrive back in San Juan until 6 A.M. on December 31.

On the morning of December 31, Jerry Hill filed a flight plan with the FAA at San Juan International Airport, giving his destination as Managua, Nicaragua. The relief supplies had been loaded aboard the DC-7 at various times during December 30 and 31, without keeping any accurate records of the total weight put aboard or its relation to the airplane's center of gravity. Under Part 121 of the regulations, those steps were supposed to be supervised by a licensed pilot or dispatcher but Rivera had no such procedures or personnel, and so the supplies were put aboard haphazardly.

At 4:05 P.M. Rivera filed a customs declaration at San Juan International Airport listing the "crew," passengers, and cargo aboard the flight. At 5:30 P.M. Hill taxied out for takeoff, but he experienced engine trouble and received a taxi clearance from the tower to return to the cargo area for engine repairs. FAA personnel in the tower could see that the DC-7's nose gear was hardly touching the ground (indicating probable overloading) when the 5:30 takeoff was cancelled due to engine trouble.

Since Rivera had no maintenance staff or facilities, it took him nearly four hours to have the malfunctioning engines checked and some of their sparkplugs replaced. At 9:11 P.M. Hill taxied out to runway 7 and was given a clearance by the FAA tower to take off at 9:20 P.M. Witnesses at the airport noticed that the DC-7 took an exceptionally long takeoff run (an estimated 7,000 to 9,000 feet), that it was barely able to climb after takeoff, and that its engines were backfiring and trailing flames as it left the runway. One of the mechanics who had worked on the plane watched the takeoff and was convinced from the sound and sight of the engines that there was an engine failure on takeoff. As the aircraft struggled off the ground, the pilot started a left turn toward the north. At 9:23 P.M., the San Juan tower received a transmission from the plane that it was "coming back around," indicating that the pilot was returning and would try to land, having lost the power of one or more engines. Right after that transmission, the aircraft crashed into the Atlantic Ocean approximately one and a-half miles offshore, two and a-half miles from the airport. Killed aboard the flight were pilot Jerry Hill, "copilot" Arthur Rivera, Roberto Clemente, and two friends of his who had worked with him on the relief committee: Angel Lozano and Francisco Matias.

While the rest of the world was getting ready to celebrate New

Year's Eve, Roberto Clemente lay at the bottom of the Atlantic Ocean, among the relief supplies he had collected from his own people. The news that Clemente had been aboard the crashed airplane shocked Puerto Ricans and his many admirers throughout the world. On New Year's Day, hundreds of people flocked to the beach area nearest the site of the crash, milling around dazedly. It seemed as though some of them expected Roberto Clemente to free himself from the airplane wreckage and walk ashore to greet them.

Clemente's body was never found. Only the body of Jerry Hill was recovered by Navy divers, who also brought up the wreckage of engines No. 1, 2, and 3 from the crash site 120 feet beneath the surface. The propeller of the No. 2 engine was found in the "feathered" position, an indication that the No. 2 engine had failed before the crash and had been shut down.

One of the purposes of having four engines on an airplane is to enable the plane to fly despite a loss of power in one or two of its engines. Even if an engine fails on the takeoff, a DC-7 is normally able to fly safely on three engines. But the post-accident investigation showed that Roberto Clemente never had a chance. The aircraft had been overloaded by 4,193 pounds. In such an overloaded condition, the best of flight crews would have found it difficult to keep the DC-7 in the air or to return it safely to San Juan Airport. It would have required the highest skills of airmanship—the coordinated skills of a qualified captain, copilot, and flight engineer, trained to work throttles and controls together in prescribed emergency procedures. But Roberto Clemente did not have such a flight crew. As the FAA said in its report of the accident:

> There were a number of factors that contributed to cause this accident. The aircraft was overloaded by at least 4,193 pounds. . . . The crew had not had adequate rest; there was no certificated flight engineer; and the copilot had no real experience in a DC-7 . . . The No. 2 engine failed shortly after takeoff and the propeller was feathered. . . . Weather was not a factor; however, the takeoff was made out over the ocean on a relatively dark night with no visual horizon. Crew coordination must have been nil. For all practical purposes, the Captain was flying solo in emergency conditions.

The Investigation

Within a few days after we were retained to represent the families of Roberto Clemente and his fellow passengers Angel Lozano and Francisco Matias, we knew that we had an open-and-shut case against Arthur Rivera, his estate, and his company. The problem was that his "American Air Express Company" did not exist, there were no assets in his estate, and there was not a nickel's worth of liability insurance covering him, his airplane, or the fatal flight. Therefore, even though we could have proved a textbook case of negligence (or even gross negligence) against Rivera, this would have brought no compensation to the families of the three deceased passengers. In a perfect tort system, we would not have had to search for any other prospective defendants. But in the real world, we faced one of the most difficult problems of tort practice: proving liability on the part of a defendant whose negligence merely contributed to an accident that was primarily the fault of another person who is unable to pay adequate damages.

We looked into the possible liability of the engine manufacturer, since the DC-7 model had experienced more than its normal share of engine problems even when operated by leading airlines. But we soon found that we could not prove a case against the engine manufacturer because Rivera had exceeded the engine design limits. The excess load of more than two tons put extra strain on the engines and would tend to make the pilot "overboost" them by pushing them beyond their stops in the struggle to get the airplane off the ground. The probability of overboosting was particularly strong because there was no flight engineer (the crewman who would normally monitor the throttles and engine instruments to guard against overboosting).

There was only one other possible defendant: the Federal Aviation Administration, whose negligence would be the legal responsibility of the United States government. Rivera had obviously violated dozens of FAA regulations, but normally the government is not responsible for such violations unless it has undertaken a duty to prevent them. We made a searching investigation, and we found that the FAA had indeed undertaken a special duty to prevent exactly the type of travesty that ended the life of Roberto Clemente.

Ever since World War II surplus multiengine aircraft had become available to the public at cheap prices, the FAA had been plagued by tramp operators of the "cockroach corner" variety. During the 1960s, the FAA struggled to develop procedures to protect the public from such operators. Unfortunately, the tramps were able to hide behind "leasing" deals under which the unwary passengers or chartering groups became the legal operators of the aircraft. Thus, a "dry lease" took the owner of the aircraft out of the category of a commercial operator and made it difficult for the FAA to enforce safety regulations. Many of these leases were phoney because the tramp operator would actually supply the crew and the gasoline under separate contracts, which really made it a wet lease rather than a dry one. FAA lawyers ran around in circles trying to make their way through the maze of paper corporations and multiple contracts in a vain effort to protect the public. FAA safety inspectors found themselves engaged in complicated economic investigations which were needed to prove that the aircraft was actually being operated for hire by an unqualified organization. As a result, there were many fatal accidents caused by unqualified operators who were able to hide behind fake dry leases, and the FAA was usually unable to take action against these killers until they had done their damage.

The situation came to a head in 1970 when 37 members of the Wichita State University football team were killed in the crash of an overloaded multiengine aircraft operated by unlicensed persons in violation of FAA regulations. The aircraft had been leased to Wichita State University, which found itself in the position of being the "operator," even though it knew nothing about the operation of aircraft. At that point, the FAA decided to take affirmative action to protect the public from illegal operators of multiengine passenger flights. Instead of waiting until an accident had happened and then going into court to set phoney leases aside, the FAA decided to let its safety inspectors do the job for which they were best qualified: keeping the questionable operators under surveillance and stopping their unsafe operations *before* there were any repetitions of the Wichita State tragedy.

After a careful study of the problem and the available manpower, the Flight Standards Division of the FAA directed that such operators be kept under continuous surveillance; that their aircraft be inspected before takeoff; and that if the inspection turned up any dangerous or illegal conditions, the persons chartering the service were to be notified immediately, so that they could cancel the flight. This order was put into effect in all of the FAA regions, including its Southern Region, which encompassed Miami and San Juan and was headquartered at Atlanta, Georgia. The Southern Region issued several surveillance orders in 1971, and on September 25, 1972, it issued an updated order which was in effect at the time of the Rivera-Clemente flight. This order, SO 8430.20C (which we will call the "Southern Order") contained the following key provisions:

ORDER   Department of Transportation
FEDERAL AVIATION ADMINISTRATION
                    Southern Region   SO 8430.20C
                                                        25 Sept. 72

Subj: Continuous Surveillance of Large and Turbine Powered Aircraft

    1. PURPOSE. This order outlines procedures for a continuous surveillance program of large and turbine powered airplanes. . . .

2. DISTRIBUTION. This order requires action by Air Traffic field facilities and General Aviation, Air Carrier, and Flight Standards District Offices. . . .

3. ACTION. Flight Standards ACDOs, GADOs, and FSDO will coordinate with Air Traffic facilities to establish the method for notification of arriving and departing large aircraft and turbine powered aircraft that cannot be readily identified as bona fide air carriers, commercial carriers, travel clubs, air taxis, or executive operators. Representative of these are: . . . DC-7 . . . To accomplish this program effectively, consideration should be given to night and weekend surveillance with the use of irregular or modified work week, as necessary.

* * * * *

5. BACKGROUND. Several accidents/incidents involving noncertificated operators disclosed that these operators were transporting specialized groups for compensation or hire without an appropriate operating certificate, and little regard to air-worthiness safety standards on their aircraft. During the special 60 day surveillance program completed by Flight Standards offices, it was discovered that a considerable number of such noncertificated operators of large aircraft and turbine powered aircraft are engaged in passenger and cargo commercial operations contrary to applicable provisions of either part 121 or 135 of the Federal Aviation Regulations.

6. SURVEILLANCE PROCEDURES. ACDOs, GADOs, and FSDO will provide continuous surveillance of large and turbine powered aircraft to determine noncompliance of Federal Aviation Regulations. At least the following actions will be taken:
a. Contact noncertificated operators of large and turbine powered aircraft within your area of responsibility, and advise them of certification requirements, as appropriate.
b. Conduct airport surveys to determine the number, type and status of large and turbine powered aircraft on airports. . . .
c. Continue efforts to encourage . . . specialized groups to contact the nearest Flight Standards office prior to engaging operator for air transportation.
d. In cases when information is known in advance of flights:
(1) Interview operator/owner, flight crews, and others including passengers to determine whether the proposed flight is a commercial or private operation.
(2) If noncompliance with applicable regulations is indicated, advise the operator and flight crew accordingly.

7. ON SITE INSPECTION
a. Conduct ramp inspection with at least the following emphasis to determine that the crew and operator comply with regulatory requirements for safety of flight.

*   *   *   *   *
(6) Airworthiness of the aircraft.

*   *   *   *   *
(8) Weight and balance.

*   *   *   *   *
(10) Pilot qualification . . .
d. . . . Clear indication of alleged illegal flight should be made known to flight crew and persons chartering the service.

8. ENFORCEMENT INVESTIGATION PROCESSING
A. When noncompliance of any kind is found, investigation and violation action shall be given priority second only to aircraft accident investigation . . .

Since the FAA Flight Standards District Offices did not have enough inspectors available to keep such aircraft under surveillance around the clock, Section 3 of the Southern Order established a method of using Air Traffic Control personnel to alert the FSDO inspectors about the imminent departure of a dangerous operator. It was a simple matter to weed out the dangerous operators from the bona fide air carriers, commercial carriers, travel clubs, air taxis, and executive operators, especially in a small aviation community such as San Juan. A notorious illegal operator such as Arthur Rivera would be the easiest of all to keep under this type of surveillance, since he was well known to the FAA employees at San Juan, and his lightning-bolt-emblazoned aircraft was the only DC-7 parked at the airport. All that the San Juan FSDO had to do to comply with the Southern Order was to establish a procedure whereby the Air Traffic Control (ATC) personnel would advise them of any proposed flight by Rivera. Rivera first filed his flight plan for the Managua flight with ATC in the early morning of December 31; so there was a period of more than nine hours in which the ATC personnel could have alerted the Flight Standards personnel that Rivera was about to conduct a flight. He could not have departed from San Juan without first getting an ATC clearance.

If the ramp inspection required by the Southern Order had been carried out, the inspector would have known immediately that the operation was illegal, since Rivera did not have a Part 121 certificate and had neither the training, the maintenance, nor the operational organization required for passenger flights with large aircraft like the DC-7. The inspector would also have learned that Rivera did not have a qualified crew aboard, and that nothing had been done to make sure the aircraft was properly loaded and balanced. Paragraph 7d of the Southern Order required the FSDO inspector to make these conditions known to Roberto Clemente, who would certainly not have flown on that plane and would probably not have entrusted his cargo to such a flagrantly illegal, unqualified, and unsafe operation.

Since the FAA itself had mandated this duty of continuous surveillance of questionable operators through the combined efforts of ATC and FSDO personnel, and since Arthur Rivera was the most notorious outlaw operator at San Juan, how did he ever get off the ground on December 31, 1972? The shocking answer is that the San Juan FSDO had never paid the slightest attention to the Southern Order. They had *never* established the coordination between Air Traffic personnel and Flight Standards personnel required by Section 3 of the Southern Order. The DC-7 was a lethal weapon in the hands of Rivera, and he was the personification of the illegal operator described in Section 5 of the Southern Order. But Rivera or any other Wichita-State-type operator who wanted to make an illegal flight could obtain takeoff clearance from San Juan Air Traffic Control without any notification to Flight Standards, even when the ATC tower personnel could see the nose wheel riding high because of overloading and when they had been advised by the pilot that the engines were malfunctioning (as was the case with Rivera's DC-7).

While Roberto Clemente was rolling down the runway toward his death sentence, some of the FSDO inspectors who could have saved his life were at a New Year's Eve party near the airport. They had never lifted a finger to implement the FAA's own lifesaving order, which was specifically designed to prevent the type of avoidable accident that killed Clemente.

Our investigation convinced us that the FAA had undertaken a duty to inform unsophisticated one-time charterers like Roberto Clemente about the illegal and dangerous nature of operations like Rivera's. There was no way to interpret the Southern Order other than as a deliberate assumption of duty by the FAA to protect the traveling public from one of the gravest dangers in aviation: the irresponsible unlicensed charter operators of large aircraft.

Thus we plunged into the morass known as the Federal Tort Claims Act, which gives every person injured through fault of the United States government or its employees the right to sue for damages—with some strings attached.

The Law

The United States inherited and adapted from English law the principle that the sovereign was immune from suit, for the king could do no wrong. Therefore, whoever was injured by a government employee here had only two possible remedies. First, they could sue the federal employee personally, but this was not likely to result in collecting substantial damages because the employee would have to pay the judgment out of his own money, if any. Second, they could request Congress to pass a private relief bill awarding them damages. Congress was therefore inundated with requests for private relief bills, and as early as 1832, our sixth president, John Quincy Adams, complained about this situation:

> There ought to be no private business before Congress. There is a great defect in our institutions by the want of a court of Exchequer or Chamber of Accounts. It is judicial business, and legislative assemblies ought to have nothing to do with it. One half of the time of Congress is consumed by it, and there is no common rule of justice for any two of the cases decided. A deliberative assembly is the worst of all tribunals for the administration of justice.

In 1855 Congress passed the Court of Claims Act, which provided some relief from the situation described by President Adams. It established a tribunal for *contract* claims against the government, but it contained no provisions for suing the government on tort claims, which continued to be presented to Congress as private relief bills. As we moved into the automobile age, Congress was inundated with the claims of people injured in accidents that involved postal or Army vehicles. Thousands of tort claims were presented to Congress each year, and they became the subject of influence peddling and lobbying. There were "claim brokers" who tried to push these private bills through Congress. Most of them were never acted upon, and some were presented year after year until the claimants passed away.

In the early part of the twentieth century Congress began serious consideration of legislation which would permit tort suits against the government. Some legislators feared that such suits might interfere with government operations, and there was also concern about excessive handouts of the sovereign's money. In 1928, Congressman Ramseyer, opposing tort claims legislation, said on the floor of the House:

> If you thrown down the bars you might make the sovereign, which in this country is the people, liable not only for hundreds of millions but billions of dollars, which might threaten the life of the sovereign and the very existence of the Government.

The overwhelming need for compensation and the blatant unfairness of letting political influence govern the amounts awarded in private bills finally overcame the inertia of Congress, which passed the Federal Tort Claims Act (FTCA) in 1946, after more than thirty years of debate. Because of the difficulty of getting it passed, the Tort Claims Act contains many compromises. It makes the United States liable for negligent or wrongful acts or omissions of federal employees in the same manner and to the same extent as private persons, but there are important exceptions. The one that most concerned us in this case is the so-called discretionary function exception, which provides that the United States may not be sued for any claims based upon the performance of a discretionary function or duty, regardless of whether such discretion has been abused.

In more than thirty years of court decisions following the 1946 enactment of the FTCA, we have yet to learn the full meaning and exact boundaries of the discretionary function exception. Its first test in the U.S. Supreme Court came in the claims arising out of the Texas City disaster of 1947. Under a federal program designed to increase food production in Europe, ammonium nitrate fertilizer, manufactured and shipped according to U.S. government specifications, had been loaded in Texas City aboard a ship owned by the French government. Ammonium nitrate is a very dangerous substance which is used in explosives. This fertilizer caught fire in the port of Texas City and exploded, killing 506 people, injuring more than 3,000 others, and causing millions of dollars in property damage. In a test case brought by the family of one of those killed, the U.S. district court in Texas held that the Federal Tort Claims Act applied, and that the government had been negligent in the manufacture, packaging, and shipment of the fertilizer.

The U.S. Supreme Court held in a 4 to 3 decision that the FTCA did not apply to the Texas City case because the acts in which the government had allegedly been negligent were discretionary functions. The court emphasized that the acts alleged as negligence in the fertilizer manufacturing process were found to have been "formed under the direction of a plan developed at a high level under a direct delegation of plan-making authority from the apex of the executive department," with final approval by the entire cabinet, and that the alleged negligence of the Coast Guard was based upon the failure of the Coast Guard to adopt regulations, which the Supreme Court characterized as a legislative function. The court emphasized that government discretion had not been exhausted at the time of the explosion, and that the acts complained of took place during planning rather than operations. This made it clear that the Supreme Court would protect high-level decisions and policy making, but unfortunately the four majority justices also made the very broad statement that "all employees exercising discretion" were covered by the blanket of the discretionary function exception, which was intended to "protect the government from claims, however negligently caused, that affected governmental functions." If you took those words literally, there would never be any liability under the Tort Claims Act, since virtually every human activity involves some judgment or discretion. In a bitter dissenting opinion, Justice Jackson concluded:

Surely a statute so long debated was meant to embrace more than traffic accidents. If not, the ancient and discredited doctrine that "The King can do no wrong" has not been uprooted; it has merely been amended to read, "The King can do only little wrongs."

Fortunately, later Supreme Court cases largely ameliorated the broad language of the Texas City decision, and by the time of the 1972 Clemente accident, it was clear that one could hold the government liable for failure of its employees to carry out duties that had been assumed by agency officials who had exercised their discretion in issuing directives to lower level agency employees. Since the Southern Order had been mandated by the director of Flight Standards of the FAA in Washington, and since it had been issued in Atlanta by the Southern Region pursuant to directions from Washington, it was our conclusion that all government discretion had been exercised prior to the receipt of the Southern Order at the Flight Standards District Office at San Juan, and that the failure of FSDO personnel at San Juan to carry out orders from above would not be protected by the discretionary function exception. But we knew that—as in all tort claims involving regulatory activities—the government attorneys would try to get the case thrown out on the grounds of discretionary function.

By the time of the Clemente trial in 1975, there had been a long line of decisions holding the federal government responsible for acts and omissions of FAA employees, particularly for failure to issue warnings about bad weather, wake turbulence (turbulence following in the wake of large aircraft), and traffic conflicts. The courts had moved away from the strict interpretation of the Texas City case and had held the government liable for the failure of its employees to carry out the well established, clearly enunciated policies and duties which were listed in government operating manuals.

As you will recall from Chapter 3, in 1956 I had reached the conclusion that the federal government was not legally responsible for the Grand Canyon collision under the FTCA because it had never assumed the duty of warning pilots about traffic conflicts off the airways. However, under the Southern Order, the FAA had clearly assumed the duties of keeping Rivera under surveillance, of conducting a ramp inspection of his aircraft prior to departure, of setting up a notification procedure between ATC personnel and FSDO personnel and of warning the charterer, Roberto Clemente. There were dozens of cases which held that the FAA assumed whatever duties were specified in the operating manuals of its employees, and that these were duties to the flying public as far as the Tort Claims Act was concerned. In preparing the Clemente case for trial, we concentrated on the evidence which would show that the Southern Order was adopted at the highest levels of the FAA, and that after the order had become effective, it was a mandatory directive which left no discretion to the FSDO employees at San Juan.

Our discovery and preparation for trial were handled by two lawyers experienced in discretionary function problems, Donald W. Madole and Philip Silverman. Don Madole is a tall, husky, affable man who resembles comedian Bob Hope, except that Don's jokes are even older than Hope's. Don claims to have starred in athletics at Winfield (Kansas) High School and in debate at Kansas State Teachers College— claims that I have not been able to verify. His education was interrupted by five years of active duty as a Naval Aviator, which he completed in 1957. He also served for fifteen years as a "weekend warrior" in the Naval Reserve, emerging with the rank of commander. In 1959 he received his law degree at the University of Denver and went to work as a trial attorney for the FAA, then left in 1962 to spend the next year and a-half as an attorney (house counsel) for American Airlines. In 1963 he joined the Civil Aeronautics Board, which was then in charge of investigating airline accidents. For three years he served as chief of the CAB's Hearings and Reports Division, Bureau of Safety, which made him the government officer in charge of airline accident hearings and reports. During his tenure with the CAB, Don taught at the government's Aircraft Accident Investigation School and served as U.S. delegate to the International Civil Aviation Organization's meeting at which the international rules on accident investigation were established. In 1966 Don received the Jump Memorial Foundation award as one of the outstanding young officials (under 40) in the federal regulatory agencies. He joined our firm in 1966 and took charge of our Washington office.

Phil Silverman began law practice in his native Brooklyn in 1949. In 1960 he became an assistant U.S. attorney in the Eastern District of New York and represented the government in civil cases there for two years. Then he moved to Washington to become a trial attorney in the U.S. Department of Justice Aviation Litigation Unit, defending aviation cases under the FTCA. He served in that unit for ten years, becoming its chief in 1970, and leaving it in 1972 to join our Washington office. Don and Phil had dealt with the discretionary function exception from both sides of the fence, using it as a shield against liability while serving as government attorneys, and avoiding it on behalf of plaintiffs in private practice. Throughout the depositions of all the FAA employees involved in the Clemente case, they concentrated on showing that there was no discretion left to the San Juan FSDO inspectors.

The Trial

The Clemente case was assigned to U.S. District Judge Juan R. Torruella, who set it down for trial in San Juan on November 13, 1975. One of the compromises made to get the FTCA through Congress was that such cases would be tried by federal district judges without juries; therefore Judge Torruella would decide the case by himself. He was then 42 years old and had been educated at the University of Pennsylvania and Boston University Law School. He decided to try the issue of liability first. If he found that the government was not responsible, the separate liability trial would spare the parties and the court the waste of hearing three death damage claims. If he held the government liable, we could then try the damage issues separately.

Our trial team was headed by Chuck Krause and Don Madole, assisted by Don's lovely wife, Juanita, who had practiced law in Washington as a member of the Aviation Litigation Unit of the Department of Justice before marrying Don and joining our firm. She had graduated with honors from Tulane University and magna cum laude from the University of Houston Law School.

The first witness Chuck Krause put on the stand was Roberto's widow, Vera Zabala Clemente, who described the events leading up to the charter of Rivera's DC-7. She had been present at the airport on December 30 when Rivera approached Roberto with the idea of taking a fourth load of supplies to Nicaragua in his DC-7. She testified that Rivera's airplane looked fine to her and to Roberto. It looked just like "Super Snoopy," the plane that Roberto had chartered for three successful round trips between San Juan and Managua during the preceding week. Neither of the Clementes had any previous experience in chartering large aircraft.

She described the work of the "Comité Roberto Clemente Pro Nicaragua," starting with a televised appeal for aid on Sunday, December 24. She related how ham radio operators in Nicaragua had kept them informed about the needs of their stricken people for food, medical supplies, and blankets, which were not coming through to them from government aid programs. Then she described how the departure of Rivera's airplane had been delayed, principally because Rivera's pilot had not returned from Miami until 6 o'clock on the morning of December 31.

Mrs. Clemente was cross-examined by the government's trial attorney, Michael J. Pangia of Washington, D.C., a member of the Aviation Litigation Unit of the Department of Justice who also held a commercial pilot's license. Pangia was aware of Mrs. Clemente's attempt to talk Roberto into delaying the flight until January 1, so that they could spend New Year's Eve together. On cross-examination Pangia probed Mrs. Clemente, hoping to establish that she had asked for this delay because of concern over the safety of the flight.

> Q. by Mr. PANGIA: But you asked him to go the next day rather than on New Year's Eve? A: I didn't insist on him not going, or anything like that.
> Q: But you asked if he would wait? A: The day before we were talking about him being away from home so much on holidays, and then he told me, "You know, every day is the same; when you are healthy and you are happy, every day of life is the same." I understood him because we always used to think the same way. Then I didn't tell him to stay, I didn't insist that he stay.

The gracious and beautiful Mrs. Clemente was an ideal witness. Her testimony, along with various flight documents, covered the events leading up to the fatal flight. Now we moved to the crucial part of the case. We had to establish exactly what the Flight Standards District Office (FSDO) at San Juan had done to carry out its duties under the Southern Order. At that time the FSDO office consisted of Chief Leonard Davis and eight other inspectors. As trial witnesses we called Chief Leonard Davis and the three inspectors who had been most closely connected with the surveillance of Rivera.

Through the testimony of the key FSDO witness, Chief Leonard Davis, Don Madole set out to establish that Davis and all of his inspectors were familiar with the Southern Order; that this required them to keep operators such as Rivera under surveillance and stipulated their cooperation and communication with the Air Traffic Control personnel at the airport; that they had never established any coordinating procedures with ATC personnel; that therefore they had completely failed to implement the Southern Order, not only for Rivera's fatal flight but for any other flight by the dangerous and irresponsible operators identified in the Southern Order. Davis testified that he was familiar with the Southern Order and knew it required action on his part; but he insisted that it gave him discretion as to how he would carry it out, and that he had exercised this discretion by establishing a policy by which ATC advised the FSDO only of *incoming* flights. Despite the language of the Southern Order requiring "notification of *arriving and departing* large aircraft," Davis had apparently determined as a matter of policy that he was not interested in the notification of illegal flights (such as Rivera's) that were about to depart in dangerous and unairworthy condition. Don Madole struggled with this incredible story.

> Q. by Mr. MADOLE: Well, in doing your job in December of 1972, did you require that there be surveillance put on large aircraft? A: I had a policy established for that period, yes, sir.

Q: You had a policy?   A: I am a field facility chief and I establish policy for implementing working programs.
Q: Did you have a policy in relation to the Southern Region
Order, Exhibit 56?   A: I had a policy, yes, sir.
Q: What was that policy?   A: We were to examine, when manpower was available, all aircraft on the airport and aircraft that
were arriving. That would be a suitable way of getting knowledge
of this.
Q: What about departing aircraft?   A: We did not handle normally departing aircraft except on opportunity. If the inspector
was there, and the aircraft was in position for departure, that is
when we did it. . . . Had this order said to me, "You must," I
would have understood it to mean that I would have to do
every arriving and every departing aircraft. This order didn't say
that. This order established a working program and I am a facility
chief and I established a policy for implementing an order.

The battle lines of the trial were now staked out. Despite the very
clear language of the Southern Order and the life-and-death nature of
the activity involved, the government was claiming that it permitted
local chief Leonard Davis to make a policy interpretation that San Juan
would only implement the order with incoming aircraft—thus making
it impossible to prevent the type of disaster described in the Southern
Order. Don Madole banged away at this defense, which we considered
to be a complete fabrication. Don showed that despite numerous conferences and written communications about the policy and management
of the FSDO station, there was not a single memorandum or note of any
discussion about Davis's alleged "arriving aircraft only" implementation
of the Southern Order. In fact, the government did not produce any
ATC personnel as witnesses, and apart from Davis's testimony, there
was no scrap of evidence to show he had ever spoken to ATC about
implementing the Southern Order for either arriving or departing
aircraft.

Davis admitted that he and the other FSDO inspectors at San Juan
were quite familiar with Rivera and his history of illegal operations. He
also admitted that Rivera came squarely within the description of dangerous operators spelled out in the Southern Order. His excuse for failing to inspect the DC-7 on December 31 was simply that he had made
a discretionary policy decision to arrange ATC notification only for arriving aircraft, and as for departing aircraft, he did not have the manpower to check every one. He did not explain how the failure to require
ATC notification of departing aircraft would help his manpower problem. Clearly, the ATC notification procedure specified in the Southern
Order would require less manpower than random surveillance, since an
FSDO inspector could be summoned by radio or telephone on those few
occasions when an illegal flight was scheduled to depart.

After Davis had been on the stand for the better part of two days,
Don Madole was satisfied that he had done everything possible to dis-

credit the "arrivals only" story. He would attack Davis's claim of policy-making discretion later, through higher-level FAA witnesses.

Don Madole also examined the other three FSDO inspectors whom we called as trial witnesses. Each of them was familiar with the Southern Order and admitted that Rivera with his DC-7 clearly belonged to the class of dangerous and illegal operators which the Southern Order described. They were also familiar with Rivera's long history of safety violations, and they knew that he could not possibly operate his DC-7 legally. Therefore, if they had received notification from ATC that Arthur Rivera had filed a flight plan or requested takeoff clearance for his DC-7, they would have known immediately that this had to be an illegal operation. They knew Rivera had none of the required equipment, personnel, or facilities to operate a DC-7 for hire legally. They knew he owned nothing but the airplane and had a long history of operating large aircraft in complete disregard of government safety regulations. None of them knew of any discussions or documents to corroborate Davis's claim that he had made a policy decision limiting the Southern Order to incoming aircraft.

Don's examination of the other three inspectors established clearly that the San Juan FSDO had simply disregarded the Southern Order requirements that coordination be established between ATC and FSDO, and that notification be given of the arrival and departure of large aircraft operated by dangerous and illegal operators. Although some inspectors claimed that they never thought Rivera would try to fly his DC-7 after his earlier taxiing accident, some knew that he had been advertising the DC-7 for lease in the San Juan newspapers during December of 1972. All the inspectors were familiar with his taxiing accident, which was still under active investigation by the FSDO when Rivera made his fatal flight.

One of the government's contentions at the trial was that even if the FSDO inspectors failed to fulfill their duties under the Southern Order, this was not a proximate cause of the accident, because the accident was caused by the obvious negligence of Rivera and pilot Jerry Hill. Government trial lawyer Michael Pangia argued that the FAA had nothing to do with overloading the airplane or operating it without a proper flight crew, and that the Tort Claims Act does not permit suits for "negligent enforcement of the law" or "negligent failure to apply sanctions." He claimed that the FSDO inspectors did not have the legal authority to ground Rivera's DC-7; and even if they had inspected it and found it unsafe, they would have to call in the Southern Region attorney and go through complicated legal procedures that would not have saved Clemente's life. But our position was that we were not concerned with the failure to ground Rivera or to apply other sanctions. We claimed that compliance with Southern Order Section 7D, "Clear indication of alleged illegal flight should be made known to flight crew and persons chartering the service," would have been sufficient to save the lives of the passengers. Don Madole was able to elicit admissions from the FSDO inspectors on this point.

FSDO Chief Leonard Davis testified that he did not think it would be necessary to inform the passengers; normally, a word to the captain would be sufficient, since he would then be on notice that the proposed flight was in violation of the regulations, and his professional career would be ended if he took off in the face of such a warning. Davis shied away from admitting that the Southern Order also required him to inform the passengers, but Don kept pressing him on this important point.

> Q. by Mr. MADOLE: Would you read the last sentence of the Southern Order, sir, that reads, "Clear indication of alleged illegal flight should be made known to flight crew and persons chartering the service." Would those "persons chartering" be the passengers?   A: "Clear indication of alleged illegal flight."
> Q: Would the flight be illegal if it were to operate in excess of the approved gross weight?   A: If I informed the captain that I had positive evidence that the airplane would be overweight, if I had positive evidence, I would have to be 100 percent sure, and if he refused to take any action, I might have told the passengers, yes, sir, I might.
> Q: Doesn't the Southern Order say you should tell the passengers?   A: It says that, that I would have to be positively sure that I am not grounding an airplane that I am not sure about. If I were sure and the captain refused—and he is the one that is the final authority on this—I would tell the passengers.
> Q: You would tell the passengers?   A: Yes, sir.

During most of his two days on the witness stand, Davis fought to keep from admitting that the Southern Order had any significance in connection with Rivera's flight. Don succeeded in exposing the fallacy of much of his testimony, but there were many lengthy government orders and manuals in evidence, and that tended to obscure the true import of the Southern Order. To establish its significance, we needed testimony from our own experts on FAA procedures. We were most fortunate in obtaining Usto E. Schulz as our chief expert. He had retired from the FAA in 1975 after a long career that culminated in the position of executive officer (No. 2 man) of the Flight Standards Division at FAA headquarters in Washington. He was the FAA official who had actually been put in charge of preventing repetitions of the 1970 Wichita State accident. As executive officer, he had been responsible for holding meetings with other FAA supervisory personnel throughout the nation to work out the best means of dealing with illegal operators of large aircraft. After many such meetings and discussions, Schulz personally directed the drafting of the Southern Order and similar orders in the other FAA regions.

Under questioning by Chuck Krause, Schulz testified that the policy of the FAA was: "Where a safety problem or violation is known to exist or is about to happen, action should be directed at that point, to the exclusion of other routine, less urgent activities." He described how the Wichita State accident had led to adoption of the Southern Order, with its requirement of continuous surveillance in coordination with ATC personnel, designed to assure FSDO inspectors the opportunity to determine the existence of safety violations before takeoff. He testified that Rivera's operation was exactly "the kind of thing we were trying to stop." Chuck Krause took him through the prior history of Rivera's operations, including the San Juan FSDO inspectors' awareness of his disdain for safety regulations. Usto Schulz gave this opinion:

> With these things known to the FAA, the field office had a
> duty to prevent that operation under the conditions then present.

Schulz's testimony established that the policy decision to keep Rivera-type operators under continuous surveillance and to take other affirmative action to prevent repetitions of the Wichita State disaster was made at the highest level of the FAA. Schulz's only superior in the FAA Flight Standards division, the director, was known as "FS-1," and it was under the authority of FS-1 that Schulz had issued a national directive requiring surveillance in coordination with ATC, ramp inspection, and warning of passengers. The national directive was the basis for the Southern Order and for similar orders in all regions of the FAA. Schulz testified that the discretion of the government was exercised in Washington at the FS-1 level of the FAA, and that nothing further was left to the discretion of lower level employees of the FAA. This was to be our sword against the government's discretionary function shield.

Chuck Krause took Usto Schulz through details of the FAA chain of command, and Schulz stated flatly that Leonard Davis had no authority to limit the Southern Order to arriving aircraft or to otherwise change its policy. Mike Pangia, the government attorney, cross-examined Schulz at length and tried to show that FSDO station chiefs were given a lot of discretion.

> Q. by Mr. PANGIA: And when latitude is given to these field officers, it was given in that area of management which in turn affected the implementation of these orders? A: Yes. But that did not give them any right to decide not to do something that was directed.
> Q: Unless he felt it was unsafe or unless he felt he couldn't do it? A: I didn't say that. He has to implement the order and if he finds out he has a physically impossible problem, he has to make judgments about that. But you have to implement it first. . . . First you implement a directive, and by that I mean you start doing what the directive asks you to do. This particular one said, "Here is the required action." The only really required action to start with was to be notified.

Q: To be notified? A: Yes. Arriving and departing aircraft.

Q: So, whether or not there is priority has to be up to the judgment of the person down here running the Flight Standards office
who knows of his own problems. He knows his area and he
knows his manpower limitations? A: He has to make judgments about where he is going to put his manpower. But he cannot do it outside the limitations of the basic policy that the agency
sets. We have 85 field offices, sir. If each set their own policy it
would be chaotic. We couldn't make a decision in Washington
that made any sense at all.

Pangia kept banging away at manpower problems and the wide geo-
graphical area that the San Juan office had to cover. But Schulz insisted
that he (and the other FAA officials at Washington headquarters who
worked with him in setting the policy of surveillance) had taken manpower problems into consideration, and that the Southern Order's requirement of notification from ATC was a means of using their manpower in the most effective way. He testified that if Leonard Davis had
any difficulty in complying with the Southern Order, his only recourse
was to get the chief of Flight Standards for Southern Region to modify
the order. There was no testimony that any modification had ever been
requested or even discussed.

Our second expert witness was Robert H. Jackson, who had been
an FSDO inspector at Miami and San Juan prior to his retirement in
1973. He complemented Usto Schulz's testimony by giving the court a
view of the Flight Standards service and the Southern Order from the
standpoint of the local inspector. His experience was particularly valuable because he had participated in the surveillance of illegal and unsafe operators at "cockroach corner" on Miami International Airport,
and had been assigned to San Juan on several occasions while the Southern Order was in effect. He testified that he had personally conducted
surveillance of large aircraft pursuant to the Southern Order. Under
questioning by Don Madole, he described how he had conducted the
ramp inspections required by the Southern Order.

Q. by Mr. MADOLE: During that month of December 1972 when
you conducted ramp inspections, did you check weight and balance? A: Yes, sir.

Q: And did you require the pilot to prove to you that the plane
was loaded within proper limits? A: Yes.

Q: Did there ever come a time when you were suspicious of the
loading of an aircraft? A: Yes.

Q: What did you require the pilot to do? A: Show me.

Q: Did you ever require the plane to be unloaded? A: Yes.

Q: And that the items be weighed? A: Yes.

Q: And did you have authority to do that? A: Yes.

* * *

Q: Would you have told the passengers? A: I would.

Q: Would you have warned them? What specifically would you have told them? A: I would have told them that this aircraft does not meet the requirements established by the Federal Regulations, and any operation therefore would constitute a violation of the regulations.

Q: And if the captain said, "We are going to go anyway," what would you do? A: I would immediately call the regional attorney and have him take action on amending their airworthiness certificate and grounding the aircraft.

Q: Would you tell the regional attorney or would you request of the regional attorney that emergency action be taken? A: I would.

Q: And did you have provisions under that order to request emergency action? A: We did.

Q: What is the reason for emergency action? A: It is to prevent an accident and also in keeping with the public safety.

Q: It is to save lives, isn't it? A: Absolutely.

Now it was the government's turn. Their case was based on the claim that implementation of the Southern Order was at the discretion of San Juan FSDO Chief Leonard Davis. The principal defense witness was Gordon W. Becker, Chief of the Flight Standards Division, FAA Southern Region, stationed at Atlanta. He was the man who actually issued the Southern Order under the national directive adopted by FS-1 in Washington. Under questioning by Mike Pangia, Gordon Becker tried to minimize the significance of the Southern Order.

Q. by Mr. PANGIA: Sir, what did you mean by that order? A: We meant the order to be a general guidance to our field facilities to use their judgment in setting up a large aircraft surveillance program within the limits of their resources and considering the other priorities of their task.

Q: Do you see the word "will" in the third paragraph, sir? A: Yes sir.

Q: Does that have any special meaning for Flight Standards? A: It means that it is discretionary as to whether they do it or not.

Q: Is there any word that the FAA uses to your knowledge that means mandatory? A: Yes sir. We use the word "must" or "shall."

Becker's testimony took only a few minutes, but it was designed to destroy the case we had built around the Southern Order. If the court accepted his testimony that the Southern Order was discretionary rather than mandatory, the discretionary function would completely bar our claims. In the crucial cross-examination of Gordon Becker, Don Madole struck first at Becker's claim that the word "will" was not mandatory. He was armed with another Southern Region order which he handed to Becker soon after he started his cross examination.

Q. by Mr. MADOLE: Mr. Becker, you said you put in a mandatory order in Miami? A: Yes, sir.

Q: You used the word "must" in it, did you? A: I don't have that order.

Q: How many times did you use the word "must" in that mandatory order? A: I don't know.

Q: How many times did you use the word "shall"? A: I don't know.

Q: How many times did you use the word "will"? A: I don't know.

Q: [handing document to the witness] Is this the order? A: Yes, sir.

Q: Show me the "shalls," the "musts," and then read me the "wills." Where are they? A: I don't see the use of the word "shall" or "must" here.

Q: May I read something to you? A: Yes, sir.

Q: I would like you to look at this exhibit, 56.6, "Action: the chief Miami Air Carrier District Office *will* operate a special office." Did you just testify to Mr. Pangia that that word in this order meant it was mandatory, is that what you meant to say to him? A: Would you say that again, sir.

Q: Didn't you just mean to tell Mr. Pangia that this Miami order was mandatory, and that in anything that is mandatory, you use the word "must" or "shall," but you would not use the word "will"? A: That is what I said.

Q: You intended this [Miami order] to be mandatory? A: Yes, sir, it was.

Q: And you wrote this? A: Yes, sir.

Q: And to make it mandatory you used the word "will": "the chief of the Miami office *will* operate a special office"? A: That is rather obvious. We did in that case.

Q: It *is* rather obvious. You said the chief of the Miami district office *will* monitor conditions of the space, etc? A: Yes, sir.

Q: And didn't you also say in procedure, "surveillance *will* be conducted on a twenty-four hour seven day a week basis including holidays"? A: Yes, sir.

Q: Did you mean by the word "will" in this order that it was mandatory? A: I have to say yes.

Q: Was there any discretion in carrying this out? A: No, sir.

Q: You are going to tell me, then, for purposes of this litigation, that you wrote one order with the word "will" and that is mandatory, and another order that is not mandatory [the Southern Order], is that going to be your testimony? A: That is it. Yes, sir.

Becker had gone about as far as technical bureaucratic jargon could take him. After Don Madole confronted him with documentary evidence that "will" was used in mandatory orders, he was not willing to stick his neck out any further. Don then turned to the chain of authority from FAA headquarters in Washington to the Southern Regional Office that Becker headed.

Q: Now, when FS-1 asks you to do something, you have to do it?   A: FS-1 or the Flight Standards Service in Washington sets up the national policies for air carrier general safety programs, yes.

Q: Do you have a right to change those policies?   A: No sir.

Q: Does Mr. Davis have a right to change that policy?   A: No, sir.

Q: Very well. And based on policy from FS-1, you had your staff write the Southern Order, is that right?   A: That is correct.

Q: When you wrote this order, were you trying to protect a certain class of people?   A: Well, "protect a class of people," I don't know. We were trying to increase the surveillance over flights of large airplanes that are operating outside of the certificate holder.

Q: Were you doing that for safety?   A: Certainly.

Q: Were you trying to save lives?   A: Yes, sir.

Now Don was getting into the area of duty assumed by the FAA. One of the government's arguments was that even if they had breached the Southern Order it was not actionable because the order created only a duty within the FAA itself—a duty on the part of the inspectors to comply with the orders of their superiors—but not a duty to protect the public. Don followed up on Becker's admission that he had written the Southern Order in an attempt to save lives.

Q: Just one more time, was the purpose of this order to protect people like Roberto Clemente from getting on this airplane?   A: To protect the lives of people.

Q: Like Mr. Clemente and Mr. Lozano?   A: Yes, sir.

Q: People who were not operators in aviation?   A: Right.

Q: People who were not professionals in aviation—they saw a nice painted airplane down there, and they needed to go to Nicaragua, and it is on the airport, and so they hired it—it is those sort of people that this order was really intended to protect, wasn't it?   A: Yes, sir.

The government also contended that the San Juan FSDO did not have sufficient manpower to keep all dangerous planes under surveillance. It was not explained why they would put a further burden on their manpower by failing to implement the Southern Order's requirement of a notification procedure from ATC, which would have made it a simple matter to conduct predeparture ramp inspections without having to keep parked airplanes under surveillance. In this case, the uncontroverted evidence was: Jerry Hill had filed his flight plan with ATC for the San Juan–Managua flight on the morning of December 31, at least nine hours prior to departure; at 4:05 P.M. he had filed a customs declaration listing the crew, passengers, and cargo; and at 5:30 P.M., nearly four hours before the actual departure time, he had taxied out for takeoff before returning to the ramp because of engine trouble. Therefore, ATC personnel had at least four hours' notice of the intended departure of the Rivera DC-7. The testimony showed that there was one FSDO inspector on duty on December 31, although a number of other inspectors were attending a New Year's Eve party near the airport.

In his questioning of the San Juan FSDO inspectors, Mike Pangia brought out that it would have taken quite a long time to make a complete ramp inspection of Rivera's DC-7 in accordance with the Southern Order. They admitted, however, that they all knew Rivera's history and the fact that he had no organization whatsoever. Therefore the FSDO inspectors would have known that an illegal and hazardous flight was about to take place the moment ATC informed them of a clearance request from Rivera's DC-7. Furthermore, they would have determined in less than ten seconds that he did not have a copilot or flight engineer aboard, which automatically made the flight illegal, regardless of whether the aircraft was within weight limits and properly loaded. In any event, the government's claimed shortage of manpower was a nonsequitur. San Juan had never implemented the notification procedure required by Section 3 of the Southern Order, and thus there was no way in which ATC could have alerted the available FSDO manpower to the need for a ramp inspection.

The trial ended on November 21, 1975. Judge Torruella requested both sides to submit briefs supporting their arguments with references to pages of the trial transcript. But the court reporters in the Puerto Rican courts had a backlog of work, so there was a long delay in getting the trial testimony transcribed. For that reason Judge Torruella's decision was not issued until November 24, 1976, a year after the trial ended.

We were delighted to learn that Judge Torruella had ruled in our favor on liability. He held that the Southern Order was mandatory, and that in conjunction with the general safety functions assigned to the FAA under the Federal Aviation Act of 1958, it created a duty on the part of the FSDO inspectors at San Juan to set up the ATC notification procedure, to conduct a ramp inspection of Rivera's DC-7, and to warn Clemente and the other passengers of the dangers involved in the illegal flight. He held that the failure to conduct the ramp inspection and to warn the passengers was a proximate cause of the passengers' deaths, since it was reasonable to infer that had they been notified of imminent danger, they would not have signed their own death warrants by remaining aboard. He found Clemente and the other passengers to be within the class of persons the Southern Order sought to protect, which means that the Southern Order had made it the FAA's legal duty to warn these passengers.

In holding that the Southern Order was mandatory rather than discretionary, Judge Torruella wrote:

We have no difficulty in concluding that this order was a clear exercise of policy judgment as to how the public interest was best to be promoted. Furthermore, we are not persuaded by the testimony presented in support of the proposition that the issuing authority intended this order to be applied at the discretion of the District Office. In a trial congested by documentary evidence, Defendant failed to buttress this allegation in any credible manner.

At this late hour such a contention smacks of litigation-oriented reasoning, particularly when we consider that the language in paragraph 2 of the order "requires action by . . . Flight Standards District Offices . . ." In our opinion it is self-evident that this order is mandatory in nature. Any possible residual discretion left to the District Office as to the operational implementation of this policy can hardly grant license to the mind-boggling logic whereby arriving aircraft are given preference over those about to depart, such action being in clear contravention to the basic policy established by higher authority.

Thus Judge Torruela swept aside the attempt by Leonard Davis and Gordon Becker to rewrite the Southern Order as discretionary rather than mandatory, and he rejected the outrageous explanation of Davis that he had implemented the Southern Order by arranging for notification of arriving aircraft but not departing aircraft.

As to duty, Judge Torruella held:

It appears to us to be undisputable that by the enactment of the Federal Aviation Act of 1958, 49 USC §1301 et seq, Congress intended to impose a duty on the FAA to promote maximum safety in the use of the nation's air space. . . . In the exercise of duties established by the above mentioned statute, the director of the Southern Region of the FAA on September 25, 1972, issued [the Southern Order]. . . . It would seem that the [Southern Order] is applicable to the flight here in question, and that Plaintiffs' decedents are within the class of persons sought to be protected thereby.

In this case we are concerned precisely with neglect of duty, a duty created in a general manner by Congress when it enacted the Federal Aviation Act of 1958 (49 USC §1301 et seq) and thereafter in a more precise fashion, as a result of the experiences of the FAA, by that Agency's promulgation of [the Southern Order]. . . . There are several other cases in which internal agency directives have been held to establish an actionable duty by those intended to be benefitted by the directive. . . . The existence of [the Southern Order] in substantially the same form since April 5, 1971, not only establishes a standard of duty but clearly brings forth the foreseeability of the present situation, particularly when the facts previously stated are taken into consideration.

As to the discretionary function argument, he reviewed the principal authorities, including the Texas City case, and he concluded that

since the Southern Order was a policy decision adopted at the highest
level of the FAA, any discretion was exhausted at that level, and there
was none left when the Southern Order reached the level of the FSDO
at San Juan. He distinguished the planning or discretionary level of the
FAA in Washington from the operational level at San Juan. Judge
Torruella concluded:

> Therefore, not being concerned with the exercise of a dis-
> cretionary function but rather the performance of duties within
> the framework of a regulation, the "exercise of due care" stand-
> ard contained in the first part of Section 2680 (a) is applicable.
> It follows that in violating its own orders, the FAA demonstrated
> a failure to exercise due care and that, as previously expounded
> herein, by said misfeasance contributed to the death of Plaintiffs'
> decedents. In view of the above we find for Plaintiffs on the issue
> of negligence.

The judge found that there was a complete failure of the FSDO
at San Juan to implement the requirements of the Southern Order. He
rejected Leonard Davis's fantastic yarn about implementing it for arriving aircraft, calling it "mind-boggling logic." As to the direct cause
of the crash, Judge Torruella found:

> From the evidence adduced at the trial, we are of the opin-
> ion that the failure of No. 2 engine was caused by an "over-
> boosting" of the engine upon takeoff. This in turn was caused
> by the lack of a proper flight crew.
> The inadequacy of the flight crew, in particular, the lack of
> a trained co-pilot and the total absence of a flight engineer (both
> crew members whose functions are of prime importance in pre-
> venting "overboosting"), together with a gross takeoff weight
> which exceeded the maximum allowable limits by more than
> two tons, created a situation wherein . . . "for all practical
> purposes the Captain was flying solo in emergency conditions."

The statement about the Captain flying solo in emergency conditions was quoted from the FAA's own report as to the cause of this accident. Thus it was undisputed that the airplane was operated with an
improper and insufficient crew and in an overweight condition. Overloading of the aircraft placed extra strain on the engines, and in the
absence of a qualified flight engineer to monitor the engine instruments
and to properly position, adjust, and monitor the throttles they could
be pushed too far forward and thus overboost the engines and cause
engine failure on takeoff. This probable sequence of events, leading to
the failure of the No. 2 engine and the doomed attempt to return to the
field in an overloaded condition, was agreed to by the government
through Mike Pangia's questioning of Leonard Davis. The government

not only admitted that the absence of a flight engineer and a copilot were causal factors, but they actually alleged this themselves, seeking to put the blame entirely on Rivera. But the court found that the flouting of the Southern Order was a direct contributing cause of the accident:

> . . . most assuredly upon the performance of a ramp inspection of the aircraft, the lack of a proper flight crew and the gross overweight would have become apparent to the inspecting authority. Upon such a "clear indication of illegal [and unsafe] flight" being made known to Plaintiffs' decedents, it is reasonable to presume that they would not have participated as passengers in this dubious enterprise.

> In our opinion, the failure of the FAA to meet the duties established by an Order which had the force of law, was *a* cause of the accident here in question. Even if not the *only* cause, the Defendant is responsible in this jurisdiction for his fault because the damages which resulted from the breach of duty were a natural, probable and foreseeable consequence of Defendant's omission. The intervening negligence or fault of third parties, if such were the case herein, does not relieve a defendant from liability in this jurisdiction where, as in the present case, the intervening party was aided by the Defendant's fault, or where the actions of said party were foreseeable within the chain of circumstances set in motion or contributed to by Defendant.

Thus, even though Rivera and Hill were obviously negligent, it was foreseeable to the FAA that if its personnel failed to conduct the ramp inspection and thus allowed the fatal flight to take off, then the negligence of Rivera and Hill was likely to result in an accident. Therefore, the chain of causation was clearly established.

Mike Pangia made a motion for reconsideration of the decision, which Judge Torruella denied. However, he did grant the government the right to appeal the liability decision before trying damages. This interlocutory appeal under 28 U.S. Code §1292 (b) is often used when liability is tried separately. So it was that the Clemente case was taken up to the U.S. Court of Appeals for the First Circuit, since that court had also granted permission for the interlocutory appeal on liability.

The Appeal

After their splendid job on the Clemente trial, Chuck Krause and the Madoles turned the task of preserving their verdict in the appellate courts over to me. They worked with me in replying to the government's appellate brief and in preparing for argument, which was scheduled for hearing in Boston on October 5, 1977. Although appellate arguments do not often produce the immediate thrills of the trial arena, they are exciting intellectual challenges. The preparation is intensive, for you must cram your mind with all the facts in the trial record and all the legal principles involved in dozens of court decisions—several thousand pages of material, any part of which you may have to recall during the fifteen to thirty minutes on your feet.

The Court of Appeals for the First Circuit has the shortest calendar delay of all our federal appellate courts. It hears appeals from the district courts of Massachusetts, New Hampshire, Rhode Island, Maine, and Puerto Rico. It might seem more appropriate for appeals from the district court of Puerto Rico to go to the Second Circuit in New York, since New York has a large Puerto Rican population. But when Puerto Rico became part of the federal judicial system, the Second Circuit was already a very busy court, and it was therefore more convenient to assign that island's appeals to the First Circuit.

In the fall of 1977, there were only two active judges on the First Circuit court. Since the court had to sit in panels of three judges, they often used a senior (semi-retired) judge or a district court judge as the third panel member. On the day of the Clemente argument, the court consisted of Chief Judge Frank M. Coffin of Portland, Maine, Circuit Judge Levin H. Campbell of Boston, and Senior District Judge E. Avery Crary of Los Angeles. The court session was held in Boston's John McCormack Post Office and Courthouse.

Pangia was the first to argue since he represented the losing party in the court below. He had submitted a long brief outlining all of the arguments that he had made in the district court. His first point was that the case fell within the discretionary function exception of the Federal Tort Claims Act because it involved investigative, enforcement, and prosecutorial acts of the government. He devoted most of his brief to this point, which had also dominated his trial defense. Another argument was that FAA's surveillance, enforcement, and prosecutorial functions were not responsibilities to the public but only internal duties of FAA personnel to their superiors. His brief also included a point relating to the "policy considerations" of Judge Torruella's decision. He claimed that holding the FAA liable for failure to warn the passengers about the dangers of the flight would serve to diminish the operator's responsibility, would have a deterrent effect upon aviation safety, and would make the government a party in every aviation accident lawsuit. In his brief, Pangia argued:

> If the government is held to have an actionable duty to prevent or warn against all such violations, it will become the

"deep pocket defendant" in all such cases, thereby rendering the government an insurer of all private aviation activities in the United States.

Moreover, the creation of such a duty would likely produce shock waves far beyond aviation. Indeed, the precedent of imposing such duty upon federal surveillance and enforcement personnel of regulatory agencies would spawn new causes of action in respect of all the other myriad of situations where members of the public are injured as a result of private activity which regulatory agencies have failed to prevent or warn against. At the federal level alone, such new litigation could change the results in cases involving the enforcement efforts of, for example, the Securities and Exchange Commission, the Occupational Health and Safety Administration, the Coast Guard, the FBI and other police agencies, and others. This is not to mention the potential effect upon the liability of literally thousands of state and local law enforcement agencies which heretofore have generally been held not to be liable for negligent enforcement of law. Recognition of any new cause of action is capable of increasing the administrative burden of courts to some degree; but when the new theory of action is negligent enforcement of law, the problem is particularly acute.

Pangia also mentioned in his brief that Chief Leonard Davis of the San Juan FSDO had never been disciplined by the FAA for failing to carry out the requirements of the Southern Order. He argued:

> In any event, this is further indication that whatever duties were imposed upon Mr. Davis by the Order, those duties were owed to his superiors in the agency, and not to the public at large.

In his oral argument Pangia had only spoken a few sentences when he was interrupted by the judges. This is the most exciting part of an appeal. I had laid out a complete argument and had run through it several times on a tape recorder, making sure that it fitted within the thirty minutes allotted to me. But few appellate judges are interested in listening to a rehearsed presentation; they know that all of the major points will be covered in the briefs which they have either read before the argument or will be reading after. Therefore they interrupt frequently with questions, and all of the time taken by the questions and answers is deducted from the time allotted for argument, so that appellate lawyers rarely get to finish their entire argument as planned.

From the very first questions put to Pangia by the judges, I could tell that we were in trouble. They wanted to know what the effect of this decision would be on government agencies—would the FAA and other agencies continue to issue mandatory orders for inspection or warning if they knew that this might lead to tort liability? They were particularly concerned with the new government agency spawned by Ralph Nader's efforts, the Occupational Safety and Health Administration (OSHA), which had undertaken responsibility for inspecting thousands of work places for conformance with federal safety standards. Would the Clemente decision open the way for government responsibility every time workers were injured after OSHA had inspected a factory and found safety violations without making these known to the workers?

From the questions asked of Pangia, it seemed that the court was not concerned with the discretionary function issue. They concentrated on the precedent the Clemente case might set. Would it broaden the liability of the federal government to include thousands of cases of government inspection, investigation, and enforcement proceedings?

By the time that I stood up to argue it was clear that the judges were deeply concerned about the policy implications of this decision. I started off by stating that the facts of the case fell within the legal principles laid down by the First Circuit itself in two recent FTCA decisions dealing with failure to warn and the legal duties of the FAA. I said that the only unusual thing about the Clemente case was the rather startling fact that the FAA admittedly ignored its own mandatory safety order, an order that was aimed at protecting the public from illegal operators of large aircraft who deliberately ignored FAA safety regulations. That was as far as I got in my prepared argument. The judges immediately bombarded me with questions about the doors that would be opened by holding the government responsible for "negligent law enforcement."

I pointed out that the FAA itself had recognized the emergency that existed after the Wichita State accident, and had taken the duty of affirmative action upon itself to save the passengers' lives by the only means available: ramp inspection and the warning mandated in the Southern Order. We were seeking damages for failure to warn the passengers rather than for negligence in the enforcement of sanctions against Rivera. I argued that the Clemente decision, if affirmed, would not broaden government liability because it was limited to cases in which the agency itself had recognized an emergency and found that the only way of protecting the public was to assume the duty of warning the potential victims. Here the action of the FAA was the public's first, last, and only line of defense against illegal operators who could not be regulated in the usual way because they made a practice of flouting government safety regulations. I said the uncontroverted trial testimony showed that the policy decision to impose such a duty on FAA personnel was made by the FAA itself at its highest level after due consideration of possible manpower and budget problems. I pointed out that the fact situation in the Clemente case was so bizzare that we were not likely to see its equivalent very often, unless our government agencies are full of employees who disregard mandatory emergency safety duties, in which event the deterrent effect of tort liability would assume even greater importance.

Again the judges asked whether government agencies would undertake life-saving functions in the future if they might lead to tort liability. I answered that the duties of the agencies were fixed by Congress, and if the agencies shirked those duties, Congress would direct them to protect the public properly. I was asked whether the FAA would continue to try to screen out these illegal operators in view of the potential liability. I answered that the Southern Order was still in effect, and it was common knowledge in aviation circles that the Clemente trial and decision had actually resulted in stepped-up efforts by the FAA to ferret out irresponsible operators of large aircraft. In our brief I had pointed out that in the first three months following publication of the district court's decision in the Clemente case, FAA inspectors had grounded 42 large aircraft and 30 pilots.

Because Pangia had raised this policy argument in his brief and had mentioned that Leonard Davis had not been disciplined by his superiors (even though this was not in the record of the trial), I had felt it necessary to point out in our brief that the actual effect of the Clemente decision was to increase aviation safety by making the FSDO inspectors in the Southern Region more conscious of their duties to protect the public. Now, as a result of the Clemente decision, they were not sitting back and hoping that their surveillance procedures would prevent illegal flights. They were going out and grounding irresponsible operators and dangerous airplanes *before* they could kill more members of the public. Thus the direct effect of the Clemente decision was to fumigate cockroach corner, something the FAA had been talking about for years but had never accomplished before Judge Torruella's decision in the Clemente case.

The judges' questions consumed most of my thirty minutes. There was very little discussion of the facts of the case, negligence, causation, or the discretionary function exception. Although the three judges had indicated by their questioning that they were doubtful about Judge Torruella's decision, I left the Boston courthouse hoping for the best. It is difficult to guess the outcome of an appeal from the questions asked during argument. Sometimes the judges bend over backwards to explore all the weaknesses of one advocate's arguments before deciding in his favor, so that they cannot be accused of ignoring the arguments of the losing side. That's what I told myself as we awaited the decision, but it didn't turn out that way. On December 16, 1977, the First Circuit unanimously reversed Judge Torruella's decision and dismissed our suit.

The judges' concern about the broad implications of Judge Torruella's decision was apparent in their opinion, which included the following language:

> To hold otherwise would be to interpret every command
> made as an exercise of discretion by the supervisory or adminis-
> trative staff of any federal agency as creating a duty of the fed-
> eral government to the beneficiaries of that command such that
> the government would be liable to the beneficiary if the command
> was not carried out. We do not believe the Federal Tort Claims
> Act was intended to expose the government to such limitless lia-
> bility and would not so hold unless we were required to do so by
> established precedent. Indeed, because the policy implications of
> finding liability on the grounds suggested here would be so severe,
> and because the surrender of sovereign immunity by the govern-
> ment should be interpreted narrowly, we must subject to critical
> scrutiny the cases cited by the district court to support its con-
> clusion that the Federal Aviation Act and the Southern Region's
> order created an actionable duty on the part of the federal gov-
> ernment.

The opinion went on to discuss these "policy implications" as applied
to the Occupational Safety and Health Administration (OSHA) and
other federal agencies that perform safety inspections. The court also
articulated its concern about the effects of such liability on government
safety functions:

> Moreover, to attempt to expand the relief available to vic-
> tims and their families through the Federal Tort Claims Act in
> circumstances similar to those of this case would, we believe,
> have an unfortunate inhibiting effect on government safety mea-
> sures. The end result of attaching liability to government attempts
> at all levels to supplement the safety precautions of private indi-
> viduals and businesses, even when there is no reliance on the
> government's assistance, is far more likely to increase the reluc-
> tance of the government to involve itself in such matters than it
> is to install a higher quality to performance in the federal em-
> ployees assigned to carry such functions out. We do not believe
> that the expanded role of the federal government in the safety
> area through such legislation as OSHA indicates an intent of
> Congress to make the United States a joint insurer of all activity
> subject to inspection under the statute or others. Nor do we be-
> lieve that there is any sound policy basis for requiring that gov-
> ernment attempts to protect the public must be accompanied by
> per se tort liability if they are unsuccessfully carried out.

Since policy decisions about government safety measures are supposed to be made by Congress rather than the courts, the First Circuit
had to base its reversal upon errors of law committed by Judge Torruella. It did so by holding that the FAA had no legal duty to the passen-

gers aboard Rivera's airplane to warn them of the dangers and the illegal nature of Rivera's operation:

> It is obvious that one of the purposes of the Federal Aviation Act was to promote air travel safety; but this fact hardly creates a legal duty to provide a particular class of passengers particular protective measures. While the Federal Aviation Act empowered the administrative staff of the FAA to issue an order such as [the Southern Order], the Act itself does not require this conduct. The agency, in issuing the order, was acting entirely gratuitously and was under no obligation or duty to Plaintiffs' decedents or any other passengers.
>
> *   *   *
>
> Not all acts and orders of United States government are so sovereign that they must be treated as commands which create legal duties or standards, the violation of which involves breaking the law. A considerable part of the government's conduct is in the context of an employer-employee relationship, a relationship which includes reciprocal duties between the government and its staff, but not necessarily a legal duty to the citizenry.
>
> *   *   *
>
> This duty to comply with the directives of their superiors is owed by the employees to the government and is totally distinguishable from a duty owed by the government to the public on which liability could be based. The failure to perform the order may be grounds for internal discipline, but it does not follow that such conduct necessarily constitutes the kind of breach cognizable by tort law.

In my admittedly biased view, the First Circuit's efforts to justify its reversal of Judge Torruella's decision led to some strained analysis. They misstated the basic statutory provisions under which the Southern Order was issued. In their opinion they cited Section 313 of the Federal Aviation Act (49 U.S.C. §1354) as the basis for the Southern Order. That section empowers the FAA to issue orders, but as the court said, it does not require them to issue such orders. However, Judge Torruella found and declared in his opinion that the Southern Order was based upon three other sections of the Federal Aviation Act which *required* the FAA to issue such orders to "reduce or eliminate the possibility of, or recurrence of accidents" (49 U.S.C. §§1302, 1303 and 1421). The First Circuit opinion did not mention Sections 1302, 1303, or 1421, even though the government (throughout the trial and appeal) never denied that those three sections were the ones under which the Southern Order was issued. Thus, the First Circuit appears to be incorrect in stating that the Federal Aviation Act did not require the administrator of the FAA to issue the Southern Order when he found an emergency to exist.

The First Circuit decision also ignored the undisputed testimony of Usto E. Schulz, the former executive officer of the Flight Standards Service who said that the Southern Order was issued after careful consideration of manpower and other requirements. Schulz had given a detailed description of the emergency that was facing the FAA, with the public at the mercy of irresponsible operators who were making a regular practice of flouting the safety regulations. Under those circumstances, it is difficult for me to understand how the First Circuit could find that in its issuance of the Southern Order, the FAA "was acting entirely gratuitously and was under no obligation or duty to Plaintiffs' decedents or any other passengers." One can only wonder what the FAA inspectors are being paid for, if they are acting gratuitously in carrying out an order which their own superiors found was necessary for the protection of the public. Furthermore, there was also the undisputed evidence of all the FAA inspectors, including those produced by the government, stating that the purpose of the Southern Order was to save the lives of unsophisticated one-time charterers like Clemente who had no means of knowing whether an aircraft operation was safe.

If the government had any basis on which to contest Schulz's trial testimony to the effect that manpower requirements had been taken into consideration, they could easily have produced the director of Flight Standards or the FAA administrator himself to refute this. But they produced no such evidence, and they never tried to refute Schulz's manpower testimony.

The First Circuit was absolutely correct in stating that not all acts and orders of the government create legal duties to the public. While the FSDO personnel at San Juan did owe a duty to their superiors in Atlanta and Washington to comply with the Southern Order, it would seem that there was also a duty (if not the primary duty) to those whose lives were supposed to be protected by proper execution of the order.

In this connection, the First Circuit described the Southern Order as an attempt to "supplement the safety precautions of private individuals and businesses." However, the very basis of the Southern Order was a recognition that there were private individuals and businesses who were taking no safety precautions and thus required continuous surveillance and government intervention to curb their life-threatening activities. If the First Circuit had been confronted with an OSHA inspection of an industry in which most of the operators were making some attempt to comply with the law, then their statement about the government inspection being a supplement to private safety precautions would make some sense. But the Southern Order did not "supplement the safety precautions" of Arthur Rivera any more than the homicide bureau "supplements the safety precautions" of hired assassins. Rivera would never have told Clemente that the flight was illegal or dangerous. Clemente's only chance to learn this was FAA performance of its duties under the Southern Order.

The First Circuit was confronted by more than two dozen prior court decisions holding that the FAA had assumed the duty to comply with its own regulations, orders, and manuals—a duty that ran to individual members of the public who were injured by the failure of FAA personnel to comply with FAA orders. The First Circuit attempted to distinguish these decisions by stating that they involved Air Traffic Control functions rather than safety inspection or other FAA functions. Most of the cases dealing with negligence of Air Traffic personnel that we had cited in our brief (and Judge Torruella had cited in his decision) involved advisory services such as weather and turbulence information rather than traffic separation or control. Of the eighteen major decisions we called to the court's attention, only four involved collisions. Here the First Circuit made an erroneous statement:

> The remaining cases cited by the district court all involve accidents resulting from the negligence of air traffic controllers.

Actually, Judge Torruella's decision cited three precedents in which it was held that the United States was legally responsible for the negligence of FAA safety inspectors (rather than air traffic controllers) and that the duty of safety inspectors to comply with their own agency's orders ran to the injured persons. Two of those decisions were federal district court cases, and one, *Arney v. U.S.,* 479 F.2d 653, was a 1973 decision of the Ninth Circuit Court of Appeals. Those three precedents, and especially the Ninth Circuit decision, were directly contrary to the First Circuit's holding that only air traffic controllers owe a duty to the public.

The First Circuit's decision in the Clemente case is the only one that calls the FAA's safety duties gratuitous. It is the only decision in an FAA case that discusses duty in any detail. Every other FAA negligence decision either assumed that the legal duty was automatic once the FAA ordered its personnel to perform public safety functions, or it disposed of the duty question by assuming the traveling public *must* be able to rely on the FAA's performance of the safety functions it has undertaken. Almost without exception the other FAA negligence decisions merely established the existence of an order or a provision in an FAA manual which directs FAA employees to perform certain functions. Then the courts assumed automatically that the public must rely upon the FAA's performance of those functions, because the FAA has preempted the field of aviation safety and there is no other authority to perform them. There were dozens of cases that held the FAA negligent, and in every one of them there was also an operator or a pilot who had a duty to take safety precautions. But this did not lessen the duty of the FAA to carry out such functions as its own senior officials have deemed necessary for the protection of the flying public. Obviously, passengers are as likely to be killed by the FAA's failure to warn of an overloaded aircraft lacking a proper flight crew as by the FAA's failure to warn of hazardous weather conditions, wake turbulence, or conflicts in air traffic.

The irony of the First Circuit's attempt to distinguish between ATC personnel and FSDO inspectors is that the Southern Order required coordination between ATC and the FSDO. Judge Torruella found on undisputed evidence that this coordination was never established for departing aircraft. Thus the Clemente case involves a failure by ATC as well as FSDO personnel to carry out prescribed duties. Judge Torruella found negligence on the part of "the San Juan FAA personnel." He did not limit it to the FSDO personnel; he also included the ATC personnel. There was no dispute as to these facts, but the First Circuit treated this case as if it did not involve ATC at all.

The First Circuit's decision required us to prove that Clemente had relied upon the FAA to perform its duties under the Southern Order—an impossible burden, since Clemente was dead, and an unrealistic one, since he would have had to read hundreds of pages in the manuals to learn what services the FAA was supposed to provide. In reality, Clemente could not have learned of his imminent danger without receiving the warning required by the Southern Order. Like any other passenger, he was forced to rely on the FAA's preemption of safety regulation for warning of hazards—a warning that he would never receive from the illegal operator. The natural reliance of the traveling public on the FAA is further strengthened by the FAA airworthiness certificate which, according to statute, must be displayed on every aircraft where it can be seen by crew and passengers. The trappings of FAA approval are everywhere: every civil aircraft has an FAA registration number painted on it; every pilot must have some kind of FAA license; a flight plan must be filed with the FAA, and clearance must be obtained from the FAA tower for takeoff. All of this could only lead Roberto Clemente and others like him to assume that the FAA was doing whatever its senior officials had found necessary to assure the safety of the flight.

While I feel that the First Circuit reached the wrong decision, I do not question their right to decide a case of this type on public policy grounds. Such policy questions were supposed to be decided by Congress when it enacted the FTCA and the Federal Aviation Act, but it is impossible for legislators to anticipate all future problems. Times change and the courts must consider public policy in making important decisions. If it were not for courageous policy-making judges, the Federal Tort Claims Act would still be limited to claims arising from the reckless operation of mail trucks.

My quarrel with the First Circuit's policy decision is that it was wrong on the facts of this safety policy situation. During the fall of 1977, while this case was pending in the appellate court, FAA officials reporting to their Congressional overseers confirmed that during 1977 their safety policy had shifted from attacking the legality of leases to stricter surveillance of airworthiness, and that this shift had resulted in grounding a number of illegal and unsafe operations, especially in the Southern Region. Thus the FAA was proudly proclaiming to its Congressional overseers that immediately following the Clemente decision it had stepped up surveillance of tramp operators of the type mentioned in the Southern Order.

Since the job advancement of government safety officials is dependent on the performance of statutory safety duties, it is not apparent how government liability for flouting directives such as the Southern Order would inhibit safety performance. If high-level FAA personnel ever tried to rescind the Southern Order without solving the tramp operator problem in some other way, there are experts on the Congressional committees which oversee the FAA who would jump on them very quickly. Senators and representatives spend a lot of time on airplanes. Anyone who has watched or read the transcript of a congressional hearing on FAA oversight would have no doubt about the legislators' will to hold the FAA to its statutory mission of air safety. Other organizations, too, watch FAA performance: the National Transportation Safety Board (NTSB), an independent agency that often criticizes the FAA; committees of the Association of Trial Lawyers of America (ATLA); Ralph Nader's Aviation Consumer Action Project; and the aviation industry's own organizations that are concerned about irresponsible operators who give the industry a bad name. With so many watchdogs looking on, any attempt by the FAA to shirk its duties and withdraw from emergency functions such as those detailed in the Southern Order would result in the loss of jobs of those who shied away from protecting the public. In my opinion, therefore, while the judges of the First Circuit were right in considering the safety and policy implications of the Clemente decision, they reached the wrong policy decision, one for which they did not cite any basis other than their own feelings.

Indeed, they did not mention any of the trial evidence which bears upon this point. Usto Schulz's testimony was the only evidence on the question of how the Southern Order was developed, the nature of the emergency it was designed to deal with, and the manpower needs that were considered by the FAA. Schulz's testimony that the Southern Order was adopted after full consideration of any possible manpower problems was unquestioned and uncontroverted. As Judge Torruella stated in his decision:

It would seem that if an Order was issued by an agency with the expertise of the FAA, that impossible tasks would not be required of its personnel.

I believe that the First Circuit should have affirmed Judge Torruella's decision. They could have avoided policy problems by confining their decision to the Rivera situation: an emergency directive aimed at a persistent life-threatening problem which could be solved only by surveillance and warning. Thus limited, affirmance of the Clemente decision could not have become the basis for indiscriminate liability of OSHA or other government inspecting agencies. Our clients had the misfortune to be in the vanguard of a concept that is just beginning to develop—a concept best described in *The Duty to Act: Tort Law, Power and Public Policy* (University of Texas Press, 1978), a book by one of the great torts professors, Marshall Shapo of Northwestern University Law School.

The First Circuit's reversal of Judge Torruella's decision was a hard blow to me, all the more so because it was the first appellate argument I had ever lost. As the appellate advocate who stands before the court alone and is named for his clients in the official reports, I had to take full responsibility for the loss, just as I would have been cited as the winner of this case even though Krause and the Madoles had done the really difficult work. What made this reversal especially hard to take was to know, as did the FAA people involved at San Juan, Miami, Atlanta, and Washington, that the great Roberto Clemente would still be alive if the FAA had not failed him by flouting its own life-saving order. His needless death must rest heavily on the conscience of those inspectors who were aware of Rivera's deadly potential and sat at a New Year's Eve party while Roberto was trying to help his unknown brothers in Nicaragua. Judge Torruella knew, and the appellate court did not dispute his findings on the facts or causation. Everyone knew, yet we lost the case.

Evidently the First Circuit felt that this was a case on which the United States government could not simply turn its back. In a Solomon-like attempt to aid the plaintiffs while overturning a decision which they considered too broad in its implications, the First Circuit concluded its opinion as follows:

> The passengers on this ill-fated flight were acting for the highest of humanitarian motives at the time of the tragic crash. It would certainly be appropriate for a society to honor such conduct by taking those measures necessary to see to it that the families of the victims are adequately provided for in the future. However, making those kinds of decisions is beyond the scope of judicial power and authority. We are bound to apply the law

and that duty requires the reversal of the district court's judgment in favor of the plaintiffs.

It appears that the First Circuit was referring to Congressional legislation when it stated that it would be appropriate for a "society to honor such conduct by taking those measures necessary" to compensate the families of the victims. Although the Federal Tort Claims Act was designed to end private relief bills, it did not void the right to apply to Congress for private relief in special situations which fell outside the FTCA. The Justice Department itself recognized the Clemente case as one suitable for private relief. In his brief to the First Circuit, Mike Pangia pointed out that Congress could assume "compassionate responsibility" to the families of the deceased passengers in this case. (Phil Silverman, who had served in Justice's Aviation Litigation Unit for 10 years, had never seen such a statement in a government brief.) We were indebted to the First Circuit for recording the appropriateness of legislation. We were unable to find a similar holding in any other FTCA case, and we decided to follow up on this one; but first we had to exhaust our appellate remedies by petitioning the U.S. Supreme Court for a writ of certiorari.

Our chances of getting to the Supreme Court were fairly slim. The court receives close to 4,000 petitions a year for writs of certiorari. Since the court can handle only about 150 cases per year, and some of them are appeals which it is legally required to hear, the odds against a successful petition are pretty long. The majority of cases accepted by the court involve criminal law, civil rights, or regulatory policy issues. Few tort cases are selected, and in the entire history of the FTCA only one decision directly involving FAA negligence (a 1949 mid-air collision case) has ever been reviewed by the Supreme Court.

The justices have frequently stated that they do not have time to correct all the errors of the lower federal courts. They must be highly selective. Nevertheless, we felt that we had to run out the string. At a cost of $3,000, we printed and filed a petition for writ of certiorari. This was denied on May 1, 1978, and thus the reversal by the First Circuit became final.

It was my sad duty to inform Mrs. Clemente and our other clients that we were out of court. Perhaps it should be some consolation to reflect that we did everything we possibly could to win the case. There was no evidence we could have produced in the trial court that would have changed the result, and there was no conceivable argument in the appellate court that was not made in the brief or in oral argument. The appellate court simply did not agree with us. That sort of thing happens every day, but that doesn't make it any easier to take.

Having exhausted our remedies in court, we turned back to the process so decried by John Quincy Adams: the private relief bill in Congress.

The Private Bill

Since Congress passed the Federal Tort Claim Act in 1946, a few private bills have been passed, notably where the government was grossly at fault but the FTCA afforded no remedy. When the Texas City disaster litigation ended with the Supreme Court's dismissal of all the claims under the FTCA, Congress passed a special bill assuming "compassionate responsibility" for the losses sustained, thereby allowing the claims to be determined by the Secretary of the Army and to be paid by the Treasury. A more recent example was the case of Dr. Frank Olson, who was driven to suicide because he was being fed LSD in a government experiment. He never knew it, and his family only found out about the LSD factor twenty-two years after his death. In 1976 Congress awarded his family $750,000.

Immediately after the Supreme Court denied our petition for certiorari on May 1, 1978, we started work on a private bill. We drafted the proposed act and attached to it a memorandum giving all of the facts of the Clemente case. We pointed out that both the Justice Department and the First Circuit Court had stated that this was a case calling for special consideration of private compensation. We described an especially ludicrous result of the First Circuit decision:

> Ironically, the finding of no legal duty by the First Circuit reduced the widows and children of Roberto Clemente and his fellow passengers beneath the status of federal prisoners, because even federal prisoners can sue the United States under the Federal Tort Claims Act for violation of duties imposed upon their jailers by federal statutes and regulations as held by the Supreme Court in *United States v. Muniz,* 374 U.S. 150, 164–165 (1963).

Although Congress permits attorneys to charge fees of up to 10 percent of the amounts collected in private bills, we decided to forego all legal fees in an effort to enhance the prospects for adequate compensation. We asked only for reimbursement of our actual out-of-pocket expenses, which came to about $50,000. The private relief bill was introduced in 1979 by Baltasar Corrada, Resident Commissioner of Puerto Rico in the United States. Known as H.R. 2434 of the 96th Congress, this bill will have to work its way through the judiciary committees of both houses, where recommendations regarding the bill are also received from the FAA and the Department of Justice. Sticking to its guns despite all of the shocking evidence of negligence found by Judge Torruella, the FAA has reported to Congress that there was no basis on which its personnel could have been responsible for this accident. As this is written, we are awaiting the recommendations of the Justice Department, which in its brief to the First Circuit suggested that this was a matter for a private compensation bill. If the bill makes its way through committee, it will come to a vote before the entire Congress. Should you feel, as we do, that this case cries out for "compassionate responsibility" by the government in view of all that has befallen these three families, please write to your representative in Congress and ask him or her to support the Clemente private relief bill, H.R. 2434, 96th Congress.

The Equalizers

The Clemente case is an illustration of the need for substantial contingent fees in tort cases. Many cases we are asked to take on are like this one on which we worked for seven years without collecting any fees. We will be lucky if we get our expenses back through the congressional private bill. Even then, we will certainly go unpaid for the thousands of hours spent on this case by half a dozen lawyers in our firm who worked on it all the way from Puerto Rico to Boston to Washington.

Sooner or later all tort lawyers get involved in cases where they fight losing causes through trial and appellate courts and wind up without any fees. Even when you win a case under the Federal Tort Claims Act, it will often produce inadequate fees for the effort involved. The FTCA prohibits jury trials of claims against the government, and it limits attorney's fees to a maximum of 25 percent regardless of the amount of work done and the difficulty of the case. Congress made it tough to sue the federal government under the FTCA, riddling the act with broad loopholes, such as the discretionary function exception. The government is not subject to the usual leverage forces of litigation, so there is virtually no prospect of settlement of an FTCA case in which there are questions about liability or damages. Moreover, the Justice Department has many promising attorneys on its staff who are eager to try cases and to establish their reputations. They are under no pressure to settle cases, and they have the mighty federal apparatus at their disposal, including the Federal Bureau of Investigation, whose agents are used routinely to investigate claimants and witnesses.

The Clemente case is a striking illustration of the bureaucratic
tyranny that the public faces in claims against the government. The San
Juan Flight Standards District Office was required to complete FAA
Form 3660, "Aircraft Accident Data Report," shortly after the fatal
Rivera crash. The first item to be filled in was entitled "FAA Responsi-
bilities," and here is what FSDO Inspector Thomas D. Coupland wrote:

> FAA personnel, facilities, procedures and/or services were not
> involved.

Thus, any lawyer searching the public records on behalf of Clemente
would be confronted with a false but official denial that the Southern
Order existed or was applicable to Rivera. During discovery, when the
government was required to produce the FAA manuals, orders, hand-
books, and instructions relating to the FSDO's surveillance, inspection,
and enforcement activities at San Juan, they handed us a loose-leaf
manual which did *not* include the Southern Order. It was only the FAA
experience of our own lawyers and experts that alerted us to the existence of the Southern Order. Then came the shocking trial testimony
of San Juan Chief Leonard Davis, who swore that he had implemented
the Southern Order for incoming flights only—a statement that Judge
Torruella officially characterized as incredible and mind-boggling. And
after the First Circuit had ruled in favor of the government, the FAA
persisted in denying any involvement, even for purposes of the "compassionate responsibility" recommended by the Justice Department and
the First Circuit. Thus the bureaucracy does not hesitate to use the
labyrinth of federal procedures to defend itself and cover up its mistakes.
Even if the First Circuit had upheld Judge Torruella's finding of liability
and we had gone on to collect generous damage judgments, I doubt that
the Clemente litigation would have been profitable for us. We would
have had to try all three claims on damages, and then most likely would
have had to argue appeals contesting the measure of damages.

While the FTCA gave the American people the right to sue their
government for tort damages, that right would be meaningless without
the equalizers, the plaintiff's tort lawyers who are willing and able to
tackle the government on a contingent fee basis. Such cases are usually
not profitable for plaintiffs' attorneys unless they come in large groups
arising out of the same accident. Yet there is an entrepreneur-lawyer,
an equalizer, available to every injured person with a legitimate FTCA
claim, regardless of the tremendous investment of time and working
capital that is required to combat the massive litigation power of the
government. The equalizers serve as a public resource, although they
receive no subsidies or assistance from public funds, which in FTCA
cases are actually mobilized against them.

As we have seen in other places throughout this book, the plaintiff's tort lawyer must often blaze new legal trails, exploring the frontiers of liability and damages in claims against giants, whether it be the federal government as in the Clemente case, or General Motors, or major industries such as aviation, chemicals, or automobiles. The thrust into new territory is the one that meets with the strongest opposition, and it is likely to cast the plaintiff's lawyer as David in a long and costly fight against Goliath. We shall return to the financial aspects of these demands upon the plaintiff's lawyer in Chapter 8, when we look at the money dynamics of tort litigation.

In Memoriam

Roberto Clemente's memory lives on and continues to be an inspiration to millions of Americans. In August 1973 he was voted into the Baseball Hall of Fame—the only time that the rule requiring five years to pass after retirement was waived. He also was honored posthumously with the Presidential Citizen's Medal, the first ever presented. More than five years after his death, the National Endowment for the Arts supplied the Washington, D.C. bus system with a poster on which the following poem by Tom Clark was printed:

Clemente (1934–1972)

won't forget	no olvidaré
his nervous	su nerviosa
habit of	costumbre de
rearing his	alzar la
head back	cabeza muy
on his neck	alta
like a	como un
proud horse.	caballo de raza.

Chapter 7

WORLDWIDE EFFECTS OF AMERICAN TORT LAW

ERMENONVILLE FOREST: THE TURKISH AIRLINES DC-10 CRASH

On March 3, 1974, a nightmare became reality. The first crash of a fully loaded jumbo jet—a Turkish Airlines DC-10 carrying 333 passengers and a crew of 13—occurred on that beautiful spring Sunday in the forest of Ermenonville, just outside of Paris. The plane had taken off from Paris's Orly Airport at 12:30 P.M. and was still in its initial climb, when it suddenly plunged to the ground, killing all aboard. A traffic controller at Orly, following the DC-10's progress on his radar screen, saw it climb past 11,000 feet and watched in horror as its image disappeared from the screen.

The French government began an investigation immediately, assisted by personnel of the U.S. National Transportation Safety Board (because the DC-10 was American-built). Soon after the crash, the DC-10's rear cargo door and six bodies were found about 9 miles from the location of the main wreckage. To the American investigators, this was a smoking-gun clue to the cause, for this was not the first DC-10 that had lost its rear cargo door in flight. Given this clue, it was relatively simple to reconstruct the accident. A DC-10 rear cargo door that was not properly locked would be subjected to about five tons of air pressure when the aircraft climbed past 10,000 feet. It would blow open and be ripped from its hinges by the plane's slipstream. This would quickly be followed by explosive decompression. In the DC-10, the rear cargo door is located below the floor of the passenger cabin, so with the air escaping from the rear baggage compartment, the cabin floor would be at the mercy of the air pressure in the passenger cabin. This would cause the cabin floor to collapse, severing or jamming the vital control cables that run underneath the cabin floor from the pilot's cockpit to the tail section. The pilot would lose rudder, stabilizer, and elevator control, and the plane would go into an immediate nosedive. With a fully loaded aircraft, the pilot would have no chance to recover before smashing into the ground.

Bryce McCormick's Windsor Blowout

The first loss of a DC-10 cargo door in flight occurred on June 12, 1972, on an American Airlines passenger plane bound from Detroit to Buffalo, New York. Captain Bryce McCormick had taken off from Detroit and had climbed to about 11,500 feet near Windsor, Ontario, when he heard a loud bang. He found that he had suddenly lost rudder and stabilizer control, most of his elevator control, and his control of the No. 2 engine (which is located in the tail). His plane was in a dive that he could not stop with conventional control movements. Two things saved McCormick's DC-10: his own training and discipline, and the fact that he had only 56 passengers aboard, all of them seated forward of the rear passenger compartment.

This light load gave him a fighting chance to maintain some control. Had he been carrying an additional seven tons of weight on the rear compartment floor (as the heavily loaded Turkish Airlines flight had done) he would probably not have been able to pull out of the dive. Even with this advantage, he would not have been able to save the ship if he had not trained himself on the DC-10 simulator to fly and steer on engine power alone. Because of his concern about survival in the event his flight controls failed, he had gone beyond the regular airline training curriculum and worked out his own methods of dealing with such emergencies. He had become so adept at using differential engine power that he was able to take the DC-10 simulator through an entire flight (except for takeoff and landing) without touching any controls other than his throttles.

McCormick brought his DC-10 out of the dive by increasing power on his two outboard engines. Then he flew the crippled ship back to Detroit in a slow descent, struggling for control by toying gingerly with his throttles. His emergency landing at Detroit without rudder or elevator control must rank as one of history's greatest feats of airmanship. He only just managed to bring the airplane down to the runway without losing control, and he had to maintain very high landing speed. As he touched down, the plane veered off the runway on to the grass, heading toward the airport buildings. McCormick and First Officer Peter P. Whitney succeeded in bringing the plane to a stop by pushing the left engine beyond its full reverse thrust position. But there was no time to lose in celebrating this narrow escape. Fearing a fuel explosion, McCormick ordered an emergency evacuation, and the DC-10's occupants slid to safety on emergency chutes.

Captain McCormick's miraculous feat was followed by intensive NTSB and FAA investigations. It was obvious that the rear cargo door had opened and had been blown away after the aircraft reached an altitude of 10,000 feet. Most of the doors on pressurized aircraft are of the "plug" type, which opens inward and cannot spring open in flight; but the jumbo jet cargo doors are rather large for practical use of the conventional plug design. McDonnell Douglas Corporation, the builders of the DC-10, and General Dynamics Corporation, the subcontractors for its fuselage, floors, and doors, devised a locking system for the rear cargo door that was supposed to make it foolproof. There was a vent door which was designed to prevent pressurization of the aircraft if the cargo door was not safety locked, and there was a cockpit warning light which was supposed to stay on to warn the flight crew that the door was not properly locked. But in McCormick's Windsor incident, the cargo handler at Detroit who closed the door had followed his instructions properly; the cockpit warning light had gone off after he closed the door; the aircraft had pressurized; and yet the door could not have been locked or else it would not have blown out in flight.

What the Windsor investigation revealed was serious deficiencies in the design of the DC-10 cargo door locking system. The entire safety backup system could be rendered inoperative by applying a force of only 80 to 120 pounds (the normal strength of a cargo handler) to the handle, so that the door would appear to be locked even though the locking pins were not fully engaged. Obviously, the locking system design had to be changed to avoid repetition of the Windsor emergency. McDonnell Douglas quickly came up with a proposed three step solution: modification of the lock pins to provide more overlap of the latches in the closed position; installation of a new support plate which increased the pressure required to force the door shut without locking it properly to 400 pounds (beyond normal human strength); and modification of the locking pins to prevent the transmission of such false signals as had turned the warning light off in McCormick's cockpit.

Since there were dozens of other DC-10s flying around with the defective door locking system, it was expected that the FAA would issue an Airworthiness Directive (AD), ordering all DC-10 operators to make this three-step modification immediately. However, McDonnell Douglas was in hot sales competition with other manufacturers and did not want a frightening AD on its record at that point. Jackson McGowen, president of the Douglas division of McDonnell Douglas, convinced FAA Administrator John Shaffer that Douglas itself would take care of these problems. According to their gentlemen's agreement, Douglas would issue its own service bulletin to its own customers and would supply them with modification kits, so that the hazards could quickly be removed by industry action and without government intervention. Nixon appointee Shaffer preferred this method, and so the Los Angeles office of the FAA, which had already started to draft an AD, was ordered to abide by this gentlemen's agreement on June 16, 1972, four days after Bryce McCormick's Windsor blowout. The FAA and the aviation industry assumed that the DC-10 cargo door problem had been solved—until the world's worst air disaster killed 346 people at Ermenonville forest on March 3, 1974.

On March 25, 1974, John Brizendine (who had succeeded McGowen as president of the Douglas division) announced to the public that the Ermenonville DC-10—which had been sold to Turkish Airlines long after the Windsor blowout and was supposed to have been modified by Douglas itself—did not in fact have the required support plate, so that its cargo door could have been closed by normal force without locking it. It was apparent that Ermenonville was a carbon copy of Windsor, except that the Turkish Airlines pilots had a fully loaded rear passenger compartment and probably lost all their flight controls.

How was it possible that one of the world's leading aircraft manufacturers failed to execute its own three-step modification on a DC-10 that was right in its own plant when the modification was adopted? Brizendine told the press that the company's records showed that the modification *had* been made. He could not explain the discrepancy between those records and the clear evidence at Ermenonville that the modifications had *not* been made. He promised a vigorous investigation to find out how such a bizarre thing could happen.

Hands Across the Sea

Most of the passengers aboard the ill-fated DC-10 had not planned to fly Turkish Airlines. Due to a strike of ground personnel, all flights of British European Airways had been cancelled, and it was difficult to book passage from Paris to London. As a result, more than 200 passengers boarded the Turkish DC-10 at Paris when it stopped there on a through flight from Istanbul to London. They were citizens of 24 different nations, the largest groups being from Great Britain, Turkey, Japan, France, and the United States. Hardest hit of all was Great Britain, with 177 passengers.

The crash occupied the center of news coverage in England for weeks. Many of the British passengers had been prominent in their fields, including law, medicine, science, government, and labor. Perhaps most poignant of all was the impact on historic Bury St. Edmunds, site of the Benedictine abbey where in 1214 the English barons struggling against the tyranny of King John took the oath that led to the Magna Carta. Bury St. Edmunds, called "the nicest town in the world" by William Cobbett in his *Rural Rides,* lost 25 players and officials of its rugby football club who had been in Paris for the annual Rugby Union football match with the French team.

In their shock and bereavement, few if any of the British families thought about financial compensation. The British tradition was to accept whatever compensation was established for such cases. As we saw in Chapter 2, it had long been the custom for European carriers to limit their liability in the small print section of passenger tickets, and this tradition was perpetuated by the 1929 Warsaw Convention, limiting damages to $8,291 per passenger on international flights. By the time of the 1974 Turkish DC-10 crash, the Warsaw Convention had been modified to bring maximum damages up to $20,000 per passenger. However, it was a rare English case that qualified for the maximum of $20,000, because the English method of calculating damages for wrongful death put a very low value on human life. The damage calculation was based strictly upon proof of *net* financial loss, with no allowance for future inflation or loss of society.

Soon after the accident, British newspapers and broadcasts informed the families that they would be limited to as little as £750 (about $1,500) for the death of a relative who left no direct dependents, and that the Warsaw Convention would restrict all claimants to $20,000 or less. Airline accident cases were never litigated in England. The Warsaw Convention and its domestic English counterpart, the Carriage by Air Act, made the airlines liable without proof of negligence, and the insurance carriers were happy to pay the small amount of compensation permitted under English law and the Warsaw Convention. Apart from a government investigation, there would be no public inquiry into the cause of the crash, and in this case, the investigation was in the hands of the French government, which was not noted for publishing any findings that might embarrass the aviation industry.

One young widow was shocked when she learned that in addition to losing her husband, she and the other passengers' families would have practically no chance to bring the responsible parties to court in England, and would have to accept the pitiful compensation that was decreed by a statutory scheme which provided no safety incentive. As it happened, she was better off financially than most of the other widows. Her husband had been a prominent journalist and broadcaster; she, too, had worked for BBC and commanded a good salary in broadcasting and journalism. But it incensed her that the archaic English system would leave most of the other families devastated financially as well as emotionally. She refused to accept the idea of settling for fixed compensation which would preclude any searching inquiry into the cause of the accident.

When it became known that the faulty cargo door locking system had probably caused the accident, the journalist's widow learned that there was a possibility of suing the DC-10's manufacturers in the United States. At her request, I met her in London and told her that in my opinion there was an excellent chance of recovering adequate compensation for all the passengers' families in the United States, where the Warsaw Convention (which applies only to carriers) would not limit damages against the manufacturers. There was no possibility of suing the manufacturer in England: the costs of preparing and trying such a case without contingent fees (which are prohibited in England) would be beyond the means of the claimants; there was no discovery procedure through which the plaintiffs' lawyers could assemble a strong case; there was a good chance that the plaintiffs would lose, and in that event, they would also have to pay the defendants' legal costs, which would wipe out practically all the passengers' families. I also told her that we would take the case on a contingent fee basis.

After seeking the advice of her family solicitors, she decided to go ahead. This was a brave step for a lone English widow to take, for it went against the British tradition of accepting misfortune and disdaining pursuit of full compensation in accident cases. In Britain, people at all economic levels were conditioned to limited accident compensation. The poor would recoup some of their unpaid losses through schemes established by social welfare legislation; the rich would fall back on their savings. Many in Britain looked upon large damage claims as a lawyers' racket.

It was clear to me that the journalist's widow was not motivated by a desire to collect large damages for herself and her infant daughter, but by her concern for the other families and her determination to bring the cause of the accident to public light. I warned her that filing the first suit in the United States would make her the center of controversy, and that her motives might be misunderstood. But she was prepared to accept that burden, and she directed us to file the suit as soon as possible, so that the other families would be alerted to the possibility of avoiding the cruel limitations of English law. Her late husband's fame and her own position in British communications would serve as a beacon for the other families. She was prepared to tell them all, through newspapers, radio, and television, that they had an alternative to the paltry compensation that was offered to them.

So it was that we filed the first DC-10 suit in the Los Angeles federal court on March 18, 1974, 15 days after the accident. Our courageous client immediately issued a statement to the press and appeared on television, explaining why she had sued in America and encouraging the other families to consider that alternative. The early filing of her suit had the desired effect: none of the bereaved English families settled for the proposed compensations. If the journalist's widow had not come forward and put herself on the line, I am certain that many of the English families would have settled for whatever was offered. It took the prestige of a prominent English family to create serious interest in the strange idea of suing for adequate damages in the United States.

The journalist's widow was innundated with letters and telephone calls from passengers' families and their solicitors who sought more detailed information about her lawsuit. Don Madole and I spent a good part of April and May in meetings with these solicitors which we held in the office of an American lawyer in the Mayfair section of London. Don explained the failure of the DC-10 cargo door locking system (using schematic diagrams) and the background of Bryce McCormick's Windsor blowout. I answered questions about American procedures and the level of damages that might be expected if we were successful. Most of these Mayfair meetings were group sessions with a dozen or more solicitors at a time, since it was not possible to arrange a private meeting for each case. All of us benefitted from the group sessions, where the questions asked by some solicitors triggered questions by others.

This was our first experience with group meetings of such magnitude. Indeed, the entire process was a novel meeting ground for English and American law practice, and it produced some pointed philosophical discussions. It was clear that some of the more conservative solicitors were put off at first by the concept of the contingent fee and the quest for what seemed like astronomical damages, which some considered almost immoral. It reminded me how in the early nineteenth century Americans had rejected life insurance, which many regarded as an obscene (if not sacrilegious) commercialization of human life. This resistance to placing a monetary value on human life is rooted in the Roman concept that the life of a slave has pecuniary value, but "the life of a free man can have no monetary estimate." It was on this basis that French law used to prohibit any contract involving the termination of human life, including life insurance.

As American life insurance became acceptable in the 1870s, damages for wrongful death developed into an important form of compensation. Rugged individualism and Puritan preoccupation with personal salvation gave way to social concern for widows and orphans. But when we met with the English solicitors in the spring of 1974, wrongful death suits in England and Europe were no more than a partial legal remedy, shortchanging the victims badly despite the lip service paid to the concept of repairing the financial damage done. There was provision for some compensation where fault was shown, but the amount could never approach the real financial damage done when the breadwinner was cut down in the prime of life. The same people whose strong sense of justice provided full redress for a lost painting or an injured racehorse, took refuge in charges of commercialization when it came to compensation for personal injury or wrongful death.

They did not seem to realize that they were placing much of the financial burden of injury and death on the innocent parties who had already suffered irreparable emotional losses. They had never asked themselves why children of deceased airline passengers should have to give up chances for education and advancement, and why widows should be forced to surrender their dignity, thus compounding their terrible losses; nor could they explain why the guilty parties should be allowed to escape without paying full financial compensation, except that it was culturally unacceptable to "profit" from such misfortunes. Centuries of traditional protection of property rights were giving way very slowly to recognition of personal rights. When the two clashed, as in the 1974 Turkish Airlines crash, the Old World courts would still make the devastated victims shoulder most of the loss, despite the multimillion dollar insurance coverage which all international airlines and aircraft manufacturers carried routinely and wrote off as a business expense (about one percent of their operating costs) because of the possibility of American litigation.

As I started to describe the American tort system to the solicitors assembled in Mayfair, I could feel the chill of moral disapproval in the air. But they listened intently, and even though centuries of English legal tradition stood in the way of their accepting the American philosophy immediately, they did not let this prevent them from considering a course that might benefit their clients. We began to make headway when Don Madole described the reasons why the Turkish Airlines DC-10 had crashed. By the time that Don had finished his dramatic presentation, I felt that we were starting to work as a team with the solicitors. They entered into the discussion with great spirit, and they seemed to be convinced that there was a need for the full inquiry and the deterrent that only an American lawsuit could produce.

Many of the solicitors asked for examples of American wrongful death awards, particularly those involving claims by foreign plaintiffs. We described a case that we had settled only a few weeks before, in which the family of a 35-year-old foreign citizen who had been working in the United States as a janitor received $650,000 compensation for his death in the world's first jumbo jet catastrophe, the 1972 crash of an Eastern Airlines Lockheed L-1011 in the Florida Everglades. Through comparison of such American awards with those described by the English solicitors, we were able to reach the joint conclusion that the probable compensation in the United States would be about 8 to 10 times the English awards in dependency cases, and about 25 times the English awards in cases that did not involve surviving dependents.

When they asked about our credentials, we were able to tell them that we were the oldest and largest firm of lawyer-pilots in the United States; that we had never lost an airline passenger case; that Don had served with American Airlines, the CAA, and the CAB (the latter as the officer in charge of the government's airline accident hearings and reports); and that I was the author of 12 volumes of textbooks on aviation and tort law, some of which had been cited as authorities by the U.S. Supreme Court and other appellate courts. But I doubt that those qualifications would have convinced many of the English solicitors to sue in California if it had not been for the leadership of the journalist's widow who filed the first suit and then broadcasted to the world that each of the claimants had a chance to recover full compensation without any cash outlay.

As to contingent fees, we explained that we were perfectly willing to serve any clients who wished to retain us on an hourly fee basis, but we did not recommend this because the legal work involved would take thousands of hours. In the end, even the most conservative solicitors agreed that it would be impossible to undertake such a suit without contingent fees. They were prepared to recommend that their clients pay contingent fees for American legal services, but of course their own work would have to be done on the noncontingent basis required by English law.

As the meetings ended, we felt that we had broken through some of the ice formed by centuries of tradition. There was, however, no rush to retain us. Many of the solicitors sought opinions from barristers as to the comparative merits of suing in the United States and in England. Some even engaged other American lawyers and law professors to advise them how best to proceed. Also, many solicitors wanted to be convinced on one point: that the American courts would allow foreigners to sue there for damages arising out of a foreign accident. We told them that the defendants undoubtedly would raise the issue of *forum non conveniens,* and that we were prepared to deal with it. We expected it to be argued and decided in the suit filed by the journalist's widow. Most of the solicitors decided to await that decision, for there was no point in filing suit in America if the courts would not accept the case.

While we were holding the London meetings in April of 1974, the insurers made an unprecedented move. On April 19, McDonnell Douglas issued a press release in England (published in many newspapers) stating that they had appointed a firm of solicitors in London and had given them "instructions to take immediate steps to proceed to prompt settlement in England of all claims by dependents and relatives of English passengers according to English law for the excess of the amount payable by the Airline under the appropriate International Agreements, and without the necessity of filing any formal lawsuit, notwithstanding that pending the completion of investigations no liability is admitted by either party." Then on April 22, the English solicitors appointed by McDonnell Douglas sent a letter to the solicitors for each English family, enclosing a copy of the press release and pointing out that the press announcement was made by McDonnell Douglas "to counter any view that McDonnell Douglas were indifferent and showing no concern for the relatives and dependents of passengers, and to make clear their decision that despite the absence of any findings of the cause of the crash and resulting liability therefore, claims would be settled promptly and on a generous basis assessed according to English law."

The letter went on to say that the official accident report was unlikely to be published by the French authorities for a considerable time, and that "plainly no decision on the issue of legal liability can be expected for a substantial period of time after the full Report becomes available." As to the length of time it would take the American courts to decide the issue of liability, the letter said, "It seems that there is almost certainly to be a period of considerable delay and it was with a view to ameliorating distress and hardship that the proposals by Mc-

Donnell Douglas Corporation had been made." The McDonnell Douglas solicitors also wrote:

> Furthermore, in those cases where action has not and is not going to be taken by claimants against McDonnell Douglas Corporation in the United States, we are authorized to indicate that our Clients will be prepared to make a general payment on account of damages in the form of an interim sum in any case of financial hardship.

Here was the first offer ever made by an aircraft manufacturer—in any country outside of the United States—to pay damages above Warsaw Convention limits. It was made despite the fact that McDonnell Douglas probably could not have been sued in England, and that none of the passengers' families could have afforded the costs and risks of such a suit in England anyway. On its face it seemed a generous offer, and under ordinary circumstances it would have been taken up eagerly by the bereaved families. But these were not ordinary circumstances. The offer was made after we had filed suit in California for the journalist's widow, and after the insurers knew that many other English claimants were considering such a suit. They promised immediate cash advances to needy claimants who were *not* going to file suit in America. Thus, the McDonnell Douglas offer was seen by many of the English solicitors as confirmation of our opinion that the DC-10 manufacturers faced the probability of large damage awards in the United States, and as evidence that the insurers were eager to settle under English damage rules for a fraction of what they might have to pay in America. Why else would the insurers at Lloyd's of London break with the long-standing British tradition of limiting compensation by instruments such as the Warsaw Convention?

It is to the great credit of the British families and their solicitors that none of them accepted the McDonnell Douglas offer. Some of them decided to file suit in California immediately. But most awaited the court decision on the right of the English plaintiffs to sue in the American courts.

Enter:
Judge Peirson M. Hall

We filed suit in the federal court in Los Angeles because the DC-10 had been designed, manufactured, and sold to Turkish Airlines at the McDonnell Douglas plant in Long Beach, located in the district covered by the Los Angeles court (the Central District of California). Since the case was to turn almost entirely on the evidence of witnesses and documents located at the Long Beach plant, we thought that the Central District court was the most convenient location for all parties. However, another New York law firm representing an American plaintiff filed suit in the Southern District of New York. This created a multidistrict situation and brought into play an ingenious method of dealing with complicated litigation.

In 1968, Congress established the Judicial Panel on Multidistrict Litigation (JPMDL), a panel of five federal circuit and district judges chosen by the Supreme Court to deal with related cases that were filed in different federal district courts. Though most of the cases that came before the JPMDL were antitrust suits and complicated business claims, the panel had quickly established jurisdiction over airline accident claims, assigning each group of related actions to a single district judge. Technically, the MDL assignment was limited to pretrial activities such as discovery, after which the MDL judge was supposed to return each case to the district of filing. In practice, however, it was found that MDL judges could be most effective in disposing of complicated aviation litigation by retaining the cases for trial on liability, and sometimes on damages as well.

Instead of the chaotic Grand Canyon type litigation that you saw in Chapter 3 (with plaintiffs and defendants bearing the burden of many sets of depositions and repeated trials of both liability and damages in different courts from coast to coast), there was a more sensible procedure now: only one set of depositions, and only one trial on liability. If the plaintiffs were represented by different lawyers, they would get together and select "lead counsel," a committee of lawyers to do the job for all the plaintiffs. There were provisions for reasonable fees to be paid to lead counsel by all the plaintiffs' lawyers who benefitted from their services. After liability was determined, each plaintiff would have the right to an individual trial of damages before a separate jury, using his own lawyer. Thus the best features of modern group litigation and the old system of individual claims were combined in the MDL procedure, which has helped to dispose of many major aviation cases in less than two years from the date of accident.

When the DC-10 litigation was brought before the JPMDL in April of 1974, we requested the panel to transfer all the cases to the Central District of California, as did other plaintiffs' lawyers who had filed suits there. The defendants argued for the Southern District of New York, but the panel went along with us and unanimously ordered transfer to Senior U.S. District Judge Peirson M. Hall of the Central District of California.

It was not happenstance that the DC-10 cases were assigned to Judge Hall. He had been the chief judge in the Los Angeles district court until he reached the mandatory retirement age of 70 (for chief judges) in 1964. He remained on the bench as a senior district judge, although he could have retired at full pay to his beloved Palm Desert and spent his time playing golf. Many senior federal judges stay on the bench to help with the backlog of cases and to maintain some activity, but for Peirson Hall it was the beginning of a new career. He let it be known that he wanted to be as active as ever, and he had developed a special interest in complicated airline accident cases, which were often a burden to regular district judges who had to handle many other civil and criminal cases at the same time. Soon his colleagues were transferring all the Southern California airline crash cases to him, and after the Judicial Panel on Multidistrict Litigation was created in 1968, it was a foregone conclusion that any California MDL aviation cases would be assigned to Judge Hall. By the time of the 1974 Ermenonville crash, he was within a few months of his 80th birthday, but he was eager to take on the most complicated air crash case in history.

Peirson Hall was a stocky, cheerful, white-haired man who reminded me of a clean-shaven Santa Claus. He had a bulbous red nose, rosy cheeks, and wild, bushy white eyebrows. But his affable appearance was not the product of an easy life. Born in rural South Dakota in 1894, his father had died when he was 14 months old. His mother was not able to support her three children on her wage of $3 per week, so young Peirson was sent to an orphanage. He came to Los Angeles in 1912 at the age of 18, determined to make himself a lawyer. The early years of his career were best described in a 1977 *Los Angeles Times* feature article:

> He attended USC law school at night, and supported himself by working as an office boy for the *California Outlook,* a weekly political magazine which supported liberal reformer Hiram Johnson, governor of California from 1910 to 1918. At other times he earned money milking cows, working as a janitor, as an usher in a theater, selling vanilla extract door-to-door and pushing a hand plow in the farm fields that then dotted Los Angeles, at that time a community of just 300,000.
>
> Hall was bitten by the political bug early and was a precinct watcher at Union Station for the 1912 presidential election between victor Woodrow Wilson and losers William Howard Taft and Teddy Roosevelt. Thirteen years later, Hall won election to the Los Angeles City Council in 1925 on a liberal platform of lowering streetcar fares and telephone rates. He called himself the enemy of the public utilities in town.
>
> During his first two terms on the council, Hall fought successfully for a comprehensive traffic and street plan for the city and authored legislation regulating flying over the city and providing for the licensing of pilots. He also helped sponsor statewide legislation which provided for municipal ownership of

airports. "I guess from the very beginning of aviation I've been interested in the field," Hall said.

After losing a race for city attorney, Hall practiced law until 1932, when President Franklin D. Roosevelt appointed him U.S. attorney for Southern California. A thorough, independent prosecutor, Hall successfully prosecuted a California District Court of Appeals judge on a charge of obstructing justice and handled a celebrated espionage case involving a former U.S. Navy yeoman accused of selling military information to a Japanese naval officer. He was not reappointed to a second four-year-term in 1937, however, because of a run-in with a law partner of the then U.S. Sen. William G. McAdoo (D—Calif.).

Later that year, Hall announced his candidacy for the U.S. Senate seat held by McAdoo, only to withdraw midway through the race in favor of fellow liberal Sheridan Downey. Hall feared the two would split liberal votes and allow McAdoo to win. His strategy of withdrawal worked, and Downey subsequently won the election.

*   *   *

Hall returned to private law practice, but not for long. In late 1939, then Gov. Culbert Olson, describing Hall as "a militant fighter against entrenched special interests, appointed him to the Los Angeles Superior Court Bench. A year later, when the nation was gearing up to enter World War II, Olson named Hall to head up draft registrations in Los Angeles under the new Selective Service System.

Because of the falling out between Hall and former Sen. McAdoo, Roosevelt for several years had refused Sen. Downey's efforts to have Hall named a federal judge. Finally, on Feb. 18, 1942, Roosevelt set aside his differences with Hall and nominated him to the post he has held since then. Upon being sworn in to the then $10,000-a-year job, Hall said: "I don't particularly want to be a profound judge, so that I lose my sense of values. I pledge myself to be always alert to see that justice is gentle yet firm; justice that abhors hypocrisy."

In his 37 years on the federal bench, Peirson Hall performed as he had pledged. He always tried to make justice gentle yet firm; he made war on hypocrisy; and to those who practiced before him he was a profound judge despite his disclaimer of intellectual pretensions. Because he was uncompromising in matters of principle, he continued to make enemies throughout his career, and in his later years he was engaged in a running battle with his superiors on the Ninth Circuit Court of Appeals. Most of this friction was caused by Judge Hall's innovations in aviation accident cases.

He was assigned to his first major airline crash case in 1958—the suits arising out of the mid-air collision between a United Airlines DC-7 and an Air Force F-100F jet fighter over Las Vegas that year. Using the established pre-MDL methods of handling mass disaster litigation,

Judge Hall found himself continuously frustrated by rules designed for simple automobile cases. It took him eight years to complete the Las Vegas litigation, with many trials and appeals. He was particularly sensitive to the effects of such delays on the lives of widows and young children because he had experienced the devastation wrought by loss of the breadwinner in his own youth. Thus he resolved that the next time he was assigned a complicated aviation case, he would use some ingenuity to close it out in much shorter time.

By 1974, he had presided over eight other major air disaster cases and had closed each of them out within two years from the date of accident. He was aided in this by the MDL procedures, which came into effect in 1968, and by his senior judge status (starting in 1965), which allowed him to devote most of his time to aviation cases. But he also developed some rules of his own under a guiding principle which he expressed in these words:

> Above all, the judge must take charge of the case, and in doing so be guided not by what is specifically permitted by Rule or Statute, but *do what is not prohibited* as long as constitutional rights are preserved and the case moves forward.

It was this homemade Peirson Hall recipe for justice which sometimes made his courtroom a storm center of controversy. I was drawn into such a Peirson Hall courtroom battle early in 1974 as, of all things, a witness.

Judge Hall was presiding over claims growing out of another mid-air collision, this one between a Hughes Air West DC-9 and a U.S. Marine Corps Phantom jet fighter plane over Duarte, California, in 1971. By that time his special savvy in handling mass disaster cases was finely developed. He had broken a logjam in the case when he discovered that an intransigent government attorney was holding up settlement by insisting on a liability trial, even though the government and the airline attorneys had reached a secret agreement to pay fixed percentages of damages. Judge Hall called in the government lawyer and showed him a little-used section of the Judiciary Code that empowered the judge to hold the lawyer personally responsible for the extra costs caused by "frivolous delay." Shortly after that conference, the liability issue was disposed of by agreement, and the case went on into the damage phase. It was typical of Judge Hall that while he improvised a tool to cut through delay, it was based upon an existing provision of law. No judge did his homework more thoroughly than Peirson Hall. Not only did he read all the briefs that lawyers submitted, but he also read (without the use of eyeglasses) every case the lawyers had cited, and then he started the search for his own authorities. He always had a solid case precedent or statute as a jumping off point for his innovative tactics, for he knew that many would be challenged in the appellate courts.

When all the Duarte cases had been settled (again in record short time), a bitter dispute arose among the plaintiffs' lawyers. Early in the litigation, Judge Hall had approved the selection of a four-man committee of lead counsel. Later on, many of the plaintiffs' lawyers who were not on the committee challenged its authority. It was one of the few times that plaintiffs' lawyers were not united in their approach to an aviation case, and it is not likely to occur again, but it did happen in Duarte. When the lead counsel applied for their fees, more than a dozen plaintiffs' lawyers objected and demanded an evidentiary hearing. Judge Hall scheduled what amounted to a full-scale trial on the issue of the work done by lead counsel and its value to each of the plaintiffs' lawyers.

After lead counsel had put into evidence all of the work done on liability, Judge Hall felt that expert testimony was required to appraise the value of that work. He called on Frank Belcher, a patriarch of the Los Angeles bar renowned for more than 50 years of litigation practice, and he also called on me. We had to read through all of the depositions and discovery taken by the committee of lead counsel, form an appraisal of it, testify under oath to that appraisal, and then face cross-examination by more than a dozen of California's leading trial lawyers. Frank Belcher and I went through that ordeal, and the valuation that we put on the services of lead counsel was adopted by Judge Hall and finally approved by the Ninth Circuit Court of Appeals. The litigation over attorneys' fees actually took longer than final disposition of all the passengers' claims. I believe that the entire bar learned from the Duarte case that mass disaster litigation goes much more smoothly when the plaintiffs' lawyers agree at the outset on a voluntary plan of lead counsel activity.

By the time that Judge Hall took on the MDL assignment in the Turkish DC-10 cases, he was in his 80th year; he had an electronic pacemaker installed in his chest to overcome recurrent heart trouble; and he was soon to be told that he had cancer. Almost any other judge would have withdrawn from the case, but those events only strengthened Judge Hall's resolve to overcome the challenges of the world's worst air disaster and the most complicated choice-of-law problems in the history of tort litigation. Above all, he wanted to complete the case in his usual record time. He did not have much time left, and he was always driven by his compassion for widows and orphans. This compassion never led him to push for excessive compensation; indeed, he was known as a conservative judge on damages. But he would never permit any delay that might rob a child of education or happiness if there was any way in the world that he could prevent it.

A Convenient Forum

The first order of business before Judge Hall in the DC-10 litigation was a motion made by McDonnell Douglas to dismiss the complaint of our client, the journalist's widow, on the grounds of *forum non conveniens*. They argued that California was not a convenient forum for a lawsuit brought by the widow of an English passenger who was killed in the crash of a Turkish airliner which was flying between France and England and had crashed in France. They claimed that it would be much more convenient to litigate this case in England, and they made this statement in their motion papers:

> In order to eliminate any doubt on the subject, this defendant hereby agrees to voluntarily appear in the courts of the alternate forum, England, on condition that this Court first grants this motion to dismiss.

McDonnell Douglas's lawyers contended that our only reason for suing in California was to shoot for a higher award of damages than the English widow could collect in England. They claimed that this was unfair, since there was no reason why the families of passengers should collect more money than they would by bringing their suits in their own country's courts. Our journalist's case stood alone at that point, being the only case of a non-American passenger which had been filed when McDonnell Douglas made the *forum non conveniens* motion.

Knowing that the fate of more than 300 families hinged on the outcome of this motion, we went to work on our answering brief. If Judge Hall granted the McDonnell Douglas motion, the English journalist's case would be dismissed, and all the other cases involving non-American families would also be barred from American courts.

Al Gans and I worked together in drafting a 36-page brief to answer the 16-page brief submitted by McDonnell Douglas. We sent it on to our Los Angeles colleague James Butler, whose firm (Butler Jefferson Fry & Dan) was co-counsel on the DC-10 cases. Jim Butler and Michael Dan put the brief into final form, and the motion was argued by Jim Butler. Our main argument was that the cases of the 23 American passengers could not possibly be shunted to another nation, and since McDonnell Douglas would have to defend those cases in Los Angeles, it was more convenient for all of the parties to have the issues determined in a single trial in one court. For McDonnell Douglas, there could not be a more convenient forum than the place in which their home office, plant, witnesses, and documents were located. If the claims of the foreign plaintiffs were dismissed in Los Angeles, suits arising out of this accident would have to be filed in at least a dozen different nations. As Al Gans wrote in our brief:

> There would be dozens of scattered lawsuits. The lone families of survivors, each litigating on its own, would not have the resources or facilities, in Turkey or Japan or other nations, to prepare the product liability issue against this huge defendant with enormous resources located many thousands of miles away. The plan would be for the defendant, a huge northern pike, to gobble up separately each small sunfish or blue gill. This court should not aid perpetration of such a wily and cunning strategy of "divide and conquer."

In reply to the offer of McDonnell Douglas to allow itself to be sued in England, we pointed out that the plaintiff has the choice of forums, and that this choice will not be disturbed by the courts without some compelling reason. There was no prospect that English courts would provide the same kind of a remedy as American courts. It is a prerequisite of dismissal for *forum non conveniens* that there be another forum which is more convenient and affords plaintiffs a remedy comparable to the one they are seeking in the court where they filed their suit. As the New York Court of Appeals said in defining *forum non conveniens,* it assumes that there is another forum "in which the plaintiff may obtain effective redress," not just another place where some kind of a lawsuit can be brought. Since there was no contingent fee system in Great Britain, it would have been impossible for the plaintiff to carry on such a massive case in the English courts. McDonnell Douglas had failed to mention any such suit that had ever been undertaken in Great Britain against an aviation manufacturer, and I inserted the following argument into our brief:

> Therefore, any claim by this defendant that "the plaintiffs have an adequate remedy in the alternative forum of England" reminds one of the statement by Anatole France, "The rich and poor have equal rights to sleep under the bridges of Paris."

As to the claim that we were unfairly seeking higher damages than our client could obtain in her native England, we replied that McDonnell Douglas should not complain about being judged by the law of their home state, where they had obviously been able to insure themselves against product liability claims quantified according to California standards. It was a California airplane that had killed our client's husband, and there was nothing inequitable about her seeking damages according to California standards.

The *forum non conveniens* motion was argued before Judge Hall on June 5, 1974, and he did not keep us waiting long. On June 11, 1974, he rendered his decision:

> The defendant's motion to dismiss the plaintiff's Second Amended Complaint on the ground that it is an inconvenient forum for the maintenance of this action is denied.

Thus he established the right of all of the 346 families from twenty-four different nations to bring their actions in a Los Angeles court. It was a typical Peirson Hall decision—practical, fair, and designed to keep the ungainly litigation moving toward a just conclusion. *Forum non conveniens* motions involve some judicial discretion, and hard-pressed judges are sometimes tempted to grant them in order to give local litigants preference in allotting precious court time. But instead of creating many separate suits that would plague courts throughout the world, Judge Hall saw the need for resolving all 346 cases in one place.

In another aspect of the case, Judge Hall used one of his home-made remedies to keep the litigation in one piece. All of the passengers' families sued Turkish Airlines (THY) as well as the two manufacturers, McDonnell Douglas and General Dynamics (who had built the fuselage, floors, and doors). There was a knotty legal problem in the suits of foreign passengers' families against THY, since Article 28 of the Warsaw Convention restricted such suits to four places: the domicile of the carrier (Turkey); the carrier's principal place of business (Turkey); the carrier's office through which the ticket was issued (Paris for most passengers); or the flight's destination (London). Even the American families could not sue THY in the United States unless the passenger's ticket had been purchased here. THY's lawyers made a motion to dismiss all the claims against them, alleging that Article 28 prevented Judge Hall from assuming jurisdiction over such claims. But Judge Hall knew that in the final reckoning, THY would have to pay each passenger's family some damages, even if limited to the $20,000 Warsaw ceiling. If he let the airline out, he would no longer have all the parties before him that he needed to dispose of the entire case in one legal swoop.

Peirson Hall's remedy was simply to sit on THY's motion. He saw no reason to decide it until he had given the natural forces of litigation a chance to end the case by payment of reasonable compensation to all plaintiffs by all defendants. He never did decide THY's motion. This way of resolving the issue was similar to the way he had dealt with the doctor who told him that he had to slow down and avoid protracted cases. He had simply changed doctors.

When the news of our victory on the *forum non conveniens* issue was published in England, the last barrier to suit by the other English families fell, and every one of the 177 English families joined in the California litigation. We represented the majority of them, although many retained other American law firms. We were also retained by the lawyers for families from 15 other nations: Argentina, Belgium, Brazil, Canada, Chile, France, Germany, Hungary, Italy, New Zealand, Portugal, Spain, Switzerland, Turkey, and the United States. In all, we were retained by the lawyers for 164 families, the largest group of claimants in this or any other aviation disaster to date.

Liability

With the case now firmly lodged in Judge Hall's court, the next order of business was liability. With all the evidence of a cargo door blowout as the cause of the accident, it was clear that eventually someone would have to compensate the plaintiffs. But who, and in what percentages? McDonnell Douglas's president Sanford McDonnell announced to the press at the company's annual meeting on April 17, 1974, that the accident had been caused by human failure—failure by the Paris baggage handler to close the cargo door properly. McDonnell Douglas, THY, and General Dynamics each blamed the others for the cargo door failure. There was no NTSB hearing or report to draw upon, since the accident had been investigated officially only by the French government, which had not released any useful information. Brief hearings had been held in Washington by two congressional committees, but they concentrated on the FAA gentlemen's agreement and other regulatory matters rather than the facts that plaintiffs needed to prove their liability case. Obviously, thorough discovery was needed on liability.

Judge Hall quickly approved the appointment of a plaintiffs' discovery committee which was chaired by Don Madole. It included six or seven other plaintiffs' lawyers from time to time, and eventually more than a dozen plaintiffs' lawyers made substantial contributions to its liability discovery. Many defense lawyers, too, were involved in the discovery, and since the defendants were freely blaming each other, their discovery work helped to put together the total liability picture.

The discovery started in April of 1974 and continued for more than a year. It included production of documents, interrogatories, and extended depositions. During much of that time, including the summer months, the lawyers worked on a schedule of two weeks of depositions and one week off, the "off" week being spent in studying past transcripts and preparing for the continuing testimony. It produced a record of the design, manufacture, and operation of the DC-10 that covered more than 50,000 pages, the most minute legal examination of an aircraft history ever made. While the plaintiffs' lawyers were dealing with a foreign accident and had no NTSB hearing record to use as a starting point, they did not have the problems Billy Hyman and I had faced a quarter of a century earlier in the Air France Azores cases. They did not have to reconstruct the accident remotely by written interrogatories; their two American defendants could be examined directly with all their records and witnesses.

The evidence that emerged from this concentrated discovery showed that the main points of contention would be the safety of the DC-10 cargo door locking system design (which involved both manufacturers) and allegations that THY had modified the system on its own and made it even less safe. McDonnell Douglas was forced to admit that it had not made the three-step modification which was mandated by their own service bulletin issued after the 1972 McCormick Windsor blowout, although Ship 29 (the one eventually involved in the Ermenonville disaster) had been sitting at the Long Beach plant and was supposed to be modified. Indeed, Ship 29's documentary history, produced on discovery, showed the official signature stamps of three McDonnell Douglas inspectors affixed to records indicating that all three modification steps had been completed on July 18, 1972.

Each of the three inspectors was deposed at great length. None of them could recall working on any DC-10 cargo door at any time in 1972. Each inspector testified that he had *not* worked with the other two on July 18, 1972; indeed, none of them could recall having worked with the others at *any* time. The affixing of the inspectors' stamps—normally a solemn act surrounded by tight security—was not explained by any of the witnesses. All three inspectors denied having loaned their stamps out or having lost them. The conclusion we drew from this baffling evidence was that later in 1972, when McDonnell Douglas was anxious to deliver Ship 29 to THY in response to a rush order, somebody decided to fill in the blank places retroactively. Whoever did that condemned 346 people to die at Ermenonville.

From the discovery, it was clear that the gentlemen's agreement with the FAA to avoid issuance of an Airworthiness Directive played an important part in the fatal mishandling of Ship 29's papers. Issuance of the modification order as one of many manufacturer's service bulletins removed the aura of urgency and necessity that was inherent in an FAA Airworthiness Directive. As a result, many DC-10s that were already in airline operation at the time of the July 1972 service bulletin did not have their cargo door locking systems modified until months (or in some cases *years*) after the Windsor incident. Many continued to fly hundreds of hours with the unsafe system. If the modification order had been in the form of an FAA AD, I doubt that anyone at McDonnell Douglas would have undertaken to affix three inspectors' stamps to a lifesaving modification that was never accomplished.

The discovery also produced a remarkable document known as the Applegate memorandum, authored by F. W. Applegate, director of product engineering of the Convair division of General Dynamics. It was written on June 27, 1972, just 15 days after Bryce McCormick's miraculous escape from disaster at Windsor. Its subject was "DC-10 Future Accident Liability," and it included this language:

> The potential for long-term Convair [General Dynamics] liability on the DC-10 has caused me increasing concern for several reasons.
> 1. The fundamental safety of the cargo door latching system has been progressively degraded since the program began in 1968.
> 2. The airplane demonstrated an inherent susceptibility to catastrophic failure when exposed to explosive decompression of the cargo compartment in 1970 ground tests.
> 3. Douglas has taken an increasingly "hard line" with regards to the relative division of design responsibility between Douglas and Convair during change cost negotiations.
>
> *   *   *
>
> My only criticism of Douglas in this regard is that once this inherent weakness was demonstrated by the July 1970 test failure, they did not take immediate steps to correct it. It seems to me inevitable that, in the twenty years ahead of us, DC-10 cargo doors will come open and I would expect this to usually result in the loss of the airplane.

Applegate described the modifications McDonnell Douglas proposed after Windsor as "bandaids." He suggested that the cabin floor be redesigned to withstand explosive decompression in the cargo compartment whether it was caused by opening of the cargo door, sabotage, mid-air collision, or other hazards. His suggestions coincided with the recommendations made by the NTSB after its own investigation of the Windsor blowout: in addition to modifying the cargo door locking system, McDonnell Douglas should install relief vents between the cabin and the aft cargo compartment in order to minimize the pressure loading on the cabin floor in the event of sudden depressurization from *any* cause. But the FAA failed to follow up on the NTSB venting recommendations; the Applegate memorandum was never sent to the FAA (or even to McDonnell Douglas); and the DC-10 was left "susceptible to catastrophic failure," just as Applegate had prophesied.

In spite of the very strong liability case that was emerging from the depositions, there had been no movement toward settlement. Although Judge Hall was aiming for a liability trial by the fall of 1975, we knew by early spring that there was at least another year of intensive discovery ahead. We had completed only ten witnesses, and the issues between the defendants were so complex that each of them had asked to depose dozens of witnesses, many of them located in Europe. There are few things more complicated than the design of a jumbo jet. Thousands of engineers work on its design for years before the plane ever flies. Thus the liability trial could easily last a year, especially since Judge Hall's condition required him to limit courtroom proceedings to about four hours a day. If he was forced to withdraw, we would face a long wait for another judge who could fit such a case into his calendar.

The outlook for a quick resolution was discouraging. Yet, we knew that each of the defendants expected to pay some damages. The problem was that the stakes were so large (about $100 million) that none of the defendants would make the first move toward settlement, for fear of being asked to pick up most of the bill. Often in modern jumbo jet litigation, the principal task of the plaintiffs' lawyers is to spell out to the defendants' teams of lawyers what the relative responsibility of each defendant is. In the days of the piston engine airliners such as the DC-3, DC-4, DC-6, and Lockheed Constellation, the litigation was much simpler. The airline was usually the only defendant. Manufacturing defects were hard to find and even harder to prove before the products liability revolution and the onset of strict liability. The federal government was rarely sued, except in the few instances of a mid-air collision in controlled airspace.

Since then, this picture has changed dramatically. The airliners of this era are much more complex and of course they carry many more passengers. In addition, aviation has become so complicated that accidents of the type that occurred in the DC-3 days are comparatively rare. Typically, a DC-3 accident would involve a pilot straying off course and flying into a mountain, or trying to land in poor visibility while operating partly on instruments and partly under visual flight rules. Only rarely was there occasion to sue defendants other than the airline. But in the wide-bodied world of the DC-10, the Lockheed 1011, and the Boeing 747, it is difficult to separate the responsibilities of airline operations, aviation manufacturing, and government regulation. We now have a maze of federal aviation regulations which place concurrent responsibilities upon airlines, manufacturers, and FAA personnel in a very broad spectrum of situations.

The tendency toward multiple defendants has been accelerated by the strict liability rule in claims against manufacturers and by the expanded concept of government liability under the Federal Tort Claims Act. Another complicating factor is the huge increase in the value of aircraft. In the DC-3 days, aircraft hull values were in the range of $50,000 to $100,000, which was less than the amount involved in one passenger death claim. Today, insurance claims for the value of the aircraft may be as high as $60 million, which will in many cases approach or exceed the total compensation paid to the families of all passengers. Thus there is another party sitting in at the settlement table and holding a sizeable hand: the attorney for the "hull insurer" who has paid out millions of dollars on the airline's hull insurance policy and now seeks to recover part or all of that payment through a subrogation suit against the government or the manufacturer. With claims increasing in size because of inflation and expanded liability concepts, it is not unusual for major airline crash litigation to result in a payment total of more than $100 million. With stakes that high, and with so many parties involved, the stage is set for compromise through appropriate contributions by various defendants to the final settlement. The litigation process thus becomes the mechanism through which a satisfactory formula can be worked out to accommodate the interests of all of these parties.

Because of the size and complexity of these claims, it generally takes a year or more of extensive discovery to bring all the parties to the point where a satisfactory contribution formula can be arranged. The settlement formula itself becomes the immediate target of lawyers who are conducting this type of litigation. A trial (or the threat of a trial) on the issue of liability may sometimes be required to bring such a formula about. Once the contribution ratios have been arrived at, the logjam is usually broken, and the litigation can be terminated by payments which satisfy all of the interests involved. The combined financial resources and insurance coverage of airlines, manufacturers, airport operators, and other such parties are adequate to provide satisfactory settlements in the few hundred cases of passenger injury and death that occur each year, and they don't cost the airlines and manufacturers as much as one percent of their total operating costs. In fact, there is heated competition among the world's leading insurers to write the nine-figure policies that cover major airlines and manufacturers. Thus, with a minimal burden on commerce and on society as a whole, airline crash litigation has an economic basis for the fair compensation of all claimants and the equitable spreading of risks.

The Turkish Airlines DC-10 case was an apt example of this complicated multidefendant pattern. The hull underwriters had paid out $35 million to THY, and had then sued the two manufacturers in California to get that money back. Two giant manufacturers were involved in the design of the parts that failed; each of them sought to fix the blame on the other, and each also blamed the airline. In addition, claims were made against the FAA because of its laxity in protecting the public with regard to the design and modification of the DC-10. In such a complicated case, there is a danger that by bringing in too many defendants you make the case unsettlable, for there must be unanimous agreement among the defendants on a settlement formula. Here each defendant had two or three sets of lawyers and there were various groups of underwriters in New York and London with different interests in the liability and hull policies. In all, there must have been 15 to 20 people sitting around the table when the defendants met to discuss a settlement formula. We heard rumors that they were very far apart despite the extensive discovery already completed. How could we paint the liability picture for them, so that each party would see clearly what it was facing at trial and what its fair share of the compensation bill should be?

Don Madole came up with the answer: a motion for summary judgment on the issue of liability. Summary judgment is a drastic remedy. The judge decides the case on papers submitted by lawyers; no witnesses are heard, and the trial is eliminated entirely. It is only granted when there is a clear showing that a trial is not necessary—when there is "no genuine issue as to *any* material fact" involved in the case. Thus, even if almost all the facts are admitted or agreed upon, the existence of an issue—a genuine disagreement on even one material fact—is enough to defeat a summary judgment motion. That is as it should be, since our legal system is based upon the right to a full hearing on the facts, by a jury if desired. Usually summary judgment is successful only in suits seeking payment of an overdue promissory note, or other simple claims based upon undisputable documents. Here we had more than 50,000 pages of documents, and their implications were hotly disputed by four different defendants. We therefore had little hope of winning summary judgment, but there were other strong reasons for making such a motion.

The motion would give us the opportunity to pull all the liability evidence together and present it in a single document for the first time. In domestic airline accidents, the comprehensive report issued by the NTSB sometimes serves that purpose. It gives the defendants a picture of the kind of case that can be marshalled against them, even though the NTSB report itself cannot be used in court. But here we had a foreign accident, no NTSB report, and no other document that summarized the available evidence. We hoped that such a document would cause each defense lawyer to evaluate his client's potential liability accurately, and thus break the deadlock on the settlement formula.

The motion would also show us, the defendants, and Judge Hall where we stood in discovery. It would point up the weak and strong points of each party's case. If we had to go on with discovery, at least we would have a better picture of how to proceed. Many of the proposed witnesses could probably be eliminated, and discovery would be shortened. In addition, the motion would smoke out the defendants—it would force each of them to come forward and explain its conduct in more detail than had ever been required before. Our liability evidence was strong enough to prevent each of the defendants from simply shrugging off the motion. Many damaging facts had been admitted in the depositions and documents; indeed, the defendants' own employees and records were practically our sole source of proof. If we could put these admissions together in a strong package, the defendants would be hard put to demonstrate the existence of genuine issues. Since none of the defendants could demonstrate freedom from fault in the face of these admissions, they had to allege intervening acts of negligence by other defendants. They would almost have to put on a preview of the trial in order to avoid summary judgment.

Don prepared the summary judgment motion, which turned out to be a 210-page document. Its Table of Contents shows the depth of its organization. (MD stands for McDonnell Douglas; GD for General Dynamics; THY for Turkish Airlines.)

I. AFFIDAVIT OF DONALD W. MADOLE IN SUPPORT OF PARTIAL MOTION FOR SUMMARY JUDGMENT ON LIABILITY.

1.0 *The Direct and Immediate Cause of the Paris Air Crash Was the Inadvertent Opening of the Aft Bulk Cargo Door at Altitude.*
1.1 The Accident
1.2 Why the Cargo Door Opened
1.21 Operation of the Aft Cargo Door
1.22 Previous Accidents:
    a. Fuselage No. 1 Incident (May 29, 1970);
    b. The Orbit of Reasonable Foreseeability: Windsor Accident (June 12, 1972)

2.0 *Gross Negligence of Defendant McDonnell Douglas*

2.1 Service Bulletins—Documented Duty
2.1a Service Bulletin A52-35 (Exhibit 2016)
2.1b Service Bulletin 52-37
2.1c Service Bulletin 52-49 (MD Exhibit 10007)
2.2 MD Failed to Install Crucial Service Bulletins on the Accident Aircraft and Such Failure Was a Contributing and Proximate Cause of the Crash in Paris on March 3, 1974.
2.22 Reports Were Received from the Field Concerning the Malfunction of the Cargo Door Closing Mechanism or Malfunction Indications.
2.23 The Evidence Revealed the Incontrovertible Physical Fact That the Latch Actuator Was Not Fully Extended, and That the Latches Were Not Safe.
2.24 It Was Determined from an Examination of the Lock Pins on the Aft Cargo Door Involved in the Paris Wreckage That Three of the Four Lock Pins on the Aft

Cargo Door Latching Mechanism Had Been Adjusted
to an Unsafe Position.

2.25 Tests Done by MD Show That the Ship 29 Cargo Door
was Improperly Adjusted or "Misrigged."

3.0 *MD Failed to Comply with Certain Federal Aviation Regulations (FARS) Which Were Intended to Insure That Jet
Transport Aircraft Were Constructed in a Safe Manner for
Public Transportation, and That Such Violations Were a Contributing and Proximate Cause of the Paris Crash on March
3, 1974.*

3.1 Violation of FAR 25.1309

3.2 The Testimony Shows That MD Violated FAR
25.365(e) Which Violation Was a Contributing and
Proximate Cause of the Paris Air Crash.

3.3 The Testimony Shows That MD Violated FAR
25.783(d) Which Violation Was a Contributing and
Proximate Cause of the Crash.

4.0 *Design Defects*

4.1 The DC-10 Was Defectively Designed, Manufactured
and Developed by MD in Conjunction with GD in a
Defective Condition.

4.2 GD Jointly Manufactured, Developed and Produced
the DC-10 with Design Defects.

5.0 *Testimony, Evidence and Documents Show That the Crash
of Hull 29 Was Due to and Proximately Caused by the Wilful Misconduct of THY.*

5.1 Testimony Shows That THY Dispatched Hull 29 in
Paris on March 3, 1974, in a Defective Condition by
Wilfully Refusing and/or Neglecting To Make Use of
the Viewing Port Which Would Have Provided It With
an Indication That the Door Was not Safely Locked
and That Such Refusal Was a Contributing and Proximate Cause of the Crash.

5.2 The Testimony, Evidence and Documents Show That
THY Wilfully and Carelessly Adjusted the Locking
Pins on the Aft Cargo Door on Hull 29 in Such a Condition as To Provide No Warning Indication of an Unsafe Door.

5.3 The Testimony, Evidence and Documents Show That
THY Wilfully Installed the Aft Cargo Door Without
Making Certain Required Adjustments and That Such
Failure Was a Contributing and Proximate Cause of the
Crash.

II. MEMORANDUM OF POINTS AND AUTHORITIES IN SUP-
PORT OF MOTION FOR PARTIAL SUMMARY JUDGMENT.

1. *Preliminary Statement*

1.1 The Defendants are Jointly and Severally Liable.

1.21 Summary Judgment is Appropriate in the Instant Litigation.

1.22 Once the Party Moving for Summary Judgment Has
Demonstrated That There Is No Genuine Issue as to
Any Material Fact and That He Is Entitled to a Judg-
ment as a Matter of Law, the Opposing Party Has the
Burden of Demonstrating the Existence of a Genuine
Issue as to a Material Fact.

2.0 *The Acts and Omissions of Defendants MD and GD Contributed to and Proximately Caused the Crash.*
2.1 Admissions from Agents, Servants and Employees of
Defendants MD and GD are Competent Evidence
Against the Said Defendants.
2.2 Post Accident Tests by MD Are Admissible in California To Show That the Failure of MD to Install Certain
Service Bulletins Was a Contributing and Proximate
Cause of the Crash.
2.3 Standard of Care
2.31 The FARs
2.32 Manufacturers Strict Liability
2.33 The Omissions and Commissions of Defendants MD
and GD Were a Contributing and Proximate Cause of
the Crash.

3.0 *The Testimony, Evidence and Documents Show That Turkish Airlines (THY) Wilfully Dispatched Hull 29 on the
Morning of March 3, 1974, in a Defective Condition; Wilfully Failed to Comply with Approved Maintenance Procedures; and That Such Wilful Misconduct Was a Contributing
and Proximate Cause of the Crash.*
3.1 Wilful Conduct
3.2 THY As a Supplier of a Defective Product Is Subject
To Strict Tort Liability—Warsaw Is Not Relevant.

III. PROPOSED FINDINGS OF FACT AND CONCLUSIONS OF
LAW

IV. TABLES OF CASES AND AUTHORITIES

V. CERTIFICATE OF SERVICE

Under each heading, Don inserted excerpts from depositions and
documents that supported our arguments. He boiled down more than
50,000 pages of complicated material to a workable 200-page analysis
of the overall liability picture. The proposed findings of fact at the end
of the motion read like a grand jury indictment of the defendants.

For the public, Don Madole's summary judgment motion was the
first peek it got at what had caused the Ermenonville disaster. The
French government had not released any testimony or documents, and
at the start of the depositions in 1974, Judge Hall had made an unusual
ruling—a "gag order"—that kept all the discovery material secret. Journalists in Los Angeles had wanted to attend the depositions and had
sought immediate access to the testimony and the documents. But the

defendants objected and requested Judge Hall to seal all the discovery
material until the case was terminated. The judge wanted to give the
defendants every opportunity to work out a settlement formula without
airing all their dirty linen in public, and he was afraid that charges and
countercharges vented in the press would harden their positions and
make settlement more difficult. He also wanted to give the defendants
an incentive to avoid a trial, for they knew that he would never agree
to bar the public from a full-scale trial. So the judge had granted their
motion to seal the discovery material. If they wanted to keep the evidence secret after discovery, they would have to concede liability and
thus open the way for settlement of all the cases.

However, Judge Hall's gag order did not apply to the evidence
contained in Don Madole's summary judgment motion, for that was,
and is, a public document. Thus the Applegate memorandum and hundreds of other items of evidence became public when our motion was
filed on March 10, 1975, and it became the basis for press reporting of
specific claims of negligence. This was of considerable importance to
many of our clients, particularly the English journalist's widow who
had led the fight to bring out all the facts through litigation, only to
be stymied temporarily by the gag order.

The motion was argued before Judge Hall for nearly four days in
April of 1975. The defendants were called upon to prepare their briefs
and arguments as carefully as if they had been facing a trial jury. The
motion succeeded in smoking out their defenses and countercharges. It
showed that all four defendants were vulnerable to claims of negligence,
and it forced them to specify charges against each other. For example,
here is how General Dynamics attempted to put the blame entirely on
McDonnell Douglas in their written reply to the motion:

> The evidence further shows that apparently the crucial al-
> terations were not made by [McDonnell] Douglas upon hull No.
> 29, and instead three different Douglas employees deliberately
> did not do the tasks assigned to them and instead counterfeited
> the paperwork so that it was fraudulently made to appear that
> the changes had been made.

That statement by a collaborator on the aircraft design and a codefen-
dant in the litigation was a stronger condemnation of McDonnell Douglas than any of the plaintiffs' lawyers had ever made. We were delighted
to see that the summary judgment motion was accomplishing some of its
objectives.

On April 29, Judge Hall denied our motion for summary judgment, with leave to renew it at any time prior to trial. We hoped that
we would not have to renew it, for we had perceived some signs that the
defendants were beginning to sort out their differences after the en-

lightening experience of the summary judgment argument. We heard rumors about serious negotiations taking place in London and Los Angeles. Then on May 25, 1979, less than 30 days after the summary judgment motion had been decided, the defense lawyers announced to Judge Hall that they had reached an agreement in principle on a settlement formula. Discovery was halted so that they could draft and sign a formal agreement. It was a complicated document because it affected rights of defendants against each other, in addition to rights of the plaintiffs.

On July 8, 1975, the defense lawyers notified Judge Hall that they had executed a written agreement for the sharing of damage payments to all plaintiffs and were ready to submit this agreement privately to Judge Hall. Having agreed among themselves on a formula for sharing compensation payments, the defendants now made a proposal to all the plaintiffs. They would agree not to contest the issue of liability in any case in which the plaintiff agreed to accept compensatory damages. They would attempt to negotiate a settlement, and if that failed, they would agree to a trial of each unsettled case on the issue of compensatory damages only. In exchange for this concession on liability, they required each plaintiff to give up any right to punitive damages.

All the plaintiffs' lawyers felt that this would have been a very strong case for punitive damages if the law had provided for them. The problem was that wrongful death law had become separated from the common law of negligence through an historical error in 1808 (as we saw in the Ford Pinto story in Chapter 5), and as a result most American states (including California) did not permit punitive damages in wrongful death cases even though they were permitted in personal injury cases. There were signs that some appellate courts were leaning away from this ancient and illogical distinction. But after appraising the situation in 1975, we advised all our clients to accept the proposal and to settle or try for compensatory damages only.

We felt that each family would get a fair shake from Judge Hall and a California jury. We knew that if we went on to claim punitive damages, there would be, in addition to the legal obstacles, at least one year of further liability discovery, another year to try the case on liability, and at least another three years in the appellate courts. It would therefore take five to eight years before our clients would recover *any* money, and the odds were still against getting anything more than compensatory damages at the end of that time. Many of the young children would have missed educational opportunities, and some of our older clients would be dead or too infirm to make use of the settlement proceeds. Insistence on punitive damages would remove any chance of ever settling the case, because California law did not specify whether the punishment would be paid for by the defendants or by their in-

surers. Certainly the insurers would not agree voluntarily to pay a penny
in punitive damages, for fear of setting a precedent that would make
them responsible for something they claimed they did not insure against
For all those reasons, our clients decided to follow our advice, and we
reported to Judge Hall that our 164 cases were ready for settlement o
trial on compensatory damages.

We were exhilarated at this turn of events which brought settle
ment within sight in July 1975—just a little over a year from date o
accident. But when we sat down to negotiate with the defense lawyers
we soon realized that they were using uncertainties about the applicable
law on damages as a means of discounting the settlement value of all bu
the American passenger cases. It was clear that we needed a decision
from Judge Hall on the choice of law problem: what law would be ap
plied by a California court to calculate the damages suffered by an
English family in the Paris crash of a Turkish airliner that was built in
California? How about a French family? A Turkish family? A family
from one of the 21 other nations represented on the passenger list? I
was a perfect conflicts of law problem for a diabolical bar exam ques
tion. But we had to get the answer from Judge Hall.

Conflict of Laws

If the Ermenonville disaster had occurred ten years earlier, there would
have been no choice of law problem. Up to the mid-1960s, American
courts automatically applied the *lex loci delicti*—the law of the place o
the wrong—in tort cases. Thus, the law of France would have been
applied to all passenger claims. But in the 1960s, the disparity among
wrongful death statutes of various states (especially those that retained
19th century railroad-lobbied monetary limitations on recovery) caused
some states to depart from the fixed *lex loci* rule.

Aviation cases had led this revolt, for they dramatically presented
the courts with large groups of death cases involving families from different states, of which some limited death damages while others did not. It
started with the 1958 crash of a Northeast Airlines Convair 240 at
Nantucket, Massachusetts. Some of the deceased passengers' families
lived in New York, and they sued the airline there. Massachusetts had a
$15,000 limit on wrongful death damages at that time, while New York
had none; but under the automatic *lex loci* rule, even the New York
families would be limited to $15,000. Lawyers for the New York pas-
sengers' families tried various means of circumventing the $15,000
Massachusetts limit, such as suing for breach of contract or claiming a
common law right to sue for wrongful death. These attempts were un-

successful, but eventually the New York Court of Appeals invented its own escape mechanism: it declared that the Massachusetts limit was against the public policy of New York. The case in which they made this declaration involved a New York passenger who had left no dependents, and it was settled later for less than $15,000. Our firm had not been involved in that case, but it then fell to us to apply the new policy in two federal court Nantucket actions that involved deaths of passengers leaving dependents. It required several trips to the Second Circuit Court of Appeals, but eventually our clients became the first two American families to collect damages beyond the *lex loci* limitation. One of them was the family of a well-known former government official and investment banker, who received $760,000 (more than fifty times the Massachusetts maximum), which at that time was the largest amount ever collected in a New York wrongful death or personal injury suit.

The appellate courts in those states (now in the majority) that departed from the rigid *lex loci* rule replaced it with a flexible process, variously called weighing of contacts, determination of the center of gravity, or analysis of governmental interest. California was one of the breakaway states, and it uses the interest analysis method. Its courts must analyze the governmental interests of the states involved and determine for each issue in the case which state's law applies most appropriately. Thus, one state's law might apply on liability, while another's might be used for damages. In the Ermenonville case, the possible choices for damage law were: California, as the forum and domicile of the two principal defendants (McDonnell Douglas and General Dynamics); the various domiciles of claimants; and France, as the place of the flight's departure and its subsequent accident.

The old *lex loci* rule often led to unjust results, but at least it had the virtue of certainty. The flexible rules that replaced it are, by their very nature, uncertain in their applicability. Therefore, when the states involved in an accident have important differences in liability or damage provisions, you can expect to see a legal donnybrook on choice of law. In the Ermenonville case, it happened that the French damage law was the ideal choice for all the plaintiffs. As we saw in Chapter 1, the entire body of French tort law is based upon Article 1382 of the Napoleonic Code, its simple language unchanged since enactment in 1804:

> Any act by which a person causes damages to another makes the person by whose fault the damage occurred liable to make reparation for such damage.

Following the tradition of Roman law, France has always allowed both material and "moral" damages in personal injury and wrongful death cases as well as in all other types of tort claims. Under Roman law, as

a sign of a higher civilization, injuries were regarded in their moral and
ethical as well as their material and physical aspects. In wrongful death
cases, moral damages took the form of compensation for grief and
sorrow suffered by relatives of persons killed in accidents. This type of
solatium had been rejected by the English courts in the early cases following enactment of Lord Campbell's Act in 1846, and most American
states (including California) refused to allow it as an element of damages in wrongful death cases.

Moral damages were especially important in the Ermenonville litigation because nearly half our English cases (as well as many of the
French and Turkish cases) involved claims in which there was very little
dependency. There had been many young passengers on the DC-10 who
were unmarried, and many others who left no dependent relatives. In
such cases, the English families would get practically nothing (less than
$2,000) if English law were applied, and even under California law, the
damages would be relatively low. While California allowed damages
for loss of society as well as loss of support, its definition of loss of
society did not then include loss of love and affection or any element
corresponding to French moral damages.

Because most of the other plaintiffs' lawyers were occupied with
the liability depositions in 1974–1975, I took the most active role in
the choice of law process. First I held meetings with our liaison lawyers
in the other nations involved. In England we were fortunate to have a
liaison committee of family solicitors composed of John D. Sheerin of
the Bury St. Edmunds firm Greene & Greene; J. Bruce Brodie of Frere
Chomeley & Co., a London firm that was in active practice when America was a British colony; and Anton Bates of the Hounslow firm Owen
White & Catlin. John Sheerin had a special interest in the choice of
law question, since he (as well as Josiah Bird of the prestigious Bury
St. Edmunds firm Bankes Ashton & Co.) represented the families of
many young Rugby players who had left no dependents. Bruce Brodie
is a leading litigation specialist who made many trips to the United
States in connection with his work on the Beatles' lawsuits. Anton Bates
had extensive experience in English tort litigation, and his firm represented several English families in our group.

In France our liaison lawyer was Jean-Marc Gernigon of Paris, an
aviation and trial specialist. In Turkey it was Mordo Dinar of Istanbul,
a prominent international lawyer. Drawing upon the experience and
wisdom of this international panel, I decided that we should ask Judge
Hall to choose French law on damages. This would give us the same
basic loss-of-support damages as California in dependency cases (under
the French material damages provision) and would also allow us to
recover moral damages for the grief of survivors, which would be the
principal element of damages in nondependency cases.

The next question was, how could we get Judge Hall to rule on choice of law? Normally that issue is not decided until a conflict arises— usually at the trial, and often as late as the time when the judge is preparing to instruct the jury. This makes it very tough on the lawyers, who may go through most of the case without knowing what law applies. But American litigation procedure was designed for the average case, which does not involve conflicts of law.

I found an answer in a book called the *Manual for Complex Litigation,* designed as a guide for judges and lawyers in MDL cases. Section 1.80 of that manual provided for discretionary early determination of choice of law. Judge Hall was not bound to follow that provision, but I had the feeling he would welcome any move that might clear the way for early settlement. I decided to ask him to exercise his discretion under Section 1.80 to take on the choice of law problem immediately, so that all parties would know what damage provisions applied and could make intelligent estimates of settlement value.

I spent much of the summer of 1974 working on the choice of law motion. Under the new California conflict rules, we could not ask Judge Hall to apply French law simply because France was the place of the accident. We had to demonstrate that of all the states involved in the case, France had the paramount interest in the issue of damages. We also had to make detailed comparisons of the damage laws of all the states involved, since the court will apply forum (California) law automatically unless the parties demonstrate that there are real differences—conflicts of law—between the forum and the other states. This exercise required me to write the equivalent of a mini-textbook on comparative law and choice of law, covering every one of the domicile states of the plaintiffs as well as California and France. In addition to the valuable assistance I received from our liaison lawyers in England, France, and Turkey, I found it necessary to consult other academic and litigation experts on foreign law, to the tune of more than $10,000 in consulting fees.

When this research was completed, I boiled down thousands of pages of texts and translations to a brief of 119 pages, which was filed in October of 1974. Not every judge would appreciate a brief that long, but I knew that Peirson Hall would gobble up everything I submitted and then go looking for more to read on his own. I tried to organize the brief like a textbook. I must say here that I feel it was the best job of legal research and writing I have ever done, and also the most interesting for me. It was exciting because the entire financial outcome of the Ermenonville litigation hinged on the choice of law. We had defeated the defendants on *forum non conveniens,* and from the outset there was little question that we would prevail on liability, either through a trial or a concession by defendants. But all that would be meaningless if we wound up with a measure of damages similar to that of England or the other states which placed a low legal value on human life. If we lost on choice of law, our clients would be no better off than if they had stayed home and accepted McDonnell Douglas's April 1974 offer to settle according to the law of passenger domicile.

As we expected, the defendants' answering briefs asked for application of the law of each passenger's domicile. This meant that they were willing to pay moral damages to the families of the French passengers (as well as those from Turkey, Japan, and several other nations that followed the Roman law), as long as they were able to treat the English families according to English law. England had by far the largest group of claimants, and the defendants would more than make up for moral damage payments to families from other nations by limiting the English families to the strictures of Lord Campbell's Act as interpreted by English courts. Even in dependency cases, the English damages for loss of support would come to only a fraction of what would be awarded under French or American law, since the English courts use methods of computation that are heavily weighted in favor of minimizing compensation. Gerald Sterns, a San Francisco lawyer who represented the second largest group of English families, wrote an excellent brief on that point (in collaboration with his English colleagues, solicitors Stephen Mitchell of London and Bernard Engler of Manchester) showing how the English damage law would deprive many widows and children of meaningful compensation.

Now there came into play one of the many subtleties of that most complex subject, conflict of laws. The rules of damage law that Judge Hall had to deal with broke down into two categories: substantive and procedural. The substantive damage law consisted of the type of damages allowable (loss of support, moral damages, etc.) and the persons permitted to recover—what the English call "heads of damage." The procedural law consisted of the rules that would guide the jury in assessing damages, such as what forms of evidence were admissible, and what yardstick would be used by the court to determine whether the jury verdict was excessive. This the English lawyers called "quantum of damages." The choice of law problem related only to the substantive law, for the forum always applies its own procedural rules. Therefore, even if Judge Hall applied English substantive law to the English cases, the Los Angeles jury would have some freedom to assess damages according to its own notions of fairness. The jurors would not be told about the low awards made in English death cases. Judge Hall would have to use Los Angeles standards in determining whether each verdict was excessive.

Having done my best to explain that point, I must admit that the line between substance and procedure is often difficult to locate. The very restrictive English methods of calculating damages, including deductions for insurance benefits and disallowance of inflation, might relate either to the types of damages recoverable (substantive) or to their assessment (procedural). It would be easy to find law professors willing to support either side of the substance-procedure argument. Therefore, we wanted no part of domicile law for our clients, lest Judge Hall's jury instructions wind up as the subject of a long fight in the appellate courts. Our first choice was French law. Failing that, we wanted California law, and we would try to make the most of its provisions for loss of society to achieve adequate damages in our non-dependency cases.

The defense attorneys submitted extensive briefs, answering all the arguments that I had made, and urging that the law of each decedent's domicile should govern damages. They were able to cite several decisions in which decedent's domicile law had been applied, and if there was any recent trend discernible, it was toward domicile law on damages. The theory was that the state of the dead passenger's domicile had the strongest interest in the type and amount of damages awarded, for that state would have to support the surviving relatives if they became indigent. They argued that France had no interest in how the families of English or Turkish or American passengers were compensated, since France's connection with them was momentary and fortuitous. And they repeated their "windfall" argument—that it would be unfair to allow English families to recover higher damages in California than they could in their own courts.

Some of the other plaintiffs' lawyers submitted short briefs, but since they were engaged in the long running liability depositions, and since we had made the motion for early determination of choice of law in our group of cases, it fell to me to carry most of the argument. When Judge Hall directed me to commence the argument on January 13, 1975, his courtroom in the Los Angeles federal courthouse was more than half filled with lawyers for various plaintiffs and defendants. John Sheerin had flown over from England to advise me on any questions of English law that arose, for we had to convince Judge Hall that there were sharp conflicts between English wrongful death provisions and those of France and California.

Judge Hall listened patiently to the arguments of more than a dozen lawyers for five days. I don't know of any other judge in the world who would have allowed such extensive argument on a motion that he did not have to hear in the first place (for he could have put off the choice of law until the trial, as is customary). From his questions and statements during those five days, it became clear that Judge Hall did not like the new California choice of law rule, which required him to decide which governmental interests were strongest but gave him virtually no guidelines for such a determination. He seemed to be leaning heavily toward California as the fairest and safest choice. Since the plaintiffs had chosen to sue there, they could not complain about choice of California damage law. The main defendants were domiciled there, and so had ample opportunity to prepare and insure themselves in contemplation of California damages. He had already ruled that California law would govern liability if a trial on that issue became necessary. I had worked very hard to assemble evidence that France's interest in the payment of moral damages was stronger than California's interest in disallowing them. I tried to convince the Judge that moral damages were the very essence of French law, and that the Napoleonic Code was the cornerstone of French society, whereas California simply had not gotten around to awarding damages for grief in death cases, although several other American states had done so and the trend was in that direction.

But Peirson Hall was not buying French law. No doubt he could see some problems with the Ninth Circuit if he made the case even more complicated by bringing in a foreign legal system. He would be open to reversal for applying the *lex loci,* which was no longer the fashionable choice. No matter what he might write about France's stronger governmental interests, the principle was so vague that no judge could be sure he was on solid ground. By the fifth day of argument, I was resigned to accepting a partial victory. California law would, of course, be much better than the dreaded domicile law. But I made a final try for French law, arguing that California law still left our clients without the moral damage remedy that was so strongly mandated by the entire history of France.

Mr. SPEISER: I suggest to your Honor that in comparing the Napoleonic Code with any pecuniary loss statute, be it California, England, or any of our states, we are comparing something like the Magna Carta on one hand, and, let's say, an arbitration statute on the other hand. Every state has an arbitration statute, because it is a good mechanical means of settling disputes. Every state has an interest in that statute, maybe a strong interest, because it helps in the regulation of business and society. But it is not an interest of the quality of the Magna Carta or the Napoleonic Code, which deal with human dignity, as compared with a mechanical means of settling disputes. I submit that the dignity of life that is embodied in the Napoleonic Code is the thing that has made it live so long. It's the thing that made Napoleon say that his Code would live much longer than his reputation as a general. His prophecy has been borne out because his Code is the cornerstone of the legal systems of most of the civilized countries of the world. So you are dealing with the difference in quality of state interests.

I submit that this great difference in the quality of state interests is enough to tip the scales, if your Honor is choosing between California and France. Furthermore, on deterrence, it is obvious from what these defendants have been saying, that their first choice is domicile law. Their second choice is California. France is their last choice. Why? Because it administers a greater sting of deterrence without any punitive factor. The *Hurtado* decision tells us that this is a very important state interest—to administer the deterrent sting of compensatory damages.

As I continued to press for French law, I got the impression that Judge Hall was tiring and that I was not getting through to him. He kept talking about the recent U.S. Supreme Court decision in *Sea-Land Services v. Gaudet*. I happened to be familiar with the case because the Supreme Court had done me the honor of citing my book *Recovery for Wrongful Death* eight times. But none of the voluminous briefs on this motion had mentioned the *Sea-Land* case, and I couldn't see how it was relevant to our choice of law problem, since it involved the federal maritime remedies for wrongful death. It contained a broad new definition of "loss of society," including loss of love, affection, care, attention, companionship, comfort, and protection; but that definition was applicable only to maritime cases, not to suits under the California wrongful death statute. I kept insisting that California law would not allow us to recover for the grief and sorrow of survivors, but Judge Hall seemed to be telling me that there was no real conflict between French law and California law on that point. I was frustrated, thinking that the old judge was slipping at last, and that I had better settle for California law. But I decided to take another shot at convincing him that the *Sea-Land* decision would not help us to recover moral damages:

> Mr. SPEISER: I grant you that when you get down to a choice between California and France, you don't have much guidance in the cases themselves. I believe that for whatever—
>
> The COURT: I think that distance [between France and California] has been narrowed by the recent *Sea-Land* case, because as I regard the *Sea-Land* case, it is not just an admiralty case . . .
>
> MR. SPEISER: I believe your Honor is correct, that *Sea-Land v. Gaudet* is the highest and most recent definition of loss of society and of pecuniary loss.
>
> The COURT: Of pecuniary loss.
>
> MR. SPEISER: Yes, under a Lord Campbell-type statute, which we have in California and most of the other states. I fully agree that if your Honor applied California law it would be proper and certainly appropriate to use the *Sea-Land* definition of pecuniary loss and loss of society.

The COURT: It seems to me that under the *Sea-Land* case, they have enlarged the definition of pecuniary loss to include any damage beyond the age of eighteen, which is now the age of majority as to both men and women.

Mr. SPEISER: Yes, sir. So I agree that the *Sea-Land* decision along with California law brings it closer to the French law. But there is still the basic difference that French law allows mental anguish and California does not. That is the only conflict, really, between California and French law. Up to that point we have no conflict of law. We have no decision to make. The only real question is, does California have a strong interest in denying mental anguish damages to these claimants? Is that interest of California in denying mental anguish damages stronger than France's interest in allowing it to them? I submit, your Honor—

The COURT: Well, if under the *Sea-Land* case love and affection can be taken into consideration as an element for fixing damages, it would seem to me that the loss of love and affection would include pain and anguish to the surviving individual who has lost a relative.

MR. SPEISER: Well, with that construction of it, that brings it closer to our position, certainly.

The COURT: That isn't any final conclusion on this. I may sleep a couple of nights and turn a flip-flop.

Final conclusion or not, it was good enough for me. Peirson Hall's message had finally gotten through to me: once the *Sea-Land* definition of loss of society was accepted, with loss of love and affection as an integral part of it, then the plaintiffs would have the right to show the mental anguish suffered by surviving relatives. Otherwise, how could one measure the value of lost love and affection? How does loss of love and affection manifest itself, if not by the sorrow and anguish that it leaves behind? Although Judge Hall would have let me ramble on for another hour, I decided that it was time to sit down.

I hadn't quite figured out how Judge Hall would make the *Sea-Land* decision a part of California wrongful death law, but he had stated several times from the bench that he intended to do so, and I knew that he was ingenious enough to find the necessary legal foundation. That represented a great victory for the plaintiffs, since it would give them the benefits of three liberal damage standards: the California wrongful death statute; the federal maritime damage rules, as expressed in *Sea-Land;* and Judge Hall's interpretation of *Sea-Land* to include mental anguish of surviving relatives.

After the choice of law argument was completed on January 17, 1975, Judge Hall held off his decision and turned his attention to pushing along the liability discovery. There was no need for him to rule on choice of law until a settlement formula had been reached. When the defendants presented him with the settlement formula agreement in July of 1975, he went to work on the choice of law decision. He issued it on August 1, 1975. It was another Peirson Hall masterpiece.

He reviewed all the complications of the DC-10 litigation, characterizing it as an "Aegaeonic case," explaining in a footnote that Aegaeon was the leader of three mythological brothers who each had 100 arms and 50 heads. Describing the choice of law under the new governmental interest test as "a veritable jungle," he found that California had the dominant interest among the jurisdictions involved in the crash, since it was in California's interest to deter the aircraft manufacturers within its borders from dangerous conduct and to maintain a uniform rule of damages for those who were injured or killed because of their dangerous conduct. He also ruled that the Californian defendants should be protected against excessive financial burdens of other legal systems if they had reason to rely upon California law, especially in this case, where the plaintiffs from 24 nations had chosen to file their suits in California. Thus his choice of California law was dictated by concern for the defendants and also by the need for a uniform result in all the suits arising out of the Ermenonville disaster.

Most judges would have stopped right there, but Peirson Hall ventured on. He found that the United States had governmental interests in this litigation at least as strong as California's interest, based upon the Federal Aviation Act of 1958, which had preempted the field of aviation regulation for the federal government. Attached to his opinion were the contents of Part 25 of the Federal Aviation Regulations, which minutely regulates the design and performance of all the systems and components of transport aircraft. He also cited a number of cases holding that the federal government has exclusive control of aviation regulation. He wrote:

> . . . in view of the federal interest, this Court will adopt the liberalization over California's interpretations of the phrase "pecuniary loss" as laid down by the Supreme Court in *Sea-Land Services v. Gaudet,* 414 U.S. 573 (1974).
>
> The Court, in conclusion, for the reasons hereinbefore stated, holds that the "governmental interest" of both California and the United States, or either of them, outweighs any and all other interest of any state or nation in determining the measure of damages in these cases; that California law applies because of California's "governmental interests"; and that the California law governs damages under the Rules of Decision Act, 28 USC §1652, because of the overriding interest of the United States in the design and manufacture of aircraft.

Thus, Judge Hall had solved the choice of law problem in his wise and wonderful way. He did not want to risk a voyage into the uncharted seas of French law, since that might create grounds for reversal on appeal.

But he saw the need for tempering California law with the moral elements of the Napoleonic Code, which was the dominant legal system
among the 23 foreign nations that had interests in this litigation. This
he accomplished in his Solomonic way by invoking one of his favorite
themes: the federal regulation of aviation, which gave the United
States a very strong governmental interest. This in turn allowed him to
use the federal damage law as enunciated most recently in *Sea-Land
Services v. Gaudet.* And under his interpretation of *Sea-Land,* surviving
relatives could prove loss of love and affection through a showing of
mental anguish.

Judge Hall had read hundreds of pages of lawyers' briefs, and
had listened to five days of argument. Then he had proceeded to make
his decision on grounds not mentioned by any of the lawyers. Yet it
was a decision that dealt with every point, every interest, every argument put forward by the many parties to the case. It resolved a knotty
multination problem in a way that would have done credit to the United
Nations. It also set an important precedent for aviation and other mul-
tistate and multinational litigation: the use of the federal government's
regulatory interest and its interest in the just and speedy disposition of
federal cases to solve choice of law problems.

Damages

Three of the major hurdles in this monumental case were now behind
us. *Forum non conveniens* had been ruled out of the case. Liability for
compensatory damages was no longer being contested, and damage
law had been chosen—a combination of California and federal law
which would recompense pecuniary loss and also loss of love and
affection. The final step would be to turn this into payment of compensation, either through settlements or damage trials.

There were some settlement negotiations during the summer and
early fall of 1975. However, we were not able to settle any cases, because the defense attorneys were still sticking to lower figures in the
foreign cases than they would have offered for Americans under similar family and earnings conditions. It was still a novel idea to them to
pay American damage settlements to foreigners. We concentrated on
the English cases first, since they were the largest group and the easiest
to compare with American cases. The defendants seemed to be trying
to buy their way out of the cases at about halfway between the damage
standards of England and California, even though English law had been
ruled out by Judge Hall. Perhaps they felt that it would be difficult for

plaintiffs' lawyers to bring the English families to Los Angeles for damage trials. It soon became apparent that we would make little progress on settlement until at least one English case had been tried.

The first English case to come up for trial involved the deaths of a 30-year-old businessman and his 29-year-old wife, which had orphaned their two infant daughters (aged one and two years). Both of the parents had excellent career records and strong future earnings prospects. This case was tried for the plaintiffs by Richard Krutch and Vernon Judkins of Seattle and Gerald Sterns of San Francisco. It was apparent that the defendants were out to show all of the English claimants that they would have a very rough time bringing their cases to court. The defense attorneys went to England and took very detailed depositions from relatives and other damage witnesses and delved deeply into decedents' private affairs. The damage trial itself, which in a death case normally would not take more than a week of court time, extended over five weeks, partly due to Judge Hall's physical need to limit court sessions to four hours a day, four days a week. The defense attorneys threw every conceivable roadblock in the way of the plaintiffs, reading hundreds of pages of depositions and forcing the plaintiffs to submit proof of many details about the lives of the decedents which normally would not be contested. Dick Krutch, Vern Judkins, and Gerry Sterns weathered this difficult trial and turned the defense's attrition tactics to the advantage of the plaintiffs, so much so that the jury brought in a verdict of $879,450 for the death of the husband and $630,500 for the death of the wife, more than twice the amount that the plaintiffs' attorneys had been willing to settle for prior to trial.

Those verdicts in favor of the two English orphans were handed down on February 26, 1976. We were scheduled to follow with the trial of a second case on March 9. Judge Hall was exhausted by the ordeal of the first trial, but he defied his doctor's orders and stood by the trial date for the second case. The defendants seemed prepared to use the same tactics as they had in the first trial. They had taken voluminous depositions of potential damage witnesses and seemed to be contesting even the most routine items of evidence. Jim Butler and Chuck Krause had the decedent's family in Los Angeles ready to start the trial. But apparently the defendants had learned a lesson from the first trial. On March 8, the day before the jury was to be selected, the case was settled for the highest amount paid for the death of any person aboard the Ermenonville DC-10.

This was important progress, but there still remained many knotty problems in appraising the damages in the rest of the cases. Many of them involved earnings records and careers that would be unfamiliar to Los Angeles jurors. If each plaintiff would have to go through weeks of damage depositions and then appear in Los Angeles ready for trial, the cost to plaintiffs, defendants, and the court would be burdensome. But how would both sides reach a consensus on the amount of compensation that a Los Angeles jury would award for the death of an East Anglia farmer, a Turkish journalist, or a French banker? Again it was Judge Hall who came up with the innovative solution. He announced that he was appointing a panel of nine retired California Superior Court judges, who had agreed to sit in groups of three as special masters to hear informal presentations of damage data in each case and would then give the court and the parties their estimates of what a Los Angeles jury would award.

There was no rule under which Judge Hall could force any of the parties to bring their cases before the panel of special masters. It was all done by agreement, with the defendants agreeing to pay the fees of the special masters, and most of the plaintiffs agreeing to present their cases to the panel for evaluation on compensatory damages. Neither side was bound by the findings of the panel, and each case could be brought on for a separate damage trial if it had not been settled through the panel procedure. The defendants were not bound to pay the amounts that the special master judges predicted juries would award. Judge Hall ordered the panel sessions to begin on April 6, 1976, and then he entered a hospital for 10 weeks of enforced bed rest (during which he continued to exasperate his doctors by running his court from his bed).

The April 6 date created a problem for us, since Chuck Krause, who was most familiar with the damage aspects of our 164 cases, was engaged in a long trial in New York. Cast in the unfamiliar role of defense attorney, he was representing Mitsubishi International Corporation, a unit of Japan's largest trading company, in a New York suit brought by Federal Steel Corporation to seek $25 million damages for breach of contract. Federal Steel was represented by Al Julien, one of New York's outstanding tort lawyers. The case went on for five weeks before it was submitted to the jury on May 3. Meanwhile the panel hearings were already under way in Los Angeles, so Chuck had to sweat out a New York jury with $25 million at stake with his mind half absent in California. At 8:15 P.M. the jurors came back with a 5 to 1 verdict in Chuck's favor. The next morning he was on the first plane to Los Angeles to join our damage panel team.

In Chuck's absence, the brunt of the early settlement hearings had been carried by Jim Butler, aided by Jim Jefferson and Michael Dan of the Butler firm, and also by Frank Granito and Hedy Voigt of our firm. The sessions of the special master panels were held in the Los Angeles Federal Court House. No clients were present and no formal evidence was taken. The attorneys for both sides were allowed to present documents, calculations, photos, films, arguments—anything that would help the judges to decide what a jury would award. Many of the family lawyers from England, France, and Turkey participated, and they were able to convey to the panel the essence of each family relationship in a way we could never have done without them.

The results were spectacular. The special masters broke the deadlock and helped to settle the majority of the cases during 1976. Often the special masters went beyond their appraisal function and took an active part in settlement negotiations. First they would hear both sides and then confer privately among themselves. Then they would bring back the plaintiffs' and defendants' attorneys separately, telling each what they thought a jury verdict would be. Often they would use their hundreds of years of combined experience as mediators to iron out remaining differences. Some of the more difficult cases went back before the panels two or three more times until they were finally settled. Largely as a result of Judge Hall's special masters program, practically all of the DC-10 cases were settled, most by the end of 1976, and others by early 1977.

The appraisals by the special masters accomplished another purpose also. They reassured all of the foreign claimants that they were getting fair settlements under American damage standards, for they provided the claimants with the careful assessments of experienced judges to augment the recommendations of their own American and local lawyers. In a little over two years from the date of accident, the 164 families whom we represented and all the other foreign claimants received compensatory damages that were many times what they would have received under the miserly compensation systems of their own nations.

If you think it unfair for English claimants to collect more in the United States than they would in England, remember that the goal of tort litigation is deterrence as well as compensation. The American defendants, McDonnell Douglas and General Dynamics, had arranged insurance coverage for the DC-10 under American standards, since they expected to be sued in America and to have damages assessed according to American law. Judge Hall had expressly invoked California and federal law to protect them against unforeseen foreign damage provisions. Think of the windfall those manufacturers would have received if their negligence had been responsible for 346 deaths and they had been let off with ridiculously low damage payments. Think of the inequity if the families of the American passengers had been permitted to collect damages according to California standards, while others who lost their relatives in the same crash had been shortchanged. Cheap prices for the taking of human life breed complacency, if not carelessness. The substantial damages payable under California and federal law were the economic incentive that produced the *only* searching inquiry into the cause of the accident—one that kept Douglas division president Brizendine in the witness chair for seven days. That kind of accountability will cause greater care to be taken in the design and building of the DC-11 and the DC-12.

Aftermath

None of the lawyers who participated in the Ermenonville case will ever forget that experience. It put our firm in close working touch with lawyers and legal systems of 15 other nations. Conversely, it gave most of the lawyers, solicitors, and barristers with whom we collaborated in those nations their first experience of working with the American tort system. Despite their initial doubts about contingent fees, jury trials, entrepreneur-lawyers, and America's high damage awards, they performed magnificently. One might have thought that they would not take any special interest in the amount recovered, but the opposite was true. Each family lawyer was zealous in seeking fair compensation for his clients, and when the settlement offer reached a figure that we advised them to accept, the family lawyers required us to demonstrate the fairness of the offer. Many of them came over to Los Angeles for the special masters hearings and helped to present the damage phases of their own cases. It was a two-way collaboration that produced one of the finest hours of American tort law.

For our group, we prepared a monthly newsletter that was sent to the family lawyers in the United States and 15 other countries. These newsletters were translated by the local lawyers and kept their clients posted on our progress in Los Angeles. In the newsletter of March 6, 1975, we wrote:

MR. SHEERIN SERVES BEYOND THE CALL OF DUTY. In Newsletter 8, we mentioned that John D. Sheerin was of great assistance throughout the argument of the choice of law motion. However, we omitted to mention heroic action on his part above and beyond the call of duty. One evening during the argument, he volunteered to do some special research at the Los Angeles County Law Library. Upon completing this research, he was unable to locate a taxicab, and so he undertook to walk from the library back to his hotel. This walk took him through one of the worst sections of Los Angeles, which was being preyed upon by the "Los Angeles Slasher," a modern day "Jack the Ripper" who specializes in disposing of shabbily dressed derelicts. Fortunately, Mr. Sheerin was wearing one of his more fashionable outfits, and so he survived this experience intact.

The newsletter was also used for more serious matters. In July of 1975, when the defendants had reached their settlement formula and the liability phase of the case had ended, our newsletter reported that the FAA had just ordered all American manufacturers and operators of wide-bodied (jumbo) jets to modify those aircraft (all DC-10s, Boeing 747s, and Lockheed L-1011s) by adding vent systems or strengthening the cabin floor, so that they would be able to withstand depressurization from any source. The FAA estimated that refitting the jumbo jet fleets of America's airlines would cost about $60 million. It was stated in the FAA announcement that its action stemmed from the Ermenonville disaster and was designed to prevent a repetition. In the newsletter, I commented:

> This is one of the most significant directives ever issued by the FAA in terms of preventive safety regulation and financial impact on manufacturers and airlines. Since the French government has not yet issued its definitive report on the Paris DC-10 accident, and United States government personnel participated in the investigation of the Paris accident only as unofficial observers, the timing and scope of this sweeping FAA action is all the more significant.
>
> We who have participated in this litigation as plaintiffs' attorneys have a strong feeling that the litigation itself played a significant role in bringing about this pervasive FAA action. While there was a short congressional investigation, and while the FAA is charged by law with the duty of taking such action on its own, we believe that the very extensive discovery proceedings in this litigation, and public disclosure of parts thereof through the summary judgment motion, maintained and accelerated the pressure for sweeping safety directives designed to prevent future accidents.
>
> Accordingly, to those involved in this litigation as plaintiffs, it should be a source of some solace and satisfaction that their decision to pursue their legal remedies has played a part in bringing about extensive air safety revisions which may well save the lives of other passengers in the future.

I did not mean to imply that litigation is a perfect instrument of deterrence, for as in the Nader–GM case, the plaintiffs' lawyers were prevented from making all of the facts public by the defendants' decision to settle short of trial. Lawyers must remind themselves that their primary duty is to their clients, however eager they might be to plow on and force complete disclosure. Nevertheless, I believe that the example of Douglas president Brizendine testifying for seven days and yielding 1,500 pages of evidence is bound to have lasting deterrent effect. Many governmental safety inquiries are structured merely to meet the legal requirement of making a public record, and often the testimony of airline and manufacturer witnesses is sketched out in prehearing conferences with government officials. Most witnesses read a statement prepared by the company's lawyers into the record, and the follow-up questioning is usually routine and devoid of surprise and embarrassment. It is the penetrating searchlight of civil lawsuit discovery that is feared by aviation accident witnesses, especially by witnesses at the highest level of corporate responsibility who are instrumental in making future safety policy.

Much credit for the pressure that brought about the FAA floor directive and sweeping changes in the system of issuing Airworthiness Directives (including banning of gentlemen's agreements) must go to the journalists who chronicled the Ermenonville crash and the resulting litigation. There was major coverage by the *Los Angeles Times,* the *Wall Street Journal,* the *New York Times,* the *Sunday Times* of London, and the British Broadcasting Corporation. The Insight Team of the London *Sunday Times,* headed by Paul Eddy, Elaine Potter, and Bruce Page, authored *Destination Disaster,* a penetrating, full-length book on the Ermenonville disaster that includes a concise history of air transport design and manufacture. It provides some of the answers to the riddle of the DC-10, whose troubles, unfortunately, were not to end with the strengthening of its floors.

Although most of the steps in the Ermenonville litigation were based on building blocks that had been formed during the preceding quarter century of pioneering air crash litigation, this was the first time that all the blocks had been put together. There had been foreign passengers aboard American flights whose families had sued in American courts, but nothing like this situation in which more than 300 families from 23 foreign nations had used the American courts to achieve justice. It was a products liability case that epitomized the ongoing products liability revolution and put it on a worldwide stage for the first time. It presented conflict of laws problems that would delight the meanest professors teaching that inscrutable subject. And it was fittingly presided over by *the* aviation judge, Peirson M. Hall—his last great case.

Judge Hall wrote a special report to the Judicial Panel on Multidistrict Litigation on April 28, 1978, summing up his work on MDL-172, the Ermenonville case. His report contained some interesting statistics. There were suits filed by a total of 1,123 claimants on behalf of 340 of the 346 occupants of the DC-10. The total amount paid in settlement of passenger deaths was $62,268,750, the largest amount paid in such litigation up to that time. Judge Hall added a commendation for the plaintiffs' lawyers committee "for doing the prodigious job of discovery which generated the settlements paid." He noted that plaintiffs' lawyers had advanced expenses of more than $2.25 million for their clients, and that the economies of scale resulting from the concentration of cases in the hands of experienced lawyers had saved the passengers' families about $10 million in legal fees. He also paid special tribute to his efficient and courteous clerk, Mrs. Thelma Alden, who had worked with him through what was probably the largest pile of papers ever to confront any judge in a tort case.

The $62 million total settlement figure in Judge Hall's MDL report produced a shiver of recognition in me. It was almost the same figure that the FAA had given as the cost of modifying *every* jumbo jet (the 747s and the 1011s as well as the DC-10s) so as to prevent catastrophic floor failure from any cause (not just cargo door problems, but sabotage, collision, etc.). The $60 million cost of making all jumbo jet floors safe would be shared by the entire industry; McDonnell Douglas's share (assuming that *they* paid the bill rather than their airline customers) would be only about one third, or $20 million. It was known and publicized after Bryce McCormick's Windsor blowout that the floors needed strengthening; indeed, the NTSB had recommended such modifications then, in 1972. And the Applegate memorandum brought that awareness right to the DC-10 designers—they knew the chances and the costs of catastrophic floor failure. Surely, that simple arithmetic was within the grasp of the FAA and the manufacturers: $60 million to correct a basic, industry-wide design flaw of jumbo jets, against $62 million just for passenger compensation (plus $35 million for hull compensation, and millions more for legal fees and litigation costs) for one highly predictable catastrophic floor failure. Why didn't these great corporations do that arithmetic? And why didn't the FAA order them to make the floor modification in 1972?

Remember that we are dealing with people who are highly motivated to produce a safe airplane. Their marketplace will quickly react to known dangers, as happened during the later DC-10 engine pylon troubles in 1979. And their own training and ideals would seem to rule out any laxity when it comes to safety. But as we saw in Eddie Rickenbacker's Comet story, the Ford Pinto fiasco, and John De-Lorean's insights (Chapter 5), these forces seem to be powerless to bring about admission and correction of an initial error, especially when it involves a shortcut that was taken collectively to increase sales.

I believe that many highly motivated aviation executives have a strong feeling of team loyalty. Often it starts with Little League Baseball or Pee Wee Football and grows even stronger in high school, college, military service, and at the decision tables of the business world. It has some good points—it teaches cooperation, unselfishness, consideration for (some) others—but it is limited to concern for those on the same team. It tends to cloud personal identity and weaken individual responsibility. It provides a handy excuse for team actions that many would hesitate to take on their own. The worst offense is to "let the side down," and the hardest task is to admit that you were the one responsible. So, if you goof in the original design of a cargo door locking system, there is a strong impetus to sweep it under the rug and hope that like thousands of other human errors, it will never be discovered.

Team loyalty is one of the most powerful forces in American business, and the higher up you go in corporate management, the stronger it gets. As the Insight Team of the Sunday *London Times* wrote in *Destination Disaster,* their book on the Ermenonville DC-10:

> Corporations, especially the large and complex ones with which we have to live, now appear to possess some of the qualities of nation states, including, perhaps, an alarming capacity to insulate their members from the moral consequences of their actions.

The Ermenonville DC-10 case is a graphic illustration of the need for the deterrent of civil litigation to break through that corporate insulation and establish the degree of personal responsibility that is required for aviation safety.

I could not help asking myself an ugly question: what if Bryce McCormick had crashed at Windsor in 1972? Clearly, the deaths of 56 American passengers would have triggered enough litigation to force disclosure of the whole cargo door story. All jumbo jet floors would have been modified, and the FAA would have *ordered* the DC-10 cargo door locking system changed in 1972. As it was, the lack of litigation arising out of Windsor enabled the industry to bury its mistakes quietly. Eventually the industry paid out more than $100 million for passenger and hull claims, and it also suffered from bad public relations and probably lost some airplane sales. This highly motivated and public spirited industry killed 346 people. By any standard of morality, cost-benefit analysis, or government safety regulation, those 346 people should not have died. They died because none of these forces worked as they were supposed to.

Judge Peirson Hall finally succumbed to cancer on December 8, 1979, at the age of 85. There are 1,123 bereaved persons in 24 nations who owe a great debt to this extraordinary man for shaping an unmanageable case into a triumph of justice by the force of his will and intellect.

The Ermenonville case was to have far-reaching effects on tort litigation and on our law firm. The associations that we formed with lawyers in other nations put us formally into international practice, and we established our own office in London with Hedy Voigt in residence. She had done much of the work of collecting and editing damage information from the English families and their solicitors, and had used her language abilities to work with our legal colleagues in France and other European nations.

I have outlined the principal events of the Ermenonville case as seen from the vantage point of our firm. The litigation involved tens of thousands of hours of lawyers' time, so I could not possibly cover the entire case in one chapter. Indeed, it would take a good-sized book to describe the accomplishments of all the lawyers who worked on the case. I have concentrated on the principal steps that our firm partici-pated in, such as the Mayfair meetings with the English solicitors that helped to convince the foreign claimants to sue in California; the *forum non conveniens* victory in the suit involving the death of the prominent English journalist; the liability discovery and summary judgment motion; the choice of law motion; the damage hearings; and the settlements. We were not alone in any of these steps. There were dozens of lawyers from other firms who participated in these events, and many of them made very significant contributions. There were other important events that I do not have the space to discuss. There is enough glory to be shared by all of the lawyers who worked on this case, which brought the benefits of American justice to the far corners of the earth, and did so at low cost and without cash outlay for people who could never have mounted such an effort in their own courts.

The effects of the Ermenonville case are still being felt. Thanks to extensive press coverage led by the London *Sunday Times,* judges, law-yers, and claimants all over the world have come to realize that it is possible to maintain a legal system which allocates the full cost of acci-dent compensation to the responsible parties, rather than forcing the innocent victims to carry the financial burden on top of their irre-placeable physical and emotional losses. From our new vantage point in London, we have observed a sharp rise in the level of accident com-pensation in England and on the Continent since 1975. There has been a visible closing of the gap between American levels of compensation and those of the other industrialized nations, although there is still a long way to go. We shall see some of the effects of Ermenonville in Chapter 8, when we take up the story of the 1977 Tenerife disaster— the crash that pushed Ermenonville into second place on the list of the world's worst aviation catastrophes.

THE 1973 VARIG PARIS CRASH

On July 11, 1973, a Boeing 707 operated by Varig Airlines of Brazil was nearing Orly Airport at Paris on a nonstop flight from Rio de Janeiro, when a small fire broke out in one of the rear passenger lavatories. The fire caused the lavatory's plastic wall coverings and other materials to smoulder and smoke, circulating the combustion product of the acrylic hydrocarbon material throughout the airplane. The smoke contained a poison gas composed of carbon monoxide and cyanide. Captain Gilberto Araujo da Silva and First Officer Antonio Fuzimoto put on their oxygen masks and made a successful emergency landing in a farm field short of the airport—a considerable feat in a large jet. But when they opened the cabin door to give their passengers the good news and start the evacuation, they found to their horror that all the passengers were sitting lifeless in their seats, fatally overcome by poisonous fumes. The pilots had not lowered the passengers' oxygen masks because this would have caused an immediate flow of oxygen in the cabin area, and might have fed the combustion. The pilots' own masks were of the demand type which does not feed oxygen until the wearer inhales. Thus the pilots were able to use their masks but they had to deny their passengers the lifesaving flow of oxygen.

The Boeing 707 had a cabin venting system designed to eliminate smoke and poisonous fume problems, but it was inadequate to remove the deadly vapors that overcame the Varig passengers on this flight. The Varig accident was little noticed in the United States, since there were no Americans aboard. The deceased passengers had been citizens of 14 nations, the largest groups coming from Brazil and France. Among the passengers were a famous international singer, an Indian ambassador, a former Brazilian cabinet member, and many prominent business executives. Their rights to sue Varig were limited by the Warsaw Convention. Because of the treaty limitations, the only hope the passengers' families had of recovering anything more than $20,000 in damages (the 1973 Warsaw limit) was a suit against the airplane manufacturer (Boeing) and those who manufactured the cabin fabrics and materials that turned the plane into a "gas chamber," to use the words of the Paris press. But such products liability suits were practical only in the United States, not in the domiciles of the passengers, as we saw in the Ermenonville story.

Fortunately, one of the French passengers had an American relative who got in touch with the law firm of Smiley & Lear in Washington, D.C. Bob Smiley and Jerry Lear had been government attorneys in the U.S. Department of Justice Aviation Litigation Unit before leaving to form their own firm. When the French passenger's relative contacted them in 1974, there was no precedent for suits brought in the U.S. by foreign passengers' families against American manufacturers. The task of pioneering such suits was a large order for a newly formed two-man law firm. They knew that we were in the process of dealing with the same problem in the Ermenonville litigation, and they decided to call us in. Thus, the firms of Smiley & Lear and Speiser Krause & Madole became cocounsel for the American relative of the deceased French passenger.

Although the Varig 707 crash preceded the Turkish Airlines DC-10 crash by almost eight months, it became the second products liability case involving a large group of foreign passengers suing American manufacturers in the United States. When Judge Peirson Hall ruled in our favor on the *forum non conveniens* motion in the Ermenonville case, it cleared the way for the Varig families to file similar suits in the United States. Up to that point, the local lawyers for the Varig families had questioned whether they could successfully maintain such actions, but Judge Hall's decision convinced them. So it was that our firm, along with Smiley & Lear, came to represent (through their lawyers) the families of 62 foreign passengers killed in the Varig Paris crash—all of those who sued in the United States.

Here we had a diversity of citizenship between the plaintiffs and the American manufacturers, and we also had to sue a Brazilian corporation, Varig Airlines. This destroyed federal diversity jurisdiction, since any case involving aliens as both plaintiffs and defendants falls outside the federal statute permitting diversity suits in the federal courts. Therefore we had to file the 62 cases in a New York state court—the Supreme Court for New York County, which you will remember from Chapter 1.

Our inability to file in the federal courts was a drawback, because at that time the New York state courts did not have any procedure for assigning the entire litigation to a single judge. Federal district courts assign all cases to a single judge at the outset, and under the MDL procedures, mass disaster cases are given special handling. But in New York County, we faced the prospect of the same sort of ping-pong litigation that we had gone through in the Ralph Nader case, where motion after motion was submitted to different judges, and interlocutory appeals were taken from the rulings of various judges. It had been tough enough to handle a single case in that way. Here we represented 62 families, and there were 8 defendants, since we were suing Varig, Boeing, and the various manufacturers whose fabrics and materials had produced the poisonous fumes.

We decided that it was time to ask the state court to use the streamlined procedures of the federal courts for handling mass disaster litigation. We made an application to New York Supreme Court Justice Edward R. Dudley, the Administrative Judge for the Civil Branch of the First Judicial District, which covers the area of New York City in which most of the world's airlines have their offices. Justice Dudley decided to recognize the Varig litigation as a "complex case" and give it special treatment. He assigned the entire litigation to a single judge, Justice Arnold Fraiman.

From that point on, the Varig litigation was processed much as it would have been under the federal MDL rules. As a result, it fell into the pattern of most of the airline MDL cases of the 1970s: extensive discovery leading to the adoption of a settlement formula among several defendants. Most of the cases were settled within two years from the time the first suit was filed, and eventually all of them were settled for amounts considered fair by American standards, yet far higher than any compensation attainable in European or South American courts.

Once again we had the privilege of a rewarding collaboration with foreign lawyers. Our old friend Maître Jean-Marc Gernigon of the Paris bar, who represented most of the French claimants in the Ermenonville DC-10 litigation, acted for French and European families in the Varig case. Chuck Krause and Bob Smiley flew to Brazil to arrange collaboration with Dr. J. H. Pinheiro Neto, whose São Paulo and Rio de Janeiro firm, Pinheir Neto & Cia., is one of the largest and most prestigious in Latin America. We also worked with family lawyers in Argentina, Austria, Chile, Great Britain, Hungary, India, Italy, The Netherlands, Switzerland, West Germany, and Uruguay.

The Varig case was an important one from the standpoint of air safety, and the investigation of this accident resulted in very intensive study of the materials used in passenger cabins. The FAA adopted stricter standards, so that there is now less danger of turning the passenger cabin into a gas chamber. The "NO SMOKING" signs you now see in the lavatories of all airliners were put there because of what was learned from the 1973 Varig incident. There still are some improvements to be made in passenger oxygen equipment and cabin venting systems, but I doubt that we will see a repetition of the Varig gas chamber disaster.

The availability of American courts to foreign claimants is not merely a matter of interest to the bereaved families of passengers. No Americans were aboard the Varig Boeing 707 gas chamber flight, but millions of Americans fly other Boeing 707s every year. Since most of the world's airlines fly American equipment and Americans are the largest passenger group in the world, we have a strong interest in learning the causes of all airline disasters. Very often, American litigation is a vital factor in forcing public disclosure of the causes of foreign accidents, because foreign aviation officials are notoriously secretive about their investigative data, and the U.S. government cannot force disclosure even when American passengers or equipment are involved. Often the discovery procedures of American courts are the *only* means of bringing these facts to light, as we saw in the Ermenonville DC-10 story. I have no doubt that the American litigation arising out of the Paris Varig crash helped to force disclosure and removal of the serious fire hazards involved.

McCUSKER
v. ONASSIS

On Sunday evening, January 21, 1973, Alexander Onassis spoke on the telephone from Athens to his girl friend, Fiona Thyssen, who was in London. They made a date for him to meet Fiona in London the next evening. But before flying from Athens to London, Alexander had an important job to finish for his father, shipping tycoon Aristotle Socrates Onassis. Aristotle was about to leave on a cruise aboard his yacht *Christina* from Greece to the Caribbean, and he wanted to have his Piaggio amphibian airplane on board. Aristotle used the twin-engine Piaggio for personal transportation to and from his island of Scorpios, and he also carried it aboard his yacht. When the yacht was anchored at sea and Aristotle wanted to reach shore quickly, he would simply have the yacht crew lower his Piaggio into the water, and then his personal pilot would fly him to his destination.

The regular pilot of the Piaggio was Donald McGregor, a veteran airman who had been a Boeing 707 captain for BOAC and Olympic Airways. He had been selected for the job of Aristotle Onassis's personal Piaggio pilot because he had long experience with flying boats, going back to the days of Imperial Airways' seaplane operations in the 1930s. But a few weeks before the *Christina's* departure for the Caribbean, Captain McGregor developed eye trouble and was temporarily grounded. It became the duty of Alexander Onassis to find a replacement quickly.

Alexander, a pilot himself, was the head man of Olympic Aviation, a subsidiary of Olympic Airways that operated a fleet of small aircraft like the Piaggio, carrying two to five passengers in an air taxi and charter service to the smaller Greek Islands. There were other Piaggio pilots in the ranks of Olympic Aviation besides McGregor, but none of them was anxious to become Aristotle Onassis's personal pilot. They knew that it was hectic duty to remain at the beck and call of Aristotle, who might order them to fly in any kind of weather, and they wanted no part of the job. Alexander was forced to go outside of the company for a replacement Piaggio pilot.

In 1973, Alexander was 25 years old, and his girl friend, the Baroness Thyssen-Bornemisza, was 41—nearly old enough to be his mother. She was the daughter of a British admiral and had been an internationally famous fashion model under the name of Fiona Campbell. In 1955, she married Baron Thyssen and divorced him nine years later. She met Alexander in 1967, when he was only 19, and for the next five years they shared a very close relationship.

Alexander was very much under the thumb of his iron-handed father. Fiona tried to help Alexander to develop his own personality and to assert some independence. Although he worked in his father's business enterprises, he had no salary—only an allowance. Thus he was completely dependent upon Aristotle, who also managed to crush his son emotionally, although apparently this was the father's method of preparing Alexander to take over the vast Onassis business empire. Despite the great wealth that he was born to, Alexander was very insecure. He had never finished his college education, and his father would not let him do anything which would give him any financial or emotional independence. The Insight Team of the London *Sunday Times,* in their excellent 1977 biography *Aristotle Onassis,* explained Aristotle's attitude toward his son:

> The most important human being in the world for Onassis was his only son, Alexander. For a Greek, any Greek, a son is a significant portion of himself. The fishing boat is built, the house is bought, the vines are sown, not just for the immediate needs of the family but for the future of the son. The son is his guarantee of immortality. For Onassis, with so much to bequeath and with an ego so overpowering, his son represented his own imperishable destiny.
>
> The irony was that everything Onassis did to Alexander was done with a view to grooming him for the succession, and that most things he did were counterproductive. His egocentricity made it impossible for his thinking on the subject to moderate a simple belief that the best person to inherit the empire of Onassis was Onassis. What he wanted of Alexander was for Alexander to be like him. It solved every conceivable problem.

By the early part of January 1973, Fiona and Alexander had worked out a plan to gain his independence from Aristotle. They would get together at her home in Switzerland, and with her own considerable financial means, she would help him to get private tutoring which would bring him university qualifications. Then he would have something to fall back on if he had to make a final break with his father.

With the encouragement of Fiona, Alexander became increasingly bold with his father. He was a very careful pilot and was quite concerned about the safety of the Piaggio operation. He had tried for a long time to convince Aristotle to replace the amphibian with a helicopter, which would have been much safer for landing on the *Christina* and making the short hops to the islands. Finally, at a meeting with Alexander in Paris on January 4, 1973, Aristotle agreed to have the Piaggio replaced. But they did not have time to make the change to a helicopter before the Caribbean cruise, and so the Piaggio had to be used one last time.

Alexander's Last Flight

Finding no replacement Piaggio pilot in Greece, Alexander decided to advertise for one in *Trade-A-Plane,* an American publication read by many commercial pilots. The advertisement was answered by Donald McCusker, a World War II Navy pilot and a former test pilot for North American Rockwell and other major American manufacturers. McCusker was at liberty due to the cancellation of defense contracts under which he had served as a test pilot. He had considerable flying time in amphibians and seemed to be the sort of pilot that was needed for the Piaggio. Alexander arranged his passage on Olympic Airways to Athens, where he would be checked out on the Piaggio and would be hired as Aristotle's pilot if he proved satisfactory.

Donald McCusker sat up all night on the Olympic flight from New York, arriving at Athens International Airport on Monday morning, January 22, 1973. He did not expect to get his check ride that day, but Alexander was under pressure from Aristotle to sign up the new Piaggio pilot. Alexander was also eager to get away to Fiona in London, which he could not do until the Piaggio and its pilot were ready to join the *Christina.* Since Captain McGregor had eye trouble, he could not check out McCusker in the Piaggio. Alexander had to do it himself, and he insisted that the check flight take place that afternoon, even though McCusker would not have a chance to get any sleep.

The Piaggio had been undergoing an overhaul and had not been flown since November of 1972. Before its certificate of airworthiness could be renewed by the Greek civil aviation authority, it had to undergo a maintenance test flight. Again, McGregor could not perform the flight, and so Alexander, under time pressure from his father, decided to combine the maintenance test flight with the orientation of McCusker.

McCusker reported to Olympic Aviation and was told to stand by to meet Alexander that afternoon. He and Captain McGregor spent much of the day sitting around the coffee shop at Athens International Airport, waiting for Alexander to show up. Finally Alexander appeared at about three in the afternoon and informed both pilots that they were to proceed immediately to the flight line and board the Piaggio with him.

Because Alexander was not fully qualified as a check pilot and instructor, a subterfuge was used to make the flight legal. Since Alexander was licensed to carry passengers, both McGregor and McCusker were listed as passengers and were issued tickets for the flight, even though McCusker was to sit in the left seat normally occupied by the captain and was to be instructed in the operation of the Piaggio by Alexander. McCusker had never flown a Piaggio before, although he had considerable flying experience in similar light twin-engine amphibians, and the Piaggio was much simpler than the larger and faster planes which he had been flying in recent years. McGregor would sit in the back seat during the orientation flight, and Alexander would talk McCusker through a few takeoffs and landings to make sure that he was competent to fly the Piaggio. They planned to take off from Athens International Airport, do some water landings and takeoffs at the nearby islands of Aegina and Poros, and return to the Olympic Aviation base at Athens International Airport. Then, when they all felt that McCusker was sufficiently familiar with the Piaggio, Alexander would take the late afternoon airline flight to London and would leave the rest of McCusker's orientation to Captain McGregor.

When the three pilots got to the Piaggio, they discovered that there was no preflight checklist aboard the airplane. Because Alexander had such a short time to complete the flight before boarding the airliner for London, he decided to go ahead without using a written checklist. The three pilots climbed aboard. Alexander sat in the right seat, normal for an instructor, and McCusker took the left seat as a student pilot, with Captain McGregor in the back seat as a passenger-observer. Alexander went through his mental version of the preflight checklist, explaining the various steps to McCusker as he went along.

The engines were started and McCusker taxied the Piaggio up to the takeoff runway, under instruction from Alexander. When they received their takeoff clearance from the tower, McCusker taxied the Piaggio on to the runway, lined up for takeoff, and opened the throttles. When the aircraft reached the takeoff speed of about 100 miles per hour, he eased the stick back and the airplane left the ground normally. But almost immediately after takeoff, within seconds of its wheels leaving the runway, the plane banked sharply to the right. Its right wing-tip float (which balances the airplane on water) struck the ground to the right of the runway. The plane then cartwheeled in a circle for more than 400 feet, smashing its nose, its tail, and both its wings before coming to rest to the right of the takeoff runway.

The emergency rescue equipment of Athens International Airport sped to the scene of the crash. Fortunately there was no fire and they were able to pull the three pilots from the wreckage. All of them were unconscious and bleeding badly. They were rushed to a hospital, where it was determined that McGregor and McCusker had been relatively lucky and would survive without serious permanent injuries. But Alexander was not so fortunate. Sitting on the right side at the point of the most severe impact with the ground, he had suffered crushing head injuries. Before they got him to the hospital it was clear that he had suffered extensive brain damage and that there was little hope for recovery. He underwent a three hour operation to remove blood clots and relieve the pressure on his brain, after which he was placed in an oxygen tent and kept alive through the night.

At the time of the accident, Jacqueline and Aristotle Onassis were in the United States, and Alexander's sister Christina was in Brazil. Aristotle and his wife flew to Athens immediately, bringing along a Boston neurosurgeon and a Texas heart specialist. But by the early afternoon of January 23, the day after the accident, all the doctors agreed that there was no hope. They kept Alexander alive until early that evening when his sister Christina arrived from Brazil. He died at 6:55 P.M.

Aristotle Onassis was at once inconsolable in his grief and irrational with rage. At first he refused to bury his son. When Aristotle's family and friends prevailed upon him to allow Alexander to be buried, he wanted the body to be deep frozen, on the chance that some day a brain surgeon would be able to restore Alexander to life. Finally Aristotle consented that his son be buried, but only if the casket was placed inside the chapel on the Island of Scorpios. When Aristotle was told that the Greek church would not allow this because it was only done in the case of saints, he finally agreed to have Alexander buried next to the chapel. Later an annex was built to cover the grave, so that in the mind of Aristotle, his son was actually buried inside the chapel, in the manner of the saints.

The Greek Investigation

Aristotle Onassis was convinced that the Piaggio had crashed because of sabotage, and he thought that the saboteurs had meant to kill him rather than his son, because he was the most frequent user of the plane. In his blind rage he blamed everyone from the CIA to his business rivals for the sabotage of the plane and the death of his son. He publicly offered a million-dollar reward to anyone who could produce proof of sabotage.

At the time of the accident, Aristotle Onassis owned all of the shares of Olympic Airways. It was the time of the dictatorship of the colonels in Greece, and Aristotle could have his way with the Greek government. In Greece, as in many nations other than the United States, major aircraft accident investigations are conducted through the courts. The Greek courts appointed an investigating team to determine the cause of the crash and to probe for evidence of the criminal activity that Aristotle continued to allege. Most of the members of the investigating team were Air Force officers. The Greek Air Force was the main source of aviation expertise apart from Olympic Airways, which could not very well participate, since the equipment and personnel of its own subsidiary were involved.

The investigators' report was delivered on April 20, 1973, but it was not published. However, they were said to have reached the conclusion that the cause of the accident was a reversal of the aileron controls, so that when the pilot turned his control wheel to the left, which would normally make the plane turn to the left, it caused the plane instead to turn to the right, just the opposite of what the pilot would expect. The investigators had determined that when the Piaggio was in for overhaul between November 15, 1972, and January 22, 1973, the aileron controls had been rerigged. On November 15, 1972, an Olympic mechanic had removed the control column, which was normal in this type of overhaul. It was replaced by a new control column, which had been installed by a different mechanic on November 25. On January 8, 1973 (four days before the crash), the Greek civil aviation authority had examined the airplane along with Olympic inspectors, and had granted it a certificate of airworthiness, subject to a maintenance test flight, which was normally required before the certificate became effective. But when the Greek Air Force investigators examined the control column, the aileron controls, and the cables after the accident, it was obvious that they had been installed improperly.

Meanwhile, Donald McCusker was in a Greek hospital recovering from his injuries, which consisted of a severe cerebral concussion; fractures of the jaw, hip, and three ribs; and compression fractures of two lumbar vertebrae. He was not able to help the investigators because he had suffered partial amnesia as a result of his injuries and remembered nothing from the time of the takeoff until after he awoke in the hospital later that afternoon. Captain McGregor, in the back seat, had not been able to observe what had happened in the few seconds the flight lasted. But once it was known that the aileron controls were reversed, it was possible to reconstruct the sequence of events.

There had been a slight crosswind coming from the left, which would cause the airplane to drift off to the right of the runway unless corrected by the pilot. A pilot with McCusker's experience, knowing the wind direction and seeing this drift, would automatically turn the plane slightly to the left to keep it lined up with the runway. With the controls reversed, this would cause the plane to turn even further to the right instead of correcting back to the left. Seeing the plane drift off more sharply to the right, the reaction of any experienced pilot would be to turn the controls even more sharply to the left. This further turn of the wheel to the left would cause the plane to veer so sharply to the right that, at slow air speed and low altitude, the right wing would dig into the ground and the crash sequence would follow exactly as it did. It was therefore clear to the aviation experts of the Greek Air Force and of Olympic Airways that the accident was caused by the mechanic's reversal of the aileron controls. Ordinarily, the case would have been closed at this point. But none of this satisfied Aristotle Onassis, still blinded by fury and determined to avenge the death of his son.

The investigators' report was especially hard for Aristotle to accept because it placed the blame on Olympic Airways, his own company, which had performed the faulty overhaul of the Piaggio. It also placed some of the blame on Alexander for failing to check the working of the aileron controls during performance of the preflight checklist. Perhaps Aristotle secretly blamed himself, knowing that his constant pressure on Alexander had forced him to compromise safety by conducting a combined maintenance test flight and new pilot orientation without the help of the checklist that might have saved his life. Indeed, Aristotle must have remembered that his son was wary of the Piaggio and had convinced his father to replace it with a helicopter only a few weeks before the fatal flight. But Aristotle persisted in his attempts to blame others, and he stuck arrogantly to his charges of sabotage.

Aristotle's sabotage theory with himself as the intended victim made no sense to his colleagues at Olympic Airways. They knew that the rigging of the aileron controls would have to be checked during a maintenance test flight before the certificate of airworthiness became effective. Therefore, Aristotle himself could not possibly have been aboard the plane when the crossing of the aileron controls would cause it to crash. It would kill only the test pilot and anyone who happened to be aboard with him during the test flight. It was also highly unlikely that Alexander Onassis would conduct the maintenance test flight, since he was not in the habit of doing so, and it was not known at the time the aileron cables were changed that Captain Donald McGregor, who normally did the test flights, would be disabled. Therefore, this would have been a very far-fetched method of trying to dispose of either Alexander or Aristotle Onassis.

Furthermore, the workings of ailerons are such that it is relatively easy to make this kind of mistake. One would expect that the movement of the ailerons would follow the control wheel; that is, if you turn the control wheel to the left, you would expect the left *aileron* to go down, because turning the wheel to the left makes the left *wing*

go down. But ailerons are so designed that they work in the opposite
direction. When you turn the wheel to the left to make the left wing
go down, the left aileron actually goes *up*. This is something of a trap
for mechanics who are inexperienced or inattentive to the job. It is one
of the major reasons why test flights are required after the rerigging
of controls, and why the preflight checklist should include a visual
check of the ailerons to make sure that they move in the proper direction.

Aristotle would hear none of these logical explanations. He managed to have Donald McCusker and three Olympic mechanics charged
with killing his son, and they were indicted for manslaughter. McCusker
was then flat on his back in a Greek hospital, leveled by hepatitis that
had set in during his post-accident treatment. As a result of answering
Alexander's ad and following his orders, he now found himself in a
foreign country run by a military dictatorship, under indictment for
killing the son of its wealthiest and most influential citizen, his passport
confiscated by the government, facing six months of slow recuperation
from hepatitis. He was too weak to do anything about defending himself against the criminal charges. But there was little that he could do
anyway, for although he was certain that he had not been at fault in
the accident, he could not remember anything about it, nor was he
told about the misrigged aileron controls found by the Greek Air Force
investigators.

The management of Olympic Airways persisted in their attempts
to talk Aristotle out of his mindless quest for revenge. They finally persuaded him to permit them to call in an impartial foreign expert who
would make a fresh investigation of the accident. With Aristotle's
grudging consent, Olympic hired Alan Hunter, a British aeronautical
engineer and aviation safety expert. Hunter's report, which was prepared confidentially for Olympic Airways, agreed with the findings of
the Greek Air Force investigators. The aileron controls had indeed
been reversed, and there was incontrovertible evidence of this fact.
There were marks on the leading edge of the right aileron which had
been made when it contacted the ground. These marks could only
have been made if the right aileron had been *up* at the moment of impact. It would have been in the *down* position if the controls had been
rigged properly.

Hunter delivered his report on July 6, 1973. It was not enough to
clear Donald McCusker's name because it was never made public (nor
was the report of the Greek Air Force investigators). However, through
the intercession of the American ambassador to Greece, McCusker was
given back his passport, and he was allowed to leave Greece and return
to the United States in July of 1973. But he was still under indictment
for manslaughter, as were the mechanics who had worked on the
overhaul of the Piaggio.

When McCusker left Greece, he was still weak from the aftereffects of hepatitis, although he was making a good recovery from the injuries he received in the crash. His career as a pilot, which had started auspiciously with his fine record during World War II and his services as a test pilot (including the testing of the Gemini space capsule), was now in ruins. He was known throughout the world as the pilot who had been at the controls of the airplane that killed the son of Aristotle Onassis and was still under indictment for manslaughter. He tried to take up his life again in Ohio with his wife and seven children, but there was little prospect that he would ever get another good job as a commercial pilot, the only profession he knew. He and his wife used up much of their savings before he was finally able to get a job in South Dakota, flying a 40-year-old World War II surplus Beechcraft in aerial mapping work, at a salary lower than that of a truck driver.

Negotiations in Greece

Before he left Greece, McCusker had retained a Greek lawyer to negotiate compensation from Olympic Airways for damages that he had suffered in the accident. Despite the irrational charges of Aristotle Onassis, McCusker was officially listed and ticketed as a passenger on the flight, and since the two investigation reports blamed the accident on control reversal rather than pilot error, he felt that he was entitled to some compensation for his injuries. The legal advisers of Olympic Airways agreed with McCusker, and they drew up a proposed settlement which was presented to Aristotle Onassis. The same type of agreement was drawn up for Captain McGregor, who had recovered from his injuries and retired from flying, and had returned to his home in England. Aristotle Onassis approved the settlement of McGregor's claim, since McGregor had been sitting in the back seat and could not have played any part in causing the accident. But he absolutely refused to let Olympic Airways make any payment to McCusker, even though Olympic Airways' own legal department pointed out that the two investigations had failed to turn up any evidence of sabotage or fault on the part of McCusker. Aristotle could not bring himself to close out the last avenue of revenge and expiation of his own guilt by paying money to the pilot who had been at the controls when his son was killed.

Donald McCusker and his wife Helena were to endure their nightmare for another five years. They kept corresponding with their Greek lawyer, who continued his efforts to obtain compensation, but Aristotle was adamant even though he had lost all interest in Olympic Airways after the death of his son. He refused to go to the airport or the airline's offices. Finally he sold his controlling stock interest in Olympic Airways to the Greek government in January of 1975. But McCusker remained under indictment, and his continued efforts to obtain compensation fell on deaf ears.

Donald McCusker struggled to rebuild his life in the United States, with the Greek indictment still hanging over his head. In Greece, the case was called for trial periodically, but every time it came up, it was put over to a later date. There was no evidence to support the indictment, but those behind it would not allow it to be dismissed.

After the death of Aristotle Onassis on March 15, 1975, Donald McCusker's hopes rose. He felt that he would soon be cleared and that at last he would be able to collect some compensation for his injuries and loss of earnings. But the criminal case dragged on, and it was not until November 8, 1977 that the Greek court finally dropped the manslaughter indictment against him. Even then his name was not fully cleared, because they merely dismissed the indictment for lack of proof. He remained at his low-paying job, flying the old Beechcraft in South Dakota, and renewed his request for compensation from Olympic Airways. McCusker is not an opportunist, and his request for compensation was modest, even by Greek standards. He had submitted an itemized list of his out-of-pocket expenses and actual financial losses that totalled $65,000; but he could get no definitive reply to his request for that sum, even after Aristotle's death. Finally in 1978, nearly three years after Aristotle's death and five years after the fatal Piaggio crash, Olympic Airways authorized an American lawyer to negotiate a settlement with McCusker. The lawyer was to examine McCusker's itemized request for $65,000 and advise Olympic whether they should pay that amount.

A New York Lawsuit

In April of 1978, Donald McCusker telephoned me from South Dakota and told me his story. He thought he might soon receive a firm offer from Olympic to settle his claim for $65,000, and he asked whether I thought he should settle for that amount. I told him that I would have to do some research, but if we could bring an action for him in New York (or any other place in the United States), he would be foolish to settle for $65,000, since his claim would probably produce a lot more than that in court. He was not eager to sue, but after enduring five years of bullying he was fed up, and his wife had urged him to seek a lawyer's advice. I suggested that he and his wife come to New York, where we could review all the facts and give him an idea of what we might accomplish through a lawsuit. In the meantime I started reading cases involving torts that I hadn't seen much of since law school: malicious prosecution and false imprisonment.

The big problem in the case was the statute of limitations, for the main damage had occurred five years earlier, and the New York limitation for negligence actions was three years. It was even shorter for some of the other torts involved, such as defamation. We had two ideas for tolling (extending) the statute of limitations. Settlement negotiations will sometimes extend the limitation period, but all that we had to support this extension were copies of McCusker's own letters seeking compensation, for Olympic had never put any offer in writing. Another means of extending the time was to search for a cause of action in admiralty, which has no definite statute of limitations but uses "laches," which permits suits to be brought within a time that is reasonable under the circumstances. Since the flight on which McCusker was injured was scheduled to make takeoffs and landings in the Aegean Sea, we could hang our hats on that slim peg to allege a cause of action in admiralty.

We felt that New York was the best place to file suit, since Olympic Airways had its American headquarters in the Olympic Airways Building on Fifth Avneue. Our claim against Olympic was for the injuries that McCusker suffered as a passenger and/or student pilot. He did not have a copy of his ticket, but we knew that it would contain some limitation of liability, under either the Warsaw Convention or local Greek law. To make all of our charges stick, we needed another defendant in addition to Olympic: the estate of Aristotle Onassis. We were convinced that he had been mainly responsible for the malicious prosecution, false imprisonment, defamation, and intentional infliction of emotional harm that we would allege in the complaint.

Suing the estate of Aristotle Onassis was a tricky business because technically no such estate existed in New York. While he controlled considerable property in New York at the time of his death, officially he was a citizen of Argentina. No administrator or executor had been appointed in New York, and somehow all of his property had been passed on to his beneficiaries without using the New York courts. However, there is a procedure under New York law through which you can have an administrator appointed for the estate of a deceased person that you wish to sue, even if that person's heirs have taken no steps to administer his estate. You can bring his estate to life legally by having the court appoint an administrator, provided the deceased left property in the county where you are seeking the appointment. Therefore, at the time that we started the McCusker suit in June of 1978, we also filed a petition in the Surrogate's Court for the

County of New York, asking that the Public Administrator be appointed as administrator of the estate of Aristotle Onassis.

Normally the Public Administrator is concerned with the estates of less affluent people. In fact, many of the estates that come across his desk are those of poor people who did not leave enough property to warrant expenditures by the surviving relatives for administration through the regular court procedures. But this time we were handing him the estate of one of the wealthiest and most conspicuous financiers in the world. Our petition for the appointment of the Public Administrator had to be served upon the two people who would have the right to act as administrators themselves: Jacqueline Kennedy Onassis, the widow, and Christina Onassis, the only surviving child. We arranged to have copies of the petition served on them, and the hearing in the New York County Surrogate's Court on the question of who should be the administrator of the estate of Aristotle Onassis was set for August 16, 1978.

With the action under way and the hearing date set for appointment of Aristotle's administrator, we turned to gathering the evidence we would need to support our claims. We expected to be up against top-flight law firms for Olympic and Onassis, and we might be put to our proof very quickly by motions to dismiss based upon the statute of limitations or other grounds. One of the big questions was how we were going to prove what had happened on the fatal flight. If McCusker had been responsible in any degree for Alexander's death, his own causes of action for negligence and all the other torts would be weakened, if not destroyed. McCusker's post-accident amnesia blanked out his memory of the entire flight. Alexander Onassis was dead. The only other eye-witness, Captain Donald McGregor, was in England; he had been compensated by Olympic; he was an unknown quantity. This led me to consider a desperate solution: the use of truth serum (sodium amytal) to restore McCusker's memory of the events leading up to the crash.

I recalled that the Civil Aeronautics Board had used sodium amytal in its investigation of the crash of a Lockheed Constellation at Canton Island in 1962. The entire crew and one of the passengers were killed, leaving as sole survivor a government doctor who had been sitting in a cockpit observer seat just behind the pilot. The doctor was seriously injured and unable to recall details, even though he had closely observed the entire sequence of the emergency that led to the crash. Readings of the instruments, engine controls, and tab settings yielded nothing that could be directly related to the accident, and since this happened before the days of the "black box" flight recorder and cockpit voice recorder, the CAB had great difficulty in establishing the cause of the crash. After sodium amytal was administered to the surviving doctor with his consent, he recalled many details of the flight, including the actions and words of pilot and copilot, right down to the exact levers which they pulled in their desperate struggle to avoid the crash. On the next day, a tape recording of the interview was played back for the survivor, and he was able to verify his independent recollection of all these important details. The CAB investigators went on to establish the probable cause of the Canton Island accident to the unanimous satisfaction of the board. Their findings were consistent with the testimony that was given under sodium amytal.

Many courts would reject such testimony even if the witness stated that he independently recalled the events now, when not under the influence of the drug. Although one is allowed broad latitude to refresh the recollection of a witness at trial by practically any means, the courts have not treated narcosynthesis as the refreshing of recollection. In view of the wide acceptance of narcosynthesis in medical circles and its use in such sensitive fact-finding tasks as military intelligence, it seems that the time has come for reappraisal of the exclusionary rule. Some courts have expressed fear of manufactured evidence, but I doubt that many perjurers would be willing or able to obtain the necessary medical connivance to construct a fictitious recollection through truth serum. It would be simpler to lie in the first place and claim perfect recall without the use of drug and doctor. In any event, with all that Donald McCusker had been through, I decided to put off the idea of truth serum. I would try to interview Captain McGregor and learn his version of the crash sequence.

In July of 1978 I arranged to meet Captain Donald McGregor in London. He turned out to be a delightful old salt whom you would immediately have to call Mac—a character right out of an Ernie Gann flying novel. He had many stories of the old days with Imperial Airways (ancestor of BOAC and British Airways) for whom he flew giant Short Sunderland four-engine flying boats. He was one of the first airline pilots to participate in midair refueling, which permitted the lumbering Sunderlands to cross the Atlantic nonstop in the days before World War II.

He wanted to help McCusker and felt that our client had been given a raw deal. He freely told me his entire recollection of the accident, which he believed to have been caused by Aristotle Onassis, who pressured his son into actions which Alexander would ordinarily not have taken. It was well known throughout Olympic Airways that whenever Aristotle gave an order to Alexander, the son felt intimidated and under compulsion to comply, even if it compromised air safety. McGregor and McCusker didn't know that they were going to fly that day until the very last minute. They were not told that a maintenance test flight was being combined with McCusker's checkout. There was no time for a proper preflight procedure, and there were no checklists aboard.

McGregor gave me copies of the checklists for the Piaggio, some of them in the handwriting of Alexander Onassis. None of these checklists had anything more than "full and free" as the response to checking the ailerons. That is, there was no item on any of the checklists which required the pilots to determine visually the up or down position of the ailerons when the wheel was turned. All they were required to do was to make sure that the *control wheel* turned "full and free," all the way to the left or right without obstruction. This was an important piece of evidence, because the Greek indictment of McCusker (which we attached to the complaint in the New York lawsuit) had charged:

> 1. Prior to takeoff you should have checked through the appropriate devices and with your eyes the good operation of the ailerons, but you omitted to do so; also because you failed to obtain the indispensable checkoff list.

The actual checklists in the handwriting of Alexander showed that even if they had been aboard, they would not have called upon McCusker to check the position or rigging of the ailerons. McGregor also confirmed that Alexander was in charge of the flight (and therefore responsible for the checklists), contrary to the Greek indictment, which named McCusker as commander of the Piaggio.

McGregor is one of nature's noblemen. He received only nominal compensation himself, for he was shown a Warsaw Convention ticket that had been made out in his name, and was told his rights were limited by the ticket. Yet, he wanted to do everything possible to help McCusker. He had volunteered to return to Greece to testify if McCusker's manslaughter trial ever took place. And at our meeting, he refused to accept reimbursement for his train fare between London and his home in Oxford, although he had come to London especially to meet with me.

While I was traveling in Europe after the meeting with Captain McGregor, I received a message from my office that the lawyers for Olympic Airways and the Onassis estate had called and asked to arrange a settlement conference. I returned to New York and met with them. In short order, the case was settled for $800,000. I mention the amount (with the permission of Donald McCusker) because it is significant in itself. It stands as a clearance of his name and a vindication of his performance during the fatal Piaggio flight—actions that should have been taken by the Greek government but were never forthcoming. By the time of the settlement in August of 1978, he had recovered sufficiently from his injuries to meet the rigid requirements of the commercial pilot physical examination. Considering his restored health and all of the legal problems (statute of limitations, Warsaw Convention, etc.), the case would not have warranted a settlement of more than $200,000 if the defendants had not been afraid that an American jury would punish them for intentional defamation and the completely unjustified burdens they had placed upon a man who had always done his duty and had led an exemplary life.

We were proud to represent Donald and Helena McCusker. Their Greek nightmare of five years ended happily for this wonderful family because the American legal system gave them the weapons they needed to overcome the arrogance of a tyrant who could manipulate the legal system of his own nation at will.

THE RAID ON ENTEBBE

On July 4, 1976, the day of America's bicentennial, one of the most amazing feats of arms in all of history took place at the Entebbe airport in Uganda. The daring rescue of the passengers held hostage by terrorists at Entebbe after the hijacking of an Air France A-300 Airbus is a story too well-known to require repetition. Here it concerns us only because of the litigation that arose out of that hijacking. Because it is still pending at this writing and our firm represents the plaintiffs, it would be improper for me to comment on the merits of the case. I shall therefore confine myself to questions of law that are already before the courts. To understand these legal questions, you should know some of the allegations in the plaintiffs' complaint, but please note that these are merely allegations at this point, and the defendants have denied responsibility for any injuries received by the plaintiffs.

The 93 plaintiffs whom we represent are all of the hostages who are suing in the United States. They are citizens of the United States (6), Israel (64), France (20), and Canada (3). They are suing the three airlines whom they consider responsible for the hijacking: Air France, the operator of the hijacked airplane; Singapore Airlines; and Gulf Air. The latter two airlines did not carry any of the hostages, but the plaintiffs allege that the four terrorists who hijacked the Air France plane had been passengers aboard Gulf and Singapore earlier on June 27, 1976, the day of the hijacking; that the terrorists were permitted to board both Gulf and Singapore carrying hand grenades, dynamite, and firearms, without being searched as required by international regulations; that as continuing passengers they made their way into the "sterile" transit lounge at Athens International Airport, thus avoiding a more thorough search that would have been made had their passage originated at Athens; that at Athens they boarded an Air France Airbus which had arrived from Israel (carrying many Israeli passengers) and was scheduled to fly to Paris; that the four terrorists had debarked at Athens from a Singapore Airlines flight which was bound for Paris, but if they had really desired to reach Paris that morning, they would have stayed on the Singapore airplane, which was scheduled to arrive in Paris much earlier than the Air France plane; that the terrorists were never properly searched by any of the three airlines that carried them on June 27, so that they were able to board the Air France Airbus with enough weapons to take over the airplane and hold all of its occupants as hostages; that the hostages were held captive under cruel conditions and under threat of violent death, and suffered various injuries ranging from gunshot wounds (some of them fatal) to miscarriage, to emotional trauma. Again, all of these statements are merely allegations which the plaintiffs will have to prove at trial.

At the present writing (1980), the suits that we filed in the New York Supreme Court are being attacked on the ground of *forum non conveniens,* a familiar phrase now that you have been through Ermenonville. Most of the plaintiffs in the Ermenonville DC-10 litigation were citizens of foreign countries, and so are the plaintiffs in the Entebbe case; but Entebbe differs in that all the defendants are foreign airlines, whereas in Judge Hall's court the principal defendants were two California aircraft manufacturers. Therefore Entebbe presents more difficult questions of law and policy.

In its *forum non conveniens* motion, Singapore argued that New York was not a convenient trial forum for a case involving plaintiffs who are (mostly) foreigners, defendants who are all foreign corporations, and allegations of negligence that allegedly occurred entirely in the foreign countries where the terrorists boarded the three flights on June 27, 1976. Since a *forum non conveniens* motion requires the defendants to establish the existence of a more convenient forum, Singapore alleged that England would be more convenient than New York, because England is the only place (outside of the United States) in which all three airlines can be sued. We argued that there is no forum in the world that is entirely convenient for trial of a case involving events and parties in many different nations, and for that reason England would not be any more convenient than New York. Indeed, England had absolutely no connection with the case, since none of the parties reside there and none of the events occurred there. Singapore might well claim that it was somewhat inconvenient for them to defend this type of case in any of the 25 nations to which its planes fly.

In addition to the fact that six of the plaintiffs are Americans (four of them citizens of New York), we argued that the defendants had failed to show that the English courts would accept the case, and even if they accepted it, they could not furnish "effective redress" as required by New York law, because they did not provide trial by jury (a constitutional right in New York) and they did not permit plaintiffs to engage lawyers on a contingent fee basis. We called the court's attention to the Treaty of Friendship, Commerce and Navigation between Israel and the United States, which requires American courts to grant Israeli citizens the same access to courts that American citizens enjoy under like circumstances. There are similar treaties with France, Canada, and many of the nations with whom we enjoy diplomatic relations.

We also made the policy argument that the United States is the only place where hostages can obtain effective legal redress. The United States is a party to two international treaties aimed at deterring aircraft hijacking, but we cannot depend upon all signatory nations to live up to their treaty obligations. We argued that American courts should implement our strong national policy against terrorism by providing its victims with a forum for effective redress when they cannot find it elsewhere. We pointed out the large volume of business that the defendants obtained through their presence in New York, and the need to give all airlines (including foreign airlines that carry American passengers) a strong financial incentive to maintain tight security, as required by treaties and other international agreements.

The Entebbe case dramatizes a dilemma facing our courts. It is easy to understand why hard-pressed trial court judges are tempted to get rid of litigation involving foreign parties or incidents. All of our state and federal courts are groaning under an oppressive burden of criminal and civil cases, and the same judges who are called upon to keep criminal calendars current must deal with the growing delay in civil cases. In New York and in other states they are making heroic efforts to reduce the backlog of civil cases that has built up as the result of explosion of urban crime. It might seem unfair to make local residents wait longer for civil trials by keeping the courthouse doors open to foreigners. Yet, as we have seen throughout this book, the benefits of American civil justice greatly enhance the image of the United States abroad.

We spend billions every year on foreign aid, for which the recipients rarely show any gratitude. Keeping our courts open to claims of foreigners who cannot obtain justice elsewhere would, in my view, be a much better investment than foreign aid. This high opinion of the value of such suits is shared by the U.S. Departments of Justice and State.

Both of them supported legislation in the 95th Congress that proposed to keep our federal courts open to alien plaintiffs. Even though they supported the termination of diversity jurisdiction for American citizens, they insisted that aliens continue to have access to American justice because of the adverse effect on foreign relations if we closed our courts to them. Thus, even in situations where American citizens would not have the right to sue in our federal courts, both State and Justice believe that it is in the best interests of the United States that aliens be permitted to sue here.

If you talked with any of the families involved in the Ermenonville or Varig cases, you would have no doubt that their access to American courts created tremendous good will for the United States, not only among the families involved but also among the thousands of foreign citizens who read their local newspaper's accounts of the equal treatment and fair compensation foreign claimants received in our courts. And Donald McCusker could tell you about the desperate need of Americans (such as the six American Entebbe hostages) to enforce their legal rights against foreign parties in American courts, a need that cannot be met by access to any other court system.

I believe that we should use American justice as a good will generator and provide enough judges and courtrooms so that anyone who needs our courts in order to achieve justice can have access to them. I cannot think of any better way to spend the taxpayer's money. In the end, the foreign cases repay much of the cost of court access, for they produce travel by foreign lawyers and litigants, which pumps money into the local economy. Depositions and trials are like miniconventions. And the fees that American lawyers earn (on both sides of the case) remain in the American economy, generating jobs and economic activity that would otherwise not be part of our gross national product.

In 1979, United Nations Secretary General Kurt Waldheim formally took possession of a $500 million Vienna office complex built for the U.N. by the Austrian government. Despite the half-billion-dollar cost, the U.N. will pay a rent of only one schilling (7.5 cents) a year. The Austrian government was willing to foot the bill for the new office center because it will bring international prestige as well as money spent locally by U.N. officials and others who visit the center for conferences. If little Austria (population 8 million) regards the U.N. office center as a good investment, is it not worthwhile for American courts to keep their doors open to foreigners and act as a center for human rights and justice on a much more personal level than the United Nations? New York City justified its expenditure of millions of dollars to refurbish Yankee Stadium by the hope that it would attract tourist expenditures. The same amount of money spent on the expansion and improvement of New York's courts could make New York a center of worldwide litigation that would yield rich dividends.

For the U.S., especially, it is important to allow individual foreigners with legitimate claims to sue here, since it is widely known that huge foreign business corporations have ready access to American courts. Indeed, foreign governments have been permitted to sue American exporters in our courts for treble damages under the Clayton Antitrust Act, even when their own laws permit the type of conduct they are complaining of. But if our hard-pressed judges succumb to the temptation to reduce calendar backlogs by shutting the courthouse doors to individual foreign plaintiffs, we will be projecting the worst image of American capitalism. Instead of advertising the strong point of our legal system—that it equalizes the power of the large corporation and the individual—we will be putting our worst foot forward by permitting multinational giants and governments to sue, but shutting out the individual foreign plaintiff. What good does it do to spend billions on faceless foreign aid, if we then fail to make one of our best products— civil justice—available to those who need it?

While trial court judges have some discretion in deciding a *forum non conveniens* motion, there are basic principles of law which they are supposed to follow. The U.S. Supreme Court laid down the rules in 1947:

> It is often said that the plaintiff may not, by choice of an inconvenient forum, "vex," "harass," or "oppress" the defendant by inflicting upon him expense or trouble not necessary to his own right to pursue his remedy. But unless the balance is strongly in favor of the defendant, the plaintiff's choice of forum should rarely be disturbed.

In cases involving airline passengers from several nations, there is nothing vexatious about bringing them together to dispose of all claims in one court. Indeed, this is actually a convenience for all the parties, including the defendants.

Of course, it is most convenient for defendants if they are not sued at all, and that is what is behind many *forum non conveniens* motions. If the plaintiffs are relegated to a forum where they cannot afford to hire lawyers, or where no such suit has ever been brought, then the defendants are going to wind up settling the claims for shockingly low sums based upon the inability of the plaintiffs to enforce their legal rights. Clearly, this is not a question of "convenience." It is the total defeat of justice, especially when the real beneficiary is a multinational insurer such as Lloyd's of London, which does the major part of its annual $5 billion business in North America and maintains a $2 billion trust fund in New York to pay judgments rendered by American courts. It is particularly ludicrous for airlines insured by Lloyd's to claim *forum non conveniens,* since the corps of expert lawyers that defends them so skillfully is centered in the United States. There is little aviation trial expertise available to plaintiffs or defendants outside the United States, for the simple reason that the Warsaw Convention and the traditional ticket limitations have made such litigation meaningless in other nations.

Chapter 8

THE SCIENTIFIC TORT LAWYER

TRAGEDY AT TENERIFE

Thirty-five years of dealing with almost every type of aviation accident have conditioned me to the possibility that a crash can occur under almost any conditions. Yet, when I look back at the world's worst air disaster, I have trouble believing what happened at Tenerife in the Canary Islands on March 27, 1977.

Here were two of the world's legendary airlines, Pan American Airways and the Dutch line, KLM, operating their flagships—great Boeing 747 jumbo jets—with crack crews aboard each aircraft. The Pan Am flight was a charter trip that had departed from Los Angeles, carrying a vacation tour group bound for Las Palmas, the main airport in the Canary Islands. The KLM flight had departed from Amsterdam that morning, also bound for Las Palmas. While both planes were en route, there was a bomb explosion in the Las Palmas airport terminal, and the airport authorities received a threat that a second might be set off. So they diverted all incoming planes to the nearby island of Tenerife, where they could await clearance to fly on to Las Palmas after the danger of bomb explosions had passed. Los Rodeos airport at Tenerife was much smaller than the Las Palmas airport, having only one runway with narrow taxi strips and a small parking area that was hardly suitable for jumbo jet operations. Situated at the base of a mountain, the airport was notorious for low-lying clouds and strong winds that caused rapid changes in ceiling and visibility, which often went to zero with little advance warning. In the past 21 years, there had been six major accidents at Los Rodeos, accounting for 252 deaths. Along with other large airliners diverted from Las Palmas, the Pan Am and KLM 747s had to sit on the ground at Tenerife for more than two hours after their early afternoon arrival. What happened after that is set forth below as described in the accident investigation reports of the Dutch and Spanish governments (the latter reporting because the Canary Islands are Spanish territory).

The KLM flight was also a charter trip, carrying 234 passengers bound for Easter holidays in the Canary Islands. Its captain was the airline's 50-year-old chief of pilot training, Jacob Veldhuyzen van Zanten, whose photo was featured in some of KLM's advertisements. He headed a highly qualified 747 crew including as first officer (copilot) Klaas Meurs, who had been a DC-8 captain himself. They were concerned about exceeding their 12-hour limit on flight time, for the Dutch regulations were so strict that offenders faced the possibility of fines and prison terms. The crew had already been on duty for nine hours, and they were scheduled to return to Amsterdam from Las Palmas the same day. If they had to wait much longer at Tenerife for their takeoff clearance to Las Palmas, they would have to remain at Las Palmas overnight instead of returning to Amsterdam the same day. This would disrupt KLM's schedules, and Captain van Zanten wanted to avoid that if possible.

The Pan Am crew was commanded by veteran captain Victor Grubbs, 56, who had over 21,000 hours of flying time and 546 hours as a 747 captain. His first officer was 39-year-old Robert Bragg, whose total of 10,800 flying hours included 2,796 as a 747 copilot. The Pan Am plane was almost fully loaded, carrying 380 passengers who were on a $2,000 package holiday trip that was to include a twelve-day Mediterranean cruise aboard the M.S. *Golden Odyssey,* starting at Las Palmas.

Due to congestion at Los Rodeos airport, the KLM plane was parked in the holding area at the beginning of Runway 12. The Pan Am 747 was parked behind the KLM plane and could not pass it, because the taxiing area was too narrow. After the airport at Las Palmas was reopened to traffic, the Pan Am and KLM crews prepared for departure, but the treacherous Tenerife weather intervened. The visibility deteriorated quickly from 10 kilometers (6.2 miles) to 1½ kilometers (0.9 miles). The KLM captain therefore took on additional fuel, so that he could return to Amsterdam in case the weather prevented a landing at Las Palmas. In the meantime, the Pan Am crew had to wait out the long delay caused by KLM's refueling, for they could not taxi past the KLM 747.

When KLM had completed its refueling, both KLM and Pan Am advised the tower that they were ready to depart. Because there were so many large aircraft diverted from Las Palmas, the regular taxi strips were clogged with parked planes. The tower cleared KLM to taxi down Runway 12—the one to be used for takeoffs—and cleared Pan Am to taxi behind KLM down the same runway. KLM was instructed to taxi to the takeoff end of the runway and to make a 180-degree turn there. Pan Am was instructed to leave the runway at the third intersection, which would require them to make a sharp left turn of about 150 degrees on to a narrow taxi strip.

Visibility had deteriorated to 300 meters (984 feet) by the time both aircraft started taxiing. The prescribed minimum takeoff visibility for KLM was 300 meters, while it was 800 meters (2,624 feet) for Pan Am. As a result of the poor visibility, the tower and the crews could not see one another.

Two clearances were required before departure; a takeoff clearance from the tower, to ensure that the runway was clear of other traffic; and an Air Traffic Control (ATC) clearance, specifying the route to be flown after the plane was airborne. Both clearances were to be obtained by radio from the tower. While the KLM plane was taxiing down the takeoff runway, the tower offered to read the ATC clearance, but KLM asked the tower to hold off because the crew were occupied with details of the pretakeoff checklist. As a result, when the KLM plane reached the takeoff end of the runway, both the ATC clearance and the takeoff clearance had yet to be requested and obtained.

The Pan Am crew, too, were busy with the checklist during taxiing, and at the same time and in heavy fog, they were trying to find the intersection at which they were ordered to leave the runway. The intersections were not indicated by markers, lights, or any other identification. The Pan Am crew missed the third intersection and taxied farther down the runway than the tower had instructed. Neither the Pan Am crew nor the KLM crew or the tower were aware of this.

When the KLM aircraft was lined up in the takeoff direction and the checklist had been completed, the first officer said to the captain, "Wait a minute, we don't have an ATC clearance." The captain affirmed that he was aware of this and ordered the first officer to request it. The first officer then requested both the takeoff clearance and the ATC clearance in one sentence. The tower controller replied by giving the ATC clearance: "KLM 8705, you are cleared to the Papa beacon, climb to and maintain flight level nine-zero, right turn after takeoff, proceed with heading zero-four-zero until intercepting the three-two-five radial from Las Palmas VOR."

While the first officer read back the ATC clearance, the captain, believing that he had received a *takeoff* clearance, said: "We gaan" (We go). He released the brakes and increased power to takeoff thrust. At the end of his read-back of the ATC clearance to the tower, the first officer added: "We are now-eh-taking off," or "We are now at take-off." According to the tower controller's statement, he understood this last message to mean, "We are at takeoff position," and thus he concluded that the KLM plane was stationary, in postion to start the take-off. He replied, "Okay," and added after a pause of about two seconds: "Stand by for takeoff, I will call you." By this, the tower controller intended to convey that KLM had read back the ATC clearance correctly and that KLM now had to wait for a separate takeoff clearance from the tower.

The Pan Am crew was alarmed by the way in which the ATC clearance was issued. The captain feared that the KLM crew might take the ATC clearance as a takeoff clearance. After the tower controller had said "Okay" and had paused for almost two seconds, the Pan Am captain and first officer cut in on the radio transmissions to inform the KLM crew that the Pan Am plane was still taxiing on the takeoff runway. This Pan Am transmission coincided with the message of the tower controller, who was at that moment telling the KLM aircraft to wait for takeoff clearance. In the KLM cockpit, these coinciding transmissions on the same frequency resulted in a strong squeal. Because of this, both vital messages were barely audible to the KLM crew. No squeal was heard by Pan Am or by the controller, who then called Pan Am and asked them to report when they were clear of the runway. Pan Am replied that they would report when clear.

These last two messages were audible in the KLM cockpit, but apparently only the flight engineer paid any attention to them. He asked the pilots: "Is hij er niet af dan?" (Hasn't he gone off, then?) The captain, who was concentrating on the takeoff roll, did not understand him and asked, "Wat zeg je?" (What do you say?), after which the flight engineer repeated: "Is hij er niet af die Pan American?" (Hasn't he gone off, that Pan American?) Both the captain and the first officer replied "Jawe" (Yes) and continued the takeoff roll.

The Pan Am's cockpit voice recorder (CVR) shows that as the plane taxied down the live runway, its officers were irritated by the extra delay caused by KLM's refueling. They went past their assigned exit, Intersection C3, which was unmarked. They were working from a very small map of an unfamiliar airport, and as they passed Intersections C2 and C3, some of their attention was focused on complying with the instructions of the detailed 747 pretakeoff checklist. When they passed C3 without sighting it, the fog was so thick that they could not see the KLM 747, which was now bearing down on them, but they knew from the radio transmissions that they were in danger. At that point Pam Am's CVR reads:

> Pan Am Captain: Let's get the hell out of here.
> Copilot: Yeh, he's anxious, isn't he?
> Captain: There he is—look at him—goddam—that son of
> a bitch is coming!
> Copilot: Get off, get off, get off!

The captain immediately increased power on all four engines and started to turn the aircraft to the left in order to leave the runway as quickly as possible.

Approximately two and a half seconds before the collision, at a distance of about 160 meters (525 feet), the KLM captain suddenly saw the Pan Am aircraft in front of him on the runway. He pulled the control wheel all the way back in an attempt to lift off the ground and fly over the Pan Am plane. He had just wrenched his 747 off the ground when the collision occurred. The raised nose section and the nose wheels of the KLM plane cleared the Pan Am fuselage, but the heavy center sections of both aircraft collided. The KLM plane fell back on the runway, and as it slid over a distance of approximately 450 meters (1476 feet), it gradually disintegrated. Meanwhile, fuel from the ruptured tanks of both aircraft ignited. Both planes and the entire area between them were on fire.

Due to the thick fog, the tower controller could not see the runway and was not aware of what had occurred 500 meters (1,640 feet) away from him. In fact, even after he heard two separate explosions and was told by crew members of aircraft parked on the apron that there was fire on the runway, the tower controller was not able to see the two huge aircraft burning almost under his windows. So heavy was the fog that neither he nor the crew members of parked aircraft were able to give the ground rescue vehicles any sightings to direct them straight to the crash scene, which the rescue crews had to find on their own. When they reached the collision site, it was already too late to help anyone aboard the KLM plane. It had exploded and all of its occupants were dead within seconds after the collision. Seven crew members and sixty-one Pan Am passengers were taken alive from the crash site, but nine of the passengers died subsequently. Many of the Pan Am survivors were flown in a U.S. Air Force C-130 to the U.S. Army Burn Center at Brooke Army Medical Center, San Antonio, Texas, where they received expert care that saved their lives.

If you are wondering how all this could have happened to two of the world's greatest airlines, you will get no comfort from the 1979 report of the director general of Dutch civil aviation, which contains this statement:

> Besides the misunderstanding arising from the radio communication, it has been established that the coincidence of a number of circumstances had a direct influence on the occurrences. It has been found that the coincidence of these circumstances made the accident almost inevitable. If either of these circumstances had not been there, it is almost certain that the accident would not have occurred.

The Dutch report then goes on to list the following "coincidences" that made the accident "almost inevitable": the fog; the airport congested by diverted aircraft; the KLM request for two clearances at once while lined up for takeoff; the garbling of radio messages; and the fact that "in busy moments, certain procedures are frequently cut short." Presumably this last statement was supposed to explain why KLM took off without ever receiving a takeoff clearance from the tower, and why the tower never asked for or received confirmation of its instruction to KLM to hold its position and wait for a takeoff clearance. Also listed among the "coincidences" is the fact that KLM did not listen to the tower's radio communication with the Pan Am plane [even though the KLM crew knew that Pan Am was taxiing into their faces]. And finally, what the report called "the predominant coincidence":

> . . . the premature takeoff of the KLM aircraft coinciding with the taxiing too far of the Pan Am aircraft.

Having ascribed the accident to these coincidences, the Dutch report reached this conclusion:

> None of the persons involved can be blamed for negligence of his duties. Each of these persons separately may perhaps be criticized; however, this criticism must be limited to the observation that they all, in the normal performance of their duties, had not functioned in an optimal way in a particular aspect.
> In the case of none of them can I point to a serious error. The situation in which they functioned was not exceptional to such an extent as to cause an unacceptable risk of accidents.

In other words, we are asked to believe that the situation on Runway 12 at Tenerife created an accident risk that must be accepted by passengers. The remarkable Dutch report is, to my mind, compelling evidence that the deterrent of civil litigation is needed to assure the safety of the airline passenger. As we shall see, the Dutch report was published in 1979 when it was known that there would never be any depositions of the

Tenerife witnesses in American litigation. It was assumed that the matter would be put to rest in the government report which assured the public that the 644 casualties (including 583 deaths) at Tenerife were caused by coincidences that did not create unacceptable risks.

The most superficial analysis of the "coincidences" cited in the Dutch report reveals that instead of making the accident inevitable, each one of them was a *flashing red danger signal* that would have made the accident *impossible* if the crews had taken the slightest care for the safety of their aircraft. If you visualize each takeoff safety factor as a building block, you start out with a solid wall that includes: good visibility, with the tower able to see all aircraft on the field and the aircraft crews able to see each other; airport radar, to alert the tower to any sudden movements toward the takeoff runway; wide taxi strips, which make it unnecessary to use the active takeoff runway as a taxiway; well-marked and lighted runway intersections; large parking aprons, suitable for jumbo jets; crew familiarity with the airport; tower personnel experienced in handling heavy jumbo jet traffic and unhampered by language limitations; plenty of time to request and clearly receive separate ATC and takeoff clearances; plenty of time to complete pretakeoff checklists; and the final safety factor that supersedes all other considerations: *DON'T GO* UNLESS YOU ARE SURE THAT YOU HAVE BEEN CLEARED AND THAT THERE IS NOTHING IN YOUR WAY.

Now, take each of those blocks away one by one, and you will then have produced the series of "coincidences" which made the Tenerife collision "almost inevitable." Consider one additional factor: the runway's center-line lights, which would have helped both crews as they moved through the fog, were out of service, and both airlines had been advised of this long before their 747s taxied out on to the runway. Then ask yourself whether the Pan Am captain should have been going through the pretakeoff checklist while he was taxiing blindly into the face of the KLM plane (knowing that it was out there in the fog, but not knowing where) and groping in the fog for an unmarked runway exit that required an extremely difficult turn onto a strange, unlighted, narrow taxi strip. And then put yourself in the place of the KLM captain. Would you open your throttles without knowing exactly where the Pan Am plane was, when you did not receive a positive takeoff clearance from the tower controller, who was obviously struggling with unfamiliar problems and in addition could not see either aircraft and had not received or sent any clear message about the position of either plane? Would your hand move the throttles forward more steadily if you also heard in the background of the tower transmissions something that sounded like the radio broadcast of a soccer match?

If the act of taking off a jumbo jet with hundreds of passengers aboard requires the highest degree of care under ordinary conditions and with all the safety blocks in place, then it required *exquisite* care under the conditions at Tenerife. I would go so far as to say that even if Pan Am had clearly reported that it had exited at Intersection C3, and if its message had been acknowledged by the tower and heard by KLM, and if thereafter KLM had been given a takeoff clearance by the tower, then proper care under existing circumstances would still have required all three parties—Pan Am, KLM, and the tower—to verify that Pan Am was clear of the runway by such visual means as the flashing of lights or even the firing of a flare, so that *somebody* on the island of Tenerife would have ascertained visually that the KLM plane could start its takeoff without hitting any part of the 231-foot-long Pan Am 747. But none of this was done, and unbelievably, the crews of both giant aircraft went through half a dozen stop signs to collide and cause the world's worst—and most unnecessary—aviation disaster.

A Christmas Gift to Holland

Most of the passengers aboard the Pan Am plane were Californians, including many married couples in their 60s and 70s. Dozens of the injured survivors, and many families of the dead Pan Am passengers, filed suits in the California courts against Pan Am and KLM. These could be filed in the federal courts, since there was a diversity of citizenship between the passengers (mostly Californian) and the defendant (Pan Am, a New York corporation).

The majority of the KLM passengers had been Dutch, and their cases were not eligible for the federal courts because the defendant, KLM, was a Dutch corporation, and suits in which both plaintiff and defendant are aliens do not qualify as diversity cases. The lawyers for thirty Dutch families had retained us, in association with the Amsterdam firm of Boekel Van Empel & Drilling, to bring suit in the United States. Twelve American families also had asked us to represent them, three from the KLM plane and nine from the Pan Am plane.

We decided to file the American families' suits in the federal district court for the Southern District of New York, and the Dutch families' suits in the Supreme Court for New York County. There was no way of keeping them all in one court, but we hoped that the Judicial Panel on Multidistrict Litigation would transfer all the federal cases to the Southern District of New York, having learned from experience that a federal MDL judge can keep the federal and state cases moving as a unit if they are filed in courts located in the same state.

This problem had come up in the very first MDL aviation case, which arose out of the 1967 mid-air collision at Hendersonville, North Carolina, between a Piedmont Airlines Boeing 727 and a Cessna 310 operated by Lanseair, Inc. Piedmont Airlines was a North Carolina corporation, and most of the passengers were North Carolina citizens. Because of this lack of diversity, their families had to sue the airline in the North Carolina state courts. Along with our North Carolina counsel, Warren C. Stack of Charlotte, we represented the largest group of claimants. Some of the passengers had been from other states, including John McNaughton, who had been killed in the accident soon after President Lyndon B. Johnson had named him Secretary of the Navy. We decided to file the suits of the non-North Carolina families in the federal courts. When all the federal cases were assigned to an MDL judge, U.S. District Judge Woodrow W. Jones of the Western District of North Carolina, he quickly solved the problem of the split litigation. In collaboration with Judge Harry C. Martin of the Superior Court for Henderson County, Judge Jones treated the federal and state court cases as one piece of litigation. Judge Jones and Judge Martin held joint hearings on important motions and coordinated all the pretrial discovery of their respective cases. In the end, a settlement formula was reached, and all of the state and federal cases were settled. The same procedure was used by U.S. District Court Judge Peter T. Fay when he received the MDL assignment in the first jumbo jet crash case, the Eastern Airlines Lockheed 1011 Florida Everglades accident of December 29, 1972. Based on those precedents, we hoped that if the Tenerife cases were assigned to an MDL judge in the Southern District of New York, he would be in a position to collaborate with the New York County judge in charge of our Dutch cases, so that we would be able to proceed almost as smoothly as if all the cases had come before a single judge.

On August 16, 1977, the Judicial Panel on Multidistrict Litigation transferred all the federal Tenerife cases to U.S. District Judge Robert J. Ward of the Southern District of New York. Judge Ward was then 51 years old, a *cum laude* Harvard graduate who had spent eleven years as a state and federal prosecutor before becoming a partner in the prestigious New York firm of Aranow Brodsky Bohlinger Benetar Einhorn & Dann. He was appointed to the federal bench in 1972. Tenerife, which produced the largest number of casualties in aviation history, was his first assignment to an MDL airline case.

Judge Ward scheduled his first pretrial conference for November 11, 1977, in New York. This set the stage for a meeting of plaintiffs' lawyers, which was held on November 10 in the Charles A. Lindbergh

Room of the Wings Club at the Biltmore Hotel in New York. The main purpose of the meeting was to reach a consensus on the list of lawyers who would act as lead counsel for the plaintiffs. More than a hundred law firms were involved in representing the Pan Am passengers and their families, and about an equal number of Dutch law firms represented the KLM families. At the time of this meeting at the Wings Club, our firm represented all of the Dutch claimants who had filed suits in New York; and collectively, our Pan Am and KLM cases formed the largest single group of plaintiffs. Most of the attorneys attending the meeting represented Pan Am families; many of them were leading aviation tort lawyers, and they came from all parts of the country.

As we met in the Lindbergh Room of the Wings Club during the 50th anniversary year of Lindbergh's great flight, it occurred to me that there was a parallel between his role as the Lone Eagle and the plaintiffs' position in the early airline crash cases. Lindbergh was not the first to fly the Atlantic Ocean, but he was the first to do it alone. Probably that's why he became the hero of the century, and why his tiny Ryan monoplane is still the leading attraction in the world's most frequently visited building, the National Air and Space Museum of the Smithsonian Institution in Washington. Just as the Ryan monoplane was designed for a single pilot, so our legal system was designed for the individual case, handled separately by each plaintiff's lawyer. In the early days of commercial aviation, this put most plaintiffs at the mercy of superior forces—the airlines, their insurers, and their unified attorneys. Sometimes witnesses were deposed five or six times by different lawyers, and they didn't always give the same answers, but only the defendants' lawyers knew this. Sometimes a witness was deposed by airline lawyers with no lawyer showing up to represent the plaintiff, as in the Grand Canyon case. Sometimes one plaintiff won and another lost in cases arising out of the same accident. Often plaintiffs' lawyers were forced to accept settlements that reflected the superior leverage of their adversaries.

But all the legal developments we have reviewed in the preceding chapters—from the group effort in the Grand Canyon cases to the federal procedures used by the Judicial Panel on Multidistrict Litigation—have helped to equalize the scales of justice. As I looked around the large meeting table in the Lindbergh room at the lawyers who had come from far and wide to collaborate on seeking compensation for the victims of history's worst air disaster, I felt that their skills and resources were a force that equaled the litigation power of the huge airlines, manufacturers, and insurers that were arrayed against the plaintiffs.

As a result of the Wings Club meeting and others that were held at the federal courthouse, the plaintiffs' lawyers submitted to Judge Ward a list of proposed members of the committee of lead counsel.

After considering these recommendations, Judge Ward appointed six firms: Speiser & Krause of New York, with Chuck Krause as chairman of the committee overall; Kreindler & Kreindler of New York; John J. Kennelly of Chicago; Severson Werson Berke & Melchior of San Francisco; Magana Cathcart & McCarthy of Los Angeles; and Richard F. Gerry of San Diego. He also appointed our firm as liaison counsel for all of the plaintiffs. We considered it a great honor to be selected by our own peers and by Judge Ward to assume these responsibilities.

At the first pretrial conference, the defendants asked for a delay of liability discovery in order to explore settlement possibilities. Chuck Krause, on behalf of the committee, opposed this on the ground that it would be a license to drag out the case interminably, and that the plaintiffs were willing to continue settlement discussions while the liability discovery was going on. He argued that no delay be allowed unless the defendants were prepared to concede liability. The defendants refused to make this concession, and Judge Ward then wisely set up a discovery timetable, with the key documents to be produced by Pan Am and KLM within thirty days. Just prior to the end of the thirty-day period, the defendants decided to throw in the towel. They advised Judge Ward that they were not going to contest liability.

This cut off the plaintiffs' access to the airlines' records and testimony of their personnel. The defendants were especially anxious to avoid public testimony by the two Pan Am pilots, who had survived. They realized that there was no possible excuse for the Tenerife collision, and if they fought the plaintiffs on liability, the jurors were likely to be much harder on them in this inflammatory case. So they wisely decided to offer settlements to all claimants, reserving the right to go to trial on damages in cases that could not be settled.

If they had followed the pattern of the Turkish Airlines DC-10 case, the defendants would have written letters to the Dutch families' lawyers, stating that they were willing to settle immediately and pay them generous compensation calculated under Dutch law. They would have warned that those Dutch claimants who ventured to seek higher damages in the United States would face the long delays, uncertainties, and heavy expenses of American litigation. But the insurers had learned some lessons in the Turkish DC-10 and the Varig Paris case. This time they did what had never been done before: they made each Dutch family an offer on the basis of *American* law, which meant that in many cases they would be paying ten to fifteen times more than the claimants would be awarded in the Dutch courts.

These offers were made shortly after the defendants had announced in New York that they would not contest liability, and they were designed to keep the large group of Dutch families who had not done so from filing suit in New York. The insurers knew that the families suing here would probably collect even higher compensation after a trial or on the eve of trial in New York, and they were anxious to settle quickly in order to avoid further legal expenses as well as the effects of a New York jury verdict on the unfiled Dutch claims. They also made excellent settlement offers in the Dutch cases that had been filed in New York. The result was that every one of the KLM passenger cases was settled quickly, without trial, and under American damage standards.

By Christmas of 1977, many of the Dutch families had received gifts in the form of compensation at a level that was unheard of outside the United States at that time. For this they can thank, among others, Dr. A.F.X. Drilling of the Amsterdam law firm, Boekel Van Empel & Drilling, who made the courageous decision to commit his clients to suit in New York. We also felt a sense of pride that our efforts had helped hundreds of bereaved Dutch relatives to achieve the justice that was not available to them in their own courts. Although we represented only the thirty Dutch families that sued in New York, in one sense we felt that our efforts and those of Dr. Drilling and his firm had made it possible for nearly two hundred other Dutch families to achieve just settlements. These were the claims of people who may never have heard of us, but if our thirty Dutch cases had not been filed in New York, chances are that all the Dutch claimants would have had to settle for the archaic European standards of compensation.

By the summer of 1978, 530 of the 644 potential claims had been settled. Most of the 104 unsettled cases involved American passengers on the Pan Am plane. While the insurers were quick to settle the Pan Am death cases that involved little or no dependency, there was harder bargaining in the cases involving younger Pan Am passengers. As in the Turkish Airlines DC-10 case, it became apparent that a jury verdict was needed to establish the current level of damages for such claims, and it fell to Chuck Krause to try the pacemaker case.

The First Trial

The first Tenerife trial was a suit brought by the husband and four sons of a 41-year-old Oregon housewife, whom we shall call Barbara Jepson. Her husband, David, was 42 at the time of the accident; the four sons were 19, 18, 17, and 15. Barbara had given her mother a *Golden Odyssey* tour as a gift, and had herself gone along on the trip. Both women died on the runway at Los Rodeos airport in Tenerife.

David Jepson was a successful timber executive. He had his personal Oregon lawyers conduct the preliminary settlement negotiations. They were able to settle the claim arising from the death of Barbara's mother, who left no dependents. Because Barbara had earned about $5,000 per year in two of the three years prior to her death by working as a part-time nurse, the defendants made a settlement offer of $200,000. (Here I depart from the usual practice of keeping settlement negotiations confidential because these negotiations have been disclosed in newspaper articles.) This offer was rejected by David Jepson on the advice of his Oregon lawyers. After further negotiations, the defendants increased the settlement offer to $220,000, but Jepson and his Oregon lawyers found this unsatisfactory and decided to take the case to trial, since the defendants had informed them that $220,000 was their final pretrial offer.

The Oregon lawyers decided to bring us in as trial counsel, and so the Jepson case was set to commence in the federal courthouse in Manhattan on August 21, 1978, before Judge Ward and a jury. During the early summer of 1978, Chuck Krause went out to Oregon to meet the family lawyers, the widowed husband and his four sons, and the potential trial witnesses. He interviewed relatives and friends of the family who could testify to Barbara's strong family relationship and household services, for both were elements of damage that the jurors would be asked to include in their award. Chuck also met with officials and co-workers at the Oregon clinic where Barbara Jepson had worked as a nurse.

After conferences with the family lawyers, who knew more about the potential Oregon witnesses than one could learn merely by interviewing them, Chuck decided on his trial strategy. He would bring in Theresa Morgan as a trial witness. She had been a close friend of Barbara Jepson's and a former teacher of the Jepson children, so she knew many details of their close family relationship, and she impressed Chuck as someone who conveyed sincerity and truthfulness. Two other witnesses whose testimony would be useful were Vernon Jackson, administrator of the clinic where Barbara had worked, and Arlene Baker, the clinic's supervisor of nurses. Since they could not get away easily for a trial in New York, Chuck decided to take their depositions and thus get the facts of Barbara's nursing career before the jury. Then Chuck decided on a final Oregon witness, one who had never met Barbara Jepson: Professor Michael Haynes, chairman of the department of economics at Southern Oregon State College—and thereby hangs a tale of the scientific tort lawyer.

In the two decades between Grand Canyon and Tenerife, wrongful death litigation had developed an entirely new specialty: the consulting economist, available to testify as an expert witness on the valuation of human life and lost earnings. I was deeply involved in this movement because many of the airline crashes involved large groups of death cases that had to be evaluated as scientifically as the law permits. I wrote the first book on this subject, *Recovery for Wrongful Death Economic Handbook,* published in 1970. In its preface, I said:

> While the use of economic data and economic expert witnesses has been commonplace in some types of commercial litigation, it was virtually unheard of in accident litigation until a few years ago. Judges and juries have been guessing about the future, while ignoring mountains of economic data which can remove much of their guesswork. Ignored in personal injury lawsuits, these data are nevertheless considered reliable enough to guide momentous financial and governmental decisions relating to huge sums of money—sums which dwarf the amounts involved in individual accident cases.
>
> The purpose of this book is to advance this more scientific approach to the calculation of damages in wrongful death cases. Death cases are the focus of the discussion and examples in the text, but the same principles can be applied to personal injury cases involving protracted loss of earnings.
>
> As shown in the text, there are striking similarities between the factors underlying valuation of the assets of a business, and those involved in determination of pecuniary loss arising from the death of a human being. Indeed, many business decisions (such as those involving purchase of automated equipment) require immediate parallel determinations of the value of a man's work as against the value of a machine. Therefore, there is no reason why economic data and economists' forecasts should be used for determining the value of a business or a machine over the next 40 years, and then be ignored when trying to determine the value of a man's earning power over the same period in the same economy.

By 1977, the use of economists as expert witnesses had become almost universal in wrongful death cases. They were particularly valuable in quantifying the value of household services and educating the jury on the effects of consistently high rates of inflation. One of the problems for the plaintiff in a wrongful death case is that most states permit judges to instruct jurors that any sum awarded now to replace future earnings must be reduced to present value, because the lump sum given in advance will earn interest that would cause the jury's award to exceed the amount of the lost earnings if this reduction were not made. Thus, in a case where the person killed had earning power of $15,000 per year and 20 years of working life left, simple arithmetic would produce an award of $300,000 ($15,000 times 20). But because the lost future earnings are paid in a lump sum, the interest that can be earned on the lump sum must be considered. For example, $172,050 invested at 6 percent interest will permit the annual withdrawal of $15,000 for 20 years, thus producing the "present" equivalent of $300,000. This, however, completely ignores the effects of inflation, which has more than offset the interest on prudent investments such as savings bank accounts since the 1960s. Thus, the way in which interest rates and inflation are handled in the economist's trial testimony can cause large changes in jurors' calculations, especially in cases involving high earnings. And the plaintiff's lawyers in wrongful death cases had no choice but to become scientists in the presentation of economic data.

On the eve of the trial, after Chuck Krause had visited Oregon and had taken the depositions of witnesses there, the defendants perceived that the case was ready for presentation to a jury and that it represented an immediate economic threat to them. At that point, the insurers raised their settlement offer from $220,000 to $300,000. Chuck conferred with the family lawyers and with David Jepson, and they all decided to reject the offer because it did not represent full compensation. They were ready for trial and felt they could do better in the courtroom. During the week before the trial, the $300,000 offer was raised to $325,000, but this, too, was rejected just before the trial started.

Opposing Chuck Krause were trial lawyers from two of the nation's leading aviation defense firms. Pan Am was represented by the New York firm of Haight Gardner Poor & Havens, whom you may remember from the Grand Canyon case in Chapter 3. Haight Gardner compiled an outstanding record in aviation litigation, thanks largely to the achievements of William J. Junkerman, a pioneer aviation specialist who has probably won more cases for airline defendants than any other lawyer in history. Bill Junkerman is a former Navy pilot who was the commanding officer of the naval air base at Johnston Island in the Pacific during World War II. By the summer of 1977 he was past the age of 72 and was starting to slacken off his trial work. One of his leading protégés at Haight Gardner, Walter E. Rutherford, drew the trial assignment for Pan Am and was assisted by Randal Craft, one of Haight Gardner's promising junior lawyers. Walter, then 45 years old, is of medium height, has greying blond hair, and wears neat, vested suits. His style is on the aggressive side, and he takes every opportunity to put plaintiff's lawyers on the defensive.

KLM was represented by Condon & Forsyth, a New York law firm of long standing in the representation of foreign airlines. Their senior partner, Cyril Hyde Condon, started law practice in New York in 1931. He soon became the American lawyer for British airlines and was eventually decorated with the Order of the British Empire. The firm's traditional representation of foreign airlines continued to flourish under the direction of George N. Tompkins, Jr., a 1956 graduate of Notre Dame University Law School. Tompkins directed the defense of Turkish Airlines in the Ermenonville DC-10 litigation, and was prominently involved in many major aircraft accidents of the 1960s and 1970s, particularly those involving foreign airlines. To try this case, Condon & Forsyth sent in a formidable young litigator, Stephen J. Fearon, a 1963 graduate of Fordham Law School. Steve Fearon is formidable in more ways than one. He stands about six foot five and weighs about 240 pounds. He has wavy white hair and gets great courtroom mileage out of his good looks and attractive personality. In contrast to Rutherford's more aggressive style, Fearon is soft-spoken, but this low-key approach does not detract from his ability to make the plaintiff's lawyers squirm. As Chuck Krause squared off against the Rutherford-Fearon one-two punch, it reminded me of the hard and soft Betts-Tilson combination of the Los Angeles Grand Canyon trial. It was almost exactly 20 years from the time of the jury selection in that first Grand Canyon trial. Betts and Tilson were dead, but Rutherford and Fearon carried on in their style. There were to be other similarities between these two landmark cases involving collisions of major airlines, and also some striking differences.

As Judge Ward called the courtroom to order, the first step was the selection of a jury composed of six jurors and two alternates (who would be discharged unless some of the jurors became ill or otherwise unable to serve). Normally each party has three peremptory challenges, but since there were two defendants who had the same interests, this would have been unfair to the plaintiffs. Accordingly, after discussion with the trial lawyers, Judge Ward ruled that David Jepson, the plaintiff, would have four peremptory challenges, and the two defendants, Pan Am and KLM, would have four peremptory challenges between them. Judge Ward then proceeded to conduct the voir dire himself. We saw a lawyers' voir dire in the Grand Canyon case (Chapter 3), but many federal judges prefer to do the questioning themselves. Plaintiff's trial lawyers are often unhappy when they are cut off from this direct contact with prospective jurors and thus prevented from conditioning the jurors to keep their minds open to the plaintiff's side of the case, and from learning something about the jurors by asking them personal questions. However, in keeping with the practice of many federal judges, Judge Ward confined his voir dire to such routine questions as possible relationships between the jurors and any of the parties; whether they ever had made a claim against an airline; and whether for any reason they could not serve as fair and impartial jurors. The judge allowed the lawyers to submit proposed questions to him, but in the end the questions he asked were routine and impersonal compared to those that lawyers usually ask when they conduct the voir dire.

With the limited voir dire, it took only about two hours to select the jury of six. Both sides exhausted their peremptory challenges in the process. The jury stacked up as follows:

Number One was a married man in his early thirties with two

young children, living in Rockland County, a rural suburb of New York City. He worked as a videotape editor.

Number Two was a housewife in her fifties who had six children. Her husband was an attorney who had worked for an insurance company at one time. She lived in Westchester County, an affluent suburb of New York City.

Number Three was a middle-aged widow who lived alone in the Gramercy Park section of Manhattan. Her late husband worked in social services, and her son-in-law worked for a major airline.

Number Four was a middle-aged spinster, employed as a secretary by a machine tool manufacturer in White Plains, New York (Westchester County).

Number Five was a middle-aged divorced black woman who lived in Mount Vernon (Westchester County) and was employed by the Westchester County Department of Social Services. Her 30-year-old daughter was employed by Pepsi-Cola, and her 31-year-old son was married and lived in California.

Number Six was a single young woman who lived with her parents in Rockland County. She was employed as a customer representative for a utility company.

Apart from gender, this jury represented a cross section of the residents of the Southern District of New York, which includes the New York City boroughs of Manhattan and the Bronx, and the suburban counties of Westchester and Rockland. Each side used its peremptory challenges to get rid of jurors whom they expected to favor the other side. Thus the defense lawyers excused a woman who had been a nurse (as Barbara Jepson had been) and also seemed to have very close family ties. Chuck Krause used his challenges to excuse people who appeared to have come from broken homes or who lacked close family ties, since much of the case would turn upon the close relationship between Barbara Jepson and her surviving husband and sons.

It was agreed that the case would be governed by Oregon law, which permitted three categories of damages: the lost future earnings of Barbara Jepson as a nurse; the loss of her future services as a housewife; and the least tangible but most important item: the loss of society, companionship, care, advice, and guidance suffered by the husband and sons. As Judge Ward put it in his charge to the jury:

> In determining the amount of compensatory damages, you may also consider loss of companionship, society, and services of Mrs. [Jepson] . . . you may consider . . . what instruction, moral training, and education Mrs. [Jepson] might reasonably have been expected to give her children had she lived.

When I met David Jepson and his four sons in our office before the trial started, they impressed me as a fine group—an all-American family who were obviously proud of one another. At the same time, I could not help noticing that the four sons looked big and husky enough to resemble the defensive line of the Pittsburgh Steelers football team. This would not help Chuck Krause to convince the jury that these sons needed much more in the way of care or services from their mother. They were obviously boys who could take care of themselves. That's the way it goes in any lawsuit. Rarely does any family fit all the categories of damages that the law provides.

Chuck Krause used the first three days of the trial to paint a picture of the Jepsons' family life. David Jepson, the first witness, gave some of the family history and sketched the working career of his deceased wife. Chuck filled in other details through the live testimony of Theresa Morgan, the close family friend, and the deposition testimony of Barbara's co-workers at the clinic.

After graduating from high school, Barbara had attended nursing school for three years and received a degree in nursing care. She had earned about $5,000 per year as a part-time nurse in two of the three years prior to her death. Vernon Jackson, business manager of the clinic, testified in his deposition that he had offered Barbara a full-time job with the clinic at $12,000 per year, to commence after she returned from her vacation trip to the Canary Islands. The airline defense lawyers had cross-examined the witness on this point, trying to show that no agreement was made and there was no certainty that Barbara would have gone to work full time. They pointed out that Barbara had worked part-time for only two of her twenty-one years of marriage, and had used the money both times to take her mother on vacation trips; that she had expressed interest in continuing her education rather than working full time; and that her husband was a successful timber executive. Thus, there was conflicting testimony as to whether she would have increased her income from $5,000 a year as a part-time nurse to $12,000 as supervisor of the Ob-Gyn department. It was a classic question of fact to be decided by the jury.

The last family witness was Mark Jepson, the oldest son, who testified to the loving care and training that Barbara had given to him and his brothers. The other three sons were present in court, but Chuck felt that it would not be appropriate to parade them before the jury as witnesses. Mark was a fine witness. Although his voice cracked as he told how sorely his mother would be missed as a family member and as a person, it was obvious that he was sincere and was not trying to play on the emotions of the jurors.

Finally the case got down to the main battleground: the testimony of the plaintiff's economist. Chuck had worked with Professor Michael Haynes for many days prior to the trial, going over all the subjects he would cover in direct testimony, bombarding him with every conceivable question the defense lawyers might ask on cross. At the trial, Chuck took him through all of his academic qualifications and brought out the fact that he had been a consultant for lawyers in about a hundred cases, mostly for plaintiffs' lawyers but sometimes for defendants' lawyers. Then Chuck went right to the heart of the case: projecting the lost future earnings of Barbara Jepson.

Q. by Mr. KRAUSE: Did you calculate for me the lost future earnings of Mrs. [Jepson] in this matter from the time of her death? A: I have done so, yes.

Q: And would you please tell the Court what you did? A: I utilized the services of a Harris S–210 computer. I made a program myself which is called EARN, which I devised about five years ago. I utilized this program to project the lost income of Mrs. [Jepson]. I made certain assumptions with regard to this projection. I assumed at the time of her death Mrs. [Jepson] was forty-one years of age. I assumed that Mrs. [Jepson] had a life expectancy of thirty-eight years. I got that data, life expectancy of thirty-eight years, from a well-known source, the Statistical Abstract of the United States, 1977, which is the latest one. It's a table called Expectation of Life and Mortality by Race, Age and Sex, 1975. In that table, a female age forty-one has 38.5 years life expectancy left. I used 38. I also assumed that Mrs. [Jepson] would retire at age 65. I assumed that she was of normal health and that she would be earning a salary of $1,000 a month, or $12,000 a year.

Q: On June 1, 1977, is that correct?

A: That's correct.

Q: And from those assumptions, sir, how did you determine the lost future earnings? A: As I said, I put this data into the computer, into my own program which I devised. I projected ahead for 24 years. Since Mrs. [Jepson] was 41 years of age at her death, adding 24 years would give us 65 at age of retirement.

Q: In determining what those future earnings would be, did you look at a historical rate of increase in earnings? A: I did, yes.

Q: Would you tell us what you looked at to determine what rate of increase in her earnings you would use in your computations? A: Yes. It is my opinion that we have to look historically at what has gone on with prices over the past, that is, to look historically at inflation. I have done so. I looked at the historical past with regard to inflation. I prepared a chart to show that.

Q: What is that chart that you prepared? Would you please tell us? A: It is a chart that shows the growth in the Consumer Price Index from 1967 up to the present time. It shows the actual plots for that time, plus it shows a trend line which I have calculated.

Q: What is the Consumer Price Index? A: The Consumer Price Index is data collected by the Bureau of Labor Statistics throughout all of the United States. It includes the north, the south, the east and the west. It includes large cities and small cities, urban and rural cities. It's a marketbasket of all goods you and I buy,

and it is then computed to see how much prices increase on a per-
month basis. So when we look at the Consumer Price Index, we
are looking at the rate of inflation.

Q: What was the annual growth rate during the period from
1967 through 1977? A: Over that period of time the actual rate
of growth was 6.18 percent per year.

The COURT: Mark that as an exhibit for identification. (Plaintiffs'
Exhibit 5 marked for identification.)

Q: Professor Haynes, would you please explain the chart that
you prepared? A: Yes. What you are looking at is a graph, if you
would like to call it that, of the growth in prices from 1967
through 1977. The red line connects the dots together. The dots
are the actual statistical Consumer Price Index numbers. I started
this in 1967. The way the Bureau of Labor Statistics does it,
1967 is the base year. That is 100. Everything from that time
increases. So what we are looking at then is over time, that is,
from 1967 through 1977, the red line shows the actual changes
in the Consumer Price Index. The black line that is on there is
what statisticians and economists call a trendline. That trend line
is the measurement of growth connecting all those dots together.
Statistically, that can be called a least square sum, if you wish to
call it that, but it is actually the rate of growth over time.

Q: The black line shows the trend line and is 6.18 percent, the
growth over those years. Is that what it is? A: The black line is
the trend line and it is the rate of growth per year from 1967
through 1977 of the Consumer Price Index.

Q: But 6.18 is the average growth over those years?
A: It is.

Chuck then took the professor over another inflation index, published by the U.S. Department of Commerce, which showed that between 1939 and 1970, median family income had grown from $1,000
to $8,500, an average annual growth rate of 6.6 percent. Then he had
Professor Haynes apply his inflation calculations to Mrs. Jepson's future
earnings of $12,000 per year:

Q: Professor Haynes, did you consider any other data in arriving at what figure you would use to project the future earnings of
Mrs. [Jepson]? A: Not with regard to her future earnings. I have
used a base of $12,000 and a growth rate of 6.18 per cent.

Q: How did you select the 6.18 per cent? A: The 6.18 per cent
is the historic inflation over the past we have been looking at.
Wages are closely associated with inflation; that is to say, wages
rise based upon the expectation of inflation. Therefore, it is my
judgment that we should look at past inflation to see how much
we can expect wages to grow in the future.

Q: Then, sir, how did you make the computation of her future
earnings? How did you go about doing that?

A: I used the computer model I described. I started with a base
of $12,000. I projected it ahead for 24 years. That would be for
Mrs. [Jepson] to age 65. I let that income grow at a rate of 6.18

percent, which is a very conservative growth rate by today's standards.

Q: Sir, what was the figure that you computed then for her future earnings on that basis?

MR. RUTHERFORD: Objection, your Honor.

The COURT: Overruled. I want to be very clear on something, Professor. You are basing your calculations, as I understand it, on the past rate of inflation, the so-called historical rate. You are not guessing what the inflation would be in the future. Is that correct? The WITNESS: That's correct, your Honor.

The COURT: Under those circumstances, I am going to allow it and, of course, it will be for the jury to make the final determination, because I would suggest that the jury may consider that inflation rates may change, they may go up, they may go down. The jury is going to have to call upon their own experience in this matter and exercise their good judgment in regard to this question.

Q: Professor Haynes, what is the figure that you calculated for her gross future earnings based on the assumptions that you have made? A: The figure is $663,307.

Q: In calculating that figure, did you include any factor in there for any promotion that she might get? A: I did not include any other facts. This started from a base of $12,000, and a growth rate of 6.18, projected for 24 years. Nothing else was considered, promotion or advancement.

Q: Sir, did I then ask you to calculate for me what the present value of those future earnings would be as of the date of Mrs. [Jepson's] death? A: That's correct, you did.

Q: What is present value? A: Present value is sometimes referred to as discounting. What it means is to look at a sum of money and to say how much would that sum of money be worth to have today, rather than wait until the future to get it. A very simple example would be if someone owed you one dollar one year from now and the interest rate was 5 percent, you would be willing to take about 95 cents today, rather than wait one year for your dollar. So the present value of one dollar at an interest rate of 5 percent is 95 cents.

Q: Just a little bit over 95 cents; it that right?

A: Just a little bit over, that's correct.

Q: Did you make that present value calculation?

A: I have made the calculation, yes.

At this point, Chuck Krause placed into evidence three charts which had been prepared by Professor Haynes on slides and were projected for the jury on a screen set up in the courtroom. The first chart, Exhibit 7, portrayed the changes in long-term and short-term interest rates from 1900 through 1970. It showed that there was a strong correlation between interest rates and inflation rates. Professor Haynes had consulted a number of basic economic sources and had arrived at an average interest rate of 5.08 percent for the period from 1948 to 1978. Exhibit 8 was another chart which showed the trends in recent interest rates on government bonds, corporate bonds, and short-term bonds. Then in Exhibit 9, he had made a study of long-term low-risk bonds from the 1930s up to the time of trial. His testimony described the various sources he had consulted in making up that chart. After detailed testimony on these charts and their sources, Chuck used all of them to establish another important point in our case:

Q: What is the interest rate you decided would be an appropriate rate to use? A: It is my judgment that a conservative low-risk interest rate that we should use for discounting is 5 percent.

Q: Then in calculating the present value and using that 5 percent and the gross earnings that you testified to before, what was the present value figure that you arrived at? Mr. RUTHERFORD: Objection, your Honor. The COURT: This is a calculation that he has made. I don't quite understand the basis of your objection. I thought you made an earlier objection which was ruled upon. Now he is making a calculation which just follows, it seems to me, from the other. Maybe I am missing something.

Mr. RUTHERFORD: We object to using the five percent rate.

The COURT: Of course, that is his opinion. I think if the jury can understand that—it's going to be up to the jury what present value or rate of discount to apply. The witness is giving his opinion as to the rate of discount which he says is 5 percent. The jurors may choose to apply a different rate based on either their accepting in part or rejecting in part or in whole this witness's testimony and applying their own understanding of such matters as interest rates. The expert is here, ladies and gentlemen, to assist you. But his judgment is certainly not determinative. You may accept his views; you may modify his views to accord with your own; or you may reject them. I want you to understand that.

* * *

Q: by Mr. KRAUSE: Would you tell the jury the present value of the future gross earnings that you calculated? A: The present value of the future gross earnings of Mrs. [Jepson] based upon work expectancy of 24 years, starting with a base income of $12,-000 with a growth rate of 6.18 percent, is $332,168.

Then Chuck went on to another calculation: a deduction for income taxes. Some states do not require or permit such a deduction, on the ground that the future tax rate is speculative, but it was required by Oregon law, and so Chuck and Professor Haynes had to go through the calculations:

Q: Did you arrive at a percentage that you felt would be an appropriate sum to deduct from that present value figure for taxes that she might pay on those earnings? A: That's correct, I have.

Q: And would you tell us what you did in arriving at that figure? A: Well, I researched this area very carefully. The latest data that I have available is some work done by Pechman and Okner. It comes out of the Brookings Institution. It is, in my opinion, one of the best works we have on what taxes are being paid in the American economy today. I have noted that in the income range of $50,000, which is what the [Jepson] family would have been in, that the total tax liability is 24.4 percent. That's all taxes. That's federal, state, and local. So the total tax liability is 24.4 percent. I therefore deducted from the present value figure this amount to adjust for taxes.

The defendants were entitled to another deduction: the total amount of Barbara Jepson's personal consumption. Under the pecuniary loss theory of wrongful death damages, the surviving relatives are not entitled to recover any sums that would have been expended by the decedent herself, since this does not represent a financial loss to any living person. Chuck questioned Professor Haynes:

> Q: And with regard to her own consumption, did you calculate what she would use for her own consumption? A: I have, yes.
> Q: What percentage rate did you come to there?
> A: 27 percent.
> Q: How did you do that? A: Work done by Earl Cheit, which is a standard work, *Injury and Recovery in the Court of Employment*. It indicates on page 78 that an adult individual consumes 27 percent of their income over life. This is a weighted average; that is, when we are younger, we consume more. As we get older and get married, we consume less. As we have children, we have to share and consume even less individually. The overall weighted average for an adult is 27 percent.

Then Chuck put together the deductions for taxes and personal consumption and continued his questioning:

> Q: Fine. After deducting that percentage figure that you mentioned for taxes and the percentage figure that you mentioned for her own consumption, would you tell us what you calculated to be the sum that would remain available for contribution to the family? A: That sum is $183,316 after all deductions.
> Q: And that would be the present value figure of those future earnings, deducting the things we have mentioned; is that right? A: That's exactly correct.

Having given the defendants the benefit of these deductions, Chuck went back to add in another of the financial losses suffered in this case:

> Q: Now, sir, did I also ask you to calculate for us the present value of a Keogh contribution of 10 percent of her salary over the 24-year work period that we have been discussing? A: That's correct, you have.
> Q: And would you tell us how you did that? A: Yes. I started with a base salary of $12,000. The Keogh Plan Mrs. [Jepson]

was under provided 10 percent. So each year, I applied 10 percent into a fund called a Keogh Plan throughout her work expectation to age 65. I allowed that fund to grow at 5 percent, using the concept I have stated earlier of long-term, low-risk investment. And I have discounted 5 percent to arrive at my calculations.

Q: And what did you calculate to be the total contribution to the Keogh Plan before you reduced it to present value? A: The contribution to age 65 is $114,036.

Q: And when you reduced it to present value, what was the figure? A: $66,330.

Then Chuck went on to another key item of financial loss, the value of the household services of Barbara Jepson:

Q: Did I also ask you to prepare yourself to calculate for us at this trial the figure in dollars for the lost household services that would be performed by Mrs. [Jepson] for her family for the remainder of her life? A: That's correct, you did so.

Q: And what functions and household activities did you take into consideration in making such calculation? A: The functions that I used were dietician, food buyer, cook, dishwasher, housekeeper, and chauffeur.

Q: And did you arrive at a computation as to the average number of hours that would be worked by a housewife on a weekly basis? A: I did, yes.

Q: For a working housewife? A: Yes, I did.

Q: One holding down a full-time job? A: That's correct.

Q: How did you come to that figure? A: I have taken three sources for that. The first source is work done in 1972 by the Chase Manhattan Bank here in New York, where they calculated that a working housewife worked approximately 24 hours a week part-time, that is, a little over three hours a day on a seven-day week basis.

*   *   *

Q: Did you arrive at a dollar value for an hour of household and housekeeping work?

A: Yes.

Q: And what was that figure that you used?

A: That figure is $3.50 an hour.

Q: How did you arrive at that figure? A: I researched the figure myself in the state of Oregon. I tried to obtain data from the state of Oregon and found that the state of Oregon, the Department of Human Resources, Statistical Section, does not keep data for housewives and that type thing. So I then investigated the Oregon State Department of Employment. I personally researched it out and found out that the base figure that is being paid now in southern Oregon is $3.50 an hour. It may run as high as $5.70 an hour for housekeepers, cooks, laundresses, those types of menial household tasks.

Q: What figure did you use? A: I used $3.50 an hour.

Q: Why was that? A: It is the low end of the figure. It is a base figure.

*   *   *

Q: What is, then, the gross value of those future services for that period of time? A: $474,278.

Chuck Krause had the professor discount the $474,278 figure to present value at 5 percent, which came to $189,851. Then he brought together all three categories of damages to be considered by the jury under Oregon law, reduced to present value, in another chart that was admitted into evidence as Plaintiff's Exhibit 11:

Q: Would you please tell us, sir, what that chart shows? A: This chart is simply a summary of all that I have just testified to. It is the adjusted present value of lost income, which is the income less taxes and personal consumption, retirement at age 65. The present value of the lost income is $183,318. For the housewife services, the present value is $189,851. And for the Keogh plan, the present value is $66,330. The total of the three is $439,497.

Chuck also asked him to calculate the same three items based on the assumption that Mrs. Jepson worked to age 70 instead of 65, and the professor calculated that adding those five years of employment would increase the total damages to $514,679. Chuck then went over some of the variables that Professor Haynes had dealt with, and made it clear to the jury that the figures in the professor's charts were not carved in stone:

Q: Now, Professor Haynes, I would like to ask you, is this figure you are testifying to with regard to her future earnings until age 65, is that a fixed and finite figure, in your judgment? A: No, it is not, in my judgment.
Q: Would you tell us what are some of the variables that can come into play in that regard? A: What I have testified to is an attempt to show, using my expertise to the best of my ability, what we can expect to have in the future based upon trends from historic past. Some of these trends may be slightly lower, some may be slightly higher, but this is my judgment as to what a conservative look would be with regard to Mrs. [Jepson], with regard to her economic value.

Chuck then established that all of the professor's calculations had been double checked through computer readouts, and that he had these readouts with him in court. This got the point across to the jury that if the defense lawyers wanted to attack any of these calculations, they had only to ask him for his computer readouts. At that point, Chuck turned the witness over to Walter Rutherford for cross-examination on behalf of Pan Am.

Rutherford started out with the accepted method of attack on a plaintiff's economist—the concept of a windfall:

> Q: by Mr. RUTHERFORD: Mr. Haynes, do I understand that your conservative point of view is that if Mrs. [Jepson] worked to 65, her family has lost $439,497; and if she worked until 70, her family has lost $514,679? A: Yes, that is my view.
>
> Q: Okay. And if we took that money right now today and we walked down the street and put it in the savings bank and got 6 percent interest, that $439,000 would bring in about $25,000 a year, and that $514,000 would bring in about $30,000 a year. And at the end of these life expectancies, not only would the family have the benefit of a yearly income of $25,000 or $30,000 a year at the end of this time, they would still have the whole pie of a half million dollars. Is that right? A: What you are saying is correct, but that's not what I testified to.
>
> Q: Do you think today that Mrs. [Jepson] would have left an estate of a half million dollars to her sons? A: In my mind, based upon the calculations—
>
> MR. KRAUSE: I would object to that question, your Honor, I think it is irrelevant to this case.
>
> The COURT: Sustained.

Rutherford's attack utilized a defense-oriented view of lost earnings. While high interest rates may yield enough income to replace lost earnings in the early years of the life expectancy without invading the principal, the opposite is true in later years when the effects of long term inflation drain the remaining principal. The economist's computer printout sheets show the real pattern year by year, and in the end there is nothing left. Chuck Krause would explain this later to the jury.

Rutherford, a tenacious bulldog at cross-examination, then questioned all of Professor Haynes's qualifications very carefully, going into details of his teaching career and particularly hitting on his prior court testimony (which had been mostly for plaintiffs). He then probed in great detail how Professor Haynes came to be called into the case by the Jepson family's lawyers. About a year before the trial, the professor had sent the family lawyers a written report that contained some lower figures than those to which he had testified in court. Under the discovery rules, we had to provide the defense lawyers with copies of this earlier report, even though it was contradictory in some respects to the professor's court testimony. Naturally, Rutherford banged away at these discrepancies, zeroing in on the changes made after Chuck had conferred with him about his prospective trial testimony:

> Q: And at that time, did you then prepare a new analysis? A: No, not a new analysis. I updated the figures but not greatly. It is not as if I changed everything. I changed very little. I updated the figures. The specific changes I made were very slight.

Q: I can think of one offhand. You certainly used a different income tax rate? A: That's one I changed.

Q: You also changed the rate per hour for the housewife? A: I testified earlier why I did that.

Q: When did you run this computer printout—that, I assume, reflects what you have testified to here today? A: That's correct.

Q: When did you run those printouts? A: About two and a half weeks ago. As soon as I was made aware by Mr. Krause that he wished me to come to New York and testify, I told him that I wished to look at the whole thing again, to very carefully check the figures, make sure they were correct, and make any modifications I felt were necessary to update the preliminary analysis. I ran it then, it must be fifteen days ago, sixteen days ago. I don't know.

Q: After being contacted by Mr. Krause, the end result is, you have upped the figures from your first report; haven't you? A: The figures that have been modified because of the tax situation, but that's all.

Q: But you have upped the figures? A: They are slightly higher, yes.

Rutherford went on to question the life expectancy tables used by Professor Haynes, pointing out that if the tables of *work* expectancy were used instead, her span would be reduced to about 20 years. Then he attempted to minimize inflation, using some Consumer Price Index figures that covered years of little or no price increases. For example, if you go back from 1976 to 1946, the average rate of increase is 3.8 percent per year, and if you reach all the way back to the beginning of the CPI in 1913, the annual rate falls to 2.9 percent—all of which would be ammunition for Walter to use in his final jury argument.

Having minimized inflation, Walter turned to the item he wanted to maximize: the interest rate that would be used to reduce damages to present value. He went into great detail about investments such as corporate bonds with AAA ratings that were yielding 10 percent or more, in an attempt to establish a higher discount rate than the 5 percent that Professor Haynes had used in his calculations. Then Rutherford attacked the figures Professor Haynes had used for income taxes and personal consumption, again stressing the differences between his early analysis and his trial testimony:

Q: What did you use for the income tax deduction for Mrs. [Jepson]? A: 24.4 percent.

Q: Sir, when you prepared your first report, did you use a different figure for income tax deduction?

A: Yes, I did.

Q: And at that time when you prepared your first report, did you use a figure of 31.6 per cent?

A: That's correct. What you are reading from is the preliminary
report.

                        *   *   *

Q: Now, you also used, besides income tax, a deduction of 27
percent for personal consumption?
A: Yes.
Q: That was the same figure that you referenced in your initial
report; isn't that true? A: That's correct, yes.
Q: As authority for that 27 percent, you cited Speiser, *Recovery for Wrongful Death Economic Handbook,* 1970, page
149; is that correct?
A: That's correct.
Q: In arriving at the percentage figure for personal consumption, did you make any analysis of the personal finances of the
[Jepson] family in terms of what they actually spent, where and
on what? A: No, Mr. Rutherford, I did not personally look at
the [Jepson] family. That statistic is a well-known national statistic that can be used for adult members of a family.

At this point, Walter executed one of the most sophisticated maneuvers available to defense counsel in death cases: he used the plaintiff's economist to make on-the-stand calculations that were beneficial
to the defendants. He asked Professor Haynes to assume some changes
in the figures that he had used to calculate lost earnings of $477,878:
reduce the span from 24 years of life expectancy to 20 years of work
expectancy; use an interest rate of 8.5 percent instead of 5 percent to
discount the earnings to present value; and use 31.6 percent for income
taxes (as the professor had done in his earlier report) instead of 24.4
percent. Cranking in those seemingly slight changes, Walter forced the
professor to calculate a new total earnings loss: $79,399, which was
only about 25 percent of the $325,000 that the defendants were then
offering to settle the case. This illustrates the hazards of assuming the
burden of proof on statistical matters. Whoever brings in the expert
automatically exposes him to confrontation with such variables. That
is why defense counsel usually do not put their own economic experts on
the stand. They would be cannon fodder for skilled plaintiff's lawyers,
who could feed their own variables into the calculations and make the
defendant's own experts admit the possibility of very high damages. Of
course, the plaintiffs have no choice. They have the burden of proof
on all issues, and if economic statistics (such as the effects of inflation)
are to be considered by the jury, they must be put into evidence through
testimony of the plaintiff's economists.

Walter Rutherford had carried the main brunt of the technical
cross-examination of Professor Haynes. His aggressive style was appropriate for the attack on the mountain of economic evidence that
Chuck Krause had elicited on direct examination. Now it was time for
the affable Steve Fearon to deliver the second part of the one-two

punch. He did not go over the same ground that Rutherford had covered so effectively; instead, he zeroed in on some of the more personal elements of the trial testimony:

> Q: by Mr. FEARON: Professor Haynes, one of the things that I wanted to learn was whether or not you ever knew Mrs. [Jepson]? A: Mr. Fearon, I did not know her, but I knew of her since she graduated magna cum laude from school and she was well known at Southern Oregon State College. But I never knew her.
> Q: Was she ever a student of yours or ever in any of your seminars? A: No, she never was.
> Q: Did you know any members of the [Jepson] family prior to March 1977? A: No, I never met them.
>
>   *   *   *
>
> Q: I would assume, Professor, that it would be helpful for you or any other economist in doing an economic projection for someone to have as much information as you could about that person, whether it's a man or woman, that person's earnings history and employment history; is that a fair observation?
> A: That is a fair observation, and in most cases I do have that kind of data.
>
>   *   *   *
>
> Q: Weren't you curious when you were first retained in this matter to find out what the earnings history of Mrs. [Jepson] was prior to the accident in March 1977? A: In this actual case, I was not interested in that as you are suggesting particularly—
> Q: I am only asking, were you curious about what her actual earnings history had been prior— A: I did not look into the past earnings records because it was absolutely clear in my mind that Mrs. [Jepson] would have come back and started at $12,000 at the clinic. Therefore, there was no point in seeing what she might have earned part-time as a nurse because she had a job waiting.
> Q: So the answer is, you weren't concerned at all about what her past earnings history had been; is that correct? A: I did not look into it, yes, sir.
>
>   *   *   *
>
> Q: Limiting my question to employment only, did they [the Jepson's lawyers] tell you at that time, if you recall, Professor, that during the period 1968 through 1975, she had no full-time employment outside the home? A: No, we did not discuss that fact.
> Q: Did they, if you recall, Professor, tell you that in the year 1975, her gross earnings were $5,435? A: No, I did not have that information.
> Q: Did they tell you, if you recall, Professor, that in 1976, her gross earnings were $5,185? A: No, I did not have that information.
> Q: Were you informed at that time, Professor, that she had quit her job on June 14, 1976, and was unemployed outside the home until November 1976? A: No, I did not have that information.

Q: Were you told at that time, Professor, that during the period
of 1960 to 1968, her income from her nursing profession ranged
from $61—a low of $61.54 in 1964—to a high of $618 in 1967?
Did they tell you that? A: No, sir, I did not know that.

Q: And therefore, the projections which you have testified about
in response to Mr. Krause's questions, are not based at all on the
actual earnings history or the actual employment history of this
lady; isn't that correct?

A: No, they are to some degree, Mr. Fearon. Not on any numbers, but on the basis that she was a registered nurse, that she
was a very highly qualified person, she was very highly liked by
everyone that knew her that I could find out.

Having planted doubts about the $12,000 base earnings figure, Steve
Fearon went on to force the professor to calculate the effects of lower
earnings:

Q: So if you used a salary of $6,000 instead of $12,000, the discounted figure is $91,658; is that correct? A: Yes, sir, that's
correct.

Q: In fact, the $6,000 we now know was a sum in excess by
almost a thousand dollars of her gross pay in 1976, which was
$5,185? A: I testified I did not see those figures. You have the
figures.

Q: Did you learn at the time what her actual earnings had been?
A: No, sir, I didn't talk with her employer about what her earnings had been. I talked with her employer about the fact she had
a job waiting for her at $12,000. I made that very clear.

Then Steve went into the discrepancies between Professor Haynes's
preliminary report and the changes he made after he discussed the case
with Chuck Krause:

Q: Mr. Rutherford asked you some questions about the Keogh
plan, and it is correct to say that no reference at all is contained
in Exhibit I [the earlier report] to a Keogh plan; is that correct?
A: Yes, sir, that is correct. In my original work, I did not inter-
ject any ideas about the Keogh plan. I found out about that later.

* * *

Q: When did you decide, in preparing to testify in this case, to
calculate in your projections a loss for this Keogh plan of some
$66,000? A: After I had been contacted by the firm of Mr.
Krause, I began updating the data I had. I then looked into it
further to find out if there were any fringe benefits because I had
not looked into that with the preliminary report. It was simply to
look at her income, that was all. Then I went ahead and did that
data.

Q: In other words, Mr. Krause telephoned you a few weeks
ago, is that correct, and told you this matter was coming on for
trial in New York? A: He called me from New York long-
distance and told me it was coming on for trial.

Q: Did you discuss with him at that time throwing in the Keogh plan damages of $66,000? A: No.

Q: With whom did you confer, if anyone, prior to deciding to include the Keogh plan as an element of damages in your testimony? A: When Mr. Krause came out to Oregon, I met with him in the office of [the Jepson's lawyers].

Q: Prior to that time, had you discussed including the Keogh plan loss with anyone else? A: No. At that time when Mr. Krause met with me, he and I discussed this case for, I think, almost three or four hours that afternoon the first time I saw him. At that time, I inquired if there were anything further that I should know about the case. He asked me if I had looked into the fringe benefits in terms of retirement. I advised him I had not. I advised him that we ought to look into that. And then I went ahead and looked into it and looked into the Keogh plan.

Q: Did you go back to the clinic at that point and find out anything about the Keogh plan? A: Yes, I did.

Chuck Krause then took over for redirect examination, and tried to clear up some of the uncertainties that had arisen during the vigorous cross-examination by the two airline lawyers. Chuck wanted to be able to argue the higher figures that were obtained by using a working span to age 70. He asked Professor Haynes:

Q: Do you know of anything that is going to change the amount of time or can change the amount of time that a person can work? A: Yes. A law has just been passed that extends—

Mr. RUTHERFORD: Objection.

The COURT: Sustained.

Mr. KRAUSE: May I ask the basis for that? Is my question bad?

The COURT: Yes. He is not here to advise the jury on the law.

Mr. KRAUSE: I ask that the Court take judicial notice of 29 U.S.C. Section 631, and Section 623, which is entitled "Prohibition of Age Discrimination."

The COURT: I take judicial notice that Title 29 of the United States Code, Section 623, which was enacted in 1967, prohibits discrimination on account of age, and Section 631, which was passed in 1978, and as I understand it, is now law, permits employees to work without discrimination on account of age, up to the age of 70. As I understand this law, employers may still require compulsory retirement at age 65. However, there must be no discrimination between and among the employees. If anyone wishes me to supplement that brief comment, I would be prepared to do so.

Mr. RUTHERFORD: Your Honor, for the record, we would object to that as being totally irrelevant to this case.

Then Chuck went on to take the last shot in the running battle between interest rates and inflation. The plaintiff's lawyer must make certain that the evidence of inflation is clearly before the jury, so that it can be used to offset the evidence of interest rates which will reduce the award to present value. Often the plaintiff's lawyer can show a widening gap between the discount rate and the inflation rate. Chuck turned his attention to the means by which Walter Rutherford had forced Professor Haynes to reduce the total loss to only $79,399. One of the key adjustments was the use of an 8.5 percent discount rate, which was then being paid on some savings accounts. But Walter had cleverly left the growth rate (inflation factor) at the long-term historical rate of 6.18 percent, instead of using the actual rate at the time of trial. This was a comparison of apples with oranges, and Chuck moved in to clear it up:

> Q: Yesterday, you referred to a differential between your projected growth rate based on historical information and the discount rate. Do you remember that? A: Yes, I do.
> Q: Your historical growth rate was 6.18 and your interest rate was 5 percent? A: Yes.
> Q: And the difference then is what? A: 1.18 percent.
> Q: In fact, you used a lower differential than the current differential between the 8.5 percent rate that was suggested [by Mr. Rutherford] and the current Consumer Price Index information; is that right? A: That's correct. I used 1.18 and currently it would be 2.30.

Thus, as the discount rate went higher, so did the growth or inflation rate, and the gap in favor of the plaintiff would be 2.3 percent instead of the 1.18 percent that the professor had used on direct examination. It is this gap that the plaintiff's lawyer must keep in focus, no matter how many bewildering economic data find their way into the case. Unless the discount rate is fully offset by the inflation adjustment, the jury may reduce its award drastically.

Chuck then went back to the differences between Professor Haynes's preliminary report and his trial testimony, and demonstrated that the changes had been made by the professor on his own. He wanted to dispel the notion that the professor's conclusions had been dictated by lawyers. He closed on this note:

> Q: Yesterday, he [Mr. Rutherford] asked you about your reference to the Speiser Economic Handbook contained in your preliminary report. Do you recall that? A: Yes, sir, I do.
> Q: Did you ever meet me or Mr. Speiser prior to using that handbook? A: No, the first time I saw you was three weeks ago.
> Q: Why did you use the Speiser Economic Handbook? A: I have been using this for eight years. It is a well-documented source.
> Q: Did I ask you to refer to that book in any way, to write this report, back in 1977? A: No, you never did.

That ended the crucial testimony of the economist. Now the case was ready for final argument and submission to the jury. Walter Rutherford summed up first for Pan Am. He admitted that Barbara Jepson had been an excellent person, a good wife, and a good mother. But the question before the jury was a monetary issue: how much money did Mr. Jepson and the boys lose as the result of her death? He argued that Barbara's life pattern indicated more interest in getting a postgraduate degree than in going to work full-time, and that the $12,000-a-year job was just talk—she intended to keep working until all the boys finished college, but there was nothing to indicate that she was going to work to the age of 65 or 70. He also pointed out that Barbara had spent $4,000 for the Canary Islands trip ($2,000 for her mother's passage and $2,000 for her own) out of a total of $5,000 that she had earned in the preceding year. Therefore he challenged the concept that she would be contributing most of her earnings to the family rather than consuming them herself. He reminded the jurors of the $79,399 figure that he had extracted from Professor Haynes as one version of the total financial loss. He did not request the jury to award a specific amount of damages, but simply asked that they consider all of Pan Am's arguments including the $79,399 calculation.

Steve Fearon followed Walter Rutherford for KLM. He pointed out how highly theoretical all of Professor Haynes's calculations had been. Each one was built on a prior assumption which might or might not come to pass. He said:

> In a sense, this whole case seems to me to be a conflict of what really happens in life and in this family, and what happened to a hypothetical woman with a hypothetical job, giving all of her hypothetical money to this family.

Then he reviewed these hypothetical assumptions and argued that all were heavily weighted in favor of the plaintiff; the award would be much lower if the defendants were given the benefit of the doubt as to any one of the hypothetical factors. He stressed the fact that the family's breadwinner had not been killed; David Jepson had testified that he did not need an extra salary in the house and that he was in a position to support his wife and four boys very well. As to loss of companionship, society, and guidance, Fearon pointed out that the boys were very independent and were past the age when they had to look to their mother for guidance and nurture. He did not put a specific value on the case. He said that Judge Ward would charge them that they could not bring in a verdict based on guesswork or sympathy: it would have to be based on reality.

Then Chuck Krause had the final word for the plaintiffs. To begin with he said:

> I want to remind you that this is the one day in court that the [Jepson] family has regarding the death of [Barbara Jepson].

Tomorrow, when you deliberate, I ask that you take all the time you need after the judge has given you his instructions to render a fair and just verdict. They can't come back. This is their only time here. They can't come back next year or five years from now and tell you it wasn't right, or it wasn't enough.

He pointed out the devastating effects of inflation, and how they had to take it into consideration because the award was going to have to stretch out for more than 20 years into the future. He asked them to recall what had happened to the cost of food, clothing, and entertainment during the past 20 years. Then he summarized all of the proof, taking it witness by witness. He hit hard at the defendants' failure to produce any evidence:

> I suggest to you that there is no question about the preponderance of the evidence in this case. I am the only one who put any evidence in on behalf of my clients. The defendants didn't like our statistics, but you notice that they didn't bring in an economist—they didn't bring in a table on nurses' earnings.

He felt that it was important to counter Steve Fearon's "hypothetical" argument:

> There has been a silent witness in this courtroom, by reason of the fact that [Barbara Jepson] is dead—*not hypothetically dead,* but dead. She is never coming back. Although she didn't get on that stand, I think she testified a little bit through her husband and a little bit through her son Mark and possibly through the other witnesses.

He went on to explain the function of the jury in setting a value on the case:

> I am going to be talking about the value of life. We can look to several comparisons and find that our society demands that the value of human life be held very high. Frankly, I am proud that I live in a country that values life as highly as we do. I don't think there is another country in the world that does. I believe that it is a mark of our civilization that we hold the principle of life to be most precious and such an expensive commodity.
>
>   *   *   *
>
> Another thing I think is significant is that we have a way in this country of spending a lot of money to protect life. If you think back to our early space age, how many billions of dollars were spent to make sure that John Glenn and his fellow astronauts were brought back? We even sacrificed putting somebody up in the air first because we wanted them to be safe.
>
> Frankly, I had hoped that Mr. Rutherford and Mr. Fearon

would tell you what they thought about this case and what they thought it was worth. Mind you, they can do that. Mr. Fearon seemed to suggest that he couldn't do that. He can. He can tell you exactly the dollar value that he thinks this case is worth. Rather, they are saying only that our claim is wrong—that whatever we are saying is wrong.

Then Chuck reviewed the basic figures that Professor Haynes had used in his calculations. He showed that they were reasonable middle-range figures for all of the values involved, rather than the highest values that could be argued or supported by expert testimony. They added up to $439,497, which Chuck had adopted as a reasonable estimate of the actual financial loss. To this he added an estimate of $200,000 for loss of society, companionship, training, nurture, and guidance. He said to the jury:

> I asked David to bring the boys here for this trial. They have to have their day in court. There is going to come a time fifteen years from now when they say, "Mom is gone a long time. What about my mother?" It will be something on their minds and they should know about this experience. So I asked Dave, and he concurred. That is why we have them here. They should know when they grow older what happened these few days in the courtroom. It is your duty, and I want you to tell them what their mother was worth to them.

While he had explained the financial damages in great detail, he merely sketched loss of society. He said that there were no firm guidelines, and they could award anything that they felt was reasonable, given the circumstances of the Jepson family.

The summations ended late in the afternoon of Thursday, August 25, 1978. Judge Ward told the jury that he would instruct them the next morning. Before the court adjourned for the day on Thursday, the defendants decided to make a final offer of settlement. They offered to pay $375,000. This figure really put Chuck Krause on the spot, because it was a little above the middle of the probable range of jury verdicts that he could visualize in this case. Given the wide variations that depended upon whether Barbara was going to work full-time; whether she would continue to keep house full-time for the rest of her life; and which discount and inflation rates were used, the jury could reasonably award something between $200,000 and $500,000 in damages. This wide range was inherent in jurors' valuation of human life, particularly in a case where the person killed was not the breadwinner, and where the father and sons obviously were able to take care of themselves.

Chuck called me at home that evening and told me about the $375,000 offer. He asked my opinion because I was more detached from the give-and-take of the trial. Since he had just completed his summation and was still tingling with all of the positive drive that must be generated to project the case properly to the jurors, he felt that I might be able to help him to evaluate the settlement offer objectively. We discussed the case for nearly an hour on the telephone. We had to put aside our natural inclination to let the case go to the jury. Once the lawyer has done all of the work of presenting the case and summing it up, there is a great deal of momentum in favor of letting the jury decide it, particularly when liability has been conceded and the only question is the amount of damages. There was also the excitement that we felt at being selected lead counsel in the largest case that had ever come up in our field of practice, and the anticipated distinction of trying and winning the first jury verdict. On the other hand, we both honestly felt that the $375,000 offer had crossed the line beyond which the interests of the clients would be better served by settling. Even if the jurors empathized completely with the family and decided to be generous, they could still bring in a verdict of less than $375,000. And if they awarded much more than $375,000, there was always the chance that Judge Ward would reduce it by remittitur. Therefore, Chuck and I agreed that he should recommend to Dave Jepson that the $375,000 offer be accepted.

Chuck met with Dave early the next morning and gave him our appraisal. Dave thought about it carefully and discussed it with his four sons. Finally they decided that since they had come all the way across the country to try the case, they would prefer to let the jury have the final word. Perhaps it was partly an emotional decision, based upon a desire to do justice to Barbara's memory. Maybe a settlement seemed like an unsuitable way to end the case when Dave and his sons had presented the story of Barbara's life to the jury. It had been an emotional experience for them, and rather than placing their own value on Barbara's life, they wanted justice to run its course. Whatever the reasons, Dave Jepson told Chuck to reject the offer and let the case go to the jury.

After hearing some final arguments about the proposed instructions, Judge Ward began his charge to the jury at 10:30 A.M. At 11:37 A.M., Judge Ward completed his instructions. Then he had the U.S. Marshall sworn, and turned the jurors over to him, saying:

> The jury is placed in charge of the Marshall. From now on you will communicate with the Court only through the Marshall by notes. The Court and counsel remain available and we will await your verdict.

It was that magic moment in American justice when the jury was exercising its power. It was a power not only to compensate one family, but to fix the future insurance rates for jumbo jet accidents, and in the process to establish the price of being careless about the safety of others. It is a process that takes place nowhere else but in the United States. If left to the systems of other countries, it would be very cheap to be careless; the insurance costs would be negligible; and one of the main incentives for safe operation of aircraft would be removed. But now two of the greatest airlines in the world were being judged by a young videotape editor and five New York women who were in no way connected with the disaster at Tenerife, or with the rate-making system at Lloyd's of London, or with any other phase of air transportation. They were six people chosen at random to deliver the judgment of an entire society as to what value is placed on human life.

At 12:45 P.M., the marshall brought a note to the judge requesting all of the exhibits used during the trial. The judge arranged for this to be done, and also sent the jurors out to lunch, to return at 2:15 P.M. At 3:30 P.M., the marshall handed the judge a note from the jury to say that they had reached a verdict. They returned to the courtroom, and the first Tenerife verdict was about to be announced.

> The CLERK: Mr. Foreman, please rise. Has the jury agreed on a verdict?
> The FOREMAN: Yes.
> The CLERK: How do you find?
> The FOREMAN: The total amount will be $375,000.
> The COURT: You find for the plaintiff in the amount of $375,000, is that correct?
> The FOREMAN: Yes, sir.
> The COURT: And so say you all?
> The JURORS: Yes.

Judge Ward thanked the jurors for their service and then he turned to the trial lawyers and the plaintiffs. He closed out the first Tenerife trial with these words:

> The COURT: I would not want to close these proceedings without saying to Mr. [Jepson] and the [Jepson] boys that you came east here, you submitted your case to a New York jury, and I can only suggest to you that to the best of our ability we gave you a full and fair hearing and in my judgment, at least, I believe that although one can never compensate totally for the loss of a wife and mother, you did receive justice here in the spirit of our own system of administering justice.
> As I said when I charged the jury, one can never put a value on these things, but I know you had six people who listened, and I am certain from observing them that they performed their function as jurors in a conscientious fashion.
> We who sit as judges try our best to give litigants a fair

trial and hope that a jury will do its job in a conscientious fashion. I have tried to do my job. I believe the jury has done its job. I want to wish you, Mr. [Jepson], and your boys a safe trip and good luck.

Mr. KRAUSE: On behalf of the [Jepson] family, I am sure they believe they have received a fair trial here in New York. They have expressed that to me.

The COURT: Mr. Krause, you are the chairman of our plaintiffs' committee, and I know of no one who could have done a better job representing the plaintiff in the first case to be tried, and I just want to make note of that.

I want to say the same to Mr. Rutherford and Mr. Craft, and Mr. Fearon for KLM. At all times this case was tried in a fashion which I believe comports with the American system, which is to do justice fairly among people, whether they be individuals or corporations, domestic or foreign. I think the manner in which this case was conducted should serve as an example.

I just want to close by thanking you all for the hard work that you have put in in preparing on relatively short notice this important case and on the manner in which it was presented.

The Court is adjourned.

Aftermath

The verdict in the Jepson case reinforced our faith in the jury system. The jurors had been bombarded with conflicting arguments and complicated theories upon which very few economics professors can agree. Yet their damage calculation was almost exactly what we and the specialists on the defense side estimated as the final value of the case. David Jepson and his sons were well satisfied with the result. Even though their decision to let the case go to the jury was based partially on the hope that the verdict would exceed the $375,000 final offer, it was, as we have seen, an emotional decision. They felt a sense of fulfillment, which they could not have achieved through a settlement on the eve of jury deliberations.

I could not help contrasting the Tenerife verdict with the result of the 1958 Grand Canyon trial in which Mel Belli had represented the family of Mildred Harkness, a woman strikingly similar to Barbara Jepson. Mildred Harkness had died at 40, one year younger than Barbara Jepson. Mildred had earned $5,080 as a full-time schoolteacher in the last year of her life, and was scheduled for automatic raises to a level of $7,100, according to the testimony of her supervisor. Barbara Jepson had been working part-time as a nurse; had earned approximately $5,000 a year in the two years that she worked; and there was testimony that she intended to take a full-time job at $12,000. Mildred Harkness had left three young children (all of them less than 14 years old), two of whom required special care, while Barbara Jepson had left four husky, self-reliant sons, all of them above the age of 14. And while Barbara was survived by her husband (the successful timber executive who was well equipped to carry on the family life) Mildred Harkness's husband had been killed with her in the Grand Canyon crash, leaving the three children without the support, guidance, or companionship of either of their parents.

Comparing all of these damage factors, one would expect most juries to award higher damages to the Harkness family, whose children suffered a demonstrably greater economic loss. Yet the Grand Canyon jury awarded the Harkness children only $20,000 for the death of their mother, while the Tenerife jury awarded $375,000. Of course, the 20 years separating the two verdicts was a time of rapidly escalating inflation. However, even if we triple the Harkness award as a generous allowance for the effects of inflation, we still have only $60,000—less than one-sixth of the amount awarded by the Tenerife jury. The Harkness case had been tried expertly by Mel Belli, the teaching master of tort law. The defendants in the Grand Canyon case had considered the $20,000 verdict so high that they made a motion to have it reduced. While the trial judge denied the motion, he did reduce the amounts awarded for the deaths of Mildred Harkness's husband and the other male passenger whose case was tried with theirs, which indicates that the Grand Canyon jury was inclined to be on the generous side according to 1958 standards. Since inflation explains only a small fraction of the difference, what accounts for this great change in the short span of 20 years? The substantive law has not changed. The new factor is the emergence of the scientific tort lawyer, who has become a scientist in the discovery and presentation of facts and arguments which can educate judges and jurors to a full awareness of the devastating impact of personal injuries and the taking of human life.

These changes were epitomized by the economist's testimony that dominated the Tenerife trial. Twenty years earlier, no plaintiff's lawyer was able to present this kind of compelling, enlightening, scientific evidence. The earlier tort lawyers were reduced to appealing to the sympathies of the jurors, only to clash head on with the judge's instructions that jurors were not to consider personal feelings or sympathies. Now, thanks to two decades of pioneering by scientific tort lawyers, death cases routinely involve evidence of the value of household services, the effects of inflation, and other sophisticated calculations by professional economists. Publications such as *The Statistical Abstract of the United States, The Consumer Price Index,* and specialized collections of economic statistics are handled routinely by judges and lawyers; and in the Tenerife trial, the jurors understood this complicated testimony so well that they were able to calculate the damages to the exact dollar that all the parties agreed was the proper measure of damages.

Despite the great advances since 1950, we were just starting to explore the use of the computer to calculate damages. Professor Haynes had made his adjustments for inflation and other economic variables by using a computer program designed for that purpose. At that time I was working on the second edition of my *Recovery for Wrongful Death Economic Handbook*. When I completed it in 1979, it included a section entitled, "Using the Programmable Hand Calculator in the Calculation of Damages." In that section, I set out detailed instructions for programming a hand-held calculator, using the Texas Instruments models TI57, TI58, and TI59 as examples. This computer program was designed to enable lawyers and economists to calculate within seconds all of the variables needed for determining wrongful death damages. Many scientific tort lawyers throughout the country were using computers, small and large, to amass, digest, and present the information needed to take the entrepreneur-lawyer's revolution into its next stage.

The Jepson trial set a standard which helped to settle many of the remaining Tenerife cases. Judge Ward stayed with the Tenerife assignment all the way. He went to San Francisco and Los Angeles to conduct settlement conferences and trials in those suits that had been filed in California and were returned for damage trials there. In all, Judge Ward conducted seven more damage trials after the Jepson case —five in California and two more in his own courtroom in the Southern District of New York. By the time he completed his second year as MDL judge on the Tenerife cases on August 16, 1979, only nine cases remained to be disposed of. In March 1980, the last of the Tenerife cases was settled, completing a remarkable achievement by Judge Ward and the federal court system.

Because of the dramatic background of the Tenerife accident, the Jepson trial received national publicity. With one of the highest verdicts ever rendered for the death of a housewife, it also brought the financial value of a housewife's services to the attention of the public. In her syndicated column of September 21, 1978, the financial writer Sylvia Porter used the case to illustrate the monetary value of a housewife and suggested that wife-insurance was among the most neglected areas of insurance coverage. "It is no more than common sense for a wife to be insured so her major services could be replaced if necessary," she said, and suggested that the value of housewives' services should be included in the calculation of the Gross National Product, since their labor is recognized by the law as a basis for awarding damages in case of death.

Tenerife had some effects on the entrepreneur-lawyer and on tort law as a whole, and we shall return to these shortly. But let us first examine the position of the tort lawyer at the start of the 1980s.

TORT LAWYERS OF THE 1980s

You may recall my saying in Chapter 2 that the trinity of torts—jury trials, contingent fees, and entrepreneur-lawyers—distinguish American tort practice from that of other nations, and that it was not until entrepreneur-lawyers emerged as a strong force that tort plaintiffs achieved equality in the courts. We caught a few glimpses of the post-1950 entrepreneur-lawyer in the cases examined in Chapters 3 to 8; now we can fill in some of their history, and I will try to document the importance of the entrepreneur-lawyer.

Some writers credit the advent of the automobile and its accompanying liability insurance for bringing on the tort revolution, citing the fact that there were very few tort suits back in the time when most tort feasors were uninsured and impecunious. It is true that there was not much point in suing the average driver of a horse and wagon, since the chances of collecting a judgment were negligible. But in giving auto liability insurance major credit for the tort revolution, they are, in my opinion, putting the cart before the horse.

Liability insurance arose from the need for coverage. It could not be sold without the threat of a large judgment, for it produces nothing positive for the buyer. Unless the buyers are concerned about an effective lawsuit that can deprive them of considerable money, no insurance salesman is going to get inside their door to sell them a policy. Liability insurance developed on a large scale only *after* tort lawyers broke through on their own and started to get awards that threatened the solvency of careless motorists. For proof of this, you have only to look at other nations. Insurance underwriting started in England, and English underwriters are still far more sophisticated than American insurers, as demonstrated by the worldwide preeminence of Lloyd's of London. Yet the English tort system, lacking the entrepreneur-lawyers, jury trials, and contingent fees, still falls far short of providing the compensation that victims can get in the United States. All industrialized nations have automobile liability insurance schemes, and many of them are compulsory. But outside the United States, there is no fully developed court system for adequate accident compensation. I do not believe it is a coincidence that the United States is also the only place that has entrepreneur-lawyers.

Probably the best starting point for the history of the entrepreneur-lawyer is the post-1950 development of that unique bar association which we first met as the National Association of Claimants' Compensation Attorneys (NACCA) and then under its new name, the Association of Trial Lawyers of America (ATLA).

ATLA as the Catalyst

I described in Chapter 3 how Sam Horovitz of Boston, a worker's compensation specialist, founded NACCA in 1946 and hooked it to the tail of the California comet, Melvin Belli, in 1949. Sam would have made a great film producer, for he knew how to pick stars and put them together in a working team. It was during Mel's presidency from 1950 to 1951 that NACCA blossomed forth to attract tort lawyers throughout the country. After he got Belli going on a nationwide crusade, Sam pulled his greatest coup in 1953 by signing up Roscoe Pound, former dean of the Harvard Law School, to become the editor of the *NACCA Law Journal*. There is no greater name than Roscoe Pound in all the history of American jurisprudence. His enormous prestige and scholarship established the *NACCA Law Journal* as a serious professional publication which judges throughout the country read and cited.

Roscoe Pound was renowned as the chief American advocate of sociological jurisprudence, which required old legal precedents to be adjusted to contemporary social conditions. He and his colleagues, including Felix Frankfurter, were credited with inspiring and providing the legal underpinning for much of Franklin D. Roosevelt's New Deal legislation in the 1930s. Pound was in his early eighties when Sam Horovitz recruited him. He stayed on for two years until his eyesight began to give out. Then Sam Horovitz came up with the impossible: a replacement for Pound that was to prove as important to NACCA-ATLA as the great dean himself. His choice was Professor Thomas F. Lambert, Jr., who was recommended by Dean Pound as his successor in 1955. Before that, Tom Lambert had already piled up enough accomplishments to last most lawyers a lifetime. He had served as professor of law at Boston University, at New York University, and at John B. Stetson College of Law in Florida, where he became the youngest dean of any law school in the United States. As an undergraduate at U.C.L.A., he was an honor student with a spectacular record as a debating champion and was awarded a Rhodes scholarship to Oxford University, where he received bachelor's and master's degrees in jurisprudence. During World War II, he served as a naval officer at General Omar

Bradley's headquarters and was decorated for his participation in the planning and operation of military government in Europe. During the Nuremberg trials, he was trial counsel on the staff of the chief American prosecutor, Justice Robert H. Jackson. Tom prepared the American trial brief against the Nazi party leaders and delivered the trial summation address against party chief Martin Bormann.

Tom Lambert has extraordinary powers of expression, both written and oral. He can make the most routine fender-bender case seem dramatic by investing it with biblical significance and grandeur. He has applied his great gifts to his work with tireless devotion. Although he was hired as the editor-in-chief of the *ATLA Law Journal,* he did not confine himself to editorial work, even though he would have given ATLA its money's worth three times over through his writing skills alone. On top of writing the *ATLA Law Journal* almost single-handedly, he barnstormed all over the country for more than twenty years, speaking to gatherings of judges, legislators, and lawyers. He opened the minds and hearts of many judges and legislators to the needs of plaintiffs and their lawyers. The entrepreneur-lawyer could not have found a more inspired prophet. One of his most valuable contributions was to inspire the plaintiff's lawyers themselves. He raised our self-esteem many notches by his laudatory descriptions of the work that we were engaged in. Our egos were receptive to praise from any quarter, but it took the expressive powers of Tom Lambert to make us *believe* that we were engaged in a noble crusade, and to give us the emotional lift that pushed us toward making this image a reality. Take, for example, some excerpts from a Tom Lambert speech delivered to law students and later published in the *Harvard Law Record* and the *Congressional Record:*

> On the threshold I would say to young law students that it is imperative early in their legal studies to fix in their souls some images of magnificence, and to be alert to the hazard that, in the moral erosions of the market place and the dilemmas of actual practice, all too often the "world's slow stain" can get them. The reassurance may, therefore, be timely that a lawyer can put his powers to the full at the personal injury bar, and without glossing or poeticizing the raw realities involved in litigating the claims of those who have been victimized by accident, he can find self-fulfillment without irony, disdain, quiet desperation, or bitterness. He can even earn his way into the surtax brackets and enjoy creature comforts in amplitude and yet make himself, if he is so minded, into a civilized man. The point that needs accenting is that this kind of enriched professional life can be achieved in personal injury practice, and the only awful kind of aging, the slow desertion of ideals, can be avoided. It is good to be able to record that, on both sides of the counsel table, the young personal injury lawyer will find men of accomplishment, cultivation,

high and unimpaired principle—men of new ideas and old valor. Certainly the writer has found a trove of these qualities among the rank and file, editors, and officers of NACCA, and everywhere in it, has felt the vivid presence of a heart.

*   *   *

It is important to distinguish between monuments and ruins and not to abandon jury trial in the drive to do away with avoidable delay. The prediction here is that the anvil of jury trial will outlast the hammers of its critics. The intractable personal injury problem today, more acute even than delay in trial or settlement, is the age-old quest for a financially responsible defendant. Inroads will be made on that problem and on reducing our court congestion without hurling the jury system into outer darkness. Jury trial (with acknowledgment and apologies to Mr. Thurber) should be more abundant, not moribundant.

*   *   *

Certainly jury verdicts have increased in modern times. The basis of our economy shifted from the ox plough and the cave to the industrial revolution, from that to the age of electricity and now to the atomic era. Why should we have gaslight verdicts in the atomic age?

*   *   *

If you set the common law, like man, against the stars, you see both immemorial age and ever-renewing youth, and you come to see that even equilibrium is dynamic.

Here are a few more Lambert gems:

(*On the deterrent effect of tort litigation*) Immunity breeds irresponsibility. . . . Safety is the religion of us all. . . . The therapeutic and prophylactic effect of tort law is unquestioned. . . . A fence at the top of a hill is better than an ambulance in the valley below.
(*On torts and the common law process*) The tort signature is harm, and compensation for that harm, coincident with effecting safety, is what tort law is all about. . . . The common law is never finished. *Stare decisis* does not mean the sanctification of ancient fallacy.
(*On products liability*) The best place to eliminate product-related injuries is on the drawing board. . . . Brakeless cars are not best, even if carefully made.

With Horovitz, Belli, Pound, and Lambert leading the way, thousands of other lawyers who had been ready to be galvanized into action made NACCA-ATLA a phenomenal success. It went way beyond the normal functions of a bar association. It became the command post of the entrepreneur-lawyers' revolution, by teaching techniques as well as law, and by organizing plaintiff's lawyers into action groups to cooperate in pending cases. You may recall from Chapter 3 that I used NACCA as the catalyst for forming a group of plaintiff's lawyers in the Grand

Canyon litigation, which I believe was the first time that any bar association served that purpose. Today, there are more than a dozen ATLA-based action groups, most of them devoted to cooperation among lawyers representing the victims of products that have allegedly caused widespread injuries. Often these groups hold meetings in conjunction with ATLA's annual conventions.

One of ATLA's great creations was the Products Liability Exchange, a lawyers' clearinghouse for information on specific product defects. As I write this, I am looking at a package of papers our firm received from ATLA's Products Liability Exchange in response to our inquiry for all their data on injuries caused by a particular medical device that is implanted in the body through surgery. They provided us with a nationwide list of cases that involved these products and have either been tried or settled. Many of these cases were not reported in any legal publication, but were gathered by ATLA through reports of its own members. The package also included the names of other ATLA members who had contacted the exchange on this subject and had requested or contributed information. The exchange is a two-way street, where ATLA members willingly contribute much of the vital information that they gather in the course of products liability cases. Also included in the package were articles from medical journals relating to these devices, and technical literature published by manufacturers. In all, this kit of more than fifty pages furnished us with information which would have taken hundreds of hours for us to compile on our own. Indeed, I doubt that we would have found all this material no matter how much time we devoted to searching, for it represents the efforts of many lawyers and the fruits of years of litigation.

ATLA has grown from a few dozen worker's compensation lawyers in 1946 to a 1980 membership of over 30,000 lawyers practicing throughout our 50 states and in Canada. It now has a large staff that serves its members effectively from its headquarters in Washington. In addition to the *ATLA Law Journal,* a scholarly hardcover book that appears every other year, ATLA now publishes the *ATLA Law Reporter* ten times a year. This digests more than a thousand significant new cases a year from all parts of the nation, thus giving ATLA members early notice of new developments in the law.

ATLA's educational programs continue to expand. On its own and in collaboration with state and local bar organizations, ATLA sponsors and organizes high quality teaching seminars for practicing lawyers. In recent years, ATLA has produced audio and video tapes of trial demonstrations and lectures, so that lawyers can learn at home or while driving their cars. Thousands of ATLA members have contributed their time and talents, often traveling to the seminars at their own expense to divulge techniques that have won cases for them. This gesture is not entirely philanthropic, for in addition to the ego gratification that goes with being recognized as a teacher by one's professional peers, it can also produce referrals of cases from lawyers in the audience.

Today the presidency of ATLA is almost a full-time job, requiring incumbents to give up much of their law practice so that they can appear at ATLA functions throughout the nation and testify before Congress and state legislatures on matters of interest to the trial bar. Four firms have each provided two presidents of ATLA. Lou Ashe succeeded his partner, Mel Belli, as ATLA president in 1959. Then Samuel Langerman of Phoenix became president in 1967, followed by his partner, Robert Begam, in 1976. Perry Nichols of Miami served as president in 1957, and his partner Bill Colson became president in 1964. Al Cone of West Palm Beach, Florida, was president in 1967, followed by his partner, Ward Wagner, Jr., in 1975.

At first ATLA was treated as an outcast by other bar associations. Perry Nichols made a great breakthrough as president in 1957, when he persuaded Charles Rhyne, then president of the American Bar Association, to speak at the ATLA convention and to open the way for cooperation between the two major national bar organizations. Here I was also able to help. My good friend Jim Donovan (the New York lawyer who engineered the Abel-for-Powers spy swap and the liberation of Cuban Bay of Pigs prisoners) was one of the main legal spokesmen for the insurance industry. Jim felt that insurance lawyers should work together with ATLA to improve the tort system, and at his request, I introduced him to ATLA officials with whom he worked effectively toward that end.

The spectacular effects of ATLA's educational programs gave birth to a new industry. Commercial publishers jumped in to produce a gusher of ATLA-inspired books, newsletters, medical atlases, charts, models, seminars, audio tapes, and videotape cassettes. Most of this material was on the practical side, stressing methods of proof and medical education for attorneys. Several medical-legal encyclopedias were published, summarizing basic medical literature in language more readily understandable by lawyers. Then came large colored charts and plastic overlays of parts of the body, not only for the education of lawyers but also for courtroom use in describing injuries to judges and juries.

Lawyers starting out in the 1980s to educate themselves for tort practice have a far easier task than their predecessors of the 1930s or even the 1960s. In one single volume called the *Lawyers Desk Reference,* written by Harry M. Philo, Dean A. Robb, and Richard M. Goodman (three Michigan lawyers who were among the pioneers of the ATLA movement), there is presented more useful information on the handling of tort cases than one could find in all the law books published in this country prior to 1950. Its 1,700 pages of technical sources for conducting personal injury actions include: the names and addresses of expert witnesses in all the major fields of tort litigation; sources of medical and environmental information; lists of technical safety publications, safety films, and safety standards; and another two dozen chapters filled with important references which it would take a lawyer thousands of hours to hunt down.

The practical effects of this information explosion were brought home to me strikingly in January of 1980. Kenneth P. Nolan, one of the young lawyers in our firm, was ready to try his first Supreme Court jury case, even though he had been admitted to the bar for less than two years. We represented a woman who was injured in a New York bus terminal. Liability was hotly contested. Not until Ken had completed his presentation of the plaintiff's case was there any settlement offer, and then it was only $7,500, which Ken judged to be way below the actual damage incurred. The case went through to completion, and the jury returned a verdict of $75,000 (then reduced to $50,000 because the jury found that the plaintiff was one-third to blame for the accident). When I heard that news, I thought back to my own level of knowledge during my second year of law practice. Nobody would have trusted me with a Supreme Court jury trial at that stage of my career. But thanks to many extracurricular courses that Ken Nolan took under the Practicing Law Institute and various ATLA programs, and also to the availability of *American Jurisprudence Trials* and *American Jurisprudence Proof of Facts* (two encyclopedic sets with graphic question-and-answer formats contributed by noted specialists in all types of tort cases), Ken had achieved a level of knowledge that equipped him to take on such responsibilities at a much earlier stage of his career. He had also profited from sitting through trials conducted by other lawyers in our firm, but in the main it was his extensive postgraduate education and the published guides to sources of proof and trial technique that had readied him for a Supreme Court trial.

There are so many educational post-admission programs today that it would be possible for a tort lawyer to spend every working day of the year at a seminar somewhere in the United States. During 1979, there were three seminars on "The Art of Making Objections" alone. Often the trial of only one or two cases in new fields such as sports and recreational liability will give rise to seminars. In 1979 there was one that had speakers on topics such as sledding, tobogganing, and ice skating; football helmets; and racquet sports. There are many seminars and educational materials on methods of selecting juries, and there are even consultants to help trial lawyers screen prospective jurors.

In the continuing search for more scientific means of proving liability and damages, ATLA and its educational offspring have fostered the development of almost every conceivable type of expert witness. I think the pinnacle of expert testimony was reached in a Nebraska criminal case in which the trial judge allowed the state to call a burglar as an expert witness on burglary. The burglar's expert testimony helped to convict the defendant, who appealed to the Nebraska Supreme Court. In their 1977 decision, the Justices wrote:

> Defendant strenuously objected to the testimony of an admitted burglar called on behalf of the State. This witness testified as to the use to which the items found in the defendant's possession might be put in perpetrating a burglary. The witness, who testified he was a retired burglar, had been convicted on at least five occasions. Defendant argues the testimony of this witness interfered with the decision-making process of the jury and was prejudicial to him. While two police officers testified as to the probable use of the items, it would be hard to find a person more qualified as an expert witness on the subject at hand than the witness to whom defendant objects.
>
> [The pertinent Nebraska statute] provides as follows: "If scientific, technical, or other specialized knowledge will assist the trier of fact to understand the evidence or to determine a fact in issue, a witness qualified as an expert by knowledge, skill, experience, training, or education, may testify thereto in the form of an opinion or otherwise."

Finding no fault with the expert burglar's scientific opinion, the Nebraska Supreme Court affirmed the conviction.

The education, inspiration, and cooperation fostered by ATLA helped enormously to further the tort revolution. But in the end it was the tort lawyer who determined what use would be made of the ammunition supplied by ATLA. And the breed had changed a lot since the pre-1950 early American era.

The New Breed

The dramatic advances in tort practice between 1950 and 1980 have changed the makeup of the tort bar. Plaintiff's tort practice is no longer dominated by those who cannot find a better way to make a living. Today you may see any kind of lawyer handling a plaintiff's tort case, and many lawyers who have opportunities for success in other branches of practice are specializing in tort cases by choice. Even the large general practice firms who derive most of their income from large business corporations may well have one or more lawyers who specialize in plaintiff's tort cases. Let's look at a few examples of tort lawyers in the 1980s.

Swift Currie McGhee & Hiers of Atlanta, Georgia, is a good example of a firm that was not part of the early American tort scene but became attracted to it when it had developed into a respectable scientific specialty. Swift Currie, with its own building in the business section of Atlanta, has twenty partners and eighteen associates. Its list of corporate clients reads like a Who's Who of American industry, including major manufacturers, insurers, and financial organizations. Glover McGhee, a Swift Currie senior partner who began his law practice in 1949, is a licensed pilot and devotes much of his time to major aviation accident cases throughout the southern states. Glover is known as an eminent specialist in representing aviation tort plaintiffs, though if you asked him to name his main claim to fame, he might tell you that he is considered one of the finest homemade (legal) winemakers in northern Georgia.

The town of Stamford, Connecticut boasts one of the largest and most prestigious law firms in all of New England: the 100-lawyer firm of Cummings & Lockwood. It was founded by Homer Cummings, Franklin D. Roosevelt's first attorney general. Cummings's integrity as a lawyer was immortalized in the Dana Andrews film *Boomerang,* which showed how Cummings proved the innocence of a man whom he himself had prosecuted for the murder of a Stamford priest. One of Cummings & Lockwood's senior partners is Morgan P. Ames, a six-foot eight-inch former Yale basketball player and Phi Beta Kappa member who has been in practice since 1948. While the firm represents the cream of Connecticut business and society, Morgan Ames devotes much of his time to personal injury litigation. Morgan has brought the unfamiliar bindings of medical textbooks and the rattle of a courtroom skeleton to the staid halls of Cummings & Lockwood. Between his busy practice and his work as a captain in the Naval Reserve, he has also found time to lecture on torts throughout the United States.

Another Connecticut firm with a blue-ribbon list of corporate and banking clients is Schatz & Schatz, Ribicoff & Kotkin of Hartford, which is the product of a merger of the firm founded by Nathan and Lewis Schatz at the turn of the century, and the firm of former U.S. Senator Abraham Ribicoff and his brother Irving, which Abraham left when he was elected to the Senate. Arthur Schatz, the son of one of the founders, started practice in 1942 and seemed destined to distinguish himself in the representation of banks, manufacturers, and retailers that had been the keystone of the Schatz & Schatz practice since the early days of the 20th century. Nevertheless, Arthur became interested in personal injury litigation in the late 1940s, when it was in its infancy as a specialty in Connecticut. He became a founding member and trustee of the Law-Science Academy Foundation of America, and he attended many domestic and international conferences on legal medicine. Arthur combines encyclopedic medical-legal knowledge with a rare trait for a plaintiff's tort lawyer: a strong financial background built on experience in the representation of banks and finance companies.

You will recall Arthur Schatz's role in the settlement of the case involving the brain-injured boy which was described in Chapter 4. Arthur did a prodigious job of "stacking" various insurance policies and arranging for strategic investment of the settlement proceeds, which resulted in raising the true financial value of that settlement by several million dollars. His years of training as a financial lawyer and the resources of his business-oriented Hartford law firm were a great boon to the family of the brain-injured boy. Arthur's imaginative handling of the settlement proceeds received favorable comment in both legal and financial publications.

In Cincinnati, Ohio, plaintiffs' tort specialist Stanley M. Chesley is now a senior partner of Waite Schneider Bayless & Chesley, a firm that was founded in the 19th century by Judge Morrison Remick Waite, a grandson of the Chief Justice of the United States under President U. S. Grant. Waite was solicitor general of the Baltimore & Ohio Railroad, and his firm was noted for its defense of railroad and insurance companies until Stan Chesley started practice in 1960. Stan has moved the firm into the forefront of Ohio's plaintiff's practice and is best known for his magnificent work as plaintiff's lead counsel in the litigation arising out of the 1977 Memorial Day fire at the Beverly Hills supper club in Covington, Kentucky, which resulted in 165 deaths and 100 injuries. Like many of the new breed, Stan is a part-time professor (at Salmon P. Chase College of Law).

William Marshall Morgan is senior partner of the Los Angeles firm of Morgan Wenzel & McNicholas, best known for its long roster of insurance defense clients. But like Glover McGhee of Atlanta, Marshall Morgan became an outstanding plaintiff's aviation tort specialist. Marshall began practice in California in 1950 after serving as a military pilot during World War II. He has used his aviation experience to good advantage in major aviation litigation, playing a prominent role on the plaintiffs' side of the Turkish Airlines DC-10 litigation before federal judge Peirson Hall. As we saw in Chapter 2, even in the early American tort period it was not unusual for outstanding defense lawyers to handle some of the larger and more difficult plaintiff's claims, but what has changed since 1950 is that lawyers like Marshall Morgan and Glover McGhee, senior partners in prominent insurance defense firms, have become *specialists* on the plaintiff's side.

Let us turn now to some of the more traditional plaintiff's firms that existed before 1950. How has the tort revolution affected them? A good starting point is an Alabama firm that bridges the gap between the early American tort lawyer and the entrepreneur-lawyer of the 1980s. Hare Wynn Newell & Newton of Birmingham is headed by Francis Hutcheson Hare, whose writings are sprinkled throughout this book. Francis started practicing in 1927 and became one of the pioneers of scientific tort litigation and medical-legal education. In his book of memoirs, *My Learned Friends,* he tells the story of one type of claim, the neck injury, which epitomizes the changes brought by the professionalization of tort practice:

> A doctor [in the old days] would answer truthfully that a plaintiff with an injured neck had no fracture of the bone. That would have been the end of the matter before medicolegal training taught the lawyer to bring out from the doctor the information that fracture of the cervical spine was actually less dangerous than a dislocation. We did not know that a dislocation would almost certainly put pressure on the spinal cord whereas a fracture might or might not.

Francis pioneered the description, measurement, and presentation of pain in the courtroom. As he said in his memoirs:

> Very few people who have been the victim of intense and prolonged pain ever receive a jury verdict that is anything like adequate for what they have suffered. Pain is not only unpleasant to endure; it is unpleasant to think about. The only chance of gaining a fair trial on the issue of pain and suffering is to persuade the jury to steel themselves to the disagreeable task of looking at the shocking reality of what pain is and what it does to a person.
>
> *   *   *
>
> Look at the law's attitude toward pain wherever it arises outside of an action for damages. The law forbids cruel and unusual punishments. The law says to the State: "You can inflict capital punishment, but you cannot use the lash on any man. You can take a man's life so long as you do it without pain. You can kill him, but you may not hurt him."

Francis H. Hare, Jr., who started practice in 1959, is now a partner in his father's firm. The Hare firm has always blended the scientific approach with the traditional folksy manner of the southern trial lawyer. Francis Jr. has helped to carry on this blending process. He was deeply involved in assembling the devastating liability evidence in the Ford Pinto civil litigation, working in cooperation with Arthur Hews and Mark Robinson of California. In keeping with the style of the new breed, Francis Jr. is the author of several books on torts and is an associate professor at the Cumberland School of Law, Sanford University, in Birmingham. In addition to the two Hares, the firm includes more than half a dozen other highly skilled tort lawyers.

The Hare firm is an example of an older tort firm that has renewed itself and continued to blossom in the era of the modern entrepreneur-lawyer. Another is the legendary Richmond, Virginia, firm of Allen Allen Allen & Allen. The practice was founded by George Edward Allen in 1910. His three sons, George E. Jr., Ashby, and Wilbur, became members of the firm, and today George E. Allen III, a member of the Virginia bar since 1973, is a third-generation Allen partner. On his mother's side George Allen traced his ancestry to William Marshall, Earl of Pembroke, one of the chief architects of the Magna Carta. The Marshalls of Virginia included John Marshall, the first great Chief Justice of the United States. On his father's side, George Allen's forebearers served in the colonial militia during the French and Indian War and fought with George Washington in the Revolutionary War at Valley Forge and in the crossing of the Delaware. George became a member of the Virginia State Senate in 1916 and served there until 1920. As a pioneer Virginia courtroom lawyer, he tried every kind of case. When the scientific tort lawyer movement started, George was one of its leaders. He was one of the earliest lecturers at the seminars which ATLA and local bar groups sponsored to educate trial lawyers on tactics.

In 1949, he took on one of the early automobile products liability cases, a marathon suit against the Ford Motor Company that was tried twice and went to the U.S. Court of Appeals for the Fourth Circuit twice before it was finally settled. The Allen firm pioneered the use of demonstrative evidence in complicated products liability cases. In his memoirs, George relates the following about the trial of the early Ford case:

> There was mounted on a huge display board before the jury the entire steering linkage, together with individual parts making up the assemblies, with large identification cards by each, and lines indicating the parts comprising each of the assemblies. Hence, each juror could, at any time during the trial, by glancing at the display board, refresh his or her memory as to the technical term and function of each of the individual parts and assemblies.
>
> Micrographs producing a magnification of eleven times on the original negative showed that the marks under the heads of the bolts and under the nuts on the clamps around the left turnbuckle were far less extensive than those on the right turnbuckle, which had been properly tightened.

In 1963, George Allen was confronted with the greatest challenge of his career. A young black Harvard law student was facing trial in Prince Edward County, Virginia, on charges of resisting arrest. It was a time of high racial tension in Prince Edward County, and the law student was unable to find a white lawyer to represent him. The dean of the University of Virginia Law School was asked for suggestions by the Lawyers' Committee for Civil Rights under Law, and he suggested George Allen. George, then 78 years old, took on the case, although Prince Edward County was some distance from his office and he was not able to get any white lawyers to work with him as local counsel. With great patience and fortitude, George avoided a racial confrontation. He worked out a compromise under which the felony charges against his client were dismissed and three misdemeanor charges were satisfied by the payment of a $100 fine. George's client wrote him a letter which George published in his memoirs. Here is an excerpt:

> I, of course, owe you my life and my future. Without your help, I have little doubt that I would now be in jail and that all the years of my training would be wasted. I was willing to bear this prospect because my pride would not permit me to be intimidated by those people in Prince Edward into admitting something that I had not done. This was the first time in my life that I have been trapped. I have learned a lot about myself during the encounter and I have learned a lot about the decency of other human beings through your example.
>
> I will not belabor the subject for I do believe that you understand. Words have a way of washing out the substance of any emotional communication between people and I do not wish to cloud the intensity of my admiration for you with unnecessary verbiage. It is not sufficient, but I do thank you and I am grateful for what you have done. There certainly can be no recompense; but, if there is anything I can ever do for you, I would feel honored if you would ask it of me.
>
> My only hope is that I can prove worthy of the faith and interest you have shown in me.

The Allen firm was a pioneer in the representation of blacks in tort cases, often arguing such cases successfully to all-white juries. George Allen, Jr., who started practice in 1935, became senior partner on his father's death in 1972, and carried on the firm's great traditions. Since 1952, he has served as a member of the Virginia State Legislature, where he led the long fight to remove the ceiling on damages that had been part of the Virginia wrongful death statute since its enactment in the 19th century. The ceiling was repealed in 1974, thanks mainly to his efforts, and now Virginia has one of the most comprehensive wrongful death statutes that includes damage provisions for "sorrow, mental anguish and solace which may include society, companionship, comfort, guidance, kindly offices and advice of the decedent."

Another second-generation scientific tort firm is Charfoos & Charfoos of Detroit, with a staff of more than a dozen tort lawyers headed by Samuel Charfoos, who began practice in 1929 and is now semiretired, and his son Lawrence, who joined the firm in 1960. In

Milwaukee, Habush Gillick Habush Davis Murphy Kraemer & Kranitz is headed by Jesse Habush, who began practice in 1930, and his son Robert, who joined the firm in 1961. Then there is the San Francisco firm of Lewis Rouda & Lewis, headed by Marvin E. Lewis, who began practice in 1929 and was joined by his son Marvin K. Lewis in 1971. Marv Lewis, Sr., one of the bar's greatest raconteurs, is most famous for his representation of the plaintiff in a suit against the National Broadcasting Company which arose out of a rape scene in a television program. The television performance allegedly was copied by assailants who attacked a nine-year-old girl with a glass bottle. Along with his regular practice of serious physical injury and death cases, Marv Lewis pioneered claims for emotional injuries, and as one of the first plaintiff's lawyers to attain important political office, he helped to establish the scientific tort lawyer in political circles. He was acting mayor of San Francisco in 1947, and later served as San Francisco's legislative representative in Washington.

The development of political clout was an important breakthrough for tort lawyers and their clients. As we saw in Chapter 2, the early plaintiffs were often deprived of a fair chance for adequate compensation by the superior political clout of the railroads and the insurance companies and their lawyers. This political leverage was used to block needed changes in the law (such as repeal of wrongful death damage limitations), and it also played a part in the selection of judges, whether by popular election or by appointment. Some of the other plaintiff's tort lawyers who achieved political prominence were: Howard Metzenbaum of Columbus, now a United States senator from Ohio; William S. Cohen, United States senator from Maine, who worked for ATLA under Tom Lambert before entering private practice; Vance N. Hartke of Indiana, who served as a U.S. senator from that state for three terms; Orville Freeman of Minnesota, who held important posts, including that of secretary of agriculture, in the John F. Kennedy administration; Sidney McMath of Little Rock, Arkansas, a major general in the U.S. Marine Corps Reserve who served as governor of Arkansas from 1949 to 1953; Stanley Preiser of Charleston, West Virginia, who served as chairman of the West Virginia State Election Commission from 1964 to 1973; and Leon RisCassi of Hartford, Connecticut, who was a Connecticut state senator from 1940 to 1946, Senate majority leader in 1945, and a member of the state commission to revise the Connecticut general statutes during the 1940s.

It was also important for paintiff's lawyers to develop clout in state and national bar associations, since the bar's recommendations are often influential in the selection of judges and in the progress of remedial legislation. Outstanding examples of tort lawyers who attained influential positions in bar associations were Joseph Schneider of Boston, who was born in Russia in 1901 and elected president of the Massachusetts Bar Association in 1955; Raymond H. Kierr of New Orleans, one of the nation's leading maritime lawyers, who served as chairman of the American Bar Association Committee on Marine Insurance Law from 1970 to 1971; and David S. Casey of San Diego, who became president of the State Bar of California in 1975. The section of insurance, negligence, and compensation law of the American Bar Association was controlled by insurance lawyers from its inception. Few plaintiffs' lawyers took the time to attend their meetings, much less to seek office or committee appointment. But this began to change in the second half of the 20th century when the ABA in general and this section in particular opened its doors to plaintiff's lawyers. As a result, two outstanding plaintiff's tort lawyers have served as chairmen of the section: Louis Davidson of Chicago from 1969 to 1970, and Walter Beckham of Miami from 1974 to 1975. Phillip Corboy of Chicago, one of the nation's leading plaintiff's tort lawyers, was elected chairman of the ABA Litigation Section (its fastest growing section) in 1979.

With this new political power, some leading plaintiff's tort lawyers themselves ascended to the bench. Outstanding examples were the late, great James A. Dooley of Chicago, who became a justice of the Illinois Supreme Court in 1976, winning election to that post by a margin of almost 2 to 1; Jacob D. Fuchsberg, who was elected to New York's highest court, the New York Court of Appeals, in 1975; Donald P. Lay of Omaha, Nebraska, who serves as a judge of the U.S. Court of Appeals for the Eighth Circuit; Richard M. Markus, judge of the Cuyahoga County (Ohio) Court of Common Pleas; and Orville Richardson, now retired from service as a circuit judge for St. Louis County, Missouri.

There are hundreds of other lawyers in all parts of the nation who helped to establish the individual on an equal footing with the corporation and the government in our civil courts. In my opinion, this movement was no less important than the so-called equal protection clause of the 14th Amendment to the U.S. Constitution, which prohibits the states from denying "to any person within its jurisdiction the equal protection of the laws." The 14th Amendment was ratified in 1868, but it meant little to the civil litigants of that time because few of them could afford lawyers who were capable of making the law work for the individual. It remained for the entrepreneur-lawyer to breathe life into the equal protection clause. Until the strong plaintiff's lawyer came along, millions of individuals were denied equal protection of the laws simply because they were represented by weak lawyers.

Further proof of the decisive role of the entrepreneur-lawyer is the record of Richard Grand of Tucson, Arizona. Dick, who was born in 1922 in what was then the free city of Danzig, emigrated to Tucson and established his own practice there in 1958. At that time it was considered a low-verdict area, but within a few years Dick was winning verdicts as high as those in urban centers such as New York, Chicago, and Los Angeles. Dick was helped by the pioneering work of Stewart and Morris Udall, who had preceded him as Tucson's leading plaintiff's lawyers. Another example in the same area is Tom Anderson, who practices in two small California desert towns, Indio and Palm Springs. Tom has brought urban sophistication to what was formerly a backward area for tort plaintiffs. Such regional differences in the outlook on tort damages fade away wherever there is an entrepreneur-lawyer strong enough to make the initial breakthrough and to consolidate it by legal statesmanship.

The success of Dick Grand and Tom Anderson reminds us that tort practice is probably the only field of law in which the individual practitioner is not at a disadvantage against large firms. There are very few plaintiff's tort firms with more than fifteen lawyers, and most have fewer than ten. For the most part they are small firms or individual practitioners with a few associates supporting them. An exception is the San Francisco area, which has long boasted some of the finest plaintiff's tort firms in the nation. Among those who have compiled outstanding records and built large organizations are Walkup Downing Shelby Bastian Melodia Kelly & O'Reilly of San Francisco, a 15-lawyer firm headed by Bruce Walkup; Boccardo Lull Niland & Bell of San Jose, San Francisco, and Irvine, a 23-lawyer firm headed by Jim Boccardo; and Cartwright Sucherman Slobodin & Fowler of San Francisco, an 11-lawyer firm headed by Bob Cartwright. But unlike general practice firms, tort firms do not grow steadily. Often the existing firms spawn new ones, as young stars seek to make it on their own. Frequently, senior tort lawyers cut back on their activity (and the size of the firms they dominate) in their later years. Even in the successful younger firms, lawyer strength will fluctuate with the case load, which is not as predictable or steady as in other fields of law.

In the Chicago area, the tradition has been for an individual practitioner to build an organization around himself without partners. Before he was elected to the Illinois Supreme Court in 1976, Jim Dooley operated in that way, building a large staff of competent associates under his own name. John J. Kennelly, who would get many votes as the greatest living plaintiff's tort lawyer, operates as an individual, with his supporting staff employed as associates or counsel. Phillip Corboy, who once worked for Jim Dooley and then set up his own highly successful practice, also operates as an individual, with eight associates filling out his organization.

In New York City, the pattern is mixed. There are many strong individual tort lawyers, some practicing alone and others employing a small staff of associates. There are also larger firms with three or more partners and five to ten associates. Let us now follow the currents of post-1950 change in tort practice through a particular law firm: Speiser Krause & Madole, which is a useful example here because it operates in Washington and Los Angeles as well as New York, and because I am a competent witness to its history.

One Firm's History

At the time of the Grand Canyon accident on June 30, 1956, my office was a one-room affair at 545 Fifth Avenue. Two young lawyers who worked for me shared the single room, and although we had no secretaries, we did have three chairs. Both lawyers had flying experience and were also good typists, the two prerequisites for employment in my firm at that time. By the fall of 1958, when the first Los Angeles Grand Canyon trial took place, we had moved our three-man firm to a relatively sumptuous five-room office at 501 Fifth Avenue, directly across the street from the New York Public Library.

In 1958, our practice consisted almost entirely of aviation accident cases. At that time, there were few pilot-lawyer tort specialists available to the plaintiffs, and there was a nationwide need for services of the type we supplied in the Grand Canyon case. I decided to expand the firm to take on more of the aviation counsel work that was available to us throughout the country. Accordingly, all of the lawyers who entered our firm during the 1950s were fliers. At one time, we were a firm of eight lawyers, all of whom had prior flying experience either in military service or with the airlines or government aviation agencies.

In sticking to that formula, I was not under any illusions that one had to be a pilot-lawyer in order to win an aviation accident case. Many plaintiff's lawyers without flying experience have won such cases. But practically all of our cases were referred to us by other lawyers, who were for the most part litigation specialists themselves. I felt that they were bringing us in as counsel because we knew more about aviation than they did, and that as a specialist firm, we had to maintain expertise in the technical details of aviation operations. Of course, pilot-lawyers must know the techniques of litigation to be effective. Fortunately, we were often retained by top-flight litigation firms from whom we were able to learn a great deal.

To counteract the defendants' natural advantages in aviation cases, I tried to recruit lawyers with particular qualifications: those with military, naval, or airline flying experience, trained in the heavy, fast jets and multi-engine aircraft that private pilots generally do not get the opportunity to fly. I also wanted lawyers who had worked for government aviation agencies. Aviation regulations are involved in every phase of air crash cases. They cover the manufacture, testing, and certification of the aircraft; the training and licensing of pilots; control of air traffic; maintenance, and surveillance of airline operations. Indeed, the wording and practical application of a single obscure aviation regulation became the central focus of the Grand Canyon litigation, as we saw in Chapter 3.

Sticking to the pilot-lawyer formula helped us to keep down the expenses of preparing cases, since we were able to avoid the cost of hiring pilots for investigation and analysis. Of course, our pilot-lawyers could not testify as expert witnesses at trial. However, it takes quite a bit of technical knowledge to determine when an expert is needed, and what qualifications the expert should have. The trial lawyer also needs a strong grasp of technical details to prepare his own expert witnesses properly and to undertake cross-examination of the defendants' experts. A good example is the Alouette II case described in Chapter 5. If the trial lawyer lets his expert testify to whatever the expert deems appropriate, he may well find himself out on a limb.

One of the lessons that I learned from successful tort lawyers such as Billy Hyman, Harry Gair, and Perry Nichols was that an ideal way of expanding a plaintiff's firm rapidly is to draw upon the defense bar for personnel. In fact, Hyman, Gair, and Nichols themselves had started out on the defense side. Defense lawyers, whether they work for insurance companies or the government, have more cases assigned to them and accumulate litigation experience more rapidly than lawyers on the plaintiff's side, since there is less delegation of responsibility from the highest levels in plaintiff's firms. This was one of the considerations that led me to select David C. Quinn as the first partner in our post-Grand Canyon law firm. He came to me with the highest recommendation possible: he was a negligence defense lawyer whom plaintiff's lawyers wanted out of their way. I learned this in December of 1958, when Al Averbach dropped in to see me. Al was one of the salty old characters of tort practice. His office was in the small town of Seneca Falls, N. Y., but the whole country was his oyster, because Al was dedicated to writing, lecturing, living, and breathing the tort revolution. He had trunks full of medical-legal literature in his atticlike office at Seneca Falls. He was a lonely bachelor who lived for the seminars of ATLA and the Practicing Law Institute that took him around the country where he could enjoy the companionship of his fellow tort lawyers.

When Al visited me in December 1958, he complained about a beating that he had just taken from a young assistant attorney general who had defended New York State against an accident claim made by

Al's client. Al said that he was the toughest trial lawyer that he had run up against in years, and that other plaintiff's lawyers who had tried cases against him felt the same way. "I wish there was some way of getting him out of Albany," said Al. "You know, he was a World War II navy pilot, and he might want to get into aviation cases. Why don't you take him on?" That half-serious suggestion led to Assistant Attorney General David C. Quinn joining our firm early in 1959, starting an association that continues to this day. Dave was our first airline captain, for he had briefly served in that capacity with Guy Lombardo's Long Island Airlines, which flew commuters between Manhattan's East River and the resort towns of Long Island in navy surplus Grumann amphibians. Dave's first assignment was to take over the final stages of the Grand Canyon litigation, a chore that kept him traveling to courtrooms around the country for more than a year.

In 1959, Chuck Krause, who was then attending Rutgers Law School, became the first in a succession of jet pilots who would work in our office as clerks and then join our firm after graduation. When we got up to six flying lawyers in 1961, we outgrew our Fifth Avenue space and moved to the Norway House at 290 Madison Avenue. In the early 1960s, we were busy working on aviation cases all over the country, and practically all of our cases were referred to us by other lawyers. We noticed one change, however. We found that once we had established a satisfactory relationship with a referring lawyer on an aviation case, he would consider us for other types of litigation, and he would also recommend us to other lawyers. Apparently some referring lawyers reasoned that if we could handle the most complicated type of tort case, we should be able to do as well with the simpler cases such as automobile and building accidents. Also, the products liability revolution started in the 1960s, and we were involved in some of the first aviation cases that developed the right of passengers and pilots to sue manufacturers. As a result, we found that lawyers were calling us in on complicated products liability cases, whether they involved aviation products or others.

This moved us to diversify somewhat. Instead of limiting our staff to those experienced in aviation, we took on lawyers who had experience in other fields of tort litigation. Al Gans and Paul Rheingold joined us in 1963. Paul had graduated from the Harvard Law School with honors and had worked under Tom Lambert as an assistant editor of the NACCA publications in Boston. He also supervised the NACCA Products Liability Exchange. Paul's job with us was his first in a law firm, and it was to turn out to be his only one. As soon as he joined us, he started concentrating on the newly emerging field of products liability.

We quickly outgrew our quarters in the Norway House, and in 1963 we were among the first tenants to move into the newly constructed Pan Am Building on Park Avenue. We felt that it was appropriate for a plaintiffs' aviation firm to be located in the Pan Am Building, even though it meant that we would often be suing our landlord. As befits an airline building, even the chief barber in the Pan Am Building barbershop was a pilot. He was also a Lindbergh buff, and my stature was raised in his eyes when I commissioned a painting of Charles Lindbergh and donated it to the National Air and Space Museum. Juan Trippe, the legendary founder and chairman of Pan American Airways, was a customer of the pilot-barber. One day I happened to walk into the barbershop when he had Trippe in his chair, and he enthusiastically introduced me to Juan as "one of the world's leading aviation attorneys." Juan was sitting there helpless, wrapped in the barber's haircutting sheet, looking as though he expected me to serve him with a summons. Although known as a cold, aloof man who rarely spoke to some of his own vice-presidents, Juan graciously extended his hand out from under the sheet and managed a sportsmanlike smile as we shook hands.

Since most of the information about the aviation industry is located in Washington and government accident investigation is directed from there, we felt the need for a Washington office. In 1965 we started using the office and part-time services of a Washington aviation attorney. We soon outgrew those facilities, and in 1966 we opened our own office in Washington's National Press Building and took on Don Madole to run it.

I wish that I had the space to mention all of the lawyers who were with our firm in the 1960s and 1970s. Many of them contributed greatly to our progress, especially William F. X. Geoghan, Jr., who tried many important aviation cases for us between 1961 and 1969, later leaving to set up his own firm. However, the purpose of this section is to illustrate the developments that have taken place within tort firms between the 1950s and the 1980s. I will therefore jump a few years at this point to describe the present structure of our firm.

As we began the 1980s, our practice was still concentrated in torts. While our staff of about twenty lawyers fluctuates from time to time, it usually consists of about twelve pilot-lawyers and about eight lawyers with general litigation experience but no flying qualifications. This ratio of 60 percent pilot-lawyers does not mean that exactly 60 percent of our work is in aviation cases. Often it will run higher than that, but our pilot-lawyers also work on non-aviation cases, and our nonpilots work on some phases of our aviation cases. Overall, our practice is an extension of what we started to build after the Grand Canyon experience. Practically all of our cases are referred to us by other lawyers. Most of them are tort cases involving complicated problems of liability or damage, although sometimes (mercifully) we get a simple one. They may come from any place in the world, and they may have to be tried anywhere in the United States. However, in cases that must be tried in places where we do not have our own offices, we usually are associated with an experienced local tort lawyer.

Frank Granito joined our New York office in 1967. Frank is a former Navy pilot with a commercial pilot's license, who served as an attorney for the Federal Aviation Administration's Eastern Region, based at John F. Kennedy International Airport from 1962 to 1966. Then he was an associate of the late John G. Reilly, one of New York's leading airline defense lawyers, whose principal client was Associated Aviation Underwriters. In 1976, Frank became the first member of a plaintiff's firm to be appointed chairman of the Committee on Aeronautics of the Association of the Bar of the City of New York. Frank is one of the pioneers of a new technique: the submission of a scientific engineering brief to the trial judge. It is designed to explain technical matters that will arise during the trial, just as the legal brief or memorandum covers points of law. In the litigation arising out of the crash of Eastern Airlines Flight 66 at John F. Kennedy International Airport on June 24, 1975, Frank himself drafted most of the material that was included in the plaintiffs' scientific engineering brief submitted to Judge Bramwell, the trial judge in the federal court for the Eastern District of New York. Frank was assisted by Paul Zahn, a younger lawyer in our firm who is a qualified airline jet pilot, holds an airline transport rating and flies for a large international airline. Paul's airline experience in the Boeing 727, the aircraft involved in the Eastern 66 crash, was useful to the plaintiffs' discovery group in the drafting of the scientific engineering brief and in the subsequent trial. Following is the table of contents of the 100-page plaintiffs' scientific engineering brief:

TABLE OF CONTENTS

The Eastern 66 trial, which was conducted by Frank Granito of our firm and Milton Sincoff of Kreindler & Kreindler, lasted nearly five weeks. It resulted in a jury verdict for the plaintiffs on the issue of liability.

The qualifications of some of the lawyers who joined us in the 1970s give the flavor of today's scientific tort practice. Our newest pilot-lawyers were coming in with much stronger aviation credentials than their predecessors. In addition to Paul Zahn, there is Dan Hayes, a U.S. Air Force Vietnam veteran who saw active pilot duty from 1968 to 1973 and emerged as a captain. Dan also holds an airline transport rating, which qualifies him to fly airline jet equipment. Our non-pilot lawyers include Larry Goldhirsch, who was a former associate of New York tort lawyer Harry Lipsig, served as an instructor at the Academy of Aeronautics at La Guardia Field, and also taught product liability law at the University of Dijon in France; Fred Heller, whose special skill in videotape presentations was mentioned in Chapter 4; Hedy Voigt, whose language abilities and love of travel made her the logical choice as the first resident at our London office, where she took postgraduate courses in international aviation law and continued her liaison work with European lawyers; and Roger Moak, a Cornell and Georgetown graduate who worked in our Washington office during his law school days, and then in 1972 joined our New York office, where he concentrates on commercial litigation and helps with the administrative management of the firm.

By 1975, we had outgrown our four-room Washington office in the National Press Building. At the urging of Don Madole, we bought a small nineteenth-century brick building on Sixteenth Street in down-town Washington. We were not worried about security because the building was located halfway between the Russian Embassy and the National Rifle Association. We converted the building to a law office, preserving its charming antique features, including fireplaces and a sep-arate carriage house. Phil Silverman's top floor office has a portico from which he can see the White House. There is a large sun deck adjacent to Don Madole's office, and on warm days he can be seen there prac-ticing law (or tending tomato plants) under a beach umbrella. The sun deck did not appear in any of the plans that were sent to the New York office, but the building's restoration under Don's direction turned out so well that the unscheduled sun deck was taken in stride.

The new building enabled us to increase our Washington staff, most notably by adding Juanita M. Madole, Don's charming wife. In addition to having soloed a Cessna 150, Juanita is a *cum laude* graduate of Tulane University and a *magna cum laude* graduate of the University of Houston Law School. She was an attorney in the Department of Jus-tice Aviation Litigation Unit before joining our firm. We also added Michael Sconyers, a helicopter pilot who served with the U.S. Marine Corps for six years during the Vietnam era and emerged as a major.

During the 1970s, Southern California became an important cen-ter of aviation accident litigation. Even in cases which did not involve California passengers, it was often necessary to file suit in the Southern California courts against major aviation manufacturers whose plants were located there, such as McDonnell Douglas, Lockheed, and General Dynamics. The FAA office in Los Angeles is the headquarters of the FAA Western Region, and through it pass most of the certification data and airworthiness directives relating to large transport aircraft. Since we had found it necessary to shuttle lawyers between New York and California ever since the Grand Canyon case, we decided in 1979 to open our own office there. As the partner in charge we selected Joseph T. (Tim) Cook, an Annapolis graduate and naval aviator who had seen active duty in Vietnam. Tim had worked as a clerk in our Washington office during his law school days at George Washington University. He then served as a trial attorney for the U.S. Department of Justice Avia-tion Litigation Unit, and finally became an assistant United States attor-ney for the Southern District of California, with the principal task of defending the government in Federal Tort Claims Act suits on the West Coast. As a part-time counsel at our Los Angeles office, we added Ned K. Zartman, who had retired in 1975 after a quarter century of service as a government aviation attorney. In the 1950s, he had acquired trial experience in the General Counsel's office of the old CAA, and had served as regional counsel and member of the Airworthiness Board of the FAA Western Region in Los Angeles from 1961 to 1975.

Our offices in New York, Washington, Los Angeles, and London

keep us in touch with aviation and tort developments in some of the
world's major litigation centers. They also put demands upon our organization which are typical of those faced by the tort lawyers of the
1980s. Although aviation is considered one of the more complicated
fields of tort practice, our experience, facilities, and personnel are by
no means unique. There are many other firms that keep themselves in
a state of readiness to handle complicated aviation cases. And other
tort specialists who are heavily involved in such fields as medical malpractice, products liability, and environmental damage, have to keep
up with their rapidly changing technologies and swelling litigation
source material.

The transitory nature of modern tort litigation makes traveling a
constant burden for our staff. We found that as we gained more experience with the preparation and trial of complicated tort cases, we were
able to settle a higher percentage of cases before trial than we did in
the 1950s and 1960s. However, the trials themselves were becoming
more complicated because of burgeoning technology. Investigation of
aviation accidents has been improved by read-outs of the flight recorders
and cockpit voice recorders installed in today's airliners. But other factors have made the cases more complicated than they were in the 1950s.
There are more instruments and systems, most of them very complicated. There are many more manuals and government regulations.
There are more prospective defendants and more potential witnesses.
There are more ways in which an airline can place the blame on a
manufacturer, or one manufacturer can blame another, so that we have
to spend much more time studying the possible liability of peripheral
defendants than we did in the simpler days of the DC-3 and the DC-4.
And of course there have been more complicated choice-of-law questions since the departure of the rigid *lex loci* rule. Now we have to consider the laws of the many different states and nations which might
apply to a single airline crash.

This expanded practice and the increased demands of each case
require that many of our lawyers be qualified to try cases, whereas prior
to 1950 a tort firm would usually have only one lawyer who tried all the
cases, while the other lawyers did the supporting paperwork. Today
the pace of trials is grueling enough to wear out lawyers who undertake
too many. By 1980, our five most active aviation trial lawyers—Chuck
Krause, Don Madole, Phil Silverman, Frank Granito, and Tim Cook—
had tried to completion and won major aviation cases in many states
from coast to coast. Larry Goldhirsch and Fred Heller are our principal
non-aviation trial lawyers who have completed and won jury trials,
in addition to Chuck Krause. Again, this is not a unique attribute of
our firm. Many tort firms throughout the country have five or more
experienced trial lawyers, because the burden of trying tort cases in
busy firms today is often too great to be carried by one or two lawyers.

Some idea of the burden on firms like ours can be gained from the MDL assignments that we have taken on during the last ten years (the 1970s). Along with lawyers from other firms, lawyers from our firm were members of the MDL plaintiffs' committee in the cases arising out of the following major aviation disasters: the Wichita State University football team crash in Colorado, 1970 (Frank Granito); the Alaska Airlines Boeing 727 crash at Juneau, Alaska, 1971 (Don Madole); the Apache Airlines crash at Coolidge, Arizona, 1971 (Frank Granito); the Eastern Airlines Lockheed 1011 Tri-Star crash in the Florida Everglades, 1972 (Don Madole); the Delta Airlines crash at Boston Airport, 1973 (Chuck Krause); the Turkish Airlines DC-10 crash at Ermenonville, France, 1974 (Don Madole); the TWA crash in the Ionian Sea off Greece, 1974 (Chuck Krause); the TWA crash on approach to Dulles Airport, Virginia, 1974 (Phil Silverman); the Eastern Airlines Flight 66 crash at Kennedy International Airport, New York, 1975 (Frank Granito); the Pan Am-KLM collision at Tenerife, Canary Islands, 1977 (Chuck Krause); the Southern Airways crash at New Hope, Georgia, 1977 (Don Madole); and the American Airlines DC-10 crash at O'Hare Airport, Chicago, 1979 (Don Madole). This list includes only appointments to the plaintiffs' committee of lead counsel in federal MDL cases. It does not cover dozens of other major aviation accident cases that engaged us during the 1970s, such as the Varig Paris crash and the Entebbe raid, where the suits were filed in state courts.

MDL assignments usually consume the better part of a lawyer's working time for two years, leaving little energy for other large projects. In the Turkish Airlines DC-10 case, Don Madole was spending so much time in Los Angeles that eventually he leased an apartment there. Later he leased an apartment in Atlanta for his frequent trips in connection with the Southern Airways 1977 Georgia crash.

As a result of the 1979 American Airlines Chicago DC-10 crash, U.S. Transportation Secretary Neil Goldschmidt appointed a committee of aviation experts to review the FAA's certification procedures for large airliners. This committee, appointed in December of 1979, functions under the auspices of the National Research Council. Don Madole was appointed to the committee, the only lawyer so honored. The other members are representatives of all facets of the airline and aviation manufacturing industries. The committee's report is expected to shape the future direction of FAA certification procedures for large airliners during the 1980s.

Opportunities for public service in a nonlegal capacity are one of the fringe benefits of tort practice. In 1960, Dave Quinn and I felt that there was a need for an organization that represented the interests of airline passengers in their dealings with airlines and the government. While all of the other parties in the air transport business—airlines, manufacturers, labor unions, and insurers—had strong representation in Washington, there was no spokesman for the passengers. We organized the Airways Club, which later changed its name to the Airline Passengers Association. Dave Quinn became its president and set it on a course of crusading for important passenger benefits. He zeroed in on the limit of 40 pounds of checked baggage per passenger, which had been set in the days of the Curtiss Condor, a wood and fabric biplane operated by our airlines in the 1930s. At that time the passengers had to be weighed along with their baggage because weight was so critical to performance of the underpowered aircraft of the 1930s. In the jet age, the great lifting power of the engines makes it unnecessary to restrict baggage weight, but the airlines kept the 40 pound limit as long as there was no group capable of challenging it.

As a result of Dave Quinn's campaign, the airlines were forced to drop their 40 pound limit in favor of the present practice, allowing passengers to check two bags regardless of weight. Dave also brought the Airways Club into other safety controversies, such as the one over the JP4 jet fuel that was then being used by some of our airlines. Again as a result of Dave's work, most of our airlines discontinued the use of JP4 fuel, which is more flammable than pure kerosene. The work that Dave Quinn pioneered is being carried on by the Airline Passengers Association in Dallas, Texas. One of the original benefits was year-round flight insurance of up to $250,000 at rates much lower than those available in the market. Today APA has over 60,000 members in 133 countries, with billions of dollars worth of low-cost insurance in force, some members being covered for as much as $1 million.

Dave Quinn retains his association with our firm, although he spends most of his time in his own office at Katonah, N.Y., a quiet suburb of New York City. Paul Rheingold, who became a partner in our firm in 1968, left us briefly in 1973 to establish his own practice. He returned to our firm as counsel in 1974, devoting most of his time to his own independent practice but collaborating with us on specific cases. He has continued a heavy schedule of writing, lecturing, and crusading for progress in tort law. In 1969, he collaborated with me in writing a book called *Handling the Big Negligence Case,* published by the Practicing Law Institute.

In order to do an effective job for our clients in the damage phase of wrongful death cases, we had to become amateur economists. We found ourselves dealing with all sorts of sophisticated economic indicators and measuring rods, as you saw in the Tenerife trial earlier in this chapter. A close study of our economy over several decades made me acutely aware of defects in the system, which is supposed to be based upon free enterprise but seems to combine some of the worst features of capitalism and socialism. I became interested in ways of improving the system, and in 1977 I wrote *A Piece of the Action,* a book that examines the possibility of combining the *best* features of capitalism and socialism under a concept called universal capitalism, which was first expounded by San Francisco lawyer Louis Kelso and the noted philosopher Mortimer Adler. As a result of that book, I was asked to join the honorary board of editors of *The Journal of Post-Keynesian Economics,* a publication started in 1978 by Professors Galbraith of Harvard, Davidson of Rutgers, and Weintraub of Wharton (Pennsylvania). I have continued to work on the theory of universal capitalism, realizing that changes of such magnitude will not be accomplished quickly or easily.

Like many other members of ATLA, I have often been called upon to testify before congressional committees which are considering changes in the law. ATLA considers it one of its functions to produce witnesses with practical litigation experience who will travel to Washington or other places of legislative inquiry at their own expense.

As I look back on three decades of tort practice, I feel that our firm has made some contribution to the revolutionary changes since 1950. Our work as pilot-lawyers in all parts of the nation has helped to develop the concept of the scientific tort lawyer. We pioneered the group handling of mass disaster cases, which has resulted in such benefits to the public as the $10 million savings in legal fees cited by Judge Peirson M. Hall in his report on the Turkish Airlines DC-10 litigation. Along with many other tort lawyers of the era, we helped to open the door for the products liability revolution. We were and are in the forefront of the movement to open American courts to foreign plaintiffs suing American manufacturers for injuries suffered outside of the country—a means of making one of our finest products, American justice, available to citizens of all nations. We did not accomplish any of these things alone. We were merely part of the group that helped to bring them about, and we were part of an even larger group that made ATLA a respected educational organization which can also mobilize tort lawyers as a task force.

The Money Dynamics of Tort Litigation

As we have seen, tort law has become more egalitarian, more scientific, and more lawyer-oriented. It has also become more money-oriented, as have nearly all types of litigation. The only difference in tort cases is that the money which is so critical to success comes from the plaintiff's lawyers, not from their clients.

At Columbia Law School, I got the impression that litigation was a quest for the Holy Grail of truth. Nobody told me that it was also a financial contest, and that in order to succeed, either you or your client must have the economic staying power to weather the stormy seas of litigation. Since the average plaintiff in a tort case does not have the money or the staying power to enter the arena against a giant opponent, it is the entrepreneur-lawyer who must supply these requisites, and must furnish the services of an organization for which the plaintiffs themselves could not afford to pay. This is the exact opposite of the defense situation, where the defendant corporations and their insurance companies dwarf the economic power of the law firms who work for them on a non-contingent basis.

It is not enough today to be a good trial lawyer or legal researcher; you must also be a scientist. You can't prepare your cases on the way to court or rely on the sympathy of jurors, as the early tort lawyers did. You must also be a good business manager, able to generate enough capital to make a large investment in each case. You must have a highly mechanized operation, including photocopiers, word-processing machines, videotape cameras, and courtroom models. You must have an extensive medical library, which may cost you almost as much to keep up as your law library. And even if you lack the imagination to invent new methods of gathering and presenting evidence, you must have the capital, time, and organization to take advantage of the thousands of new information sources that have been developed since 1950.

Today, with the rapidly escalating costs of tort litigation, it is not unusual for plaintiff's lawyers to lay out six-figure sums for processing a single case. Indeed, in the Turkish Airlines DC-10 litigation, the plaintiffs lawyers as a group laid out more than $1 million in expenses, for which they received no interest while their money was at risk in a commitment which no bank would finance. Today, there can be as much at stake in a single injury case involving paralysis as there was in all of the 128 deaths at Grand Canyon in 1956. Such a case can involve $5 million or more in damages, because of inflation and because the courts are now dealing realistically with all of the human effects of injuries that cripple the body, the pocketbook, and the personality. Unless the plaintiff's attorneys have staying power, the defendants will try to buy them out cheaply or starve them out by stalling the litigation.

Managing tort litigation is something like producing a show or a movie, where the producer packages the enterprise and pays all the actors, writers, directors, and technicians. Tort lawyers perform similar functions as they prepare their client's case for trial, but there are major differences. Producers commonly finance their capital risk by selling equity, obtaining bank loans, and selling auxiliary rights, such as record albums and publications. They can also offer tax benefits to those who want to assume the risks of the enterprise. Usually the producers wind up with a large percentage of ownership although they have invested little or no money of their own. No such gravy train is available to the tort lawyers. They must finance everything themselves. Once launched, the play or film runs on in theaters and on television, whereas the trial is a one-shot performance which must pay its own way on the day that it goes to the jury. Though films and plays are considered very risky investments and most of them return little or nothing to their backers, there is still a ready market for equity offered by experienced producers. However, no such financing or tax shelter advantages are available to plaintiff's tort lawyers, no matter how experienced or successful they may be.

After more than 30 years of building a law firm, I looked forward to easier times in the 1980s. But the capital required to run a firm of twenty lawyers with overhead expenses of more than $1 million a year (not including cash advanced to prepare cases) is greater than ever. Defense lawyers have added to their natural financial advantages by establishing their own bar organizations, equal to ATLA in their ability to educate and mobilize lawyers. Yet the plaintiff's lawyers must be ready to take on the insurance establishment at a moment's notice, laying out their own money every step of the way, whereas opposing lawyers are financed by their well-heeled clients. And as we saw in the Clemente case, sometimes you pay the expenses and the salaries of a team of lawyers working on a case for seven years, and all that money is lost.

The high cost of maintaining specialist facilities is illustrated by our Washington office, a four-story building that accommodates six lawyers and an equal number of law clerks and secretaries. While much of their work concerns cases pending in the Washington area and the southern states, they also devote a lot of time to gathering evidence and source material for use in aviation cases pending throughout the United States. Washington is the information center for all phases of aviation, and so we have found it worthwhile to maintain our own information center there. It costs as much to maintain this as does the running of a fairly good-sized tort litigation firm, but without it we could not hope to stay on equal footing with the airlines and the aviation manufacturers and their attorneys, who have thousands of engineers and experts at their beck and call, as well as vast technical data which we have to compile anew for each case.

Throughout this book we have encountered expenditures that must be made for plaintiffs, such as fees for economists, expert witnesses, and construction of models. Let us take a closer look at one expensive but

vital item that today's tort lawyers must consider in every serious injury case: the use of a videotape camera to portray "A Day in the Life
of—" (the disabled plaintiff). In Chapter 4 I described the dramatic
use of the videotape camera which resulted in a multimillion dollar
breakthrough. But even without the original discovery drama of that
videotape, every day dozens of such tapes are made by lawyers all over
the country to provide a graphic record of the changed circumstances
under which victims of serious injury have to live their lives. This is
important because individual jury members are not likely to have
known anyone who was paralyzed or suffered brain damage. The mere
sight of an accident victim sitting next to the tort lawyer at the counsel
table in court is not very instructive. The real devastation wrought by
such injuries lies in the inability to do a hundred everyday tasks the
way one used to. The jurors would have to watch the plaintiff at home
or at work for days on end to grasp the full measure of disability. A
videotape camera can capture that over a period of days and then present it to the jury in a few minutes.

This is what a day in the life of a male paraplegic plaintiff might
look like on videotape: A bedroom door is opened and someone enters
the victim's room to wake him up. He will probably be lying in a specially equipped bed, and may have to pull himself up by overhead bars.
Dressing is accomplished with help from another person, as is washing.
At some point during the day the tape will show, as discreetly as possible, the special toilet arrangements that have to be made for a paralyzed person (because of the loss of bowel and bladder control that is
often experienced). The victim will then be assisted into the wheelchair
that has become his primary tool in dealing with the world, and he will
have breakfast with his family. He will then be wheeled down a special
ramp built onto the side of his house after the accident, and will have a
driving lesson in a car which he can operate without using his feet in
any way (including some kind of lifting device for getting him and his
wheelchair into the car or van). Then he might go on to physical therapy, where he will be taught to make the maximum use of the parts of
the body that can still be controlled. A physical examination by a doctor
might be recorded, and this might include some mention of the drugs
a paraplegic must take to avoid infecting the urinary tract by the regular
use of catheters and urine bags. If the plaintiff can return to work,
that will also be shown. The day will end with his return home, spending an evening with his family and being helped to make his way to bed.

Such videotapes are not made simply to get the sympathy of the
jury. Indeed, the images they portray frequently arouse less sympathy
than a real-life demonstration would. They are designed to show jurors
the whole picture of devastating injuries. The jurors are made to squirm,
but only in this way can they reach a full realization of what damage has
been done to the life of the person whose financial future they must

decide. This type of demonstration, coupled with a detailed account of the cost of continuing medical care, nursing help, and rehabilitation, explain why there are a lot of seven-figure verdicts in the courts now. It is simply a fact of life that when someone is paralyzed or crippled, the financial cost alone is enormous, without considering the emotional impact of having one's life shattered by the carelessness or selfishness of another person. Multimillion dollar awards are not breathtaking when they are considered one minute at a time, as the juries have to do when they watch a videotape and when they add up the costs of the special care the victim needs just to carry on life for one day. These tapes are expensive because they require professional planning and execution. A plaintiff's lawyer may spend $5,000 to $10,000 for videotapes, but they are of priceless value to the client's cause.

Another weapon in the arsenal of the scientific tort lawyer is the legal treatise that supports his position on liability or damages. Treatises will not be accepted by prestigious publishers or cited by the courts unless they are well reasoned and deal adequately with relevant precedents. It may take years of research to turn out a work that will be cited by the courts—years of research and writing that are costly to the busy tort lawyer. But in the 1950s and even today, tort lawyers have found it necessary to write their own treatises, lest they be left to the mercy of commentators such as Professor Cooley, who (as you saw in Chapter 2) was still espousing a $5,000 limitation on wrongful death claims in the 1930s.

In Chapter 3 I pointed out how important Belli's "Adequate Award" articles and books were in bringing tort awards into line with the financial realities of the 1950s. Perhaps the most important application of these writings is at the point when a plaintiff's lawyer has achieved a breakthrough verdict, especially one involving a type or amount of damages not previously awarded. At that point one has to reach back and document the history that led up to the breakthrough. It is then that the common law of torts is most flexible and most responsive to the influences of treatises. Most of tort law is common law rather than statute law, and therefore it is malleable in the hands of judges. As Roscoe Pound wrote in the 1954 *NACCA Law Journal:*

> In the law of torts the role of *stare decisis* is limited. Judicially established rules here do not affect the economic order. Titles do not depend on them. Legal transactions are not entered into on the face of them. Enterprises are not set up in reliance upon them. In particular, *stare decisis* has no legitimate application to remnants remaining in the law of torts after the principle behind them has been given up.

These factors give a greater opportunity to shape the law to tort lawyers than to advocates in other fields of practice. But the absence of treatises and authorities can put the tort lawyer's hard-won verdicts in great jeopardy. As an example, take the case of Ken Strong, a famous athlete of the 1930s. He was a unanimous all-American football selection as a halfback in 1928, his senior year at New York University, in which he set a collegiate record of 2,100 yards gained. At that time, there was more money in professional baseball than in football, and Strong was equally talented in baseball. He signed a contract with the Detroit Tigers after he had set a minor league record of 41 home runs in 1930. With a brilliant major league baseball career ahead of him, Strong underwent a wrist operation in Detroit, during which the surgeon removed the wrong bone. What should have been a routine surgical procedure that left Strong in perfect condition for major league baseball did, in fact, end his career because it stripped him of the ability to throw a baseball properly.

Strong sued the surgeon in the Detroit federal court. On July 21, 1933, after hearing two weeks of testimony, a Detroit jury awarded Strong $75,000 in damages—an unprecedented amount, and an unprecedented finding of negligence against a prominent surgeon, despite expert testimony produced by the surgeon's lawyers which supported his view of the case. At that point, the defense lawyers moved for a new trial or dismissal of the case. Strong was represented by Stevens T. Mason, one of the leading insurance defense lawyers in Detroit—a common situation in the 1930s, when plaintiff's specialists were generally too weak to take on such a case. Mr. Mason always wore a swallowtail coat and striped black trousers when he appeared in court. He was dressed that way when he stood before federal judge Ernest A. O'Brien to justify the $75,000 verdict and defend against the motion for a new trial.

Mason pointed out to Judge O'Brien that the surgeon had admitted his error in writing, and that there was ample testimony from Strong's New York doctor that the operation, of questionable utility in the first place, had not been performed in accordance with ordinary surgical skill and care. He argued that the jurors (led by Number 12, who was an accountant) had calculated Strong's loss of earnings over a prospective 15-year baseball career almost to the penny, since his average future earnings of $7,780, reduced to present value at 5 percent, came to $77,022. But when the time came to cite precedents for the $75,000 verdict, Mason had no authorities to back him up. First he argued logic and experience rather than law:

> To the average person of the white collar class such an injury as that suffered by this plaintiff would not be serious. Therefore, to compare this verdict with other injuries is unfair to the plaintiff. A slight injury to a vocal cord of Caruso, Schuman-

Heink and very many other opera singers would have caused a loss of more than a million dollars.

It must be remembered that this is a most unusual case on account of the great athletic ability of the plaintiff. The evidence is undisputed that the plaintiff took part in eighty baseball games after the original injury, with the same batting average as he always had. This meant that he was really hitting better, since the baseball witnesses all said that pitchers do better work in the last half of the year. The testimony showed conclusively and the defense offered no evidence in contradiction that Kenneth Strong is out of baseball for all times. It is a well known fact that for the past generation earnings of baseball players have steadily increased and have stood up far better during the depression than the earnings of individuals in any other profession.

At the same age, with the identical injury, a verdict of $1,000,000 would have been inadequate for Babe Ruth, Jack Dempsey, Gene Tunney, Ty Cobb, John McGraw, Connie Mack, Fritz Kreisler [the violinist], Paderewski, and many others whose identity anyone may recall. To hundreds of ballplayers in similar circumstances a verdict of $250,000 would have been inadequate, including Mathewson, Eddie Collins, Hornsby, Frisch, Gehrig, Terry, Moranville, Grove, Simmons, and others.

During the course of the trial, defendant's attorney admitted in open court that the plaintiff, Kenneth Strong, was one of the greatest football players that ever lived. Great football ability is the stuff that great baseball stars are made of. Mathewson, the great Bucknell fullback, became the greatest pitcher that ever lived. Eddie Collins, Columbia quarterback, became baseball's greatest second baseman. Frisch was All-American halfback at Fordham in 1918 and after fourteen years is still the best second baseman in the National League. Gehrig was a star football player at Columbia and has not missed a game in eight years with New York and is now the American League's best first baseman. Rixey was a star football player at Virginia twenty-five years ago and is still pitching for Cincinnati at age 42.

Seeing that his unprecedented $75,000 verdict was slipping away, Mason made a desperate attempt to get Judge O'Brien to look at it as a contract case, knowing that the courts rarely disturbed jury verdicts for breach of contract if the amount awarded was supported by evidence:

This case resembles a breach of contract case more than a personal injury case, because all the plaintiff is claiming practically is loss of his ability to perform his contract with the Detroit Baseball team and the loss of the prospect of his ability to perform future contracts. His earning power was tremendous and it was destroyed. Who can say that $75,000 was an excessive estimate of the future earning capacity of Kenneth Strong? He was popular with the fans and the testimony is uncontradicted that he could pull the crowds through the gates as few ballplayers could.

No matter what the injury was, if it destroyed that tremendous
earning capacity it could not be said that $75,000 was excessive.

But Mason's valiant efforts to remove the curse of the tort label were
in vain. Judge O'Brien set the verdict aside and ordered a new trial.
Knowing that there was no hope of obtaining full compensation, Mason
convinced Strong that he should settle for $15,000 rather than go
through another trial, which might be lost.

Fortunately, Ken Strong's stiff wrist did not prevent him from
becoming one of professional football's greatest runners and kickers.
He was the star player of the New York Giants in the 1930s. When he
retired after the 1940 season, he had scored more points than anyone
in the history of professional football, and he was later elected to the
Pro Football Hall of Fame. But in those fledgling days of professional
football he did not earn nearly as much as he would have in baseball.

Today, lawyers representing clients like Ken Strong would be able
to cite many authorities in support of their arguments. One of the important functions of the scientific tort lawyer is defending the ground
won in jury trials. Here the technique books and seminars don't help
as much as legal treatises. The greatest source of satisfaction that I
have found in law practice is the acceptance of some of my writings by
the courts. It is probably as thrilling as winning a trial for your own
client when something you have written helps to win a case for someone
you have never met. The most satisfying such case for me was one that
has become famous as "the case of the two nuns."

In *Goheen v. General Motors Corporation,* the Supreme Court of
Oregon was faced with a dilemma. Two nuns, Sisters Margaret Mary
O'Donnell and Mafalda Maria Zucca, had been killed in a 1971 accident
that was allegedly caused by a manufacturing defect in the automobile
in which they were riding. Both nuns had taken a vow of poverty, had
never received any pay for their work, and left no dependents. Oregon's
wrongful death statute provided for such damages as "will reasonablv
and fairly compensate the spouse, dependents, or estate for the actual
pecuniary loss, if any."

Suit was brought by the executrix of the estates of the two nuns
and also by the Sisters of the Holy Names of Jesus and Mary, the religious order to which they belonged. If one interpreted the wording of
the Oregon statute literally, there was no "actual pecuniary loss," and
so the trial court dismissed the case on the ground that no pecuniary
loss had been shown. But the plaintiffs appealed to the Oregon Supreme
Court, which reversed the trial court, holding that "all human life has
pecuniary value in terms of either actual or potential earning capacity,"
and that it was basically unfair to permit a defendant who has negligently killed a human being to escape liability merely because the vic-

tims were contributing their services to a nonprofit organization. They wrote:

> It follows, in our opinion, that in adopting [the Oregon wrongful death statute] the Oregon legislature intended to continue to leave to the courts the question of defining the circumstances under which recovery will be permitted in wrongful death cases involving "loss to the estate," including the measure of damages to be applied in determining the pecuniary loss to the estate of a decedent in such a case.
>
>   *   *   *
>
> We believe that this result is in accord with the present trend to liberalize the rule of "pecuniary loss" in wrongful death cases and to respond to "new emergencies" in this often perplexed and tortured field of the law.

Fighting its way through the jungle of wrongful death law to achieve a just result, the 18-page opinion of the Oregon Supreme Court cited my book *Recovery for Wrongful Death* twelve times.

I have continued to devote considerable time to writing. By the start of 1980, these writings amounted to 18 volumes, including the definitive *Res Ipsa Loquitur* and *Attorneys' Fees.* Probably the most ambitious undertaking was a three-volume work entitled *Aviation Tort Law,* with Chuck Krause as coauthor. In 1978, when the weekly *National Law Journal* was established, I became its regular columnist on torts.

In addition to writing textbooks, it is important for the scientific tort lawyers to keep their message before judges and lawyers in legal periodicals. Articles for law reviews are even more arduous to write than textbooks, because the editorial staffs of the law reviews are composed of eager young law students who are often more exacting in their requirements than the lawbook publishers. Law review editors will insist on getting almost every point documented or annotated by footnotes, and they do not hesitate to argue their views—sometimes to the point of nitpicking. It takes several months of research and writing to turn out a major law review article; but once published, it flows into the mainstream of jurisprudence and may produce radiation effects like those in the case of the two nuns.

Continuing our firm's emphasis on legal research and scholarship, we added James E. Rooks, Jr., to our staff in 1978. At that time, Jim Rooks was the editor of the *ATLA Law Reporter* and a protégé of Tom Lambert. Following in the footsteps of Al Gans, he is accustomed to reading most of the reported tort cases in the United States as a regular exercise.

Such facilities for shaping the law, like the capability for handling specific claims, must be maintained at the tort lawyer's own expense.

Even though these facilities serve as a public institution, tort lawyers get neither government subsidy nor tax shelter. They have to use what money is left after paying taxes on past earnings to keep their firm ready to serve the public and go into action the moment they are called in by a client, who is usually helpless. They must be ready to investigate an accident at any time—even at night or over a weekend, when there is danger of the evidence disappearing—and they must keep their money available to pay for such investigations. Sometimes they even have to secure medical treatment for their clients.

Because of the risks of tort litigation, it is usually the last choice of the star law students who have alternative job offers. In order to compensate for these risks, tort cases are supposed to produce a higher hourly income than other legal work; but even if the tort firm is successful, it is difficult to accumulate the working capital needed to keep a large organization running between collections. There is no way of raising capital for such an organization except from the lawyers themselves. Like most plaintiff's tort lawyers, I started out with virtually no capital of my own. Had I been sitting on a large pile of capital, then the last thing I would probably have invested it in was a self-perpetuating sponge such as a plaintiff's tort firm.

A large organization creates a certain momentum which tends to increase operating expenses. If you are regularly called in on large damage cases that are complicated, and you want to maintain a reputation for thoroughness, your staff falls into the habit of spending a lot of money to prepare cases—or even to study cases that are finally rejected. We have often laid out $5,000 to $10,000 for preliminary investigation of a case, just to decide whether or not we think the claim would be successful. This does not include such overhead expenses as rent, library, or the salaries of the lawyers, clerks, and secretaries who work on the case. It only includes the hard cash paid out for specific case expenses—travel, photographs, experts' opinions, literature searches, laboratory tests, and the like.

Plaintiff's tort lawyers are small businessmen, subject to all of the disadvantages of that status, plus a few that are unique. There is practically no business credit available to them. There are no tax breaks, not even substantial depreciation or investment tax credits, which other small businessmen benefit from. Other businesses of our size are able to get some capital from banks, or to sell stock to the public, or to get assistance from government agencies. But no such help is available to us. If you think that tort practice is a gravy train, go to your bank and try to borrow money against a tort case. No bank will lend money to a tort lawyer beyond the personal assets that the lawyer can put up as security, because the bank cannot step in and finish up the job if something happens to the lawyer.

This creates constant pressure on the proprietors of tort firms to maintain their personal assets in highly liquid form, since they may need them on short notice to keep their practice going. Thus, they are deprived of the opportunity to make equity and real estate investments, which other lawyers are free to engage in without fear of tying up funds needed for law firm capital. This heavy financial penalty is never discussed publicly, but it is one of the reasons why the profits of a successful tort practice must be higher than those of lawyers paid by the hour.

Corporate law firms and those that do not depend on contingent fees do not have this capital reserve problem. They can bill their clients within a few months after rendering services, and they are not called upon to advance large amounts of cash for clients. They can grow to any size—like the 250-lawyer giants of the late 1970s—without running into capital problems. Most lawyers who start out with savings or inheritances are attracted to business law rather than torts. When they become partners, they are usually willing and able to contribute capital to the firm. Tort lawyers, for the most part, start out with little or no savings, and so their newly created partners will rarely have much capital to contribute.

While our large business corporations are subsidized in various ways by the tax system (such as the $19 billion annual gift of the investment tax credit, and the tax deductibility of interest on the huge borrowings available from banks and insurance companies), and even our small entrepreneurs (such as farmers) are eligible for government assistance, the tort lawyer goes it alone. Even doctors are subsidized by government health programs. They don't have to advance money for their patients or to perform services on speculation, and the same goes for dentists, accountants, and other professionals. Tort lawyers are really the last of the true entrepreneurs, putting their skills and capital on the line, and reaping profits in proportion to their performance.

Having read this far, I hope you are convinced that plaintiff's tort lawyers earn every penny they take in. Competition among highly qualified tort lawyers all over the country keeps fees at reasonable levels. Today, most serious tort cases are referred to the specialists by family or business lawyers, so that the tort lawyer's client is actually a very sophisticated lawyer. Such lawyers would not refer these cases if the specialists had not established a track record for adding much more to the client's net recovery than they take out of the case. Thus the cost of hiring a tort specialist is self-liquidating. Tort lawyers' fees are built into the system. Judges and most jurors are aware that tort cases are handled on a contingent fee basis. Jurors usually allow for the fact that the plaintiff will not get all the money—that they must add something to cover fees and expenses. Judges reviewing awards take this into consideration, and so do insurance companies and defense lawyers when they make settlement offers. Thus there is no public outlay for the huge apparatus that now exists for the public's benefit: the facilities maintained by plaintiff's lawyers. Nobody has to pay anything until these facilities have been used and have benefitted the user; and when the tort lawyer's fees are paid, they reflect the exact value of the facilities to the beneficiaries. How many other facilities of this nature do we have? Health care? Financial advice? Accounting? Government services? All of those services must be paid for regardless of results, and many are heavily subsidized by tax dollars, as are our huge industrial concerns.

In order to be useful to its helpless clients, the tort firm must have a financial base. Billy Hyman, who was described in Chapter 2, built such a base on his subrogation practice for an insurance company, but most other successful tort lawyers have had to build their own bases from scratch, using after-tax dollars to maintain their facilities at readiness. So the next time you read about a "big" contingent fee, remember what was needed to keep the lawyer's facilities in readiness to produce the client's compensation, and what would have happened to that client's claim if there had been no such facilities.

This brings me to a sore point: the treatment of contingent legal fees by the press. Almost every journalist who has interviewed me concerning a large settlement or verdict has questioned me closely about the legal fees. I usually take some time to explain all the work that we had to do to make the case a success, and all the facilities we had to maintain in order to give the plaintiff any chance of getting fair compensation. As a rule I decline to state the amount of the legal fee, because experience has taught me that either the journalist or the editor will delete all mention of our work and our facilities, but will highlight a six-figure legal fee as though it were a windfall.

Unless plaintiff's lawyers can collect substantial fees in large cases, there will be no plaintiff's bar capable of carrying on the fight to balance the scales of civil justice. Yet, the very success of plaintiff's lawyers creates a threat of interference with legal fees, and that could remove the incentive for maintenance of the entrepreneur-lawyer institution. Sometimes well-meaning law professors write articles for law journals or newspapers, stating that proof of liability has become a routine matter which does not require any extraordinary legal services and therefore does not involve any "contingency"; therefore, plaintff's lawyers should be paid by the hour, or their percentage fees should be regulated, lest they take advantage of the public. This theory ignores the fact that at the time the tort lawyer is retained, it is impossible to determine how much work will be needed on liability. Thus, the plaintiff may be committed to pay hourly fees that will add up to much more than he or she can afford. In most courts where statistics are available, the defendants actually win more tort trials than do the plaintiffs. And were it not for the strength of modern entrepreneur-lawyers, plaintiffs would be back where they were before 1950, when most tort lawyers took 50 percent fees, had no money to spend on preparing cases for trials, and were so weak that they accomplished little or nothing for their clients. Today, the fee percentages are much lower, and expenditures for clients are much higher. I have never heard plaintiffs who recovered large damages complain about the fact that their lawyer's fees also added up to a large sum of money. It is only professors and journalists who examine these figures in the abstract and then attack them without having the proper background information.

Let us take the Tenerife trial described earlier in this chapter as an example. The insurers decided not to contest liability because the culpability of both airlines was blatant, and they knew that the plaintiffs' lawyers were strong enough to prove this, even if they had to seek out the evidence in the Canary Islands. It is only when defendants want to take the sting out of an inflammatory case that they concede liability. In that way, they prevent the damaging liability evidence from entering the jurors' minds, and they appear to be sympathetic, if not magnanimous. Most experienced tort lawyers agree that where liability is conceded, the plaintiff's lawyers may well have to work harder to achieve adequate compensation. We saw in the Jepson case that the highest offer the defendants made before the case was ready for trial was $220,000, although they had assessed its fair value at $375,000. They were confident that Walter Rutherford and Steve Fearon could hold the award down and that they were not risking much by going to trial on damages only.

The insurance group that decided to concede liability in Tenerife was at the same time vigorously contesting liability in other major accidents, such as the Eastern Airlines Kennedy Airport crash of 1975; the 1974 Eastern Airlines DC-9 crash at Charlotte, North Carolina; and the 1974 Pan American Airways Boeing 707 crash at American Samoa. In each of these cases, they required the plaintiffs to try the issue of liability to completion after years of preliminary work, and then they took the case on to appellate courts, contesting it to the very end because they thought they had a chance of being exonerated. In the Eastern Airlines Charlotte litigation, one trial witness the defense lawyers brought in was Frank Borman, the former astronaut who is now president of the airline. This was in keeping with their consistent practice of parading impressive witnesses before the jury when seeking exoneration. Thus this highly selective process leaves it up to the insurance companies to determine whether there is a "contingency" involved in an aviation case. If they convinced the press and the public that there is no contingency (no question of liability) in major airline cases, they could destroy the economic foundation of the entrepreneur-lawyer, and aviation cases would be back in the dark ages of the *Titanic* and the Triangle Shirtwaist fire. They have it within their power to contest these cases vigorously, and when they choose not to do so, it is only because they feel that experienced and efficient plaintiff's lawyers would make a hash of their defenses, and then the jury would make them pay more than if they had admitted liability.

Even where liability has been conceded or disposed of in a prior trial, plaintiff's lawyers must often do a great deal of work to develop the damage evidence properly. We saw in Chapter 7 how our firm did months of work and spent more than $10,000 on law professor's consulting fees, just on the question of what law would apply to the *damage* phase of the Turkish Airlines DC-10 cases. On that decision hinged the fate of practically all of the plaintiffs, for if it had gone against them, they could not have recovered anything approaching adequate compensation. Even after choice of law has been decided, there remain interviews with business and family witnesses, analysis of financial data, and preparation for economists' testimony. The plaintiff's lawyers must master all the economic data that economists on *both* sides of the case might use in court. In the Tenerife Jepson trial, the plaintiff's own economist was led to fix the loss within a range of $79,399 to $439,497, depending upon how he was questioned.

It is easy for journalists and the public to form a "fat cat" image of the plaintiff's contingency fee lawyer, since no previous author has described the obstacles to be overcome and the facilities that must be maintained to serve the public. You will not find any plaintiff's lawyers in *Fortune's* list of multimillionaires. Tort lawyers cannot amass any fortunes comparable to those of fried chicken entrepreneurs, real estate developers, oil drillers, entertainers, professional athletes, and dozens of other groups whose income is accepted as part of our free enterprise system, even though most of them do not undertake the degree of public service or responsibility that every tort lawyer assumes. There does not seem to be any public resentment about the contingent fees of real estate brokers, who regularly take a large percentage bite out of the largest investment most people ever make. Real estate brokerage commissions take much more out of our gross national product than do contingent fees of tort lawyers. Brokers need little professional training, and in some instances they do no more than to insert newspaper advertisements that the homeowners themselves could compose. Yet their billions in annual commissions are not questioned, since they perform a useful service that is partly self-liquidating because its cost is built into the structure of the real estate market. There is little or no price competition among real estate brokers, though there is among tort lawyers. The public must either pay the fees established by brokerage groups or sell their houses themselves.

Another threat to the institution of entrepreneur-lawyers (and to the clients they represent) is the so-called "big" verdict or settlement. Journalists make a seven-figure award seem like a windfall, without considering that the injured have lost all their senses or seen their lives go completely down the drain. We have represented clients from all walks of life who have received seven-figure compensation, and I cannot think of one—rich or poor—who was pleased with the tradeoff or who celebrated a windfall. How many journalists would take that amount of money in exchange for permanent paralysis or loss of all of the useful and pleasant sensations of life? How many would trade it for the loss of their husbands or wives? But in the quest for a juicy headline that will titillate the readership, this question is never asked. I have never seen a newspaper article about a seven-figure verdict which explains to the public that the amount will be reviewed by the trial judge and appellate courts, and will be reduced or set aside completely if it does not conform to the legal requirements for proof of actual damages.

Journalists often comment on zooming insurance costs in areas such as medical malpractice and products liability, where the instruments of damage are capable of inflicting devastating permanent injuries or death. These fields of litigation have only begun to develop since 1950. They had a century of catching up to do, which caused huge percentage increases in the cost of liability insurance, because liability was practically nonexistent a few years ago and the insurance, if they bothered to carry it at all, was dirt cheap. This is in contrast to a field such as aviation, in which the insurance costs have been kept below one percent of operating expenses for the airlines and the manufacturers despite steady increases in the amounts awarded. There is brisk competition for the huge multimillion dollar aviation risks. In 1979, Mr. E. O. Walklin, chairman of Lloyd's Aviation Underwriters Association, reported:

> The last ten years have produced steady aviation profits and this has attracted a new market, very often to the detriment of the existing market . . . . There is now so much capacity that brokers can complete their slips without the support of major sections of the market, and this has actually happened in the last few weeks. The prospect of any major and lasting improvement in our market therefore depends on some contraction in capacity.
>
> *   *   *
>
> I suppose the biggest problem we have can be summed up in one word—greed. Where sections of a market corner too much of the business, then it is inevitable that the have-nots will compete, perhaps too keenly, to retain a reasonable account.

And at the end of 1979, *Business Insurance,* reporting on the 1979 DC-10 crash at Chicago's O'Hare Airport (which cost 273 lives and was the worst aviation disaster to occur in the United States) stated that "tremendous capacity in the aviation insurance market is holding hull and liability rates low" despite the impact of the O'Hare disaster.

Thus the insurance business is profitable and the rates can be held down when there is an orderly development of liability. But when manufacturers have been getting away with causing injuries or deaths for many generations, and liability is suddenly thrust upon them, it is not surprising that their insurance costs will escalate sharply. Concentration on making *safe products* will bring insurance rates down within manageable limits, and as in aviation, insurance costs will not add up to a significant portion of operating expenses or annual profits.

It seems that journalists (and sometimes law professors) are unconcerned about the damage that they might do by turning the success of the entrepreneur-lawyers against them, claiming that it has now become easy to prove liability and that verdicts are too high. Every tort lawyer I have spoken to agrees that each year the practice becomes more demanding and the facilities more expensive to maintain. And I do not know of any large damage award that was not closely scrutinized by one or more judges before it was finally paid by a defendant or an insurance company. Certainly the professors and the press owe it to the public to mention these facts along with their opinions.

Role of the General Practice Firm

Law practice as a whole is more specialized now than ever before. Most American lawyers are engaged in business or tax counseling and advisory work, and generally perform these services in their offices rather than in the courtroom. Therefore the practice of referring personal clients to tort specialists, which (as we saw in Chapter 2) helped to professionalize tort practice, is stronger than ever. In the earlier days, many large general practice firms would disdain any participation in tort cases, even if important personal clients were injured in accidents. They would simply give their clients the names of one or more tort lawyers whom they considered competent and suggest that their client call the tort lawyer directly. At that point they would bow out without taking any responsibility for the progress of the case or participating as cocounsel.

However, due to the recent advances in scientific tort practice, large general practice firms have shown an increasing tendency to participate in tort cases even after referring them to tort specialists. We have often collaborated as cocounsel with general practice firms whose clients had been killed in airplane crashes. In these and other wrongful death cases where they are already involved as attorneys for the estate, general practice firms often participate as cocounsel. Yet some such firms are still reluctant to participate as cocounsel in other types of accident cases. We have always believed that they should participate and should share in the fees, since they have important functions in the selection of tort specialists, the conduct of the litigation, the appraisal of settlement offers, the final decisions on settlement, and the investment of the proceeds.

Making it legal for lawyers to advertise was intended to aid the public, but it actually makes the selection process more difficult in tort cases. In urban areas, seriously injured accident victims may be deluged with advertisements from dozens of prospective tort lawyers and could easily make the mistake of choosing a lawyer who is not fully equipped to handle their case. They might base their decision entirely on quotation of a low percentage fee, without realizing that the lawyer in question may intend to settle the case for whatever he can get without spending the time and money needed to get it ready for trial. And there is always the chance of ending up with a zero verdict. While the client might have difficulty in sorting out the qualifications of various tort lawyers and thus might go along with the lowest bidder, the general practice lawyers have more reliable methods of making the selection. They can negotiate with the tort specialist for a reasonable fee arrangement, using their leverage as continuing colleagues who refer other cases to the specialist.

Having the general practice firm as personal lawyers and the tort specialist as consultant gives the client the best possible combination of legal services, drawing upon the strengths of both firms. General practice firms are used to retaining other lawyers for their clients in locations where they do not practice and they know how to monitor the work of attorneys and follow the progress of a case. They also know how to evaluate settlement offers and recommendations, even in the relatively unfamiliar field of torts. Since more than 90 percent of tort cases are settled before trial, careful appraisal of settlement offers and the leverage of each party is required. The general practice firm, with its own litigation department, can objectively appraise the information given to them by the specialist and make a professional analysis of the settlement posture at all stages in the case, so that the client has the best chance of settling the case at the right time for the right amount. Or, in those cases which *should* go to trial, the general practice firms can assure the clients that it is in their best interests to reject settlement, and that a trial is really necessary. Otherwise, the clients must rely entirely on the specialists. Even if the specialists do their job perfectly, the clients can never learn enough about tort practice to be sure that every useful step has been taken.

Some people have been brainwashed by articles in magazines and newspapers about the "personal injury racket," and they approach tort lawyers with trepidation. Compared to the personal attention they get from a large general practice firm—whom they pay by the hour— they may feel that their treatment in a busy tort specialists' office is brusque. We try to avoid this, but it is sometimes inevitable. Tort practice is more oriented toward dealing with judges, jurors, insurance adjusters, and defense lawyers than toward the personal counseling of clients. Often the senior members of specialist firms are busy in court or traveling on depositions and do not have much time available for client counseling. During the preparatory stages of the case, the client's contacts are often with junior lawyers, who may not inspire as much confidence in the client as the familiar counselors at the general practice firm. Therefore, the personal lawyer has an important role to play in keeping harmonious relations between the client and the specialist, and in making sure that the client understands each step in the litigation. For that reason, progress reports are best made from the specialist to the personal lawyer, who will then relay them to the client in a manner which will satisfy the client that each necessary step in processing the case is taken properly. The plaintiff is probably engaged in a once-in-a-lifetime relationship with the specialist, whereas the personal lawyer is a source of potential future referrals for the specialist. As in the matter of fixing fees, the personal attorney has much more leverage than the plaintiff when it comes to getting timely progress reports from the specialist.

Two items that require careful explanation to a tort plaintiff are the delays of litigation and the chance of losing the case entirely. The general practice lawyer can help to condition plaintiffs for delays to be expected in the normal course of litigation, so that they do not lose confidence in the tort specialist or come to feel that their case is being neglected. As to the chances of losing, very few plaintiffs understand the fault system; most think only in terms of damages. In considering a settlement offer, they will often concentrate on comparing the dollar amount to their actual losses and disregard the possibility of losing the case at trial. They may compare the settlement they are offered with amounts collected by some other plaintiffs who may have had much stronger liability cases, or may have been forced to run the risk of losing on liability at trial. In such situations, the combined services of the personal lawyer and the specialist can avoid the risk of being forced to trial in a case which has already been won by a good settlement.

Furthermore, the general practice firm is intimately familiar with the business and personal life of the client. Even the most conscientious specialist is not likely to learn as much about the tort victim's family, career, and business prospects as the personal lawyer who has worked with that person on estate planning, family problems, or other legal matters over a long time and may be very familiar with the organization which employed the person and governed this employee's future income and career advancement. Many important pieces of evidence have been turned up through the participation of general practice firms in all phases of the litigation.

This intimate knowledge of the client's affairs is also important at the final stages of the case. Awards today are often large enough to require estate and investment planning—functions that a tort specialist does not usually undertake. Indeed, the client may have been offered a large settlement in "structured" form—part being in cash and the ballance in annuities or other deferred payments—and this, too, requires expert financial analysis.

During the 1970s, many large general practice firms revised their attitudes about referring tort cases. They came to realize that by using some of their litigation and counseling skills, they could help their clients to achieve adequate compensation and personal satisfaction in tort suits, and at lower cost and lesser risk than the clients would encounter on their own. Recognizing that this is a very valuable professional service to their clients, they do not hesitate to participate in contingent fees.

Large general practice firms have become more interested in acting as participating counsel since the recoveries in tort cases increased during the 1970s. The contingent fees in serious injury or death cases are usually sufficient to pay the general practice firm fees comparable to those they would charge on an hourly basis. At the same time, the collaboration is favorable to the client, because it produces better results, and in the end it costs the plaintiff nothing to have the additional services of the general practice firm. Of course, this is only practical in cases of serious injury or death, for only where the damages are substantial is there room for truly professional services by the general practice firm and the specialist. The leading specialist firms are not geared to handle cases involving small damages, because they simply cannot do them justice. In such instances, the general practice firm will probably help the client to select a tort lawyer who is willing to handle smaller cases, or they may be able to settle the case by negotiating directly with the insurer. Some tort specialists will help general practice firms to settle such cases by providing an appraisal of settlement value at nominal cost.

Kicking in Rotten Doors

As Dean Pound said so aptly, "*Stare decisis* has no legitimate applica-tion to remnants remaining in the law of torts after the principle behind them has been given up." This is a parallel to John Kenneth Gal-braith's observation that most of the progress toward economic equality has come about through the "kicking in of rotten doors." There still are a lot of rotten legal doors that need to be kicked in, and the best wea-pons are the legal treatise and the law review article. In the long fight to overcome the archaic privity defense that protected manufacturers against having to pay for the damage done by their faulty products, Dean William Prosser's writings were a potent force. Prosser elegantly described this battle as the "assault on the citadel of privity." One of the helpful assault weapons was an oft-cited annotation by Al Gans—written in 1946, when he was editor of *American Law Reports*—in which he pointed out that the exceptions had swallowed up the privity rule. When seen in that light, privity was no longer a citadel but merely a rotten door that barred the way to justice. A few years after Prosser and Gans had attacked it, it was kicked in by the courts.

Despite the great strides made by the scientific tort lawyer, some ancient inequities persist. As we have seen, the remnants of Lord Ellenborough's infamous decision in *Baker v. Bolton* continue to plague the relatives of deceased accident victims. There is no logical, legal, or moral reason to treat personal injury damages differently from those in wrongful death cases; and yet, as we start the 1980s, most states permit punitive damages in personal injury cases but not in wrongful death cases, and they permit damages for mental anguish in personal injury cases, but deny them to the aggrieved relatives of persons killed in accidents. There is still much to be done to make our courts world-wide centers of litigation, so that harried judges do not have to worry about their crowded calendars in making decisions on *forum non con-veniens*. Property is still given greater protection than human life and limb. You saw in Chapter 2 that in the very first American aviation trial—the 1822 case of the balloonist who damaged the field of rad-ishes—the property owner was protected by the law because the damage was forseeable. Yet, in many personal injury and death claims—such as the Roberto Clemente case—it remains difficult to get the courts to apply this standard of foreseeability when liability is not based upon ancient precedents or the ownership of property.

One of the rottenest doors remaining to be kicked in is the one that bars plaintiffs in tort actions from recovering interest from the date of injury, while such prejudgment interest is awarded to plaintiffs in nontort cases such as those involving contracts. As you saw in Chapter 5, American Airlines' successful suit against Ford for breach of contract relating to the overhaul of their Ford Trimotor in 1931 brought the airline a judgment for $30,000 (the value of the airplane) plus $13,489 in interest; but the families of the passengers killed in the accident were barred from recovering interest on their losses. The ancient principle that is supposed to justify this distinction is that damages are "liquidated" in contract actions, whereas they remain "unliquidated" in tort actions. If this is true, then courts throughout the world have wasted thousands of trials to determine the value of the damages suffered in breach of contract cases. Where there is a dispute between the parties that requires a trial, the damages are no more liquidated or predetermined in a contract action than they are in a tort action. Indeed, many times the *only* issue in dispute in a breach of contract action is the amount of damage.

Another ancient maxim which was supposed to support this distinction is that prior to the suit, there is a "preexisting obligation" to pay in a contract action, while in a tort action, there is no obligation until the injury is suffered. This ignores the preexisting legal obligation in every tort action: the duty of the defendant to exercise reasonable care for the safety of the public, including the plaintiff. Furthermore, since the plaintiff's suffering begins at the moment of the injury, that distinction is illogical and indefensible from the standpoint of deterrence as well as compensation. Nevertheless this ancient distinction has been preserved in our law. It has been questioned in legal texts and has nothing left to support it—save inertia. In a leading legal encyclopedia, *American Jurisprudence 2d,* the distinction is held to be without substance:

> Such decisions are difficult to justify on the distinction between liquidated and unliquidated claims. The four elements generally compensated in a personal injury action . . . can be referred to an objective standard in the same manner as damages for breach of contract.

The specious distinction which robs tort plaintiffs of the right to recover interest from the date of injury has a disastrous effect on our courts. It encourages (and indeed subsidizes) defendants who wait until the very last minute to settle tort cases. Why should they rush to settle cases—even those in which their liability is clear—when they can earn 10 to 20 percent a year on the money for several years while waiting out calendar delay? If they had to pay interest to the plaintiffs from the date of injury, it would not be profitable to withhold this money, and it would give them an incentive to settle meritorious cases earlier.

Since the distinction between tort and nontort cases for prejudgment interest purposes is a judge-made rule, it can be unmade by judges. This is one of the joys of the common law of torts—it is not totally ossified. A giant step in that direction was taken in the cases arising out of the 1979 crash of an American Airlines DC-10 at O'Hare Airport in Chicago. In that litigation, we have the privilege of collaborating with John J. Kennelly of Chicago in the largest group of plaintiffs' cases filed as of this writing. In one of those cases, we made a motion requesting that the judges in charge of the case hold American Airlines and McDonnell Douglas Corporation liable for interest from the date of the accident. The defendants opposed this motion on the grounds that the wrongful death statutes of Illinois and California (the plaintiffs' residences) did not provide for prejudgment interest, and that it was not available at common law in tort cases. Judges Robson and Will of the U.S. District Court, Northern District of Illinois, Eastern Division, presiding over all the federal cases arising out of this accident by order of the Judicial Panel on Multidistrict Litigation, decided on December 6, 1979, that they would include prejudgment interest as an element of damages in all instructions to juries in the O'Hare cases.

Judges Robson and Will refused to be bound by ancient precedents stemming from the property-oriented seventeenth-century jurisprudence of England. The court found that there were legal grounds for including prejudgment interest as an element of "fair and just compensation" required by the applicable wrongful death statutes. But it also based its decision on an equitable ground which may have very far-reaching effects on the entire law of torts and the calendar congestion problem in our courts. The court stated that the huge amounts of interest which the insurers would be collecting on the prospective compensation represented "a real incentive for the defendants to postpone paying the plaintiffs," thus defeating the court's responsibility "to insure the fair, just, and speedy disposition of cases." These equitable grounds seem to be equally applicable to personal injury cases and all other tort claims. How many of the legion of tort cases that are left unsettled for two, three, or four years would stay that way if the defendants had to pay prejudgment interest?

The memorandum that we submitted in support of our motion for prejudgment interest was written mostly by Jack Kennelly, a master of the Brandeis brief. To dramatize the injustice of denying interest to the O'Hare widows, Jack Kennelly dug up ten cases—some of them going back nearly a hundred years—in which Americans were allowed to collect prejudgment interest for the deaths of animals, including a bull, a mule, cattle, a horse, a colt, sheep dogs, sheep, goats, a cow, and a pig. If the courts could impose the obligation of prejudgment interest in such cases, why should the loss of human life be taken more lightly and its redress be treated with less concern?

In many other ways as well, property rights are favored over personal rights. Thus the statute of limitations for personal injury and wrongful death claims is shorter in most states than the statute of limitations for property damage, even when both losses arise out of the same accident. Kentucky has a one-year statute of limitations for personal injury, but five years for property damage. Illinois, Pennsylvania, Oregon, and New Jersey allow two years for personal injury and six years for property damage. There is no logic or justice in this discrimination.

The same type of discrimination is shown by the fact that in property cases the courts can impose procedural safeguards (such as liens that protect creditors against the sale of assets or the bankruptcy of the defendant), but in most tort cases nothing can be done to protect the compensation of an injured person until a judgment has been entered—by which time property may have been disposed of or the defendant may be in bankruptcy. Even though the transfer of property or the insolvency of defendants may cause accident victims to lose their only chance of compensation and a decent life, there is no protection; whereas they would have had all sorts of ancient devices for their protection if they had engaged in property transactions with the defendants.

Such are the challenges facing the scientific tort lawyer in the last quarter of the twentieth century. It will probably take the rest of the century to bring tort victims to a place of equality with property owners in our courts. And a doughty band of entrepreneur-lawyers will be leading the way, noisily kicking in rotten doors as they go.

Chapter 9

INTERVIEW WITH A TORT LAWYER

I asked several people (including journalists, lawyers, and students) to read the manuscript of this book with a view to questioning me about the topics covered in the preceding chapters. Following is a compendium of their questions and my answers. The page numbers in parentheses refer to sections of the first eight chapters in which more detailed information can be found.

Q: You present a very rosy picture of modern tort practice and the whole civil litigation system. Do you really think it's that great?

A: It has lots of defects and problems, but I think it fits Winston Churchill's appraisal of democracy: "It's the worst system except for all the others that have been tried from time to time."

Q: Since you cited Ambrose Bierce's uncomplimentary definitions of lawyers and litigation in the preface, how do you reply to them?

A: Bierce was confusing the weaknesses of human nature with those of the legal system. Most lawsuits are brought to counteract dishonesty, stupidity, infidelity, recklessness, greed, lack of consideration for others—the whole catalogue of human failings. Neither courts nor lawyers can turn these raw materials into a product that is attractive to the people involved. All they can hope to do is provide some measure of relief, and their efficiency in providing relief is limited by what society is willing to pay for that service.

Q: If this is so, then why are lawyers so unpopular?

A: Lawyers are the natural scapegoats for society's dissatisfaction with the limitations of legal remedies. Moreover, they are forced to make themselves unpleasant to the opposition in the course of fighting for their clients' rights.

Q: Why does the settlement of disputes have to be unpleasant? Do we really need the adversary system?

A: Yes, I'm afraid it is the only way to achieve truth and justice in the present state of human nature. Legal rights are not self-executing, and people do not always tell the truth when money is at stake; if they did, there would be few lawsuits. You might be only 51 percent convinced that you, the lawyer, should represent a client, but once you undertake the case, you must shift gears and use 100 percent of your skills to try to win, for then you have complete responsibility for the client's cause. Centuries of experience have shown that the best way to achieve justice is to have both sides present the strongest possible case and let the judge and jury (not the lawyers) decide who should prevail.

Q: That doesn't explain to me why litigation has to be so unpleasant. Why can't it be a high-level intellectual quest for the truth that leaves both winner and loser satisfied?

A: The real world doesn't work that way. Most people come into litigation convinced that they are right; many actually erase from their mind facts that will hurt their case. America is already known as a litigious society. If litigation were pleasant and inexpensive, we would have even more of it. Lawyers on both sides must question every statement that is damaging to their clients' cause. In the end, the losers are publicly branded as liars and ordered to pay the winners, who feel imposed upon all the same, because they have to pay their own lawyers for obtaining what they were entitled to in the first place. This is not an ideal system, but its very unpleasantness helps to force pretrial settlement of more than 90 percent of civil lawsuits. Litigation is a form of warfare, not the gravy train that is sometimes pictured. People should settle their disputes without litigation whenever possible.

Q: Don't you feel rather shabby about playing the role of one who will take money to argue either side of a cause?

A: That doesn't apply to me, since I have been almost exclusively on the plaintiff's side throughout my career, but it is not a valid criticism of any lawyer. It misconstrues the role of the lawyer. The lawyer's job is to make the legal system work by assisting people on either side of a controversy to have their rights adjudicated through a fair trial.

Q: Why are Americans so litigious?

A: We've always been very independent and jealous of our rights. De Tocqueville observed in 1834 that we were litigious. We seem even more litigious today because some of our other means of settling disputes (such as family, church, school, community, and legislature) are losing their authority, while the courts have become stronger and are open to many more people, thanks to contingent fees and the availability of a lawyer for any legitimate claim. Also, while legislatures study, debate, and compromise to avoid decisions on the merits, the courts *must* decide every dispute presented, even when Congress has ducked an economic policy issue, as in the *Bakke* reverse discrimination case.

Q: Doesn't that mean that lawyers are reshaping society according to their own notions?

A: No. Lawyers can only respond to the need for enforcement of legal rights; they cannot invent disputes.

Q: Don't we have too many lawyers bringing suits now?

A: Again, lawyers don't invent lawsuits. If we want a government of laws rather than of personalities, we have to put up with a large lawyer population. The societies over which Hitler, Stalin, and Idi Amin presided did not need many lawyers. Nor did we ourselves have many lawyers when the courts were preoccupied with enforcement of property rights. But now that the emphasis has shifted toward the personal rights of over 200 million people, it will obviously take more and more lawyers to enforce these rights. Our insistence upon attempting to achieve perfect justice for each individual is the main reason why we have almost two-thirds of the world's lawyers.

Q: So you are in favor of a litigious society?

A: I'd rather live in a place where justice was automatic, but I haven't been able to find the address. In the meantime, settling our disputes by litigation is fairer, more democratic, and less violent than any other means I know. Other democracies try to settle many competing demands by social legislation, but it doesn't seem to be working well anywhere, because it is inflationary and human nature turns it into exploitation by political power groups.

Q: Public opinion polls show that most people think the legal system favors the rich and powerful over everyone else. Does it?

A: It used to, but as we have seen in this book (e.g., pp. 341–372), that situation has changed dramatically in the second half of the 20th century largely due to the rise of the entrepreneur-lawyer. If you took a poll of the rich and powerful, they would probably list the legal system and contingent fee lawyers among the greatest threats to them. Ambrose Bierce's 1911 definition of wealth as the equivalent of impunity certainly doesn't hold true in lawsuits of the 1980s.

Q: Do you mind being unpopular?

A: I've become resigned to it, although I hope that this book will make me and other lawyers less unpopular. Richard (Racehorse) Haynes, the famous Texas lawyer, has some comforting thoughts on that subject:

> I do not believe that lawyers as a class—the legal profession—*ought* to be popular. If you ask the citizen on the street about lawyers, he will tell you that lawyers generally ought to be taken out and shot down like dogs. But ask him about his own personal lawyer: "There is a great person, dedicated, intelligent, who will go to the courthouse and make sure that my claims are satisfied and that my wrongs are righted." As long as we can satisfy our own clients, I think maybe we are doing all right.

Q: Do our courts really achieve equal protection of the laws?

A: No, because there is a basic conflict between our economic system and the ideal legal system envisioned in the Constitution. While the Bill of Rights mandates equal protection, it is silent on the economic system, which continues to create unequal portions of wealth, income, and power. However, despite the automatic inequality caused by the economic system, we are getting closer to equal protection because in many cases now, lawyers of equal ability are available to the rich and the poor.

Q: That sounds like an attack on capitalism. Do the socialist nations come closer to equal protection?

A: No, they don't even try to supply many individual legal remedies. They reduce the populace to the lowest common denominator and make it practically impossible for most individuals to bring civil claims to court. I think the socialist concentration of economic and political power in the same hands is the worst possible system. Capitalism is full of flaws, but it has permitted the growth of an egalitarian legal system that is constantly advancing toward equal protection.

Q: In his famous 1978 Harvard commencement address, Alexander Solzhenitsyn condemned America's legalistic society:

> **Any conflict is solved according to the letter of the law and this is considered to be the supreme solution. If one is right from a legal point of view, nothing more is required. . . . The letter of the law is too cold and formal to have a beneficial influence on society.**

Do you agree?

A: It is obvious that Dr. Solzhenitsyn knows little about the workings of the American legal system. The existence of jury trial alone assures that the conscience of society will mitigate the law's harshness and clumsiness. In addition, I would suggest that he read Judge Peirson Hall's choice-of-law opinion in the Turkish Airlines DC-10 case (pp.

450–460) and the Oregon Supreme Court's decision in the case of the two nuns (pp. 566–567) as examples of the moral basis of American law.

Q: In the same address, Solzhenitsyn gave some examples of the immorality of American law:

> An oil company is legally blameless when it purchases an invention of a new type of energy in order to prevent its use. A food manufacturer is legally blameless when he poisons his product to make it last longer; after all, people are free not to buy it.

Any comment?

A: I wish Dr. Solzhenitsyn would send those two cases to a contingent fee lawyer, preferably me. He must have been reading some nineteenth-century textbooks when he wrote those words.

Q: To avoid the expense and delay of civil lawsuits, could many disputes be settled by administrative bureaus or legislative schemes?

A: Efforts along these lines have had disastrous results, and the public has lost confidence in politicians and bureaucrats. Would you prefer to have your financial future decided by politicians, by bureaucrats, or by a jury of your neighbors who have heard the evidence given under oath in open court? Would you like the final statement of your legal rights to come in the form of a press release from the legislative or executive branch, or as a reasoned legal opinion based on our Constitution and our laws and signed by the judges who wrote it?

Q: But isn't it possible to streamline procedures by getting away from the courts, with their formal rules of evidence?

A: The 1970s trend toward dismantling administrative agencies is the best answer to those who would substitute administrative procedures for the courts. Efforts to fix legal rights through administrative bureaus are likely to end up in a Kafka scenario such as the Internal Revenue Code, which now has more than 38,000 pages of regulations appended to it, in language that is mystifying even to most lawyers. Experience has shown that taking claims out of the courts does not speed up disposition unless legal rights are sharply curtailed.

Q: What about the no-fault automobile insurance system?

A: Basically, it is a system for paying out more money to compensate minor injuries at the expense of some victims who have been damaged more seriously. It also eliminates the deterrent aspect of tort suits, and it tends to decrease individual responsibility in favor of a lowest-common-denominator approach. It also opens the door to more fake claims, and in the 24 states that have no-fault legislation, it has not brought the promised reduction in auto insurance rates. It was suggested by two prominent torts professors (Keeton and O'Connell) who were concerned about claimants who receive no compensation for injuries sustained in auto accidents. I believe it is a worthwhile experiment at the level at which it operates (the least serious injuries and wage losses sustained in auto accidents) because it has become difficult for the tort system to do justice to claims of that size.

Q: Do you think that no-fault should be extended to more serious injuries and to nonautomobile accidents?

A: No. I think it has a long way to go to prove its effectiveness even in minor auto injury cases. It would be disastrous to extend it to areas such as products liability, where the deterrent aspect is as vital as compensation. It goes against the grain of American justice, which has moved away steadily from the archaic principle that victims of accidents should subsidize those who inflicted the injuries by absorbing economic losses on top of their physical and emotional losses. Professor Keeton (now a federal judge) does not recommend extension of no-fault to other fields, and Professor O'Connell has given up the idea of extending it by legislation.

Q: What about worker's compensation? Doesn't it supply compensation for accidental injuries without the delay and expense of lawsuits?

A: It does supply limited compensation for injuries suffered on the job, but like most systems based on competing political demands rather than justice, it falls below the level of compensation needed to maintain human dignity. I daresay that most employees would gladly exchange their miserly worker's compensation benefits for the right to sue employers in court, even if it took longer and required payment of higher contingent legal fees. I know that to be true of railroad and maritime workers. They are *not* covered by worker's compensation. Instead, they must retain contingent fee lawyers and sue their employers in court. But when they were offered a worker's compensation scheme they turned it down flatly, accepting some inconvenience rather than give up their right to adequate compensation for serious injuries.

Q: Can the worker's compensation scheme be extended to other accidental injuries, such as auto and products liability cases?

A: The scheme's benefits are fixed by state legislation, which is a product of lobbying power. Despite its tremendous political power, organized labor has not been able to lobby worker's compensation benefits to decent levels. Most seriously injured workers are financially ruined for life, unless they were fortunate enough to have been injured on the job by a third party (such as machine manufacturer) who can be sued in court and forced to pay adequate damages. Since the labor lobby has fared so poorly, you can imagine what benefits motorists and consumers (two of society's least politically organized factions) would get from the legislatures.

Q: Are you arguing for the "status quo," or do you have some changes to suggest?

A: I think that we should hang on to our basic system of civil litigation, but keep working at improving it, as we have been doing steadily during the past 30 years.

Q: What specific improvements do you have in mind?

A: The biggest need is to devote more of our resources to the courts, even if that means decreased expenditures on the legislative and executive branches. We've seen massive growth in congressional expenses, which now support a total staff of 18,400 "aides," whose main function seems to be to produce tons of documents which are not read or turned into legislation. We have invested untold billions in education and foreign aid, with limited returns. We know that every dollar spent on judges and courtrooms produces some justice—the best brand of justice that human nature can muster in a democracy whose people have diverse backgrounds and a strong taste for personal freedom. But our per capita expenditure for the legal system is much less than that of most industrial nations. We are way behind West Germany, Sweden, Italy, and France in the number of judges per million population, and our total expenditure on the federal court system is about $250 million per year—less than the cost of one Trident submarine, and not even one-half of one percent of the total defense budget.

Q: Is our court system really inadequate?

A: Yes, and here I must depart from the subject of this book to get over into the criminal field. In most courts, the same judges preside over both civil and criminal cases. The crime explosion of the 1970s has put tremendous strain on the entire court system, criminal and civil. Criminal trials must take priority because society must be protected immediately and the defendants are entitled to speedy trial after indictment. The result is that civil cases are put on the back burner, and the waiting time for civil trials increases even though lawyers and judges have become more efficient in dealing with large case loads.

Q: How can this situation be changed?

A: I think the American people have to appreciate the value of our legal system, which Alexander Hamilton called "the cement of society." They must be told that while the end result of the 18,400 congressional staffers' work is only 700 pieces of legislation, our courts are handling 12 million new civil suits and 11 million new criminal cases (not including 65 million traffic violations) each year. They must come to appreciate that the judicial branch is the one arm of government in which the people can still participate fully, since their influence on the legislative and executive branches has been blunted by the very narrow choices available in the voting booth.

Q: Why do you say that the people can participate fully in the judicial system?

A: Because jury trials give ordinary citizens the power to judge great corporations and set our standards of morality and justice. Jefferson said that if he had to choose between giving up the vote and the right to serve on juries, he would rate jury trials as the more important. This is reflected in the Declaration of Independence, which listed deprivation of jury trial as one of the main grievances against the Crown, and in the Bill of Rights, which guarantees jury trials in both civil and criminal cases.

Q: Aren't jurors susceptible to emotional arguments?

A: Yes, but in the end all of us are. Just as the corporate boardroom seems to nourish mob psychology and shirking of individual responsibility (pp. 364–365), so the jury room seems to bring out the best in people. Jurors will hold themselves and the parties in the case to much higher moral standards than they use in their own affairs; they are privileged to control the levers of power for a brief moment, and they usually rise to the occasion.

Q: Couldn't judges do the job faster and better without juries?

A: On that one, let me quote Jim R. Carrigan, former justice of the Colorado Supreme Court and now a federal district judge:

> While recognizing that most trial judges are fair, honest, and well-motivated, I submit that the *least* reliable of factfinders is the old, experienced, callous, cynical trial judge. He thinks he has heard the same case a thousand times before, and his most urgent desire is to get it over with. But the typical juror approaches each case with a freshness and a dedication to accomplish justice.

English author G. K. Chesterton put it another way: "I would rather trust twelve ordinary men than one ordinary man." Judges are isolated somewhat from the mainstream of life. They are not usually experts on everyday affairs, or on scientific or financial matters. The collective knowledge and conscience of the jury is bound to be more representative of our society. Juries are particularly adept at handling intangible concepts such as good faith, reasonable care, dangerous design, pain, suffering, and loss of society.

Q: Doesn't the use of a jury slow the trial down?

A: Yes, but it's worth the extra expense and trouble to maintain the last opportunity for our citizens to participate directly and personally in self-government. We've turned over most of our lives to politicians and bureaucrats who are increasingly controlled by lobbyists. The residual power of our democracy now rests in the jury system.

Q: Shouldn't juries be limited to simpler cases?

A: No. It is important that we keep juries sitting at the highest level of business regulation, in the complicated cases that involve large sums of money and set standards of conduct for the whole nation. The mere existence of juries helps to maintain higher standards of compliance with the law. As De Tocqueville said:

> Now, the institution of the jury raises the people itself, or at least a class of citizens, to the bench of judges. The institution of the jury consequently invests the people, or that class of people, with the direction of society . . .

When De Tocqueville wrote those words in 1834, the "class of citizens" that held the power levers of the jury system was limited to male property owners in many cases. Today, practically all our adult citizens are eligible for jury duty, so that this great power is even more broadly diffused than it was when De Tocqueville marveled at it. And in a 1977 survey of more than 3,000 state trial judges, 92.5 percent favored retaining juries for determination of both liability and damages. The Tenerife trial (Chapter 8) is one of many examples of the manner in which jurors can grasp technical data and reach a fair and logical result.

Q: Don't juries often hand out money too liberally?

A: Occasionally, jurors get carried away and award damages that are beyond the legal standards. But those damages are never collected, because the verdict is reviewed by the trial judge and is reduced or set aside if it does not conform to the legal standards of proof, as we have seen numerous times in the preceding chapters. Beyond that, appellate courts will set aside jury verdicts where there is evidence of passion or prejudice.

Q: But aren't verdicts too high now? How can you justify multimillion dollar awards in tort cases?

A: Multimillion dollar awards that are actually collected always have a strong financial underpinning, such as the astronomical cost of daily care for a paraplegic, or the loss of support suffered by the widow of a successful businessman. The courts have never hesitated to affirm large awards based on the value of property, such as works of art. Now we have finally recognized—as the rest of the world has not—that it is possible to do as much damage to a human being as to a piece of canvas.

Q: Don't these huge awards threaten the existence of manufacturers and the thousands of jobs that their products represent?

A: No; the deterrent of tort litigation threatens the existence of unsafe products but not the existence of manufacturers. There is no useful product that cannot be made safe or substituted for. If manufacturers devoted more funds to product safety research and less to lobbying and public relations attacks on the tort deterrent, the problem would disappear. We are past the age when manufacturers can ask their victims to forfeit their legal rights in order to subsidize the continued irresponsible marketing of hazardous products. We now allocate the full cost of compensation to the responsible party (pp. 341–372).

Q: Don't you think it is repulsive to put a price tag on human suffering and to exploit misfortune by suing for huge damages?

A: I think it is repulsive to allow anyone to ruin the life of another person through carelessness or greed, and then make the victim bear the financial loss in addition to the physical and emotional losses that can never be erased. Large damage awards reinforce individual responsibility and deter future repetition of this antisocial conduct, as well as furnishing compensation to the victim to the extent that money can accomplish this. I am not ashamed of the fact that such lawsuits also give me the opportunity to profit in direct proportion to the compensation and deterrence my efforts may produce.

Q: Can you demonstrate that tort liability is a deterrent force?

A: Yes, I have given specific examples such as the safety changes that followed the Turkish Airlines DC-10 (pp. 465–468) and Varig Paris (pp. 469–472) crashes, compared to the lack of action after the Tenerife (pp. 498–500) and De Havilland Comet (pp. 345–347) accidents, which were not followed by liability litigation; the Mohawk 600 rifle (pp. 348–355); and the Ford Pinto (pp. 355–366). Deterrence is strongest when insurance coverage and rates are tied directly to claims experience, as in aviation and products liability.

Q: How do you justify contingent fees professionally—aren't you destroying your professional detachment by taking a piece of your client's compensation?

A: No. I find that being paid strictly on the basis of results you achieve for your client is a professional challenge of the highest order. I started out with a Wall Street law firm that had no contingent fee clients, and I didn't feel any more or less professional than I did while working on a contingent basis. The corporations that we represented bought our services, used them to help their business, and then passed the cost along to the public. We were part of the corporate production process, just as tort lawyers are part of the compensation process. As to detachment, I am not sure it has any value in litigation. If I needed a tort lawyer, I would want him or her to be deeply involved in my problems. The contingent fee is ideal for that purpose.

Q: Doesn't the contingent fee create a conflict of interest between you and your client?

A: No; just the opposite is true. Our financial interests are completely attuned, more so than in any other type of fee relationship. Often when I have recommended to a client that a settlement offer be accepted or rejected, my explanation has been cut short by the client saying: "Well, we're in the same boat; whatever I collect, you're going to get part of, so I'll certainly go along with your recommendation." Another advantage is that the clients always know where they stand. When a settlement offer is made, the clients can calculate exactly how much money *they* will get. That is not usually the case when the fee is non-contingent.

Q: Don't contingent fees encourage groundless lawsuits?

A: No; once again the exact opposite is true. If I were interested in wiping out plaintiff's tort lawyers, I would feed them thousands of groundless lawsuits, so they could spend their time and money on losing causes. Defense lawyers are well trained to spot groundless claims, and would be delighted to carry such cases all the way through trial and appeal. It makes them look good in their clients' eyes, and they are well paid for their efforts. There may be lawyers who bring vexatious small claims, hoping to profit from nuisance value settlements; but it is cheaper and wiser in the long run for insurers to force such cases to trial and nip such practices in the bud. I don't know of any lawyer who has built a successful practice out of groundless lawsuits. In fact, even a meritorious case on a contingent basis is no picnic, as you saw in the story of our five-year struggle with *Nader v. General Motors* (Chapter 1).

Q: You mentioned a fee of about one-third of the recovery in Ralph Nader's case against GM. Isn't that rather high?

A: As it turned out, it was rather low (p. 102). There was so much work to the case that we didn't come out well on an hourly basis: about $30 an hour, much less than the lowest hourly fees in New York for litigation. But we never know at the beginning of the case how much work there will be. It averages out over the long run if you have a successful practice, but you must commit yourself to each client to go all the way if necessary.

Q: Suppose that it turns out to be easier than you expected, and you settle a case for a large sum after very little work. Do you reduce the fee then?

A: That rarely happens in a large case because even if liability is clear, the defendants will examine damage evidence minutely through discovery before paying out large sums. Futhermore, the plaintiffs do not buy a fixed number of hours from us—they could not afford to do so. What they are interested in is a favorable result, and if we achieve that in one case with 100 hours work, and in another case with 2,000 hours work, it makes no difference to the clients. So we can't afford to adjust fees to the actual number of hours worked, because we are not being paid on that basis, and we agree in advance not to increase the fee when we do more work than was contemplated. Also, noncontingent fees are not necessarily calculated on an hourly basis. In the United States and many other nations, noncontingent fees take into consideration the amount of money involved, the result obtained, the skills required, and other criteria as well as hours worked.

Q: But you did reduce the fee in Ralph Nader's case, didn't you?

A: Yes, but not because we did less work than we expected—

just the opposite happened. We reduced it because of the purpose for which Ralph used the money: to launch his consumer activist movement.

Q: Why don't you give your clients the option of paying an hourly fee or a percentage fee, whichever turns out to be cheaper?

A: That would be the equivalent of getting the services of an expensive computer that has been programmed to respond to your needs, and paying only for the electricity it uses when it solves your problem.

Q: Aren't contingent fees too high in serious accident cases? How do you justify taking hundreds of thousands of dollars in fees from a person crippled for life or a widow who has lost her lifetime financial support?

A: They are not too high, *especially* when they are up in the hundreds of thousands, because it means that you have produced many more hundreds of thousands for your client. A contingent fee of $100 might be too high, because it means that the client probably did not net more than $200. To answer your question more fully, I'd have to explain the money dynamics of tort litigation (pp. 559–574).

Q: Can you summarize the money dynamics?

A: As a tort lawyer today, you must maintain expensive facilities in readiness for the needs of your clients, who could not begin to pay for them. You must be a scientist and a good business manager, able to finance your organization and the special expenditures needed for each case. You must do this out of after-tax profits, without the help of tax breaks, bank loans, and equity financing, which are available to business and industry. And the fees in successful cases have to sustain your organization through the losing cases (pp. 417–419). You must be able to take on giant corporations, insurers, and well-financed law firms that are many times the size of your own.

Q: Why is so much capital required?

A: Hundreds of new sources of evidence and methods of presentation have been developed for tort cases (pp. 534–549). In large cases, plaintiff's lawyers must often advance $100,000 or more in special preparation expenses. Sometimes they will spend $5,000 to $10,000 just to investigate a claim they turn down eventually. All these expenditures are necessary if they are to set their clients on equal footing with wealthy insurers and defendants, who can be expected to take advantage of all the latest investigation and presentation techniques. The money must come from lawyers because the plaintiffs cannot usually afford to lay it out in the aftermath of their devastating financial and physical injuries.

Q: What sort of items make up the "special preparation expenses"?

A: The biggest items are charges made by shorthand reporters for depositions of witnesses and trial transcripts; travel expenses of lawyers during investigation and discovery; copying and duplication of documents, such as operating and maintenance manuals, log books, and other records kept by defendants; charges of experts and consultants (such as engineers, economists, and physicians) for analysis, advice, and court testimony; and the making of videotapes, models, photographs, and enlargements for use as evidence. There are also routine items such as telephone calls, local transportation, postage, and express delivery. None of these involve payments to regular employees of the tort lawyer's office, or overhead expenses such as rent and library costs. They are extraordinary expenditures made for a particular client.

Q: When you spend $5,000 or more to investigate a claim that you turn down eventually, what sort of items are involved?

A: That depends on the type of case. In an aviation accident, it would usually involve a trip to the site of the crash; analysis and testing of parts of the wreckage; and consultation with experts. In a products liability case, it might involve testing of the product involved; research into the quantity and nature of past malfunctions; and consultation with experts. In cases involving medical questions, the principal costs are copying of medical records; research and compilation of medical authorities; and consultation with medical experts.

Q: Journalists usually portray the plaintiff's tort lawyer as a fat cat. How do you feel about that?

A: I picture the fat cat as one who lives off the work of others, reaping large profits through financial leverage. Like most of the clichés you have thrown at me, this one is quite inapplicable to the tort lawyer's position. Tort practice is usually the last field selected by the bright law students who want to make a lot of money—they will go for the chance of partnership in a large general practice firm that does *not* work on contingent fees.

Q: So you are not a fat cat?

A: No. Whatever I make is a small percentage of the benefits that I bring to the people in need of my services, and if I don't help them substantially, I make nothing. Indeed, my share costs the plaintiff nothing, because tort lawyer's fees are built into the system and are self-liquidating. Without them, we would need a government-financed structure like medicare or social security, but the institution that I help to maintain for the public's benefit costs the taxpayers nothing.

Q: What are the alternatives to the contingent fee?

A: We'd need some kind of government-financed program, such as expanded legal aid. This would create a new bureaucracy, and you can well imagine the quality of legal services and the level of compensation that would result. Here are some of the existing advantages we would lose: the screening process by which self-interested tort lawyers weed out unmeritorious claims; the chance for adequate compensation against strong defendants; and the deterrent effect of tort litigation (pp. 341–372).

Q: Suppose we kept the private lawyer concept but restricted contingent fees to lower percentages or to amounts fixed by the court at the end of the case?

A: You would probably eliminate the huge investment of skill and capital that is maintained by today's entrepreneur-lawyers. It would not pay to assume such risks if the rewards were arbitrarily restricted. There is no public support for such measures. Have you ever met a seriously injured person who laments the payment of a large sum to a tort lawyer, when it represents a fraction of what the tort lawyer accomplished for the accident victim? Often such restrictions are suggested by insurers, manufacturers, and other interested parties who want to push the tort system back to the days of the *Titanic* and the Triangle Shirtwaist fire (pp. 128–138), when defendants could literally get away with murder. Sometimes restrictions are suggested by well-meaning law professors who have never analyzed the money dynamics of tort litigation; this is understandable because no study of those dynamics has ever been published before. But such restrictions are never suggested by the millions of helpless people who have benefitted or stand to benefit from contingent fees.

Q: Have contingent fees been going up with inflation?

A: No; the percentages have actually been going down with the expansion of tort practice and the intervention of general practice lawyers who use their leverage to get the best deal for their personal clients. Remember that in the earlier days of tort litigation, 50 percent fees were standard, and the tort lawyers had little skill or money with which to help their clients (pp. 144–151). I can't think of any other service that has improved so much in quality, gone down in cost, and sustained itself without any government or bank assistance.

Q: You describe contingent fees, jury trials, and entrepreneur-lawyers as the trinity of torts. Are all three elements necessary to put the plaintiffs on equal footing with their adversaries?

A: Yes. We have had jury trials since colonial days and contingent fees since the 1880s, but as we saw in pre-1950 cases like the *Titanic, Eastland, General Slocum,* Triangle Shirtwaist and Iroquois Theatre (pp. 128–138), the plaintiff's cause was practically hopeless until the entrepreneur-lawyer came along.

Q: You paint a rather heroic portrait of entrepreneur-lawyers as champions who boost their individual clients to equal courtroom footing with huge corporations, insurers, and the government. Is this an accurate picture?

A: Of course I am biased, but I believe it is accurate. There is nothing else to explain why Ralph Nader could bring a successful suit against General Motors; anywhere else in the world, a large corporation could invade the privacy of a critic without fear of such a result (pp. 112–118). None of the other major cases described in this book could have been won without entrepreneur-lawyers. And the 14th Amendment guarantee of equal protection of the laws was meaningless when there were no lawyers strong enough to represent the individual against the establishment.

Q: Are you suggesting that England and other nations adopt the contingent fee system?

A: Not necessarily. I don't know enough about their legal systems to propose radical changes. I hope that this book will demonstrate the importance of the contingent fee in the American system. Beyond that, it is a question of what each nation hopes to accomplish through its courts. If they are satisfied with the social legislation approach and do not wish to use their courts as we do, then there is no need to adopt the contingent fee. In the United States, social legislation has not been very effective, and our egalitarian philosophy demands individual legal remedies to rectify injustices, which in turn require the contingent fee.

Q: One hears a lot of questions about the competency of trial lawyers today. Is that a big problem in tort cases?

A: There are thousands of competent firms with adequate facilities and personnel to handle tort cases today, and there is no reason why any injured person should be poorly represented. Every conceivable type of tort case is covered by textbooks, technique books, seminars, audio cassettes, and videotapes.

Q: But let's suppose that I was seriously injured in an accident, and that I don't know any tort lawyers. How can I be sure that I choose the right lawyer for my case?

A: I'd advise you to go to your personal or family lawyer. If you don't have one, then seek one out whom you trust and feel comfortable with. See if this lawyer can solve your problem, and if not, then ask the lawyer to help you to select a suitable specialist.

Q: Won't that cost me a lot more money, since I'll have to pay two lawyers instead of one?

A: No. It will probably be cheaper for you to have the assistance of a good general practice lawyer in choosing a specialist (pp. 574–577). The specialist will look forward to other referrals from your lawyer, who will have more leverage than you in working out a fee arrangement consistent with the ability of the specialist to do a thorough job. If you try to find the specialist on your own, there are many ways in which this can cost you more than working with your personal lawyer.

Q: For example?

A: First of all, it is not easy for a lay person to select the proper specialist. Today, when lawyers are permitted to advertise and to use public relations counselors, it is relatively easy for them to get their names before the public in ways that seem to indicate that they are well qualified to handle certain types of cases. But they may not be the best choice for your particular problem. Your personal lawyer will have much greater insight than you in screening prospective specialists.

Q: Do personal lawyers get part of the fee for sending a client to a specialist?

A: They will usually get a share of the ultimate contingent fee, but not just for sending you to a specialist. Selecting a specialist involves a lot of responsibility, for if they choose the wrong one and the case turns out badly, their clients may blame them for it and may well cease to be their regular clients.

Q: What else do they do to earn a share of the fee?

A: They negotiate an appropriate fee arrangement and then follow through to make sure that the specialist gives the case proper attention. They help to round up important evidence that the client or the specialist might miss, such as personal and business information about the client which they may remember or have in their files. They confer with the specialist throughout the case and keep the client advised of what is going on. And when it is time for the crucial decision—whether to settle or go to trial—the specialist will have to convince the personal lawyer first, and then the client will have two professional opinions to rely upon.

Q: Apart from more money to be spent on expansion of the courts, what suggestions do you have for improving the administration of civil justice?

A: I agree with Chief Justice Warren Burger and Ralph Nader, who have suggested that every piece of federal legislation be accompanied by a "judicial impact statement," a counterpart to the environmental impact statement now required. Many federal statutes create new rights and obligations, giving rise to waves of new litigation that engulf our already hard-pressed courts. The judicial impact statement would help to educate Congress and the public to the needs of the court system, and would either inhibit legislation that creates new lawsuits or provide funds to expand the courts as needed.

Q: Anything else?

A: I am in favor of experiments with arbitration of claims up to $50,000, like those which are now conducted in three federal district courts. It would be wonderful if we could maintain the right to a jury trial of every legitimate claim, but inflation and the realities of court budgets make it difficult to provide this service in smaller cases. I was tremendously impressed with the results of the quasi-arbitration that Judge Peirson Hall used in the Turkish Airlines DC-10 cases (pp. 460–464) and I think that we should try experiments of that type, using panels of retired judges as forecasters of jury verdicts.

Q: Do you have any suggestions for changes in tort law?

A: I have mentioned them in previous chapters: the use of products liability law to overcome the gun lobby (pp. 369–372); eliminate all distinctions between damages recoverable in wrongful death and personal injury cases, and thus finally lay to rest Lord Ellenborough's monstrous 1808 decision in *Baker v. Bolton* (pp. 578–579); and most important, put an end to the archaic discrimination against tort plaintiffs' right to prejudgment interest, a step that will remove thousands of cases from our trial calendars (pp. 579–581). All of these changes are already under way, and can be accomplished by judges without any new legislation. Another change I would welcome would be a more general recognition of American civil justice as one of our nation's finest products, which should be made available to foreigners suing Americans here, without the threat that calendar congestion may result in a *forum non conveniens* dismissal of meritorious claims.

Q: On your last point, how can we take on cases like the Entebbe raid and the Alexander Onassis crash, which happened overseas and involved foreign parties, when our courts are straining under the burdens of purely domestic cases?

A: Keeping our courts open to foreigners who cannot obtain justice elsewhere is one of the best investments we can make. It creates tremendous goodwill and advertises one of our best products: American justice. The Departments of Justice and State regard this as an important national policy. The slight extra burden on the courts is offset by the increase in our Gross National Product which comes from the fees and travel expenditures generated by such cases. Travel by foreign lawyers and litigants pump money into the local economy (pp. 487–492).

Q: Are you hopeful about the future of civil justice?

A: Yes, but I think it is tied in with a basic American problem which I would characterize as a breakdown of self-control. Our permissive society, strained by Watergate, Vietnam, inflation, television violence, drug addiction, and waning respect for government and law itself, is in deep trouble. These problems, epitomized by the 11 million criminal offenses that our courts must deal with each year, might overwhelm our entire legal system unless it is strengthened. Therefore, I think it is appropriate to end with the prophetic words of the seldom sung second verse of "America the Beautiful," written in 1893:

> America! America!
> God mend thine every flaw
> Confirm thy soul
> In self-control
> Thy liberty in law!

Notes

Following are citations of major cases, books, and articles mentioned in the text, as well as others which may be of interest. Case citations always begin with the volume number. Thus "71 U.S. 2 (1886)" refers to a decision of the United States Supreme Court in 1886, appearing at page 2 of volume 71 of the official *United States Reports*. Names of publishers of legal textbooks are not customarily given, since they are available in law libraries.

Chapter 1

Page 3: R. Nader, *Unsafe at Any Speed: The Designed-In Dangers of the American Automobile* (New York: Grossman Publishers, 1965).

Page 19: C. McCarry, *Citizen Nader,* 13 (New York: Saturday Review Press, 1972).

Page 26: *Ex Parte Milligan,* 71 U.S. (4 Wall.) 2 (1866).

Page 32: W. Prosser, *Handbook of the Law of Torts* 802–803 (4th ed. 1971); *Roberson v. Rochester Folding Box Co.* 171 N.Y. 538 (1902).

Page 34: *Cohen v. Marx,* 94 Cal.App. 2d 704, 211 P.2d 320 (Cal.App. 1949).

Page 36: W. Prosser, *Handbook of the Law of Torts* 808 (4th ed. 1971).

Page 37: The English practical joker case is *Wilkinson v. Downton,* (1897) 2 Q.B.D. 57.

Page 83: The Appellate Division's affirmance of Justice Streit's decision is reported at 292 N.Y.S.2d 345.

Page 86: Justice Brust's decision is reported at *Nader v. General Motors Corp.,* 292 N.Y.S.2d 514 (Sup. Ct., Special Term 1968).

Page 90: The Appellate Division decision is reported at *Nader v. General Motors Corp.,* 298 N.Y.S.2d 137 (App. Div. 1969).

Page 94: *Pearson v. Dodd,* 410 F.2d 701 (D.C.Cir. 1969).

Page 95: The Court of Appeals decision is reported at *Nader v. General Motors Corp.,* 25 N.Y.2d 560, 307 N.Y.S.2d 647 (1970).

Page 98: W. Prosser, *Handbook of the Law of Torts* 816 (4th ed. 1971).

Page 106: J. Wright, *On a Clear Day You Can See General Motors* 53 (Grosse Point: Wright Enterprises, 1979).

Page 112: On the world's legal systems, the landmark work is J. Wigmore, *Panorama of the World's Legal Systems* (1928). A more recent treatise covering the legal systems discussed in Chapter 1 is H. de Vries, *Civil Law and the Anglo-American Lawyer* (1973).

Chapter 2

Page 121: W. Churchill, *The Birth of Britain* (vol. 1 of *A History of the English-Speaking Peoples*) 217, 219 (New York: Dodd, Mead 1956).

Page 123: *Muller v. Oregon,* 208 U.S. 412 (1908); *Lochner v. New York,* 198 U.S. 45 (1905).

Page 125: J. Dooley, 1 *Modern Tort Law* 436 (1977).

Page 126: The judge's observation on loss of a leg is found in *Hamilton v. The William Branfoot,* 48 Fed. 914, 917 (D.S.C. 1892).

Baker v. Bolton, 170 Eng. Rep. 1033 (1808).

Page 127: The decision placing property ahead of life and liberty is *Children's Hospital v. Adkins,* 284 F. 613 (D.C.Cir. 1922), affirmed in *Adkins v. Children's Hospital,* 261 U.S. 525 (1923).

Page 128: B. Schwartz, *The Law In America* 112–113 (New York: McGraw-Hill, 1974).

Page 132: The decision of the U.S. Supreme Court in the *Titanic* litigation is reported at *Ocean Steam Navigation Company Ltd. v. Mellor et al,* 233 U.S. 718 (1914).

Page 141: On the history of contingent fees, see F. MacKinnon, *Contingent Fees for Legal Services* (1964); and S. Speiser, 1 *Attorneys' Fees* Chapter 2 (1973).

Page 144: F. Hare, *My Learned Friends* 7–8 (1976).

Page 152: S. Behrman, *Duveen* 107–109 (New York: Random House, 1952).

Page 158: R. Davies, *Airlines of the United States since 1914* (London: Putnam, 1972)

Page 163: *Guille v. Swan,* 1 CCH Aviation Cases 1 (1822).

Page 167: The Conklin case is reported at *Conklin v. Canadian-Colonial Airways, Inc.,* 266 N.Y. 244, 194 N.E. 692 (1935).

Page 169: McLarty, *Res Ipsa Loquitur in Airline Passenger Litigation,* 37 Va. L. Rev. 55 (1951). See also S. Speiser, 1 *Res Ipsa Loquitur* Chapter 10 (1972).

Page 185: W. Hyman, *The Magna Carta of Space* (Amherst: Amherst Press, 1966).

Chapter 3

Page 258: L. Nizer, *My Life in Court* 383 (New York: Doubleday, 1961).

Judge Ridge's ruling on the CAA's failure to warn is quoted from *McClenny et al. v. United Air Lines, Inc.,* 178 F.Supp. 372 (D.Mo. 1959).

Page 261: Belli, *The Adequate Award,* 39 Cal.L.Rev. 1 (1951).

Page 262: The Chancellor Kent quotation is from *Colman v. Southwick,* 9 Johns 45, 52 (N.Y. 1812).

Page 263: The quotation on demonstrative evidence is from M. Belli, *My Life On Trial* 107–108 (New York: William Morrow, 1976).

Page 265: Cooley's appraisal of wrongful death damages is taken from the first edition of T. Cooley, *Treatise on the Law of Torts* 274 (1880). The language was unchanged through the three succeeding editions, appearing in the last edition (1932) at page 168.

Page 268: On the Ruby trial, M. Belli, *My Life On Trial* 289 (New York: William Morrow, 1976).

Chapter 4

Page 294: *Botta v. Brunner,* 26 N.J. 82, 138 A.2d 713 (N.J. 1958). For an exhaustive annotation on the per diem or mathematical basis for fixing pain and suffering damages, see 60 A.L.R.2d 1347.

Chapter 5

Page 306: *MacPherson v. Buick Motor Co.,* 217 N.Y. 382 (1916).

Page 308: Justice Steuer's decision in the Ford Trimotor case is reported at *American Airways, Inc. v. Ford Motor Co.,* 10 N.Y.S.2d 816 (N.Y. Co., 1939). It was affirmed by the Appellate Division for the First Department in 1940 (17 N.Y.S.2d 998) and by the Court of Appeals in 1940 (284 N.Y. 807).

Henningsen v. Bloomfield Motors, Inc., 32 N.J. 358, 161 A.2d 69 (1960).

Greenman v. Yuba Power Products, Inc., 59 Cal.2d 57, 377 P.2d 897, 27 Cal.Rptr. 697 (1962).

Escola v. Coca-Cola, 24 Cal.2d 453, 150 P.2d 436 (1944).

Page 309: The first appellate decision permitting an airplane passenger to sue a manufacturer for breach of warranty was *Goldberg v. Kollsman Instrument Corp.,* 12 N.Y.2d 432, 240 N.Y.S.2d 592 (1963).

The New York decision extending strict manufacturer's liability to an aircraft accident on the high seas was *Middleton v. United Aircraft Corp.,* 6 CCH Aviation Cases, 17,975 (S.D.N.Y. 1960).

The contrary 1962 Delaware decision was *Noel v. United Aircraft Corp.,* 7 CCH Aviation Cases 18,082.

For the present state of the law of products liability in aviation cases, see S. Speiser & C. Krause, 2 *Aviation Tort Law* Chapters 19–20 (1979).

Page 342: W. Prosser, *Handbook of the Law of Torts* 654–655 (4th ed. 1971).

Section 402A, probably the best-known section of the American Law Institute's Second Restatement of Torts, reads as follows:

§402 A. Special Liability of Seller of Product for Physical Harm to User or Consumer.
(1) One who sells any product in a defective condition unreasonably dangerous to the user or consumer or to his property is subject to liability for physical harm thereby caused to the ultimate user or consumer, or to his property, if
   (a) the seller is engaged in the business of selling such a product, and
   (b) it is expected to and does reach the user or consumer without substantial change in the condition in which it is sold.
(2) The rule stated in Subsection (1) applies although
   (a) the seller has exercised all possible care in the preparation and sale of his product, and
   (b) the user or consumer has not bought the product from or entered into any contractual relation with the seller.

Page 345: The quotation on improved machine safety is from National Safety Council, *Accident Prevention Manual* 796 (7th ed.)

The De Havilland Comet story is quoted from E. Rickenbacker, *Rickenbacker: An Autobiography* 414 (Englewood Cliffs: Prentice-Hall, 1967).

Page 363: The Eighth Circuit crashworthiness case quoted from is *Larsen v. General Motors Corp.,* 391 F.2d 495 (8th Cir. 1968).

Page 365: *Baker v. Bolton,* 170 Eng. Rep. 1033 (1808).

As of the time of this writing, the Appellate Division for the Third Department had refused to allow punitive damages in the Ford Pinto wrongful death case, leaving that decision to the New York Court of Appeals or the state legislature. *Robert v. Ford Motor Co.,* 417 N.Y.S.2d. 595 (St. Lawrence Co. 1979), reversed at 424 N.Y.S.2d 747 (App.Div. 1980). On the other hand, in a 1980 case, the Supreme Court of Idaho permitted punitive damages in a wrongful death action: *Gavica v. Hanson,* 608 P2d 861, citing as authority S. Speiser, 1 *Recovery for Wrongful Death* §3:4 (2d Ed. 1975).

Page 370: The absurd and patently unconstitutional Army program for gun sales to NRA members was finally terminated by a 1979 decision of the U.S. District Court for the District of Columbia (*Gavett v.*

Alexander, 477 F.Supp. 1035). The National Coalition to Ban Handguns instigated the suit, and the Defense Department, which is charged with the duty of defending charges of unconstitutionality of such statutes, refused to do so, thus ending 75 years of subsidizing the NRA.

Page 371: The machine-readable codes are called "bar codes," and can be used to keep track of virtually anything by computer. Many libraries now use them to control circulation—an operation exactly like one that could be used to trace guns.

Page 372: The Rodino bill's designation is H.R. 5823, 96th Congress. Identical legislation was introduced in the Senate as S. 1936 by Senators Kennedy, Javits, Ribicoff and others.

Chapter 6

Page 386: The Federal Tort Claims Act was enacted as part of the Legislative Reorganization Act of 1946, 60 Stat. 812. It now appears, for the most part, in 28 U.S.C. §§ 1346(b), 2671–2680. For its legislative history, see L. Jayson, 1 *Handling Federal Tort Claims* Chapter 2 (1964). For its application to aviation cases, see S. Speiser & C. Krause, 2 *Aviation Tort Law* Chapter 15 (1979).

Page 387: The Supreme Court decision in the Texas City disaster case was *Dalehite v. United States,* 346 U.S. 15 (1953).

Page 388: Justice Jackson's famous remark appears at 346 U.S. 60. Apparently Congress agreed with his sentiments, for on August 12, 1955 it passed Public Law 378, 69 Stat. 707, recognizing and assuming "the compassionate responsibility of the United States" for the losses in the disaster, and setting up a procedure for evaluating and settling claims arising from the event.

Page 400: Judge Torruella's decision is reported at *Clemente v. United States,* 422 F.Supp. 564 (D.P.R. 1976).

Page 408: The First Circuit's decision is reported at *Clemente v. United States,* 567 F.2d 1140 (1st Cir. 1977).

Page 415: The report of the Supreme Court's denial of the certiorari petition appears at 435 U.S. 1006 (1978).

Chapter 7

Page 437: The New York Court of Appeals *forum non conveniens* decision quoted from is *Varkonyi v. Varig,* 29 N.Y.2d 356, 292 N.Y.S.2d 670 (1968).

Page 451: The New York Court of Appeals decision declaring the Massachusetts limit to be against the public policy of New York is

Kilberg v Northeast Airlines Inc., 9 N.Y.2d 34, 211 N.Y.S.2d 133 (1961). The two Second Circuit cases in which the recovery exceeded the Massachusetts limit are *Pearson v. Northeast Airlines Inc.,* 309 F.2d 553 (2nd Cir. 1962) and *Gore v. Northeast Airlines Inc.,* 373 F.2d 717 (2nd Cir. 1967).

Page 457: *Sea-Land Services v. Gaudet,* 414 U.S. 573 (1974).

Page 459: Judge Hall's decision on choice of law is reported at *In re Paris Air Crash of March 3, 1974,* 399 F.Supp. 732 (C.D.Cal. 1975).

Page 466: P. Eddy, E. Potter, B. Page, *Destination Disaster* (New York: Quadrangle, 1976).

Page 474: N. Fraser, P. Jacobson, M. Ottaway, L. Chester, *Aristotle Onassis* (Philadelphia: J. P. Lippincott, 1977).

Page 491: The case permitting a foreign government to sue an American exporter under the Clayton Antitrust Act is *Pfizer v. Government of India,* 434 U.S. 308 (1978).

The Supreme Court decision laying down the *forum non conveniens* rules is *Gulf Oil Corp. v. Gilbert,* 330 U.S. 501 (1947).

Chapter 8

Page 532: The instructions for programming hand-held calculators will be found at S. Speiser, *Recovery for Wrongful Death Economic Handbook,* Appendix B (2d Ed. 1979).

Page 543: F. Hare, *My Learned Friends* 8–9, 19 (1976).

Pages 544–545: G. Allen, *The Law as a Way of Life* 97, 103 (1969).

Page 566: The case of the two nuns is *Goheen v. General Motors Corp.,* 263 Or. 145, 502 P.2d 223 (1972).

Page 578: The annotation on the privity rule written by Al Gans in 1946 is "Manufacturer's liability for negligence causing injury to person or damage to property of ultimate consumer or user," 164 A.L.R. 569.

On the denial of damages for mental anguish in wrongful death cases, see 1 S. Speiser, *Recovery for Wrongful Death* §§3:52–3:55 (2d Ed.1975); and S. Speiser & S. Malawer, *An American Tragedy: Damages for Mental Anguish of Bereaved Relatives in Wrongful Death Actions,* 51 Tulane Law Review 1 (1976).

Page 579: The statement about the specious distinction between liquidated and unliquidated claims is from 22 Am.Jur.2d §191.

Page 580: The motion to allow prejudgment interest was made originally in *Kamhi v. McDonnell Douglas et al.,* No. 79 C 2272, U.S. District Court, Northern District of Illinois, Eastern Division. Judges Will and Robson made their decision applicable to all of the cases assigned to them as MDL judges in the O'Hare litigation (MDL No. 391). It is reported at *In re Air Crash Disaster Near Chicago, Illinois, on May 25, 1979,* 15 CCH Aviation Cases 17,835 (N.D. Ill. 1979). See also the comments at 23 *Trial Lawyer's Guide* 536 (1980).

Chapter 9

Page 583: On the unpopularity of lawyers, see M. Mayer, *The Lawyers* 3–13 (New York: Harper & Row, 1967).

Page 584: The reverse discrimination case is *Regents of the University of California v. Allan Bakke,* 438 U.S. 265 (1978). Quotas for admission to medical schools are largely an economic policy issue which Congress has left to the courts.

INDEX